FACULTY OFFICE
REGISTERS
1534–1549

Letter of dispensation for marriage without banns issued by the Faculty Office, 1 July 1536

(See Introduction, pp. xxv, xxvii, xxviii)

FACULTY OFFICE REGISTERS

1534-1549

*A Calendar of the first two Registers
of the Archbishop of Canterbury's
Faculty Office
edited with an Introduction
and Index*

BY

D. S. CHAMBERS

OXFORD
AT THE CLARENDON PRESS
1966

Oxford University Press, Ely House, London W. 1

GLASGOW NEW YORK TORONTO MELBOURNE WELLINGTON
CAPE TOWN SALISBURY IBADAN NAIROBI LUSAKA ADDIS ABABA
BOMBAY CALCUTTA MADRAS KARACHI LAHORE DACCA
KUALA LUMPUR HONG KONG

PRINTED IN GREAT BRITAIN

PREFACE

ACKNOWLEDGEMENTS must be made to Mr E. G. W. Bill, Lambeth Librarian, without whose initiative and encouragement none of this work would have been undertaken, let alone have been published; to Dr A. B. Emden and Mrs A. E. B. Owen for reading the typescript and giving much advice and particularly helpful suggestions about the identification of place-names; and to the British Academy and the Faculty Office for grants of money towards the cost of publishing. If a dedication is appropriate for this sort of work, it should probably be made to the staff of Lambeth Palace Library, as one of whom I started work on the registers in 1960.

Department of Mediaeval History
St Salvator's College, St Andrews
1965

CONTENTS

ABBREVIATIONS

(excluding those for christian names)

acol.	acolyte
affin.	affinity
arb.	arbitratur (arbitrated payment)
archbp	archbishop
archdcn	archdeacon
B.A.	Bachelor of Arts
B.C.L.	Bachelor of Civil Law
B.Cn.L.	Bachelor of Canon Law
B.M.	Bachelor of Medicine or (in Introduction) British Museum
B.Th.★	Bachelor of Theology
benef.	benefice
bp	bishop
Cant.	Canterbury
Carth.	Carthusian
cath.	cathedral
ch.	church
chapl.	chaplain
cl.	clause
clk	clerk
coll.	college
consang.	consanguinity
D.C.L.	Doctor of Civil Law
D.Cn.L.	Doctor of Canon Law
D.Th.★	Doctor (Master or Professor) of Theology
dau.	daughter
dcn	deacon
dio.	diocese
disp.	dispensation
f., ff.	folio, folios
fr.	friar
gent.	gentleman
gentw.	gentlewoman
h.o.	holy orders
hsehld	household

★ These forms for B.D. or D.D. (Bachelor or Doctor of Divinity) have been preferred here since they are given in the register.

K.G.	Knight of the Garter
Kg	King
l.d.	letters dimissory
Lamb. Pal. Lib.	Lambeth Palace Library, London
Ld	Lord
Ly	Lady
M.A.	Master of Arts
M.D.	Doctor of Medicine
nr	near
non-res.	non-residence
O.C. fr.	Order of Carmelite friars (white friars)
O.Cist.	Cistercian Order
O.F.M.	Franciscan Order of Friars Minor (grey friars)
O.P.	Dominican Order of Friars Preacher (black friars)
O.S.A.	Order of St Augustine
O.S.B.	Order of St Benedict
p.a.	per annum
P.R.O.	Public Record Office, London
p.s.r.	pro sigillo regis (taxed for the Great Seal)
par.	parish
permut.	permutation
Premonstr.	Premonstratensian (Order of Prémontré)
Qn	Queen
r.	rector
reg.	register
sch.	scholar
sec. pr.	secular priest
subdcn	subdeacon
suppr.	suppressed
Trin.	Trinity
v.	vicar
yr(s)	year(s)

INTRODUCTION

THE first two registers of the Faculty Office, in Lambeth Palace Library Archives, are among the earliest administrative records of the Church of England after Henry VIII's breach with Rome. They provide an important source of material for historians and genealogists, and one which has hitherto been very little used.[1] In these introductory pages an attempt has been made to describe and interpret the contents of the registers, but clearly such an introduction cannot claim to be exhaustive and the main intention in this work has been to provide a calendar and index for the use of others.

By the Dispensations or Peter's Pence Act of November 1533[2] a new office machinery was set up to replace the departments of the Roman curia which had issued 'licences, dispensations, faculties, compositions, rescripts, delegacies, instruments and other writings': miscellaneous privileges, in brief, of which dispensations from the letter of the canon law were by far the most common. The foundation of a court or office of faculties[3] is itself a good illustration of the transference of ecclesiastical authority rather than reform which occurred in the 1530's: it contrasts with the root-and-branch attitude towards the canon law and dispensations of Luther and Calvin. Nevertheless, if the Faculty Office was papal in character, its records during this early period (1534–49) do reflect some of the changes which the Church gradually underwent, and the Office's own decline after a powerful beginning.

The first register, Lambeth Palace Library Archives F I/Vv, runs from 12 April 1534 (f. 7ᵛ) to 27 December 1540 (f. 352ᵛ). It is a large paper volume, measuring 15 × 11 inches, re-bound in leather but with the stamped design of a bird, a dog, and a bee[4] of the original binding preserved. It contains 379 folios, now numbered consecutively in the top right-hand

---

[1] W. Hooper, 'The Court of Faculties', *E.H.R.* xxv (1910), 670–86 refers briefly to the registers and some of their contents. The first register has recently been used by G. A. J. Hodgett, 'The Unpensioned Ex-Religious in Tudor England', *Journ. Eccles. Hist.* xiii (2), (1962), 195–202. Austin's friars' names extracted from it have also been used by F. Roth, O.S.A., *The English Austin Friars 1249–1538*, ii, *Sources* (New York, 1961), 514*–17*, though this list contains some misreadings. The second register was used to provide lists of marriage dispensations, but without full data, in J. L. Chester and G. J. Armytage, *Allegations for Marriage Licences . . . 1543–1869*, Harleian Society Publications, 24 (London, 1886).

[2] 25 Henry VIII, c. 21; text in *Statutes of the Realm*, iii (1817), 464–71; E. Gibson, *Codex Iuris Ecclesiastici Anglicani*, i (London, 1713), 102–11 gives a slightly edited text.

[3] The change of system is discussed (but without reference to the registers) by I. J. Churchill, *Canterbury Administration* (S.P.C.K., 1933) i. 508, 586–8; E. F. Churchill, 'Dispensations under the Tudors and Stuarts', *E.H.R.* xxxiv (1919), 409–15; W. Sparrow Simpson, *Dispensations* (S.P.C.K., 1935), pp. 94–96.

[4] Hodgett, art. cit., p. 197, n. 7, refers for this to J. B. Oldham, *English Blind-Stamped Bindings* (Cambridge, 1952), p. 42.

corner;[1] ff. ii–xxiv at the beginning are blank, and there are several blank
folios separating one year of the register from the next. It was made up of
groupings within years, probably to facilitate the division of revenues at
the end of each year. The fees charged for each dispensation were given
beside each entry, and the total on every folio added up at the bottom (a
detail which has been omitted in this edition). The erratic chronology,
recurrence of entries, and long stretches of uniform handwriting, suggest
that the register was entered up infrequently, perhaps at the end of the year
from a rough dossier of fiats. The first 'year', however, runs from April
1534 until December 1535, almost covering two calendar years, and the
entries are often confusedly dated. Sometimes after a retrospective entry
the formula 'anno predicto' is used, which may refer to the year of the
preceding and exceptional entry, or to that of the general run of previous
entries. Mr. Hodgett has demonstrated the confusion of 'anno predicto' used
near the beginning of the register, when the scribe did not recognize
the new regnal year, beginning on 22 April, until some entries later.[2]
Register Vv has had a less settled history than the rest of the Faculty Office
records in Morton's Tower, as it disappeared for a while[3] and only returned
there in 1955.[4] Two almost complete transcripts of it also exist. One of
these was made towards the end of the nineteenth century by E. H. W.
Dunkin, and survives among his papers bequeathed to the British Museum.[5]
It is a single notebook written in pencil, and the order of pages is in some
confusion; the entries have not been interpreted (original abbreviations
and spelling of place-names are retained, for instance), nor are the fees
included. The other transcript was made by Canon Claude Jenkins, formerly Lambeth Librarian, on eight writing pads; it has now been presented
to the Bodleian Library.[6]

The second register, Lambeth Palace Library Archives F I/A, has some
scattered entries from 1539–43,[7] but its main sequence runs from November 1543 to April 1549. It is also written on paper, but is a much smaller
volume than its predecessor, measuring 12×8 inches, and has only its
modern binding. It contains 347 pages, with the original numeration, and
3 blank pages at beginning and end. Unlike Register Vv, it does not give

---

[1] The original Roman numeration within each annual grouping is therefore obsolete.
The references given by Mr. Hodgett, art. cit., *passim*, should be revised according to the
new foliation.

[2] Hodgett, art. cit., p. 97.

[3] G. Baskerville in *Essays Presented to R. L. Poole*, ed. H. W. C. Davis (Oxford, 1927),
p. 439 n. 4.

[4] Lambeth Palace Library Report, 1955.

[5] B.M. Add. MS. 39401; used by L. F. Salzmann, 'Sussex Religious at the Dissolutions', *Sussex Archeol. Collections*, cii (1954). From later registers Dunkin transcribed
only Sussex entries.

[6] Information from the Lambeth Librarian.

[7] F I/A, pp. 84, 101 (1539); p. 17 (1541); p. 35 (1542); pp. 2, 9, 14, 16, 17, 25, 27
(1543).

the sum of fees at the bottom of each page, nor the general annual divisions, and the charges entered against each dispensation represent only the portion of the fee paid to the archbishop's commissary.[1] The term 'dispensation' is often replaced by alternatives such as 'concession' or 'licence', and in the later sections of the register entries are often carelessly written down, without date or full details.[2] A classified index to F I/A was made in 1847 for the Faculty Office by William Hardy, and is deposited at Lambeth; the following Register, F I/B, which does not start until 1568, was indexed in the same way.[3] This Elizabethan register (1568–91) has now been transcribed on to a card index at Lambeth, and is the only other one surviving before the main series begins in 1660.

Both F I/Vv and F I/A are written in Latin, and contain thousands of entries; as the entries are abbreviated and do not give the full text of the original except in a very few cases,[4] 'register' is perhaps an inaccurate term for these muniment books, though they will be referred to as such here. In paraphrasing and condensing the entries, the form and particular information of the original has been followed as closely as possible. Archaisms in the spelling of place-names have been modernized where identification is obvious; where it is hypothetical, the original spelling is given in brackets. 'Dispensation' has been used to describe all entries so described in the original; the variant terms such as indult, faculty, concession, licence, capacity, &c., are similarly followed.

The following chapters will attempt to outline the theory and general practice of 'dispensing' before 1534, to examine the new faculty administration after that date, and to analyse and discuss the different classes of dispensation found in the registers, and the financial basis of the system.

---

[1] See below, pp. lxii–lxiii.   [2] e.g. F I/A, pp. 272–7, 324–7.
[3] F I/Index A–B.
[4] F I/Vv, ff. 56ᵛ, 116ʳ, 130ʳ, 208ʳ, 255ʳ, 256ᵛ–7ʳ, 273ʳ, 301ʳ–2ʳ, 336ᵛ–7ʳ, 340ʳ–1ᵛ. F I/A, pp. 19–20, 72–74, 139–40.

I

DISPENSATIONS: THE PAPAL BACKGROUND

THE classical definition of a dispensation, a relaxation of the canon law in a particular instance, goes back not to Gratian but to another twelfth-century commentator, Rufinus. The canon law not being revealed or divine law, but received traditions and decrees, it was held that the vicar of Christ, or his authorized deputy, might in approved cases loosen or dispense with it. Later commentators (Albertus Magnus and Guillaume Durand, for example) added that dispensations should only be granted where their end was useful, necessary, and inclined to advance the common good.[1] These concepts were certainly still current at the time of Henry VIII's breach with Rome: they had been restated, for instance, by Cardinal De Vio ('Cajetan') in his Commentary on Aquinas, and in a short tract on dispensations by Pietro Andrea Gambara, one of Clement VII's auditors of the Rota.[2] The granting of dispensations by the pope can be traced back to remote instances, but it is unlikely that they were issued on any considerable scale until the centralization of papal authority from the eleventh century onwards, and particularly as an effect of the codification of the canon law: unofficially by Gratian (c. 1140) and officially in the *Decreta* issued under Gregory IX in 1234, and later additions.[3] They must be clearly distinguished from privileges of the confessional such as pardons and absolutions.

The majority of papal dispensations can be divided for convenience into three classes: two of them applying only to the clergy, and one only to the laity. Those limited to the clergy were, first, concerning the procedure of taking holy orders: relaxation of the rules for ordination at one of the four Ember seasons, and after presentation of letters dimissory from the candidate's bishop, or of the impediments of illegitimate birth, deformity, or age if under 25. Secondly, there were dispensations concerning the tenure

---

[1] A. Van Hove, *Commentarium Lovaniense in Codicem Iuris Canonici*, i, Tom. 5 'De Privilegiis, De Dispensationibus' (Mechlin and Rome, 1939), especially pp. 297–349, is followed here; see also R. Naz, 'Dispense', in *Dictionnaire de Droit canonique*. There are chapters on the theory and history of dispensations in W. J. Sparrow Simpson, *Dispensations* (S.P.C.K., 1935), and the report of the Archbishop of Canterbury's Commission, *Dispensation in Practice and Theory* (S.P.C.K., 1944), is valuable.

[2] The tractatulus *De Dispensationibus* forms Lib. X of Gambara's *De Officio Legati de Latere*, printed in *Tractatus . . . Illustrium Iurisconsultorum*, xiii (ii) (Venice, 1584), pp. 221ᵛ–30ᵛ.

[3] G. Le Bras, 'Canon Law' in *The Legacy of the Middle Ages*, ed. C. G. Crump and E. F. Jacob (Oxford, 1926), pp. 321–61. A. Friedberg, *Corpus Iuris Canonici*, 2 vols. (Leipzig, 1879), is the standard edition of the canon law.

of benefices: a vast range of instances. There were 'capacities' releasing regular clergy from their vows, to hold benefices while remaining within their Order, or to become secular priests abandoning the regular life altogether. There were licences for non-residence, usually due to alleged illness or the wish to study, and many sorts of dispensation for holding incompatible benefices in plurality.[1] The papacy had for long tried to enforce the restrictions upon tenure of more than one benefice with cure of souls, though dispensations to hold two in plurality were common, and certain exceptions were allowed for the *élite*, noble and lettered members of the clergy. In the mid thirteenth century the Cardinal Legate Ottobuono had laid down the rule, confirmed by the Council of Lyons in 1274, that diocesan bishops should refuse institution to incompatible benefices unless valid dispensations were shown, but further exceptions were allowed in Urban V's decree *Consueta* of 1366: no secular clerk should be dispensed to hold more than two incompatible benefices with cure of souls, and the fruits should not exceed £120 p.a., but noblemen in orders could hold three up to a maximum of £200 p.a. and doctors of divinity or professors of canon law could hold four, up to £300 p.a. in value.

The third main class of dispensations, which applied only to the laity, were those concerning marriage, 'the sacrament by which the Church exercised the widest influence upon general social life'.[2] The largest class of these concerned the prohibited degrees of consanguinity (relationship of blood) and affinity (relationship through marriage) beyond those laid down in Chapter 18 of the Book of Leviticus.[3] Marriage within the second, third, and fourth degrees of consanguinity and affinity (i.e. back to the great-great-grandparents) were prohibited in the Fourth Lateran Council (1215); there were also impediments of 'spiritual degree', incurred through godparents and sponsors in the sacraments of baptism and confirmation.[4] Spiritual genetics were exacting: not only was a dispensation necessary to marry a godchild or confirmation protégé, but also if a parent or former spouse had been the godparent or sponsor of either party to the marriage, or of the latter's offspring by a previous marriage. Such dispensations might also be obtained after marriage, if it had already taken place in spite of impediments. But a severe attempt to abolish this practice was made in

---

[1] A. Hamilton Thompson, 'Pluralism in the Mediaeval Church', *Reports and Papers of the Associated Architectural Societies* (Lincoln, 1915), pp. 42–69, is followed here.

[2] G. Le Bras, op. cit., p. 344. A comprehensive discussion of the teaching of the mediaeval Church on marriage is given by A. L. Smith, *Church and State in the Middle Ages* (Oxford, 1913), pp. 57–100.

[3] See A. Esmein, *L'Histoire du Droit canonique privé: Le Mariage* i. (Paris, 1891), 335–402, ii. 316–68; also the short articles by R. Naz and others in the *Dictionnaire de Droit canonique*, 'Affinité', 'Cognatio Spiritualis', &c.

[4] These are laid down in Gregory IX's *Decreta* Lib. IV, Tit. XI–XIV, 'De Cognatione Spirituali' (Friedberg, cols 693–704), and Boniface VIII's 'Sexti Decretalium', Lib. IV, Tit. III (ibid., cols 1067–8).

1524 by Pope Clement VII, who announced that in future he would only issue absolutions with an order for separation in such cases.[1] As well as the causes for dispensations to marry which are listed above, there were a number of others. A dispensation was needed to dissolve the validity of betrothals or pre-contracted childhood marriages, since violation of these was an offence against *publica honestas* even if no physical relations had occurred to constitute affinity. The reading three times of the banns (another enactment of the 4th Lateran Council), or the obligation for marriage within one or other party's parish church, and during certain prohibited seasons, notably Lent and Advent, could also be excused by dispensation.

Besides the three main classes of dispensation, there was a range of positive concessions, miscellaneous faculties or licences, which either clergy or laymen might seek: for instance, to eat flesh and the so-called 'white meats', eggs, milk, butter, cheese, &c. during Lent and at other fast times, to permit the celebration of offices in chapels of ease and private oratories, or the provision of portable altars. The granting of degrees and licensing of preachers and notaries also come under this miscellaneous heading.

In practice the papal authority to issue dispensations was much delegated. In the curia the official concerned with most classes of them was the cardinal penitentiary,[2] or his office, and letters in his name directed to diocesan bishops, authorizing them to release dispensations, can be found in many episcopal registers. Dispensations concerning benefices, however, would normally have to go through the usual procedure for the issue of papal letters either through the papal chancery or chamber. This meant that the petitioner would have to commission, if not specially dispatch, an experienced proctor, who would see the matter through all its stages until the drawing up and payment for the sealed letters. Unfortunately, it is not yet possible to estimate the volume of papal letters of dispensation applied for, and arriving in England, Wales, and Ireland from Rome in the forty years preceding the breach. Extracts from the papal registers of supplications have not been calendared beyond 1421,[3] and the *Calendar of Papal Letters* (bulls and briefs) does not go beyond 1492.[4] It may be objected that

[1] Papal letters of 7 Sept. 1524, to Wolsey and to the Archbishop of St Andrews, order publication of the new restrictions (*L.P.* iv. i. 640–1, D. Hay, *Letters of James V*, p. 104).
[2] This delegation was begun by Nicholas IV (1288–92); see E. Göller, *Die päpstliche Pönitentiarie, Bibliothek des Kgl. Preußischen Historischen Instituts in Rom* (1907–11), i. 25.
[3] W. H. Bliss, *Calendar of Entries in the Papal Registers, Petitions to the Pope, 1342–1419* (London, 1896). L. Macfarlane, 'The Vatican Archives, *Archives*, iv. 21–22 (1959), p. 99, states that all English, Welsh, and Irish entries from Reg. Supp. 635–78 have been microfilmed for deposit in the National Library, Dublin; these registers only cover the years 1469–72, however.
[4] The last volume contains the final transcripts of J. A. Twemlow, edited posthumously: *Calendar of Entries in the Papal Registers Relating to Great Britain and Ireland: Papal Letters (1484–92)*, xiv (1959). Microfilms of British and Irish entries from 1432–1513 in Reg. Vat. 775–990, and from 1484–1503 in Reg. Lat. 841–1127 are deposited in the National

even if the series went up to 1533, the evidence could not be considered complete, since not all papal letters were entered into the registers. However, the published volumes include many letters of dispensation for plurality and non-residence, and contribute some evidence in the later fifteenth century of abuses of the system by unscrupulous proctors, who returned from the curia pretending that they had been unable to obtain the letters their clients required, and so were sent back with a second commission and fee.[1] Transcripts of papal letters of dispensation are sometimes found in bishops' registers,[2] and a number of the original letters from Rome have also survived. Among the very last of these before the breach must be one in Lambeth Palace Library, dated at Rome 11 July 1533, which dispenses Thomas Vyvyan, M.A., vicar of St Petroc, Bodmin, to hold two incompatible benefices.[3]

As well as issue direct from the curia, minor dispensations could sometimes be obtained from specially delegated persons. Papal legates *a latere* were empowered to issue certain classes of them, and generally had their own office machinery for doing so.[4] Particularly interesting as an illustration of this are Cardinal Wolsey's legatine faculties: in their extension of

Library of Ireland, Dublin. (L. Macfarlane, art. cit., p. 99). Unfortunately the proposed continuation of the Calendars (ibid., p. 34 n. 17) has been abandoned. For the pontificate of Leo X (1513–21) there is a summary calendar of registered bulls by J. A. G. Hergenröther, *Regesta Leonis X* (Freiburg im Breisgau, 1884).

[1] *C.P.L.* xiii (ii), 600; xiv. 217, 226, 230–1.

[2] The early sixteenth-century York registers (Reg. Savage, Bainbridge, and Wolsey, in the Borthwick Institute, York) are particularly rich in dispensations. The most common are those permitting marriage in the prohibited degrees, though a number dispense clerks from defects of birth or physical deformity in order to take holy orders. Usually the letters are directed by the cardinal penitentiary to the archbishop or his vicar-general, and the latter's fiat is included in the register. A dispensation to hold three incompatible benefices for a canon of York, dated 29 Nov. 1520, however, is registered in the form of a bull in the pope's name, Reg. Wolsey f. 127ʳ, and so is a dispensation for marriage despite third-degree affinity in 1504, Reg. Savage, f. 105ʳ. Similarly, in the London register of FitzJames there is a dispensation in Pope Julius II's name, dated 3 Nov. 1509, for a canon of Blackmore to hold a benefice with or without cure, and another of Pope Leo X permitting the Abbot of Tiltey to hold an additional benefice, 7 Nov. 1519 (Guildhall Library, London, MS. 9531/9, ff. xii, cxlii). A dispensation from Leo X in 1515 to Robert Heggys, O.Cist., monk of Bruerne, to hold a benefice with or without cure and wear his habit beneath that of a secular priest, appears in Reg. Gigli II, ff. 126ᵛ–7ᵛ (Worcester Diocesan Record Office).

In the formulary of T. Oughton, *Ordo Judiciorum*, ii (London, 1738) a number of examples of dispensations are given, including some in the pope's name. The last example given (p. 86) before the breach with Rome is inadequately cited, however, without details of the supplicant's name, date (beyond the year 1519) nor provenance: it is a dispensation of Leo X for ordination despite the loss of an eye.

[3] Lamb. Pal. Lib. Papal Documents 126 (formerly MS. 643, f. 37). There are other late letters of dispensation in the same collection, also among the Stowe Charters of the British Museum. A papal dispensation dated as late as 29 Oct. 1533 is noted below p. xlv n. 2.

[4] F. Wasner, 'Fifteenth Century Texts on the Ceremonial of the Papal Legatus a Latere', *Traditio*, xiv (1958), esp. 342–3. Lesser emissaries than cardinal legates also held faculties to dispense, e.g. James, Bishop of Imola, in 1485 (*C.P.L.* xiv. 23–25).

6 January 1521 the authority to issue certain dispensations was included.[1] Though practically all records of Wolsey's legatine jurisdiction have been lost, there are some fragments of a register or extracts from a register of dispensations issued in 1525–6.[2] These include dispensations for marriage within the prohibited degrees, holding of benefices in plurality, and for ordinations outside the statutory time and age. A few original letters of dispensation issued by Wolsey have survived, having been endorsed as valid under the new régime in 1537,[3] and various bishops' registers contain transcripts of others.[4] It may be that this department of Wolsey's administration, in which Edmund Bonner[5] and Dr. John Hughes[6] were employed, had some influence in the organization of the new Faculty Office: and its existence during most of the 1520's may suggest that the clause in the Dispensations Act of 1533 about grievous and excessive expense and inconvenience in sending to Rome draw some of its power from a regret for the recent disappearance of Wolsey's Faculty Office.

Limited numbers of specified dispensations might also be issued, according to special papal delegation, by papal collectors[7] and bishops returning from Rome. Diocesan bishops were also permitted, under Boniface VIII's constitution 'Cum ex eo', to license clerks to be absent from their benefices to study,[8] and by tradition to dispense for various minor matters, such as ordination or marriage outside the statutory time, marriage without the banns being read more than once or twice, or in a private chapel, also for celebrations of mass in private oratories, and licensing of portable altars. Thus a certain number of dispensations in the Faculty Office registers are admittedly for causes which the archbishop as diocesan had been able to dispense for during the past two centuries; some bishop's registers contain long lists of such dispensations.

Finally, under the Pluralities Act of 1529,[9] which severely restricted the

[1] Rymer, *Foedera*, xiii. 734–5.　　[2] P.R.O. SP I/39, ff. 19–29.
[3] Lamb. Pal. Lib., Papal Documents 131–4 (133 is a capacity for an Augustinian to hold a benefice with cure of souls, 14 Apr. 1527). There are also dispensations issued by the papal nuncios Gianpietro Caraffa and Lorenzo Campeggio (Papal Documents, 130, 135).
[4] e.g. disp. dated 6 Feb. 1528 for Richard Sheperd, O.F.M., pr. of Bridgnorth, to hold a benef. 'et etiam deferre habitum dicti ordinis sub veste sive chlamide presbiteri secularis quoad vixeris'(Worcester Diocesan Record Office,Reg. Gigli II bound with de' Medici and Ghinucci, f. 2ᵛ). Wolsey's own York register contains some examples (Borthwick Institute, York, Reg. Wolsey, ff. 109, 130ʳ, 132ᵛ). Longland's register at Lincoln and Campeggio's at Salisbury contain others (information from Mr Michael Kelly).
[5] Churchill, *Canterbury Administration*, i. 505–6.　　[6] See below, p. xxvii.
[7] For instance, in 1491 Adriano Castellesi was empowered to create 15 notaries, dispense 12 men and 12 women for marriage despite third and fourth or fourth only degrees of kindred and affinity; 12 persons under age to hold benefices in their 23rd year; 15 persons to take holy orders despite illegitimate birth; and an indult for 10 clerks to have the fruits of their benefices while studying (*C.P.L.* xiv. 54–55).
[8] Churchill, *Canterbury Administration*, i. 505–7.
[9] 21 Henry VIII, c. 13: *Statutes of the Realm*, iii. 292–6; edited in Gibson, *Codex Iuris*, ii. 945–9. See also below, pp. xxxvii sqq.

acquisition of dispensations to hold more than one benefice with cure of souls, or for non-residence, the king asserted the right to license his own chaplains for pluralities and non-residence (cl. XVII). The Act did not presume to challenge the pope's dispensing power, however, but merely revived claims which had been made long before by Edward I.

One may ask what motive—apart from conscience—compelled supplicants to sue for dispensations? As regards the two classes of dispensation restricted to the clergy, the question is easily answered: a dispensation was equivalent to a title-deed, charter, or patent, a legal weapon and testimonial: without it, ordination or institution to a benefice would be refused; embarrassment could be caused in visitations or litigation; reduction of status, or even excommunication, were risked. Dispensations extending to the laity, particularly those concerning marriage and eating prohibited food during Lent and other prescribed fasts, similarly must have been a judicious precaution against excommunication, as well as a means to silence scandalmongers: in the case of marriage, there was the risk of later allegations which would prove the contract invalid. To have all one's papers in order is a strong urge in a Hobbesian world: and it may be that there was also an element of clerical espionage in inquiries made into family backgrounds (though links of kindred through the fourth degree of affinity must sometimes have been difficult to prove or disprove). Yet it is difficult to find evidence suggesting that dispensations were obtained under pressure, rather than voluntarily. It is also difficult to discover what exactly were the first steps taken in seeking them. Did one apply to the bishop or his official, who referred cases to a known proctor in the Roman curia? It seems unlikely that direct contact could be made with proctors or couriers except perhaps in London, and a few other larger towns and seaports. Here, the want of knowledge is daunting: but it is clear that there was a formidable traffic of couriers and proctors travelling between England and Rome, even in the early sixteenth century, and notwithstanding the curious lack of notaries of English birth working in the curia during this period.[1]

[1] See my unpublished thesis 'English Representation at the Court of Rome in the Early Tudor Period' (Oxford D.Phil., 1962), pp. 89–91, in the Bodleian Library.

II

THE FACULTY ADMINISTRATION, 1534–1549

T HE new system for issuing dispensations came into effect on 12 March 1534: after this date any received from Rome were declared invalid under the Act. However, in 1536 another Act, much more anti-papal in tone, extended the date since, it asserted, papal dispensations had still been 'temerously and ignorantly receyved used and erroniusly exercised'. This Act conceded all papal dispensations for marriage up to 3 November 1534; all other papal dispensations would become invalid after Michaelmas 1537, when application should be made for their confirmation under the Great Seal.[1] Some evidence remains of these confirmations, though not in the registers.[2] Meanwhile, the first Faculty Office dispensations were issued in April 1534. The machinery of issue was complicated, and must be discussed here in some detail.

Archbishop Cranmer was not invested absolutely with the former papal power: the transference was conditional, for ultimately the power to loosen and bind rested with the king. While the archbishop and his successors

> . . after good and due examynacion by theym had of the causes and qualities of the persons procuring for licenses, dispensacions etc . . . shall have full power and auctoritie by theym selff or by theire sufficient and substanciall Comissarye or deputye by theire discreacions, from tyme to tyme, to graunte and dispose by an instrument under the name and seale of the seid Archebisshop . . . (cl. III)

only dispensations costing less than £4 ('whiche he mattiers of no great importance') could be issued under the archbishop's seal; others, costing more, could not

> . . . in any wyse be putt in execucion till the same . . . be fyrst confirmed by your Highness . . . under the greate Seale, and inrolled in your Chauncerie in a Roll by a Clerke to be appoynted for the same. . . . (cl. IV)

The cheaper dispensations 'of no greate importance'

---

[1] 28 Henry VIII, c. 16: *Statutes of the Realm*, iii. 672–3; Gibson, *Codex Iuris*, i. 111–14. The cost of confirmation by the archbishop and under the Great Seal was 25s. 6d. A special commission was set up to examine these called-in dispensations, in Nov. 1536: *L.P.* xi. 1217 (22).

[2] A number of papal letters granting dispensations and endorsed in 1537 survive at Lambeth (Papal Documents 108–26). These endorsements are not made by recognizable officials of the Faculty Office, however: maybe the signatures are those of chancery clerks. Other papal dispensations were redrafted and confirmed in the king's name (CM xi. 65–71; xii. 44–45, 50, 54). There is an entry in F I/Vv, f. 289ᵛ dispensing for holy orders despite defect of age, confirming a previous dispensation 'by the pretended authority of Rome'.

... shall not of any necessitie be confirmed by the greate seale onles the procurers of such licence, faculty, or dispensation desire to have theym soo confirmed; in whiche case they shall pay Vs.

However, the chancery clerk of the faculties

... shall also intitle and note particulerly and dayly in hys boke ordeyned for that purpose the nombre and qualitie of the Dispensacions etc. which shalbe sealed only with the seale of the said Archebisshop, and also which shalbe sealed with the seid seale and confirmed with the greate seale. (cl. VI)

In F I/Vv there are various entries recording that confirmation in chancery was sought, particularly in the case of dispensations for non-residence, by the marginal note 'pro sigillo regis Vs'. As there are no dispensation books or rolls of chancery surviving in the Public Record Office before Elizabeth's reign, the two faculty registers are the only comprehensive record of all classes of dispensation granted, despite this provision for a double administration.

The cumbersome sharing of authority with chancery was not the only limitation upon the archbishop's power. On his refusal to issue a dispensation, appeal could be made to the king, and should the archbishop or his deputy remain intractable, their authority might be taken away altogether.

Your Highness . . . shall have power and auctoritie in every suche case, for the default negligence and wylfulnes of the seid Archbishopp or gardiane, to sende your wrytt of Injuncion under your greate seale. . . . And yf the seid Archibishopp or gardiane, after the recept of the seid wrytt, refuse or denye to graunt suche licences faculties or dispensacions as shalbe inyoyned hym by vertue of the said Wrytte, and shewe and prove before your Majestie your heires or successors noo juste or resonable cause whye he shuld soo doo, then the seid Archebisshopp or gardyane . . . shall suffer lose and forfayte to your Highnes etc. suche payne and penaltie as shalbe lymytted and expressed in the seid wrytt of Injuncion; And over that it shalbe lawful to your Highnes . . . to geve power and auctoritie by commission under your greate seale to suche two spirituall prelatts, or persons to be named . . . as woll doo graunt suche licences etc. (cl. XI)

⋆   ⋆   ⋆

This erection of a sort of 'two-handed engine' for dispensations must not be forgotten when one speaks of the archbishop's Faculty Office. It has a special significance as the means whereby Thomas Cromwell was able to control the machine. In May 1534 he became Master of the Rolls, which gave him power over the clerks of chancery, second only to Lord Chancellor Audley; while Audley, in his more confined legal role, has been described as Cromwell's 'rather subservient partisan'.[1] Only a month or two earlier, Cromwell had become Principal Secretary, with

---

[1] G. R. Elton, *The Tudor Revolution in Government* (Cambridge, 1953), pp. 22–23, 129–33 *passim*, 260.

command over the signet clerks;[1] in January 1535 he was appointed the King's 'Vice-Regent, Vicar-General, and Special Commissary in Matters Spiritual':[2] 'the highest Ordinary in England under the King' one applicant for a dispensation called him.[3] In 1536 he became Lord Privy Seal.[4] In all these offices his authority was contingent to the faculty administration, and his hand can be detected in it from the beginning. The very first dispensation in F I/Vv, a plurality for Bishop Salcot of Bangor, was obtained after application to him.[5] A protégé of Cromwell, Stephen Vaughan, was appointed by patent in April 1534 the clerk responsible for writing and enrolling all the confirmations of dispensations in chancery.[6] Vaughan was often absent in the Low Countries, where he had commercial interests, and intermittently he held government commissions there; eventually, in 1544, he became the King's official financial agent at Antwerp, when he delegated the clerkship of the faculties to a young man called Griffith ap Vaughan,[7] probably a relation. It may be that in practice Vaughan's clerkship was little more than a sinecure; however, there is other evidence besides this of Cromwell's influence over dispensations. The many marginal notes in Register Vv of exhibition of warrants, ordering the free issue of dispensations, probably reflect his initiative, whether the warrants were under the signet or (from 1536 onwards) privy seal, though in some cases these warrants are described as warrants 'of the lords': perhaps they signify 'the lords of the council'. In 1535–6 the usual abbreviation in the margin is 'ost(enso) bill warranto'; from early in 1538 'per bill warrantum dominorum ostens(um)' is more common. In several cases there is even record of personal letters of Cromwell ('per litteram domini Crumwell'),[8] of the

---

[1] Elton, op. cit., pp. 123–6.

[2] Wilkins, *Concilia*, iii. 784; abstr. *L.P.* viii. 75.

[3] Tho. Megges to Cromwell, 8 Apr. 1536; abstr. *L.P.* x. 634.

[4] Elton, op. cit., pp. 133–4.

[5] See Salcot's letter as Abbot of Hyde to Cromwell, 4 Nov. 1533 in *State Papers*, i. (London, 1830), p. 410 (abstr. *L.P.* vi. 1396): '. . . I perseve the Poopys Hollynes wyll, in noo wysse, grawnte me the Bulle, accordynge to the tenor of my supplycacyon to hym made. . . . I beseeche yower Mastershypp to calle to yower remembrans, that ye devysyde, and thowght ytt goode, the Kynges Highnes to gyve me the temporaltees of the sayde Bysshoppryche; wheer on to I humbelly desyre yow to be a meene for me, yff ytt may stand. . . .'

[6] P.R.O., C. 66/663 m.37, cited by Elton, op. cit., p. 260 n. 2 (inadequate abstr. *L.P.* vii. 587, no. 13). Cromwell wrote to Vaughan in Sept. 1535 that he could not expect more from the King than his £20 salary and 'the office which his highnes latelie gave you of the Facultees', R. B. Merriman, *Life and Letters of Thomas Cromwell*, ii. 43 (abstr. *L.P.* x. 376). On Vaughan, see W. C. Richardson, 'Stephen Vaughan, Financial Agent of Henry VIII', *Louisiana State University Studies, Social Science Series*, iii (Baton Rouge, 1953); pp. 16–17 give evidence of personal friendship with Cromwell.

[7] Richardson, op. cit., pp. 82–83, n. 5. Vaughan's request for this in a letter of 22 Apr. 1544 (abstr. *L.P.* xix. i. 379) was followed by a patent dated 12 May (ibid. 610, n. 83). Vaughan wrote approvingly of this substitute, who was his own general agent (*L.P.* xix. ii. 652, 745, 751, 757). The clerkship continued in his own name until 1551 (*Cal. Pat Rolls, Edw. VI*, iv. 153).

[8] F I/Vv, ff. 91^r, 193^v, 201^v.

King[1] or Lord Chancellor.[2] The issue of warrants is noted against entries for every year in Register Vv except, curiously, 1537.

Cromwell's influence is traceable most of all in connexion with the issue of 'capacities' for monks and friars to hold benefices, especially, of course, during the dissolutions. This will be discussed more fully in a later chapter: but it may not be out of place to quote here a letter written to him by a Carthusian wanting to wear the habit of a secular priest and leave his Order in April 1534. This letter reveals that there was a decided confusion caused by the new system, and the dual control between the archbishop's Faculty Office and chancery. Peter Watts, Carthusian monk of Witham, was dismayed to find that his application to the former would not suffice:

Right honorable in my most humble manner I hartely commennde me unto yor honorable m(aster)ship mekely beschinge the same for the love of Jhu Chryste to tendre my necessitie and to obteyne the kyngs gracious consent and licens concernyng my capacitie and discharge from the charterhous men. Whereunto I founde my lordes good grace our metropolytane gracious and favorable in so much that his grace had fully granted me my capacitie the which was writen and sealed and mony payde therfore. And now when I shuld have inioyed it: it was witholden for what consideration I cannot tell, but I understonde because yt lacked the consent and licens of the kyngs noble grace that was required to be had unto the same under the brod seale. The which yff it wold please yor honorable m(aste)rship to speke unto the kyngs noble grace for: yow shuld bynd me and my poere friends to pray for yor goodnes. Wher as we be not able otherwys to do any suche licke pleasure or make recompens. I wold a put myself hertofore in prece [sic] to a ben poere sewter unto yor honorable m(aste)rship: but I fered taching [sic] and so by the counsail of mr Wodall secretary unto the same, I sewed unto my lord of canterburye thinkyng that his grace had had sufficient autoritie & poere to a dispached my busynes withought to be autorized of any higher poere. . . .[3]

This confusion may have been largely owing to the newness of the whole procedure in April 1534: but there is some further evidence to suggest that the requirements for confirmation in chancery did sometimes slow down the issue of a dispensation. Watts, for instance, had to wait till March 1535—nearly a year—before his dispensation was released.[4] That dispensations were ever refused confirmation in chancery is unlikely: at any rate, it must be assumed that their entry in the Faculty Office registers, with a note of the fee paid, signifies a valid expedition. On the other hand, the date in the registers should be treated with caution, as technically the dispensation would not be valid until it had also received the dated fiat of the chancery

---

[1] Ibid., ff. 208ʳ, 326ᵛ. [2] Ibid., ff. 8ʳ, 43ᵛ, 326ᵛ.
[3] P.R.O. SP 1/83, f. 192 (abstr. *L.P.* vii. 577); mentioned by G. Baskerville, *English Monks and the Suppression of the Monasteries* (London, 1937), p. 153.
[4] F I/Vv, f. 29ʳ.

clerk of dispensations. In two cases where letters of dispensations have survived, there has been a discrepancy of dates.[1]

★ ★ ★

As well as this 'two-handed engine' of chancery and archbishop's Faculty Office, dispensations could still be issued from various other sources, under the provisions of the Act of 1533.

The king himself, besides his rights under the Pluralities Act, had in theory the power to issue any dispensation, though he did not exert the royal supremacy outrageously in this field. His general dispensations for eating 'white meats' in Lent will be discussed more fully in a later chapter;[2] otherwise the royal dispensing power seems to have been limited to its indirect authority in chancery confirmations, special warrants, and Cromwell's initiative as vicar-general. The Archbishop of York and diocesan bishops were still permitted to dispense in cases admitted previously (cl. IX) and evidently did so; for instance, Edmund Bonner as Bishop of London put his experience in Wolsey's faculty office to good use;[3] Foxe's register at Hereford also contains lists of dispensations for marriage after one reading of the banns, as well as licences for friars to preach.[4] However, it is striking how the Faculty Office encroached upon the diocesan's authority; not only was its formal confirmation sought, but in some cases its direct licence for preachers,[5] celebration in chapels of ease,[6] new graveyards,[7] unions of churches,[8] the collection of alms,[9] delegation of an archdeacon's duties,[10] &c.: cases which had not formerly required application to Rome.

Cranmer himself probably left much of the routine work of dispensing to his office staff, rather than sit himself in a special court of audience or (on the papal analogy) *segnatura*. In the most important cases, for instance that of Henry VIII's dispensation from third-degree affinity and reading of the banns to marry Jane Seymour, the letters were signed by Cranmer himself;[11] but normally his name would simply appear at the formal head of

---

[1] See below, p. xxix. [2] See below, p. xxxix.

[3] e.g. licence for marriage after one reading of the banns, 17 Apr. 1541 (Reg. Bonner, Guildhall Museum, London, MS. 9531/12, f. xiiv) and a licence to eat meat in Lent, 12 Mar. 1540 (ibid., f. xviii).

[4] Ed. A. T. Bannister, *Cant. & York Soc.* xxviii (1921), pp. 372, 380. The registers for Bath and Wells, Winchester, and Durham during this period are also printed; they do not include dispensations, but one cannot infer none were issued. Archbishop Lee's register at York contains several marriage dispensations concerning banns (f. 85ᵛ, 101ʳ) during 1534–6, and two licences for beneficed clerks to study in 1536 (f. 107). Preachers are licensed in 1534 (f. 85ᵛ).

[5] F I/Vv, ff. 9ʳ, 44ʳ, 58ʳ; F I/A, p. 8.

[6] F I/Vv, ff. 6ʳ, 32ʳ, 70ʳ, 215ᵛ, 263ᵛ, 275ᵛ, 295ʳ; F I/A, pp. 252, 254.

[7] F I/Vv, ff. 70ʳ, 139ᵛ, 209ʳ, 299ᵛ, 300ʳ; confirmations, ff. 229ᵛ, 273ʳ, 274ᵛ, 374ᵛ.

[8] Ibid., ff. 15ʳ, 43ʳ, 193ʳ. [9] Ibid., ff. 7ʳ, 8ʳ.

[10] Ibid., f. 138ᵛ. [11] P.R.O. E 30/1472/1 (abstr. *L.P.* x. 915).

the letters. Yet there may have been a certain amount of personal super-vision. The Carthusian Peter Watts, whose letter has been quoted above, seems to have applied to Cranmer himself, not to any intermediary; and Cranmer's personal refusal to issue several marriage dispensations can be documented.[1] Possibly it was when the grounds of supplication were not straightforward that he took a case into consideration, or when it was made through influential channels.

There is little evidence to illustrate the early working of the Faculty Office. It has not even been established who was the first 'sufficient and substanciall Commissary or deputye' or 'gardiane' of the faculties (as the Dispensations Act variously described this officer). There is no record of such an appointment in Cranmer's episcopal register until that of Dr Nicholas Wotton in 1538.[2] This does not, however, constitute evidence that no appointment was made; for Cranmer's register does not in any case include any other of his appointments before 1538 (we cannot discover from it who were his first vicar-general, commissary, and official, either). There is a literary tradition that the first commissary, deputy, guardian, or master (the term later adopted) of the faculties was none other than Edmund Bonner,[3] fresh from his experiences of this sort of work under Wolsey; but this has not been confirmed. There is, however, some more convincing evidence that the office was held by a clerk called Roger Tonneshend or Townsend, at any rate by 1536. His signature, as 'Rogerus Tonneshend Commiss.', appears on two early letters of dispensation which survive in their out-going form: one of 1 July 1536 permitting the marriage without banns of Lord Henry Manners and Lady Mary Nevell,[4] and another of 20 July 1536 to Richard Sampson, Bishop of Chichester, permitting him to hold the deanery of St. Paul's *in commendam*.[5] There is also extant a letter from Wriothesley to Tonneshend, of the following month, asking him to make out capacities for the religious of Bittlesden Abbey.[6] Tonnes-hend was described as in Cranmer's service (in which he was allowed to remain) by a patent appointing him a royal chaplain in August 1537.[7]

Nicholas Wotton's appointment on 16 October 1538 specifically bestowed in his care the seal of the faculties, and the right to a share in the fees

---

[1] See below, pp. xxxiii–xxxiv.

[2] Lamb. Pal. Lib. Reg. Cranmer, f. 217. On Wotton's career see *D.N.B.*, article by A. F. Pollard.

[3] J. Strype, *Memorials of Archbishop Cranmer* i (Oxford, 1812), 102.

[4] Lamb. Pal. Lib., CM vi. 69. See frontispiece, and below, pp. xxvii–xxviii.

[5] Hatfield House, Salisbury MSS. I 49 (abstr. *H.M.C. Reports*, 1883, p. 11; *L.P.* xi. 125). There is a microfilm in the B.M. MSS. Dept. (M 485/i).

[6] Abstr. *L.P.* x. 1248.

[7] Ibid., xii. ii. 617 (6). A dispensation describes him as D.C.L. and King's chap-lain in F I/Vv, f. 147ʳ, though not as commissary of the faculties, but nor is Wotton so described in 1544, F I/A, pp. 72–73. Tonneshend's signature also appears in a formal renunciation of papal supremacy in 1534, B.M. Add. MS. 38656, f. 1; for reproduction, see D. Hay, *The Italian Renaissance* (Cambridge, 1961), plate xxiv.

specified under the statute. Previously Wotton had been the Official of Tunstall, Bishop of London; he had sat in the Legatine Court hearing the Divorce in 1529, and had canvassed foreign universities with Edward Foxe, seeking support for the king. Wotton was clearly a man of the régime, and in Cromwell's confidence. It was he who fetched from Cleves the notorious portrait in 1539 and despite the inauspicious outcome of the affair, he continued to serve frequently as a diplomatist during the next decade. However, the office of commissary of the faculties was one of the few where Cromwell had to suffer a set-back of his patronage. For when he proposed another protégé, William Petre, instead of Wotton, Cranmer replied with a fairly crushing refusal:

My veray singular good Lorde After my most harte Commendacons theis shalbe to advertise yor Lordeship that I have receyvid your Lres for the preferment of Mr Doctour Peter under Doctor Wottons rowme of the faculties whan it shall channce by the promotion of the said Doctour Wotton to be voide/ Suerly my Lord I woulde be as gladde of Mr Peters preferment as of any maniys lyving to that Office, for suche good qualities as I knowe in hym of olde. But in dede my lorde I have promised it unto my Commissarie Doctour Nevynson, who hat of me xxti marks by yere and can spende no penye with condition that he should surrender it unto my handes Whan I hadd gyvin hym a benefice/ Wherfore if your Lordeship of your goodnes will provid sume benefice for my Commissarye, I shall both satisfie your lordeships request and deliver myself of my promyse. And this I wryte bycaus I have many to provid for and litle to provide theym of. As concernyng the kings maiestie I will not strive with his highnes. howbeit I suppose the gifts should apperteigne unto me, considering Mr Wotton hath it, but only at my pleasour.[1]

In fact no vacancy occurred, and Wotton continued in name to be commissary or guardian of the faculties throughout the period covered by the two first registers, despite his long absences abroad on diplomatic missions. He appointed as surrogate James Rokeby, an Auditor of the Court of Augmentations, from 26 March 1543;[2] and on 18 February 1545 the seal and book of faculty charges were handed over to Dr William Coke,[3] who on 28 February 1545 became Dean of the Court of Arches.[4]

[1] P.R.O. SP I/83, f. 192 (abstr. *L.P.* vii. 577); referred to by Hooper, art. cit., *E.H.R.* xxx (1910), 682–3, and, in a misleading context, by F. G. Emmison, *Tudor Secretary, Sir William Petre* (London, 1961), p. 43.

[2] F I/A, p. 50, Memorandum by Anthony Huse of moneys received on 31 May 1544 from James Rokeby, surrogate for expediting faculties, since Mar. 1543. There are many references to Rokeby in *L.P.*, and he was also a doctor of laws of the Court of Arches (Reg. Cranmer, f. 40).

[3] F I/A, p. 106.

[4] Churchill, *Canterbury Administration*, i. 595. He was probably the Wm Coke who was elected a fellow of All Souls in 1525, B.C.L. Feb. 1528, r. of Elmley, Kent, on 9 Jan. 1532 (Reg. Warham, f. 414), and later a chief agent in Bonner's persecutions. I am grateful for this information to Dr A. B. Emden.

The Dispensations Act had also laid down that the archbishop should appoint a clerk in the Faculty Office, and this clerk in practice must have done most of the work:

. . . the seid Archebishop and hys successours shall have power and auctoritie to ordeyne make and constitute a Clerke, which shall (wrytte) and regestre every suche licence dispensacion facultie wrytyng or other instrument to be graunted by the seid Archbishop and shall fynde parchment, waxe and sylken laces convenyent for the same. . . . As well the seid Clerke appoynted by the seid Archebishop as the seid (chancery) Clerke to be appoynted by your Highness, your heirs or successors, shall subscribe theire names to every suche licence, dispensacion, faculty, or other wrytyng. (cl. v)

The likeliest holder of this office is Anthony Huse, Cranmer's registrar. His signature appears on some of the confirmations of the papal and legatine dispensations mentioned above.[1] There is a letter of 25 April 1539 from Cromwell jointly to Wotton, Vaughan, and 'Hewis', asking them to issue capacities for the White friars (Carmelites) of Northampton,[2] thus linking them as the three persons most concerned with the practical side of issuing dispensations. Anthony Huse is also noted in F I/A as Wotton's proctor, receiving money on his behalf.[3] The identification of Anthony Huse is slightly confused, however, by the existence of an official with the name of John Hughes, who had served in Wolsey's Legatine Faculty Office. His signature appears on two of Wolsey's outgoing letters,[4] and also on the two surviving letters of the new Faculty Office in July 1536.[5] Possibly he was then serving Vaughan as a clerk of chancery, rather than Tonneshend in the Faculty Office. For his signature in the 1536 marriage dispensation appears on the opposite side to Tonneshend's, and beneath the formal signature of Vaughan.[6] The 'Mr Hewis' of Cromwell's letter could, of course, refer to either individual. As well as Huse and Hughes, there may have been yet other assistants who did the physical work of copying, sealing, and registering the dispensations; Cromwell's letter to Wotton, Vaughan, and Huse was also addressed 'in their absence to their depute'.

The way the early Faculty Office conducted its business, the procedure of applying for a dispensation, the hearing of evidence, drawing up of allegations, employment or not of proctors or of influential patrons[7] to

---

[1] Lamb. Pal. Lib., CM iv. 8, 10, 11; xi. 65–67, 69, 71. (See also above, p. xviii n. 3, p. xx n. 2).

[2] R. B. Merriman, *Life and Letters of Thomas Cromwell* (Oxford, 1902), ii. 222 (abstr. *L.P.* xiv. i. 852). See also below p. lii.

[3] Below, p. lxiv.

[4] Lamb. Pal. Lib., Papal Documents, 133–4. On the former he signs as 'actuarius et commissarius'. There is certainly no question of Huse and Hughes being the same person; quite apart from the difference of names, the signatures are distinctly different.

[5] Above, p. xxv.   [6] Not visible in frontispiece.

[7] This seems to have been the case of the canon of Bodmin who fell foul of his prior for obtaining a capacity in May 1535 (see below, p. xlvi). The prior complained in a letter to

hasten a suit, whether it was summary routine or could be quite protracted, established at Lambeth, or itinerant with the archbishop, eludes us. In the later seventeenth century the suitor had to present a petition giving details, which would receive the archbishop's fiat with his signature and then be forwarded to the Faculty Office for the letters of dispensation to be drawn up.[1] Office routine tends to be conservative so this may well have been the practice from 1534 onwards. Few of the letters survive: presumably because they were valid to the holder at longest only for his life: there was little motive for preservation. However, it is still conceivable that others may be lying in muniment rooms all over the country.

The Manners–Nevill marriage dispensation, signed by Tonneshend and Hughes, and (formally) by Vaughan, showing that chancery confirmation was sought, has already been mentioned. It is written on parchment and bears the battered remains of its seal suspended on a cord: unfortunately the seal is in too bad a condition to be recognizable as the seal of the faculties. The survival of this dispensation may be due to the fact that only a day before (according to the register) the parties had obtained a different faculty: dispensing with a spiritual degree of relationship:[2] so it is likely that another letter was drafted to cover both. The seal of the faculties is also missing from Henry VIII's dispensation to marry Jane Seymour, and from Richard Sampson's dispensation to hold the deanery of St Paul's. There also survives a 'capacity' addressed to Thomas Pope, Abbot of Hartland, to become a secular priest and hold a benefice; it is dated 21 April 1539, endorsed by 'Nicholas Wotton Commissarius' and bears a couple of fragments of seal on red strings attached to it ('.ACULTATES.' is the only portion of the legend remaining). A most interesting feature of this dispensation is that a royal letter patent, separately confirming it, is attached by means of the tag of the letters patent, which also bear a large battered piece of the Great Seal.[3] Besides these originals, three capacities for ex-religious of the diocese of York are entered in full, with royal confirmation, in Archbishop Lee's register there.[4] Such entries are most

W. Loke, a London mercer, 'I am sore thretynyd with won master Roger Arundell, a gret berar and mayntynar of my bretherne agenst me, and the procurar of there capacites' (T. Wright, *Letters Relating to the Suppression of the Monasteries*, Camden Soc., xxvi. 1843. 130–1).

[1] Information from Mrs. Jane Houston, who has worked on the later Faculty Office records in preparation for the Guide to Lambeth Palace Library Archives.

[2] F I/Vv, f. 77ʳ, dated 29 June. The second dispensation is dated 30 June in the register (f. 77ʳ) though 1 July on the outgoing letter (see frontispiece).

[3] Dean and Chapter Library, Exeter, D. & C., Exeter, 1036–7. I am very grateful to Mrs. Audrey M. Erskine, for this description, and for checking as correct the text of the letters printed in G. Oliver, *Monasticon Diocesis Exoniensis* (Exeter, 1846), p. 216.

[4] Borthwick Institute, York, Reg. Lee, f. 105ᵛ, for James Hicks, O.C.Fr., 20 Mar. 1536 (F I/Vv, f. 59ᵛ); f. 111ʳ for William, canon of Guisborough 15 Oct. 1538 (F I/Vv, f. 219ʳ); f. 111ʳ–111ᵛ for Robert Hull, alias Tomsone, canon of Thornton, 23 Oct. 1538 (F I/Vv, f. 220ᵛ).

exceptional. A study of registers of the period might show, however, that they are not unique. Lee's register also contains a Faculty Office licence, with royal confirmation, for the inhabitants of Elstanwicke in Holderness to use a new graveyard at a chapel of ease.[1]

In form, it seems that the letters issued by the Faculty Office corresponded very closely to those previously issued from Rome, though they are not written in an Italianate humanist script. Anti-papal polemics apart (and the Dispensations Act, passed in 1533, really ante-dated the climax there), the basic difference between the old and new systems was supposed to be that the latter would be cheaper and more rapid. The question of cost will be kept for a later chapter, but about quickness of dispatch something may be said here. The Act stated

. . . some tymes the spedyng of suche dispensacions etc. at Rome have byn soo longe differred that the partyes laboryng for the same have suffered great incommodities. . . . (cl. VI)

It cannot be shown in general how lengthy the procedure was between the initial application and delivery of the letters, but certain cases of considerable delay can be proved. The example of Peter Watts, the Carthusian, has already been given;[2] that of the Abbot of Hartland was just as slow. His Faculty Office dispensation, signed by Wotton, is dated 21 April 1539; but its entry in the register[3] and the confirming letters patent out of chancery[4] took nearly a year later to come, being dated 17 April 1540. More evidence will be shown later of the troublesome delays which the religious suffered before receiving their capacities.[5]

On the whole, the new system set in motion by the Dispensations Act seems to have been clumsy, if not ramshackle, with its division of authority, absentee officials, and jurisdiction overlapping that of the diocesan bishop.[6] It extended throughout England and Wales, even to Calais, Guernsey, Guisnes, and Boulogne, and must have been intended to apply to Ireland: but there were different views on the propriety of this. Ireland presented a special problem. A letter from Sir Thomas Audley to Cromwell in 1535 expresses the view that the system should apply there:

. . . My poor advise ys that concernyng the Act for Dispensations, that the subgettes of Irlond shuld take their dispensations here, in Englond, at the handes of the Archebisshop of Canterbery, with confirmation under the Gret Seale, as

---

[1] Reg. Lee, ff. 106ʳ–106ᵛ, dated 18 July 1536. This does not appear in F I/Vv.
[2] Above, p. xxiii.   [3] F I/Vv, f. 322ᵛ.
[4] The date is Apr. 17 ann. 31 Henry VIII. Mrs. Erskine confirms that this discrepancy in the dates of the two documents is correct.
[5] Below, pp. li sqq.
[6] '. . . the granting of Dispensations was continued, although in a desultory way, without any proper study of the principles, and in the absence of any clearly defined system', W. Sparrow Simpson, *Dispensations* (S.P.C.K., 1935), p. 96. This judgement, though reached without any study of the Faculty Office registers, still seems fairly valid.

the Kynges Inglische subgettes now do; by cause Englond ys the chife part of the Crown, and Irlond a membir appendaunt to it. And me semyth this way were honerable for the kynge, and not to enhabill eny Primate of Irlond to graunt such dispensations.[1]

But in January 1537 a letter to Cromwell from Archbishop George Brown of Dublin gave quite different advice:

I have advertized your Lordeschip, dyvers tymes, what inconvenience mought fall for lake of dispensacions; for, in that poynte, they be compelled to sew to Rome, Wherfore I think good, that, with all celeritie and spede, it were necessary that we had dispensacions, a Vicar Generall, and a Master of the Faculties. . . .[2]

There can be little doubt that Brown was right: the Irish were still applying to Rome. There are a certain number of dispensations for Irish suitors entered in both registers,[3] but they cannot correspond to all the cases for which they must have been required during this period. Nevertheless, Brown's advice seems to have gone unheeded until, in 1546, a commission was granted to the Bishop of Meath, assisted by 'a temporal man', one Dr Rede, to issue dispensations 'as my Lord of Canterbury does, the lack whereof drives many to seek them at Rome'.[4] But it is worth bearing in mind that the Irish had preferred to apply to Rome even in the days of Wolsey's legatine faculties, which it could be argued did not explicitly refer to Ireland. The Irish were said to obtain financial concessions at the curia, and Wolsey was advised to make similar concessions in order to gain their custom.[5] Perhaps the new Faculty Office would also have had more success there had it adjusted its tariff.

[1] *State Papers*, i (London, 1830), pp. 438–9; abstr. *L.P.* ix. 41.
[2] *State Papers*, ii (London, 1834), p. 540; abstr. *Cal. Carew Papers (1515–74)*, 114, mentioned by Hooper, art. cit., *E.H.R.* xxv (1910), 684. Hooper seems to have invented a statute whereby the faculty administration was extended to Ireland, possibly by misreading a note in the *Cal. of Irish State Papers*, p. 35.
[3] F I/Vv, ff. 34ᵛ, 105ᵛ, 193ʳ, 196ʳ, 248ᵛ, 269ᵛ, 272ᵛ, 274ʳ, 320ᵛ, 330ʳ, 331ᵛ, 332ᵛ, 338ᵛ, 339ʳ; F I/A, pp. 29, 31, 45–46. A marriage dispensation (consanguinity) for a couple from Drogheda, dated 9 Jan. 1539, in the Archbishop of Canterbury's name, appears in the early part of Archbishop Dowdall of Armagh's register; A. Gwynne, *The Medieval Province of Armagh 1470–1545* (Dundalk, 1946), p. 254. This seems significant as there is no corresponding entry in F I/Vv.
[4] *State Papers*, iii (London, 1834), p. 580; abstr. *L.P.* xxi (2), 156. Irish 'Rome runners' were said to be passing by way of Scotland in 1538–9 (*L.P.* xiii. ii. 159; xiv. i. 1245).
[5] John Alen to Wolsey, 1 June 1523? or 1529?: '. . . Abought the degrees of consanguinitie and affinitie, your Gracis bulles be not verraie cleare for this countrie which hurtith. . . . For many partes under the Kinges obeysaunce ther been penall statutes, that no Inglishman shall marie with thIrish, so that they be so intricate in consanguinitie or affinitie, and besides that, the people of themselff be propine to evill, they wold marie withought dispensacion, orelles be infourcid to sue to the Courte of Rome. Wherof hath insued the decaie of the churche of Irelonde; for whan an idill person gooth to the Courte of Rome, the compositions be to Irishmen so small for ther povertie, that by him many other exorbitant matiers be sped. So that, in this lande, your Graces dispensations be necessarie to be graunted with lesse difficultie, than elles wheare for thavoiding of con-

In England and Wales, however, applications for, and issue of, dispensations seem to have been very regular. Presumably much the same motives and scruples caused them to be sought as before, and the procedure was slightly less tedious than it had been under papal supremacy. Nevertheless, it would be hard to show that this particular change of Henrician 'reformation' was much appreciated. John Husee, Lord Lisle's steward, commented after difficulties about a marriage dispensation, 'I pray God send me little ado with any spiritual men':[1] he probably expressed an attitude that was fairly general.

tempte of holy canons, and thoccasion of theinconvenience that foloith of their Rome runners. And over that, the maner of the compositions in this lande for ther povertie, shulde be reduced from sterling money to the money of this countrie; wherby I suppose we shulde spede thre dispensations than to oon nowe' (*State Papers*, ii. 102; abstr. *L.P.* iv. 5625).

[1] Abstr. *L.P.* xiii. 227.

III

DISPENSATIONS ISSUED BY THE FACULTY OFFICE, AND THEIR SIGNIFICANCE

1. *Continuity*

UNDER the Dispensations Act the power was assumed for issuing every species of dispensation previously issued from Rome. There was no hint of a reform on principle: in fact it was represented as a tightening-up: not

> ... to declyne or vary from the congregacion of Christis Churche in any thynges concernyng the veray articles of the Catholyke Feith of Christendome ... only to make an Ordynaunce by policies necessary and conveyente to represse vice, and for good conservacion of this Realme in pease unytie and tranquyllitie from (ravyne) and spoyle. (cl. XIII)

Similarly, the Act for the Submission of the Clergy had enforced the continued application of the canon law and although a committee had been established to study its revision[1] the committee's successive proposals never came to anything.[2] In the course of time, however, two drastic changes were made, affecting very radically the scope of the Faculty Office. One of these, of course, was the dissolution of the monasteries and friaries, which (once the spate of 'capacities' accompanying the suppression had passed) meant that the large range of dispensations which had affected the regular clergy no longer existed. The other was the alteration of the marriage laws in 1540, 'The Act for Marriages to stand notwithstanding Precontract'.[3] This swept away not only dispensations invalidating pre-contract, but all the prohibited degrees except those originally laid down in the Book of Leviticus. These changes explain why F I/Vv is so much larger and more varied in its contents than F I/A, and why the Faculty Office, after a flourishing start, declined so rapidly in power and revenue.[4] It is certainly a misfortune that no register at all survives for the very period of this climacteric: for three years from the winter of 1540 to that of 1543. One wonders was there a breakdown in the administration, due to Wotton's absence, and perhaps reflecting Cromwell's disappearance from the scene: or was a short register kept for the intervening period which has since been lost?[5]

---

[1] 25 Henry VIII, c. 19: *Statutes of the Realm*, iii. 460–1.
[2] J. Ridley, *Thomas Cranmer* (Oxford, 1962), p. 331.
[3] 32 Henry VIII, c. 38: *Statutes of the Realm*, iii. 793.   [4] See below, pp. lxiii–lxv.
[5] The backlog in F I/A might strengthen the view no register was kept, though it would be more convincing were the backlog larger.

Despite these modifications in scope, the Faculty Office was still regarded by some as a disgraceful instance of the Scarlet Woman's survival. In his *Complaint of Roderyck Mors* (c. 1542), the ex-Franciscan, Henry Brincklow, complained the bishops

... wold have made the Kyng their pope, and they gave hym auctoryte to doo all things in England that the pope dyd in Rome: as, to forbyd maryage certen tymes in the yeare, and than to sell licencys for the same, to selle lycence to eat flesh in Lent, non residencys, and such other.[1]

2. *Dispensations for marriage*

Since Henry VIII's case against Catherine of Aragon was based on the proposition that marriage with a brother's widow was unlawful, and a dispensation for this invalid, dispensations for marriage within the prohibited degrees were a topical subject in the 1530's. It is not surprising that at first policy favoured reinforcing the prohibitions. On the other hand, that there would be some relaxation seems to have been expected in certain clerical as well as lay circles. A too-progressive priest called William Glynn even wrote to Cromwell in November 1535 inquiring whether the 'popish law' still stood whereby marriages within the fourth degree or connexion by affinity were invalid; his glee that there was a reduction in 'the sale of abusions and mart of vice' seems a little premature.[2] Cromwell himself that year had drafted a memorandum for an Act 'that all persons shall marry at their liberties in all degrees and cases not prohibited by God's Law'.[3] Nevertheless, a glance at F I/Vv will show the formidable number of dispensations for marriage within the prohibited degrees issued by the Faculty Office during its first six years of existence: by far the largest single class of entries.[4]

Cranmer himself took a fairly rigid line over the prohibited degrees. He personally refused an application made with Cromwell's own backing for marriage with a deceased wife's niece, and wished the divine prohibitions laid down in the Act of Succession in 1533[5] had been more comprehensive: he wrote in September 1536:

... And whereas your lordship writeth to me in the favour of this bearer, Massey, an old servant to the King's highness, that being contracted to his sister's daughter of his late wife deceased, he might enjoy the benefit of a dispensation in that behalf, specially considering it is none of the cases of prohibition contained in the statute, surely, my lord, I would gladly accomplish your request herein,

---

[1] *Henry Brincklow's Complaint of Roderyck Mors*, ed. J. M. Cowper, Early Eng. Text Soc., Extra Series xxii (London, 1874), 35.

[2] B.M. Harl. MS. 604, f. 75; abstr. *L.P.* ix. 748.

[3] Abstr. *L.P.* ix. 725.   [4] See below, p. xxxvi for figures.

[5] 25 Henry VIII, c. 22: *Statutes of the Realm*, iii. 472 (cl. II); the prohibitions were extended in 28 Henry VIII, c. 7 (ibid., p. 658).

if the word of God would permit the same. And as touching the act of parliament concerning the degrees prohibited by God's law, they be not so plainly set forth as I would they were. Wherin I somewhat spak my mind at the making of the said, but it was not then accepted. . . .[1]

There is some evidence that Cranmer was even inclined to stick over granting minor marriage dispensations. It was difficulty about 'a licence to marry with once asking' that had provoked John Husee's acid remark about 'spiritual men':[2] maybe, in the reactionary atmosphere of 1539, Cranmer was becoming alarmed by reports of abuses caused by a too liberal dispensing of the rules about banns.[3] Stephen Vaughan himself implied in March 1546 that Cranmer could be difficult, when asking Paget to obtain a licence directly from the king for him to marry his second wife at Calais,

. . . And if yor plesur wer to signifye that the Kings Majeste gevith me lycence to mary there without banys or askyng, so shuld I not be troublyd to sue to my lorde of Canterbury for a lycence, who therein woll make no small scruple. . . .[4]

It appears from this that Cranmer retained a considerable initiative over the more strictly spiritual dispensations. Perhaps he saw his part as equivalent to that of the cardinal penitentiary. Having himself been English penitentiary at Rome for a short time,[5] Cranmer would have been well aware of the distinction in the dispensing power.

There is, however, an unpleasant note of hypocrisy or subservience in contrast to this rigidity, when one considers how the system of marital dispensations was tailored to the King's convenience. This went much further than the affair of Catherine of Aragon, and the dispensation to marry Jane Seymour. For it was by casuistry over dispensations that Henry was relieved of his contracts both to Anne Boleyn and Anne of Cleves. In the Boleyn case, one allegation was of a pre-contract between her and the Earl of Northumberland; this had been denied on oath by the latter in 1532 when Henry was about to marry her, and he repeated this in 1536 in a letter to Cromwell;[6] nevertheless, there is still a possibility that it was this impediment Anne was prevailed upon to confess to Cranmer when he was 'sitting judicially'. More convincing, however, is the way out emphasized by Cranmer's recent biographer:[7] the ban upon marriage to the sister of

[1] E. Cox, *Miscellaneous Writings and Letters of Thomas Cranmer* (Parker Soc., Cambridge, 1846), pp. 328–9; abstr. *L.P.* xi. 416.

[2] See above, p. xxxi.

[3] N.B. the supplication complaining about 'persons who avoiding the ordinary's jurisdiction go to privileged places . . . and there without banns asked, by virtue of licence from the archbishop of Canterbury confirmed under the Great Seal, procure marriages with others, who are often lawfully contracted already' (abstr. *L.P.* xiv. i. 870).

[4] P.R.O. SP/I/215, f. 19 (abstr. *L.P.* xxx. i. 347). Nevertheless, a Faculty Office dispensation was issued for him, not mentioning Calais (F I/A, p. 195).

[5] Ridley, *Cranmer*, p. 31.   [6] Abstr. *L.P.* x. 864.

[7] Ridley, *Cranmer*, pp. 106–9.

one's mistress hastily added to the second Act of Succession. The Pope's dispensation of 1527 permitting Henry to contract such a marriage was, moreover, invalidated by that Act of 1536 already mentioned which cancelled, or at any rate called in for confirmation, all dispensations previously received from Rome. In any case, Cranmer's judgement, which he never publicly expounded, was one of the most sinister instances of 'doublethink' of his career. In the Cleves case, the whole affair from beginning to end was Faculty Office jobbery. Nicholas Wotton himself, Commissary of the Faculties, had been sent to Cleves in the summer of 1539 to investigate the possibilities of the marriage, and had reported that Anne was not bound by previous marriage covenants with the Duke of Lorraine,[1] and Stephen Vaughan was also involved in entertaining her in Antwerp and bringing her to London.[2] Nevertheless, six months after Henry's marriage with Anne in January 1540, this pre-contract was brought up again as valid grounds for invalidating the marriage. Cranmer went back on his opinion of the contract's technicalities: before he had pronounced it *de futuro*, now he pronounced it *de presenti*.[3] In the farcical proceeding before Convocation in June, Anthony Hughes read out the deposition in Cranmer's presence.[4]

Perhaps the most cynical touch of all was that the Act for Marriages to stand Notwithstanding Pre-contract[5] was passed the same year. It was represented as a moral reform: too many divorces had been made possible by these allegations:[6]

. . . heretofore divers and many persones after longe contynuaunces togither in matrimonye, without any allegation of either of the parties, or anny other at their mariage, whie the same matrimony should not be good, juste and laufull, and after the same matrimony solemnised and consummate by carnall knowlege . . . have nevertheless by an unjuste law of the Bishop of Rome, whiche is that uppon pretence of a former contracte made and not consummate by carnall copulation, for profe whereof two witness by that lawe were onely required, been divorsed and separate, contrarie to Goddis lawe and so the true matrimony . . . clerely frustrate and dissolved; Further also by reason of other prohibitions than Goddis lawe admitteth, for their lucre by that Courte invented, the dispensation whereof they alwaies reservid to themselfis, as in kynnerede or affinitie betwene cousyngermaynes, and so to fourth and fourth degree, carnell knowlege of anny of the same kynne or affinitie bifore in suche outwarde degrees, which elys were lauful, and he not prohibited by Goddis lawe, and all bicause they wolde gett monney by

[1] Abstr. *L.P.* xiv. ii. 33. Wotton in his letter had judiciously underpraised Anne, noting that she could neither sing nor play, and was dominated by her mother.
[2] W. C. Richardson, *Stephen Vaughan*, p. 41.
[3] Ridley, *Cranmer*, p. 205. [4] Abstr. *L.P.* xv. 860.
[5] 32 Henry VIII, c. 38: *Statutes of the Realm*, iii. 792.
[6] Allegations of consanguinity could also, of course, be used as an escape route. In the case of Sir Henry Everingham, the Archbishop of York wrote to Cromwell in May 1538 that Lady Everingham had vowed there was no consanguinity between the parties, as alleged (abstr. *L.P.* xiii. i. 960).

it, and kepe a reputation to their usurped jurisdiction . . . mariages have been brought into suche an uncertainty thereby, that no mariage coulde be so surely knytt and bounden, but it shulde lye in either of the parties power . . . to prove a precontracte. . . . From July 1 1540 no reservation or prohibition, Goddis Lawe except, shall trouble or impeach any marriage without the Levitical degrees.

The revolutionary change, or contraction of scope, that this imposed upon the Faculty Office will at once be appreciated, though strange to say F I/Vv shows that the issue of such dispensations did not cease altogether on 1 July 1540. In fact, on that very day one of the most elaborate and expensive dispensations for marriage in the whole register is recorded, for an Irish couple:[1] probably they were unaware of the new law, at any rate it is on record that they paid £12. 10s. unnecessarily. There are eight other dispensations for marriages despite the abolished degrees during that month of July, and one as late as 24 October.[2] It is a nice question whether the Faculty Office was being outrageously dishonest in continuing to issue them, or whether the people who applied did not trust the new law or their consciences, and insisted on having (redundant) letters issued. However, such entries were exceptions; the difference made by the Act is at once clear from a comparison of figures for this class of dispensation in 1540 with the previous years. All that were left, and which still occur in Register A, were the dispensations concerning banns, choice of churches, and the prohibited times. It is remarkable how the number of these tended to rise.

Marriage Dispensations

Prohibited degrees	1534/5	1536	1537	1538	1539	1540
4th consang., affin.	134	46(1)	58(3)	67(3)	67(1)	35(3)
3rd	26	6(1)	8(2)	9	9	9(1)
4th and 3rd	94	34(1)	48(1)	60	57	27(1)
3rd and 2nd	10	4	2	5	5	4
2nd and 4th	1	2	2	1	..	1
Relationship through godparents	43	20	42(1)	40	23	19
Relationship through sponsors at confirmation	8	3	5	5	11	7
Pre-contract validated	3	2	2	1	1	..

Other causes	1534/5	1536	1537	1538	1539	1540	1543/4	1545	1546	1547	1548/9
No banns	22	48(1)	61	50	75	89	69	99	103	107	102
Banns read once only	9	10	6	12	12	5	8	8	7	13	5
In any ch., by any pr. &c.	17	6	16	10	26	60	78	61	60	97	92

Note: Brackets indicate dispensations validating marriages already contracted despite impediments as above.

[1] F I/Vv, f. 338ᵛ.   [2] Ibid., f. 345ᵛ.

3. Dispensations concerning benefices (pluralities and non-residence) and ordination, eating in Lent, and other miscellaneous causes

Dispensations for pluralities occur frequently in the registers. The Pluralities Act of 1529[1] had followed the papal tradition of distinguishing between benefices with cure of souls and those without, and the system of special concessions to the *élite* of 'noble and lettered persons'. Most of these dispensations are therefore pluralities for the privileged clergy, though there are a certain number also for clergy unqualified under the terms of the Act:[2] some, of course, are only to hold extra benefices with cure up to the maximum of £8 p.a. The table below shows the respective figures. The *élite* clearly did well: royal, episcopal, and noblemen's chaplains, 'spiritual men of the King's council', chaplains of various office holders, doctors and bachelors of divinity and the canon law were all among this class; (not least of the registers' values is the evidence they give of so many chaplains' names). The Commissary of Faculties himself benefited from the system: Tonneshend held a dispensation to hold benefices up to the value of £300 p.a. in 1537,[3] and in 1544 the outrageously generous dispensation made to Nicholas Wotton by the archbishop's special authority was to enable him to hold the deanery of York together with that of Canterbury.[4]

	1534/5	1536	1537	1538	1539	1540	1543/4	1545	1546	1547	1548/9
Élite	47	34	38	49	44	32	83	62	70	64	40
Unprivileged	23	10	14	14	8	13	6	6	2	9	4
Ditto up to £8 p.a.	11	11	9	10	18	12	19	9	20	15	4
Others	5	5	2	..	..	1	4	..	..	..	..

The rules against the tenure of benefices with cure by those unentitled to them seem to have been followed fairly strictly. Cranmer took as firm a stand here as he did over marriages. John Husee can again be quoted in protest against this. He wrote on 30 April 1537 to Lord Lisle:

... and as ffor a capacyte for Mr Jaymes my lorde of Canterbery hathe made Mr Kyngston playne answer that he never granntyd anny suche nor never wyle do/ so that it is in vayne to labor anny more for the same/ he sayth that he hathe denyed the Kyng of lycke requests and the most part of the pyres of the reallme.[5]

Husee referred this to Cromwell, for he wrote next February:

And wher yor lordship hathe wryten unto my lorde prevy seall for lycens for Mr Jaymes to taike a benefyce of yor patronage and my ladyes/ he wyll in no wise here of it/specyally when the mater is tuchyng charge of sowlles/ ne yet the same pertaygneth unto my lorde of Caunterbury who hathe denyede the same to the

[1] 21 Henry VIII, c. 13: *Statutes of the Realm*, iii (1817), 292–6, and see above, pp. xviii, xix.   [2] e.g. bishops, archdeacons, regular clergy, &c.
[3] F I/Vv, f. 147ʳ.   [4] F I/A, pp. 72–73.
[5] P.R.O. SP 3/4, f. 80ᵛ (abstr. *L.P.* xii. ii. 1068).

best of this realme so that yor lordship sholde but frustrat your sywt to wryt or labour anny more in it/ but my lorde prevy seall saythe if you can spye a prebende or ffre chapell he wylbe ffrendly in it/ So that by thadvice of all yor ffrynds here your lordship shall wryt no further in this mater seing it is taken so vehemently here and so unlawfull.[1]

Non-residence was also quite strictly regulated by the Pluralities Act; it was only to be allowed where good reason was shown, illness, senility, or study, for instance. An Act of 1536 condemned absentees more stringently, however, and forbade persons over the age of forty from taking dispensations to study, except a few in privileged positions.[2] As the statute law was so closely involved in dispensations for non-residence, the slightly paradoxical situation arose of Cranmer himself having to submit his recommendations to the secular power. For instance, he wrote to Cromwell on 16 March 1538:

And whereas there is suit made unto me for one Sir William Chevenay, parson of Kyngston besides Canterbury, which being a very impotent man, above fourscore years of age, and also blind, is not able in his own person to discharge his cure and would very gladly have licence to abide with his friends and kinsfolks, and would find an honest priest in the meantime to discharge his cure; forasmuch as he is not able, besides the finding of the priest, to keep house of the same and the benefice being so small value, as I am informed that it is: these shall be, therefore, to desire you to be good lord unto the said parson in this his suit unto your lordship, that he may be discharged of the act concerning residence, if it may be. And he shall pray during his life, for the preservation of your good lordship. . . .[3]

Dispensations for non-residence are not very often found in the registers, except where the 'non-residence clause' accompanies the plurality dispensations for privileged clergy. They were sometimes obtained in response to special allegations, about which the entries in the register provide details. The following table shows the number of dispensations granted specifically for absence from a cure:

Alleged cause	1534/5	1536	1537	1538	1539	1540	1543/4	1545	1546	1547	1548/9
Illness or old age	3	9	13	10	..	1	1	1	..	2	1
Study	..	2	..	..	1	..	1	..	..	..	1
Parsonage uninhabitable	..	..	..	2	1	..	..	..	..	..	..
No cause shown	19	13	8	3	..	..	..	1	..	..	2

The great number of dispensations from the various rules governing ordination do not seem of sufficient significance for analysis here, but the small class of them permitting bastards to take orders and/or hold

[1] P.R.O. SP I/129, f. 12 (abstr. L.P. xiii. 226).
[2] 28 Henry VIII, c. 13: Statutes, iii. 668–9.
[3] Cox, Writings of Cranmer, pp. 364–5 (abstr. L.P. xiii. 516).

benefices are of some interest, also those concerning deformed priests and ordinands. Of the former, it may be worth mentioning, there was a Cistercian monk in 1536,[1] and a Gilbertine canon the following year,[2] and a nun was also dispensed to be abbess of the Minories, London, despite defective birth.[3] Fourteen dispensations concerning bastardy have been counted in Register Vv, and six in Register A;[4] two of these (in 1545 and 1546) were priest's sons.[5] The dispensations about deformity were more rare: only five have been counted, and none after 1538. The causes for these include being lame or deformed in one foot, one-eyed, and having lost two fingers or the thumb of the right hand: in the latter it is specified that this was not the victim's own fault.[6] Such dispensations are of interest as survivals of the rules enforced by the papal curia.

The dispensations to eat prohibited food during Lent and other prescribed times of fast describe a significant pattern: in their way they are almost as reflective of changes in ecclesiastical policy as the capacities for ex-religious.

In F I/Vv there are very few cases. In 1534–5 three dispensations are registered for the eating of meat, eggs, butter and other milk and fat foods, or 'white meats': all of them for monastic dignitaries. The Abbot of Walden, and the priors of Norwich and St Pancras, Lewes, each paid £4 for this privilege, which in each case included four favoured monks whom they might invite to their tables.[7] No apology is offered as cause for these dispensations, and without much doubt one can accept them as crude concessions to monastic gluttony. There is no such dispensation registered in 1536, and one only, on medical grounds, in 1537: to Sir Nicholas and Lady Jane Poyntz for which they paid £2;[8] the only other in the register is in 1540, to Lord Wentworth, his wife, and three others, at £2 a head.[9]

Until 1537 it would appear that all the traditional eating taboos were rigidly enforced;[10] but in that year, half-way through Lent, a notable change was made: the first of Henry VIII's proclamations of a general dispensation for the eating of 'white meats'. The change was not always welcomed. There were riotous scenes at Salisbury[11] when the proclamation was posted, and one citizen was in spite of it denounced to the Bishop's

---

[1] F I/Vv, f. 55ʳ. A previous dispensation for a Benedictine sub-prior was also referred to (f. 24ᵛ).

[2] Ibid., f. 165ʳ.   [3] Ibid., f. 138ᵛ.

[4] Several more, i.e. than Hooper noticed (art. cit., *E.H.R.* xxv (1910), 680).

[5] F I/A, pp. 121, 215.

[6] F I/Vv, f. 78ᵛ. The tariffs of the papal penitentiary (see below, pp. lx–lxi) allowed a dispensation costing 16 grossi for 'ille qui amputavit sibi duos digitos ex simplicitate'.

[7] Ibid., ff. 38ᵛ, 39ᵛ, 40ʳ.   [8] Ibid., f. 159ʳ.   [9] Ibid., f. 325ʳ.

[10] For instance, Richard, Abbot of Winchcombe wrote to Cromwell on 7 Dec. 1535 that he had placed two monks in custody for eating meat during Advent and refusing penance (abstr. *L.P.* ix. 934).

[11] References to its posting in Coventry and Lichfield diocese in a letter to Bishop Lee (abstr. *L.P.* xii. i. 679) and Salisbury (*L.P.* xii. 746, 755).

Chancellor for eating eggs.[1] A year later at Windsor a conservative baker boasted to a chanter: 'By the grace of God no eggs shall come in my belly before Easter': but he was assured by the priest: 'The restraining of white meat to be eaten is but a tradition of the bishop of Rome of whom every man for money might redeem to feed at large, but the King, God preserve his Grace! hath freely given licence to all his subjects and without money.'[2] However, the limitations of this indulgence must be recognized: it did not apply to meat. Prosecution for the eating of flesh seems, in fact, to have been severe. In 1538 a group of Oxford scholars were in trouble with the Bishop of Lincoln's Chancellor over this,[3] and in 1539 a man was even reported to have been hanged for eating flesh on a Friday.[4] In 1542, and 1543, there is record of a new and perpetual proclamation:[5] justified on the grounds of a scarcity of fish, and because 'to abstain from milk, butter, eggs, cheese, and other white meats is but a mere positive law of the church and used by a custom within this realm'. Observance of a fast of the spirit was enjoined instead, i.e. of the 'carnal affections'. Nevertheless, there was still nothing in this proclamation to permit the eating of meat. Prosecution for this offence still continued. In Lent 1543 arrests were made in London, including Henry Howard, Earl of Surrey, and two other young bloods, all three of whom alleged they had licences,[6] which the gap in the Faculty Office registers cannot disprove. London butchers were even raided and ordered to supply lists of their customers.[7]

Greater laxity at the beginning of Edward VI's reign was not suffered for long. In January 1548 a new proclamation was issued 'For the Abstaining from Flesh in Lent time' which complained 'at this time nowe late, more than at any other time, a great part of (the King's) subjects do break and contemn that abstinence which of long time hath been used'. The spiritual benefits of abstinence were again rehearsed, with also the 'wordly and civil' arguments of benefit to fishermen and stock breeders; while the eating of 'white meats' was still permitted, meat eating was to be punished by imprisonment on the testimony of two witnesses.[8]

These developments are reflected in F I/A. Flesh is the only prohibited food in the dispensations of the 1540's. At the beginning of the Register, medical reasons are given more often than not,[9] but their pro-

[1] Abstr. *L.P.* xii. 756. The plaintiff complained to Cromwell.
[2] Ibid. xiii. i. 686.
[3] Ibid. 811; the scholars nevertheless protested to Cromwell they 'for their health did use the liberty of the gospel and ate flesh' (ibid. ii. 819).
[4] *L.P.* xiv. i. 967.
[5] Wilkins, *Concilia*, iii. 867; mentioned *L.P.* xvii. 85 and note.
[6] J. R. Dasent, *Acts of the Privy Council*, N.S., vol. i. 1542–7 (London, 1890), p. 104. Cf. p. 114 for other victims. [7] Ibid., pp. 108, 112.
[8] Wilkins, *Concilia*, iv. 20; J. E. Cox, *Writings of Cranmer*, pp. 507–8.
[9] Some of these are thin. What benefit was eating meat likely to afford someone suffering from 'dropsy, indigestion, excessive wind, and various other ailments'? (F I/A, p. 23).

portion diminished. There was a leap in numbers of dispensations in 1548, which suggests that the proclamation did not represent much more reaction than an enforcement of the rules by which the rule could be broken. The view that Lenten fasting, even from flesh, was meritorious but not divinely ordained, had been preached by Cranmer's own Commissary in March 1547, and seems to have been expressed in the Injunctions of the following September.[1]

	1544	1545	1546	1547	1548	1549 (incomplete)
Medical causes . .	13	8	11	6	1	..
No specified cause .	9	5	15	16	51	5
Total . . .	22	13	26	22	52	5

In terms of persons, the figures should be even higher than those given here, since in about a dozen cases individual dispensations were extended to a number of guests at the suitor's table. Those dispensed included Cranmer's brother, the archdeacon, in December 1545,[2] and in 1548, Bishop Goodrich of Ely,[3] and in an undated dispensation, probably the following year, Archbishop Holgate of York obtained one free.[4] There are several other cases where fees were not charged,[5] and one of cancellation because the supplicant was unwilling to pay.[6] The boom in these neo-papal licences was paradoxical, since the Church was moving in a protestant direction; but a boom was much needed by the Faculty Office, for its revenues had steadily declined since 1540.[7]

★   ★   ★

There are a number of miscellaneous faculties or dispensations in the registers which do not come under any of the headings already discussed. The minor licences for new graveyards, preachers, &c. usually issued by a diocesan have been mentioned in an earlier chapter,[8] and the confirmation of letters bearing the seal of other authorities. These confirmations are generally for diocesans' decrees and dispensations,[9] but there are some peculiar cases. For instance, in 1536 the Prioress of Marrick was confirmed in possession of her office;[10] in 1537 the relaxation of censures was confirmed for a clerk who had had an affair with a married woman,[11] and the grant of Walden to Lord Audley is curiously included.[12] As well as these, are letters

---

[1] Ridley, *Cranmer*, p. 264. Froude's statement that Cranmer himself ate meat in Lent 1547 is disputed here.

[2] F I/A, p. 171.   [3] Ibid., p. 294.   [4] Ibid., p. 338.

[5] Ibid., pp. 192, 202, 311.   [6] Ibid., p. 305.

[7] See below, pp. lxiv–lxv.   [8] See above, pp. xviii, xxiv.

[9] As well as cases noted above, p. xxiv, e.g. confirmations of institution to benefices F I/Vv, ff. 39ᵛ, 221ʳ, 256–7ʳ; of a composition, ff. 180ᵛ, 183ᵛ; of a decree about tithes, f. 233ᵛ; of the statutes of collegiate churches, f. 194ʳ, 226ʳ; one further peculiarity is the confirmation of a divorce judged by Nicholas Wotton, f. 340ᵛ.

[10] Ibid., f. 28ᵛ.   [11] Ibid., f. 214ʳ.   [12] Ibid., f. 208ʳ.

creating public notaries, conferring degrees,[1] and licences for the practice of medicine.[2] Finally, there are a number of dispensations which are pure curiosities: several permitting clergy to wear the cathedral canon's almuce, a grey fur scarf or lining between the hood and outer vestment;[3] one for a hermit to enter a poor house although not of the prescribed age;[4] even one for an elderly Welsh parson to have a woman look after him who must be over 60 and known to be free from the vices of the flesh.[5]

4. Capacities for the regular clergy to hold benefices or leave religion

These dispensations, coinciding with Henry VIII's visitations and dissolutions of religious houses, are undoubtedly the most significant, historically, of those contained in the first register of the Faculty Office.[6] A 'capacity'—the word was currently used, but it hardly appears at all in the register[7]—signified a release from vows, and might enable the holder to leave his or her Order altogether for the secular life, and (except for nuns) to hold a benefice for which a secular priest was eligible, either remaining within the Order, or leaving it completely.

The evidence in the register must nevertheless be treated with some caution. In the first place, it is no guide to the population of the religious orders; not every house can be traced here, and the lists are only of those inhabitants who applied for the formal letters of the Faculty Office. Nuns, with a very few exceptions,[8] are not listed at all after the middle of 1537. Perhaps they gave up taking capacities when evicted *en masse*; in any case, capacities for nuns, permitting them to live without the veil,[9] were much more limited in usefulness than those for men in religion: there can have been little prospects outside the cloister for a nun except marriage or a secluded dependence upon relatives. In 1536 the names are given of 44 nuns leaving religion on account of suppressions, and 56 in 1537. These lists of nuns are unique, however, for as pensions were not paid to them at

---

[1] D.C.L., F I/Vv, f. 175ᵛ; master of grammar, f. 202ᵛ; B.A., F I/A, p. 92; confirmation of D.Th., F I/Vv, f. 255ʳ. Licences for notaries are not detailed here as they are so numerous.

[2] F I/Vv, f. 104ʳ (confirmation); ibid., ff. 107ᵛ, 145ʳ (both for monks); f. 226ᵛ (for a clerk); F I/A, p. 266.

[3] F I/Vv, ff. 86ʳ, 157ᵛ, 177ᵛ; F I/A, p. 127. Despite the Latin here 'amictus griseus' instead of 'almutium', almuce seems the correct rendering, not amice, which was a square of white linen worn during celebration of Mass.

[4] F I/Vv, f. 28ᵛ. [5] Ibid., f. 214ʳ.

[6] There are also three capacities entered in F I/A, pp. 84, 88, 101.

[7] The word only appears in entries on the following pages: F I/Vv, ff. 120ᵛ, 122ʳ; F I/A, p. 101.

[8] Two nuns of Malling in 1538, one of the Minories, London, in 1539 (F I/Vv, ff. 227ʳ, 286ʳ).

[9] The Latin formula most used in the text runs: 'ad seculum se conferre ac ibidem extra velum et habitum vivere possit', though there are variants.

this stage they are not listed in the pension books of the Court of Augmentations. The pension books duplicate the lists of names of most monks
from the winter of 1537–8 onwards which are found here; on the other
hand, for the unpensioned ex-religious, i.e. those leaving religion before
1537–8, and the friars throughout, the register is an unrivalled source. It has
recently been used by Mr Hodgett to demonstrate his thesis that there were
many more redundant ex-religious in the country, with neither benefices
nor pensions, than had recently been supposed.[1] The only other sources
which provide any of these names are the reports of the Commissioners,
such of them as survive,[2] and the deeds of surrender, which are also far
from complete,[3] and in any case were demonstrably not signed by all the
members of a community. A look at these records in comparison with the
register is nevertheless useful and slightly sobering. It shows in some cases
the wildly variant forms in which the names of the religious might be given
(besides variant spelling, this includes the problem of surnames being
confused with names in religion taken from place of birth).[4] It also reveals
that in some cases, even at the final dissolutions, some of the religious did
not apply for capacities,[5] or cases where they did apply, but eventually
(according to the register) were not granted them.[6]

The Faculty Office register therefore complicates, at the same time as it
illuminates, the historical problems connected with the ex-religious. In the
following sections, some of these problems will be discussed further, but
obviously much more will remain to be said. Firstly, some points about the
differing forms of 'capacity' will be considered, and the extent to which they
were issued before the final suppressions, also the problem of preferment
for the unpensioned ex-religious: the substance, in fact, of Mr Hodgett's
recent article. Secondly, some of the administrative difficulties and shortcomings involved in the mass production of capacities for ex-religious,
and their possible significance, will be examined.

★   ★   ★

[1] G. A. J. Hodgett, 'The Unpensioned Ex-Religious in Tudor England', *Journ. Eccles.
Hist.* xiii. 2 (1962), 195–202.

[2] M. D. Knowles, *The Religious Orders in England*, iii. 306 gives a list of these.

[3] J. Hunter, *A Catalogue of the Deeds of Surrender of Certain Abbeys &c. 8th Report of
the Deputy Keeper of the Public Records* (London, 1847), pp. 1–51.

[4] Compare, for instance, various names at Bardney (F I/Vv, f. 252ᵛ: Jo. Ponfrett, Rob.
Cambridge, Peter Barton, Ric. Furisbye; *8th Report*, p. 8: Jo. Tomson, Rob. Oda, Peter
Reyns, Ric. Wolay).

[5] For instance, even if the Surrenders are incomplete, names appear in them not in
the register: three more Austin friars at Tickhill, for instance (*8th Report*, p. 45, cf. F
I/Vv, f. 252ʳ); three more Dominicans and Franciscans at Cambridge (*8th Report*,
p. 14, F I/Vv, ff. 237ᵛ) &c.

[6] For instance, at Boxgrove in July 1536, 8 monks told the Commissioners they wanted
capacities (*L.P.* xi, App. 2) but only 6, including the prior, are entered in F I/Vv, f. 129ʳ. On
the other hand, at St Denys (Hants) 3 are entered by the Commissioners (P.R.O. SC 12/33/
27), whereas 5 are listed in F I/Vv, f. 86ᵛ.

Various sorts of capacity were issued to the religious before the suppressions. Differences in the wording of entries indicate this, and it is confirmed by differences in the fees charged (so the possibility that the registrar was being inconsistent or careless in the form of words used is unlikely). Suppression capacities were, of course, uniform; each monk or friar wanted both a release from vows, and (if in orders) entitlement to a benefice such as a secular priest might hold. This we might call a 'full capacity'; in the register, the abbreviated formula runs 'ad recipiendum beneficium cum integra habitus mutacione', to hold a benefice with complete change of habit. Its complete form in the outgoing letters may be read in the capacity issued to the Abbot of Hartland, already mentioned.[1] Such a dispensation cost £12,[2] though the more normal fee seems to have been £8, and reductions by arbitration were frequent; upon suppression, of course, no fee was charged. There were also lesser or limited capacities issued to voluntary applicants: for instance, simply to hold a benefice (which might still depend on the consent of the prior), or to hold a benefice and continue to wear the habit of the religious order: either of which cost £4. An example of the former sort of letter is available in the case of Robert Hull *alias* Tomsone, a canon of Thornton.[3] There were also capacities to hold a benefice wearing the habit beneath that of a secular, which cost £8 (it is not quite clear whether this double clothing was obligatory in the physical sense or merely figurative; if the former, it may only have applied during celebration of the Mass).[4] The formula for such a capacity usually ran as follows: 'ut quodcumque unum beneficium ecclesiasticum clerico seculari assignari solitum recipere / nec non habitum dicti ordinis regularem sub honesta veste presbiteri quoad vixerit deferre et gestare valeat et possit.' There were also capacities which made no mention of the right to a benefice, but simply a release: 'ut religionem quam professus est exire et ad seculum se conferre ac ibidem de cetero in veste presbiteri secularis vitam agere et finire possit', or 'ut habitum dicti ordinis mutare possit'. The text of one of these also survives in the case of William Piers, Canon of Guisborough.[5]

The emphasis placed upon these distinctions may seem slightly laboured, but it has importance in an introduction to the register; and so far as possible, the entries have been transcribed in this edition to correspond as closely as possible to the variants in the text. The importance is particularly clear in the distinction between capacities which permitted the suitor to leave religion, and those which permitted him to stay within, while

---

[1] Oliver, *Monasticon Diocesis Exoniensis*, p. 216; see above, p. 25.

[2] See F I/Vv, ff. 14ʳ, 28ᵛ; but cf. f. 40ʳ for instance.

[3] Borthwick Institute, York, Reg. Lee, f. 111ᵛ (see above, p. xxviii n. 4).

[4] e.g. F I/Vv, f. 26ʳ, 29ʳ; the formula for some change of habit ('aliquali mutacione') presumably implies the same (e.g. f. 14ᵛ).

[5] Reg. Lee, f. 111ʳ (see also above, p. xxviii n. 4).

holding a benefice. For there was nothing new in monks or friars being allowed to hold benefices, while remaining in their Orders. Warham had complained in August 1529 'if ther bee any good vicareige, diverse of the said religiouse howses optainethe dispensations of the See Apostolike to kepe them in ther own hands, and bee served by religiouse men, and so they have almost al good parsonages and vicareiges in ther hands'.[1]

As an example of this, one of the very last dispensations to be issued from Rome before the new system came into operation must have been the capacity for a canon of Mottisfont to hold a benefice, dated 29 October 1533.[2] In September 1535, a letter to Thomas Cromwell from John Placett, a sycophantic monk of Winchcombe who played the part of royal apologist, illustrates well the monastic mind as benefice-hunter, wanting the best of both worlds:

. . . y moste mekely besyche yow in visceribus Jesu Christi to helpe me and grante me be yor hye auctoryte withowte scrip . . . of concyens to be capax beneficii nat changing my habyte. yff my master or any man can see in my wrochidenes syche lernyng conversacon or aptytude to take cure as mynister (wyche y am unworthy), my lorde off Chester knowythe where y myght have hade a lyving to good for me yff I wolde have take hyt . . . yett y have fryndes that promyse me hylles off golde but my truste ys gode and youre grett goodenes and in my master the father abbot whyche hathe cownsellyde me thys rudely to scrybl to yor gracius goodeness, affyrmys that he wyl be to me ever ful lovyng and myche the better for yor sake to whom y pray yow gyve thank. y have the cure under hym off a lytil vyllege where ys nat paste xl persons. syche a thynge were meste qwyet for me whyche y may serve and kepe my bede and borde and go to my boke yn the monasteri, nen the lacer. the yerely value of thys lytil cure ys nat iiii £ be the yere. . . .[3]

This letter raises again the subject of Cromwell's initiative, particularly as Vicar-General: might a limited capacity even be issued independently of the Faculty Office? Or—even more unpleasant a possibility—might the register be incomplete? Placett's name does not occur in the register, and although he might have been unsuccessful in his suit, nor does that of the Carthusian Rawlyns, of whom a fellow monk, Jasper Fyllols, wrote assuring Cromwell in September 1535

Dan Nycholas Raulyns hath his Capacyte sealyd but he hath borowed all hys secular vestments off a prest of his acquentance.

Fyllols went on to inform Cromwell,

Dan Thomas Salter and Dan John Darley wold fayne be owt off the cloyster by the favor of yor mastyrshyppe. Dan John Darley is provyded of a servyce at Salesbury.[4]

---

[1] H. Ellis, *Original Letters*, 3rd series, ii. 29–30 (slightly misleading abstract in *L.P.* iv. 4631 quoted by Baskerville, *English Monks and the Suppression*, p. 157).

[2] *Register of Stephen Gardiner, Bp of Winchester*, ed. H. Chitty, *Cant. & York Soc.*, xxxvii (1930), 28–29.   [3] P.R.O. SP I/96, p. 128 (abstr. *L.P.* ix. 322).

[4] P.R.O. SP I/96, p. 92 (Jasper wrongly transcribed as James Fyllol in *L.P.* ix. 284).

Letters for these are not entered in the register either. However, these are problems which, while noting, we cannot take further in the present context. They do, nevertheless, serve to re-emphasize that the register must be used with caution.

Another case of what was apparently an application for only a limited capacity might be worth mentioning. This concerns an Austin canon of Bodmin, John Bandon, who according to the register obtained a dispensation to hold a benefice conditional on his prior's consent on 7 May 1535: for this he paid £4.[1] His prior, however, denied consent. In a letter dated 25 May, which almost certainly has been wrongly calendared under the year 1536, the Prior of Bodmin wrote to a London mercer called Lok:

> Syr, I am sore disquietid with a sett of unthryfty chanons, my convent and there berars, which of longe contynuans have lyvyd unthriftili and agene the gode order of relygyon . . . the buschope yn hys late visitacyon gave certayne and dyvers injuncions, commaundyng me straytle to see observyd and kept, which are noo harder thane ower owene rule and profession byndis us, and as alle other relygyus men use and observe where god relygioun is observid and kept; wherewith they be sore grevid, and yntend the most parte of them to depart with capacitise withowt my concent and wylle, and won of them hathe purchesid a capacyte in the last terme withowt my lycence, which is agene the wordes of his capacite, wherfor I have restraynyd his departyng, for no gret los that I showld have of hym, but for the yl exemple to othere; for yf I showld suffer this man to depart yn this maner, I shall have never a chanon to byde with me.[2]

In view of the character of Bandon's dispensation, the prior certainly seems to have been exaggerating the situation's gravity: moreover, his efforts at restraint failed. For on 7 June an additional dispensation for Bandon is entered in the register, overriding the regulation that he should obtain his prior's consent.[3] The benefice which he was to hold was evidently that of Broadwoodwidger in Devon.[4]

Another instance where the register seems to contradict literary evidence, is that of the monk Richard Skydmore, of St Peter's, Gloucester. In a visitation much later in the century he alleged that he held a dispensation to obtain an ecclesiastical benefice and to change his habit for that of a secular priest, dated 20 November 1535.[5] In the register, however, this appears only as a dispensation costing £4 to hold a benefice; and it is

[1] F I/Vv, f. 32ʳ.
[2] Wright, *Suppression of the Monasteries*, pp. 130–1. See also above, p. xxvii n. 6.
[3] F I/Vv, f. 45ʳ.
[4] Hodgett, art. cit., p. 198 n. 17 from *Valor Ecclesiasticus*, ii. 386. Mr Hodgett here gives the date of Bandon's dispensation as 1534 instead of 1535.
[5] G. Baskerville, 'The Dispossessed Religious of Gloucestershire', *Transactions of the Bristol and Gloucestershire Archaeological Society*, xlix (1927), 65. A transcript of the dispensation is reported (ibid., n. 10) to be among the Hockaday papers in Gloucester public library: file RUDFORD.

dated 20 October.[1] Such dispensations, not surprisingly, become more rare after 1536, in the face of 'full' capacities, but they are still found. In January 1538, for instance, a Carmelite friar paid £4 to hold a benefice while retaining the habit of his Order.[2]

All these differences in the form of capacities have been shown in the statistical table (pp. lvii–lviii): a table which, it must be emphasized, does not include figures for the gratuitous 'full' capacities mass-produced when religious houses were suppressed. This amplified statement and analysis of the pre-suppression capacities, which can be checked against entries in the register, suggests that Mr Hodgett's recent estimates were over optimistic, and demand a slight revision. In his summing up of the evidence from the first 'year' of the register, he writes: 'Between May 1534 and December 1535, 38 monks and canons regular, 3 hermits and 14 friars obtained capacities, a chantry priest was permitted to hold a cure with his chantry, 4 were allowed to hold cures while almost certainly remaining in religion and 4 were granted permission to hold cures *in commendam*. Of this total, 15 were Benedictines, 11 Austin canons, 7 Premonstratensians, 3 Carthusians, and 3 Dominicans, with a similar number of Carmelites, Franciscans, and Observant friars.'[3]

It is not quite clear why a chantry priest should be included in this list of regular clergy, and in reality the number of religious who can definitely be said to have applied for capacities to leave religion (i.e. hold the 'full' capacity both for change of habit and tenure of a benefice, or just for change of habit) was less high than Mr Hodgett estimated. In 1534/5 the total amounted to 16 monks and canons, and 10 friars; one monk also obtained a capacity to change his habit without mention of a benefice, i.e. a simple release. In 1536 there were 24 monks or canons with full capacities, and an additional 15 with simple releases; 26 friars with full capacities (2 of whom had still to obtain their superior's permission) and 12 more for releases. In 1537 there were 11 monks or canons and 11 friars. All these figures are set out more intelligibly in the accompanying table, and an additional table shows the numbers of religious who paid fees for their various capacities. The proportion who continued to do so in spite of everything is not negligible; generally they paid the full amount, though sometimes this was reduced. A Carthusian paid the maximum £12 for a full capacity in 1536,[4] and two Benedictine monks of Westminster paid the same high fee the following year.[5] At Norwich, in order to become Dean and Chapter of the new cathedral foundation, the Prior and 17 former monks of the Benedictine priory paid respectively £10 and £6. 13s. 4d. a head for special capacities.[6] Although the friars were more often granted capacities free, as late as 1538 two Franciscans and two Dominicans paid

[1] F I/Vv, f. 39ʳ.   [2] Ibid., f. 172ᵛ.   [3] Art. cit., pp. 197–8.
[4] F I/Vv, f. 61ʳ.   [5] Ibid., f. 125ʳ.   [6] Ibid., ff. 199ʳ–200ʳ.

the reduced fee of £4,[1] and an Austin friar £12,[2] for full capacities. Some of the remissions of fees that year are stated to be on account of the suitors' poverty;[3] which sounds slightly ironical when one reflects that the friars, at any rate, were supposed to be mendicant.

Mr Hodgett infers from his figures 'it would appear from the number of those seeking capacities, that many were reading the writing on the wall'. There may well be something in this, especially as the majority of full capacities issued in 1534–5 were in fact issued after the commissioners had made their first rounds and had imposed injunctions (though Mr Hodgett does not make this point) and admittedly the numbers rose in 1536. But the metaphor is perhaps too vivid: this was no Belshazzar's feast. The figures are not astonishingly high, and even if they reflect reaction against severe injunctions, this is not the same thing as apprehension about imminent dissolution. It might be borne in mind, without irrelevance, that as late as September 1536 the Abbot of the Cistercian house of St Mary Grace's, London, considered the future of the monasteries still a good enough proposition to pay £125. 11s. in order to hold the monastery of St Mary's, Coggeshall, in commendam.[4] Moreover, this final point may be worth making: that we have no standard of comparison for the number of capacities, either limited or 'full', which had been issued from Rome in any year before 1534. The Vatican archives may contain evidence[5] which would make the 'writing on the wall' look like a quite familiar phenomenon, if not just a mirage.

* * *

The second, and major, conclusion of Mr Hodgett about the ex-religious in the register concerns the much-discussed problem of their later careers. It is, as he owns, a fairly tentative conclusion. By comparing the evidence of F I/Vv with the pension books of the Court of Augmentations and certain other available sources, he surmises that a surprisingly large number of religious were, after all, thrown upon a bleak world with neither pensions nor preferment: nearly a thousand monks and canons (mostly before the winter of 1537–8) and over a thousand friars, to say nothing of 86 nuns. 'Only about 50 of them can be found in livings', he writes, 'and . . . some had to wait almost fifteen years before obtaining preferment.'[6] However,

[1] F I/Vv, ff. 186ᵛ, 196ᵛ, 207ᵛ.   [2] Ibid., f. 202ʳ.
[3] Ibid., ff. 190ᵛ, 194ᵛ (O.S.B.); 196ᵛ (O.F.M.); 194ᵛ (observant); 186ᵛ, 192ʳ, (O.P.).
[4] Ibid., f. 98ᵛ.
[5] The remarks of a contemporary, Thomas Solmes, canon of St Osyth's, to Cromwell, would support this: 'Nonnullis religiosis licenciam mutandi habitum, ante hac (cessante causa) romanus pontifex concessit' (B.M. Cotton MS. Cleop. E IV, f. 26ʳ; abstr. of letter, L.P. ix. 1157). Cf. also H. Jedin, A History of the Council of Trent, i. (trans. E. Graf, Edinburgh, 1957), 414: '. . . the dispensation, so fatal to regular discipline, which permitted monks to live outside their monasteries had become a simple administrative measure granted without previous examination of the reasons alleged.'
[6] Art. cit., pp. 201–2.

as he admits, only limited sources have been consulted in order to establish this: five bishops' registers which are in print, lists for the dioceses of London, Chichester, and Canterbury, the *Valor Ecclesiasticus*, which only gives incumbents' names up to 1535, the index of the Composition Books for First Fruits (but this only up to 1541), and some unspecified parish registers. It would clearly be a very long job to carry the investigation further: identification of names is itself a hazardous business, with the confusion between secular surnames, and monastic names according to place of origin. But until all the episcopal and parochial registers and the later index to the Composition Books have been combed, the surmise seems hardly a fair one. There will be no short cuts to answering the questions 'Where did the ex-religious go? What did they do? How did they gain a livelihood?' Mr Hodgett goes on to suggest that perhaps 'some entered the houses of the nobility and gentry. These unpensioned ex-religious were certainly those who had the least sense of vocation for the cloistered life and it would seem they were absorbed into lay society.'[1] This may be so: but the likelihood of their remaining in ecclesiastical life, or at least on its fringes, is still great: they must have intended to remain within, or they would not have wanted capacities. There were minor chaplaincies (in the sense of both private chaplaincies and assistant curacies) or places as chantors, sacristans, almoners, doorkeepers, &c. One canon of Bourne, William Newton, eventually became town clerk and organist at Edenham[2] but it is very difficult to obtain evidence about most of these minor appointments. Henry Brinklow, himself an ex-Franciscan, declares in the 'Complaynt of Roderyck Mors':

> Where thei [the monasteries] had alweys one or other vicar that eyther preached or hyred some to preach, now is there no vicar at all, but the fermer is vicar and person all together, and onely an old cast away monke or fryre, which can scarsely say his matens, is hyred for xx or xxx shillings, meat and drinck; yea, in some place, for meat and drinck alone withowt any wages.[3]

Part-time employment like this for ex-religious would obviously not reach the records. There is also the possibility that many of them were old or ill at the time of suppression, and did not long survive the shock of eviction: like the Grey friars of Reading, of whom Dr London wrote to Cromwell on 31 August 1538: 'The most partt of them be very agede men and be nott of strength to go moch abrode for ther lyvinges.'[4]

★   ★   ★

[1] Ibid., p. 202. 'Those remaining in the friaries were the proletariat of their class', Knowles, *Religious Orders*, iii. 365.

[2] Lincolnshire Archives Office, Anc/3/3/173. I am grateful to Mrs A. E. B. Owen for this reference.

[3] Ed. J. M. Cowper, *Early English Text Society*, Extra Series xxii (London, 1874), 34.

[4] Wright, *Suppression*, p. 218 (abstr. *L.P.* xiii. ii. 235).

d 2

The faculty administration was strained by the dissolutions, and in-conveniences were undoubtedly suffered by the religious who sought capacities.

The confusion of authorities concerned with dispensations, particularly the part played by Thomas Cromwell, has already been mentioned. Appli-cations addressed to him for capacities have been illustrated before the suppressions in the cases of Peter Watts and Jasper Fyllols, both Car-thusians, and the Benedictine, John Placett.[1] There are cases of quite candid voluntary applications for full capacities. For instance, in 1536 one Richard Beerly, a monk of Pershore, wrote to him:

> Most reverent lord yn God, second person yn this rem of Englond, ynduyd with all grace and goodnes, y submytt my selfe unto your grace and goodnes. . . . Now, most gracyus lord and most worthyst vycytar that ever cam amonckes us, helpe me owt of thys vayne relygyon . . . and save my sowlle, wych sholdbe lost yf ye helpe yt not, the wych ye may save with on word speckyng. . . .[2]

It may be that there was more likelihood, in a successful application to Cromwell, of having the fee for the capacity reduced or remitted.

As the visitations and suppressions advanced, more and more reference to Cromwell seems to have been made, though the Commissioners' in-structions implied that the normal procedure of the Faculty Office would operate. They were to find out from the monks

> . . . how many of them will go to other houses of that religion, or how many will take capacities . . . the residue of them that go to the world to send them to my Lord of Canterbury and the Lord Chancellor for their capacities, with the letter of the same commissioners. To them that will have capacities some reasonable reward. . . .[3]

However, a canon of St Osyth's sued to Cromwell for a licence to leave his Order 'on Dr Legh's advice' rather than to Cranmer or the Chancery;[4] and other cases are recorded of the normal channels being by-passed. Legh was even reputed to issue capacities himself, which his colleague Bedyll found embarrassing; he wrote to Cromwell on 15 January 1536 in a state of confusion about who could license what:

> Here in this monastery of Ramsey be two brethern whiche have gyven thes billys enclosed unto me, very affectuously desiryng to have liberte to go from thaire cloyster by the Kinges grace authorite, or els to have licence to repair to my lord of Cauntrebury to sue thaire capacites. I have steyed thaim as wel as I

[1] Above, pp. xxiii, xlv.

[2] Wright, *Suppression*, pp. 132–3 (abstr. *L.P.* xi. 1449); mentioned by Knowles, *Reli-gious Orders*, iii. 341.

[3] See the Act of Suppression, 27 Henry VIII, c. 28 (cl. VIII) in *Statutes of the Realm*, iii. 575 sqq.; also quoted by Baskerville, *English Monks and the Suppression*, p. 144 from Burnet.

[4] Abstr. *L.P.* ix. 1157.

can, with suche counsels and exhortations as I could gyve thaim; but I fere, if they can have no liberte graunted thaim, they wol take it of thaire owne auctorite. I beseche you to write a word or two how I shal use me self towardes thaim and al other whiche wol make like suyt, in no smal number as I think, whereof som occasion hath growen by that docter Lee now at Christmas gave liberte to half the house at Sawtre to depart (as I am informed), which Sawtre is within v. myles of Ramsey. The religious men thinketh that I have like auctorite as doctor Lee. . . .[1]

The Commissioners themselves in sending for capacities seem to have applied to Cromwell as a matter of course. For instance, those who visited Sibton in 1536 made notes to obtain from the Vicar-General a capacity for the abbot to hold two benefices with cure and be non-resident, as well as a similar licence from the Lord Chancellor.[2] Normally, however, it must be assumed that these capacities, even if granted through Cromwell's authority, found their way on to the Faculty Office, and are recorded in the register. On the other hand, he did reserve to himself or to the Commissioners the issue of the special dispensations for the religious to infringe the strict letter of the visitors' injunctions (e.g. to leave the confinement of the cloister):[3] these did not count as faculties at all.

The issue and distribution of capacities on a large scale must have presented many practical problems. Delivery finally into the religious' own hands of their capacities may have taken a long time; perhaps some never received them at all. A monk of Louth Park alleged that he had received on 14 September 1536 from a canon of Bourne a capacity for himself to wear the habit of a secular priest and 76 others, which he delivered to Markby, Hagnaby, and Grimsby, and for certain canons of Wellow.[4] Did they all reach their destinations safely, one wonders, and did perhaps both the ex-canon of Bourne and ex-monk of Louth Park demand a fee as middle men? The records of the later commissions and suppressions, from the winter of 1537/8 onwards, illustrate most fully the sort of thing that was going on. The Commissioners appear to have sent in their reports to Cromwell by messenger, expecting by return the capacities according to their lists of names;[5] but the process demanded a lot of office work, and

---

[1] Wright, *Suppression*, p. 99 (misleading abstr. *L.P.* x. 103). Legh's capacities were evidently rather suspect. The Archbishop of York considered one which the Abbot of Fountains claimed he had received was insufficient for his collation to a benefice (abstr. *L.P.* x. 521).

[2] P.R.O. SP I/104, ff. 274–5 (abstr. *L.P.* x. 1247).

[3] e.g. Legh wrote to Cromwell on 24 Aug. 1535 he had given orders 'none should go out . . . without your and the king's special licence . . . that they might the more know the king's supreme ecclesiastical power in seeking to him or you for relief' (abstr. *L.P.* ix. 167). Several heads applied to Cromwell (e.g. *LP.* ix. 211; 880), but Legh was licensed to issue these concessions (Wright, *Suppression*, p. 65; abstr. *L.P.* ix. 265).

[4] Abstr. *L.P.* xii. i. 380.

[5] e.g. Dr. Petre wrote to Cromwell from Lanthony on 17 Mar. 1538 'This berar can certefye your lordeshipp whow farre wee have procedyd hitherto, by whom wee have send

passage through different departments. For a pensionable ex-monk a warrant for a free capacity evidently had to be obtained through the Court of Augmentations;[1] though for others a warrant in Cromwell's name sent down to the Faculty Office seems to have been sufficient. There are even marginal notes in the register about letters from Cromwell for two capacities obtained early in 1539 apart from the suppression. One of these was for a Franciscan,[2] and the other for William Knotton, a renegade of Sion who had made an unsuccessful bid for release eighteen months earlier.[3] But the usual directive for the Faculty Office to issue capacities after suppression came from Cromwell: this seems clear from his letter of 25 April 1539 to Wotton, 'Hewis', and Vaughan, already mentioned in an earlier chapter. In this he wrote:

... hereafter ensue the names of the white freres in northampton for whom the kinges Maiesties pleasour and commaundement is that ye shall make out capacities in due forme after thaccustomable maner with lycence to take one benefice with cure and that frely without requiring any thing for the same. . . .[4]

Great batches of orders for capacities for religious in a particular region of the country as it was covered by the Commissioners, must have been forwarded all at once to the Faculty Office, judging from the register.[5]

The friars suffered most from the shortcomings of the administration. They experienced difficulty in obtaining capacities quite apart from exclusion from the pension lists and the struggle to obtain preferment. The Commissioners themselves expressed pity, and were irritated at their own inability to provide quicker dispatch or relief.

At first it seems that the friars were even expected to pay for capacities if they wanted them. This was hard, considering their genuine poverty. Richard Ingworth, Bishop of Dover, and himself an ex-Dominican, wrote to Cromwell:

...yt ys pety to knowe the penury of the howseys and I thynke ther kowldd no better

the names of the chanons for the making of ther capacities' (Wright, *Suppression*, p. 178; abstr. *L.P.* xiii. 531).

[1] Cromwell wrote to Rich, Chancellor of the Court, on 23 May 1538 about Tho. Lacoke, an ex-monk of Kingswood: 'Thies shalbe therfor to desire you to make hym foorth aswell thassurance for the said pension as also a warrant for his capacitie to be had free', Merriman, *Life and Letters of Thomas Cromwell*, ii. 143 (abstr. *L.P.* xiii. i. 1051). Lacoke's name does not appear in the register however. There are also some warrants for canons of Notley and others among the Miscellaneous Books of the Augmentations Office (abstr. *L.P.* xiv. i. 105).

[2] F I/Vv, f. 193ᵛ.

[3] Ibid., f. 201ᵛ. Knowles, *Religious Orders*, iii. 220 refers to Knotton's arrest by the watch on 10 June 1537 on the way to obtain a release from Cromwell (reference in *L.P.* xi. 67).

[4] Merriman, op. cit. ii. 222, and see above, p. xxvii.

[5] e.g. many friars from Wales and the Welsh borders (ff. 236ʳ–7ʳ) followed by Cambridge, Thetford, and Lynn friars (ff. 237ᵛ–8ᵛ).

dede be don/ than to set every man at lyberte that wolde goo/ for they have no thynge to purches ther capacyts with and leve in misery.[1]

In another letter he added:

. . . yt war a charytabull dede yff capacyt[es] war chepar, so that freers myght make shyfte to have them for non can gett them but priors that sell the convents goods or lemytors that with ther lemytacyons purches them.[2]

In fact, the register proves that all friars' capacities were issued free upon dissolution of their houses, but both Ingworth and London kept up their protests at the burdensome delays caused by having to send up long lists of names to London for separate concessions of free capacities, instead of being empowered to issue them on the spot. Ingworth protested in July:

yff that I myght know that I shulde not offende the kynges grace nor yower lordeschype, I koulde by juste and fayer menys, and do no wronge, dyspache a gret part off the fryers in Ynglonde, or my yere off vysytacyon was endeyd, so that I myght have sum lyberte to lycens them to change ther habetts after ther howsys wer gyffyn up. For off trewth ther harttes be clene from the relygyon the more parte, so they myght change ther cotes, the whyche they be not abull to paye for, for they have no thenge. I harttely beseche yower lordeschype be good lorde to theys pore men that have gyffyn up ther howsys that they have have sum dyscharge. I sende ther namys here incloseyd.

He suggested in a postscript:

if that ye wold be so gode lord to me to send to me a hunderyd worans for the dely-verans of a hunderyd ffreeres that schall gyff up ther howseys in thys progresse, and leve a space for ther nameys, I woll brynge yow the nameys and place at my returne.[3]

Early in August he wrote from Lichfield:

The copy of thys Inuentory I sende mekely besechynge yowr Lordschype to be so goode Lorde to me to sende to thes Fryers ther warantts to change ther habetts, by this bryngar; and my good Lorde, I beseche yow be so goode Lorde to me to sende me yowr pleasur whether I shall kepe styll thys order with the Fryers or no. . . . I harttely beseche your Lordeschype to sende me yowr plesur what I shall do for the warrants for the Fryers that I shall put owt, for who that I am fare from London yt shall be to gret a charge to sende for ther warrantts, and than sende them agayne to the place wher they dwell.[4]

Ingworth wrote several petulant letters to Cromwell on his tour of the west midlands and Welsh border in August. From Shrewsbury he wrote on 13 August:

I receyvyd non word from yower lordschyp sythe that I receyvyd yower letter by my servants, wretyn in Petworth, the xxviii. day of Julii. I make promes to the

---

[1] P.R.O. SP I/134, f. 242ᵛ (abstr. *L.P.* xiii. i. 1456).
[2] P.R.O. SP I/134, f. 244ʳ (abstr. *L.P.* xiii. i. 1457).
[3] Wright, *Suppression*, pp. 197, 199–200 (abstr. *L.P.* xiii. i. 1484).
[4] Ellis, *Original Letters*, 3rd Series, iii. 191–2 (abstr. *L.P.* xiii. ii. 49).

freeres that gyff up ther howseys that I shall send to them waranttes ffor ther abettes before Myhelmas, and in the tyme I gyff them letters to vesyte ther frynddes.[1]

On 23 August the complaint was repeated:

I have note harde from yowr lordschype but on letter sythe that I departeyd from youe the whyche make me hevy/ & my servant hathe beyn seke so that I had non to sende but thys next weke I woll sende my servant with sum boks of certeyn convents trusteynge that ye woll be goode lorde for the warents for suche fryers as gyve up ther housys to be had at my cymynge. . . .[2]

Finally, he wrote from Hereford on 27 August:

Goode my lorde, I pray yow be good lorde to me that the waranttes for ther habettes maye be had accordeynge to my promes, for they may not be sufferyd to saye masse abrode in chyrchys tyll they have ther exempcyons. I have wreten to dyverse of the byschoppes, and with dyverse I have spokyn, to lycens them tyll after Mychelmas, & at that tyme I have promyseyd to sende ther lycens to certen placeys wher they shall have them fre, for the more parte of them have no peny to paye for the charge of them. . . .[3]

Similar complaints of delay and confusion occur in Dr London's letters during his tour of the friaries. The capacities were particularly slow in arriving for the friars of Oxford. He forwarded in his own hand a petition to Cromwell from the Carmelites:

. . . It may lyk yowr gudde lordeschippe for that tendre pytie yow do bere towards all indigent persons we may by yor charitable supplication made unto the kings maiestie in our behalf obteyne for everyoon of usse licens under hys grace is seale and writing to channge our habitts payng nothing therfor and of hys most gratiose pytie and liberalitie to grannt unto usse som vesture convenyent at the tyme we shall by hys most gratiose pleasure putt of thys habytt We do now we(ar) and that we being of honest conversation gudde litterature and other acceptable qualities mete for the same may have lycens in wryting undre hys grace ys seale to receyve such lyvings as secular priests do enioy payng also no money in consideration of our extreme povertie for the same.[4]

London also put several questions to Cromwell:

It may like yor lordeschipp to acerten usse of yor pleasur. . . . Item wher we have sent uppe all the namys of such as hath made submission of your lordeschippe will accept itt then that with spede we may have ther capacyties ffor the longer they tary the more they will wast Item to have yor pleasur how yow will have the guddes kept when they have ther capacyties. . . .[5]

---

[1] Wright, *Suppression*, p. 206 (abstr. *L.P.* xiii. ii. 92).
[2] P.R.O. SP I/135, f. 215 (abstr. *L.P.* xiii. ii. 169).
[3] Wright, *Suppression*, pp. 210–11 (abstr. *L.P.* xiii. ii. 200).
[4] P.R.O. SP I/134, f. 115 (abstr. *L.P.* xiii. i. 1335, no. 2).
[5] P.R.O. SP I/134, f. 125ᵛ (abstr. *L.P.* xiii. i. 1342).

Although the capacities for all the orders of friars in Oxford are entered up in the register under the date 31 July,[1] it seems that there was still a serious delay in delivering them. London wrote on 14 August:

As yet we have nott ther capacities and therfor be at the chardge in fyndyng them mete and drink I do perceyve that residew abrode do lok for lyke dimission whose coots and maner of lyving as they be monstruose and full of dissimulation and ypocrisie so be they acceptyd of the people. and few do geve any almys to them Wherfor yor lordeschipp schall do a gudde dede to reduce them with other to that conformable fasschon of lyvinge as other honest prests do use.[2]

By the end of the month his patience, like Ingworth's, seems to have been running out. He reported:

I have causyd all our fower ordre of fryers to chaunge ther cotes and have dispacchide them as well as I can till they may receyve ther capacities for the wiche I have now agen sent uppe thys berar doctor Baskerfelde, to whom I do humblie besek your lordeschippe to stonde gudde lorde. He ys an honest man, and causyd all hys howse to surrendre the same and to chaunge ther papistical garmentes. I wrote to your lordeschippe specially for hym to have in hys capacitie an expresse licens to dwell in Oxford altho he wer benyfycyd. And your lordeshyp then wrote that yt wasse your pleasur he and all other shulde have ther capacities acording to ther desyer . . .[3]

These delays, this congestion of the machinery, must certainly have aggravated the problems of the unpensioned religious. Possibly there is here another cause which should be related to Mr Hodgett's argument, discussed in the earlier part of this chapter. Delays in the issue of capacities are proved by comparing the dates of the surrenders, and the Commissioners' reports, with the dates in the Faculty Office register, but not even the latter record on what date the letters eventually reached the ex-religious individually. One cannot help asking the questions: in some cases did they never arrive? or had the religious sometimes despaired and dispersed before their arrival? Were patrons sceptical of the validity of capacities, and contemptuous of the disreputable poverty of the friars? Dr London was still insisting on their particular difficulties in a letter from Godstow, which has been dated 6 November:

Oon of your lordeschips injunctions geven in the kinges name ys that no ffryar schalbe admytted to serve any cure. Now they be dismissed owt of ther howses no man will admytt any of them to be curattes, unlesse they do bring ther capacyties; wherfor I besek your lordeschippe we may have them with spede, ffor in the mean tyme the power men be withowt lyvinges, and now I have sett many abrode.[4]

---

[1] F I/Vv, ff. 210ᵛ–11ᵛ.   [2] P.R.O. SP I/135, f. 84ʳ (abstr. *L.P.* xiii. ii. 94).
[3] Wright, *Suppression*, p. 217 (abstr. *L.P.* xiii. ii. 235).
[4] Ibid., p. 228 (abstr. *L.P.* xiii. ii. 767).

In February 1539 Ingworth, then at Lincoln, repeated this point:

besecheyng yower lordschyp to be good lorde for the pore ffreyrs capacytes; they be very pore and can have lytyll serves withowtt ther capacytes. The byschoyppys and curettes be very hard to them withowtt they have ther capacytes.[1]

Writing from the north of England the following month Ingworth drew attention to yet another difficulty put in the way of the friars:

... in these parts, within the Dyocese off Yorke, the pore men that make surrender off ther Houses, be hardely orderyd by the Byschops Offycers att the Byschops commandement, so that they can nott be sufferyd to synge, nor saye in Paryshe Churche withoute they shewe ther Letters off ther Ordres; my letters or ther capacytes, notwithstondynge; and the charges off these Letters off ther Ordres be so grett that the pore men be nott abull to bere ytt; some muste goo an hunderyd myle to seke them, and when they come ther the cherges of sergyng the regyster ys so grett that they be not able to pay ytt, and so they come home ageyne confowndyd.

I have bene with my Lorde of Yorke, and shewyd to him your Lordeschypps letter, that your commandemente ys that they wyche so have surrenderyd ther Houses, shulde be suffryde withoute interrupcon to synge and saye in anye churche. The Byshope made many obieccions, and sayd that ytt muste be knowne whether they ware prysts or no, and I certefyde hym that wee that receivyd the Houses make dewe serge wyche ware prysts and whiche ware none, and so made certyfycate to yowr Lordeshyps, and yor Lordeshype to the Kyngs Grace, so that by that meane ther capacytes ware grauntyd, wherfore I desyred hym to accepte ther capacytes from the Kyngs Grace with so moche favor as the Byshops off Romes capacytes before had ben receyvyd, for the wyche ther was never serche made, butt streyghte obeyd. . . . Yor Lordeshype sholde do a charytable dede to wryghte your letters to the Byshope that he streyte att the syghte off yowr letters myghte sende thoroughe hys Dyocese that all curats myght have warnynge to suffer soche pore men that have gyff upe ther Houses, to synge in ther Churches, for they all have before commaundement of the Byshope that they shall not suffer them to synge withoute they shewe ther Letters off ther Ordres, the wyche ys not possyble for them to doo. . . .[2]

Supposing that some could not produce capacities nor proof of ordination, it would help to explain why so few can be traced holding benefices. In any case, this letter raises another point; it implies that to 'sing and say' as assistant curates was about the most that the unpensioned ex-religious could hope for.

---

[1] Wright, *Suppression*, p. 193 (abstr. *L.P.* xiv. i. 348).
[2] Ellis, *Original Letters*, 3rd Series, iii (1846), 186–8 (abstr. *L.P.* xiv. i. 494).

Table Showing Distribution of Capacities among the Religious (Excluding Those Issued upon Dissolution of Houses)

N.B. Parentheses indicate that Superior's permission must first be sought

	O.S.B.	Cluniac O.S.B.	O.Cist.	Austin canons	Pre-monstr. and Gilb.	Carth.	O.C. fr.	O.F.M.	O.P.	Austin fr. or hermits	Observ. fr.	Other friars	Hermits
1534/5													
Full capacity	10	..	1	3	..	2	2	2	3	1	3	..	..
Capacity to change habit	..	1	1	2	..	..	1	..	..	..	..	..	..
Capacity to hold benef.	6	1(2)	(3)	4(3)	(4)	..	1	(1)	..	..	..	1 Crutched fr.	1
Do. with habit beneath that of a sec. pr.	..	1	..	1	..	1	..	2*	..	1	..	..	..
Transference to another Order	..	..	..	..	..	..	..	2*	..	..	..	..	1
1536													
Full capacity	9	..	..	12	2	1	4	9(1)	4	5	1	2 Crutched fr.	..
Capacity to change habit	9(2)	..	1	3	2	2	2	3	..	3	2(1)	1	..
Capacity to hold benef.	4(2)	1	4(1)	8(2)	2	..	1	..	..	2(1)	..	1	..
Do. with habit beneath that of a sec. pr.	3(2)	1	..	4(2)	1	..	2(1)	3	..	..	..	..	..
1537													
Full capacity	6	..	..	..	1	..	..	5	1	..	..	..	..
Capacity to change habit	2	1	..	..	1**	..	..	1	1	..	..	1	..
Capacity to hold benef.	..	..	2	..	..	..	..	..	3	..	..	..	..
Do. with habit beneath that of a sec. pr.	3(1)	..	3	..	..	1	1	1	5	1	1	..	..

* One to become an Austin canon (f. 13ᵛ); the other to become a hermit of St Anthony (f. 36).

** Unspecified canon.

Table Showing Distribution of Capacities among the Religious (Excluding Those Issued upon Dissolution of Houses) (cont.)

	O.S.B.	Cluniac O.S.B.	O.Cist.	Austin canons	Pre-monstr. and Gilb.	Carth.	O.C. fr.	O.F.M.	O.P.	Austin fr.	Observ. fr.	Other friars	Sion
1538													
Full capacity	28†	..	..	4	..	..	..	4	2	2	..	..	1
Capacity to change habit	2	..	..	2	1	..	3	7	8	1	1	2	..
Capacity to hold benef.	1	..	..	1	1	..	..	..	2	..	..	..	..
Do. wearing habit beneath that of a sec. pr.	2	..	..	..	2	..	..	1	2	..	..	..	..
Transference	..	..	..	..	..	..	..	1††	..	..	..	..	..
1539													
Full capacity	1	..	..	..	1	..	..	..	..	..	..	..	..
Capacity to hold benef.	..	..	..	1	..	..	..	..	..	..	..	..	..

† 18 of these from Norwich.   †† To become hermit of St Paul (f. 197ᵛ).

Table Showing Payment for Capacities

(N.B. This does not include pluralities for regular clergy)

	1534/5		1536		1537		1538	
	Monks and Canons	Friars	Monks and Canons	Friars	Monks and Canons	Friars	Monks and Canons	Friars
Full capacities	14	10	16	4	5	..	7	5
Capacity to change habit	1	..	4	1	2	1	4	6
Do. to hold a benef.	23	5	18	4	2	1	3	2
Do. wearing habit beneath that of a sec. pr.	4; 1 hermit	4	16	6	6	4	4	3
Do. without benef.	3	1	..	..	..	..	..	..

IV

FINANCIAL ASPECTS OF THE FACULTY OFFICE

HENRICIAN propaganda denounced the Court of Rome for venality (the Act of 1540, for instance, asserted that marriage dispensations within prohibited degrees were 'for their lucre by that court invented'), but the Faculty Office also charged high prices for dispensations. In this chapter an attempt is made to compare the prices, and also to analyse the economy of this new department of government, the rise and decline of its revenues.

The Dispensations Act represented the new system as a genuine reform: there was, of course, some truth in this.

And for as moche as the charges of obteynyng the said licences, dispensacions, faculties and other rescriptes or wrytynges afore named at the Courte of Rome, by the losses and exchanges, and in conductyng of currours, and wagyng solicitours, to sue for any suche licences, dispensacions, faculties, instruments, and other rescripts or wrytynges, have been grevous and excessive to your people, and many times greatter sommes have byn demaunded for the spedy expedicions in the Courte of Rome then be expressed in the olde taxe lymyted to be payd for the said expedicions, wherby your people (hath) byn brought to an incertentie upon the payment for expedicions of suche thynges, and by reason therof have byn constrayned to pay more than they were wont to doo, to the great impoverishing of this Realme/ And sometymes the spedyng of suche dispensacions etc. have byn soo longe diferred, that the partyes laboryng for the same have suffered great incommodities and losse for lacke of quycke spede . . . to thintent that all ambiguytie and incertentie of payments . . . may be taken away, that noo fraude or exaccion shalbe exercised uppon your people. . . .

Be it enacted . . . that there shal be two bokes drawen up and made of one tenour: In whiche shalbe conteyned the taxes of all customable dispensacions etc. wonte to be (spede) at Rome; which bokes, and every lefe of those bokes, and both sides of every lefe, shalbe subscribid by the Archebisshop of Caunterbury, the Lord Chaunceler of Englond, the Lord Treasourer of Englonde, and the ii chefe Justices of both Benches for the tyme being; to the whiche bokes all Suters for dispensacions etc. shall have resource yf they require hit; And one of the seid bokes shall remayne in the handes of him which shalbe appoynted to regester and scribe of the said dispensacions etc. and the other boke shall remayne with the Clerke of the said Chauncerie. . . . (cl. VI)

. . . no man suing for dispensacions etc. . . . shall paye any more . . . then shalbe conteyned taxed and lymitted in the said Duplicate bokes of taxes onely; composicions (except) of which being arbitrarye noo taxe can be made; Wherfore the

taxe therof shalbe sett and lymytted by the discreacion of the seid Archebishop
of Caunterbury and the Lorde Chaunceler of Englond or the Lorde Keeper of
the greate seale for the tyme being: And that suche as shall exacte or receyve of
any suter more for any dispensacion etc. then shalbe conteyned in the seid bokes
of taxes, shall forfett ten tymes so moche as he shall soo extorciously exacte and
receyve. . . . (cl. VII)

Neither of these books of taxes, made up in the prescribed manner, seems
to have survived, though one still existed in the early eighteenth century.[1]
There are some undated sheets of what may have been either a draft or
early copy of it in the P.R.O.,[2] but this document is not complete; many
types of dispensation are excluded from it, and some of the fees it quotes
do not correspond with those entered in Register Vv.[3] A more authentic
copy of the tariff survives from the mid seventeenth century;[4] this excludes
the abolished classes of dispensation (those affecting regular clergy, and
the prohibited degrees for marriage), and includes later revisions by Archbishop Parker, but the first section of it (Nos. 1–98) seems to correspond
exactly with the original Henrician tariff as charged in Register Vv.

It is difficult to make a valid comparison between these fees and the
charges of the papal curia. Some papal tariffs for dispensations survive,
but these do not, of course, allow for all the superfluous expenses, 'losses
and exchanges, and in conductyng of currours and wagyng solicitours',
nor for the disregard in practice of the tariff, an abuse to which the Act
refers, and which Pope Leo X had hoped to reform.[5] It is probable that
the fees in the tariffs are purely nominal; a collection of proctors' accounts,
if only they could be brought to light, would be necessary to show the
truth.[6]

One such papal tariff, published in 1520,[7] includes some of the fees
charged in the chancery for pluralities and other causes, as well as the more

---

[1] Gibson, *Codex Iuris*, i. 105 n.

[2] P.R.O. SP I/104, ff. 316ᵛ–29. It is not clear why this document should be dated 1536
in *L.P.* x, App. 4, p. 538, where it is only briefly noted.

[3] For instance, a capacity for a non-mendicant regular to hold a benefice and retain the
habit of his Order beneath that of a secular is quoted at £12. 10s. (f. 322ᵛ), whereas in the
Register it usually costs £8; a dispensation for marriage in third and fourth degrees of
consanguinity is quoted at 15s., and in third degree at £7. 5s. (f. 326ᵛ) compared to 30s.
and £6 respectively in the Register.

[4] P.R.O. SP 16/499, ff. 223–30ᵛ, noted in *Cal. S.P. Dom. 1641–3*, p. 545; reference
by E. F. Churchill, art. cit., *E.H.R.* xxxiv (1919), p. 410.

[5] E. Göller, 'Die päpstliche Pönitentiarie', *Bibliothek des Kgl. Preußischen Historischen
Instituts in Rom* (1907–11), Band II, part I (1911), p. 172; part II, p. 139.

[6] H. C. Lea, 'The Taxes of the Papal Penitentiary', *E.H.R.* viii (1893), 435–6 produces
the interesting case of Abbot Whethamstede of St. Alban's dispensation for eating meat in
Lent in 1423. In theory he should have paid 10 grossi, in fact he paid about 462 grossi, or
£7. 14s.

[7] *Taxe Cancellarie apostolice e taxe sacre Penitentiarie itidem apostolice*, Paris, Foussains
Denis, 1520. (B.M. pressmark 1022. c. 28. There are a number of earlier printed tariffs
also in the B.M., catalogued under the heading 'Rome, Cancellaria Apostolica').

spiritual classes of dispensation restricted to the penitentiary, to which these lists are usually confined. Prices are quoted in papal grossi or carleni, of which there were 10 to the ducat, which in turn was worth about 4s. 6d. of English currency.[1] This 1520 tariff also states some of the supplementary charges payable for the drawing up of the letters granting the dispensation. The scriptors received 1 ducat for every 10, or 25 quatrini for every carleno; 1 ducat 2 carleni were payable to the sinecure office of janissaries for all dispensations costing less than 30 ducats. It candidly points out that dispensations are a class privilege: the poor could not obtain them at all.[2] On the other hand, the nobility had to pay more, generally double the statutory fee. The fees quoted are much lower than those of the Faculty Office. A dispensation to hold two incompatible benefices cost 30 grossi or about 13s. 6d., whereas the Faculty Office charged £6. 10s., excluding the non-residence clause which cost another £1. 3s. 4d. A licence to eat meat in Lent cost 10 grossi or 4s. 6d., against £2 charged by the Faculty Office. For a regular to transfer from one order to another is quoted at 16 grossi or about 7s. 2d., while an unfortunate Franciscan had to pay £3 to the Faculty Office for this in 1534.[3]

The most recent of these papal tariffs before the English breach with Rome is dated 1525 and restricted to the dispensations issued by the penitentiary.[4] It quotes the fees in grossi of Tours ('Turonenses') but these were equivalent to papal grossi.[5] The list is much the same as that of 1520, but gives some further details of supplementary charges. For instance, while the basic fee for a dispensation to marry despite fourth degree of consanguinity was 7T, or about 3s. 2d., another 7T had to be paid to the scriptors, and 5T for the seal, making the total about 8s. 7d.; the Faculty Office charged 26s. 8d. For the third degree of affinity or consanguinity the difference was greater still: 39T or about 18s. in Rome, compared to £6 in England.

A glance down the fees entered in the Faculty Office registers confirms that, the current value of money considered, they were far from cheap. The prices charged for Wolsey's dispensations fluctuated slightly, but were usually about the same, or a shilling or two cheaper; there were a few striking differences. He charged 20s. (f. 23) for a marriage without banns instead of 10s.; and in one case a regular canon was charged £6 to wear his habit beneath that of a secular (f. 20ᵛ); in another only 30s. (f. 22ᵛ) but this

[1] E. Martinori, *La Moneta* (Rome, 1915), p. 56; Göller, op. cit., Band II (1), p. 156 n. 2, p. 176; F. C. Dietz, *English Government Finance 1485–1558* (Univ. of Illinois Studies in Social Sciences, ix. 1920), App. i, p. 215.
[2] p. xxiii: 'et nota diligenter quod huiusmodi gratie et dispensationes non conceduntur pauperibus qui non sunt ideo non possunt consolari'.
[3] F I/Vv, f. 13ᵛ.
[4] Biblioteca Vallicelliana, Rome, MS. I 78, ff. 1–24ᵛ, quoted by Göller, op. cit., Band II (II Teil), App. C, pp. 146 sqq.
[5] Martinori, *La Moneta*, p. 205.

was probably a case of remission by special grace. Even allowing for the large supplementary costs of obtaining dispensations from Rome, which probably rose still higher after the sack of 1527,[1] the possibility still seems tenable that Baskerville was right in his statement that Rome had been cheaper than the system which replaced it.[2]

The system of dividing the fees laid down in the Dispensations Act[3] was complicated.

If the fee was £4 or above, it was divided into the following fractions (in brackets are shown the sum this would be in the case of a £4 fee): two-thirds (£2. 13s. 4d.) to chancery, and one-third (26s. 8d.) to the archbishop's office. Of the former, three-quarters (£2) went to the king, and a quarter (13s. 4d.) to the Lord Chancellor, who had to pay a third of this (4s. 5d.) to the clerk of the faculties 'for his pains travail and labours' (which included collecting the money). Of the archbishop's share, two-thirds went to that prelate personally 'to his use'; the remaining third (about 8s. 11d.) went to his officers, of which one-half (4s. 5½d.) to the clerk or registrar and the other half to the commissary. If the fee was under £4 the Lord Chancellor, of course, lost his share. Fees between £2 and £4 were divided into two-thirds for the king (3s. 4d. of which he gave to the chancery clerk of the faculties) and one-third for the archbishop: a half of this went to the latter personally and the other half was equally divided between scribe and commissary. Fees below £2 down to 26s. 8d. were again differently divided (in brackets are shown the divisions for a fee of 26s. 8d.). Half went to the king (13s. 4d.) of which 2s. was paid to the clerk; and half to the archbishop, who kept half of this (6s. 8d.) himself and split the rest (3s. 4d. each) between scribe and commissary. Fees below 26s. 8d. down to £1 were also halved, but the archbishop was only entitled to a third of his half, the other two-thirds being equally divided between scribe and commissary (3s. 4d. each for a £1 fee). Below 20s. the fee was supposed to be halved between the chancery clerk and the archbishop's commissary.

This system of division provides the clue to the striking difference in the entries of fees between Register Vv and Register A. At first sight one assumes there must have been an astonishing reduction of faculty charges in the 1540's (a very unusual phenomenon for anything to be going down in price during that decade, especially the fees of a declining office). But it soon becomes clear that the fees in the second register only represent a fraction of what the suitor was paying: the fraction due to the archbishop's commissary. This is illustrated, for instance, by the fees charged for eating meat in Lent: £2 in Register Vv, 3s. 4d. in Register A; or that to hold two

<hr/>

[1] H. Jedin, *A History of the Council of Trent*, i (trans. E. Graff, Edinburgh, 1957), 416.
[2] *English Monks and the Suppression*, p. 152.
[3] Cl. VIII. The draft tariff in the P.R.O. already mentioned (SP I/104, ff. 316ᵛ–29) indicates the respective shares paid to each party for the dispensation it quotes.

incompatible benefices, £6. 10s. in Register Vv, 7s. 2d. in Register A. The lower fees (under £1) do not correspond so exactly to the rules, however, and it looks as though the archbishop was probably demanding his share as well. For instance, marriage without banns is charged at 10s. in Register Vv, and marriage with one reading at 6s. 8d.: the corresponding fees in Register A, however, are 3s. 4d. and 2s. 2d.

As well as these fixed charges, the registers (especially Vv) reveal that fees were sometimes reduced by a process of arbitration, or remitted altogether. This has already been noted in the case of capacities for the religious, and dispensations for eating in Lent;[1] but except for these, and a number of miscellaneous cases,[2] such concessions most often applied to marriage in the more expensive prohibited degrees. In a few cases, a marginal note indicates that poverty was the cause for remission of the fee;[3] however, for the most part, no cause is shown, nor even who authorized the remission. Cranmer's own initiative is occasionally revealed,[4] also the Lord Chancellor's;[5] and from 1538 onwards it is often signified that remissions or reductions were according to warrant, which may (as in the case of capacities) mean that Cromwell was the power behind them. In the 1540's there are very few gratuitous dispensations recorded,[6] but then there were far less cases for which payment might have been an unreasonable hardship. The following table will show the scale on which gratuitous or arbitrated letters of dispensation were issued (excluding capacities for the religious): in brackets are shown the number from each total where poverty was the cause:

	1534/5	1536	1537	1538	1539	1540	1543/4	1545	1546	1547	1548/9
Gratis	3 (1)	1	7 (2)	7 (4)	15 (5)	10 (4)	2	2	7	2	3
Arbitrated	15	8	8	12	5	5	..	..	..	..	..

The annual revenues of the faculty administration are entered in Register Vv and (except that roman numerals have been turned into arabic) are shown in the table overleaf.

The striking drop of the revenue in 1539 shows that the suppression of the monasteries and friaries had an immediate effect. The continued

---

[1] Above, pp. xli, xlvii.

[2] There were a number of pluralities for privileged persons for which no charge was made: the persons including the Lord Chancellor himself, and Nicholas Wotton, Commissary of Faculties; also the king's secretary Vannes, and Cromwell's chaplain. (F I/Vv, ff. 32ᵛ, 77ʳ, 130ʳ, 173ᵛ, 208ʳ, 326ᵛ, 374ʳ; F I/A, pp. 72–74.) There were three concerning ordination (F I/Vv, f. 185ᵛ, for a bastard, f. 222ᵛ; F I/A, p. 150); several for notaries (F I/Vv, f. 9ʳ. F I/A, pp. 146, 217, 218); preachers were not charged.

[3] Excluding the religious: F I/Vv, ff. 34ᵛ, 117ʳ, 135ᵛ, 176ʳ, 179ʳ, 186ʳ, 194ʳ, 274ʳ, 275ʳ, 280ʳ, 299ʳ, 300ʳ, 310ʳ, 328ʳ, 333ʳ, 333ᵛ.

[4] Ibid., ff. 26ʳ, 27ʳ, 28ᵛ, 42ʳ.   [5] Ibid., ff. 8ʳ, 43ᵛ, 336ʳ.

[6] However, four of them were for marriage without banns (F I/A, pp. 202, 231, 237, 272) for which in F I/Vv fees were not remitted.

	King	*Chancery*	*Archbp's office*	*Total*
f. 44^{v}, 1534/5	£940. 10*s*. 9½*d*.	£243. 18*s*. –	£726. 15*s*. 10½*d*.	£1,911. 4*s*. 8*d*.
f. 109^{v}, 1536	£670. 7*s*. ½*d*.	£224. 6*s*. 6¼*d*.	£527. – 6¾*d*.	£1,421. 14s. 2*d*.
f. 165^{v}, 1537	£555. 7*s*. 1½*d*.	£187. 7*s*. 10½*d*.	£463. 5*s*. –	£1,206. – –
f. 243^{v}, 1538	£659. 7s. 3½*d*.	£112. 11*s*. 8½*d*. (1*d*. chan.) £103. 11*s*. 11*d*. (clk.)	£301. 9*s*. 1½*d*. (archbp.) £239. 4*s*. 3½*d*. (comm. and scribe)	£1,416. 4*s*. 4*d*.
f. 304^{v}, 1539	£396. 19*s*. 1¾*d*.	£63. 16*s*. 3*d*. (1*d*. chan.) £74. 1*s*. 5½*d*. (clk.)	£187. 14*s*. 7½*d*. (archbp.) £174. 14*s*. 2¼*d*. (comm.)	£897. 6*s*. 8*d*.
f. 352^{v}, 1540	£354. 6*s*. 11*d*.	£57. 18*s*. 8*d*. (1*d*. chan.) £64. 8*s*. 10¾*d*. (clk.)	£160. 18*s*. 8*d*. (archbp.) £157. 9*s*. 6*d*. (comm.)	£795. 2*s*. 7¾*d*,[1]

reduction in 1540 must also be due to the revision of the marriage laws, affecting the latter half of the year.[2] It will also be noticed from these figures that Cranmer derived from the faculties an appreciable new source of income, and the King, of course, did even better: this was a supplementary item of crown revenue which historians in general have not recognized.[3] It is paradoxical that the most lucrative sources of this revenue were so soon renounced by the authority which had enjoyed them.

In Register A there are no regular entries of the total revenues year by year, and only an occasional memorandum of the sums which Anthony Huse picked up from the archbishop's office to send on to the absentee Commissary Nicholas Wotton,[4] and the salary paid to Coke as surrogate.[5] The latter was not provided for under the terms of the Dispensations Act, but fixed payments were made to him of £6. 13*s*. 4*d*. a year: not an over-generous salary. It is difficult to estimate from the register what were the total annual revenues; to the Commissary's fee entered in the margin one must add the shares which went to the other authorities, for each dispensation. It is not easy to calculate what was charged for some of the more expensive plurality dispensations, or the more complicated combinations of causes dispensed with for marriage. However, a rough estimate for the

1 In the register, the total for this year is incorrectly added up to £799. 1*s*. 8*d*.

2 Above, pp. xxxv–xxxvi.

3 For instance, F. C. Dietz, op. cit.

4 26 Mar. 1543/4–31 May 1544 £64. 9*s*. 4*d*. (F I/A, p. 50); 18 Feb. 1545–7 June 1545 £20. 10*s*. (p. 131); 11 July 1545–10 Sept. 1545 £8. 1*s*. 10*d*. (p. 148); 7 June–9 Oct. 1545 £21. 11*s*. 2*d*. (p. 155); 9 Oct. 1545–31 July 1546 £51. 2*s*. 2*d*. (p. 209); 31 July 1546–11 July 1547 £77. 17*s*. 9*d*. (p. 270); 11 July 1547–10 Sept. 1548 £77. 0*s*. 9*d*. (p. 329).

5 7 June 1545 'paid to the master oon quarter for his paynes accordyng to the agrement 33s 4d' (p. 131); 9 Oct. 1545 'paid to Mr Coke for his paynes for oon quarter 33s 4d' (p. 155); 31 July 1546 'paid to Mr Choke for 3 quarters of a yeres stipende . . . fyve pounds' (p. 209); 11 July 1547 (p. 270) and 10 Sept. 1548 (p. 330) 'paid to Dr Coke £6. 13s 4d'.

years 1545 and 1548 suggests a figure somewhere between £500 and £600. The mainstay of the office were the plurality dispensations, but these of course fluctuated very much in number from year to year, as the table already has shown. 1548 was not so good a year for pluralities as 1545; but the revenues were helped by the dispensations for eating meat in Lent. In 1545 the latter yielded only £26; in 1548 they contributed £124. 10*s*. This estimate of somewhere above £500 as the income from the faculties indicates that the department was continuing to decline. It confirms what Stephen Vaughan wrote to the King in 1544 (a year during which it looks from a rough calculation that the revenues were even lower): 'thoffyce, like as yor majeste knowithe ys fallen into a great decaye and ys veray letle worthe to hym that shall occupie it';[1] to Paget the same month he revealed 'thoffyce ys like as yow know in a great decaye and ys not worthe to me xx li a yere, and yet am cowntable to the kyngs Ma[jes]te'.[2]

[1] P.R.O. SP I/187, f. 6ᵛ (abstr. *L.P.* xix. i. 379), quoted also by Richardson, *Stephen Vaughan*, p. 84 n. 5.
[2] P.R.O. SP I/187, f. 11 (abstr. *L.P.* xix. i. 380); Richardson, loc. cit.

REGISTER Vv (1534–1540)

f. 1ʳ

1534 Apr. 15 Jo. Salcott *alias* Capon, abbot of St Peter's, Hyde. Disp. also to hold the bpric of Bangor. £100.

May 14 Ann Castelforth, O.Cist., nun of Gokewell, Linc. dio. Disp. to be head of a religious hse despite being in her 27th yr. £5.

12 Edm. Cranmer, archdcn of Canterbury. Disp. to hold 2 benefices with cure with the archdcnry, or 2 without it; permut. & non-res. cl. £9.

19 Giles Kaye & Agnes Beaumonte, York dio. Disp. for marriage (4th & 4th degrees consang.). 26s 8d.

Tho. Blenerhaset, acol., Norw. dio. Disp. to take h.o. from any bp, 2 on the same day. 26s 8d.

3 Tho. Rokewoode, acol. Disp. to take h.o. at any times despite being in his 23rd yr. £3 6s 8d.

f. 1ᵛ

18 Tho. Carden, M.A., Cant. dio. Disp. to take h.o. at any times, 2 on the same day, from any bp. 26s 8d.

19 Ric. Willyams & Marg. Morgan, Lland dio. Disp. for marriage (4th degree consang.). 26s 8d.

Jo. Brokhols & Helen Sherborn, York dio. Disp. for marriage (3rd & 4th degrees affin.). 30s.

Ric. Walwyn & Dorothy Leyghton, Heref. dio. Disp. for marriage (4th degrees consang. & affin.). 50s.

Hugh Awborne & Janet Frende, Carl. dio. Disp. for marriage (3rd & 4th degrees affin.). 30s

Tho. Kent, acol., Bath & W. dio. Disp. to take h.o. at any time, 2 on the same day, from any bp. 26s 8d.

Apr. 14 Jo. Cheswright, r. of Baldock & Wisbech, Ely dio. Disp. to hold a benef. with the above, or 2 without; permut. & non-res. cl. £13 6s 8d.

f. 2ʳ

May 20 Geo. Greves, reg. canon, recently sub-prior of Holy Trinity & Christchurch, London. Disp. to hold any benef. with or without cure; permut. cl. £4.

May 20 Jo. Lyngfeld, prior of St Jas, Tandridge, Winton dio. Disp. to hold any benef. with or without cure with the above; permut. cl. £10.

21 Hy Shawe, Cov. & Lich. dio. & Alice Homes, York dio. Disp. for marriage (4th & 4th degrees consang.). 26s 8d.

Rob. Atkynson & Janet Scott, Carl. dio. Disp. for marriage (4th & 4th degrees affin.). 26s 8d.

23 Wm Symson & Agnes Walkar, York dio. Disp. for marriage (4th & 4th degrees affin.). 26s 8d.

f. 2ᵛ

25 Stephen Sketter & Marg. Nelson, Linc. dio. Disp. for marriage (3rd & 4th degrees consang.). 30s.

30 Wm Archer & Agnes Byrkhede, York dio. Disp. for marriage (3rd & 4th degrees consang.). 30s.

Ric. Coxe, acol., M.A., Linc. dio. Disp. to take h.o. at any times, 2 on the same day, from any bp. 26s 8d.

Jas Wysse & Eliz. Howmes, Lond. dio. Disp. for marriage without banns. 10s.

Mich. Browne & Joan Denys. Disp. for marriage in any ch. or chapel, the banns read once. 6s 8d.

June 3 Jas Whitacre, r. of Quarley, Winton dio. Disp. to hold another benef. with cure with the above, or 2 others or any eccles. office etc. without; permut. & non-res. cl. £7 13s 4d.

f. 3ʳ

Tho. Norwoode & Eliz. Woodestocke of Croydon, peculiar of Cant. dio. Disp. for marriage (2nd & 3rd degrees affin.). Arb. £4.

6 Geo. Cureton & Ann Lowe, Cov. & Lich. dio. Disp. for marriage (4th degree consang.). 26s 8d.

3 Alice Cranmere, O.Cist., nun of Stixwould, Linc. dio. Disp. to join any other order or community of nuns, and act as abbess or prioress if so elected. £10.

9 Ric. Hertley & Kath. Walton, Cov. & Lich. dio. Disp. for marriage (3rd & 4th degrees affin., 3rd & 3rd and 4th & 4th equal degrees of consang.). £6; 26s 8d.

f. 3ᵛ

John ap Philippe, St David's dio. Disp. to take all h.o. outside statutory times, 2 on the same day, from any bp. 26s 8d.

8 Lawrence Shawe & Joan Hargraves, Cov. & Lich. dio. Disp. for marriage (4th degree consang.). 26s 8d.

June 10 Rob. Johnson & Alison Maltbye, Linc. dio. Disp. for marriage (Rob.'s father was Alison's godfather). 30s.

11 Nich. Hyne & Marg. Sawle, York dio. Disp. for marriage (3rd & 4th degrees consang.). 30s.

Baldwin Hyll, r. of Dowlish Wake, Bath & W. dio. Disp. to take all h.o. outside the statutory times, from any bp. 26s 8d.

12 Geo. Masson & Agnes Cawpestayke. Disp. for marriage (3rd & 4th degrees consang.). 30s.

f. 4ʳ

14 Geo. Cureton & Alice Lowe, Cov. & Lich. dio. Disp. for marriage (4th degree consang.). 26s 8d. [cf. above, f. 3ʳ]

17 Tho. Cockeson & Ann Toppan, York dio. Disp. for marriage (3rd & 4th degrees consang.). 30s.

Jo. Coventre & Janet Warton, Cov. & Lich. dio. Disp. for marriage (4th degree consang.). 26s 8d.

14 Humfrey Moryce, B.Cn. & C.L., v. of Oundle, Linc. dio. Disp. to hold a benef. with or without cure with the above, or 2 others without; permut. cl. £6 10s.

20 Nich. Bowkar & Joan Keynam. Disp. for marriage (4th degree consang.). 26s 8d.

21 Rob. Foxe & Agnes Alen, widow. Disp. for marriage without banns, & in any church. 10s.

2 Geo. Vyncent & Ann Knyght, gent. & widow, Linc. dio. Disp. for marriage, the banns read once. 6s 8d.

12 Chris. Frankelyn & Eliz. Churche, Sarum dio. Disp. for marriage (Chris.'s father was Eliz.'s godfather). 30s.

f. 4ᵛ

22 Rob. Crabtre & Joan Sothyll, Cov. & Lich. dio. Disp. for marriage (4th degree consang.). 26s 8d.

29 Edw. Mawde & Eliz. Oldefelde, York dio. Disp. for marriage (4th degree affin.). 26s 8d.

22 Ric. Hore, M.A., r. of North Tuddenham ('Northudnaham'), Norw. dio., chapl. to Archbp of Cant. Disp. to hold a benef. with or without cure with the above or 2 without; permut. & non-res. cl. £7 13s 4d.

20 Rob. Pullen & Marg. Creteham, York dio. Disp. for marriage (Marg. was godmother to a child of Rob.). Arb. £4.

27 Thrustan Wylding & Marg. Mosse, Cov. & Lich. dio. Disp. for marriage (3rd degree consang.). £4.

June 29 Rob. Hole, B.Th., r. of Nettleton, Linc. dio. Disp. to hold a benef. with the above, or 2 without. £6 10s.

f. 5ʳ

30 Rob. Colyns, M.A., v. of Felsted, Lond. dio., chapl. to Viscount Rocheford. Disp. to hold a benef. with cure with the above, or 2 without; permut. cl. £6 10s.

July   1 Wm Stanley, r. of Sutton, York dio. Disp. to hold a benef. with cure with the above, if it does not yield over £8 p.a., or 2 without. £4.

4 Tho. Crumplehere & Agnes Norton, Sarum dio. Disp. for marriage (Agnes was godmother to a child of Tho.). £6.

11 Tho. Topcliff, pr. of the coll. ch. of St Mary & All Saints, Fotheringay, Linc. dio. Disp. to hold a benef. with cure not yielding over £8 p.a. with the above, or 2 others without; permut. & non-res. cl. £4.

Edw. Eyre, B.Cn.L., r. of Eton, Linc. dio. Disp. to hold a benef. with cure with the above, or 2 without; permut. & non-res. cl. £7 13s 4d.

7 Berden, prior & Convent of, O.S.A., Lond. dio. Disp. as recently allowed use of par. ch. of St Nicholas, Berden, to provide a canon or pr. to administer it. £4.

f. 5ᵛ

14 Ric. Benet & Eliz. Bonsall, of Hartington, peculiar of Cov. & Lich. dio. Disp. for marriage (3rd & 4th, & 4th & 4th degrees of consang.; 3rd & 4th degrees affin.). £6; 30s; 26s 8d.

15 Tho. Blythe, v. of Colwich. Disp. to hold a benef. with the above, or 2 without; permut. & non-res. cl. £7 13s 4d.

June 17 Ric. Comes & Eliz. Brockes, Linc. dio. Disp. for marriage without banns. 10s.

26 Rob. Mosse & Kath. Wylding. Disp. for marriage (Kath.'s father was Rob.'s sponsor at confirmation). 26s 8d.

27 Wm Atkyns & Helen Eden. Disp. for marriage (4th & 4th degrees consang.). 26s 8d.

Wm Chester, subdcn, Ex. dio. Disp. to take the rest of h.o. in his 22nd yr. 23s 4d

Nich. Bukfast. Disp. to receive pr.'s orders in his 22nd yr. 23s 4d.

30 Baldwin Borwyke & Agnes Gylping. Disp. for marriage (4th degree consang.). 26s 8d.

f. 6ʳ

June 30 Jo. Watson & Marg. Walkar, York dio. Disp. for marriage (4th degree affin.). 26s 8d.

Oliver Herde & Kath. Richardson. York dio. Disp. for marriage (4th degree affin.). 26s 8d.

Tho. Cokayn & Eliz. Barewell, York dio. Disp. for marriage (4th degree consang.). 26s 8d.

Inhabitants of Pinner, peculiar of Cant. dio. Erection of baptistery in the chapel of St Jo. Baptist, without prejudice to the par. ch. of Harrow-on-the-Hill, or its r. & v. 13s 4d.

July 8 Ric. Wilson. Disp. to take all h.o. outside statutory times. 20s.

7 Ric. Gillett & Alice Walkar, York dio. Disp. for marriage (3rd & 4th degrees consang.). 30s.

13 Tho. Lancaster & Marg. Sanderson, Carl. dio. Disp. for marriage (3rd & 4th degrees consang.). 30s.

June 28 Geo. Medley & Mary Damet. Disp. for marriage (2nd & 3rd degrees consang., and the Countess of Dorset, Geo.'s mother, was Mary's godmother). £8; 30s.

f. 6ᵛ

July 11 Hy Moryce & Emma Smythe *alias* Toucke. Disp. for marriage (Emma's father was Hy's godfather). 30s.

10 Tho. Panton & Kath. Salisbury, St. Asaph dio. Cancelled disp. confirming their marriage already contracted. (Tho. was betrothed previously to Kath.'s sister Jane.)

13 Tho. Percevall & Eliz. Sordall. Disp. for marriage (4th degree consang.). 26s 8d.

17 Walter Wylkyns & Eliz. Rundell, Sarum dio. Disp. for marriage (3rd & 4th degrees consang.). 30s.

Wm Broke, gent., & Dorothy Nevell, gentw. Disp. for marriage (3rd & 4th degrees consang.). 30s.

21 Jo. Parker, B.A., Linc. dio. Disp. to hold a benef. in his 24th yr, be non-res., & to take all h.o. from any bp outside statutory times, & 2 on the same day. 26s 8d; 20s.

f. 7ʳ

20 Geo. Taylour, esq., & Adriana Canesforde, Winton dio. Disp. for marriage, the banns read once. 6s 8d.

22 Jo. Adams, Jo. Jordan, Nich. Shawe, Wm Chaterton, of the Guild of SS Chris. & Geo., York. Disp. to collect alms through their proctor in the province of Canterbury. 10s.

July 24 Geo. Cawpestaicke & Alice Mydleton. Disp. for marriage (3rd & 4th degrees consang.). 30s.

Edw. Wode & Janet Burton. Disp. for marriage (4th degree consang.). 26s 8d.

Ric. Smarwhat & Eliz. William, York dio. Disp. for marriage (3rd and 4th degrees consang.). 30s.

22 Tho. Ewer of London & Helen Ingham of King's Langley, Lond. dio. Disp. for marriage, the banns read once. 6s 8d.

f. 7^v

31 Jo. Elyott & Juliana Tanner. Disp. for marriage (4th degree consang.). 26s 8d.

15 Tho. Herley, M.A., r. of Clovelly, Ex. dio., Kg's chapl. Disp. to hold a benef. with cure with the above, or 2 without; permut. & non-res. cl. £7 13s 4d.

17 Elias Bodeley, D.Cn. & C.L., r. of Beckenham, Roch. dio., chapl. to Bp of Bath & W. Disp. to hold a benef. with cure with the above or 2 without; permut. & non-res. cl. £7 13s 4d.

June 5 Wm Danyell, M.A., v. of Chesham, Linc. dio., chapl. to Earl of Wiltshire. Disp. to hold a benef. with cure with the above, or 2 without; permut. & non-res. cl. £7 13s 4d.

Apr. 12 Jo. Dawson, York dio., chapl. to Duke of Richmond & Somerset, K.G. Disp. to hold any 2 benefices with cure; permut. & non-res. cl. £7 13s 4d.

f. 8^r

July 29 Rob. Dobell, B.Cn.L., r. of Silverton, Ex. dio. Disp. to hold a benef. with cure with, or 2 without, the above; permut. cl. £6 10s.

3 Tho. Portyngton, r. of Speldhurst, Roch. dio. Disp. to hold a benef. with cure with the above, or 2 others without; permut. cl. £6 10s.

Aug. 4 Edm. ap David ap Pell & Angharada verch Llan ap Pell, St Asaph dio. Disp. for marriage (2nd, 3rd, & 3rd & 4th degrees affin.). 'Nichil Regi quia remittebatur per dominum Cancellarium gratis.'

22 Jo. Barcoste & Eliz. Tatersall, Cov. & Lich. Dio. Disp. for marriage (3rd degree affin.). £6.

July 6 Jo. Lynyng & Kath. Robyns, Lond. dio. Disp. for marriage (3rd & 4th degrees consang.). 30s.

9 Wm Lysley, proctor or warden of the Poor House, Hammersmith. Disp. to collect alms. 10s. [cf. f. 44^v, below]

f. 8^v

Aug. 24 Rees Owen, v. of Mathry, St David's dio. Disp. to hold a benef. with the above, or 2 without. £4.

26 Rob. & Marg. Percyvall. Disp. for marriage (2nd & 3rd degrees affin.). Arb. £4.

Ric. & Marg. Hey, Cov. & Lich. dio. Disp. for marriage (3rd degree affin.). £4.

Morgan Mathew & Dacia Williams *alias* Herbert, Lland. dio. Disp. for marriage (Morgan was godfather to a child of Dacia). Arb. £4.

Sept. 9 Hy Newsam & Marg. Stede, Cov. & Lich. dio. Disp. for marriage (Hy was Marg.'s godfather). 'Remittebatur gratis.'

17 Roger Gelle & Kath. Wygley, Cov. & Lich. dio. Disp. for marriage (3rd degree consang.). £6.

f. 9^r

19 Ric. Mathew, B.Cn.L., v. of Lenton, York dio. Disp. to hold a benef. with cure with the above, or 2 without; permut. cl. £6 10s.

July 4 Bernard Sondeforthe, Bath & W. dio. Licence as notary. 'Nichil.'

9 Geo. Alyngton, licence as notary. 13s 4d.

Oct. 12 Ric. Hore, r. of North Tuddenham, Norw. dio., & All Saints, Lombard St., London. Disp. to preach throughout the realm, at the Archbp's pleasure. 5s. 'Tot ad usum domini.' Royal seal.

Sept. 16 Jo. Mason, r. of St Botulph of Borowe. Disp. for non-res., being in his 70th yr, and afflicted with various illnesses for which medical attention is needed. 53s 4d.

f. 9^v

22 Ric. Seggeswyke & Kath. Agrege, York dio. Disp. for marriage (3rd & 3rd & 4th degrees consang.). £6; 26s 8d.

Oct. 4 Jo. Man, r. of Hawkwell, Lond. dio., chapl. to the Earl of Wiltshire & Ormond. Disp. to hold a benef. with cure with the above, or 2 without. £6 10s.

2 Wm More, B.Cn.L., Master in Chancery, r. of Bradwell, Lond. dio., & Barnardiston, Norw. dio. Disp. to hold a benef. with cure with the above, or 3 others without. £13 6s 8d.

May 25 Emery Tuckfelde, r. of Hinton, Sarum dio., Kg's chapl. Disp. to hold a benef. with cure with the above, or 2 without. £7 13s 4d.

Oct.   5 Tho. Carpenter, pr., r. of Stoke Wake, Sarum dio. Disp. to hold
a benef. with cure, not yielding over £8 p.a., with the above;
permut. & non-res. cl. £4.

f. 10ʳ

11 Wm Jermy & Ella Mortost, Norw. dio. Disp. for marriage (3rd
degree consang. & without banns). £6 10s.

7 Baldwin Prest, v. of Knowstone, Ex. dio., chapl. to the Earl of
Wiltshire & Ormond. Disp. to hold a benef. with cure with the
above, or 2 without; permut. & non-res. cl. £7 13s 4d.

21 Jo. Colyns, B.Cn.L., v. of Stapleford, Ex. dio. Disp. to hold a
benef. with cure with the above, or 2 without. £7 13s 4d.

July   2 Edw. Brerely, pr., r. of 2 parts of the par. ch. of Rippingale,
Linc. dio. Disp. to hold a benef. with cure not yielding over £8
p.a. with, or 2 without the above. £4.

May 28 Tho. Payne, r. of Llandow, Lland. dio., chapl. to Ric. Bp of St
David's. Cancelled disp. to hold a benef. with cure with, or 2
without, the above; permut. & non-res. cl. £7 13s 4d.

f. 10ᵛ

Aug.   7 Edw. Isacke, gent., & Marg. Gryffythe, gentw., Linc. dio. Disp.
for marriage by any pr., in any ch., without banns. 10s.

Edm. Butler & Joan Storye, Lond. dio. Cancelled disp. for
marriage by any pr., in any ch., without banns. 'Vacat quia
postea.'

Bartholomew Ferys, clk. Disp. to take all h.o. outside the statutory times, from any bp. 20s.

8 Jo. Yate & Alice Benet, Cov. & Lich. dio. Disp. for marriage
(3rd and 4th degrees consang.). 30s. 'Postea.'

9 Edw. Irlham & Isabella James, Cov. & Lich. dio. Cancelled
disp. for marriage (4th degree consang.).

1536 (sic: ann. 27 Hy VIII) Apr. 6 Ric. Burton & Marg. Harrys, Winton dio.
Disp. for marriage in any ch. without banns. 10s.

f. 11ʳ

1535 (26 Hy VIII) Feb. 11 Wm Master alias Maister, dcn, Ex. dio. Disp. to take
pr.'s orders in his 24th yr from any bp. 16s.

Mar.   7 Tho. Wasdall & Eliz. Wharton. Cancelled disp. for marriage
(4th degree affin.). 'Vacat quia postea.'

Tho. Wightman & Agnes Hunchinson, York. dio. Cancelled
disp. for marriage (4th degree consang.). 'Vacat quia postea.'

Mar. 4 Rob. Nyghtingale & Agnes Marwalde. Cancelled disp. for marriage (4th degree consang.). 'Vacat quia postea.'

Jan. 27 Mich. ap Davis ap Roberts, sch., St Asaph dio. Cancelled disp. to take all h.o. outside the statutory times, 2 on the same day. 'Vacat quia postea.'

f. 11ᵛ

Feb. 27 Ormond Hill, B.A., Linc. dio. Cancelled disp. to take all h.o. outside the statutory times, without l.d. 'Vacat quia postea.'

Mar. 31 Geo. Nevell. Cancelled disp. to take all h.o. in or outside the statutory times. 'Vacat quia postea.'

? Edmund Wright, gent., & Ann Salwyn, widow of Sir Ralph Salwyn, Norw. dio. Disp. for marriage without banns. 10s.

Feb. 4 Jo. Wade & Kath. Shepeshanke, York dio. Cancelled disp. for marriage (4th degree consang.). 'Vacat quia postea.'

Jan. 21 Tho. Taylour & Agnes Brown, Cant. dio. Disp. for marriage by any suitable pr. in any ch. or chapel. 10s.

f. 12ʳ

Geo. Sely, gent., & Christobel Dawtry, of London. Disp. for marriage without banns. 10s.

July 10 Tho. Panton & Kath. Salisbury, St Asaph dio. Disp. legitimizing their marriage already contracted (Tho. was betrothed in childhood to Kath.'s sister Jane). 26s 8d.

Aug. 7 Edw. Isaac, gent. of Cant. dio., & Marg. Griffith, Lond. dio. Disp. for marriage without banns. 10s.

Edw. Butler & Joan Storye. Disp. for marriage without banns. 10s.

6 Wm Hutton & Joan Bardisaye, York dio. Disp. for marriage (3rd & 4th degrees consang.). 30s.

f. 12ᵛ

Barth. Ferys, clk, Sarum dio. Cancelled disp. to take all h.o. outside the statutory times. 'Vacat quia ante.'

8 Jo. Yate & Alice Benet, of Hartington, peculiar of Cov. & Lich. dio. Disp. for marriage (3rd & 4th degrees consang.). 30s.

13 Edw. Fulham & Isabella James, Cov. & Lich. dio. Disp. for marriage (4th degree consang.). 26s 8d.

Edw. Clynton, Cant. dio., & Eliz. Blunte *alias* Taylbusshe, Linc. dio. Disp. for marriage without banns. 10s.

10 Benedict Lethen, B.A., Ex. dio. Disp. to take all h.o. at any time, 2 on the same day. 26s 8d.

Aug. 10 Tho. ap Rhes, sch., St David's dio. Disp. to take all h.o. at any time. 26s 8d.

Jo. Hepworth & Marg. Brigge, York dio. Disp. for marriage (3rd & 4th degrees consang.). 30s.

f. 13ʳ

22 Jo. Keneston & Kath. Powys, Cov. & Lich. dio. Disp. for marriage (4th degree consang.). 26s 8d.

24 Ric. Leyver & Kath. Bolton, Cov. & Lich. dio. Disp. for marriage (4th degree consang.). 26s 8d.

Tho. Holmes & Alice Morys. Disp. for marriage (4th degree consang.). 26s 8d.

25 Hy Henley & Joan Edale, Winton dio. Disp. for marriage, the banns read once. 6s 8d.

Jo. & Eliz. Coplande, York dio. Disp. for marriage (4th degree consang.). 26s 8d.

Jo. Nicolson & Kath. Singleton, York dio. Disp. for marriage (4th degree consang.). 26s 8d.

Jo. Reynolds & Eliz. Meridith, Lond. dio. Disp. for marriage, the banns read once. 6s 8d.

28 Ric. Brokesby, r. of Ashby & of Saxilby, Linc. dio. Disp. to hold a benef. with cure with the above, or 3 without; permut. & non-res. cl. £13 6s 8d.

f. 13ᵛ

25 Jo. Northende & Sibyl Drake, York dio. Disp. for marriage (4th degree consang.). 26s 8d.

21 Tho. Pope, pr., O.F.M., of Exeter. Disp. to move to any house of reg. Augustinian canons, with change of habit. £3.

25 Chris. Ryley & Alice Mercer, Cov. & Lich. dio. Disp. for marriage (4th degree affin.). 26s 8d.

29 Edw. Cole, Winton dio., & Agnes Cosyn, Norw. dio. Disp. for marriage, the banns read once. 6s 8d.

Francis Framlingham & Ly Eliz. Tylney, widow of Sir Philip Tylney, Norw. dio. Disp. for marriage (3rd & 4th degrees affin.), without banns. 30s; 10s. 'Resp. quousque.'

Sept. 7 Jas Parson & Agnes Arnoll, Chich. dio. Disp. for marriage (4th degree consang.). 26s 8d.

13 Wm Elde, dcn, Cov. & Lich. dio. Disp. to take pr.'s orders in his 22nd yr. 23s 4d.

f. 14^r

Oct. 12 Wm Margrave, York dio. Disp. to take all h.o. outside statutory times. 20s.

Jo. Hill & Agnes Poll, Bath & W. dio. Disp. for marriage (2nd & 4th degrees consang.). 33s 4d.

10 Wm Robynson & Alice Jackson. Disp. for marriage (4th degree consang.). 26s 8d.

Martin Elde & Kath. Sheldon, Cov. & Lich. dio. Disp. for marriage (3rd & 4th degrees consang.). 30s.

12 Tho. Channt, Bath & W. dio. Disp. to take h.o. although one-eyed. 40s.

Sept. 8 Maurice Griffith, B.Th., O.P. Disp. to hold a benef. with cure, with complete change of habit. Arb. 53s 4d.

Oct. 11 Chris. Dacre & Janet Beverhaset, Carl. dio. Disp. for marriage (Chris. was godfather to a child of Janet's). £6.

15 Jo. ap David ap Rice & Joan Draper, St Asaph dio. Disp. for marriage (Jo. was godfather to a child of Joan's). £6.

Jo. Escefeld & Alice Heywood, Linc. dio. Disp. for marriage (3rd & 4th degrees affin.). 30s.

Aug. 4 Jo. Byrde, O.Cist., r. of Cooling, Roch. dio. Disp. to change his habit. £4.

f. 14^v

Oct. 18 Wm Hughe & Kath. Knava. Disp. for marriage (3rd degree affin.). Arb. £4.

Tho. Lichfeld *alias* Kirkbye, canon of St Bartholomew's in the W., Smithfield. Disp. to hold a benef., with some change of habit. £8.

25 Jo. Lewes, r. of Knolton, Cant. dio. Disp. for non-res. for 3 yrs. 20s.

28 Jo. De la Hole & Alison Deson, York dio. Disp. for marriage (4th degree consang.). 26s 8d.

Nov. 12 Jo. Roberts & Ann Cope, Heref. dio. Disp. for marriage (4th degree consang.). 26s 8d.

13 Hy Thasilwoode, Linc. dio. Disp. to take all h.o. outside the statutory times, & 2 on the same day. 26s 8d.

5 Wm Godmersham, monk of St Augustine's, Canterbury. Disp. to hold any benef. with some change of habit. £8.

Aug. 1 Geo. Vercuts, v. of Wethering, chapl. to the abbot of Glastonbury.
Disp. to hold another ch. with the above, or 2 without it; permut.
& Non-res. cl. £7 13s 4d.

4 Ric. Benet & Eliz. Bonnsall, Cov. & Lich. dio. Disp. for marriage
(3rd, 3rd & 3rd, & 4th, 4th & 4th degrees affin.). 'Vacat quia
postea.'

f. 15ʳ

20 Jo. Rissheton & Eliz. Podmere, Cov. & Lich. dio. Disp. for
marriage (4th degree consang.). 26s 8d.

Sept. 13 Jo. Griffith & Eva Fluellen, St Asaph dio. Disp. for marriage
3rd & 4th degrees consang.). 30s.

Rob. Heron & Eliz. Colyngwoode. Disp. for marriage (Eliz.
was godmother to a child of Rob.). £6. (obt. pro 5).

Wm Pare, M.A., r. of Shelden, Winton dio. Disp. to hold a benef.
with cure with the above, or 2 without; permut. & non-res. cl.
£7 13s 4d.

14 Jo. Conncister *alias* Savage, Cluniac monk of St Pancras,
Lewes. Disp. to hold a benef. with non-res., having obtained
his prior's permission; permut. & non-res. cl. £4 10s.

15 Jo. Hughes. Disp. for union of the ch. of St Peter ad Vincula nr
Ruthlin, Bangor dio., to Bangor cath. £9. 'Resp. quousque.'

17 Philip Fryer, Ex. dio. Disp. to take all h.o. & 2 on the same day.
26s 8d.

Aug. 8 Tho. Dacre & Eleanor Denton, Carl. dio. Disp. for marriage
(2nd & 3rd degrees consang.). £8.

f. 15ᵛ

Philip Fryer, B.Cn. & C.L., v. of Dean Prior, Ex. dio. Disp. to
hold a benef. with cure with the above or 2 without. £7 13s 4d.

Sept. 30 Jo. Hert, hermit. Disp. to take h.o. outside the statutory times.
20s.

Oct. 7 Roger Peny & Isotta Bury, Heref. dio. Disp. for marriage (Roger's
mother was Isotta's sponsor at confirmation). 26s 8d.

5 Walter ap Rice *alias* Watkin & Christine verch Lewes, St David's
dio. Disp. for marriage (4th degree consang.). 26s 8d.

Sept. 30 Wm Stone & Joan Rokner, Bath & W. dio. Disp. for marriage
(3rd & 4th degrees affin.). 30s.

Oct. 7 Jo. Lother & Janet Karhell. Disp. for marriage (3rd & 4th degrees
consang.). 30s.

f. 16^r

Sept. 14 Ric. Dawding, sch., Sarum dio. Disp. to take all h.o. in his 24th yr. 26s 8d.

16 Jo. Karellet, Bath & W. dio. Disp. to take all h.o. in his 24th yr at any time. 20s.

23 Wm Tempulman & Marg. Browne, Bath & W. dio. Disp. for marriage (Marg.'s father was Wm's godfather). 30s.

24 Ralph Clydrowe (son of Ric. Clydrowe) & Joan Sherbury, York dio. Disp. for marriage (4th degree consang.). 26s 8d.

27 Jas Howe & Agnes Hall, Cov. & Lich. dio. Disp. for marriage (3rd & 4th degrees consang.). 30s.

30 Wm Egerton & Jane Bromley, widow, Cov. & Lich. dio. Disp. for marriage in any chapel or ch. by any pr., the banns read once. 10s.

Oct.   5 Walter White & Jane Kyne, Winton dio. Disp. for marriage (4th degree consang.). 26s 8d.

Ric. Longmere & Alice Sowthall, Cov. & Lich. dio. Disp. for marriage (4th degree consang.). 26s 8d.

f. 16^v

Tho. Wolworth & Isabella Voule, Worc. dio. Disp. for marriage (Tho.'s mother Helen was Isabella's godmother). 30s.

Alex. Bullocke, sch., York dio. Disp. to take all h.o. at any time, from any bp, with l.d., & 2 on the same day. 26s 8d; 6s 8d.

8 Chris. Halydaye & Marg. Darnforde, Worc. dio. Disp. for marriage (4th degree consang.). 26s 8d.

12 Rob. Taylor & Eliz. Bordeley, York dio. Disp. for marriage (4th degree consang.). 26s 8d.

f. 17^r

15 Jo. Fisher & Janet Adamson, York dio. Disp. for marriage (4th degree consang.). 26s 8d.

18 Francis Howseley & Joan Parkyn, York dio. Disp. for marriage (3rd and 4th degrees consang.). 30s.

20 Jo. Sutton & Agnes Poore, Winton dio. Disp. for marriage (4th degree consang.). 26s 8d.

Jas Beanes *alias* Banes & Alice Buskell, of Kirkby Lonsdale, Archdcnry of Richmond, York dio. Disp. for marriage (4th degree consang.). 26s 8d.

21 Ric. Harryson & Alice Robynson, York dio. Disp. for marriage (4th degree consang.). 26s 8d.

Oct.   2 Edw. & Eliz. Morton, York dio. Disp. for marriage (3rd & 4th degrees consang.). 30s.

f. 17ᵛ

26 Godfrey Stephenson & Alice Redferne, Cov. & Lich. dio. Disp. for marriage (4th degree consang.). 26s 8d.

28 Geo. Heylile & Eliz. Sclaydon, York dio. Disp. for marriage (4th degree consang.). 26s 8d.

19 Philip Trygg & Alice Symon. Disp. for marriage (4th degree consang.). 26s 8d.

Wm Meder & Alice Gladfeld *alias* Soper. Ex. dio. Disp. for marriage (4th degree affin.). 26s 8d.

28 Philip Wall & Eleanor Trowe, Worc. dio. Disp. for marriage (4th degree consang.). 26s 8d.

30 Tho. Hardyn & Eliz. Watte, Cov. & Lich. dio. Disp. for marriage (3rd & 4th degrees consang.). 30s.

Nov.   2 Simon Gonby & Isabella Leven, York dio. Disp. for marriage (3rd & 4th degrees consang.). 30s.

f. 18ʳ

3 Rob. ap Powell & Eliz. verch John, widow of Jo. ap Madog, Bangor dio. Disp. for marriage (3rd & 4th degrees affin.). 30s.

Philip Atkynson & Marg. Smyth, York dio. Disp. for marriage (4th degree consang.). 26s 8d.

1535 Jan. 31 Ric. Mason & Agnes FysSher, Carl. dio. Disp. for marriage (4th degree affin.). 26s 8d.

1534 May 28 Tho. Payne, r. of Llando, Lland. dio., chapl. to Bp of St Davids. Disp. to hold any benef. with cure with the above; permut. & non-res. cl. £7 13s 4d.

Oct. 28 Jo. Whitton & Christine More, Lond. dio. Disp. for marriage (Jo. was godfather to a child of Christine, & without banns). £6; 10s.

Nov.   1 Nich. Syngleton & Marg. Portyngton, Linc. dio. Cancelled disp. for marriage (Marg. was godmother to a child of Nich.). £6. 'Vacat quia postea.'

f. 18ᵛ

5 Jo. Harrywylcoke & Marg. verch Johnsmyth, Lland. dio. Disp. for marriage (in childhood Jo. was betrothed to Kath. verch Nicholl, Lland. dio., now dead, related to Marg. in the 2nd degree). 26s 8d.

Nov.   1 Hy Byreman, r. of Beaumont, Carl. dio. (which he affirms does not yield over £8 p.a.), chapl. to Ld Dacre. Disp. to hold benef. with cure, with the above, or 2 without; permut. & non-res. cl. for study. £4.

3 Ade Hilton *alias* Hulton & Clementine Norres, Cov. & Lich. dio. Disp. for marriage (4th degree consang.). 26s 8d.

6 Jas Bordbent, York dio. Cancelled disp. to take all h.o. from any bp, without l.d. 6s 8d. 'Vacat quia postea.'

8 Jo. Cawthorn, Ely dio. Disp. to take all h.o. at any time, 2 on the same day. 26s 8d.

f. 19ʳ

4 Tho. Baghe, Lland. dio. Disp. to take all h.o. despite defect of birth, & a benef., with non-res. cl. £4.

10 Laurence Blakey & Marg. Shawe, Cov. & Lich. dio. Disp. for marriage (4th degree consang.). 26s 8d.

12 Ric. Helyar & Eliz. Sadler, Cov. & Lich. dio. Disp. for marriage (4th degree consang.). 26s 8d.

13 Jo. Bonde & Eliz. Hawthorntwyt, York dio. Disp. for marriage (4th degree consang.). 26s 8d.

9 Tho. Bayly, of Wylley, Heref. dio., & Magdalen Doy, Cov. & Lich. dio. Disp. for marriage (Magdalen was godmother to a child of Tho.). £6.

f. 19ᵛ

16 Tho. Watering & Eliz. Small, Winton dio. Disp. for marriage (Tho.'s mother was Eliz.'s godmother). 30s.

17 Humfrey Vyse & Isabella Fytton. Disp. for marriage (4th degree consang.). 26s 8d.

18 Chris. Ingham & Marg. Hurstwoode, Cov. & Lich. dio. Disp. for marriage (4th degree consang.). 26s 8d.

19 Nich. Barbour & Eliz. Bower, of Glossop, Cov. & Lich. dio. Disp. for marriage (3rd & 4th degrees consang.). 30s.

f. 20ʳ

20 Tho. Metham (son & heir of Tho. Metham esq., & Dorothy Darcy) & Dorothy Darcy (dau. of Sir Geo. Darcy), York dio. Disp. for marriage (3rd & 4th degrees consang.). 30s.

Ric. West & Cicily Mason, Linc. dio. Disp. for marriage (Cicily's mother was Ric.'s godmother). 30s.

Nov. 17 Hy Conwey, son of Hy Conwey, & Alice Salisbury, dau. of Peter Salisbury, gent. Disp. for marriage (3rd degree affin.). Arb. 26s 8d.

22 Gilbert Lancastre & Alice Fissher, Cov. & Lich. dio. Disp. for marriage (4th degree consang.). 26s 8d.

26 Jo. Hertley & Alice Mosley, Cov. & Lich. dio. Disp. for marriage (4th degree consang.). 26s 8d.

Jo. Thewe, Linc. dio. Disp. to take all h.o. at any time, from any bp, 2 on the same day. 26s 8d.

f. 20ᵛ

24 Sir Tho. Spart & Mary Skarne, Lond. dio. Disp. for marriage without banns, within the prohibited time, frcm any bp. 3cs.

28 Leonard Horsman, M.A., r. of Birkin, York dio., chapl. to the Archbp of York. Disp. to hold a benef. with cure with the above, or 2 without; permut. & non-res. cl. £7 13s 4d.

Wm Wilbore, B.Cn.L., v. of All Saints, Arksey, York dio. Disp. to hold a benef. with cure with the above, or 2 without. £7 13s 4d.

Dec. 3 Rob. Webber, Ex. dio. Disp. to take all h.o. at any time, from any bp, although not past his 24th yr. 20s; 20s.

Nov. 28 Roger Dune *alias* Don, r. of Sedgebarrow, Worc. dio. Disp. to hold a benef. with cure with the above, or 2 without; permut. & non-res. cl. £7 13s 4d.

Dec. 21 Jo. Paynter & Petronilla Ketley. Disp. for marriage (3rd degree affin.). 'Remittebatur gratis per sacr[ament]um.'

f. 21ʳ

4 Ric. Hals, M.A., v. of Buckland Monachorum, Ex. dio., chapl. to Ld Mordaunt. Disp. to hold a benef. with the above, or 2 without; permut. & non-res. cl. £7 13s 4d.

2 Ric. Grygell, M.A., r. of Hamswell, St David's dio., v. of Barking, Lond. dio., chapl. of Jo. Archbp of Thebes, of Carlisle cath. Disp. to hold a benef. with cure with the above, or 3 others without; permut. & non-res. cl. £13 6s 8d.

5 Jas Wheteley, subdcn, York dio. Disp. to take remaining h.o. in his 24th yr, at any time, from any bp. 20s; 16s.

Nov. 26 Nich. Pelham & Ann Sackoyle, Chich. dio. Disp. for marriage (4th degree consang.). 26s 8d.

Dec. 5 Jo. Wynston, v. of Awre, Heref. dio., chapl. to Sir Wm Harbert. Disp. to hold a benef. with, or 2 without, the above; permut. cl. £6 10s.

f. 21ᵛ

7 Roger Jakson, v. of Shepherdswell, Cant. dio., which does not yield over £8 p.a. Disp. to hold a benef. with the above, or 2 without, of which one must not yield over £8 p.a.; permut. & non-res. cl. £4.

1 Ant. Watson & Janet Richardson. Disp. for marriage (Janet's father was Ant.'s godfather). 30s.

Nov. 26 Rob. Stooks, M.A., Worc. dio. Disp. to take all h.o. without l.d., at any time, 2 on the same day. 26s 8d; 6s 8d.

Dec. 5 Rob. Farnwell, Sarum dio. Disp. to take pr.'s orders from any bp, although in his 23rd yr. 20s.

4 Jo. Everson & Avotta Leynton, Carl. dio. Disp. for marriage (3rd & 4th degrees consang.). 30s.

f. 22ʳ

9 Tho. Boxfeld & Matilda Lanewaye, Winton dio. Disp. for marriage (4th degree consang.). 26s 8d.

14 Jo. Fychett, r. of St Kath.'s, Whetstone, Ex. dio. Disp. for non-res. as he is about 78 & blind in both eyes. 53s 4d.

16 Tho. Curtope, M.A., Cant. dio. Disp. to take h.o. from any bp without l.d., although he has lost the nail and middle part of a finger. 50s; 6s 8d.

Oct. 5 Wm Betts, r. of Bp's Hatfield, Linc. dio., Qn's clk. Disp. to hold a benef. with the above, or 2 without; permut. & non-res. cl. £7 13s 4d.

18 Edw. Haldesworth & Isabella Croter. Disp. for marriage (4th degree consang.). 26s 8d.

f. 22ᵛ

Dec. 13 Tho. Warre & Christine Chidley. Disp. for marriage (3rd degree affin.). £6.

20 Jo. Hollonde, M.A., r. of Ashby, Linc. dio., chapl. to Bp of Linc. Disp. to hold a benef. with cure with the above, or 2 without. £6 10s.

13 Wm Blackborne, chapl. to Earl of Cumberland, v. of Skipton in Craven, York dio. Disp. to hold a benef. with the above, or 2 without; permut. & non-res. cl. £6 10s.

Sept. 17 Jo. Wilborne, recently dispensed to hold in comm. the hospital of St Mary, Strood, & par. churches of Chiselhurst & Brook ('Bryock'), all in Roch. dio. Disp. to hold a benef. with the above instead of the hospital, or 3 without these. £9.

Dec. 17 Jo. Nowell & Benedetta Towneley. Disp. for marriage (3rd & 4th degrees consang.). 30s.

f. 23ʳ

21 Wm Mason & Eliz. Dalowe, Heref. dio. Disp. for marriage (3rd degree consang.). Arb. per sacr[ament]um. 53s 4d.

22 Ric. Hawarden, r. of St Mary's, Babistocke, Sarum dio., chapl. to Jo. Bp of Bangor. Disp. to hold a benef. with cure with the above, or 2 without. £6 10s.

1535 Jan. 4 Hy Page and Matilda Bugge, of Harrow, peculiar of Cant. dio. Disp. for marriage without banns, within the prohibited times, by any pr. 20s; 10s.

2 Tho. ap Jankyn & Waldissa ap Jankyn, Lland. dio. Disp. for marriage (4th degree consang.). 26s 8d.

7 Jo. Robynson & Isabella Mytton, Cov. & Lich. dio. Disp. for marriage (4th degree consang.). 26s 8d.

2 Hy Devall, keeper of the perpetual chantry in the ch. of Mere, Sarum dio. Disp. to hold a benef. with cure with the above, or 2 without; non-res. & permut. cl. £7 13s 4d.

f. 23ᵛ

7 Tho. & Blanche Harbart, Lland. dio. Disp. for marriage (3rd & 4th degrees consang.). 30s.

Tho. ap Sutton Sayer & Helen verch Yarwarth, St David's dio. Disp. for marriage (4th degree consang.). 26s 8d.

Sir Walter Calverley & Ann Danby *alias* Hopton, gentw. Disp. for marriage (4th degree consang.). 26s 8d.

Wm Hanston & Ann Dane, Lond. dio. Disp. for marriage without banns. 10s.

Jo. Holbeme & Mary Seyntclere, Ex. dio. Disp. for marriage (4th degree consang.). 26s 8d.

Tho. Clyston & Eleanor Osbaldston, Cov. & Lich. dio. Disp. for marriage (Tho. was previously betrothed to Isabella Osbaldston, sister to Eleanor; also in 4th degree consang.). 26s 8d; 26s 8d.

Rob. Pendelburye & Jane Assheton, Cov. & Lich. dio. Disp. for marriage (2nd & 3rd degrees affin.). £8.

f. 24ʳ

11 Wm Dormer, of Linc. dio., & Mary Sydney, Lond. dio., both of gentle birth. Disp. for marriage within prohibited times. 20s.

1534 Sept. 17 Jo. Methwolde, r. of Bodney, Norw. dio. Disp. to hold a benef. with cure with the above, or 2 without, of which one must not yield over £8 p.a.; permut. & non-res. cl. £4.

1535 Jan. 18 Jas Shawe, acol., Cov. & Lich. dio. Disp. to take all h.o. & hold a benef. despite being lame in the foot. 40s.

20 Rob. Fawcett & Eliz. Potter, York dio. Disp. for marriage (3rd & 4th degrees affin.). 30s.

21 Giles Churchill & Kath. Warre, widow. Disp. for marriage within the prohibited times. 20s.

Rob. Hovell, r. of Dewerbilton, Chich. dio., chapl. to Ld Dacre. Disp. to hold a benef. with cure with the above, or 2 without; permut. & non-res. cl. £7 13s 4d.

27 Ric. Ganarde & Isabella Holte, Bath & W. dio. Disp. for marriage (3rd degree affin.). £6.

f. 24ᵛ

Jo. Denton esq., & Marg. Browne. Disp. for marriage without banns during the prohibited times. 20s; 10s.

Wm Elwey & Marg. Chapman. Disp. for marriage within the prohibited time (3rd & 4th degrees consang.). 30s; 20s.

24 Arthur Meyverell, O.S.B., sub-prior of Tutbury, Cov. & Lich. dio. Disp., as he has previously proceeded to h.o. with disp. for defective birth, to hold the office of abbot or prior of Tutbury or any other house. £12.

Feb. 3 Jas Barnarde & Ursula Maydenhede, Cant. dio. Disp. for marriage without banns within the prohibited times. 20s; 10s.

4 Jo. Wade & Kath. Shepeshanke, York dio. Disp. for marriage (4th degree consang.). 26s 8d.

Wm Harte & Eliz. Rygbye. Disp. for marriage (3rd & 4th degrees consang.). 30s.

Wm Hymerforde, sch., Bath & W. dio. Disp. to take h.o. from any bp although in his 22nd yr. 23s 4d.

f. 25ʳ

6 Ric. Grene & Joan Raynolde, Worc. dio. Disp. for marriage (3rd & 4th degrees consang.). 30s.

Jan. 26 Nich. Hethe, Kg's chapl., archdcn of Stafford, Lich. cath. Disp. to hold 2 benefices with the archdcnry, or any 3 benefices if not more than 2 are par. churches. £9.

Feb. 5 Rob. Singleton, v. of Preston in A[mou]nderness, York dio. Disp. to hold a benef. with cure with the above, or 2 without; permut. & non-res. cl. £7 13s 4d.

8 Hy [Ledar, r. of Upham, Winton dio., chapl. to the Bp of

Winchester. Disp. to hold a benef. with cure with the above,
or 2 without; permut. & non-res. cl. £7 13s 4d.

Feb.   5 Wm Chaplayne, v. of Welton, Linc. dio. Disp. to hold a benef.
with cure with the above, or 2 without, one of which must not
yield over £8 p.a. £4.

7 Tho. ap Richarde, v. of Carmarthen, St David's dio. Disp. to
hold a benef. with cure with the above, or 2 without, one of
which must not yield over £8 p.a. £4.

f. 25ᵛ

5 Rob. Rygbye & Eliz. Harte, Cov. & Lich. dio. Disp. for marriage
(3rd & 4th degrees consang.). 30s.

Jan. 26 Matthew ap David ap Robert, St Asaph dio. Cancelled disp. to
take all h.o. at any time, 2 on the same day, from any bp. 26s 8d.
'Vacat quia postea.'

Feb. 9 Rob. Prycklowe. Disp. to hold any benef. with cure; permut.
& non-res. cl. £4 10s.

1534 Dec. 20. Jo. Baylye, r. of Fenchurch, Lond. dio., v. of Rowtham, Cant.
dio., chapl. to Ld Cobham. Disp. to hold a benef. with cure with
the above or 3 without; permut. & non-res. cl. £9.

1535 Feb. 12 Stephen Wraye & Janet Halyn, Carl. dio. Disp. for marriage
(Janet's mother was Stephen's godmother). 30s.

Gerard Fenwyke & Isabella Lawson, Durham dio. Disp. for
marriage (3rd & 4th degrees consang.). 30s.

Jo. Netilton & Jane Steryng, Linc. dio. Disp. for marriage (3rd
degree consang.). Arb. 40s.

Ric. Tathewell, v. of Glentworth, Linc. dio., chapl. to Ld Burgh.
Disp. to hold a benef. with cure with the above, or 2 without;
permut. & non-res. cl. £7 13s 4d.

f. 26ʳ

20 Wm Felde, O.F.M., of London. Disp. to act as a sec. pr., wearing
the habit of his Order beneath that of a sec. pr. £4.

18 Tho. Marshe, prior of the Cluniac house of Mendham. Disp. to
hold any benef. with cure. £4.

Jo. Burkebecke, Carl. dio. Disp. to take all h.o. outside the
statutory times, without l.d. 20s.

21 Wm Baker & Agnes Foster, Durham dio. Disp. for marriage
(2nd & 3rd degrees affin.). 'Regi nichil quia remittebatur gratis
per Archiepiscopum.'

Feb. 19 Wm Felde, O.F.M., of London. Disp. to hold a benef., if given permission by his prior or provincial, & without change of habit. £4.

Jo. Vyncent, r. of Sheeply, Linc. dio. Disp. to hold a benef. with cure with the above, or 2 without; permut. & non-res. cl. £7 13s 4d.

16 Rob. Balfronte, r. of Upton, Sarum dio. Disp. for non-res., if the Kg's licence is obtained, for 5 yrs. 33s 4d.

23 Roger Conert, Observant fr. Disp. to hold any benef. with cure & to change his habit; without non-res. cl. £12.

f. 26ᵛ

Ormond Hill, Linc. dio. Disp. to take all h.o. at any time, without l.d., 2 on the same day, from any bp. 26s 8d.

27 Matthew ap David ap Roberts, sch., St Asaph dio. Disp. to take all h.o. at any time, 2 on the same day. 26s 8d.

Jan. 10 Jo. Brereton, Kg's chapl., r. of Hertford ('Hatforde'), v. of Buckland, Sarum dio. and Longstanton, Ely dio. Disp. to hold a 4th benef. £6 13s 4d.

Feb. 4 Rob. Nytingale & Agnes Marwalde, Lond. dio. Disp. for marriage (4th degree consang.). 26s 8d.

Mar. 4 Jenn ap Philip & Helen verch David, St David's dio. Disp. for marriage (4th degree consang.). 26s 8d.

5 Jas Proctor, O.Cist., of Furness, York dio. Disp. to hold any benef. with cure for life; permut. & non-res. cl. £4 10s.

8 Ric. Wylcokson, r. of Pertenhall, Linc. dio., chapl. to Ld Windsor. Disp. to hold a benef. with cure with the above, or 2 without; permut. cl. £6 10s.

f. 27ʳ

17 Laurence & Agnes Hergraves, Cov. & Lich. dio. Disp. for marriage (3rd & 4th degrees consang.). 30s.

14 Jo. Lyll, r. of Plymtree, Ex. dio., chapl. to Earl of Huntingdon. Disp. to hold a benef. with cure with the above or 2 without; permut. & non-res. cl. £7 13s 4d.

31 Jas Bordbent, acol., York dio. Disp. to take all h.o. at any time, 2 on the same day. 26s 8d.

26 Wm Watson, O.Cist., of Byland, York dio. Disp. to hold any benef. with cure, if licensed by his abbot. £4.

Apr. 3 Jo. Kyllyngworth & Marg. Frase. Disp. for marriage (3rd degree consang.). 'Arb. per sacr[ament]um per d[omi]n[um] Cant[uarensem] ad 40s.'

Geo. Nevell, sch., York dio. Disp. to take all h.o. at any time and 2 on the same day, from any bp. 26s 8d.

Mar. 31 Tho. Ratclif, Durham dio. Disp. for marriage (3rd & 4th & 4th degrees consang.). 30s; 26s 8d.

12 Jo. Russell, v. of Yetminster, Sarum dio. Disp. to hold a benef. with the above, or 2 without; permut. & non-res. cl. £7 13s 4d.

f. 27ᵛ

Apr. 8 Nich. & Marg. Thwate, York dio. Disp. for marriage (4th degree consang.). 26s 8d.

Hy Clesby & Mabel Plett, Carl. dio. Disp. for marriage (4th degree consang.). 26s 8d.

Feb. 12 Rob. Barton & Sibil Baynham. Disp. for marriage (3rd & 4th degrees consang.). Arb. £4.

Apr. 10 Tho. Vyllars, r. of Stourton, Sarum dio. Disp. to hold a benef. with cure with the above or 2 without; permut. & non-res. cl. £7 13s 4d.

9 Francis Sherley & Dorothy Congreve, Cov. & Lich. dio. Disp. for marriage (Francis was sponsor at the confirmation of a child of Dorothy's). £5.

19 Wm Hale & Helen Tatloke, Cov. & Lich. dio. Disp. for marriage (3rd & 4th degrees consang.). 30s.

Mar. 31 Tho. Bull, dcn. Disp. to take pr.'s orders although in his 24th yr. 16s.

Apr. 16 Tho. Jorden, r. of Longford Parva, Sarum dio., chapl. to Edw., Ld Stourton. Disp. to hold a benef. with cure with the above, or 2 without; permut. & non-res. cl. £7 13s 4d.

f. 28ʳ

3 Jo. Assheton, v. of Spondon, Cov. & Lich. dio., chapl. to Ld Audley. Disp. to hold a benef. with cure with the above, or 2 without; permut. & non-res. cl. £7 13s 4d.

12 Jo. Gybley & Eliz. Wylley, St David's dio. Disp. for marriage (Jo. was godfather to a child of Eliz. or vice versa). £6.

15 Leonard Hucchinson, v. of Croughton & Bladon, & by previous disp. of the adjacent chapels of Hesington & Woodstock, Linc. dio. Disp. to hold a benef. with cure with the above, or 2 without; permut. & non-res. cl. £9.

18 Jo. Flooke, v. of Portbury, Bath & W. dio. Disp. to hold a benef. with cure with the above; permut. cl. £4.

Apr. 10 Rob. Crowder & Marg. Woodhede, York dio. Disp. for marriage (2nd & 3rd degrees consang.). £8.

12 Edw. Stondon *alias* Stonton & Marg. Cole, Ex. dio. Disp. for marriage (Marg. was godmother to a child of Edw.). £6.

17 Tho. Hickeling, O.S.A., formerly canon of St Bartholomew's in the W., Smithfield, Lond. dio. Disp. to wear his habit beneath that of a sec. pr. £4.

20 Jo. Harryson & Eliz. Henman, Chich. dio. Disp. for marriage (Jo. was godfather to a child of Eliz.). £6.

f. 28ᵛ

24 Tho. Hickling, monk. Disp. to hold a benef. with cure; permut. cl. £4.

16 Ric. Gardyn, pr., Ex. dio. Disp., as he is a non-beneficed pr., & holds the par. ch. of Bp's Cheriton by farm, to have cure of souls in the same. 20s.

4 Wm Lumbarde, hermit. Disp., although between 50 & 60 yrs old, to enter the coll. or Christ's Poorhouse of Westbury-on-Trym, & receive all charities & privileges thereof. 'Remitte-batur per d[omin]um Cant[uarensem] gratis.'

17 Hy Hawte, Carth., of London. Disp. to hold a benef., as a sec. pr. and wear a sec. pr.'s habit. £12.

28 Jo. Antilbye, O.Cist., of Shipton, Norw. dio. Disp. to hold a benef. with cure if licensed by his prior. £4.

May 1 Gerard Croste, r. of Galbye, Linc. dio., chapl. to the Earl of Rutland. Disp. to hold a benef. with cure with the above, or 2 without; permut. & non-res. cl. £7 13s 4d.

f. 29ʳ

Mar. 15 Wm Felde, O.F.M. Cancelled licence to hold any benef. with cure, if licensed by his prior. 'Vacat quia ante.'

20 Peter Watts, Carth., Lond. dio. Disp. to hold any benef. with cure; also disp. to act as a sec. pr. & wear his habit under that of a sec. pr. £4; £4.

Lewis ap David ap Rhes & Marg. verch Jenn ap Howell. Disp. for marriage (4th degree consang.). 26s 8d.

17 Wm Smith, subdcn, Norw. dio. Disp. to take all h.o. at any time & 2 on the same day. 26s 8d.

4 Tho. Colepotts & Alice Horn. Disp. for marriage (3rd degree consang.). Arb. £4.

Mar. 7 Tho. Wasdall & Eliz. Wharton, Carl. dio. Disp. for marriage (4th degree affin.). 26s 8d.

Tho. Wightman & Agnes Hucchinson, York dio. Disp. for marriage (4th degree consang.). 26s 8d.

f. 29ᵛ

July 7 Wm Laceby, Premonstr. canon of Tupholme, Linc. dio. Disp. to hold a benef. with cure, if given consent by the abbot and visitor. £4.

Jan. 31 Ric. Mason & Agnes Fyssher, Carl. dio. Disp. for marriage (4th degree affin.). 26s 8d.

Apr. 13 Jo. Helmar & Joan Scraggs, of the par. of St Mary Magdalene, Southwark, Winton dio. Disp. for marriage without banns. 10s.

16 Rob. Markham, gent., & Alice Hatfield, York dio. Disp. for marriage without banns. 10s.

Ric. Askewyth & Matilda Egglyfeld, York dio. Disp. for marriage (Ric.'s father was Matilda's godfather). 30s.

23 Howel ap William & Gwenlian verch William, Lland. dio. Disp. for marriage (3rd & 4th degrees consang.). 30s.

24 Jo. Bell, sch., Linc. dio. Disp. to take all h.o. at any time, 2 on the same day. 26s 8d; 6s 8d.

26 Jo. Kenall, Ex. dio. Disp. to take pr.'s orders although in his 24th yr, & to hold a benef. 20s.

f 30ʳ

27 Hugh Pruste & Agnes Atkinson, Ex. dio. Disp. for marriage (Hugh's mother was Agnes's godmother). 30s.

22 Chris. Roper & Eliz. Bloer, Cant. dio. Disp. for marriage within the prohibited times. 20s.

May 3 Jo. Wodestall & Emma Wytter, Cov. & Lich. dio. Disp. for marriage (3rd & 4th degrees affin.). 30s.

5 Gilbert Atkynson & Alice Gye, York dio. Disp. for marriage (4th degree consang.). 26s 8d.

Tho. Atkinson & Margery Gye, York dio. Disp. for marriage (3rd & 4th degrees consang.). 30s.

Geo. Bothe & Eliz. Trafforde, Cov. & Lich. dio. Disp. for marriage (4th degree consang.). 26s 8d.

Jo. Nelson & Emma Atkynson, York dio. Disp. for marriage (4th degree consang.). 30s.

May 8 Ric. Baron & Alice Orell, Cov. & Lich. dio. Disp. for marriage (4th degree consang.). 26s 8d.

f. 30ᵛ

Edw. Lulham & Joan Lacye, Chich. dio. Disp. for marriage (Joan's father was Edw.'s godfather). 30s.

Walter Harrys, subdcn, Norw. dio. Disp. to take all h.o. at any time, 2 on the same day. 26s 8d.

Jo. Atwode & Joan Overed, Worc. dio. Disp. for marriage (3rd & 4th degrees affin.). 30s.

10 Tho. Robynson & Marg. Jackman, York dio. Disp. for marriage (3rd & 4th degrees consang.). 30s.

Wm Oxenhyrde & Joan Lowcocke, York dio. Disp. for marriage (3rd & 4th degrees consang.). 30s.

12 Roger Wade, Linc. dio. Disp. to take pr.'s orders in his 24th yr, from any bp, & to hold a benef.; non-res. cl. 20s.

13 Tho. Pache & Isabella Hobbes, Worc. dio. Disp. for marriage (Tho.'s mother was sponsor at Isabella's confirmation). 30s.

Jo. Richardson & Isabella Swetlove, Cov. & Lich. dio. Disp. for marriage (3rd & 4th degrees consang.). 30s.

14 Hy Longe & Mary Horton, Sarum dio. Disp. for marriage (3rd & 4th degrees consang.). 30s.

f. 31ʳ

Ric. ap Thomas ap Griffith Goghe & Matilda verch Jenn David, Lland. dio. Disp. for marriage (4th degree affin.). 26s. 8d.

Walter Hill & Eleanor Yearnton, Worc. dio. Disp. for marriage (3rd & 4th degrees consang., & Walter's mother or father was Eleanor's godparent). 30s; 26s 8d.

15 Rob. Horsffall & Marg. Shawe, York dio. Disp. for marriage (4th degree consang.). 26s 8d.

Rob. Waterhouse & Marg. Fayrebanke, York dio. Disp. for marriage (3rd & 4th degrees consang.). 30s.

Nich. Robynson & Isabella Shawe, Cov. & Lich. dio. Disp. for marriage (4th degree consang.). 26s 8d.

Apr. 14 Fountains, abbot and community of, O.Cist. Confirmation of letters (their content not specified) issued by Wm, abbot of Fountains, York dio., to Ric. Rypon, monk & cellarer of the same. 40s.

May 17 Notice of letters issued by the Archbp of Cant. commissioning Wm Peter, D.C.L., Hugh Vaughan, & Jo. Tendering, to examine the petition of the nun, Kath. Hutton. 40s.

f. 31ᵛ

4 Brian Russell & Marg. Banes *alias* Wyndor, York dio. Disp. for marriage (3rd & 4th degrees affin.). 30s.

5 Mich. Huccham & Isabella Goslynge, Winton dio. Disp. for marriage (Isabella's father, Wm Goslynge, was Mich.'s godfather). 30s.

1536 Feb. 17 Jo. Whitholme, r. of Laverington, Ely dio., & Walpole, Norw. dio. Disp. for non-res. for life. 53s 4d.

1535 May 3 Tho. Gresham, M.A., r. of Southrepps, Lempham & St Martin's, Cornwall, which he holds in plurality by previous disp. Disp. to hold any 4th incompatible benef. with the above, or any 3 others without them; permut. & non-res. cl. £13 6s 8d.

7 Jo. Godyn & Agnes Holbyn, Bath & W. dio. Disp. for marriage (2nd & 3rd degrees affin.). £8.

Antony Skeffington, r. of Glaston, Lutterworth & Shelton, by previous disp. Disp. to hold a 4th benef. with cure with the above, having obtained the Kg's licence. £8.

11 Wm Weston, Linc. dio., clk in minor orders. Disp. to take dcn's & pr's orders on any day within statutory times from the Bp of Linc., or any other bp. 26s 8d.

f. 32ʳ

9 Wm Parson, O.Cist., of New Manse or New[en]ham, Ex. dio. Disp. to hold a benef. with cure, if granted his abbot's licence; permut. & non-res. cl. £4 10s.

Wm Taylboys, v. of Billinghay, Linc. dio., chapl. to Earl of Northumberland. Disp. to [hold another benef.]; permut. & non-res. cl. £7 13s 4d.

7 Jo. Bandon, canon of Bodmin, Ex. dio. Disp. to hold any benef. with cure, if granted his prior's licence; permut. & non-res. cl. £4 10s.

22 Wm Awforde, r. of Holton-le-Bekering, Linc. dio., chapl. to Earl of Rutland. Disp. to hold a benef. with cure with the above, or 2 others without; permut. & non-res. cl. £7 13s 4d.

28 Ric. Catesby & Eliz. Askell. Disp. for marriage (Eliz. was sponsor at the confirmation of a child of Ric. & without banns). £5; 10s.

21 Halifax, inhabitants of. Disp. to use, & receive the sacraments in, a chapel within the par. £4.

f. 32^v

June 8 Ric. Lyghe, v. of Broxbourne, Lond. dio. Disp. to hold a benef.
with cure with the above, or 2 without; permut. & non-res. cl.
£7 13s 4d.

5 Benedict Carter, canon of Bodmin. Disp. to hold a benef. with
cure, if granted his prior's licence, & to retain his habit. £4.

10 Hugh Harrys & Joan Don. Disp. for marriage (3rd degree
affin.). Arb. £4.

9 Jo. Barett, O.C. fr. Disp. to wear the habit of his order beneath
that of a sec. pr. £4.

7 Jo. Bawscale & Helen More, York dio. Disp. for marriage (3rd
degree consang.). Arb. 20s.

Mar. 10 Jo. Thomson, York dio., chapl. to Tho. Cromwell, Kg's 1st sec.
Disp. to hold the mastership of the House of God of Austin
hermits, nr Dover, in comm. with other benefices for which he
already holds disp., viz. par. ch. of Ebberston & St Jas, Dover,
and v. of Peckham, Cant. dio. Arb. £4. 'Resp. quousque.'

f. 33^r

June 14 Ric. Turner, acol., Cov. & Lich. dio. Disp. to take all h.o. at any
time, 2 on the same day. 26s 8d.

5 Jo. Barrett, O.C. fr. Disp. to hold any benef. with cure; permut.
cl. Arb. £4.

15 Peter Bayne & Agnes Hammon, York dio. Disp. for marriage
(Peter's mother was Agnes's godmother). 30s.

16 Edw. Blankarne & Marg. Rudde, Carl. dio. Disp. for marriage
(3rd & 4th degrees consang.). 30s.

Jo. Abagworth & Agnes Philipp, Linc. dio. Disp. for marriage
(Agnes was godmother to a child of Jo.). Arb. 20s.

17 Hy Byngham & Jane Cranmer, York dio. Disp. for marriage
(4th degree consang.). 26s 8d.

Tho. Crisall & Joan Petrot, Norw. dio. Disp. for marriage (3rd
& 4th degrees consang.). 30s.

Jo. Bandon, reg. canon. Cancelled disp. to hold a benef. with
cure, if granted his prior's licence. 'Vacat quia post.'

f. 33^v

18 Philip ap Jenn ap Kynwyn & Marg. verch Jenn ap Glinn ap
Richard, St David's dio. Disp. for marriage (4th degree consang.). 26s 8d.

June 18 Walter ap Thomas ap Rhes *alias* Watkin ap Rhes & Blanche verch Howell. Disp. for marriage (4th degree consang.). 26s 8d.

3 Ld Hy Clifford & Eleanor Brandon. Disp. for marriage (4th & 4th degrees consang.) & without banns. 26s 8d; 10s.

19 Ric. Jenn, O.S.A., prior of St Mary Bradleigh, Sarum dio. Disp. to hold a benef. with cure with the above office. £10.

20 Andrew Marcyall, Cluniac monk of Farleigh, Sarum dio. Disp. to wear his habit beneath that of a secular pr. £4.

23 Jo. Hammon[d], Premonstr. canon of Leiston, Norw. dio. Disp. to hold a benef. with cure & retain his habit, if granted his prior's licence. £4.

29 Jo. Manknoll & Eliz. Robert, Cov. & Lich. dio. Disp. for marriage (4th degree consang.). 26s 8d.

27 Tho. Conyers, canon of Watton, York dio. Disp. to hold a benef. with cure & retain his habit, if granted his prior's licence. £4.

July 4 Jas Beaumonte, fellow of the coll. ch. of Greystoke. Disp. to hold a benef. with cure with the above, or 2 without, one of which must be without cure of souls. £4.

f. 34ʳ

June 25 Andrew Marcyial, Cluniac monk of Farleigh. Disp. to hold any benef. with cure, if granted the consent of his prior. £4.

July 5 Owen ap William ap Et & Agnes verch Robert ap Meredith, St Asaph dio. Disp. for marriage (3rd & 4th degrees consang.). 30s.

6 Wm Cary & Joan Snyppe, York dio. Disp. for marriage (Hy Snyppe, formerly husband of Joan, was godfather to a child of Wm). £6.

7 Wm Laceby, Premonstr. canon of Tupholme, Linc. dio. Cancelled disp. to hold a benef. with cure, if granted his abbot's consent. 'Vacat quia ante.'

8 Ric. Waldram, r. of Archingworth, Linc. dio. Disp. to hold a benef. with cure with the above, or 2 without; permut. & non-res. cl. £7 13s 4d.

13 Simon Beneson, v. of Sturminster Marshall, Sarum dio. Disp. to hold a benef. with the above, or 2 without; permut. & non-res. cl. £7 13s 4d.

12 Wm Broke, Linc. dio. Disp. to take all h.o. at any time, 2 on the same day. 26s 8d.

July 14 Hy Ravenall & Alice Grenewaye, Heref. dio. Disp. for marriage (Joan Grenewaye, Alice's mother, was Hy's godmother). 30s.

f. 34ᵛ

13 Tho. Elington, abbot of the Premonstr. hse of Wending, Norw. dio. Disp. to hold any benef. with cure with this office. £10.

8 Tho. Dowghtie. Disp. to take all h.o. & hold a benef. with cure of souls, despite defect of birth; non-res. cl. £4.

12 Jas Adams, O.F.M., of Preston in A[mou]nderness. Disp. to hold any benef. with cure, if granted his prior's licence. £4. Also disp. to wear the habit of his Order beneath that of a sec. pr. £4.

Jo. Moyne & Kath. Frayne, Dublin dio. Disp. for marriage (Kath. was godmother to a child of Jo. or vice versa). £6.

May 24 Walter Mugge, treasurer of the coll. ch. of Crediton, Ex. dio., chapl. to Jo. Bp of Exeter, v. of the ch. of the vault (de Arcus) by disp. Disp. to hold another benef. with cure with the above, or 3 without; permut. & non-res. cl. £9.

July 17 Tho. Symson & Joan Rennyer, Linc. dio. Disp. for marriage (Tho. was Joan's godfather). 'Arb. in forma pauperis.'

16 Philip Assheley, O.S.B., of Shrewsbury, Cov. & Lich. dio. Disp. to hold a benef. with cure. £4.

f. 35ʳ

12 Tho. Apulton, formerly reg. canon O.S.A. now a hermit. Disp. to hold any benef. with cure & to wear the habit of his Order beneath that of a sec. pr. £4; £4.

17 Ric. Dere, r. of St Mary's on the Hill, Cowbridge, Lland. dio. Disp. for non-res. for 3 yrs. 20s.

20 Humfrey Beyrfforde & Ann Blackwall, Cov. & Lich. dio. Disp. for marriage (3rd degree consang.). £6.

Tho. Johnson & Agnes Harstoste, Cov. & Lich. dio. Disp. for marriage (Tho. was godfather to a child of Agnes & Cuthbert Harstoste, then her husband). £6.

24 Wm Outfelde & Agnes Midelton, York dio. Disp. for marriage (4th degree consang.). 26s 8d.

19 Jo. Godman, r. of Charleton, v. of W. Harptree, Bath & W. dio. Cancelled disp. to hold a benef. with the above, not over £8 value p.a. 'Vacat quia post.'

25 Jas Hoggeson & Joan Lynsa. Disp. for marriage (4th degree consang.). 26s 8d.

July 23 Morgan Philip. Disp. to take h.o. from the bp or suffragan of his
          dio. at any time. 26s 8d.

f. 35ᵛ

       17 Rob. Warde, O.P., Ely dio. Disp. to hold a benef. with cure & to
          leave off his habit. Arb. £6.

       30 Jo. Assheworth & Joan Butterworth, Cov. & Lich. dio. Disp. for
          marriage (4th degree consang.). Arb. 20s.

          Rowland Atkynson & Eliz. Sawer, York dio. Disp. for marriage
          (3rd & 4th degrees consang.). 30s.

Aug.   3 Jo. William & Marcelina Lewys, Lland. dio. Disp. for marriage
          (3rd degree affin.). Arb. 20s.

        6 Jo. Goldisburne & Eliz. Thewe, Linc. dio. Disp. for marriage
          (4th degree consang.). 26s 8d.

       10 Tho. Hemsley, acol., York dio. Disp. to take all h.o. without
          l.d., 2 on the same day. 26s 8d; 6s 8d.

        8 Jo. Warner, v. of Wharstede, Norw. dio., chapl. to Archbp of
          Cant. Disp. to hold a benef. with the above, or 2 without;
          permut. & non-res. cl. £7 13s 4d.

          Bartholomew Michell, r. of Wooton Courtney, Bath & W. dio.,
          chapl. to Bp of London. Disp. to hold a benef. with cure with
          the above or 2 without; non-res. cl. £7 13s 4d.

f. 36ʳ

       20 Hy. Gardaile & Eliz. Fawcett, York dio. Disp. for marriage (4th
          degree affin.). 26s 8d.

          Jas. Fawssett & Helen Blande, York dio. Disp. for marriage (3rd
          & 4th degrees affin.). 30s.

       22 Tho. ap Robert ap Richarde & Janet verch Rice ap John. Disp.
          for marriage (4th degree consang.). 26s 8d.

       21 Jas Lancashere & Isabella Barlo, Cov. & Lich. dio. Disp. for
          marriage (3rd & 4th degrees affin.). 30s.

       25 Tho. Philip & Alice Morvell, York dio. Disp. for marriage (4th
          degree consang.). 26s 8d.

       26 Laurence Quitquam & Marg. Ingham, Cov. & Lich. dio. Disp.
          for marriage (4th degree consang.). 26s 8d.

       27 Ric. Barlo & Helen Hardey, Cov. & Lich. dio. Disp. for marriage
          (3rd & 4th degrees affin.). 30s.

July   5 Wm Casson, O.F.M. of Lynn, Norw. dio. Disp. to take the
          habit & rule of the hermits of St Anthony. 40s.

f. 36ᵛ

Aug. 27 Matthew Raynar & Janet Broket, York dio. Disp. for marriage (3rd & 4th degrees consang.). 30s.

18 Ric. Banester, esq., & Alice Charleton, Cov. & Lich. dio. Disp. for marriage (3rd & 4th degrees affin.). 30s.

31 Jo. More & Agnes Croste, Cov. & Lich. dio. Disp. for marriage (3rd & 4th degrees affin.).

1534 Sept. 4 Tho. Monyfolde & Cicily Watterfall, Cov. & Lich. dio. Disp. for marriage (3rd & 4th degrees consang.). 30s.

May 14 Walter Hill & Eleanor Yearnton, Worc. dio. Cancelled disp. for marriage (3rd & 4th degrees consang. & Eleanor's mother or father was Walter's godparent or vice versa). 'Vacat quia ante.'

15 Rob. Horsfall. Cancelled incomplete disp.

1535(?)Sept.10 Maurice ap William of the Kg's household & Ann Adams *alias* Studley. Disp. for marriage within the prohibited times. 20s.

May 31 Jo. Walker & Joan Pennell, Heref. dio. Disp. for marriage (3rd & 4th degrees affin.). 30s.

June 2 Hugh Purese, acol., Linc. dio. Disp. to take all h.o. at any time, 2 on the same day. 26s 8d.

f. 37ʳ

Morgan William & Alice verch John Thomas ap Jankyn, Lland. dio. Disp. for marriage (4th degree affin.). 26s 8d.

7 Bartholomew Hare & Ann Dall, Linc. dio. Disp. for marriage (3rd & 4th degree affin.). 30s.

8 Edw. & Marg. Keneston, Cov. & Lich. dio. Disp. for marriage (3rd & 4th degrees affin.). 30s.

9 Tho. Smyth & Agnes Appolgarth, York dio. Disp. for marriage (3rd & 4th degrees affin.). 30s.

10 Geo. Gibson, acol., Sarum dio. Disp. to take all h.o. at any time. 26s 8d.

11 Geo. Richardson & Marg. Horpton, of London. Disp. for marriage the banns read once. 'Nil regi.' 6s 8d.

Ric. Holgate & Eliz. Draper, York dio. Disp. for marriage (4th degree consang.). 26s 8d.

6 Jas Samson, Sarum dio. Disp. to take all h.o. at any time & 2 on the same day. 26s 8d.

June 25 Jo. James & Emota Furnes, Cov. & Lich. dio. Disp. for marriage (4th degree consang.). 26s 8d.

26 Nich. Palmer, York dio. Disp. to take pr.'s orders & hold a benef. although in his 24th yr; non-res. cl. 20s.

f. 37ᵛ

25 Jo. Shelley & Ann Markewicke *alias* Ammersam, Chich. dio. Disp. for marriage (3rd & 4th degrees consang.). 30s.

Tho. Ball & Janet Snarpe, Cov. & Lich. dio. Disp. for marriage (3rd & 4th degrees consang.). 30s.

28 Jo. Ducke & Janet Marcygall, York dio. Disp. for marriage (3rd & 4th degrees consang.). 30s.

29 Jo. Monde & Alice Symones, Heref. dio. Disp. for marriage (3rd & 4th degrees affin.). 30s.

30 Nich. Hibbarte & Joan Thornelle, Cov. & Lich. dio. Disp. for marriage (3rd & 4th degrees consang.). 30s.

July 1 Tho. Vyncent & Eliz. Crosebye, Norw. dio. Disp. for marriage (4th degree consang.). 26s 8d.

June 30 Wm Leche, Ely dio. Disp. to take all h.o. at any time & 2 on the same day. 26s 8d.

July 1 Alan Harper & Eliz. Smorthwell, York dio. Disp. for marriage (3rd degrees consang. & affin.). 53s 4d.

2 Tho. Meller & Eliz. Tedrington, Cov. & Lich. dio. Disp. for marriage (4th degree consang.). 26s 8d.

f. 38ʳ

6 Lewis ap Rhes Gwyn & Stana (?) verch Lloyd Edwarde, St Asaph dio. Disp. for marriage (4th degree consang.). 26s 8d.

June 28 Wm Wodall & Eliz. Damparde, Cov. & Lich. dio. Disp. for marriage (4th degree consang.). 26s 8d.

July 6 Lancelot Brokbanke & Janet Robynson, York dio. Disp. for marriage (4th degree consang.). 26s 8d.

2 Jo. Banke & Marg. Strykett, Carl. dio. Disp. for marriage (4th degree consang.). 26s 8d.

12 Rob. Wodless & Joan Smyth, Lond. dio. Disp. for marriage without banns. 'Nil regi.' 10s.

11 Geo. Swan & Marg. Bromesall, Cov. & Lich. dio. Disp. for marriage (Geo.'s mother was sponsor at Marg.'s confirmation). 30s.

July 17 David ap Hopkyn & Janet verch John, Lland. dio. Disp. for marriage (4th degree consang.). 26s 8d.

Aug. 11 Roger Dene & Agnes Darlington, Cov. & Lich. dio. Disp. for marriage (3rd & 4th degrees affin.). 30s. 'Enrolled int. iiiito & iii.'

10 Jo. Damparde & Kath. Manwaring, Cov. & Lich. dio. Disp. for marriage (4th degree consang.). 26s 8d.

f. 38ᵛ

11 Jankyn Thomas & Marg. Kemys, Lland. dio. Disp. for marriage (4th degree consang.). 26s 8d.

12 Rob. Baryngton, O.S.B., abbot of Walden. Disp., together with 4 monks of the same or another Order or otherwise who eat at his table, to eat meat, butter, cheese, & other fat foods throughout the yr. £4.

20 Ric. Flynt, r. of Blakenham Aquarum, Norw. dio., chapl. to Ld Tho. Howard. Disp. to hold a benef. with cure with the above or 2 without, without non-res. cl. £6 10s.

22 Nich. Gyles & Eliz. Pereson, Linc. dio. Disp. for marriage (Eliz. was godmother to a child of Nich.). £6.

Sept. 4 Matthew Herbart & Mary Gamage. Disp. for marriage (4th degree consang.). 26s 8d.

30 Jo. Pope, Bath & W. or another dio. Disp. to take all h.o. at any time, 2 on the same day. 20s.

David ap Rhes Glin & Joan verch Thomas Griffith. Disp. for marriage (3rd & 4th degrees affin.). 30s.

f. 39ʳ

Oct. 24 Roger Sadler & Joan Metcalf, York dio. Disp. for marriage (4th degree consang.). 26s 8d.

18 Griffin ap William & Kath. verch James ap Owen, St David's dio. Disp. for marriage (4th degree consang.). 26s 8d.

Nov. 1 Francis Dundye, O.F.M. Disp. to hold any benef., with change of habit; permut. cl. 'Remittebatur gratis.'

Oct. 23 Hector Assheley & Rose Mannyngton, Lond. dio. Disp. for marriage (Hector was godfather to a child of Rose, & without banns). £6; 10s.

Ralph Fearfaxe, O.S.A., prior of Kyme, Linc. dio. Disp. to hold any benef. with cure in comm. £10.

22 Ric. Cawrden, r. of St Jo. the Evangelist (place unnamed);

chapl. to Sir Wm Fitzwilliam. Disp. to hold a benef. with cure with the above or 2 without; permut. & non-res. cl. £7 13s 4d.

Oct. 22 Jo. Laurence *alias* Warde, Observant fr. Disp. to hold a benef. with cure & change his habit. 'Remittebatur gratis.'

20 Ric. Skydmore, monk of St Peter's, Gloucester. Disp. to hold a benef. with cure; non-res. cl. £4.

f. 39ᵛ

10 Jo. Roser & Agnes Ven, Chich. dio. Disp. for marriage (Jo. was sponsor at the confirmation of a child of Agnes). £5.

20 Tho. Powell, pr. Cancelled disp. to hold any 2 benefices with cure; permut. & non-res. cl. £7 13s 4d. 'Vacat quia post:' 'No[t]a si non p[rovisus] non seq[uitur].'

31 Hickling, prior of. Confirmation of letters concerning the presentation to an unnamed ch. 40s.

July 10 Wm Castelton, prior of Norw. cath. priory. Disp. together with 4 other religious to eat meat & other fat foods publicly or privately. £4.

Oct. 27 Edw. Welden, Durham dio. Disp. to take all h.o. although in his 23rd yr, at any time, 2 on the same day, without l.d. & to hold a benef. with cure after taking pr.'s orders. 26s 8d; 20s; 6s 8d.

Nov. 7 Jo. Letherlonde, r. of Covenham, Linc. dio., chapl. to Earl of Rutland. Disp. to hold a benef. with cure with the above or 2 without; permut. & non-res. cl. £7 13s 4d.

6 Tho. Mortymer & Joan Dodrydge, Ex. dio. Disp. for marriage (4th degree consang.). 26s 8d.

7 Tho. or Rob. Dyo & Agnes verch Jankyn, Lland. dio. Disp. for marriage (3rd & 4th degrees affin.). 30s.

10 Wm Hare, O.S.A., canon of Bisham. Disp. to hold any benef. with cure with change of habit. Arb. £4.

f. 40ʳ

8 Rob. Aske & Ann Sutton, York dio. Disp. for marriage (4th degree consang. & 3rd & 4th degrees affin.). 26s 8d; 30s.

10 Tho. Hunte, r. of Challacombe ('Cholachom') Ex. dio. Disp. for non-res. during illness. 30s.

Jo. Waren, prior of Pembroke at Monketon. Disp., having resigned the above office, to hold a benef. with cure & wear the habit of his Order beneath that of a sec. pr. £8.

Nich. & Agnes Keyte, Sarum dio. Disp. for marriage (3rd degree consang. & 2nd degree affin.). Arb. £6.

Tho. Griffith, canon of Elsing Spital, Lond. dio. Disp. to hold any benef. & change his habit. £8.

Nov. 12 Rob. Croham, prior of St Pancras, Lewes. Disp., together with 4 monks of his table, to eat meat, butter, cheese, & other fat foods throughout the yr. £4.

10 Edw. Payne, canon of Bisham. Disp. to hold any benef. with cure & to change his habit. Arb. £4.

Rob. Forman *alias* Madestone, monk of Roch. cath. Disp. to hold any benef. with cure & with change of habit. Arb. £4.

f. 40ᵛ

12 Tho. Sanclone & Jane Slyfelde, Sarum dio. Disp. for marriage (one of them was sponsor at the confirmation of a child of the other). Arb. 50s. 'Resp. quousque.'

16 Jo. Grymesdiche & Helen Cloughe, Cov. & Lich. dio. Disp. for marriage (4th degree consang.). 26s 8d.

14 Ralph Oldon, r. of Brydshaw, chapl. to Ld Fitzwarren. Cancelled disp. to hold a benef. with cure with the above, or 2 without; permut. & non-res. cl. £7 13s 4d. 'Vacat quia post.' 'No[t]a si non [provisus non sequitur].'

15 Jo. Henry, O.C. fr., Newcastle-on-Tyne, Durham dio. Disp. to hold a benef. with cure & change his habit. Arb. £4.

14 Rob. London *alias* Chamberlayne, monk of Roch. cath. Similar disp. Arb. £4.

17 Jo. Wyke & Marg. Dune, Ex. dio. Disp. for marriage (4th degree consang.). 26s 8d.

19 Jo. Hill *alias* Taylour, Heref. dio. Disp. to take all h.o. at any time & 2 on the same day. 26s 8d.

18 Rob. Bennett, O.S.B. Disp. to hold any benef. in Linc. dio. £4. [Probably prior of Bardney. See *L.P.* vii. 1121 (6).]

20 Jo. Pawlett, Bath & W. dio. Disp. to take all h.o. at any time & 2 on the same day. 26s 8d.

Geo. Barton, York dio. Disp. to take all h.o. at any time & 2 on the same day. 26s 8d; 6s 8d.

Edw. Philip & Agnes Stephen. Disp. for marriage (4th degree consang.). 26s 8d.

f. 41ʳ

21 Jo. Lydys & Agnes Sakvyle, Chich. dio. Disp. for marriage (3rd & 4th degrees consang.). 30s.

Nov. 15 David ap Howell Ychan & Gwentillian verch Lewys ap Jenn Eynon, St David's dio. Disp. for marriage (3rd degree affin.). £6.

20 Rob. Molyneux, Cov. & Lich. dio. Disp. to take h.o. & hold a benef. with cure, despite defect of birth & having reached his 15th yr only; non-res. & permut. cl. £4.

Jo. Butler, Observant fr. Disp. to hold a benef. & change his habit. £8.

Nich. Spelhurst *alias* Arnold, O.S.B., Roch. cath. Similar disp. £8.

23 Edm. Barton, hermit of the Order of St Paul. Disp. to wear his habit beneath that of a sec. pr. £4.

25 David Stephen & Alice Dunsey, Ex. dio. Disp. for marriage (3rd & 4th degrees consang.). 30s.

26 Ric. Alen & Joan Marten, Bath & W. dio. Disp. for marriage (3rd & 4th degrees affin.). 30s.

Tho. Bedill, archdcn of Cornwall. Disp. not to proceed to pr.'s orders for 2 yrs. 20s.

f. 41ᵛ

13 Jo. Rye *alias* Harroke, O.S.B., monk of Roch. cath. Disp. to hold a benef. & change his habit. Arb. £4.

26 Wm Mayfelde *alias* Dryke, monk. Similar disp. £8. 'Res. quo usque.'

25 Rob. Shether, v. of Hendon & Gt Waltham, nr London. Cancelled disp. to hold any benef. with cure; non-res., permut. cl. £8. 'Vacat quia post.'

28 Wm Mores & Helen Openshawe, Cov. & Lich. dio. Disp. for marriage (3rd & 4th degrees consang.). Arb. 20s.

20 Owen Hawkyns & Fortune Marler. Disp. for marriage outside the statutory time. 20s.

30 Jo. Martin de Ursanis & Marg. Soler. Disp. for marriage within the prohibited times. 20s.

27 Rob. Menysshe *alias* Nale, O.S.B., of Canterbury cath. Disp. to hold a benef. with change of habit. £8.

12 Jo. Amery, O.S.A., canon of Missenden. Disp. to wear the habit of a sec. pr. & remain in his Order. £4.

27 Nich. Smyth, Austin fr. of Norwich. Disp. to hold a benef. with change of habit. £8; 10s.

Nov. 26 Hy Dawson & Ann Warner, York dio. Disp. for marriage (3rd degree affin.). Arb. 40s.

26 Wm Hornyng *alias* Ugge, O.S.B., monk of St Benet Hulme. Cancelled disp. to hold a benef. with change of habit, & non-res. cl. £8 10s. 'Vacat quia post.' 'No[t]a si non p[rovisus] non sequitur.'

f. 42ʳ

20 Rob. Kaye, O.P. Disp. to hold a benef. with change of habit. 'Remittebatur per Dominum Cant[uarensem] gratis.'

Dec. 1 Brian Bee, Carth., of Axholme, Linc. dio. Disp. to hold a benef. with change of habit. Arb. £6.

9 Jo. Worlyche & Kath. Cokkett, Norw. dio. Disp. for marriage within the prohibited time, without banns. 20s; 10s.

Jo. Patesayne & Matilda Swyre, York dio. Disp. for marriage (3rd & 4th degrees consang.). 30s.

Wm Alen & Joan Fayth, of St Mary Magdalen par., London. Disp. for marriage within the prohibited time. 20s.

10 Raymond Thompson & Agnes Morlande, York dio. Disp. for marriage (3rd & 4th degrees consang.). 30s.

9 Jo. Cobham *alias* Stace, monk of Ryarsh ('Rierst'), Roch. dio. Disp. to hold a benef., with change of habit. £8. 'Resp. quousque.'

4 Tho. Flere *alias* Maynard, monk of Roch. cath. Disp. to hold a benef. with change of habit. £8. 'Resp. quousque.'

Nov. 27 Tho. Pyrton. Cancelled disp. concerning presentation of un-named benef. £19. 'Cancellat hic quod on[er]at postea in Compo. de anno XXIX sicut cont. ibm.'

f. 42ᵛ

Sept. 17 Francis Malet, v. of Rothwell, York dio. Disp. to hold a benef. with the above or 2 without; permut. & non-res. cl. £6 10s.

Dec. 9 Jo. Est & Joan Alan, Linc. dio. Disp. for marriage (2nd & 3rd degrees affin.). £8.

14 Edw. Whitchurche & Ann Welles. Disp. for marriage within the prohibited time. 20s.

1 Rhes ap Glin ap Lln ap Tyder & Janet verch More ap Rhes ap Howell, Bangor dio. Disp. for marriage (4th degree affin.). 26s 8d.

Ric. Badeley, Cov. & Lich. dio. Disp. to take all h.o. & 2 on the same day. 26s 8d.

Dec. 15 Tho. Sharpe. Disp. to take all h.o. & 2 on the same day. 26s 8d.

Jo. Reydon & Mary Broke *alias* Cobham, Roch. dio. Disp. for marriage within the prohibited time. 20s.

5 Jo. ap David *alias* Guithlike & Kath. Puleston, St Asaph dio. Cancelled disp. for marriage (Kath.'s father was Jo.'s godfather). 30s. 'Vacat quia post' &c.

9 Tho. Gyles, O.C. fr., of Norwich. Disp. to hold a benef. & change his habit. £8.

13 Ric. Dyrecks, prior of the Hospital of the Holy Cross (Crutched friars), Colchester. Disp. to hold a benef. £4.

16 Jo. Fitzherbert, r. of Waltham & Maper, Linc. dio. Disp. to hold a benef. with cure with the above, or 3 without; permut. & non-res. cl. £13 6s 8d.

f. 43ʳ

17 Hy Huskyn, O.Cist., of Neath, Lland. dio. Disp. to hold a benef. with change of habit. 'Remittebatur gratis.'

20 Eli Modye, O.F.M., of Canterbury. Disp. to hold a benef., with change of habit. Arb. £4.

17 Jas Rason *alias* Showler, O.S.B. of Abingdon, Sarum dio. Disp. to hold any benef., with cure; permut. cl. £4.

Rob. Debnam, Premonstr. canon of Beeleigh, Lond. dio. Disp. to hold any benef. with cure, if granted his abbot's consent. £4. 'Resp. quousque.'

16 Jo. Holme, v. of Woodford, Linc. dio. & reg. canon. Disp. to wear his habit beneath that of a sec. pr. £4.

10 Giles Honywoode, O.S.B., of Dover, Cant. dio. Disp. to hold a benef.; permut. cl. £4.

20 Nich. Sandeforde, clk. Disp. concerning unnamed benef. 40s.

10 Wm Christchurche, O.S.B., of Cerne, Sarum dio. Disp. to hold any benef. £4.

July 11 Shap, abbot & convent of. Disp. concerning union of unnamed benef. £50.

f. 43ᵛ

Dec. 20 Wm Becher, fr. Disp. to hold any benef. for life; permut. & non-res. cl. Arb. £4.

Rob. Danys, r. of Pitsea, Lond. dio. Disp. for non-res. for 3 yrs. 20s.

19 Edw. Hill & Agnes Chapman. Disp. for marriage (Edw. was godfather to a child of Agnes). Arb.

Dec. 30 Tho. Welles & Eliz. Welshe, of Luton, Linc. dio. Disp. for marriage (Tho.'s father was Eliz.'s godfather, & Eliz.'s Tho.'s). 'Remittebatur gratis per dominum Cancellarium.'

f. 44ʳ
1534   14 Jo. Fychett, r. of St Kath.'s, Whetstone, Ex. dio. Disp. for non-res., under the royal seal. 5s.

1535 Feb. 16 Rob. Balfount, r. of Upton, Sarum dio. Disp. for non-res. for 2 yrs, under the royal seal. 5s.

Jo. Whitholme, r. of Walpole. Disp. for 2 yrs non-res., under the royal seal. 5s.

May 11 Wm Weston. Disp. to take all h.o. on the same day, from any bp, under the signet. 5s.

June 9 Jo. Dale. Disp. to practise as M.D. and reside where he wishes; under the signet. 5s.

8 Tho. Swynnerton, clk. Disp. to preach throughout the realm, under the signet. 5s.

6 Tho. Garrard, B.Th. Disp. to preach throughout the realm, under the royal seal. 5s.

20 Hy Kensyke, clk, r. of Fonthill Gifford. Disp. for non-res. under the signet. 5s.

Jo. Thixstill. Disp. to preach throughout the realm, under the signet. 5s.

Wm Peterson, r. of Bonyng, Calais. Unspecified disp. under the royal seal. 5s.

July 9 Jo. Chekye. Disp. to preach throughout the realm. 5s.

1 Wm Higwaye, r. of Colmworth. Disp. for non-res. for 3 yrs. 5s.

f. 44ᵛ
7 Geo. Savage, r. of Redmarley. Disp. for non-res. 5s.

Oct. 15 Jerome Clyfforde. Disp. for non-res. for 2 yrs. 5s.

Nov. 15 Rob. Paterson. Similar disp. 5s.

14 Similar disp. for Wm Balforde, 5s; & Nich. Dundye, 5s.

23 Jo. Corye. Similar disp. 5s.

Dec. 9 Roger Conert. Similar disp. 5s.

12 Jo. Knight. Similar disp. 5s; also for Hugh ap Robert, 5s; & Wm Glyn, 5s.

15 Ric. . . ., Disp. concerning unnamed benef., under royal seal. 5s.

f. 45ʳ

1534 Nov. 3 Nich. Singleton & Marg. Portington, Linc. dio. Disp. for marriage (Marg. was godmother to a child of Nich.). £6.

1535 June 10 Jo. Bandon, reg. canon. Disp. to hold a benef. with cure although he cannot obtain the licence of his suffragan or prior, as specified in previous disp. 26s 8d.

July 19 Jo. Goodman, r. of Carleton, v. of W. Harptree, Bath & W. dio. Disp. to hold a benef. (not with cure or incompatible) with the above. £8.

Aug. 20 Tho. Powell, clk. Disp. to hold 2 benefices with cure; permut. & non-res. cl. £7 13s 4d.

Nov. 14 Ralph Oldon, r. of Bredeshaw, chapl. of Ld Fitzwarden. Disp. to hold an incompatible benef. with the above, or 2 without these; permut. & non-res. cl. £7 13s 4d. ('Nota quod omnia ista summa sequens onerant in compo[t]e de anno XXVIII in titulo disp.')

25 Rob. Shether, v. of Hendon & Gt Waltham, nr London. Disp. to hold a 3rd benef. with cure; permut. & non-res. cl. £8.

f. 45ᵛ

26 Wm Hornyng *alias* Ugge, monk of St Benet Hulme. Disp. to hold a benef. & change his habit, non-res. cl. £8 10s.

Dec. 15 Jo. ap David ap John Smthike & Kath. Puleston, St Asaph dio. Disp. for marriage (Kath.'s father was Jo.'s godfather). 30s.

ff. 46ʳ–48ᵛ blank.

f. 49ʳ

1536 Jan. 6 Wm King & Joan Lye, Cant. dio. Disp. for marriage (Wm's mother was Joan's godmother). 30s.

5 Tho. Wymbusshe & Dorothy Husey. Disp. for marriage (4th degree consang.). 26s 8d.

4 Jenn ap Howell ap John & Marg. verch David ap Jenn ap John, Bangor dio. Disp. for marriage (3rd & 4th degrees consang.). 30s.

19 Wm Meriwether & Eliz. Gill, Sarum dio. Disp. for marriage (3rd & 4th degrees affin.). 30s.

15 Jo. Both & Cicily Haryson, Cov. & Lich. dio. Disp. for marriage (2nd & 4th degrees consang.). 30s.

f. 49ᵛ

20 Fulcon Powell & Joan Butler, of London. Disp. for marriage without banns, within the statutory time. 10s.

Jan. 11 Gilbert Bowdocke & Eliz. Bowkes, Lond. dio. Disp. for marriage without banns. 10s.

21 Oliver More & Isabella Jackson, York dio. Disp. for marriage (4th degree consang.). 26s 8d.

Tho. Clayton & Kath. Punchin, Lond. dio. Disp. for marriage without banns. 10s.

24 Wm Walker & Kath. Singleton, Cant. province. Disp. for marriage without banns. 10s.

20 Rob. Latymer, sch., subdcn, Linc. dio. Disp. to take dcn's & pr.'s orders on any day. 13s 4d.

f. 50ʳ

Feb. 3 Rob. Cusse & Joan Capell, Bath & W. dio. Disp. for marriage without banns. 10s.

4 Tho. Ducke & Joan Carter, in the immediate jurisdiction of Cant. cath. Disp. for marriage the banns read once. 6s 8d.

5 Jas Carlall & Kath. Hayle, of London. Disp. for marriage, the banns read once. 6s 8d.

6 Hugh Bothewell & Grace Bolton, Cov. & Lich. dio. Disp. for marriage (4th degree affin.). 10s.

Geo. Towneshende, Norw. dio., & Alice Thurston, of London. Disp. for marriage without banns. 10s.

Ralph Haworth & Janet Taylor *alias* Hayworth, Cov. & Lich. dio. Disp. for marriage (Ralph & a certain Grace Lowe of the same dio., related in the 3rd & 4th degrees consang. to Janet, were previously betrothed). 26s 8d.

f. 50ᵛ

9 Tho. Nottingham, B.A., York dio. Disp. to take all h.o. without l.d. 6s 8d.

Rob. Aldridge & Ann Pace, of Barnards Inn, nr London. Disp. for marriage without banns. 10s.

13 Gurdion Keyne & Agnes More, Linc. dio. Disp. for marriage, the banns read once. 6s 8d.

12 Giles Tederland & Bridget Barker, Norw. dio. Disp. for marriage, the banns read once. 6s 8d.

15 Tho. Mores, subdcn, St David's dio. Disp. to take dcn's & pr.'s orders on any day, from any bp. 13s 4d.

Jan. 10 Nich. West, Cant. dio. Disp. to take all h.o. from any bp. 6s 8d.

f. 51^r

Roger ap Eynon & Eliz. Pyxley, Cov. & Lich. dio. Disp. for marriage (4th degree consang.). 26s 8d.

Jan. 11 Ant. Marten & Marg. Cotton, Cant. dio. Disp. for marriage (3rd & 4th degrees consang.). 30s.

Hy Thompson & Brigett Flemmyng, of London. Disp. for marriage without banns. 10s.

12 Hugh Longley & Agnes Cowdrey. Disp. for marriage, the banns read once. 6s 8d.

Jas Chaterton & Agnes Masterling, Sarum dio. Disp. for marriage (Jas was godfather to a child of Agnes). Arb. £4. Warrant shown.

10 Jo. Marbury, Austin fr. of Richmond. Disp. to hold a benef. with cure with change of habit. Gratis.

14 Hy Deson & Marg. Smyth, Worc. dio. Disp. for marriage (4th degree consang.). 26s 8d.

f. 51^v

12 Simon Paching & Godlina Vate, Cant. dio. Disp. for marriage (Simon was godfather to a child of Godlina). £6.

14 Ric. Devias, O.S.A., canon of St Mary's without Bishopsgate, London. Disp. to give up the habit of his order & annual service. £4.

19 Wm Page, O.S.B., of St John's, Colchester, Lond. dio. Disp. to hold a benef. with cure as a sec. clk & be non-res., if granted his superior's consent. £4 10s.

Jas & Eliz. Fell, of Furness, York dio. Disp. for legitimization of marriage already consummated (3rd & 4th degrees consang.). £6.

20 Tho. Gray, O.S.A., canon of Butley, Norw. dio. Disp. to hold a benef. with change of habit. Gratis; warrant shown.

Chris. Slee, prior of Carl. cath. Disp. to be v. of Castle Stamby (*sic* for Castle Sowerby?) as well. £4.

f. 52^r

Jo. Crostewayte, Premonstr. canon, v. of Lympnehow, Vintur, & Southwood. Confirmation of letters from the Bp of Norw. permitting him to hold these benefices in commendam. 40s; p.s.r. 5s.

Feb. 1 Ant. Moryce, O.S.B., of Peterborough, Lond. dio. Disp. to hold a benef. with cure if granted his abbot's consent, & wear his habit beneath that of a sec. pr. £8.

Jan.   7   Tho. Albaster, r. of Batheley, Norw. dio. Disp. to hold a benef. with cure with the above, or 2 without; permut. & non-res. cl. £7 13s 4d.

1535 Nov.   6   Jo. Butler, r. of Colome, in the march of Calais, Kg's chapl. Disp. to hold a benef. with cure with the above, or 2 without; permut. & non-res. cl. £7 13s 4d.

1536 Jan.   20   Rob. Sall, O.S.A., canon of Walsingham. Disp. to hold a benef. with cure if granted his superior's consent. £4.

     26   Jo. Hynton, O.S.A., canon of Shulbrede, Chich. dio. Disp. to wear the habit of his order beneath that of a sec. pr. £4.

f. 52ᵛ

1535 Dec.   11   Chris. Croste, v. choral of Ex. cath. Disp. to hold a benef. with the above, or 2 others without, one of which must not have cure of souls; permut. & non-res. cl. £4.

1536 Feb.   4   Rob. Cockthorpe, O.C. fr. of Blakeney, Norw. dio. Disp. to hold any benef. with cure. £4.

1535 Nov.   7   Tho. Smyth, B.Cn. & C.L., v. of Newchurch, Cant. dio. Disp. to hold a benef. with cure with the above, or 2 without; permut. & non-res. cl. £6 10s.

    Sept. 20   Ric. Deane, chapl. to Archbp of York, r. of Ackworth, York dio. Disp. to hold a benef. with the above or 2 without; permut. cl. £6 10s.

1536 Feb.   8   Rob. Byble & Juliana Selson, Bath & W. dio. Disp. for marriage (3rd degree affin.). £6.

f. 53ʳ

    Jan. 26   Jo. Turner, Premonstr. canon, v. of Walsall, Cov. & Lich. dio. Disp. to hold a benef. with cure with the above (previously obtained by disp. and which does not yield over £8 p.a.); permut. & non-res. cl. £4.

     21   Ric. Horwell & Eliz. Grey, of London. Disp. for marriage without banns. 10s.

     13   Edm. Moore & Alice Alman, Norw. dio. Disp. for marriage at any time. 20s.

     12   Wm Towne & Isabella Hargreaves, Cov. & Lich. dio. Disp. for marriage (4th degree consang.). 26s 8d.

       Jo. Omerode & Marg. Barecrosse, Cov. & Lich. dio. Disp. for marriage (4th degree consang.). 26s 8d.

    Feb.   8   Wm Bull, O.F.M., Lond. dio. Disp. to wear his habit beneath that of a sec. pr. £4.

f. 53^v

Feb. 6 Tho. Cornewalys, M.A., r. of Tharston ('Thandeston'), Norw.
dio. Disp. to hold a benef. with cure with the above, or 2
without; permut. & non-res. cl. £7 13s 4d.

7 Jo. Sall, monk of Norw. cath. Disp. to hold any benef. with
cure and wear his habit beneath that of a sec. pr.; permut. &
non-res. cl. £8 10s.

9 Ric. ap William & Eliz. Folkke, St Asaph dio. Disp. for marriage
(3rd degree affin.). Gratis; warrant shown.

10 Wm Morwyn, M.A., chapl. to Ld Lumley, v. of Bainton, York
dio. Disp. to hold a benef. with cure with the above or 2 without; permut. cl. £6 10s.

Tho. Roche, formerly Observant fr. Disp. to hold any benef.
with cure with complete change of habit. Gratis; warrant shown.

f. 54^r

8 Jo. Carter & Agnes Inge. Disp. for marriage (one was godparent
to a child of the other). Arb. £6; warrant shown.

10 Rob. Ryder, O.C. fr., prior of Burnham Norton, Norw. dio.
Disp. to hold a benef. with cure & wear his habit beneath that of
of a sec. pr., having resigned the above office. £8.

15 Ric. More, r. of Kellington, Linc. dio. Disp. for non-res. for
2 yrs. 13s 4d.

13 Tho. Nevell, M.A., chapl. to Earl of Rutland, r. of Knipton,
Linc. dio. Disp. to hold a benef. with cure with the above,
or 2 without; permut. cl. £6 10s.

15 Edw. Bawdewyn, O.Cist., of Robertsbridge, Chich. dio. Disp.
to hold any benef. & give up the habit of his Order. Also for
Geoffrey Iden, Jo. Hope, Jo. Cartwright. Suppr.

Ric. Goling, Cluniac monk of Lewes, Chich. dio. Disp. to wear
the habit of his Order beneath that of a sec. pr. £4.

f. 54^v

20 Jo. Salysbury, O.S.A., canon of Breamore, Winton dio. Disp. to
hold any benef. with cure & change his habit. £8.

Tho. Spalding *alias* Prest, O.S.B., monk of Spalding, Linc. dio.
Disp. to hold any benef., if granted his superior's consent. £4.

23 Edm. Whytfeld *alias* Hickeling, O.S.A., canon, r. of Horsey,
Norw. dio. by previous disp. Disp. to wear the habit of his
Order beneath that of a sec. pr. £4.

Cuthbert Scott, Durham dio. Disp. to take all h.o. at any time &
2 on the same day. 26s 8d.

Feb. 15 Ric. Wheler & Eliz. Phillips, Lond. dio. Disp. for marriage without banns, & in the prohibited time. 20s; 10s.

21 Tho. ap David ap Loyde, sch. of St David's dio. Disp. to take all h.o. outside the statutory time. 20s.

f. 55ʳ

23 Jo. ap Rhes ap Griffith, O.Cist. Disp. to hold any benef., if granted the consent of his superior, & to wear the habit of his Order beneath that of a sec. pr., & despite defect of birth. Gratis; warrant shown.

20 Roger Standford *alias* Coke, O.S.B., of Worcester. Disp. to hold a benef. & wear the habit of his Order beneath that of a sec. pr. Arb. £4; warrant shown.

16 Jo. Musgrave & Agnes Busshe, York dio. Disp. for marriage (Jo.'s father was either Agnes's godfather, or sponsor at her confirmation). 30s.

26 Tho. Bacon & Jane Mery, of London. Disp. for marriage without banns & within the prohibited time. 20s; 10s.

25 Edw. Parnell, subdcn, Linc. dio. Disp. to take all h.o. despite being in his 23rd yr. 20s.

Jan. 7 Tho. Sare, O.F.M. Disp. to hold any benef., if granted his superior's consent, & with complete change of habit. Gratis; warrant shown.

f. 55ᵛ

20 Wm Harington, O.S.A., canon, of Conishead, Warden of the Lepers' Hospital of St Leonard, Kendall, York dio., dependent upon the above priory. Confirmation of disp. from his prior & convent to hold any benef. with the above office. £4.

Feb. 20 Tho. Lord., prior of Conishead, O.S.A. Confirmation of letters exhibited for union of the par. ch. of Orton, Carl. dio., as a perpetual vicariate with the priorship. £4.

Mar. 1 Jo. ap Griffith & Janet Hughe ap John ap Madocke, Bangor dio. Disp. for marriage (4th & 3rd degrees, & 4th, consang.). 26s 8d; 30s.

f. 56ʳ

Feb. 13 Ric. Chichemell *alias* Triamell, O.S.B. of Ramsey, Linc. dio. Disp. to hold any benef. with complete change of habit. Arb. 20s, by warrant shown. Also for Tho. Benson *alias* Burton. 20s.

27 Nich. Channterell, Winton dio., & Alice Hamworth, Lond. dio. Disp. for marriage without banns & within prohibited times. 20s; 10s.

Feb. 10 Jas Myller, r. of Farleigh, Winton dio. Disp. for non-res. for 3 yrs. 20s; p.s.r. 5s.

14 Jo. Warde, O.S.B., of Ely cath. Disp. to hold a benef. with cure & with complete change of habit. £8.

24 Hy Beke, formerly prior of Crutched friars, Colchester. Disp. to hold any benef. with cure & change his habit completely. Arb. £4; warrant shown.

f. 56ᵛ

16 Rob. Wallington, abbot of Langley, Norw. dio. *Inspeximus* & confirmation of letters from the late Bp Ric. of Norw. to above, admitting his proctor, Ric. Rydman, & permitting him to hold as r. the par. ch. of St Andrew, Kirkby Ridon, or Kirkstead, provided services are maintained there. £4.

Mar. 4 Edm. Rumsey *alias* Ellys, O.S.B., of Hyde, Sarum dio. Disp. to wear the habit of his Order beneath that of a sec. pr. £4.

8 Wm Codde, acol., Linc. dio. Disp. to take all h.o. outside the prohibited times, & 2 on the same day. 26s 8d.

f. 57ʳ

Feb. 17 Wm Fawcon & Helen Clere, Cov. & Lich. dio. Disp. for marriage (Wm was godfather to a child of Helen). Arb. 40s; warrant shown.

Mar. 6 Wm Ollrington & Cecily Federstonhalghe, Durham dio. Disp. for marriage (3rd & 4th degrees consang., & Wm's mother was Cecily's godmother). Arb. 30s; warrant shown.

9 Cristobel Cowper, O.S.B., prioress of Marrick, York dio. Confirmation in possession of the above office, in response to her annual supplications. 40s.

7 Jo. Sutton, dcn, O.S.A. canon of St Bartholomew's in the West, Smithfield, London. Disp. to take pr.'s orders from any bp although in his 23rd yr. 20s.

10 Rob. Cokayne & Eliz. Barington, Winton dio. Disp. for marriage, the banns read once. 6s 8d.

f. 57ᵛ

Feb. 23 Tho. Curbett, v. of Kessingland, Norw. dio. Disp. for non-res. for 2 yrs. 13s 4d; p.s.r. 5s.

Mar. 10 Nich. Harvye, sch., Cov. & Lich. dio. Disp. to take all h.o. from any bp without l.d. 6s 8d.

1 Jo. Madewell, O.P. Disp. to hold any benef., non-res., with complete change of habit. Gratis.

Feb. 28 Jo. Scoler *alias* Coler, O.S.A., canon of Ixworth, Norw. dio. Disp. to hold a benef. with complete change of habit. Arb. £4; warrant shown.

Mar. 14 Jo. Bedman, literate, Chich. dio. Disp. to practise as a notary. 13s 4d.

8 Geo. Mownston, r. of Clayworth, York dio., chapl. to Ld Geo. Talboys. Disp. to hold a benef. with cure with the above, or 2 without; permut. & non-res. cl. £7 13s 4d.

f. 58ʳ

Feb. 14 Jo. Ruttley, M.A. Disp. to preach throughout the realm. 'Nil iuxta forma libri taxacionum.'

Mar. 7 Tho. Marten, O.F.M. Disp. to hold a benef. & wear the habit of his Order beneath that of a sec. pr. Gratis; warrant shown.

10 Jo. Hills *alias* Aston, Premonstr. canon of Stoneleigh, Cov. & Lich. dio. Disp. to hold any benef. & wear the habit of his Order beneath that of a sec. pr. £8.

12 Tho. Hall, O.S.A., canon of West Dereham, Norw. dio. Disp. to hold any benef. with cure, if granted his superior's consent, & to wear the habit of his Order beneath that of a sec. pr. Arb. £6; warrant shown.

Wm Clarke, O.S.A., canon of Christchurch, Twyneham (Hants). Disp. to hold any benef. with cure & change his habit; permut. cl. £4.

Rob. Style, O.S.A., canon of Kyme, Linc. dio. Disp. to hold a benef. & change his habit. Arb. 40s; warrant shown.

f. 58ᵛ

9 Chris. Kyrkby, Austin fr. of London. Disp. to hold a benef. with cure if granted his superior's consent. £4.

Feb. 5 Nich. Vertu, monk of Hyde, Winton dio. Disp. to hold a benef.; non-res. cl. £4 10s.

4 Nich. Williamson, sch., Carl. dio. Disp. to practise as a notary. 13s 4d.

Mar. 21 Rob. Ocle, O.S.A., canon of Latton, nr Gabchester (*sic* for Colchester?). Disp. to hold any benef. if granted the consent of his superior. £4. Also for Tho. Austen. £4.

22 Jo. Flyngaunte, O.S.B., of St John's, Colchester, Lond. dio. Disp. to give up his habit & dress as a sec. pr. Gratis; warrant shown.

f. 59ʳ

Rob. Wysedome *alias* Reason. Similar disp.

Mar. 23 Ralph Lawse, M.A. Disp. to take all h.o. at any time & 2 on the same day. 26s 8d.

18 Tho. Knollis, v. of Wakefield, prebend. of York. Disp. for non-res. for 2 yrs. 13s 4d.

Feb. 15 Tho. Hammond, formerly conventual fr., now prior of the Austin friary, London. Confirmation of letters from Geo. Browne, Bp-elect of Dublin & Provincial of the Austin friars & Dominicans, appointing him to this office by royal authority. £4.

18 Roger Williams, B.C.L., Lland. dio. Disp. to take all h.o. outside the statutory time. 20s.

f. 59ᵛ

Mar. 17 Jo. Mabelstone, D.Cn. & C.L., sub-prior of the hospital of Jerusalem at Clerkenwell. Disp. (as he asserts he already has a disp. to hold in comm. Althorpe ch., Linc. dio., & Lurgassall, Chich. dio.) to hold a 3rd benef. with cure; permut. & non-res. cl. £9.

21 Jo. Robynson, prior of St Mary Magdalen, Lanecrost. Disp. to hold a benef. as well as the above office, & the ch. of Aykan (sic) & Halton, Carl. & York dio., & Northerdenton, Carl. dio. 40s.

18 Adam Sedbarge, abbot of the Premonstr. house of ? Garwall (sic for Cartmel, O.S.A.?). Confirmation of this election to his office. 40s.

19 Tho. Welde, O.S.A., canon of Dorchester, Linc. dio. Disp. to wear the habit of his Order beneath that of a sec. pr. £4.

20 Jas Higgs, O.C. fr., York dio. Disp. to wear the habit of his Order beneath that of a sec. pr. £4.

f. 60ʳ

24 Lewis Wagar, O.F.M. Disp. to wear the habit of his Order beneath that of a sec. pr. Gratis; warrant shown.

28 Jo. Cheyny & Jane Woodman, Lond. dio. Disp. for marriage without banns. 10s.

22 Tho. Pery, acol., Lond. dio. Disp. to take all h.o., 2 on the same day. 26s 8d.

27 Wm Mores, subdcn, Cov. & Lich. dio. Disp. to take dcn's & pr.'s orders outside the statutory times. 20s.

28 Geo. Sutton, v. of St Mary's, Oxford, Linc. dio. Disp. to hold a benef. with cure with the above or 2 without; permut. & non-res. cl. £7 13s 4d.

Apr. 3 Jo. Forewarde, sch. Disp. to take all h.o. at any time, 2 on the same day. 26s 8d.

f. 60^v

Apr. 5 Tho. Smythson, v. of Watringbury, Roch. dio. Disp. if the above does not yield over £8 p.a. to hold a benef. with cure with, or 2 without, it. £4.

2 Ric. Walwoode, O.F.M., formerly Observant fr. Disp. to wear the habit of a sec. pr. & hold a benef., being non-res. Arb. £6; warrant shown.

Jan. 27 Tho. Mylton *alias* Garlande, O.S.B., of Milton, Sarum dio. Disp. to wear the habit of his Order beneath that of a sec. pr. £4.

Apr. 6 Hy Kingston *alias* Webbe, O.S.B., of Winchester cath. Disp. to wear the habit of his Order beneath that of a sec. pr., if granted his superior's consent. £4.

3 Nich. Ducke, O.S.A., canon of Shulbrede, Chich. dio. Disp. to wear the habit of his Order beneath that of a sec. pr. £4.

Feb. 25 Jo. Flere, r. of Bulbridge, Sarum dio. Disp. for non-res. for 2 yrs. 13s 4d; p.s.r. 5s.

f. 61^r

Apr. 6 Jo. Bowcher & Agnes Awardes, York dio. Disp. for marriage (3rd & 4th degrees consang.). 30s.

Mar. 12 Jo. Parker, O.C. fr., Lond. dio. Disp. to wear the habit of his Order beneath that of a sec. pr., if granted his superior's consent. £4.

Apr. 7 Stephen Browne, O.S.B., of St Augustine's, Canterbury. Disp. to wear the habit of his Order beneath that of a sec. pr. £4.

Mar. 29 Jo. Darley, Carth., of London. Disp. to hold any benef. with complete change of habit. £12.

28 Alex. Warde, pr., York dio. Disp. from penance for having taken pr.'s orders on the same day as subdcn's without disp. 10s.

f. 61^v

7 Jo. Bradeway, r. of Campe (? Campsey Ash), Norw. dio., chapl. to Ld Sandys. Disp. to hold a benef. with cure with the above or 2 without; permut. & non-res. cl. £7 13s 4d.

29 Jo. Brasebridge, acol., Linc. dio. Disp. to take all h.o., 2 on the same day, from any bp. 26s 8d; 6s 8d.

Nich. Everade, D.Cn.L. Disp. to hold another benef. with cure with the ch. of Capford, Lond. dio., or 2 other benefices without it; also the vicariate of Comeweden & par. ch. of Farnham, Lond.

dio., & canonry & prebend of Barnaby, York, for which he had
previous disp. £4.

Feb. 11 Jo. ap David, r. of More, Heref. dio. Disp. for non-res. for a
yr. 6s 8d; 5s.

Mar. 26 Ric. Woodford, r. of Gt Woolston, Linc. dio., chapl. to Ld Mordaunt. Disp. to hold a benef. with cure with the above, or 2
without; permut. but not non-res. cl. £6 10s.

22 Ric. Corbete *alias* Berall, O.S.A., of Abingdon, Sarum dio. Disp.
to hold a benef. & to change his habit completely. Gratis; warrant
shown.

30 Ric. ap Owen & Janet verch Morgan, St David's dio. Disp. for
marriage (4th degree double consang., 3rd & 4th degrees affin.).
Gratis; warrant shown.

Apr. 1 Jo. Walsch, acol., Bath & W. dio. Disp. to take all h.o. at any
time, 2 on the same day. 26s 8d.

3 Owen Godfray, r. of Elveden, Norw. dio. Disp. for non-res. for
2 yrs. 13s 4d; p.s.r. 5s.

2 Jo. Bowth, v. of Swell, Bath & W. dio. Disp. to hold a benef.
with the above, since it does not yield £8 p.a., or any 2 without
it; permut. & non-res. cl. £4 10s.

1 St John's Hospital, Sandwich. Confirmation (in full?) of liberties & privileges. £4.

Mar. 21 Jas Loge, Austin fr. Disp. to hold a benef. & change his habit
completely. £12.

Apr. 2 Wm Robynson, Gilbertine canon of Sempringham. Disp. to
hold a benef. £4.

6 Jo. Grenewood *alias* Malkins, formerly canon of Bilsington, Cant.
dio. Disp. to wear the habit of a sec. pr. Gratis; warrant shown.

7 Jo. Moys, formerly prior of Bilsington, Cant. dio. Disp. to hold
a benef. with complete change of habit; non-res. cl. Gratis;
warrant shown.

6 Tho. Stunte, O.S.B., of Battle. Disp. to wear the habit of a
sec. pr. for life. Gratis; warrant shown.

8 Jo. Wintringham, monk of St Neot's, Linc. dio. Disp. to hold
a benef., with some change of habit. Gratis; warrant shown.

Apr. 7 Ric. Browne, v. of —— Disp. to hold another with it, if this benef. does not yield over £8 p.a., or 2 without. £4.

4 Jo. Brownefelde, O.S.A., canon of Bilsington, Cant. dio. Disp. to hold a benef. with change of habit. Gratis; warrant shown.

8 Jo. & Eliz. Bawden, Cov. & Lich. dio. Disp. for marriage (3rd & 4th degrees consang.). 30s.

f. 63ᵛ

6 Chris. Shanes, sch., Carl. dio. Disp. to take all h.o. at any time, 2 on the same day. 26s 8d.

2 Wm May, acol., r. of Hatfield, Lond. dio. Disp. to take 2 h.o. on the same day. 10s.

4 Jo. Fido & Agnes Braser *alias* Stockwell, Heref. dio. Disp. for marriage (Jo.'s mother was Agnes's godmother). 30s.

12 Jo. Fletcher & Agnes Rudlawnde, Norw. dio. Disp. for marriage (Agnes's mother was Jo.'s godmother). 30s.

1 Tho. Taverner, chanter in the chantry of Roger Holmes in St Paul's, London. Disp. to hold a benef. with the above or 2 without; permut. & non-res. cl. £7 13s 4d.

14 Wm ap Thomas ap Rhes & Gwenlian verch Glin ap Morgan, St David's dio. Disp. for marriage (4th degree consang.). 26s 8d.

f. 64ʳ

12 Jenn ap Tuder & Marg. Salysbury, St Asaph dio. Disp. for marriage (4th degree consang.). 26s 8d.

Ric. Randall, v. of Talsey, Sarum dio. Disp. for non-res. for 2 yrs. 13s 4d; p.s.r. 5s.

8 Ric. Hallford, O.S.A., canon of Bruton, Bath & W. dio. Disp. to wear the habit of his order beneath that of a sec. pr. £4.

13 Chris. North, chapl. to Ld Ferrars, v. of Bethersden, Cant. dio. Disp. to hold a benef. with cure with the above, or 2 without; permut. & non-res. cl. £6 10s.

15 Geo. Whitlocke & Agnes Browne, Durham dio. Disp. for marriage (4th degree affin.). Gratis; warrant shown.

Tho. Harreson, O.S.A., of 'Rembesey' (*sic* for O.Cist., Revesby, or O.S.B., Ramsey?) Disp. to hold any benef. with complete change of habit. Gratis; warrant shown.

f. 64ᵛ

12 Jo. Dykans, r. of Eyke, Norw. dio. Disp. for non-res. for 2 yrs. 13s 4d; p.s.r. 5s.

Apr. 14 Tho. Seburne, dcn, Sarum dio. Disp. to take pr.'s orders out-side the statutory times. 10s.

11 Tho. Darneton, abbot of Egglestone. Disp. to hold the par. ch. of Thorpe Bassett in comm., as he has a previous disp. to hold a benef. with his office; permut. & non-res. cl. 40s.

14 Tho. Standewyne, literate. Disp. to practise as a notary. 13s 4d.

Dec. 3 Jo. Wawen, v. choral of the coll. ch. of 'Houydon' (Howden), York dio. Disp. to hold another benef., if the above does not yield over £8 p.a., with it or with another benef. of the same value; permut. cl. £4.

Apr. 17 Wm Lathimbre & Blanche Twyford, Cov. & Lich. dio. Disp. for marriage without banns. 10s.

f. 65ʳ

12 Jas Broughe, pr., r. of Cold Norton, Sarum dio. Disp. for non-res. for 2 yrs. 13s 4d; p.s.r. 5s.

16 Geo. Sneth, *alias* Landsall, O.S.A., canon of 'Amwyke' (*sic* for Premonstr. of Alnwick?) Disp. to wear the habit of a sec. pr. Gratis; warrant shown.

1 Jo. Vicars, O.C. fr. Disp. to hold a benef. with complete change of habit. Gratis; warrant shown.

17 Chris. Ellis & Ann Clerke, York dio. Disp. for marriage (4th degree consang.). 26s. 8d.

23 Jo. Wode, M.A., chanter in the chantry of Hy & Tho. Ryppingall in the prebendal ch. of Grantham, Linc. dio. Disp. to hold a benef. with the above, since it does not yield £8 p.a.; permut. cl. £4.

20 Ric. Hadcocke, acol., York dio. Disp. to take the rest of h.o. at any time. 20s.

f. 65ᵛ

29 Roger Hayton, Crutched fr. of London. Disp. to become a sec. pr. Gratis; warrant shown.

28 Grono ap Meryke & Marg. verch Llen, Lland. dio. Disp. for marriage (4th degree affin.). 26s 8d.

25 Jo. Skelsing, formerly monk of Ely cath. Disp. to become a sec. pr. Gratis; warrant shown.

1 Jo. Marcylis, O.F.M. Disp. to hold a benef. & for some change of habit. Gratis; warrant shown.

Wm Slye, monk of Carl. cath. Disp. to hold any benef. £4.

May 1 Wm Arundell *alias* Pemble, O.S.B., of Cant. cath. Disp. to hold any benef. & wear the habit of his Order beneath that of a sec. pr. Arb. 40s; warrant shown.

f. 66ʳ

Apr. 29 Rob. Books, O.S.A., canon of Southwark, Winton dio. Disp. to hold a benef. £4.

27 Jo. Griffith, v. of Llan Vaure (*sic*), St Asaph dio. Disp. as the above does not yield over £8 p.a. to hold another with it or with another of the same value as it. £4.

21 Ric. Varney & Eliz. Germayne, Ex. dio. Disp. for marriage, the banns read once. 6s 8d.

Jan. 28 Edm. Stretham, Crutched fr., formerly prior of ——. Disp. to hold a benef. with some change of habit. Gratis; warrant shown.

Apr. 1 Tho. Thelbold, v. of Kemsing, Roch. dio. Disp. to hold the above benef. if he takes subdcn's orders within 2 yrs. 20s.

f. 66ᵛ

23 Ric. Turner & Kath. Crabtre, York dio. Disp. for marriage (4th degree consang.). 26s 8d.

27 Tho. Hartely, monk of Furness, v. of Urswick, York dio. Confirmation of institution by Tho. Metcalfe, v. general of the archdcn of Richmond Chris. Urswick, D.C.L., ambassador abroad, & the abbot of Furness. 40s.

May 4 Tho. Ade, v. of Gt Thurlow, Norw. dio. Disp. for non-res. for 2 yrs on account of old age & various infirmities, especially gout. 13s 4d; p.s.r. 5s.

6 Tho. ap Glyn & Kath. verch Jankyn ap Griffith, St David's dio. Disp. for marriage (4th degree consang.). 26s 8d.

f. 67ʳ

3 Jo. Grete *alias* Basill, O.S.B., of Hyde, Winton dio. Disp. to hold a benef. with or without cure of souls. Gratis; warrant shown.

Martin Hall, O.S.A., canon of Southwick, Linc. dio. Disp. to hold any benef. Gratis; warrant shown.

8 Jas Atkinson of Fleet St., London, & Isabella Wright, of Westham, Lond. dio. Disp. for marriage without banns. 10s.

30 Giles Foster, esq., of the Duke of Richmond's hsehld, & Isabella Dowcray, of Sarum dio. Disp. for marriage, the banns read once. 6s 8d.

Mar. 9 Keneran Kendall, chapl. to Hy, Earl of Exeter, v. of Tyward-
        reath, Ex. dio. Disp. to hold a benef., with cure, with the above,
        or 2 without; permut. cl. £6 10s.

May   9 Tho. Jones & Eliz. Nasche, Worc. dio. Disp. for marriage (3rd
        & 4th degrees consang.). 30s.

f. 67ᵛ

      11 Jo. Aglionby & Kath. Salkede *alias* Aglionby, Carl. dio. Disp.
        for marriage (Kath. was previously betrothed to Jo.'s late brother,
        Tho.). 13s 4d.

       4 Ric. Hill, chapl. to Ric., Bp of Chich., v. of Brabourne, Cant.
        dio. Disp. to hold a benef. with cure with the above, or 2
        without; permut. & non-res. cl. £7 13s 4d.

      12 Wm Dedicot, B.Cn. & C.L., Worc. dio. Disp. to take all h.o.
        at any time, 2 on the same day. 26s 8d.

      13 Jo. Hollond, pr., Premonstr. canon of Newbo, York dio. Disp.
        to leave the religious life & become a sec. pr. Gratis; warrant
        shown.

f. 68ʳ

      14 Wm Haynys & Kath. Fawteles, Norw. dio. Disp. for marriage
        without banns. 10s.

      16 Tho. Nothingham, B.A., York dio. Disp. to take all h.o. at any
        time, 2 on the same day. 26s 8d.

       5 Stephen Templar, B.A., chapl. to the Bp of Bangor, r. of Alding-
        ton, Sarum dio. Disp. to hold a benef. with cure with the above or
        2 without; permut. cl. £6 10s.

       4 Rob. Pyper, O.S.A., canon of Westacre, Linc. dio. Disp. to
        hold a benef. with cure if granted his superior's consent; permut.
        & non-res. cl. £4 10s.

      12 Jo. Sutclyffe & Isabella Draper, York dio. Disp. for marriage
        (3rd & 4th degrees consang.). 30s.

f. 68ᵛ

      13 Jo. Holden, B.A., Cov. & Lich. dio. Disp. to take all h.o. at any
        time, 2 on the same day. 26s 8d.

      10 Ric. Creseweller, v. of Alfriston, Chich. dio. Disp. to hold a
        benef. with cure with the above, or 2 without; permut. & non-
        res. cl. £7 13s 4d.

      13 Tho. Aglionby *alias* Myckson, reg. canon, incumbent of Bew-
        castle by previous disp. Disp. to hold another benef. with cure if
        the above does not yield £8 p.a.; permut. & non-res. cl. £4.

David ap Hughe & Eliz. verch ?David, St David's dio. Disp. for marriage (3rd & 4th degrees consang.). 30s.

May 12 Jo. Viall, O.F.M., of Bedd (*sic* for Bedford?). Disp. to hold any benef. & to change his habit completely. Arb. £5; warrant shown.

f. 69ʳ

16 Jo. Mylgate, r. of Welby, Norw. dio. Disp., if the latter does not yield over £8, to hold a benef. with cure with it; or with any other benef. of the same value; permut. & non-res. cl. £4.

Confirmation of indenture by Chris., formerly prior of Carl. cath. & Edw., abbot of Swainby ('Swareby'), Carl. dio., dated St Matthew's Day, 1535, by which Edw. was provided to the par. ch. of 'Saburgan' (*sic* for Sedbergh?) with the tithe of Welton, being 6s 8d at Pentecost & St Martinstide. Witnessed by Sampson of 'Sudronbry' & Tho. Heyde, husbandman of 'Rangtonhied' in Cumberland. 40s.

f. 69ᵛ

18 Ric. Coddington, Winton dio., & Eliz. Auckman, Lond. dio. Disp. for marriage without banns. 10s.

Rhes ap Howell ap Madcocke & Guyvenonyner (*sic*) verch John ap Griffith ap Nicholas. Disp. for marriage (3rd & 4th degrees consang.). 30s.

12 Nich. Giste, Cluniac prior of Tywardreath, Cornwall, Ex. dio. Disp. to hold a benef. with or without cure of souls with some change of habit. Gratis; warrant shown.

13 Ric. Campion, M.A., chapl. to Archbp of Cant., v. of Eastry. Disp. to hold a benef. with cure with the above or 2 without; permut. & non-res. cl. £7 13s 4d.

16 Wm Ponnde *alias* Francis, B.Th., Austin fr. Disp. to hold a benef. with complete change of habit. Gratis; warrant shown.

20 Jas Thoker *alias* Ansell, pr., monk of Glastonbury, Bath & W. dio. Disp. to hold any benef.; permut. cl. £4.

f. 70ʳ

Ric. Were, O.Cist., of Ford, Ex. dio. Disp. to hold a benef.; permut. cl. £4.

22 Tho. ap John & Janet verch Thomas, St David's dio. Disp. legitimizing marriage (contracted & consummated in ignorance of 4th degree consang.). 26s 8d.

1 Parishioners of Bourton-on-the-Hill, Worc. dio. Disp. to bury their dead in a cemetery by the consecrated ch. there, on account of the unfit state of the roads, through floods & hills, to Brockley,

about 2 miles away, where they have been accustomed to go for burials. The cemetery may be consecrated by any bp. £4.

f. 70ᵛ

May 20 Hy Saxton, O.Cist., of Vaudey, Linc. dio. Disp. to hold a benef., with or without cure of souls, if granted his superior's consent; permut. & non-res. cl. £4 10s.

Apr. 6 Wm Bradye, O.F.M., of Greenwich. Disp. to hold any benef., with complete change of habit. Gratis; warrant shown.

May 20 Tho. Haywarde, r. of Clungarnford, Heref. dio., chapl. to Ric. Sampson, Dean of the Chapel Royal. Disp. to hold a benef. with cure with the above, or 2 others without it; permut. & non-res. cl. £7 13s 4d.

    24 Edm. Sharpe & Eliz. Banyll, Cov. & Lich. dio. Disp. for marriage (4th degree consang.). 26s 8d.

    26 Wm Vincent & Agnes Parker, Norw. dio. Disp. for marriage (3rd & 4th degrees consang.). 30s.

f. 71ʳ

Jo. Thuxton, v. of Hemley, Norw. dio., chapl. to Wm, Bp elect of Norw. Disp. to hold a benef. with cure with the above, or 2 others without it; permut. cl. £6 10s.

Terrington, par. ch. of St Jo. Baptist, Norw. dio. Confirmation of letters separating it from the par. ch. of St Clement, to which it was formerly attached as a chapel, on account of the distance between the 2, & difficulty of access to St Clement's in bad weather &c. £4.

f. 71ᵛ

    28 Wm Ottrey, O.Cist., of Ford, Ex. dio. Disp. to become a sec. pr. Gratis; warrant shown.

Feb. 12 Tho. Thyrley, archdcn of Ely, incumbent by previous disp. of Ripley & Cheste, York dio. Disp. to hold a benef. with the above, or 3 without them; permut. & non-res. cl. £8.

Apr. 21 Wm Fynch, Premonstr. canon of Beeleigh, Lond. dio. Disp. to hold any benef. with complete change of habit. Gratis; warrant shown.

May 29 Jo. Bingehinton, O.S.B., of Cant. cath. Disp. to hold any benef. with complete change of habit. Gratis; warrant shown.

    28 Tho. Ondlam & Marg. Helett, Cov. & Lich. dio. Disp. for marriage (3rd & 2nd degrees affin.). £8.

f. 72ʳ

    20 Jo. Dannston & Mabel *alias* Marg. Hanley. Disp. to marriage (Marg. was godmother to a child of Jo.'s). £6.

May 20 Roger Stokman, B.Cn. & C.L., r. of Jacobstow, Cornwall, Ex. dio. Disp. to hold a benef. with the above, as well as the office of sacristan in the coll. ch. of Ottery St Mary, also a prebend attached to it held by previous disp.; permut. & non-res. cl. £8.

31 Tho. Richardson & Marg. Walton, Durham dio. Disp. for marriage (4th degree consang.). 26s 8d.

Mar. 25 Wm May, D.C.L., r. of Hatfield, Linc. dio. Disp. to take all h.o. within 15 months of taking possession of the above. 12s 6d.

f. 72ᵛ

May 20 Wm Hedge, v. of Stoke, Norw. dio. Disp. for non-res. for 2 yrs. 13s 4d; p.s.r. 5s.

27 Jo. Clenchwerton *alias* Watson, O.S.A., canon of Walsingham, Norw. dio. Disp. to hold any benef. £4.

28 Ric. Topclyffe *alias* Bell, O.S.A., of Marton, York dio. Disp. to hold a benef. with complete change of habit. Suppr.

24 Jo. Mason, M.A., r. of Farthingstone, Linc. dio., chapl. to the Bp of Lincoln. Disp. to hold a benef. with cure with the above or 2 without; permut. & non-res. cl.; & since he has been in the Kg's service for a long time, not to proceed to h.o. till later. £7 13s 4d; 20s.

27 Tho. ap Morgan & Cicily Herbert, Lland. dio. Disp. for marriage (4th degree consang.). 26s 8d.

f. 73ʳ

25 Wm Bulkeley & Cicily Cocksey, Cov. & Lich. dio. Disp. for marriage (3rd & 4th degrees consang.). 30s.

June 8 Hy Marlas & Emma Proctor, Cov. & Lich. dio. Disp. for marriage (Hy was sponsor at the confirmation of a child of Emma's). £5.

May 31 Jo. Cotton & Brigett Sprinte, both of gentle birth. Disp. for marriage without banns. 10s.

24 Rob. Cople, canon of Elsing Spital, London. Disp. to hold a benef. with entire change of habit; also for Ric. Chase, Ric. Congyrave, Rob. Byggam, Wm Antony, Jo. Cole. Suppr.

June 10 Tho. Sprat, O.Cist., of Robertsbridge, Chich. dio. Disp. to hold any benef. £4.

f. 73ᵛ

Alex. Colyer, acol., York dio. Disp. to take all h.o. from any bp at any time, although in his 23rd yr, & to hold a benef.; permut. & non-res. cl. 40s; 30s.

May 31 Tho. Cesay, O.S.A., canon of Marton, York dio. Disp. to hold a benef. with complete change of habit; also for Geo. Burch, Edm. Baker, Tho. Jodson. Suppr.

June 6 Jo. Chester, O.Cist., of Sawley, York dio. Disp. to hold a benef. with complete change of habit; also for Hy Claghton, Rob. Gisburne, Tho. Bolton, Alex. Fonnters, Jo. Skypton, Tho. Herde, Hy Bradford, Ric. Clederhow, Ric. Newton, Percival Thornton, Tho. Salley, Wm Harwood, Ric. Wakefield, Chris. Stanford, Jo. Forest. Chris. Parysch, monk, who also has a disp. with permut. & non-res. cl. Suppr.

f. 74ʳ

May 20 Ric. Estgate, O.Cist., of Sawley, York dio. Disp. to hold a benef. with a stall in the choir, a seat in the chapter, & a portion in any monastery, to which the Kg may assign him. Suppr.

June 9 Jo. Baker & Joan Barrow, Cant. dio. (Marg. Baker, formerly wife of Jo., was godmother to a child of Joan). Arb. 20s; warrant shown.

May 12 Tho. ap Hughe ap Rhes ap David & Kath. verch David Lloyd, St David's dio. Disp. for marriage (3rd & 4th degrees affin.). 30s.

June 16 Tho. Powell ap John & Ann Kymys, Lland. dio. Disp. for marriage (4th degree consang.). 26s 8d.

Nich. Gyfford & Agnes Colwell, Linc. dio. Disp. for marriage without banns. 26s 8d.

f. 74ᵛ

Rob. Farnner & Marion Burton, Lond. dio. Disp. for marriage, the banns read once. 6s 8d.

12 Hugh ap John ap Ithell & Gwenlioyne verch Rhes ap Thomas. Disp. confirming their marriage already contracted & consummated despite knowledge of 3rd & 4th degrees affin. 30s.

17 Ric. Grigge & Eliz. Curlo, Lond. dio. Disp. for marriage without banns. 10s.

18 Ric. Bysley, M.A., Linc. dio. Disp. to take all h.o. at any time, 2 on the same day. 26s 8d.

16 Tho. Hammond, B.Th., prior of the Austin friary, London. Disp. to hold any benef.; non-res. cl. 'Remittitur pro rell[igione] et habitu' 10s; warrant shown. Gilbert Rose, Austin fr. Disp. to hold a benef. with change of habit; non-res. cl. 10s remitted; warrant shown.

f. 75ʳ

June 20 Jo. Symnell, formerly O.S.A., canon of Mottisfont, Winton dio. Disp. to hold a benef. with change of habit. Also for Tho. Aylworth, Tho. Geele, Tho. Edmonds. Suppr.

Wm Coppocke & Helen Alcocke, Cov. & Lich. dio. Disp. for marriage (4th degree consang.). 26s 8d.

21 Tho. Roberts, M.A., Worc. dio. Disp. to take all h.o. at any time, 2 on the same day, from any bp. 26s 8d.

Jo. Granemer & Joan Bostoke, Cov. & Lich. dio. Disp. for marriage (3rd & 4th degrees affin.). 30s.

22 Rob. Frye, B.C.L., Sarum dio. Disp. to take all h.o. despite being in his 24th yr, at any time & 2 on the same day; subsequently to hold a benef. 20s; 26s 8d.

f. 75ᵛ

21 Hugh Higdon, B.A., Linc. dio. Disp. to take all h.o. despite being in his 23rd yr, & before this to hold a benef. with non-res. cl. though having received the benef. he must proceed to h.o. 40s.

20 Ric. Thomas & Matilda verch Jenn, St David's dio. Disp. for marriage (4th degree consang.). 26s 8d.

22 Ralph Wilcoks, O.P., Cov. & Lich. dio. Disp. to leave off the habit of his Order & wear that of a sec. pr. Gratis; warrant shown.

20 Jo. ap Mores, St David's dio. Disp. to take all h.o. & hold a benef. despite defect of birth. £4.

22 Jas Coson, O.P., B.Th. Disp. to leave off the habit of his Order & wear that of a sec. pr. Gratis; warrant shown.

f. 76ʳ

27 Wm Hardware, O.S.A., canon of Norton, Cov. & Lich. dio. Disp. to hold a benef. & for some change of habit. £8.

23 Jo. Gilbert, Lond. dio., & Alice Young, Cant. dio. Disp. for marriage without banns. 10s.

Hy Byrd & Jane Tate, Lond. dio. Disp. for marriage without banns. 10s.

26 Hy Brigewoode & Angela Bromley, Cov. & Lich. dio. Disp. for marriage (4th degree consang.). 26s 8d.

Ric. Myddelmore, v. of Broadhempston, Ex. dio. Disp. to take all h.o. at any time, 2 on the same day, from any bp. 26s 8d.

28 Rob. Bybble & Juliana Selson, Bath. & W. dio. Disp. for marriage without banns. 10s.

f. 76ᵛ

Tho. Hampton, subdcn, Bangor dio. Disp. to take dcn's & pr.'s orders at any time, from any bp. 13s 4d.

June 24 Jo. Palmer, O.Cist., formerly abbot of Tilty, Lond. dio. Disp. to hold a benef. with complete change of habit; also for Jo. Chychely, Geo. Browne, Jo. Hogeson, Suppr.

26 Wm Byge, M.A., r. of Patching, Chich. dio. Disp. to hold a benef. with cure with the above or 2 without it; permut. & non-res. cl. £7 13s 4d.

28 Rob. Bothe, r. of Thornton, Cov. & Lich. dio. Disp. for non-res. for 2 yrs if a suitable pr. is found in his place, as he is 60 & suffers from colic & other infirmities. 13s 4d.

29 Jo. Spence & Alice Frere, York dio. Disp. for marriage (4th degree consang.). 26s 8d.

f. 77ʳ

Wm Burdon, prebendary of the chapel of the Holy Sepulchre, York Minster; r. of Beckingham ('Beggynham'), Linc. dio. Disp. for res. at the latter for 2 yrs as he is old & in ill-health. 13s 4d.

Ld Hy Nevell, son of Ld Ralph Nevell, Earl of Westmorland, & Ly Ann Maners, dau. of Ld Tho. Maners K.G., Earl of Rutland, Ld Ros of Hamlake, Crosebushe, & Belvoir. Disp. for marriage (Ly Ann's father was Ld Hy's godfather). 30s.

30 Rob. Wroton, B.Th., Cluniac abbot of Bermondsey, Winton dio., Bp elect of St Asaph. Disp. to hold the above monastery in comm. with the bpric. 'Remittitur gratis per ipsum Regem; ost. warranto D[omi]ni Regis.'

28 Jo. Avawton & Helen Skeret, Cov. & Lich. dio. Disp. for marriage (2nd & 3rd degrees consang.). Gratis; warrant shown.

f. 77ᵛ

24 Wm Channdeler, B.Th., Disp. to hold a 4th benef.; he asserts that he already has a disp. by the Kg's licence to hold the par. ch. of Thurlaston, also South Kilworth & Brailsford, Linc. & Cov. & Lich. dio. £8.

28 Tho. Anelme, O.S.B., of Battle, Chich. dio. Disp. to hold a benef. with complete change of habit. Gratis; warrant shown.

30 Ric. Smyth & Ann Bate, York dio. Disp. for marriage (3rd & 4th degrees affin.). 30s.

Ld Hy Nevell & Ly Ann Maners (as above). Disp. for marriage without banns. 10s.

f. 78^r

Jo. Vere, son of Ld Jo. de Vere & Ly Dorothy Nevell. Disp. for marriage in any church without banns. 10s.

July   1 Jo. Spowes & Marg. Spristaw, Lond. dio. Disp. for marriage without banns. 10s.

Jo. Paner & Kath. Woodburne, York dio. Disp. for marriage (Kath.'s father was Jo.'s godfather). 30s.

Wm Tyldisley of the Kg's hsehld & Jacomina Lytill, Sarum dio. Disp. for marriage without banns. 10s.

2 Ric. Myddlemore, v. of Broadhempston, Ex. dio., chapl. to Jo., Bp of Exeter. Disp. to hold a benef. with cure with the above, or 2 without; permut. & non-res. cl. £7 13s 4d.

3 Jo. Bery, sch., Chich. dio. Disp. to take all h.o. at any time, from any bp. 20s.

f. 78^v

1 Rob. Willis, sch., Worc. dio. Disp. to take all h.o. at any time, 2 on the same day, from any bp. 26s 8d.

Elis Linmall & Eliz. Leys, Cov. & Lich. dio. Disp. for marriage (3rd & 4th degrees affin.). 30s.

June 21 Nich. Robinson, York dio. Disp. to hold a benef. with cure of souls, although after taking pr.'s orders he was disabled by losing his right thumb, not by his own fault. 40s.

July   4 Edw. Langtre, acol., Sarum dio. Disp. to take all h.o. at any time, 2 on the same day, from any bp. 26s 8d.

May 24 Wm Lee, r. of Gawsworth, Cov. & Lich. dio. Disp. for non-res. for a yr to study letters. 6s 8d.

f. 79^r

July   5 Jo. Hollingbourne, monk of Cant. cath. Disp. to hold a benef. with complete change of habit. 'Remanet.'

June 28 Jo. Crosse, monk of Battle, Chich. dio. Disp. to hold a benef. with complete change of habit. Gratis; warrant shown.

July   5 Nich. Thorndon & Alice Newton, Norw. dio. Disp. for marriage (Alice's father was Nich.'s godfather). 30s.

6 Edw. Pynchion & Eliz. Palmer, of London. Disp. for marriage without banns. 10s.

Peter Vannes, Kg's Secretary for Latin letters. Disp. to hold the canonry & prebend of Bedwyn attached to Salisbury, with the deanery of Salisbury & other benefices obtained by previous disp. £10.

f. 79ᵛ

July   6 Jo. Studley *alias* Hayter, O.Cist., formerly of Stanley, Sarum dio. Disp. to hold a benef. with complete change of habit. Suppr.

Tho. Baby, O.S.B., of Hurley, Sarum dio. Disp. to hold a benef. with complete change of habit. Also for Nich. Crosiar, Wm Horley, Tho. Cocks, Jo. Stegge, Humfrey Colley. Suppr.

Hy Maydman, O.S.A., canon of Osney, Linc. dio. Disp. to hold a benef.; permut. cl. £4.

7 Humfrey Garden & Marg. Walgar, York dio. Disp. for marriage (3rd & 4th degrees affin.). 30s.

5 Jo. Bulkeley & Joan Winterbotham *alias* Smyth, Cov. & Lich. dio. Disp. for marriage (4th degree consang.). 26s 8d.

7 Wm Smyth & Agnes Blyth, Cant. dio. Disp. for marriage after the banns are read (?once). 6s 8d.

f. 80ʳ

Leonard Haydon, r. of Swaton ('Swarington') Norw. dio. Disp. to take all h.o. at any times, 2 on any day, & from any bp. 13s 4d.

Jo. Leake, subdcn. Disp. to take dcn's & pr.'s orders at any times on any day & from any bp. 13s 4d.

Wm Lloyd ap Edward, sch., St Asaph dio. Disp. to take all h.o. & hold a benef. despite defect of birth & being in his 24th yr. £5; 20s.

June 30 Wm Sapcotte *alias* Leycestre, O.S.A., canon of Kenilworth, Cov. & Lich. dio. Disp. to hold any benef.; permut. & non-res. cl. £4 10s.

July   7 Rob. Downing, pr., r. of Upminster, Lond. dio., chapl. to Earl of Rutland. Disp. to hold a benef. with cure with the above, or 2 without; permut. & non-res. cl. £7 13s 4d.

f. 80ᵛ

11 Tho. Fyssher & Isabella Shaw, Cov. & Lich. dio. Disp. for marriage (Tho.'s mother was Isabella's sponsor at her confirmation). 26s 8d.

12 Moryce Oliver & Alice Fletcher, of London. Disp. for marriage without banns. 10s.

Jas *alias* Jak Sarth & Marg. Sympson, York dio. Disp. for marriage (4th degree consang.). 26s 8d.

13 Hy Haynys, formerly Premonstr. canon of Lavendon, Linc. dio. Disp. to hold a benef. with complete change of habit. Also for Wm Grene, Walter Wyton, Rob. Asheburne, Wm Bedne, Ralph Parker, Jo. Howton, Jo. Downys. Suppr.

July 11 Wm Stapleton, O.Cist., of Louth Park, Linc. dio. Disp. to hold a benef., with complete change of habit. Suppr.

f. 81ʳ

4 Reg. Bysley. Inspeximus of letters issued by Nich. Evered, D.Cn.L., dated 12 June 1532, empowering the latter to act as proctor to the Archbp of York wherever he goes in the latter's province. 40s.

14 Edm. Coke & Agnes Cox, Norw. dio. Disp. for marriage (3rd & 4th degrees consang.). 30s.

13 Jo. Cotton & Isabella Spencer, Ely dio. Disp. for marriage without banns. 10s.

14 Wm Rowell, r. of Cockerington, Linc. dio. Disp. for non-res. for a yr on account of fevers & other infirmities; a suitable curate to be provided. 6s 8d.

f. 81ᵛ

15 Jo. & Joan Hogeson, Carl. dio. Disp. for marriage (3rd & 4th degrees consang.). 30s.

Geo. Webb & Dorothy Clerke, of London. Disp. for marriage in any ch., without banns. 10s.

Nich. Barton & Marg. Scott, Lond. dio. Disp. for marriage (Nich.'s father was Marg.'s godfather). 30s.

Tho. Pope, gent., & Marg. Dover, widow, of London. Disp. for marriage in any ch., without banns. 10s.

Wm Haymoy of the Isle of Thanet, Cant. dio., & Jane Wilshire, of London. Disp. for marriage in either's par. ch. without banns. 10s.

f. 82ʳ

17 Ric. Underwood, pr., O.S.B., of Norw. cath. to which he was professed in childhood by exhortation of the prior & monks before his 24th yr, & by royal decree reduced to being a sec. pr. Disp. to act as a sec. pr. & hold a benef. 40s.

31 Jo. Joseph, O.F.M. Disp. to hold a benef. with complete change of habit. Gratis; warrant shown.

Laurence Townerolde, O.P. Disp. to hold a benef. with complete change of habit. Gratis; warrant shown.

20 Rob. Knolls, O.F.M. Disp. to hold a benef. with complete change of habit. Gratis; warrant shown.

14 Wm Lyving, O.F.M. Disp. to hold a benef. with complete change of habit. Gratis; warrant shown.

f. 82ᵛ

July 14 Rob. Paynyswyke, canon of Lanthony, nr Gloucester, Worc. dio. Disp. to hold any benef., if granted his superior's consent, permut. cl. £4.

16 Jo. Walkeley, O.S.A., formerly prior of Berden, Lond. dio. Disp. to hold a benef. with complete change of habit. Also for Jo. Marler & Alex. Duke. Suppr.

14 Jo. Vyrley, formerly canon of Stonley, Linc. dio. Disp. to hold a benef. with complete change of habit. Also for Ric. Downes, Wm Colye, Tho. Dane, Edm. Bydenham. Suppr.

18 Tho. Whit, O.F.M. Disp. to become a sec. pr. Gratis; warrant shown.

Edm. Smyth, Austin fr. Disp. to become a sec. pr. Gratis; warrant shown.

f. 83ʳ

20 Edw. Phillipson & Helen Costron, Linc. dio. Disp. for marriage (3rd & 4th degrees consang.). 30s.

Wm Langley, sch., Cov. & Lich. dio. Disp. to take all h.o. at any time, 2 on the same day, from any bp. 26s 8d.

Edw. Love & Alice Hudson, Linc. dio. Disp. for marriage without banns. 10s.

23 Tho. Bulkeley, acol., r. of Llangissing (sic), Bangor dio. Disp. to take all h.o. at any time, 2 on the same day. 26s 8d.

11 Jo. Whythurst & Agnes Berdecomb, Cov. & Lich. dio. Disp. for marriage (4th degree consang.). 26s 8d.

26 Tho. Personis & Alice Mylward, Bath & W. dio. Disp. for marriage (4th degree consang.). 26s 8d.

f. 83ᵛ

31 Edm. Goddisham, Austin fr. Disp. to become a sec. pr. Gratis; warrant shown.

18 Rob. Rankin, Austin fr. Disp. to become a sec. pr. Gratis; warrant shown.

20 Tho. Darnell, pr., r. of Thorpeden or Ermondthorpe, Linc. dio., chapl. of Jo. Towchet, Ld Audley. Disp. to hold a benef. with cure with the above or 2 without it; permut. & non-res. cl. £6 10s.

23 Tho. Canbrige, Austin fr. Disp. to hold a benef. with complete change of habit. Gratis; warrant shown.

20 Rob. Hoy, O.S.A., canon of St Osyth's, Lond. dio. Disp. to become a sec. pr. 'Remanet.'

July 18 Jo. Sterman, O.C. fr., of Cambridge. Disp. to hold a benef. with complete change of habit. Gratis; warrant shown.

f. 84ʳ

16 Rob. Rande, formerly O.S.A., canon of St Botolph's, nr Colchester, Lond. dio. Disp. to hold a benef. with complete change of habit. Also for Ric. Parker, Tho. Tornor, Jo. Gibbes. Suppr.

Ric. Standon, O.S.B., prior of Hatfield Broadoak, Lond. dio. Disp. to hold a benef. with complete change of habit. Also for Wm Wright, Jas Nycolson, Wm Wade, Rob. Hastings. Suppr.

Simon Sponer, O.S.A., formerly prior of Thremhall, Lond. dio. Also for Tho. Mutford, Oliver Holden, Jo. Danyell. Suppr.

20 Rob. Smyth & Ann Howman, widow, of London. Disp. for marriage (Rob. was godfather to a child of Ann). 'Remanet.'

f. 84ᵛ

24 Jo. Olyver, D.C.L., v. of Minster in Thanet, Cant. dio.; r. of Wolstanton, Cov. & Lich. dio. Disp. to hold a 3rd benef. without taking h.o. but he must take some h.o. within 3 yrs. 30s.

20 Ric. Schut, v. of Tenbury, Heref. dio., chapl. to Ld Hy Clifford, heir to the Earl of Cumberland. Disp. to hold a benef. with cure with the above, or 2 without; permut. & non-res. cl. £7 13s 4d.

Roger Pottenne, formerly O.S.A., prior of hospital of St Mary, Elsing Spital, Lond. dio. Disp. to hold a benef. with complete change of habit. Suppr.

f. 85ʳ

Edw. Cadwell, formerly reg. canon of Breamore, Winton dio. Disp. to hold a benef. with complete change of habit. Also for Jo. Finch, Geo. Rogeris, Nich. More, Hy Pope, Hy Hollingbourn, Hy Conwey. Suppr.

22 Ric. Preston, O.S.A., prior of Cartmel, York dio. Disp. to hold a benef. with complete change of habit. Also for Augustine Fell, Jo. Rudley, Tho. Briggs, Tho. Pereson, Ric. Bakehouse, Jas Estbridge, Jo. Cowper, Wm Panell, Brian Willen. Suppr.

15 Peter Prescote, O.S.B., recently prior of St Tho. the Martyr, [Up]holland, Cov. & Lich. dio. Disp. to hold a benef. with complete change of habit. Also for Jo. Codling & Hugh Fareclought, Jo. Aynesdall, Jas Smyth. Suppr.

f. 85ᵛ

22 Hugh Huxeley, O.S.A., formerly prior of Burscough, Cov. & Lich. dio. Disp. to hold a benef. with complete change of habit.

Also for Wm Aspingwall, Ric. Castello, Hugh Woodhever, Ralph Evers. Suppr.

July 20 Warin Brampton, O.Cist., formerly of Sawtre, Linc. dio. Disp. to hold a benef. with complete change of habit. Also for Ric. Brampton & Ric. Graffon. Suppr.

Rob. Stoppin, formerly canon of the Trinitarian priory of Easton, Sarum dio. Disp. to hold a benef. with complete change of habit. Also for Wm Toppyn, Hy Bryan, Ric. Alyson. Suppr.

26 Wm Webb, r. of Claycoton, Linc. dio., chapl. to Hy Earl of Dorset. Disp. to hold a benef. with cure with the above, or 2 without; permut. & non-res. cl. £6 10s.

f. 86ʳ

26 Ant. Bayly & Marg. Gibson, York dio. Disp. for marriage (4th degree consang.). 26s 8d.

Ric. Stondon, pr., O.S.B., formerly prior of Hatfield, Lond. dio. Disp. to wear the grey almuce of a cath. canon where, when, & however much he likes. 10s. Suppr.

31 Jo. Dodge & Eliz. Careleton, Lond. dio. Disp. for marriage, the banns read once. 6s 8d.

Ric. Jones, O.P., Bangor. Disp. to become a sec. pr. Gratis; warrant shown.

Aug.   9 Jo. Scotte & Kath. Gray, Lond. dio. Disp. for marriage without banns. 10s.

f. 86ᵛ

5 Ric. Forth & Eliz. Tylney, Norw. dio. Disp. for marriage without banns. 10s.

1 Ric. Couper, formerly sub-prior of Beaulieu, Winton dio. Disp. to hold a benef. with complete change of habit. Also for Jo. Salisbury, Chris. Elkham, Ric. Stilfelde, Jo. Winchester, Jo. Warde. Suppr.

4 Jo. Lymden, O.S.A., formerly prior of Reigate, Winton dio. Disp. to hold a benef. with complete change of habit. Suppr.

6 Geo. Cleyton *alias* Rhetheram, O.S.A., formerly prior of Thornholme, Linc. dio. Disp. to hold a benef. with complete change of habit. Suppr.

1 Tho. Newman, formerly O.S.A., canon of St Denys, nr Southampton, Winton dio. Disp. to hold a benef. with complete change of habit. Also for Ric. Lynton, Tho. Austen, Hy Forest, Stephen Latemer. Suppr.

f. 87ʳ

July 13 Tho. Small, Observant fr. Disp. to become a sec. pr. Gratis; warrant shown.

20 Ric. Sampson, Bp of Chich. Disp. to hold the deanery of St Paul's in comm. £40. Taxed according to warrant shown.

13 Wm Orphen, recently Observant fr. Disp. to become a sec. pr. Gratis; warrant shown.

f. 87ᵛ

31 Ric. Bragwen, O.Cist., formerly abbot of Medmenham, Linc. dio. Disp. to hold a benef. with complete change of habit. Suppr.

20 Jo. Sympson, formerly canon of Sempringham, Linc. dio. Disp. to become a sec. pr. Gratis; warrant shown.

24 Tho. Lord, O.S.A., formerly prior of Conishead, York dio. Disp. to hold a benef. with complete change of habit. Also for Tho. Bakehowse, Geo. Carneford, Chris. Preston, Nich. Wilson, Chris. Poole, Tho. Heysam, Ric. Scotsande. Suppr.

31 Jo. Copessheffe, formerly abbot of Beeleigh. Disp. to hold a benef. with complete change of habit. Also for Tho. Willes, Tho. Harvy, Rob. Mottes, Tho. Dales, Jo. Busshe, Ric. Pyende, Roger Golding, Alex. Gates, Tho. Fraunce, Edw. Peace, Wm Shole. Suppr.

f. 88ʳ

Aug. 4 Jo. Pynker, O.S.A., formerly prior of Markby, Linc. dio. Disp. to hold a benef. with complete change of habit. Also for Wm Inglomes, Rob. Hornecastell, Jo. Lowth, Jo. Hackbey, Tho. Marom. Suppr.

Roger Browne, O.S.B., formerly of Swineshead, Linc. dio. Disp. to hold a benef. with complete change of habit. Also for Wm Cotgham, Tho. Ros, Wm Grentham, Geo. Gobston, Rob. Lake, Tho. Myddleton. Suppr.

3 Jo. Sutton, O.S.A., canon formerly of Torksey, Linc. dio. Disp. to hold a benef. with complete change of habit. Also for Hy Taylor, Jo. Raignoldson, Ric. Kempe, Ric. Gibson. Suppr

4 Wm Webure, O.S.B., formerly abbot of Vaudey, Linc. dio. Disp. to hold a benef. with complete change of habit. Also for Arthur Baynbridge, Francis Nycholson, Edw. Clerke, Wm Darton, Rob. Derham, Jo. Hemyng. Suppr.

f. 88ᵛ

Jo. Water, O.Cist., formerly of Waverley, Winton dio. Disp. to hold a benef. with complete change of habit. Also for Simon

Skyggs, Jo. Parker, Jo. Smyth, Tho. Carpenter, Jo. Heythorne. Suppr.

Aug. 20 Tho. Whiffen, formerly O.S.A., canon of Nocton Park, Linc. dio. Disp. to hold a benef. with complete change of habit. Suppr.

12 Tho. May, acol., Sarum dio. Disp. to take all h.o. at any time, 2 on the same day. 26s 8d.

20 Edm. Toser, formerly O.S.A. (*sic* for Premonstr.?), abbot of Hagneby, Linc. dio. Disp. to hold a benef. with complete change of habit. Also for Ric. Thedilthorpe, Rob. Carborow, Jo. Holte, Tho. Clee. Suppr.

2 Rob. Thomas, O.Cist., formerly of Margam, Lland. dio. Disp. to hold a benef. with complete change of habit. Also for Morgan Jones, Wm Lotewich, Jo. ap Retherth, Maurice Kydwely, Jo. Whytty, Jo. Yong, Jo. Whitlond, Jo. Hopkyn. Suppr.

f. 89ʳ

4 Jo. Small, O.S.A., recently abbot of Bourne, Linc. dio. Disp. to hold a benef. with complete change of habit. Also for Wm Gaynsforde, Rob. Baston, Rob. Haske, Edw. Boston, Jas Aslegbye, Edw. Bedford. Suppr.

6 Jo. Beves, O.S.B., recently of Humberston, Linc. dio. Disp. to hold a benef. with complete change of habit. Suppr.

20 Rob. Whytclyfe, recently abbot of Wellow, Linc. dio. Disp. to hold a benef. with complete change of habit. Also for Jo. Whaplot, Hy Parke, Wm Yong, Rob. Laurence, Tho. Wright, Wm Medeford. Suppr.

Jo. Woode, O.S.A. (*sic* for Premonstr.?), recently prior of Newsham, Linc. dio. Disp. to hold a benef. with complete change of habit. Also for Jo. Frebanke & Jo. Parson. Suppr.

Tho. Wildy, recently O.S.A., canon of Bisham, Sarum dio. Disp. to hold a benef. with complete change of habit. Suppr.

f. 89ᵛ

Chris. Turke, recently O.S.A., canon of Elsham. Disp. to hold a benef. with complete change of habit. Suppr.

4 Jo. Standerope, recently O.S.A., canon of Thornholme, Linc. dio. Disp. to hold a benef. with complete change of habit. Also for Chris. Holderness & Jo. Tykell. Suppr.

20 Wm Stephenson, recently O.S.A., canon of Newbo, Linc. dio. Disp. to hold a benef. with complete change of habit. Also for Wm Browne, Wm Wright, Rob. Mayborn. Suppr.

June 10 Ric. Sampson, D.Cn. & C.L., Kg's councillor, recently appointed Bp of Chich. & by the Kg's special will Dean of Lichfield, archdcn of Suffolk, Norw. dio., prebendary of Langford, Linc. dio., Dean of St Paul's. Disp. to hold a benef. with bpric of Chich. so long as Rob., the former Bp, is alive. £40. Taxed according to warrant.

f. 90^r

Aug. 20 Philip Gantibye, recently O.S.A., canon of Newstead, Linc. dio. Disp. to hold a benef. with complete change of habit. Suppr.

Walter Browne, M.A., r. of Harston, Master of the Hospital founded in memory of Wm Wigeston in Leicester, Linc. dio. Disp. to hold a benef. with cure with the above, or 2 without; permut. & non-res. cl. £7 13s 4d; 6s 8d.

12 Walter Jones & Ann Wemer. Disp. for marriage (2nd & 3rd degrees affin.). £8.

June 10 Ric. Sampson (as above). Disp. also to hold the deanery of the Chapel Royal, Windsor, the Treasurership of Salisbury, & archdcnry of Cornwall. £40. Taxed according to warrant shown.

f. 90^v

Aug. 14 Ric. Devereux, son & heir of Ld Walter & Ly Mary Ferrers of Chartley, & Dorothy Hastings, dau. of Geo. Earl of Huntingdon. Disp. for marriage (3rd degree consang. on one side, 3rd & 4th on the other). £6; 30s.

12 Humphrey Lymhoke & Cicily March, widow of the late Simon March, Norw. dio. Disp. validating marriage contracted in ignorance of 3rd degree affin. £6.

4 Rob. Boston, O.S.A., formerly sub-prior of Tupholme, Linc. dio. Disp. to hold a benef. with complete change of habit. Also for Edm. Burreth, Peter Tompson, Wm Newarke, Ric. Walker. Suppr.

6 Rob. Harte, O.S.B., formerly of Louth Park, Linc. dio. Disp. to hold a benef. with complete change of habit. Also for Wm Dobibee, Wm Kyrkbye, Jo. Grene, Gabriell Yambson, Ric. Banks, Jo. Wistow. Suppr.

f. 91^r

21 Ric. Mabot, D.Th., Master of the Hospital of St Tho. the Martyr, Southwark, Winton dio. Disp. to hold any benef. with cure with the above office; permut. cl. £10.

20 Jo. Hilsey, Bp of Roch. Disp. to hold the priorship and house of the Dominicans of London. Warrant shown; 'remittitur gratis per littera [m] domini Crumwe [ll]'.

Tho. Grenewood & Agnes Myggebye, York dio. Disp. for marriage (3rd degree consang.). £6.

Aug. 30 Rob. Coke, formerly Premonstr. canon of St Agatha's, Richmond, York dio. Disp. to hold a benef. with complete change of habit. Also for Jo. Tournour, Geoffrey Adamson, Jo. Raby, Jo. Alen, Wm Harland, Rob. Raynerd, Mich. Crekson, Tho. Rypon. Suppr.

f. 91ᵛ

20 Jo. Bull, O.F.M. Disp. to hold a benef. with complete change of habit.

4 Stephen Desborgh, pr., O.F.M., Ely dio. Disp. to become a sec. pr. Warrant shown.

31 Ralph Eddo & Gwen Edward, Cov. & Lich. dio. Disp. for marriage (3rd & 3rd equal degrees consang.). Arb. £4; warrant shown.

20 Wm Flatbury, pr., O.Cist., abbot of Sibton, Norw. dio. Disp. to hold a benef. with complete change of habit. Also for Wm Dunwich, Wm Boys, Peter Hichson, Rob. Bets, Tho. Hadley. Suppr.

21 Geo. Willayne & Alice Sheperd, York dio. Disp. for marriage (4th degree consang.). 26s 8d.

22 Tho. Fuller & Jane Master, Roch. dio. Disp. for marriage (Jane's father was Tho.'s godfather). 30s.

f. 92ʳ

24 Edw. Asheton & Agnes Benson, Cov. & Lich. dio. Disp. for marriage (4th degree consang.). 26s 8d.

25 Ric. Ugdene & Agnes Grene. Cov. & Lich. dio. Disp. for marriage (4th degree consang.). 26s 8d.

Wm Alsley & Marg. Barbey. Disp. for marriage without banns. 10s.

21 Ric. Waye & Grace Diconson, York dio. Disp. for marriage (4th degree consang.). 26s 8d.

22 Chris. Thornton & Ann Carr, York dio. Disp. for marriage (4th degree consang.). 26s 8d.

26 Jo. ap Thomas ap Betherch & Marg. verch Llan. Disp. for marriage (3rd & 4th degree affin.). 26s 8d., 3s 8d.

26 Tho. Doughson & Eliz. Garlyke, Cov. & Lich. dio. Disp. for marriage (4th degree consang.). 26s 8d.

f. 92ᵛ

Aug. 21 Ric. Karlell & Eliz. Hesillyed, Carl. dio. Disp. for marriage (3rd & 4th degree consang.). 30s.

25 Hugh Brathwake & Janet Byrkhede, Carl. dio. Disp. for marriage (3rd & 4th degrees consang.). 30s.

Sept. 1 Nich. Kente & Isabella Mygley, York dio. Disp. for marriage (3rd & 4th degrees consang.). 30s.

Jo. Gordon, Sarum dio. Disp. to take all h.o. at any times, 2 on the same day. 26s 8d.

2 Geoffrey Bolynannte, subdcn, Cov. & Lich. dio. Disp. to take dcn's & pr.'s orders at any times. 13s 4d.

Jo. Keton, v. of Kings Dannton (*sic* for Kingsteignton?) & Yealmpton, Ex. dio. Disp. for non-res. on account of old age, gout, & other infirmities. 20s.

f. 93ʳ

Aug. 31 Wm Matilby, recently O.S.B., prior of Snelshall, Linc. dio. Disp. to hold a benef. with complete change of habit. Suppr.

30 Rob. Higdon, B.Th., chanter in the chantry of Wm, Bp of London, in the low chapel beneath the palace (*sic*). Disp. to hold a benef. with cure with the above, or 2 without; non-res. cl. £7 13s 4d.

31 Tho. Shepey, O.C. fr., of Stamford, Linc. dio. Disp. to hold a benef. with complete change of habit. Gratis; warrant shown.

Sept. 3 Eustace Woodeford & Agnes Bayly, of London. Disp. for marriage in any ch. or chapel, without banns. 10s.

Tho. Mayligge & Helen Sympson, of London. Disp. for marriage without banns. 10s.

4 Wm Bychiat, O.C. fr., Linc. dio. Disp. to hold a benef. with complete change of habit. Arb. £4; warrant shown.

f. 93ᵛ

July 24 Tho. Cockston, pr., O.S.A., canon of Leeds, Cant. dio. Disp. to hold a benef. with complete change of habit. Arb. £4; warrant shown.

Sept. 6 Rob. Ruttill, formerly O.S.A., prior of Hickling, Norw. dio. Disp. to hold a benef. with complete change of habit. Also for Ric. Leke, Rob. Mange, Rob. Webster, Mathew Odee, Rob. Alyn. Suppr.

July 31 Ralph More, formerly O.S.A., canon of Dunmow, London dio. Disp. to hold a benef. with complete change of habit. Also for Wm Grey, Jo. Rame, Rob. Stoks, Geoffrey Shether. Suppr.

Sept. 2 Mary Cornewall, formerly nun of Castle Hedingham, Lond. dio. Disp. to leave the religious life. Suppr.

20 Jo. Penketh, formerly O.S.A., of Norton, Cov. & Lich. dio. Disp. to hold a benef. with complete change of habit. Also for Hy Barons. Suppr.

f. 94^r

3 Ellis Pecocke, formerly Celestine monk of Pill, St David's dio. Disp. to hold a benef. with complete change of habit. Suppr.

6 Rob. Benyon & Agnes Marler, of Manchester, York dio. Disp. for marriage (4th degree consang.). 26s 8d.

1 Morgan Lewis, clk, St David's dio. Disp. to practise as a notary. 13s 4d.

6 Jo. Croke, B.C.L. Disp. to practise as a notary. 13s 4d.

Tho. Clement & Jane Vernando. Disp. for marriage without banns. 10s.

8 Wm Larke & Eliz. Walshe, of Normanby, Linc. dio. Disp. for marriage (Wm's mother was Eliz.'s godmother). 30s.

19 Tho. Flatcher, r. of ?Kirk Bramwith ('Braynewich') York dio. Disp. for non-res. for 2 yrs to study letters. 13s 4d.

f. 94^v

Feb. 20 Tho. Preston *alias* Hall, v. of Preston, York dio. Disp. for non-res. for 2 yrs on account of fever & senility. 13s 4d.

Sept. 15 Ant. Sparow & Eliz. Frost, Norw. dio. Disp. for marriage (3rd & 4th degrees affin.). 30s.

16 Wm Gefferison & Eliz. Byrde, Winton dio. Disp. for marriage in either's par. ch. without banns. 10s.

19 Tho. Broke, B.A., Cov. & Lich. dio. Disp. to take all h.o. at any times from any bp, 2 on the same day. 26s 8d.

Aug. 1 Alice Cranmer, formerly prioress of the nunnery of Sheppey or St Sexburga in Minster in Thanet, Cant. dio. Disp. to leave the religious life. Also for Ursula Gosburne, Agnes Bolney, Ann Clifford, Marg. Rilers, Eliz. Stradling, Marg. Tuke, Ann Loveden, Joan Godiar, Agnes Davy, Dorothy Topclyffe. Suppr.

f. 95^r

Sept. 18 Ric. Rolneson & Agnes Holme, York dio. Disp. for marriage (4th degree consang.). 26s 8d.

24 Ric. Butfloure & Eliz. Curtes, of Wickham, Durham dio. Disp. for marriage (3rd & 4th degrees consang.). 30s.

Aug. 3 Ann Goderne, formerly prioress, O.S.A., of Greenfield, Linc. dio. Disp. to leave the religious life. Also for Marg. Pynder, Agnes Growannce, Joan Walbanke, Marg. Newcombe, Marg. Sherewood, Agnes Johnson, Agnes Crober, Cecily Stephenson, Kath. Wright. Suppr.

Jane Messodyn, formerly prioress of the O.Cist. Priory of Legbourne, Linc. dio. Disp. to leave the religious life. Also for Ann Fysswyke, Agnes Synelde, Ursula Taylwode, Joan Horsolde, Marg. Fytzwilliam, Eliz. Broune, Eliz. Cleyton, Eliz. Martyn, Ann Wright. Suppr.

Peter Ayshebury, r. of Scrayingham, York dio. Disp. for nonres. for 3 yrs. 30s. p.s.r. 5s.

f. 95ᵛ

Sept. 20 Jo. Rose, formerly monk of Malmesbury, Sarum dio., & now monk of Pilton, Ex. dio. Disp. to hold a benef. with complete change of habit. Suppr.

Wm Pyper & Geneta Walker. Disp. for marriage (Geneta was sponsor at the confirmation of a child of Wm at Furness, in the par. of Dalton, York dio.). £6.

Jo. Rigton, recently prior of Blythburgh, Norw. dio. Disp. to hold a benef. with complete change of habit. Also for Jo. Baker, Geo. Thurstan, Ralph Dale. Suppr.

Wm Parker, recently prior, O.S.B., of Eye, Norw. dio. Disp. to hold a benef. with complete change of habit. Also for Ric. Alen, Francis Raggs, Chris. Franncis, Tho. Bury, Jo. Costes, Hy Alen, Wm Walters. Suppr.

f. 96ʳ

Geo. Carleton, recently abbot of the Premonstr. hse of Leiston, Norw. dio. Disp. to hold a benef. with complete change of habit. Also for Jo. Blythborough, Jo. Sondoll, Wm Ryve, Rob. Fyske, Tho. Hycklyn, Geo. Payne, Rob. Hacon, Tho. Rowse, Jo. Marshall, Ric. Fagons. Suppr.

Wm Blome, formerly prior O.S.A., of Ixworth, Norw. dio. Disp. to hold a benef. with complete change of habit. Also for Reg. Facon, Wm Reynberd, Adam Pennder, Ric. Aldrige, Simon Fyssher, Jo. Hunte, Jo. Stoller, Rob. Baracke, Wm Seward. Suppr.

Jo. Downe, recently monk O.Cist., of Flaxley, Heref. dio. Disp. to hold a benef. with change of habit. Also for Wm Ipesley, Edw. Arlington, Gabriell Woodwarde, Tho. Parpyn. Suppr.

f. 96^v

Sept. 20 Tho. Donchaster, recently monk, O.Cist., of Rufford, York dio.
Disp. to hold a benef. with complete change of habit. Also for
Tho. Bellam, Tho. Wellis, Rob. Waterall, Tho. Artor, Edw.
Knabrough, Ric. Stonnton, Hy Baker, Ric. Pewson, Ric. Melton,
Tho. Capron. Suppr.

25 Tho. Tulley & Isabella White, of Hartfield, Chich. dio. Disp.
for marriage (3rd & 4th degree consang.). 30s.

24 Marg. Sackwill, recently prioress of Easebourne, Chich. dio.
Disp. to leave the religious life. Also for Alice Parker, Marg.
Prate, Helen Hill, Joan Sackwill. Suppr.

f. 97^r

27 Edw. Lay & Eliz. Edwards, widow, Lond. dio. Disp. for marriage
without banns. 10s.

30 Ric. Galeway, recently Cluniac monk of (Monkton) Farleigh,
Sarum dio. Disp. to hold a benef. with complete change of habit.
Also for Jo. Wynchelsey, Tho. Kysbury, Rob. Burton. Suppr.

20 Hy Austen, recently O.S.A., prior of Chacombe, Linc. dio.
Disp. to hold a benef. with complete change of habit. Also for
Tho. Payne, Tho. Stone, Edw. Done, Jo. Hareford. Suppr.

26 Jo. Hynde, recently canon of St Bartholomew's in the W., Smithfield. Disp. to hold a benef. with complete change of habit.
Arb. £4; warrant shown.

30 Peter Skellington & Jane Whitfield, of Tideswell, Cov. & Lich.
dio. Disp. for marriage (4th & 4th degrees consang.). 26s 8d.

f. 97^v

26 Jo. Whyte, recently O.S.A., canon of Ivychurch, Sarum dio.
Disp. to hold a benef. with complete change of habit. Also for
Wm Preston, Hy Verges, Wm Phillips, Wm Grene. Suppr.

31 Jo. Currey (or Crurey?) v. of Anthury (*sic* for Athelney?) Bath
& W. dio. Disp. to hold a benef., with the above as it does not
yield over £8 p.a.; permut. & non-res. cl.; or else 2 others, only
one of them with cure. £4.

20 Tho. Sheston, O.Cist., recently abbot of Garendon, Linc. dio.
Disp. to hold a benef. with complete change of habit. Suppr.

30 Peter Gonernee & Joan Manubfrete, of the par. of St Tho.
the Martyr, Salisbury. Disp. for marriage (Joan was sponsor at
the confirmation of a child of Peter's). Arb. 20s. warrant shown.

20 Wm Melton *alias* Wurmell, O.Cist., recently of Garendon, Linc.
dio. Disp. to hold a benef. with complete change of habit.
Suppr.

f. 98^r

Sept. 30 Tho. Jury, M.A., r. of Bishopstow, Sarum dio., chapl. to Jo., Bp of Bath & W. Disp. to hold a benef. with the above, or 2 without; permut. & non-res. cl. £7 13s 4d.

Wm Bowman, O.C. fr., of Sele. Disp. to become a sec. pr. Gratis; warrant shown.

27 Jo. Watkyns, v. of St Leonard's, Newcastle, at Bridgend, Lland. dio. Disp. to hold a benef. with the above, if the latter does not yield over £8 p.a., permut & non-res. cl. £4.

30 Mich. Ecclesall *alias* Bredewell, recently sub-prior of Premonstr. hse of Beauchief, Cov. & Lich. dio. Disp. to hold a benef. with complete change of habit. Also for Jo. Wilkinson, Jo. Browne, Wm Darneton, Chris. Hill, Wm Beneson, Hy Norton, Ric. Bright. Suppr.

Oct. 1 Geo. Ornne & Alice Whitfield, Cov. & Lich. dio. Disp. for marriage (Alice's mother was Geo.'s godmother). 30s.

f. 98^v

Sept. 4 ——, abbot O.Cist., of St Mary Graces by the Tower, London. Disp. to hold in comm. with the above the monastery of St Mary, Coggeshall, Lond. dio. freely resigned by Wm Love, formerly abbot; non-res. cl. £125 11s. Taxed according to warrant shown.

Oct. 2 Benedict Harward, B.A., r. of Berston, Linc. dio. Disp. to take all h.o. at any time, 2 on the same day from the Bp of Salisbury or his suffragan. 26s 8d.

Wm & Alice Goodman, of Upwilliam, Linc. dio. Disp. for marriage (4th degree consang.). 26s 8d.

Wm Marten, subdcn, Cov. & Lich. dio. Disp. to take dcn's & pr.'s orders outside the statutory time and from any bp. 13s 4d.

4 Rob. Banks, B.A., York dio. Disp. to take all h.o. from any bp at any times. 20s; 6s 8d.

1 Hy King & Esdra Holden, Roch. dio. Disp. for marriage (Hy's mother was Esdra's godmother). 30s.

f. 99^r

4 Nich. Bachon & Agnes Cosell, of London. Disp. for marriage without banns. 10s.

Wm Llan ap Jenn & Mabel verch David ap David ap Jenn ap Hoell, St David's dio. Disp. for marriage (4th degree consang.). 26s 8d.

Oct.   4 Helen Thirkill, recently Cluniac nun of Westwood, Worc. dio. Disp. to leave the religious life. Also for Ann Sawley, Agnes Banes. Suppr.

July 17 Jo. Sandall, dcn, York dio. Disp. to hold pr.'s orders and hold a benef., having, as he asserts, heard confessions of the faithful. 40s.

Oct.   6 Jo. Foston, recently O.S.A., canon of Haltemprice, York dio. Disp. to hold a benef. with complete change of habit. Also for Hy Taylor, Bartholomew Lylforth, Ric. Wagger, Rob. Colynson, Rob. Johnson, Edm. Bugge, Jo. Smyth, Jo. Hewson. Suppr.

f. 99ᵛ

Reg. Brinkisworth, pr., recently monk O.S.B., of Holy Trin., York. Disp. to hold a benef. with complete change of habit. Also for Ric. Stubbis, Ric. Staneley, Rob. Evers, Ric. Browne, Rob. Beste, Oliver Ward, Wm Grene, Jo. Killingbecke. Suppr.

Sept. 30 Wm Chamber, recently O.S.A., canon of Healaugh Park, York dio. Disp. to hold a benef. with complete change of habit. Also for Jo. Boncktrowte, Jo. Pety, Wm Oldefelde, Tho. Maneld. Suppr.

Oct.   1 Tho. Burgh, formerly O.S.A., canon of North Ferriby, York dio. Disp. to hold a benef. with complete change of habit. Also for Tho. Androw, Wm Seyman, Jo. Sey, Wm Calverd, Edw. Widall, Jo. Yonge, Jo. Bawdewyn. Suppr.

     6 Hy Colson, recently O.S.A., canon of Marton, York dio. Disp. to hold a benef. with complete change of habit. Suppr.

f. 100ʳ

Sept. 30 Jo. Bolton, recently O.S.A., canon of Warter, York dio. Disp. to hold a benef. with complete change of habit. Also for Tho. Smyth, Tho. Spruse, Jo. Jackson, Hy Hanley, Wm Modye, Rob. Seyman, Rob. Appleby. Suppr.

Ant. Mason, formerly O.S.A., canon of Drax, York dio. Disp. to hold a benef. with complete change of habit. Also for Alex. Genyns, Hy Johnson, Jo. Husey. Suppr.

  20 Tho. Wigstone *alias* Stanley, O.Cist., formerly of Garendon, Linc. dio. Disp. to hold a benef. with complete change of habit. Also for Jo. Wodwarde, Jo. Coventre, Rob. Mownsarell, Wm Hatham, Wm Eylston, Jo. Ayshby. Suppr.

Oct. 14 Geo & Marg. Fell, of Pennington, York dio. Disp. for marriage (3rd & 4th degrees affin.). 30s.

f. 100^v

Oct. 10 Ric. Page, pr., recently prior O.S.A., of Ivy Church, Sarum dio.
Disp. to hold canonry of Sarum & the prebend. of Uphaven, also
the par. ch. of Clutton, Bath & W. dio. 54s. p.s.r. 5s.

12 Nich. Marshall, formerly O.Cist., of Newminster, Durham dio.
Disp. to hold a benef. with complete change of habit. Also for
Tho. Morpeth, Tho. Ritton, Rob. Mathew, Geo. Sotheron,
Chris. Howell, Wm Goston, Gilbert Ogell, Ralph Hebstote,
Tho. Barton, Edw. Wadderell, Denis Thorlis, Lancelot Laylorn,
Ric. Caldecatts, Edw. Morphen, Hy Castell, Ric. Horton. Suppr.

f. 101^r

20 Ric. Sley, r. of Castlecarrock, Carl. dio. Disp. for non-res. for
2 yrs. 13s 4d; p.s.r. 5s.

16 Cuthbert Hutton, York dio., & Eliz. Bellingham, Carl. dio.
Disp. for marriage (2nd & 4th degrees mixed consang. & 4th
equal consang. & 4th & 4th equal of affin.). 33s 4d; 26s 8d;
26s 8d.

7 Wm Mawndesfild, v. of Fleet, Sarum dio. Disp. for non-res.
for 2 yrs on account of colic & 2 other ailments. 13s 4d.

16 Jo. Marychurch & Jane verch Jenken Lloyd, St David's dio.
Disp. for marriage (4th & 4th degrees consang.). 26s 8d.

23 Chris. Fyssher & Mary Edamy, of London. Disp. for marriage,
the banns read once. 6s 8d.

20 Tho. Awarke, O.S.A., canon of Carlisle, v. of Thoresby, Carl.
dio. Disp. to hold a benef. with the above. £4.

f. 101^v

Rob. Harwell, O.S.A., of Reading, Sarum dio. Disp. to leave
the religious life, not having taken any clerical orders and being
under 25. £4.

Wm Hall, prior of the Gilbertine priory of Haverholme, Linc.
dio. Disp. to hold any benef. with some change of habit; having
resigned the above priorship; permut. cl. £8.

31 Hy Gest, subdcn, recently monk of Rewley by Oxford, Linc.
dio. Disp. to hold a benef. with complete change of habit.
Suppr.

20 Wm Roll, B.C.L., v. of Jacobstow, Ex. dio. Disp. to hold a benef.
with the above, or 2 others without; permut. cl. £6 10s.

4 Jo. Skype, D.Th., v. of Thaxted, Lond. dio. Disp. to hold 2 benefices with the above or 3 without; permut. & non-res. cl. £9.

f. 102^r

Oct. 31 Peter Hed, O.Cist., recently of Rewley, Linc. dio. Disp. to hold a benef. with complete change of habit. Also for Nich. Austen, Jo. Bradham, Tho. Scotte, Ric. Davis, Tho. Ros, Jo. Benvell, Tho. Hoddington, Rob. Byrell, Jo. Kniston, Tho. Marbroke. Suppr.

20 Tho. Were, recently O.S.A., abbot of Flaxley, Heref. dio. Disp. to hold a benef. with complete change of habit. Suppr.

July 31 Lewis Dore, O.Cist., recently of Garendon, Linc. dio. Disp. to hold a benef. with complete change of habit. Suppr.

Oct. 20 Rob. Nichols, B.Th., r. of St Marg., Rainham, Norw. dio. Disp. to hold a benef. with the above, or 2 without; permut cl. £6 10s.

f. 102^v

Jo. Cowper, recently canon of Church Gresley, Cov. & Lich. dio. Disp. to hold a benef. with complete change of habit. Also for Jo. Okeley, Roger Joly, Jo. Dordon, Jo. Wolbard. Suppr.

Jo. Waketon, recently Premonstr. canon of Durford, Chich. dio. Disp. to hold a benef. with complete change of habit. Also for Hy Dente, Ric. Sandefeld, Roger Wheler, Hy Wyndesore. Suppr.

31 Ralph Mastey, O.F.M., recently of Southampton, Winton dio. Disp. to hold any benef. with complete change of habit. Gratis; warrant shown.

Nov. 2 Wm Malenercee & Eliz. Hopton, York dio. Disp. for marriage (3rd & 4th degrees consang.). 30s.

4 Ric. Roberts, Winton dio., & Agnes Broke, Lond. dio. Disp. for marriage without banns. 10s.

f. 103^r

6 Ric. Jefford of the Kg's hsehld & Ann Goring of the par. of Burgeton or Burton, Chich. dio. Disp. for marriage without banns. 10s.

Ric. Davy, of the par. of St Martin's, Bishopgate St., & Joan Walys, of St Augustine by St Paul's, London. Disp. for marriage without banns. 10s.

9 Wm Lyon & Eliz. Goodwyn, widow, of Norw. dio. Disp. for marriage in any ch., without banns. 10s.

Tho. Barley & Grace Colmnbell, Cov. & Lich. dio. Disp. for marriage (the banns read once; 3rd & 4th degrees affin.). 6s 8d; 30s.

Nov. 16 Nich. Gravet & Agnes Darell, of Wickham, Linc. dio. Disp. for marriage without banns. 10s.

15 Ric. Fuller & Eliz. Sharpe, Ely dio. Disp. for marriage (Ric.'s mother was Eliz.'s godmother & Eliz.'s father was Ric.'s godfather). Arb. 20s; warrant shown.

f. 103ᵛ

12 Martin Wyley, sch., Linc. dio. Disp. to take all h.o. at any times. 20s.

Jo. Blande, M.A., Fellow of St Jo.'s Coll., Cambridge. Disp. to take all h.o. at any times from any bp. 20s.

18 Jo. Marys & Kath. Gabyn, Norw. dio. Disp. for marriage (Jo.'s father was Kath.'s godfather). 30s.

Jo. Longforde, Heref. dio. Disp. to take dcn's & pr.'s orders at any times. 13s 4d.

23 Roger Storkey & Kath. Hardy, Lond. dio. Disp. for marriage without banns. 10s.

Ralph Dulfeld, B.A., Worc. dio. Disp. to take all h.o., 2 on the same day, outside the statutory time. 26s 8d.

f. 104ʳ

20 Rob. Wabington, recently O.S.A., abbot of Langley, Norw. dio. Disp. to hold a benef. with complete change of habit. Also, for Jo. Deryngham, Ric. Walker, Wm Asen, Jo. Glymlyng, Tho. Smyth. Suppr.

23 Wm Tewkisbury, O.S.A., recently of Chepstow, Lland. dio. Disp. to hold a benef. with complete change of habit. Suppr.

12 Jo. Mathew, recently O.S.A., canon of Dorchester, Linc. dio. Disp. to hold a benef. with complete change of habit. Also for Jo. Clyfton, Wm Poerch, Hugh Buntyng, Geo. Harte. Suppr.

10 Rob. Browne *alias* Broone, B.M., of Oxford, licensed to practise by the University. Disp. to confirm this & permit him to practise anywhere. 40s; p.s.r. 5s.

f. 104ᵛ

Jo. Lyrpole, recently O.S.A., canon of Maiden Bradley, Sarum dio. Disp. to hold a benef. with complete change of habit. Suppr.

20 Jo. Banberry, formerly canon of Wroxton, Linc. dio. Disp. to hold a benef. with complete change of habit. Also for Jo. Haynys, Rob. Hanly, Rob. Cocks, Ric. Clerke, Nich. Wynbyry. Suppr.

30 Tho. Poundfold, r. of Minterne, Sarum dio., chapl. to Sir Jo. Horsey. Disp. to hold a benef. with the above, or 2 without; permut. & non-res. cl. £7 13s 4d.

Nov. 10 Roger Coverte, B.Th., v. of Cowfold, Chich. dio. Disp. to hold a benef. with above or 2 without; permut. & non-res. cl. £6 10s.

20 Jo. Clerke, recently prior O.S.A., of Thetford, Norw. dio. Disp. to hold a benef. with complete change of habit. Suppr.

22 Edw. Marre, B.Th., r. of Grundisburgh, Norw. dio. Disp. to hold a benef. with above, or 2 without; permut. cl. £7 13s 4d.

26 Roger Werner, r. of ?Stretford ('Long Scredford'), Heref. dio. Disp. for non-res. during his illness. 20s.

Sept. 20 Rob. Dyxson, recently O.S.A., canon of Shelford, York dio. Disp. to hold a benef. with complete change of habit. Also for Wm Mobson, Ric. Grene, Nic. Batman, Ric. Drake, Hy Lees, Jas Bullam, Tho. Fell, Jo. Hilliun, Tho. Porter. Suppr.

Nov. 29 Rob. Nowell & Mary Asheton, Lond. dio. Disp. for marriage, the banns read once. 6s 8d.

20 Tho. Clore, M.A. Confirmation of letters (given almost in full) to hold in comm. the par. ch. of Clonmell, Lismore dio., in the patronage of the Bp of Lismore & Waterford, although claimed by Alan Mosse of the O.S.A. house of St Mary de Portu (sic), Casshel dio. This claim is supported by his prior as the benef. is united to the above hse. 40s.

10 Tho. Norwich, Cluniac monk of Prittlewell, Lond. dio. Disp. to hold a benef. with complete change of habit. Also for Wm Broke, Tho. Davy. Suppr.

Dec. 2 Jo. Carpenter & Ann Orislond, Heref. dio. Disp. for marriage (3rd & 4th degrees consang.). 30s.

Nov. 30 Ric. Wich, O.Cist., recently abbot of Tintern, Lland. dio. Disp. to hold a benef. with complete change of habit. Also for Tho. Elyotts, Ric. Wade, Maurice Burnell, Rob. Thomas. Suppr.

10 Oliver Lloyd, B.Cn.L., r. of St Mich. by the cath. of Worcester. Disp. to hold a benef. with the above, or 2 without; permut. cl. £6 10s.

Dec. 4 Ann Castelforth, recently prioress of Gokewell, Linc. dio. Disp. to leave the religious life. Also for Isabella Vavasor, Joan Osgarby, Joan Williamson. Suppr.

10 Tho. Spratte, B.Th., v. of Bodiam, Chich. dio. Disp. for non-res. for 6 months during illness. 20s; p.s.r. 5s.

f. 106ᵛ

Dec. 3 Hugh Huchinson, York dio. Disp. to take all h.o. from the Bp of
Linc. or his suffragan, without l.d., at any time, 2 on the same
day. 6s 8d; 26s 8d.

5 Wm Pynnocke & Mary Glade, of Maxstoke, Cov. & Lich. dio.
Disp. validating their clandestine marriage without banns, with
absolution. 15s; 20s.

6 Andrew Growte & Mary Poote, of London. Disp. for marriage
without banns, & during the prohibited times. 10s.

Tho. Lewis & Janet William, of ?Bury ('Browey'), St David's
dio. Disp. for marriage (4th degree consang.). 26s 8d.

Aug. 3 Ric. Hosiar, Heref. dio. Disp. to practise as a public notary.
13s 4d. Also for Wm Warmystre, literate, Heref. dio. 13s 4d.

f. 107ʳ

Dec. 10 Jo. Coke, canon of St Mary's, Osney, Linc. dio. Confirmation of
letters of Tho. Parker to the above, instituting him to the prebend of Bibury with the adjacent chapel, by resignation of Tho.
Waill, canon of the same hse & former prebendary. 40s.

Nich. Gardener, O.F.M., Worc. dio. Disp. to become a sec.
pr. Gratis, warrant shown.

Jo. Beverley, recently Premonstr. canon of Newhouse, Linc.
dio. Disp. to hold a benef. with complete change of habit.
Also for Tho. Harpeham, Jo. Skelton, Wm Floxwill, Chris.
Lackwood, Rob. Backster, Tho. Gowland. Suppr.

f. 107ᵛ

Nov. 30 Hy Thaxstede, recently O.S.B., of Walden, Lond. dio. Disp. to
hold a benef. with complete change of habit. Gratis; warrant
shown.

Dec. 10 Wm Bays, recently Premonstr. canon of Thornholme, Linc.
dio. Disp. to hold a benef. with complete change of habit.
Also for Tho. Meckesbroke. Suppr.

Rob. Moreton, O.Cist. monk. Disp. to practise medicine anywhere, despite h.o. £4.

Nov. 30 Wm Foxall, chanter in Salisbury cath. Disp. to hold a benef.
if the value of the chantry is not over £8 p.a.; permut. & non-res.
cl. £4.

Dec. 20 Jo. Fynch, recently O.S.A., canon of Bicester, Linc. dio. Disp.
to hold a benef. with complete change of habit. Also for Rob.
Gibbes, Jo. Wheler, Rob. Ellis, Ralph Alwayn. Suppr.

f. 108ʳ

Nov. 10 Tho. Bugley, chanter in the perpetual chantry for the souls of Walter Halsinghall & Rob. Burnell, Bath & W. cath. at the altar of the Holy Cross, nr the entrance to the Chapter hse. Disp. to hold a benef. as well as this chantry if the value of the latter is not over £8 p.a.; permut. & non-res. cl. £4.

Dec. 10 Edw. Pagete & Magdalene Parker, of London. Disp. for marriage by any suitable pr., in their par. ch. within the prohibited time, but after the banns are read. 20s.

18 Edw. Parceverall, acol., Worc. dio. Disp. to take subdcn's & dcn's orders within the statutory time & on the same day, from the Bp of Roch. or his suffragan. 15s.

12 Wm Kempe, O.C. fr., of Calais. Disp. to become a sec. pr. Gratis; warrant shown.

f. 108ᵛ

20 Tho. Hunte, pr., r. of Horbleton, Bath & W. dio., chapl. to Ld Wm Stourton. Disp. to hold a benef. with the above, or 2 without; permut. cl. £6 10s.

Jo. Beynston, recently Observant fr. Disp. to become a sec. pr., if granted his superior's consent. £4.

Geo. Windam, clk. Disp. to hold a benef. as well as several others he claims to have received by royal licence; permut. & non-res. cl. £10. Taxed according to warrant shown.

Wm Burlay, Austin fr., recently of Cambridge. Disp. to hold any benef. & spend the rest of his life as a sec. pr. Gratis; warrant shown.

f. 109ʳ

30 Jo. Busby, subdcn, Linc. dio. Disp. to take dcn's & pr.'s orders outside the statutory times, on the same day from the Bp of Linc. or his suffragan. 13s 4d.

20 Helen Williams, recently prioress O.S.B., of Usk. Disp. to leave the religious life. Suppr.

19 Jo. Candisshe *alias* Melford, recently sub-prior of St Jo.'s, Colchester, Lond. dio. Disp. to hold a benef. with some change of habit. Arb. £5; warrant shown.

Jo. Swale, r. of Rokeby, Cov. & Lich. dio., chapl. to Ld Geo. Tailboys. Disp. to hold a benef. with the above, or 2 without; permut. & non-res. cl. £7 13s 4d.

f. 109ᵛ

10 Hy Patenden & Dorothy Mapisden, Cant. dio. Disp. for marriage (2nd & 3rd degrees affin.). £8.

Dec. 31 Wm Brabonde, pr., recently O.S.A., canon of St Gregory's, nr Canterbury. Disp. to hold a benef. with complete change of habit. Also for Wm Hamonde, Nich. Champion, Gregory Botulphe, Chris. Churche, Tho. Welles, Jo. Sympkyns. Suppr.

ff. 110ʳ–13ᵛ blank.

f. 114ʳ

1537 Jan. 4 Rob. Kyddon & Isabella Blysse, of Whaddon, Worc. dio. Disp. for marriage (Isabella's mother was Rob.'s godmother). 30s.

Rob. Raynoldes, B.C.L., Fellow of New Coll., Oxford. Disp. (in full) to practise as a public notary. 13s 4d.

Tho. Warner & Lettice Wuscetur, Linc. dio. Disp. for marriage (Lettice's mother was Tho.'s godmother). Arb. 13s 4d.

8 Walter Dolling & Joan Downe, Ex. dio. Disp. for marriage (Walter's mother was Joan's godmother). 30s.

f. 114ᵛ

Jo. Shotter of the Duke of Suffolk's hsehld, and Marg. Petyte of St Marg.'s par., Southwark, Winton dio. Disp. for marriage without banns. 10s.

Wm Singleton of Preston, York dio. & Ann Becausall, of Croston, Cov. & Lich. dio. Disp. for marriage (4th degree consang.). 26s 8d.

10 Wm Bowlowe & Joan Bradwey, Heref. dio. Disp. for marriage (4th degree consang.). 26s 8d.

12 Wm Andrewes & Alice Hanley, Heref. dio. Disp. for marriage (Wm's father was Alice's sponsor at confirmation). 26s 8d.

10 Wm Wilbore & Alice Byrkeby, widow, of London. Disp. for marriage without banns. 10s.

f. 115ʳ

12 Tho. Rutler & Marg. Spurstow, Cov. & Lich. dio. Disp. for marriage (4th degree consang.). 26s 8d.

14 Rob. Radcliffe, 6th Earl of Sussex, Privy Councillor, & Ly Mary Arundell, Ly of the Qn's hsehld. Disp. for marriage in any ch. or chapel without banns. 10s; 10s.

10 Owen ap Thomas ap Philip esq., & Cath. verch John ap Thomas ap Harry, gentw. St David's dio. Disp. for marriage (3rd & 4th degrees affin.). 30s.

Simon Rawlyns, r. of Gt. Brickhill, Linc. dio. Disp. to hold a benef. with the above or 2 without it. Permut. cl. £6 10s.

12 Tho. Marbery of St Pancras par., & Helen Hunte, widow of the par. of St Tho. Bristol. Disp. for marriage without banns. 10s.

f. 115ᵛ

Jan. 20 Rob. King *alias* Barington, O.S.B., recently of Walden, Lond. dio. Disp. to become a sec. pr. 'Remittitur gratis.'

1536 Dec. 6 Wm Alyn & Helen Whyte, widow of Kempton, Linc. dio. Disp. for marriage (Wm was godfather to a child of Helen). Arb. £4.

1537 Jan. 8 Edw. Stokwode & Avis Morice, Lond. dio. Disp. for marriage (Avis's father was sponsor at Edw.'s confirmation). 26s 8d.

20 Jo. Chaderton, of the Kg's hsehld, & Kath. Palshide, Winton dio. Disp. for marriage without banns & outside their par. ch. 10s; 10s.

17 Wm Button, Winton dio., & Isabella Rede, Sarum dio. Disp. for marriage without banns. 10s.

20 Wm Halle & Ann Clerke, Norw. dio. Disp. for marriage (3rd & 4th degrees affin.). 30s.

f. 116ʳ

Humfrey Chesshyre & Helen Smythe, of the par. of St Clement without Temple Bar, London. Disp. for marriage, the banns read once. 6s 8d.

1536 Aug. 10 Wm More, clk, graduate. Disp. (given in full) to hold the O.S.B. hse of Walden, London dio. in accordance with the royal grace permitting him to hold a benef. together with any bpric or title. £100.

1537 Jan. 20 Jo. Clampett & Parnella Gavell of Otford, Cant. dio. Disp. for marriage without banns. 10s.

f. 116ᵛ

Jan. 22 Alex. Welles & Joan Cheseman, Chich. dio. Disp. for marriage in Joan's par. ch., the banns read once. 6s 8d.

23 Jo. Wanton & Ann Hubberde, of Sandwich, Cant. dio. Disp. for marriage without banns, but within the statutory time. 10s.

24 Ric. Leyghton & Eleanor Wigmore, of Norton, Cov. & Lich. dio. Disp. for marriage (3rd degree affin. & consang.). £6.

Jo. Tirrell, son & heir of Sir Jo. Tyrell (*sic*), esq., of Little Waverley, & Agnes Willys of the par. of St Dunstan-in-the-East, London. Disp. for marriage within the prohibited times. 20s.

23 Wm Acars, O.P. Disp. to wear the habit of his Order beneath that of a sec. pr. Gratis.

24 Jo. Byrde & Marg. Small, widow, of London. Disp. for marriage without banns. 10s.

f. 117^r

Jan. 25 Ralph Rudde, M.A., Fellow of the Qn's Coll., Oxford. Disp. to take all h.o. from any bp within the prohibited times. 26s 8d.

Mich. Lyster, esq., of the Kg's hsehld & Margery Horseman, gentw. Disp. for marriage without banns. 1os.

31 Ric. Mychell, O.P. Disp. to wear the habit of his Order beneath that of a sec. pr. Gratis.

Roger Sempere, pr., r. of Welford, Linc. dio. chapl. to Earl of Huntingdon. Disp. to hold a benef. with above, or 2 without it; permut. & non-res. cl. £6 1os.

Jo. Williams, recently fr., of Gloucester. Disp. to wear the habit of his Order beneath that of a sec. pr. Gratis.

Chris. Askew & Agnes Atkinson, Carl dio. Disp. for marriage (3rd & 4th degrees affin.). 'Conceditur gratis ob paupertatem.'

f. 117^v

Jo. Seyman, dcn, Ex dio. Disp. to take pr.'s orders although in his 24th yr & afterwards to hold a benef. with cure. 2os.

Rob. Nottell, O.S.B., of Norwich. Disp. to hold any benef. if granted his prior's consent, & to wear the habit of his Order beneath that of a sec. pr. £8.

Feb. 1 Ric. Dyson, B.A., subdcn, Worc. dio. Disp. to take dcn's & pr.'s orders within the prohibited times, on any day, from any bp. 13s 4d.

4 Jo. Irton, York dio., & Ann Dykes, Carl. dio. Disp. for marriage (4th degree consang.). 26s 8d.

Jan. 31 Wm Wydderley, r. of Barrow, Linc. dio. Disp. to hold a ch. with the above, of which the value p.a. is not over £8, or 2 others without. £4.

f. 118^r

Feb. 4 Wm Worthington & Frances Turrell, of London. Disp. for marriage within the prohibited times. 2os.

Jan. 10 Jas Longborowe, pr., recently monk of Garendon, Linc. dio. Disp. to hold a benef. with complete change of habit. Suppr.

13 Tho. Reynolds, v. of ?Pinhoe, or ?Upton Pyne ('Pyne') Ex. dio., Kg's chapl. Disp. to hold a benef. with the above, or 2 others without; permut. & non-res. cl. £6 1os.

20 Philip Brune, pr., chapl. of the free chapel of Stan[d]ford, Sarum dio. Disp. for non-res. for 2 yrs. 13s 4d; p.s.r. 5s.

Laurence Snell, pr., recently canon of Bilsington, Cant. dio. Disp. to hold a benef. with complete change of habit. Suppr.

Feb. 7 Wm Leys, acol., Cov. & Lich. dio. Disp. to take all h.o. within the prohibited times, if granted his diocesan's licence. 20s.

f. 118ᵛ

9 Gilbert Burne, M.A., Fellow of All Souls Coll., Oxford. Disp. to take all h.o. outside the statutory times & 2 on the same day & from any bp. 26s 8d.

12 Jo. Williamson *alias* Harwoide, monk of Kirkstead, Linc. dio. Disp. to hold any benef., if granted his abbot's consent. £4. Also for Jo. Wilson *alias* Mardersey. £4.

7 Jo. Deynt, acol., Cov. & Lich. dio. Disp. to take all h.o. outside the statutory times. 20s.

Jan. 17 Nich. Burton, r. of Stoke by Chichester. Disp. for non-res. during his illness, & for a month after recovery. 20s.

Feb. 28 Edw. Buxum, v. of Queensborough. Disp. to hold a benef. with the above, which does not yield over £8 p.a. £4.

13 Jo. King, sch., Sarum dio. Disp. to take subdcn's & dcn's orders (no cause given). 15s.

f. 119ʳ

14 Edw. Davys, sch., Lland. dio. Disp. to take all h.o. although in his 23rd yr & afterwards to hold a benef. 40s.

7 Jo. Pytman, acol., Bath & W. dio. Disp. to take subdcn's & dcn's orders on the same day. 15s.

12 Ric. Walton, recently canon of Norton, Cov. & Lich. dio. Disp. to hold a benef. with change of habit. Also for Roger Fletcher. Suppr.

Tho. Tolyt, canon of Bourne, Linc. dio. Similar disp. Suppr.

Ric. Toppes & Rob. Busshenden of ?Bushmead ('Bushendon'), Linc. dio. Similar disp.

f. 119ᵛ

Tho. Bulman, pr., recently prior of Weybourne, Norw. dio. Similar disp. Also for Jo. Froste, of the same priory. Suppr.

Wm Dycons, recently prior of Maxstoke, Cov. & Lich. dio. Similar disp. Also for Tho. Watts, Rob. Bushworthe, Roger Singleton. Suppr.

Arthur Seyntleger, recently prior of Leeds, Cant. dio. Similar disp. Gratis.

18 Rob. Falver, r. of Bramshott, Winton dio. Disp. for non-res. during his illness. 20s.

Reg. Hendra, v. of Cutbert, Cornwall. Similar disp.

1536 Nov. 30 Rob. Mortlake, r. of Foxearth, Lond. dio., chapl. to Viscount Lisle. Disp. to hold a benef. with the above; permut. cl. £6 10s.

f. 120ʳ

1537 Feb. 20 Wm Feylde, dcn, of London. Disp. to take pr.'s orders from any bp on any day within the prohibited times. 10s.

22 Hy Brome, acol., Lond. dio. Disp. to take all h.o. outside the statutory times. 20s.

Hy Sanderson, M.A., Fellow of St Jo.'s Coll., Cambridge. Disp. to take dcn's & pr.'s orders during the prohibited times. 13s 4d.

Wm Scollowe, acol., Worc. dio. Disp. to take all h.o. without l.d. 6s 8d.

1536 July 24 Francis Mallett, B.Th., r. of Swillington, York dio., v. of Roth-well. Disp. to hold a 3rd benef. £8.

Oct. 6 Jo. Killingbecke, recently of Holy Trinity, York. Disp. to hold a benef. with complete change of habit. Also for Rob. Evers, Wm Gryme, Ric. Stubbes, Ric. Stavele, Ric. Brome, Reg. Brinkisworthe, Rob. Beste, Oliver Warde. Suppr.

f. 120ᵛ

Sept. 30 Alex. Jennyns, recently canon of Drax, York dio. Disp. to hold a benef. with change of habit. Also for Jo. Humsley & Hy Johnson. Suppr.

Jo. Petyt, recently canon of Healaugh, York dio. Similar disp. Also for Wm Otfelde, Tho. Manelde, Jo. Buktrowte, Wm Chamber. Suppr.

Tho. Smythe, recently of Warter priory. Capacity to hold a benef. with complete change of habit. Also for Tho. Sprust, Jo. Balton, Wm Modye, Rob. Styman, Jo. Jackson, Hy Hanley. Suppr.

Nov. 1 Jo. Bawdwyn, recently of North Ferriby priory, York dio. Disp. to hold a benef. with change of habit. Also for Tho. Burghe, Tho. Andrew, Jo. See, Edw. Wydall, Jo. Yonge, Wm Calverde, Wm Seman. Suppr.

f. 121ʳ

1537 Feb. 20 Wm Basse, recently of Lethering[ham], Norw. dio. Similar disp. Also for Tho. Coke & Wm Walsingham. Suppr.

Ric. Wodill, recently monk of Quarr, Isle of Wight. Similar disp. Also for Ric. Purlee, Rob. Barkeley, Ric. Bathe, Tho. Wartham, Tho. London. Suppr.

1536 Oct.   6 Rob. Collynson, recently of Haltemprice priory, York dio. Similar disp. Also for Hy Taylor, Jo. Foston, Edm. Bucke, Rob. Johnson, Bartholomew Lylforth, Jo. Smythe, Ric. Wagar, Jo. Hewson. Suppr.

Hy Colson, recently canon of Marton, York dio. Similar disp.   • Suppr.

f. 121ᵛ

1537 Feb.   20 Tho. Aglionbye *alias* Nickson, reg. canon, r. of Bewcastle, Carl. dio. Disp. to wear the habit of his Order beneath that of a sec. pr. £4.

23 Tho. Wheler, r. of Tunstall, Norw. dio. Disp. to resign the above ch., for certain valid reasons, & to arrange for a suitable person to administer it with an annual pension.   10s.

24 Stephen Prowett, chapl. to the Duke of Suffolk; celebrant of an annual service in the par. ch. of St Peter, Norwich. Disp. to hold a benef. as well as the above, or 2 without; no non-res. cl. £6 10s.

1536 Sept. 10 Rob. Tewkisbury, recently monk of St Oswald's Gloucester. Disp. to hold a benef. with change of habit. Also for Nich. Newman, Tho. Bristowe, Geo. Evessham, Walter Abington, Tho. Alston. Suppr.

f. 122ʳ

1537 Feb.   15 Joan Stanforde, recently nun of Harrold priory, Linc. dio. Disp. to leave the religious life. Also for Eliz. Knyghton & Eleanor Hale. Suppr.

20 Hy Wydon, recently prior of Llanthony, Lland. dio. Disp. to hold a benef. with change of habit.

Wm Lakenham, recently monk of Bromholm, Norw. dio. Similar disp. Also for Wm Atwode, Jo. Marten, Humfrey Seysull, Tho. Norwiche. Suppr.

25 Jo. Collen recently monk of Ipswich ('Gypsincham'), Norw. dio. Similar disp. as above. Also for Jo. Elles, Jo. Smyth, 'Besonn' Wright. Suppr.

28 Hy Basingborne, canon of Woodbridge, Norw. dio. Capacity. Also for Wm Lycham, Tho. Spendley, Wm Pope, Wm Dawneby. Suppr.

f. 122ᵛ

Mar.   1 Tho. Tutbury, recently abbot of Stoneley, Cov. & Lich. dio. Disp. to hold a benef. with change of habit. Also for Jo. Knyver, Jo. Cotton, Hy Tanworthe, Jo. Morton, Wm Bulkington, Jo. Grace. Suppr.

Mar. 1 Agnes Lytle, recently nun of Wroxall, Worc. dio. Disp. to leave the religious life. Also for Jane Shakesper, Dorothy Brown, Eliz. Squyer. Suppr.

Jo. Adamson, recently monk of the priory of Coxford, Norw. dio. Disp. to hold a benef. with change of habit. Also for Jo. Grey & Jo. White. Suppr.

Feb. 28 Wm Dalham, recently canon of Studley, Worc. dio. Disp. to hold a benef. with change of habit. Also for Wm Coughton, Wm Warwyke, Wm Hampton, Wm Tutby, Wm Hunt, Rob. & Ric. Dewhurst. Suppr.

f. 123ʳ

Mar. 1 Wm Rypon, v. or governor of the chapel of Carisbrook Castle, Isle of Wight, Winton dio. Disp. to hold a benef. with the above, or 2 without; permut. cl. £6 10s.

5 Tho. Mason, dcn, Heref. dio. Disp. to take pr.'s orders from any bp outside the statutory times. 10s.

Ethelbert Styce, dcn, Heref. dio. Disp. to take pr.'s orders within the prohibited times. 10s.

7 Jo. Warner, M.D. Disp. to take all h.o. within the prohibited times & 2 on the same day. 26s 8d.

14 Ric. Mooke, pr., r. of Swynecombe, Linc. dio. Disp. for non-res. during his illness, & for 6 months after recovery. 20s; p.s.r. 5s.

f. 123ᵛ

9 Grace Sampson, recently nun of Redlingfield, Norw. dio. Disp. to leave the religious life. Also for Joan Smythe, Joan Deane, Alice Redlingfield, Ann Drury, Agnes Nicholas, Joan Pettewell. Suppr.

10 Wm Dale, recently prior of St Olave's (Herringfleet), Norw. dio. Disp. to hold a benef. with change of habit. Also for Jo. Meke, Jo. Piggolle, Hy Harison, Jo. Cever, Wm Rooke, Jo. Dale. Suppr. Gratis.

12 Rob. Codde, recently prior of Pentney, Nor. dio. Disp. to hold a benef. with change of habit. Also for Ric. Bongyn, Jo. Chaunde-ler, Jo. Smythe, Stephen Longe, Tho. Lytell, Gilbert Seyman, Chris. Wode, Wm Barry. Suppr.

f. 124ʳ

13 Jo. Barnardiston, r. of Gt Coates, Linc. dio., incumbent of Ketton, Norw. dio. Disp. to hold a benef. with above, or any 2 others; permut. cl. £8.

Mar. 14 Margery Studfelde, recently nun of Crabhouse, Linc. dio. Disp. to leave the religious life. Also for Agnes Smythe, Cecily Brandley, Emma Taillour. Suppr.

16 Tho. Channte, Bath & W. dio. Disp. to take all h.o. & 2 on the same day. 26s 8d.

20 Ric. Loghor & Eliz. Mathew, Lland. dio. Disp. for marriage (4th degree consang.). 26s 8d.

21 Ric. ap Edward & Sabell ap Jenn, Bangor dio. Disp. for marriage (4th degree consang.). Arb. 13s 4d.

f. 124ᵛ

Ric. Holden sch., Chich dio. Disp. to take all h.o. & 2 on the same day. 26s 8d.

20 Wm Dyngley, M.A. Disp. to take dcn's & pr.'s orders outside the statutory times & on the same day. 10s.

Ric. Furness & Agnes Made, York dio. Disp. for marriage (3rd & 4th degrees affin.). 30s.

24 Jo. Goller, pr., r. of Spargrave, Bath & W. dio. Disp. for non-res. on account of illness, & for 6 months after recovery. 20s.

27 Ant. Dale & Cristine Ferande, York dio. Disp. for marriage (4th degree affin.). 26s 8d.

Geo. Constantine, creation as public notary & tabellion. 13s 4d.

f. 125ʳ

20 Wm Paynell, B.Th., r. of Shelton, Linc. dio. Disp. to hold a benef. with the above, or 2 without. £6 10s.

Lewis Thomas, pr., recently of Margam, Lland. dio. Disp. to hold a benef. with change of habit. Suppr.

1536 Aug. 31 Wm Love, pr., recently abbot of Coggeshall, Lond. dio. Disp. to hold any benef.; permut. & non-res. cl. £4 10s.

1537 Mar. 20 Jo. Clerke, pr., M.Th., monk of Westminster. Disp. to hold a benef. with complete change of habit. £12. Also for Jo. Gorton, also M.Th. of Westminster. £12.

27 Edw. Karne, esq., & Ly Anne Raglan, widow. Disp. for marriage (3rd & 4th degrees affin.) & without banns. 30s; 10s.

f. 125ᵛ

15 Agnes Coke, recently nun of the priory of St Giles in the Wood (Flamstead), Linc. dio. Disp. to leave the religious life. Also for Agnes Verney, Agnes Weste, Alice Thorle, Joan Richards. Suppr.

Mar. 20 Edw. Barlas & Joan Bolney, of London. Disp. for marriage (2nd & 3rd degrees affin.). £8.

31 Tho. Tyntaine, monk of Tintern, Lland. dio. Disp. to hold a benef. with change of habit. Also for Wm Gloucester. Suppr.

Apr. 1 Chris. Smythe, recently prior of Whalley. Disp. to hold a benef. with complete change of habit. Also for Tho. Horowode, Jas More, Wm Chatborne, Ric. Woode, Ric. Marstyn, Rob. Parys, Jo. Foster, Wm Worlde, Jo. Holden, Ric. Moreton, Miles Whitacre, Hy Clydero, Ralph Caterwall. Suppr.

f. 126ʳ

Ric. Watson, recently of Hexham priory, York dio. Disp. to hold a benef. with change of habit. Also for Geo. Heynemers & Rob. Still. Suppr.

7 Edw. Fayrechilde & Cath. Broke. Disp. for marriage without banns. 10s.

10 Rob. Beste, r. of Metheringham, Linc. dio., chapl. to the Earl of Rutland. Disp. to hold a benef. with the above or 2 without. £6 10s.

Ric. ap Rice, pr., recently monk of Conway, St Asaph dio. Disp. to hold a benef. with change of habit. Also for Jo. Porter, Tho. Burtall, David Vaughan. Suppr.

Edw. Smythe, sch., Cov. & Lich. dio. Disp. to take h.o. & hold a benef. with cure of souls, although he is deformed in the right foot or shin. 40s.

f. 126ᵛ

Sebastian Bony & Matilda Vyncent, of London. Disp. for marriage without banns. 10s.

Tho. Pyrton, M.A., v. of Aldeburgh, Norw. dio. Disp. also to be v. of Southminster, Lond. dio. as he asserts its value is not over £8 p.a., & to hold several other benefices. £4. 'Ultra medietatem beneficii uniti medietas £5.'

11 Geo. Gower, of London dio., & Ann Statham, of Sutton, Cant. dio. Disp. for marriage without banns. 10s.

12 Rees ap Robert & Gwenlyan verch David. Disp. for marriage (4th degree consang.). 26s 8d.

Tho. Kinge, B.Cn.L., r. of Fenny Drayton, Linc. dio. Disp. to hold a benef. with cure with the above or 2 without; permut. & non-res. cl. £6 10s.

f. 127ʳ

12 Walter Thorneham, pr., recently monk of Horsham St Faith, Norw. dio. Disp. to hold a benef. with change of habit. Suppr.

Apr. 12 Tho. Mason, recently canon of Combwell, Cant. dio. Similar disp.

Hy White, pr., recently monk of St Radegund's, Cant. dio. Similar disp. Also for Jo. Russell, Wm Mercer, Hy Ham.

Jo. Haselden & Marg. Parteridge, Winton dio. Disp. for marriage without banns. 10s.

14 Alex. Fawcett & Christabelle Blande, York dio. Disp. for marriage (4th degree consang.). 26s 8d.

15 Wm Forman & Joan Eylande. Disp. for marriage without banns. 10s.

f. 127ᵛ

16 Wm Potkyn, literate, Cant. dio. Disp. to practise as notary & tabellion. 13s 4d.

17 Jo. Flecher & Joan Love, Cov. & Lich. dio. Disp. for marriage (Jo.'s father was Joan's godfather). 30s.

Tho. Starkey & Joan Hudson, of Bowden, Cov. & Lich. dio. Disp. for marriage (Joan's father was Tho.'s sponsor at his confirmation). 26s 8d.

18 Edw. Griffith, acol., Heref. dio. Disp. to take all h.o., within the prohibited times, 2 on the same day. 26s 8d.

Ric. Gostwike, B.Cn. & C.L., r. of West Thorneton & Ingatestone ('Ingreston'), London dio. Disp. for non-res. during illness & 6 months after recovery. 20s.

20 Ant. Bustarde & Melicent Hawton, Linc. dio. Disp. for marriage in Melicent's par. ch. without banns. 10s.

f. 128ʳ

10 Tho. Piell, pr., recently monk of Tintern, Lland. dio. Disp. to hold a benef., with change of habit. Also for Wm Hopkyns, Tho. Robyns, Wm Machyn. Suppr.

Walter Godlive, pr., recently monk of Horton, Cant. dio. Disp. to hold a benef. with change of habit. Also for Nich. Colles, Edw. Owtered, Jo. Myles, Wm Hudson. Suppr.

12 Rob. Game, recently monk of Clifford, Heref. dio. Similar disp. Also for Rob. Hewardyn, Nich. Hewes *alias* Thomas. Suppr.

Tho. Parks, recently monk of Buildwas. Similar disp. Also for Tho. Leydyate & Ric. Cramer. Suppr.

Mar. 20 Tho. Herman, recently novice of Buildwas. Similar disp. Also for Ric. Smythe & Tho. Hothe also novices. Suppr.

f. 128ᵛ

Apr. 24 Chris. Grene & Mary Danby, York dio. Disp. for marriage (Jane Danby, sister of Mary, was previously betrothed to Chris.). 26s 8d.

25 Tho. Bigge & Alice Fynche, Linc. dio. Disp. for marriage (Tho.'s mother was Alice's godmother). 20s.

24 Wm Cooke, acol., Cov. & Lich. dio. Disp. to take all h.o. outside the statutory times. 20s.

25 Wm Grace, pr., r. of Langham, Lond. dio. Disp. for non-res. for 2 yrs. 13s 4d.

26 Edm. Pergeter, r. of Farthinghoe ('Faringo'), Linc. dio. Disp. for non-res. for 2 yrs on account of gout & paralysis, provided a suitable pr. is put in charge. 13s 4d.

f. 129ʳ

Mar. 20 Tho. Mylis, recently prior of Boxgrove. Disp. to hold a benef. with change of habit. Also for Tho. Mason, Ric. Combys, Ric. Hedde, Jas Ryman, Jo. White. Suppr.

Geo. Walden, recently prior of Shulbrede. Disp. to hold a benef. with change of habit. Also for Jo. Stany, Laurence Weste. Suppr.

Tho. Mey, recently monk of Tortington. Similar disp. Also for Wm Bremer, Hy Ringwode, Geo. Kington, Jas Stidall. Suppr.

Tho. Holben, recently monk of Michelham. Similar disp. Also for Tho. Bucke, Edw. Pelham, Rob. Forde, Martin Cater, Rob. Motte, Wm Couper, Jo. Browne. Suppr.

f. 129ᵛ

Apr. 10 Eliz. Sydney, recently nun of Rusper. Disp. to leave the religious life. Also for Eliz. Hayes.

Tho. Gayes, recently monk of Morgan. Disp. to hold a benef. with change of habit. Also for Jo. Morice. Suppr.

6 Helen Buttery, recently nun of Campsey (Ash) priory. Disp. to leave the religious life. Also for Barbara Sheringham, Alice Cooke, Eliz. Norwiche, Marg. Backon, Eliz. Wyngfelde, Cath. Logen, Ursula Heydon, Parnella Felton, Kath. Grome, Brigitt Cockett, Ann Bardewell, Ann Wynterhey, Christine Avell, Dorothy Brampton, Kath. Blomflede, Ann Butteler, Marg. Cherke. Suppr.

f. 130ʳ

Mar. 3 Rob. Holgate, Master of the Order of Sempringham, Prior of Watton. Disp. (given in full) to retain the above offices as Bp of Llandaff, as by special royal licence & nomination, or to hold any other additional benefices provided the cure of souls is not neglected. 'Taxatur Arbitrio Domini Cancellarii Anglie et Archiepiscopi Cantuariensis ad summam £80.'

f. 130ᵛ

Apr. 20 Percival Giles & Marg. Haisgill, Carl. dio. Disp. for marriage (4th degree consang.). 26s 8d.

26 Wm Parker & Alice Thesdale, York dio. Disp. for marriage (3rd & 4th degrees consang.). 30s.

Hoell ap David ap John & Helen verch Henry, St David's dio. Disp. for marriage (4th degree consang.). 26s 8d.

28 Wm Wray & Eliz. Sympson, York dio. Disp. for marriage (3rd & 4th degrees consang.). 30s.

29 Lewis ap Rice, subdcn, Lland. dio. Disp. to take dcn's & pr.'s orders within the prohibited times. 13s 4d.

30 Hy Malerents, subdcn, York dio. Disp. to take dcn's & pr.'s orders from any bp, outside the statutory times. 13s 4d.

f. 131ʳ

Mar. 31 Tho. More, pr., recently monk of Thornholme, Linc. dio. Disp. to hold a benef. with change of habit. Also for Tho. Bushope. Suppr.

Apr. 20 Edm. Stanforde, monk of Furness, v. of Millom, York dio. Disp. to wear the habit of a reg. beneath that of a sec. pr. £4.

Jo. Turnor, recently canon of (Little) Wymondley, Linc. dio. Disp. to hold a benef. with change of habit. Also for Jo. Henley, Ric. Isode, Wm Stoketon. Suppr.

Roger Eltryngham, pr., monk of St Mary's, Stratford (Langthorne), Lond. dio. Disp. to hold any benef. & wear the habit of his Order beneath that of a sec. pr. £8.

Tho. Hayle, recently monk of Barlings. Disp. to hold a benef. with change of habit. Also for Chris. Patrike, Hy Thirnbeke, Ric. Byrkett. Suppr.

f. 131ᵛ

Mar. 20 Wm Southwell, recently prior of Hurley. Disp. to hold a benef., with change of habit. Suppr.

Tho. Basse, recently monk of Leiston, Norw. dio. Similar disp. Also for Jo. Grene. Suppr.

Apr. 20 Maurice Griffithe, B.Th., v. of Sutton, Roch. dio. Disp. to hold 2 benefices with or 3 without the above; permut. & non-res. cl. £9.

30 Chris. Greneside & Eliz. Couper, York dio. Disp. for marriage (Chris. was godfather to Eliz.'s child). £6.

May 1 Wm Willowbye & Eliz. Baskerfilde of the par. of St Mary, Lambeth, Winton dio. Disp. for marriage, the banns read once. 6s 8d.

f. 132ʳ

Edw. Smythe, sch., Cov. & Lich. dio. Disp. to take all h.o. within the prohibited times. 20s.

Reg. Keyns & Alice Harbyns, Carl. dio. Disp. for marriage, the banns read once. 6s 8d.

2 Jo. Abbott & Joan Saunders, Linc. dio. Disp. for marriage (3rd & 4th degrees consang.). 30s.

4 Reg. Williams & Eleanor Newport, Heref. dio. Disp. for marriage (3rd & 4th degrees affin.). 30s.

5 Chris. Litcott, esq., & Cath. Cheyney, gentw. Disp. for marriage without banns. 10s.

f. 132ᵛ

1 Ric. Breten, recently monk of Royston, Norw. dio. Disp. to hold a benef. with change of habit. Also for Jo. Manntre, Jo. Welles, Alex. Stokes, Ric. Alleson, Tho. Sykes, Tho. Warde. Suppr.

2 Christina Browne, recently nun of St Mary of Carrow, Norw. dio. Disp. to leave the religious life. Suppr.

4 Jo. Clerke & Agnes Barde, Linc. dio. Disp. for marriage (Jo. was godfather to Agnes' child). £6.

Ralph Jackson & Marg. Whitacre, of Prestwich, Cov. & Lich. dio. Disp. for marriage (3rd degree affin.). £6.

Nich. Lincoln, r. of Brampton, chapl. to Duke of Suffolk. Disp. to hold a benef. with the above, or 2 without; permut. cl. £6 10s.

f. 133ʳ

Tho. ap Allen & Jane verch David, of Llanbeay (*sic*), St David's dio. Disp. for marriage (4th degree affin.). 26s 8d.

Geo. (Walker), recently abbot of Louth Park, Linc. dio. Disp. to hold a benef. with change of habit. Also for Tho. Lilborne, Jo. Bydall, Wm Kelsaye. Suppr.

Apr. 20 Tho. Penell, v. of Hertbury, Worc. dio., chapl. to Jo., Bp of Carlisle. Disp. to hold a benef. with or 2 without the above; permut. cl. £6 10s.

22 Alice Femme, recently nun of Stixwould, Linc. dio. Disp. to leave the religious life. Suppr.

26 Alice Hawker, nun of Aconbury, Heref. dio. Disp. to leave the religious life. Also for Joyce Morebet, Marg. Touneshend. Suppr.

f. 133v

30 Chris. Bolton, pr., recently prior of Felley, York dio. Disp. to hold a benef., with change of habit. Also for Jas Twistfelde, Ric. Longe, Wm Leycester. Suppr.

May 4 Ric. Sutton, recently monk of Kirkstead, Linc. dio. Disp. to hold a benef. with change of habit. Also for Wm Curtes, Ric. Arnolde, Tho. Kendell, Rob. Mede, Leonard Lunde, Francis Kirby, Rob. Brikehed, Jo. Parkyn, Rob. Horsehed, Jo. Tatsall, Rob. Apley. Suppr.

10 Wm Burton, pr., recently monk of Barlings, Linc. dio. Disp. to hold a benef. with change of habit. Suppr.

Chris. Crumboke, recently monk of Whalley. Disp. to hold a benef. with change of habit. Also for Tho. Hokeson, & Jas Michell. Suppr.

11 Wm Johnson & Agnes Harys, of London. Disp. for marriage within the prohibited times and without banns. 20s; 10s.

f. 134r

May 12 Hy Burges & Alice Bettis, Norw. dio. Disp. for marriage without banns. 10s.

Jo. Laysbye & Agnes Yonge, Linc. dio. Disp. for marriage (Agnes Laysbye *alias* Scudall, sometime wife of Jo., was Agnes' godmother). £8.

Ann Smyth, recently nun of Sopwell, nr St Alban's, Linc. dio. Disp. to leave the religious life. Suppr.

Wm Tailbois, v. of Billinghay, Linc. dio. & Gisburn, York dio. Disp. for non-res. during illness. 20s.

Wm Hethroth, sch., Cov. & Lich. dio. Disp. to take all h.o. without l.d. & 2 on the same day. 6s 8d; 26s 8d.

Jo. Tyther, acol., Worc. dio. Disp. to take all h.o. within the prohibited times 2 on the same day, without l.d. from his diocesan. 26s 8d; 6s 8d.

f. 134^v

May 8 Chris. Roche, pr., O.P., recently of Bristol, Bath & W. dio. Disp. to change his habit for that of a sec. pr. £4.

9 Alice Hanker, recently nun of Aconbury, Heref. dio. Disp. to leave the religious life. Also for Ann Grow, Joyce Mores, Cecily Asshe, Matilda Apie, Marg. Touneshend. Suppr.

Edm. Huntt & Eliz. Hopkyns, Cov. & Lich. dio. Disp. for marriage (4th degree consang. or affin.). 26s 8d.

10 Kenelm Deen, M.A., r. of Stanton, Worc. dio. Disp. to hold a benef. with cure with or 2 without the above; permut. cl. £6 10s.

Roger Hughes, B.Cn.L., v. of Mathon, Worc. dio. Disp. to hold a benef. with or 2 without the above; permut. cl. £6 10s.

Tho. Merbury, v. of Feltham, Lond. dio. Disp. for non-res. for 2 yrs. 13s 4d.

f. 135^r

12 Hy Jaggis & Cecily Leonarde, Norw. dio. Disp. for marriage (Hy was godfather to a child of Cecily). £6.

10 Brian Gardner, pr., recently prior of Furness, York dio. Disp. to hold a benef. with change of habit. Also for Jo. Thorneton, Jo. Grene, Jo. Harington, Michael Thornbroe, Ric. Bussyn, Mathew Kirbie, Jo. Setell, Jo. Trougton, Holmo (*sic*) Coltram, Roger Preston, Hugh Browne, Jas Bancliff, Chris. Carre, Wm Newerke, Antony Plummer, Jas Forester, Chris. Mashorder, Wm Barwyke, Wm Ridge, Chris. Whalley, Giles Bolande, Stephen Skipton, Wm Forest, Ric. Martindale, Rob. Kechyn, Stephen Standforthe, Edw. Blomer, Tho. Snell, Roger Waller, Rob. Legate. Suppr.

f. 135^v

Edw. Downnys & Marg. Broke, Cov. & Lich. dio. Disp. for marriage (Marg. was sponsor at the confirmation of a child of Edw.). 30s.

Wm Dawson & Margery Kell, York dio. Disp. validating their marriage (contracted in ignorance of 3rd degree affin. & Wm's mother having been Margery's godmother). 'Remittitur gratis ob paupertatem.'

15 Tho. Eynsworth, acol., Cov. & Lich. dio. Disp. to take all h.o. outside the statutory times. 20s.

16 Ric. Gifforde, gent., & Eliz. Godfrey, of London. Disp. for marriage without banns. 10s.

May 17 Wm Lymbry, sch., Sarum dio. Disp. to take all h.o. within the prohibited times. 26s 8d.

f. 136^r

18 Jo. & Eliz. Mottershed, Cov. & Lich. dio. Disp. for marriage (4th degree consang.). 26s 8d.

16 Ric. Thomas & Helen verch Morgan, St David's dio. Disp. for marriage (3rd & 4th degrees affin.). 30s.

10 Jas Jacobbe & Denisa Rightwise, of London. Disp. for marriage without banns, not in their par. ch. 10s; 10s.

14 Geo. Trappys of London & Isabella Boughton, of Woolwich, Roch. dio. Disp. for marriage without banns. 10s.

Tho. Ryvett, M.A. Disp. to take all h.o. within the prohibited times. 20s.

f. 136^v

20 Ric. Abrighton, pr., recently monk of Abbey Dore, Heref. dio. Disp. to hold a benef. with complete change of habit. Also for Ric. Burforde, Jo. Dydebroke, Ralph Westbye, Wm Marbye. Suppr.

Jo. Sharp, recently prior of Birkenhead, Cov. & Lich. dio. Disp. to hold a benef. with complete change of habit. Also for Ric. Chester, Wm Lyrpole, Tho. Tassy, Wm Hereforde. Suppr.

Maurice Johne, recently prior of Pill, St David's dio. Disp. to hold a benef. with change of habit. Suppr.

Wm Stansfelde, v. of Conisborough, York dio., chapl. to Ld Windsor. Disp. to hold a benef. with the above, or 2 without; permut. & non-res. cl. £7 13s 4d.

30 Ric. Wright, pr., recently canon of Norton, Cov. & Lich. dio., v. of Burton-on-Stather, Linc. dio. Disp. to wear the habit of his Order beneath that of a sec. pr. £4.

f. 137^r

20 Roderic Johns, recently abbot of Talley, St David's dio. Disp. to hold a benef. with change of habit. Also for Jo. Grifithe, Jo. Leades. Suppr.

Wm Jerome, pr., monk of Cant. cath. Disp. to hold a benef. with complete change of habit. Gratis.

9 Rob. Cooke, r. of Freiston, Norw. dio. Disp. for non-res. for 2 yrs. 13s 4d.

26 Ric. Johns, sch., Heref. dio. Disp. to take all h.o. within the prohibited times & 2 on 1 day. 26s 8d.

May 30 Jenn ap Thomas & Joan verch Rice, St David's dio. Disp. for marriage (3rd & 4th degrees affin.). 30s.

31 Ric. Smythe & Joan Scele, Winton dio. Disp. for marriage (4th degree consang.). 26s 8d.

f. 137^v

26 Jo. Ledell, acol., Durham dio. Disp. to take all h.o. within the prohibited times. 20s.

30 Wm Overton, v. of St Alkmund, Shrewsbury, Cov. & Lich. dio. Disp. to hold a benef. with or 2 without the above; permut. cl. £6 10s.

31 Rob. Radforde, pr., recently prior of Birkenhead, Cov. & Lich. dio. Disp. to hold a benef. with change of habit. Also for Hugh Hill & Tho. Maundisley. Suppr.

June 3 Tho. Bidchell & Joan Stanbridge. Disp. for marriage (Joan's father was Tho.'s godfather). 30s.

4 Jo. Wynde & Joan Evans, Worc. or Heref. dio. Disp. for marriage (Jo. was godfather to a child of Joan). Arb. £4.

8 Tho. Gweylym & Leckye verch Hoell, Lland. dio. Disp. for marriage (4th degree double consang.). 50s.

f. 138^r

7 Rob. Strowdill, O.P. Disp. to hold any benef. while retaining his habit & profession as a religious. £4.

Jo. Foster, B.Th., v. of Steeple Aston, Sarum dio. Disp. to hold a benef. with the above, or 3 without them, provided not more than 2 are par. churches; permut. & non-res. cl. £9.

8 Jo. Williams & Alice Hughes, Lland. dio. Disp. for marriage (3rd & 4th degrees affin.). 30s.

9 Gregory Warren & Kath. Fitzjeffrey, Linc. dio. Disp. for marriage without banns & not in their par. ch. 10s; 10s.

Wm Mather & Marg. Barlow, Cov. & Lich. dio. Disp. for marriage (4th degree consang.). 26s 8d.

Tho. Sawre & Marg. Couper, York dio. Disp. for marriage (3rd & 4th degrees consang.). 30s.

f. 138^v

3 Eliz. Savage, Poor Clare nun of the Minories, Aldgate, London. Disp. to become Abbess of the above hse despite defect of birth. £4.

8 Jo. Quarrt, archdcn of Llandaff. Disp. to depute to a suitable person the office of visitor of the archdcnry; 2, 3, or 4 churches

to be visited on a single day & the usual procurations received. 40s; p.s.r. 5s.

June 9 Chris. Haryson & Mabel Holme, York dio. Disp. for marriage (3rd & 4th degrees affin.). 30s.

10 Jo. Griffiths, recently abbot of Grace Dieu, South Wales. Disp. to hold a benef. with change of habit. Suppr.

11 Jo. Newton & Joan Fuller, Ely dio. Disp. for marriage (3rd & 4th degrees consang.). 30s.

f. 139ʳ

9 Ralph Swynslerste & Alice Parker, York dio. Disp. for marriage (3rd degree consang.). Arb. 40s.

10 Tho. Elington, pr., recently monk of Wendling, Norw. dio. Disp. to hold a benef. with change of habit. Suppr.

12 Tho. Elis, O.P., of Sudbury. Disp. to hold a benef. & retain his habit. £4.

13 Hugh ap Richarde Gombey & Kath. verch John ap David. Heref. dio. Disp. confirming their marriage (contracted in ignorance of 4th degree consang.). 26s 8d.

14 Chris. Grene, Bath & W. dio. Disp. to take all h.o. outside the statutory time & 2 on the same day. 26s 8d.

15 Jo. Haslum & Joan Longworthe, Cov. & Lich. dio. Disp. for marriage (4th degree consang.). Gratis.

f. 139ᵛ

10 Inhabitants of Birlingham, a hamlet in the par. of Nafford, Worc. dio. Disp. as they are accustomed to receive the sacraments in the chapel of Birlingham, but to bury their dead at Pershore Abbey, to bury at Birlingham on account of the distance to Pershore also the bad weather & state of the roads in winter. 13s 4d; p.s.r. 5s.

15 Wm Gibson, Cov. & Lich. dio. Disp. to take all h.o. within the prohibited times. 20s.

17 Jo. Horowode & Agnes Rande, of London. Disp. for marriage without banns & not in their par. ch. 10s; 10s.

Hugh Fenne & Agnes Leson. Disp. for marriage without banns. 10s.

f. 140ʳ

20 Jo. Chayney & Marg. Rolffe, Cant. dio. Disp. for marriage (3rd & 3rd degrees affin.). £6.

June 20 Jo. Tayler, B.Th., r. of St Peter's, Cornhill, London, Kg's chapl. Disp. to hold a benef. with or 2 without the above; non-res. or permut. cl. £7 13s 4d.

Wm Bothe, r. of Cradley, Heref. dio. chapl. to Bp of Roch. Disp. to hold a benef. with or 2 without the above. £6 10s.

Wm Laken recently monk of Abbey Cwmhir, St David's dio. Disp. to hold a benef. with change of habit. Suppr.

Ric. Ewer, B.Th., r. of ?Horkesley ('Hartusey'), Lond. dio. Disp. to hold a benef. with or 2 without the above; permut. cl. £6 10s.

f. 140ᵛ

22 Wm Houldefelde & Jane Waterhouse, York dio. Disp. for marriage (3rd & 4th degrees consang.). 30s.

Jo. Carington & Helen Bothe. Disp. for marriage (4th degree consang.). 26s 8d.

23 Jo. Michell & Helen Talkys, Linc. dio. Disp. for marriage (Jo.'s father was Helen's godfather). 30s.

Wm Perpoynt, r. of Holme, York dio. Disp. to take h.o. without l.d. from his diocesan bp. 6s 8d.

24 Wm Nedeham & Marg. Garlecke, Cov. & Lich. dio. Disp. for marriage (4th degree consang.). 26s 8d.

f. 141ʳ

26 Chris. Conyers & Mary Bulmar, Durham dio. Disp. legitimizing their marriage (contracted in ignorance of 4th & 4th degrees consang.). 26s 8d.

Joyce Bikerley, recently nun of Catesby, Linc. dio. Disp. to leave the religious life. Suppr.

Laurence Coocks *alias* Maure, recently O.S.B., of Glastonbury. Disp. to change his habit. Gratis.

28 Rob. Clerke & Isabella Furthe, Lond. dio. Disp. for marriage without banns. 10s.

Jo. Philipp & Joan verch Morgan. Disp. for marriage outside Lland. dio. (4th & 4th degrees consang.). 26s 8d.

Jo. Wolseley, r. of Ecton, Linc. dio. Disp. to take all h.o., 2 on the same day, within the prohibited times. 26s 8d.

f. 141ᵛ

30 Edm. Millum & Helen Lyster, Carl. dio. Disp. for marriage (4th & 4th degrees consang.). 26s 8d.

June 30 Wm Richardson & Marg. Browne, York dio. Disp. for marriage (3rd & 4th degrees consang.). 30s.

July   1 Peter & Agnes Birkhed, York dio. Disp. for marriage (3rd & 4th degrees consang.). 30s.

       2 Rob. ap Robert ap Hoell & Marg. verch Robert ap Tuder, St Asaph dio. Disp. for marriage (4th & 4th degrees consang.). 26s 8d.

Jo. Worthall, B.Cn.L., v. of Sutton & Northiam 'Northundam', Chich. dio. Disp. to hold another benef. with Sutton, not Nordiam. £4.

f. 142ʳ

June 30 Wm Gales, pr., recently canon of Langley, Norw. dio. Disp. to hold another benef. with change of habit. Suppr.

Nich. Daws, recently canon of Wombridge, Cov. & Lich. dio. Disp. to hold a benef. with change of habit. Suppr.

Gilbert Shier, recently monk of Swineshead, Linc. dio. Disp. to hold a benef. with change of habit. Suppr.

Ric. Aston, recently prior of Ronton, Cov. & Lich. dio. Disp. to receive a benef. with change of habit. Also for Rob. Parker, Ralph Corke, Jo. Olde, Ric. Forster. Suppr.

Jo. Brasonall, recently canon of Trentham, Cov. & Lich. dio. Disp. to hold a benef. with change of habit. Also for Alex. Foxe, Jo. Elysmar, Tho. Lagart, Jo. Fysher, Jo. Copenall. Suppr.

f. 142ᵛ

July   4 Humfrey Wilks & Kath. Cooke, Heref. dio. Disp. for marriage (Kath.'s father was Humfrey's godfather). 30s.

Jo. Flemyn & Kath. Johns, Lland. dio. Disp. for marriage (4th & 4th degrees consang.). 26s 8d.

       5 Ld Rob. Ogle & Jane Radcliff, gentw., Durham dio. Disp. for marriage (3rd & 4th degrees affin.). 30s.

Jo. Knottisforde, of the Kg's hsehld, & Jane Lumbey. Disp. for marriage without banns. 10s.

Wm Sadler *alias* Jane, Sarum dio. Disp. to take all h.o. within the prohibited times & 2 on the same day. 26s 8d.

       6 Rob. Marshall, reg. canon, v. of Chatton, Durham dio. Disp. to wear the habit of his Order beneath that of a sec. pr. £4.

f. 143ʳ

       9 Ric. Couper, Durham dio., & Joan Gregory, Linc. dio. Disp. for marriage (Ric.'s mother was Joan's godmother). 30s.

July 10 Ralph Chamberleyne, son 7 heir of Edw. Chamberleyne & Eliz. Chamberleyne, Norw. dio. Disp. for marriage without banns. 10s.

Tho. Carington & Eliz. Bettye, Cant. dio. Disp. for marriage without banns. 10s.

Hy Saulpter, recently prior of Hempton, Norw. dio. Disp. to hold a benef. with change of habit. Suppr.

Tho. Day, v. of Bocking, Bath & W. dio. Disp. to hold any benef., if value is not over £8 p.a.

Jo. ap Griff & Kath verch Lewes, St Asaph dio. Disp. validating marriage (contracted in ignorance of 3rd degree affin.). Arb. £4.

f. 143ᵛ

Ric. Fenton, O.P. Disp. to become a sec. pr., & wear the habit of his Order beneath that of a sec. pr. £4.

11 Francis Stockedale & Alice Clavell, Sarum dio. Disp. for marriage (3rd & 4th degrees consang.). 30s.

Jo. Atkinson & Joan Melson, Dent, York dio. Disp. for marriage (3rd & 4th degrees consang.). 30s.

Jo. Balkehurst & Marg. Johnson, Cov. & Lich. dio. Disp. for marriage (3rd & 3rd degrees consang.). Arb. 53s 4d.

Laurence Wodewarde & Grace Tayler, Cov. & Lich. dio. Disp. for marriage (3rd & 4th degrees affin.). 30s.

Ric. Dale & Joan Low, Heref. dio. Disp. for marriage (3rd & 4th degrees consang.). 30s.

f. 144ʳ

12 Sir Wm Penyzon, of the Kg's hsehld, & Ly Ann Noris, widow of Sir Lionell Noris. Disp. for marriage in Ly Ann's par. ch. without banns. 10s.

Jo. Yonge, O.F.M. Disp. to become a sec. pr., wearing the habit of his Order beneath that of a sec. pr. Gratis.

16 Chris. Bikerdale, clk. under the jurisdiction of the archdcn of York. Confirmation of absolution for censures and relaxation of functions, on account of adultery committed with Eliz. Popley, for which he has done penance. 40s. p.s.r. 5s.

17 Jo. ap Thomas ap Gwillym & Helen verch Llan Hoell ap Richarde, Bangor dio. Disp. for marriage (4th degree consang.). 26s 8d.

f. 144ᵛ

July 17 Rob. Curson of London & Joan Noote, Winton dio. Disp. for marriage in Joan's par. ch. without banns. 10s.

Simon Kent, literate, Norw. dio. Disp. to practise as a notary· 13s 4d.

18 Wm Tutte *alias* Baker & Eliz. Edwards, Sarum dio. Disp. for marriage (Wm's mother was Eliz.'s godmother). Gratis.

Simon Betingham & Joan May, Winton dio. Disp. for marriage without banns & not in their par. ch. 10s; 10s.

Ric. ap Jenn & Gwelleana verch Walkyn, St David's dio. Disp. for marriage (3rd & 4th degrees affin.). 30s.

f. 145ʳ

Tho. Bedill, archdcn of Cornwall. Disp. to hold several cures & incompatible benefices on condition of his taking h.o. within 3 yrs. 30s.

19 Peter ap John Holante & Kath. verch Richard ap Jenn ap David ap Ithell, St Asaph dio. Disp. for marriage (3rd & 4th degrees consang.). Gratis.

20 Jo. Compton, pr., monk of Pershore, Worc. dio. Disp. to hold a benef. & to practise medicine everywhere, if granted his diocesan bp's consent. £8.

Ric. Walter, recently monk of Frithelstock, York dio. Disp. to hold a benef., with change of habit. Also for Tho. Clerke, Jo. Wyllyams. Suppr.

f. 145ᵛ

Jo. Lingow, pr., recently monk of Llanthony, Lland. dio. Disp. to hold a benef. with change of habit. Suppr.

24 Alex. Guy & Eliz. Nelson, of Dent, York dio. Disp. for marriage (4th degree consang.). 26s 8d.

Aug. 1 Rob. Baron & Joan Sherington, Cov. & Lich. dio. Disp. for marriage (3rd & 4th degrees consang.). 30s.

Rob. Griffith ap Robert Vaughan & Laura verch Hugh ap John, Bangor dio. Disp. for marriage (3rd & 4th double degrees consang.). 53s 4d.

Edm. Wetherden, B.Th., monk of Bury St Edmunds, Norw. dio. Disp. to become a sec. pr. & wear the habit of his Order beneath that of sec. pr. £4.

4 Laurence Herington, subdcn, York dio. Disp. to take h.o. outside the statutory times. 13s 4d.

f. 146^r

Aug. 6 Mich. Wentworth, gent. of the Kg's hsehld, & Eliz. Whitley, York dio. Disp. for marriage without the banns & outside their par. ch. 10s; 10s.

Rob. Scottow, of Herringfleet, & Agnes Nobbys, of Ashby, Norw. dio. Disp. for marriage without banns, in Agnes' par. ch. 10s.

10 Peter Asby, r. of ?Skreynggam, Winton dio. Disp. to hold a benef. with cure with or 2 without the above; permut. cl. £6 10s.

12 Jo. Danaster, gent., of Chobham, Winton dio., & Ann Roberts, widow, of London. Disp. for marriage in Ann's par. ch. without banns. 10s.

17 Geo. Stevenson, dcn, York dio. Disp. to take pr.'s orders within the prohibited times. 10s.

20 Mich. Federstonehaulghe & Ann Trolhoppe, Durham dio. Disp. for marriage (4th & 4th degrees consang.). 26s 8d.

f. 146^v

20 Ric. Morgan, esq., & Jane Covert, widow, of Winton dio. Disp. for marriage (Jane was godmother to a child of Ric.). £6.

Nich. Holme, chanter in York Minster. Disp. to hold a benef. with cure with the above, or 2 without, if he obtains suffragan's or royal licence; permut. cl. £6 10s.

21 Tho. Wale, of Monks Kirby & Joan Garett, widow, of Cov. & Lich. dio. Disp. for marriage without banns. 10s.

Ric. Fournes & Marg. Draper, York dio. Disp. for marriage (4th degree consang.). 26s 8d.

Ric. Grewode & Marg. Mighlay, York dio. Disp. for marriage (4th degree consang.). 26s 8d.

Tho. Panton, dcn, of Cant. dio. Disp. to take pr.'s orders within the prohibited times from any bp. 10s.

f. 147^r

6 Roger Tonneshende, D.C.L., Kg's chapl., r. of St. Mary's, North Creake, Norw. dio., & holder by disp. of various other benefices. Disp. to hold another benef. provided his total annual income from eccles. benefices does not exceed £300. £20.

10 Wm Humfrey, pr., chapl. to the Bp of London, v. of St Nich.'s, Willoughby, Cov. & Lich. dio. Disp. to hold a benef. with the above, or 2 without; permut. cl. £6 10s.

24 Jo. ap David Lloid ap David ap Llin & Eliz. verch David ap

Madocke, St Asaph dio. Disp. for marriage (4th degree consang.). 26s 8d.

Aug. 25 Chris. Thorntown & Jane Procter, York dio. Disp. for marriage (Jane's mother was Chris.'s godmother). 30s.

f. 147ᵛ

24 Edw. Asheton & Agnes Benetson, Cov. & Lich. dio. Disp. for marriage (4th degree affin. & 3rd & 4th degrees consang.). 26s 8d; 30s.

25 Tho. Robotham & Agnes Cowtrell, of Glossop, Cov. & Lich. dio. Disp. for marriage (3rd & 4th degrees consang.). 30s.

26 Jas Batman, B.A., York dio. Disp. to take all h.o. & 2 on the same day, within the prohibited times. 26s 8d.

Roger ap Jean ap Griffithe & Gwenllian verch Philipp Thomas Vichan, St David's dio. Disp. for marriage (3rd & 4th degrees affin.). 26s 8d.

Tho. ap Ritheich & Janet verch Notlym, St David's dio. Disp. for marriage (4th degree consang.). 26s 8d.

Jo. Scott *alias* Barbour, O.F.M. Disp. to become a sec. pr., & hold a benef. with cure. 'Remittitur gratis.'

f. 148ʳ

28 Ric. Parker, M.A., Winton dio. Disp. to take all h.o. 2 on 1 day, outside the prohibited times. 26s 8d.

30 Wm Andrew & Winifrid Statham, of London. Disp. for marriage without banns. 10s.

Ric. Kyste, Bath & W. dio. Disp. to take all h.o. outside the prohibited times. 20s.

Sept. 1 Lancelot Lowder of Fleming, Carl. dio., & Janet Flemyng of Worsthorne, York dio. Disp. for marriage (2nd & 3rd degrees consang.). £8.

2 Geo. Clayton, pr., r. of Broughton, Linc. dio., chapl. to Duke of Suffolk. Disp. to hold a benef. with the above, or 2 without: permut. & non-res. cl. £7 13s 4d.

f. 148ᵛ

5 Ralph Lee & Marg. Parys, Ely dio. Disp. for marriage without banns. 10s.

6 Ric. Staney *alias* Semores, & Janet verch David Lloid, St Asaph dio. Disp. for marriage without banns. 10s.

10 Leonard Reresbro, sch., York dio. Disp. to take all h.o. outside the statutory times & 2 on the same day. 26s 8d.

Sept. 10 Nich. Kipping & Alice Egleton, Linc. dio. Disp. for marriage in Alice's par. ch. without banns. 10s.

Wm Fauks, literate, York dio. Creation as notary public & tabellion. 13s 4d.

Jo. Randall, recently O.S.B. monk of the dissolved hse of Westminster. Disp. to hold any benef., having given up his habit. Arb. £6 13s 4d.

f. 149ʳ

Sept. 12 Rob. Bone, pr., Kg's chapl., r. of Hanslope ('Hampslapp'), Linc. dio. Disp. to hold a benef. with cure with or 2 without the above. £6 10s.

8 Wm Genyns & Agnes Glover, of St Bridgett's par., London. Disp. for marriage without banns. 10s.

Reg. Brysley, advocate of the Court of York. Creation as public notary. 13s 4d. Also for Tho. Walter, clk of York, & Chris. Beysley, literate, York dio. 13s 4d.

f. 149ᵛ

15 Jo. Tyxhalle, M.A. Disp. to take dcn's & pr.'s orders within the prohibited times. 13s 4d.

16 Ric. Bolde, esq., of Prescott, & Eliz. Gerarde, dau. of Sir Tho. Gerarde, Cov. & Lich dio. Disp. for marriage (3rd & 4th & 4th & 4th degrees consang. & 3rd & 4th degrees affin.). 30s; 26s 8d; 30s.

Rob. Johnys, v. of Llan carnan (sic), Lland. dio. Disp. for nonres. so long as his various illnesses last, & for 6 mnths after recovery. 20s.

20 Wm Dobyson, pr., chapl. to the Master of the Rolls, v. of Marybraden, Cant. dio. Disp. to hold another benef. if the above does not yield over £8 p.a., permut & non-res. cl. £4.

f. 150ʳ

22 Geo. Bruches, subdcn, Cov. & Lich. dio. Disp. to take dcn's & pr.'s orders outside the statutory times. 13s 4d.

20 Ric. Smythe & Joan Freglington, of Tetenhall, Cov. & Lich. dio. Disp. for marriage (Ric.'s mother was Joan's godmother). 30s.

Giles Elis & Ann Wise, of Abchurch par., London. Disp. for marriage without banns. 10s.

Edw. Pendilton, sch., Linc. dio. Disp. to take all h.o. outside the statutory times & 2 on the same day. 26s 8d.

Sept. 20 Chris. Troughton & Isabella Rokes, Linc. dio. Disp. for marriage (Chris.'s mother was Isabella's godmother). 30s.

Wm Gryndon, recently prior of Stavordale, Bath & W. dio. Disp. to take a benef. without change of habit. £4.

f. 150ᵛ

22 Tho. Morgan, B.C.L., of Kingsthorpe, Linc. dio. Creation as public notary & tabellion. 13s 4d.

25 Tho. Kydde & Kath. Brokeholes, York dio. Disp. for marriage (3rd & 4th degrees consang.). 30s.

26 Nich. Randall *alias* Wodall, M.A., holder of minor orders. Disp. to take the rest of h.o. within a yr, in order to retain a benef. 10s.

27 Ant. Pygge, acol., Lond. dio. Disp. to hold a benef. provided he takes h.o. within a yr. 10s.

Wm Biller, literate, York dio. Disp. to be recognized as both notary & tabellion. 13s 4d.

30 Rob. Browne & Agnes Makyn, of the kingdom of England (*sic*). Disp. for marriage (Agnes was godmother to a child of Rob.). Gratis.

f. 151ʳ

20 Edw. Large, O.F.M. Disp. to hold a benef. with change of habit. Gratis.

30 Jo. ——., D.Th., r. of Marlborough, Sarum dio. Disp. to hold a benef. with or 2 without the above; permut. cl. £6 10s.

Oct.   2 Ric. Bolde, esq., & Eliz. Jerarde, Cov. & Lich. dio. Disp. for marriage (4th & 4th degrees affin.). 26s 8d.

Ric. Marshe & Joan Snowe, Linc. dio. Disp. for marriage (4th degree consang.). 26s 8d.

3 Wm Wyseman, dcn, Lond. dio. Disp. to take pr.'s orders within the prohibited times. 10s.

f. 151ᵛ

7 Hy Golde, chapl. to the Bp of Chich., v. of Horndon on the Hill, Lond. dio. Disp. to hold a benef. with or 2 without the above; permut. cl. £6 10s.

Tho. Banes, subdcn, Cov. & Lich. dio. Disp. to take dcn's & pr.'s orders within the prohibited times & on the same day. 13s 4d.

3 Hy Haselwode, pr., r. of Cuddington, Linc. dio. chapl. to Ld Hastings. Disp. to hold a benef. with or 2 without the above; permut. cl. £6 10s.

Oct.   7 Jo. Isacke & Edith Deen, Bath & W. dio. Disp. for marriage (Jo.'s father was Edith's godfather). 30s.

      16 Tho. Holden & Eliz. Wadington, Cov. & Lich. dio. Disp. for marriage (4th degree consang.). 26s 8d.

      17 Augustine Augustine & Agnes Hede, Winton dio. Disp. for marriage in their par. ch. without banns. 10s.

f. 152^r

         Tho. Symson & Marg. Bereser, Sarum dio. Disp. for marriage (Tho.'s mother was Marg.'s godmother). 30s.

      18 Tho. Trotte & Matilda Keylde, York dio. Disp. for marriage (3rd degree consang.). £6.

      20 Philip ap Thomas Apell Goz & Alice verch Llin ap Thomas, St David's dio. Disp. validating their marriage (contracted in ignorance of 4th degree affin.). 26s 8d.

         Tho. ap Rice ap Thomas & Agnes verch Thomas, St David's dio. Disp. for marriage (3rd & 4th degrees affin.). 30s.

         Nich. Saunders, r. of St Andrew's, Lewes, Chich. dio., chapl. to the Bp of St Asaph. Disp. to hold a benef. with or 2 without the above; permut. cl. £6 10s.

f. 152^v

      22 Geo. Blakewall & Eliz. Ayer, Cov. & Lich. dio. Disp. for marriage (3rd & 4th degrees consang.). 30s.

June 20 Ric. Sandall, recently monk of Blyth, York dio. Disp. to hold a benef. with change of habit. Also for Tho. Graystocke, of the above hse. Suppr.

Oct. 25 Tho. Willyams, subdcn, r. of Alkrington, Linc. dio. Disp. to take dcn's & pr.'s orders within the prohibited times. 13s 4d.

      12 Jo. Ashelocke, pr., r. of Beckington, Bath & W. dio. Disp. for non-res. for 2 yrs. 13s 4d; p.s.r. 5s.

      20 Ric. Asheforthe *alias* Bochiar, pr., recently monk of Prittlewell, Lond. dio. Disp. to hold a benef. with change of habit. Suppr.

         Jo. Nicolls *alias* Marsey, pr., B.Th., recently monk of Colchester, Lond. dio. Disp. to hold a benef. with change of habit. Gratis.

f. 153^r

      22 Geo. Fitzwillyam, esq., & Mary Skipwythe, dau. of Sir Wm Skypwythe. Disp. for marriage in Mary's par. ch. without banns. 10s.

      27 Ric. Wadyngton & Alice Judde, of London. Disp. for marriage in Alice's par. ch. without banns. 10s.

Oct. 27 Warin Brampton *alias* Sawyer, pr., recently monk of Sawtry, Linc. dio. Disp. to hold a benef. with change of habit. Suppr.

26 Geo. Chidley, chapl. to Ld Windsor, r. of Lanreath ('Llandrethow'), Ex. dio. Disp. to hold a benef. with or 2 without the above; permut. cl. £6 10s.

Jo. Mabury & Marg. Wyralde, Cov. & Lich. dio. Disp. for marriage (3rd & 4th degrees affin.). 30s.

f. 153ᵛ

Ralph Forster & Marg. Veables, Cov. & Lich. dio. Disp. for marriage (3rd & 4th degrees affin. or consang.). 30s.

10 Jo. Chester, recently monk of Whalley. Disp. to hold a benef. with change of habit. Also for Francis Grene, Jo. Lawe, Tho. Blackeborne. Suppr.

31 Jo. Paty & Juliana Kempe, of Welford, Sarum dio. Disp. for marriage (Juliana's father was Jo.'s godfather). 30s.

Feb. 28 Geo. Croste, M.A., Kg's chapl. Disp. to hold an additional benef. with or without cure; permut. & non-res. cl. £12.

Oct. 31 Hy Wyntenstalle & Eliz. Pownall, Cov. & Lich. dio. Disp. for marriage (4th & 4th degrees affin.). 26s 8d.

f. 154ʳ

Hy Shawe & Eliz. Wynnyngton, Cov. & Lich. dio. Disp. for marriage (3rd & 4th degrees affin.). 30s.

Geoffrey Caye & Agnes Rothwell. Disp. for marriage (4th degree consang.). 30s.

Nov. 2 Jas Breune & Alice Done, Cov. & Lich. dio. Disp. for marriage (3rd & 4th degrees affin.). 30s.

3 Rob. Stapleton & Eliz. Malory, York dio. Disp. for marriage (4th degree consang.). 26s 8d.

28 Jo. Dysney & Eliz. Garlande, of Godmanchester, Linc. dio. Disp. for marriage (Eliz. was godmother to a child of Jo.). Arb. 20s.

Oct. 31 Tho. Rusburye *alias* Worceyter, pr., monk of St Mary's, Reading, Sarum dio. Disp. to wear the habit of his Order beneath that of a sec. pr. Gratis.

f. 154ᵛ

Nov. 2 Jo. Seys, dcn, Heref. dio. Disp. to take pr.'s orders within the prohibited times. 10s.

3 Edw. Clopton & Ann Smythe, of Lothbury par., London. Disp. for marriage without banns. 10s.

Nov. 4 Edm. Sutton & Marg. Letleton, of Dudley, Worc. dio. Disp. for marriage without banns. 10s.

Oct. 31 Tho. Mortymer, acol., Cov. & Lich. dio. Disp. to take all h.o. without l.d. from his diocesan bp. 6s 8d.

Nov. 1 Ric. Warde, r. of Manningford Abbas, Sarum dio., chapl. to Sir Wm Paulet. Disp. to hold a benef. with the above, or 2 without; permut. cl. £6 10s.

f. 155ʳ

Sept. 20 Miles Jeffys, pr., v. of Eardisland? ('Erislonde'), Heref. dio., chapl. to Earl of Worcester. Disp. to hold a benef. with the above, or 2 without; permut. cl. £6 10s.

Oct. 31 Ric. Straynge, O.F.M., of Winchester. Disp. to become a sec. pr. Gratis.

Nov. 7 Wm Gomerlande & Eleanor Eccles, Cov. & Lich. dio. Disp. for marriage (4th degree consang.). 26s 8d.

2 Jo. Crosbye, pr. of the coll. ch. of St Wm, York. Disp. to hold a benef. with cure with the above if the latter does not yield over £7 p.a. £4.

7 Jo. Webbe & Agnes Squyer, Bath & W. dio. Disp. for marriage (3rd & 4th degrees affin.). 30s.

6 Ric. Barker, B.A. Disp. to take pr.'s orders despite being in his 23rd yr. 20s.

f. 155ᵛ

7 Tho. Hollande, esq., of Linc. dio., & Joan Rogers, of Kingston-on-Hull, York dio. Disp. for marriage without banns. 10s.

8 Jo. Cottrell, chantry pr. in the chantry of Arden, Birmingham, Cov. & Lich. dio. Disp. for non-res. for 2 yrs with the founder's & patron's consent. 13s 4d.

Simon Harbyn, sch., Sarum dio. Disp. to take all h.o. within the prohibited times. 20s.

Wm Cowpelande, v. of St Sepulchre's without Newgate, London, chapl. to Earl of Worcester. Disp. to hold a benef. with cure with the above, or 2 others without; permut. cl. £6 10s.

Jo. Pychar & Helen Anderson, of Tottenham Highcross, Lond. dio. Disp. for marriage (Helen was godmother to a child of Jo.). Arb. 26s 8d.

Oct. 31 Jo. Savage *alias* Conycister, recently monk of St Pancras, Lewes, v. of Cuckfield. Disp. to change his habit. £4.

f. 156^r

Nov. 8 Jo. Collyns, M.A., chapl. to Hy Ld Montague. Disp. to hold
         any 2 benefices with cure; permut. cl. £6 10s.

         Wm Pierypoynt, B.C.L., York dio. Disp. to take all h.o. during
         the prohibited times, & 2 on the same day. 26s 8d.

      6 Geoffrey ap Jenn ap Philip & Gwenllean ap Jenn Vichan, Lland.
        dio. Disp. for marriage (4th degree affin.). 26s 8d.

      8 Wm Tewert & Alice Stokedale, York dio. Disp. for marriage
        (Alice's mother was Wm's godmother). 30s.

        Geo. Cotes, York dio. Disp. for marriage (3rd & 4th degrees
        consang.). 30s.

     13 Tho. Went & Jane Homme, Heref. dio. Disp. for marriage
        (Tho.'s father was Jane's godfather). 30s.

f. 156^v

        Ric. Wyern & Marg. Georson, York dio. Disp. for marriage
        (4th degree consang.). 26s 8d.

     10 Ric. & Alice Snowe, of Totteridge, Lond. dio. Disp. for mar-
        riage (3rd degree consang.); also Ric's father & Alice's mother
        were respectively godparents to Alice & Ric. £6; 30s; 30s.

     13 David ap David ap Meyryke & Nesta verch David ap Howell,
        Lland. dio. Disp. to validate marriage (contracted in ignorance
        of 3rd & 4th degrees affin.). 30s.

      6 Jo. Clerke & Joan Body, Bath & W. dio. Disp. for marriage (Jo.'s
        mother was Joan's godmother). 30s.

     12 Tho. Clevelond & Marg. Adlam, York dio. Disp. for marriage
        (Tho. was sponsor at the confirmation of a child of Magdalene:
        sic.). Arb. 26s. 8d.

f. 157^r

     14 Tho. Johnson & Alice Rathbone, Cov. & Lich. dio. Disp. for
        marriage (3rd & 4th degrees consang.). 30s.

      7 Jo. Holte, v. of Elm, Ely dio., & Gt Barton, Norw. dio. Disp.
        for non-res. during his various illnesses, & for 6 months after
        recovery. 20s; p.s.r. 5s.

     14 Ric. Banaster & Ann Grenehalgh. Cov. & Lich. dio. Disp. for
        marriage (4th degree consang.). 26s 8d.

     15 Jo. Bikerton & Constantine Goode, York dio. Disp. for marriage
        (4th degree consang.). 26s 8d.

     18 Rob. Dey, O.P., pr., prior of Pontefract. Disp. to hold any
        chantry or free chapel together with the above office, retaining
        the habit of his Order. £4.

f. 157^v

Nov. 16   J. ——, abbot O.S.B. of Milton Abbas, Sarum. dio. Disp. to wear anywhere the grey almuce of a cath. canon. 10s.

10   Jo. Nycolls & Eliz. Mohun, Ex. dio. Disp. for marriage (3rd & 4th degrees consang.). 30s.

16   Jo Berwyke & Dorothy Goddarde, Sarum dio. Disp. for marriage (4th degree consang.). 26s 8d.

17   Tho. Ravill & Mabel Todhunter, Carl. dio. Disp. for marriage (4th degree consang.). 26s 8d.

Jo. Frende & Agnes Heckeley, Winton dio. Disp. for marriage (Jo.'s father was Agnes' godfather). Gratis.

f. 158^r

Jo. Eton & Brigett Palmer, of London. Disp. for marriage without banns. 10s.

6   Wm Draper, B.C.L., r. of Horsted Keynes, Chich. dio. Disp. to hold a benef. with the above or 2 without, if he is granted his suffragan's or bp's licence; permut. cl. £6 10s.

13   Wm Hayball, pr., r. of St Tho., Cricket, Bath & W. dio. Disp. for non-res. on account of serious illness & for 6 months after recovery. 20s.

17   Rob. (Warton), Bp of St Asaph. Extension & amplification of disp. granted to hold the above in comm. with the monastery of St Saviour, Bermondsey. £4.

f. 158^v

18   Lancelot Robynson, O.C. fr. Disp. to wear the habit of his Order beneath that of a sec. pr. 'Gratis conceditur.'

19   Ric. Aspley & Ann Jackson, widow, of Newport, Cov. & Lich. dio. Disp. for marriage (Ric. was godfather to a child of Ann). £6.

20   Rob. Laneham, recently Observant fr. of Richmond, Winton dio. Disp. to wear the habit of his Order beneath that of a sec. pr. Gratis.

12   Jo. Newton, pr., v. of Much Cowarne, Heref. dio. Disp. for non-res. during various illnesses & for 6 months after recovery. 20s; p.s.r. 5s.

18   Tho. ap Harry ap Reynolde & Kath. verch Howell ap John, St Asaph dio. Disp. for marriage (3rd & 4th degrees consang.). 30s.

Ralph Bradshawe & Marg. Bagnalde, of London. Disp. for marriage in their par. ch. without banns. 10s.

f. 159ʳ

Nov. 17 Wm Herbert, esq., of the Kg's hsehld & Ann Parre, of the late
Qn Jane's hsehld. Disp. for marriage without banns & not in
their par. ch. 10s; 10s.

10 Jo. Thetford, suffragan Bp of Thetford with comm. (he asserts)
of the hse of rg. Premonstr. canons of Titchfield. Disp. to hold
any 2 benefices with cure with the above. £6.

20 Sir Nicholas Poyntz. Disp. to eat meat, butter, & forbidden milk
foods during Lent & other prohibited times, on medical advice
due to ill-health: also for his wife, Ly Joan. 40s.

21 Rob. Smythe, gent., of London & Eliz. Barley, of the par. of St
Olave, Old Jewry, London. Disp. for marriage without banns
10s.

f. 159ᵛ

25 Tho. Doncasse & Marg. Barlow, of Runcorn, Cov. & Lich. dio.
Disp. for marriage (3rd & 4th degrees affin.). 30s.

Wm Dalowey & Ann Elfer, Heref. dio. Disp. for marriage (3rd
& 4th degrees consang.). 30s.

16 Rob. & Eliz. Parkynson, York dio. Disp. for marriage (3rd & 3rd
degrees consang.). Arb. £4.

20 Jo. Ascott, M.A., archpr. of St Mich.'s Mount, Ex. dio. Disp. to
hold any benef. without cure, and not yielding over £8 p.a., with
the above. £4.

22 Jo. ap Thomas & Joan verch Wylym, St David's dio. Disp. for
marriage (4th degree consang.). 30s.

f. 160ʳ

20 Tho. Mason, pr., v. of Kinlett, Heref. dio. Disp. for non-res.
during illness & for 6 months after recovery. 20s.

22 Ric. Dobbys & Jane Choppyng, St Matthew's par., London.
Disp. for marriage in Joan's (*sic*) par. ch. without banns. 10s.

Mar. 10 Tho. *alias* Geo. Parker, precentor of Heref. cath. Disp. to hold
also the par. ch. of Winterborne Eastham, Worc. dio., & Marsh-
field, Heref. dio., or any other incompatible benef.; permut. cl.
£13.

Nov. 20 Jo. Magett, v. of West Shefford, Sarum dio. Disp. to hold a benef.
with the above, or 2 without; permut. cl. £6 10s.

22 Ric. Williamson & Joan Curteys, of the par. of Peakirk, Linc.
dio. Disp. for marriage (4th degree consang.). 26s 8d.

f. 160^v

Nov. 24 Ric. Warde, pr., chapl. to Ld Sandys, r. of Laverstock, Winton dio. Disp. to hold a benef. with above, or 2 without; permut. cl. £6 10s.

25 Geo. Hollande & Eliz. Lowes, of London. Disp. for marriage in their par. ch. without banns. 10s.

26 Philip Rawlyns, sch., Norw. dio. Disp. to take all h.o. within the prohibited times. 20s.

Augustine Smythe & Marg. Billing, Linc. dio. Disp. for marriage (Marg.'s mother was Augustine's godmother). 30s.

Aug. 10 Hy Saulter, recently prior of Hempton, r. of Scarning, Norw. dio. Disp. to hold another benef. with the above, or 2 without; permut. cl. £6 10s.

f. 161^r

Nov. 17 Jo. Norwiche & Ann Cobham, Linc. dio. Disp. for marriage without banns & not in their par. ch. 10s; 10s.

29 Rob. Baylye & Ann Tayler, York dio. Disp. for marriage (4th degree consang.). 26s 8d.

Wm Lett & Jane *alias* Joan Eaton, of St Leonard's par., London. Disp. for marriage, the banns read once. 6s 8d.

17 Mich. Raynolde, sch., Ex. dio. Disp. to take pr.'s orders during the prohibited times. 20s.

18 Jo. Manne, r. of Westbury, Linc. dio. Disp. for non-res. for 2 yrs. 13s 4d.

20 Wm Collys, O.C. fr., recently of Bristol, Worc. dio. Disp. to wear the habit of his Order beneath that of a sec. pr. Gratis.

f. 161^v

July 10 Ric. Cox, B.Th., r. of Kelshall, Linc. dio. Disp. to hold a benef. with cure with the above, or 2 without; permut. cl. £6 10s.

Sept. 20 Geo. Daye, D.Th. Disp. to hold any 2 benefices with cure; permut. cl. £6 10s.

Nov. 30 Wm Everest, of the Kg's hsehld, & Marg. Hunte, of St Dunstan's in-the-East par., London. Disp. for marriage without banns. 10s.

10 Jo. Barker, chanter in the chantry at the altar of the Holy Saviour, Cant. cath. Disp. to hold a benef. with the above, or 2 without; permut. cl. £6 10s.

Mar. 20 Peter Aysheton, M.A., r. of Shillington, Linc. dio. Disp. to hold 2 benefices with cure with the above, or 3 without; permut. & non-res. cl. £13 6s 8d.

f. 162^r

Nov. 29 Wm Philipp & Gwenllean verch David, St David's dio. Disp. for marriage (4th degree affin.). 26s 8d.

David Thomas ap Ridd & Marg. verch Llin ap Rys, St David's dio. Disp. for marriage (3rd & 4th degrees consang.). 30s.

Dec. 2 Geo. Trapps of London, & Isabella Boughton, Roch. dio. Disp. for marriage without banns, within the prohibited times. 20s.

May 10 Ant. Barker, M.A. Disp. to hold any number of benefices with cure not yielding over £300 p.a.; permut. & non-res. cl. £20.

Dec. 2 Humfrey Collys, esq., & Eliz. Darsaye, Bath & W. dio. Disp. for marriage without banns & during the prohibited times. 30s.

f. 162^v

Nov. 20 Jo. Antony *alias* Avery, pr., O.S.B., of Winchcomb. Disp. to hold a benef. with change of habit. Gratis.

28 Warin Brampton, pr., recently monk of Sawtry, Linc. dio. Disp. to hold a benef. with change of habit. Also for Ric. Graffeham, Jo. Pecke, Ric. Brampton. Suppr.

Dec. 1 Jo. Tayler *alias* Cardemaker, pr., O.F.M., of Exeter. Disp. to hold a benef. with complete change of habit. 'Gratis conceditur.'

Tho. Sall *alias* Growte, pr., recently monk of Norw. cath. Disp. to wear the habit of his Order beneath that of a sec. pr. Gratis.

3 Tho. Heretage, M.A., Dean of the coll. ch. of South Malling, in the immediate jurisdiction of Cant. & incumbent of the par. ch. of Stanner, united to the above. Disp. to hold another benef. £10.

f. 163^r

6 Wm Todde, pr., recently prior of the Gilbertine priory of Malton, York dio. Disp. to leave the religious life & hold a benef. £4.

1 Rob. Forster, pr., recently prior of Flanesford, Heref. dio. Disp. to hold a benef. with change of habit. Suppr.

2 Rob. Wyllsey, reg. canon. Disp. to leave the religious life. Gratis.

30 Rob. Bede, pr., O.F.M., of Cambridge. Disp. to become a sec. pr. Arb. 40s.

2 Tho. Woode, B.Th., O.F.M. Disp. to hold a benef. with change of habit. 'Condonatur gratis.'

11 Griffin Whight & Mary Perott, St David's dio. Disp. for marriage (4th degree consang.). 26s 8d.

f. 163ᵛ

Dec. 12 Arthur Dudley, r. of Bartlow, Ely dio. & holder of a mediety of the ch. of Malpas, Cov. & Lich. dio. Disp. to hold a benef. with cure with the above, or with 2 others; permut. & non-res. cl. £8.

Rob. Wylkynson, O.P., of Dunwich. Disp. to leave the religious life & wear the habit of his Order beneath that of a sec. pr. £4.

11 Tho. Hunte & Ann Heythe, of Cornhill, London. Disp. for marriage without banns & within the prohibited times. 30s.

12 Ric. Cotton, esq., & Jane Ouley, of London. Disp. for marriage within the prohibited times & without banns. 30s.

Rob. Babthorpe, B.Th., r. of Ashwell, Linc. dio. Disp. to hold a benef. with cure with the above or 2 without; permut. cl. £6 10s.

f. 164ʳ

13 Rob. Walcott, acol., Linc. dio. Disp. to take all h.o. within the prohibited times. 20s.

16 Brian Rye & Joan Syrt, York dio. Disp. for marriage (4th degree consang.). 26s 8d.

Ric. Mychelborne & Petronilla Legge, Chich. dio. Disp. for marriage the banns read once, & within the prohibited times. 20s; 6s 8d.

12 Edm. Dey, O.P. Disp. to leave the religious life. Gratis.

3 Ralph Dey, O.P. Disp. to wear the habit of his Order beneath that of a sec. pr. Gratis.

18 Jo. Faror & Isabella Quythed, York dio. Disp. for marriage (3rd & 4th degrees consang.). 30s.

f. 164ᵛ

17 Chris. Deconson & Joan Edmonson, Cov. & Lich. dio. Disp. for marriage (4th degree consang.). 26s 8d.

18 Jo. Holywell & Marg. Crane, Cov. & Lich. dio. Disp. for marriage (4th degree consang.). 26s 8d.

10 Ric. Langstar & Agnes Wardeman, York dio. Disp. for marriage (Ric. was godfather to a child of Agnes). Gratis.

20 Stephen Lufkyn, Austin fr., of Clare, Lond. dio. Disp. to wear the habit of his Order beneath that of a sec. pr. £4.

Tho. Byrkenhed, pr., recently abbot of Norton, Cov. & Lich. dio. Disp. to become a sec. pr. and hold a benef. with or without cure of souls. Also for Jas Pate, monk of the same. Suppr.

f. 165ʳ

1 Jo. Lepyngton, Gilbertine canon. Disp. to hold a benef. despite defect of birth. £4.

Dec. 12 Ric. Wright, pr., r. of Swine, York dio. Disp. to hold another benef. if the above does not yield over £8 p.a. £4.

20 Ric. Forde, r. of Acrise, Cant. dio. Disp. to hold another benef. if the above does not yield over £8 p.a. £4.

Mathew Charder, subdcn, York dio. Disp. to take dcn's & pr.'s orders within the prohibited times. 13s 4d.

31 Wybert Gilboye, monk, formerly of Stratford Langthorne, Lond. dio., now of St Mary Graces. Disp. to wear the habit of his Order beneath that of a sec. pr. £4.

f. 165ᵛ

12 Cuthbert Hardecastle, chapl. to Ld Jo. Vere, K.G., Earl of Oxford. Disp. to hold 2 additional benefices; permut. cl. £6 10s.

31 Rob. King, Bp of Rheon *in partibus infidelium*, resident in England; abbot by disp. of Thame, O.Cist.; disp. to hold a benef. in comm. with the above & take the headship of any other rel. hse to which he may be elected. £4.

Jo. Hawkyn *alias* Cristmas, chapl. to Bp of London, r. of Norton, Cant. dio. Disp. to hold a benef. with above; permut. cl. £6 10s.

ff. 166ʳ–171ᵛ blank.

f. 172ʳ

1538 Jan.   4 Jo. Ralay & Joan Thorne, of Winterborne Danvers, Sarum dio. Disp. for marriage without banns. 10s.

Adam & Eleanor Waryng, Lond. dio. Disp. for marriage (3rd & 4th degrees consang.). 30s.

Jo. Smythe & Joan Tomlynson. Disp. for marriage (Joan's father was Jo.'s godfather). 30s.

Wm Lloid ap Ritherch, sch., Bangor dio. Disp. to take all h.o. despite being in his 22nd yr & to hold a benef.; non-res. cl. £4.

f. 172ᵛ

10 Edm. Spencer & Isabella Aspden, Cov. & Lich. dio. Disp. for marriage (4th degree consang.). 26s 8d.

12 Miles Gill, pr., of the Gilbertine Order of Sempringham, Lincoln. Disp. to hold a benef. retaining the habit of his Order; permut. cl. £4.

Jo. Dys, O.P. Disp. to wear the habit of his Order beneath that of a sec. pr. £4.

Rob. Heden, M.A., Durham dio. Disp. to take all h.o. within the prohibited times & 2 on the same day. 26s 8d.

Jan. 12 Wm Longe, subdcn, of Stanford [in the Vale], Sarum dio. Disp. to take all h.o. without l.d. from his diocesan bp, as he asserts he was born in the above dio. 6s 8d.

f. 173ʳ

15 Tho. Blenerhassett, chapl. to Tho. Duke of Norfolk, r. of Solihull, Cov. & Lich. dio. Disp. to hold a benef. with, or 3 others without, the above. £9.

Miles Clyfforde, B.A., Carl. dio. Disp. to take all h.o. outside the statutory times & without l.d. from his diocesan bp. 26s 8d; 6s 8d.

Tho. Chamber & Helen Ilonde, of London. Disp. for marriage the banns read once. 6s 8d.

10 Wm Bowell, pr., r. of Collingdon, Linc. dio. Disp. for non-res. during his various illnesses, & for 6 months after his recovery. 20s; p.s.r. 5s.

f. 173ᵛ
1537
(ann. HVIII 29)

Dec. 20 Rob. King, Bp of Reon *in partibus infidelium* & abbot of Thame, Linc. dio., by royal licence, & holder of other benefices in comm. Disp. to be head of any other religious community to which he may be elected. 'Gratis remittitur per ipsum regem'; warrant of the King shown.

Giles Croxforde, pr., recently prior of Titchfield, Winton dio. Disp. to hold a benef. with change of habit. Also for Wm Godwyn, Jo. Lekar, Nich. Knyght, Jo. Baker, Edw. Bacheler, Jo. Foster, Tho. Gryme, Jo. Warde, Ric. Fawldewe Marks. Suppr.

Aug. 2 Jo. Colman, recently canon of Bridlington, York dio. Disp. to hold a benef. with change of habit. Also for Rob. Todde, Wm Mason, Tho. Paitson, Rob. Anlaby, Rob. Burdus, Wm Bromflet, Wm Walker, Jo. Skeresbeke, Jo. Lambert, Wm Toye, Mathew Charde, Sebastian Freston, Laurence Chapman, also canons. Suppr.

f. 174ʳ

31 Ric. Metcalf, recently monk of Jervaulx. Disp. to hold a benef. with change of habit. Also for Jo. Pratt, Simon Cleyslande, Tho. Sandaill, Wm Gregg, Jo. Deane, Wm Hall, Wm Ronkorne, Ric. Sawere, Ric. Staynton, Tho. Mudde, Chris. Dixson, Tho. Sharpe, Geo. Mason, Jo. Maisterman, monks of the same hse. Suppr.

Dec. 31 Rob. Croham *alias* Peterson, recently prior of Lewes. Disp. to hold a benef. with change of habit. Also for Jo. Benett, Ant. Bolney, Wm Panter, Ric. Shirborne, Jo. Marten, Simon Overy,

Denis Mychell, Tho. Atwell, Jo. Peverell, Nich. Canterbury, Jo., Canterburye, Wm Bayly, Jo. Sympson, David Frankfelde, Ric. Goleng, Jo. Halyfax, Geo. Morley, Tho. Chamblayn, Clement Browne, Wm Atherolde, Jo. Senocke, Tho. Tedman, Rob. Fiske, Wm Burton, Jo. Beetys, Jas Holman, Rob. Danyell, Jo. Howseholde, Edw. Wadnow, Rob. Batman, Jo. Skelton, Wm Ellis, Jo. Alowe, monks of the same hse. Suppr.

f. 174ᵛ

1538 Jan.   17 Wm Mylnar, dcn, Linc. dio. Disp. to take pr.'s orders from any bp within the prohibited times. 10s.

Tho Grene & Marg. Kyrbye, of the par. of St Olave's in Old Jewry, London. Disp. for marriage without banns. 10s.

Rob. Barker & Matilda Alen, York. dio. Disp. for marriage (Rob. was sponsor at the confirmation of a child of Matilda). Warrant of the lord's shown. Arb. £3 6s 8d.

21 Jo. Weekes & Kath. Colles, Ex. dio. Disp. for marriage (Jo.'s mother was Kath.'s godmother). 30s.

Jo. Thier & Isabella Lye, Worc. dio. Disp. for marriage (Jo. was godfather to a child of Isabella). £6.

22 Edw. Mawde, York dio. Disp. to take all h.o. within the prohibited times & 2 on the same day. 26s 8d.

f. 175ʳ

Nich. Lancaster & Agnes Atkynson, York dio. Disp. for marriage (3rd & 4th degrees consang.). 30s.

23 Tho. Gruffith, pr., r. of Wallington, Chich. dio., chapl. to Wm Earl of Arundel. Disp. to hold a benef. with the above; permut. cl. £6 10s.

24 Alex. Mytton & Agnes Robynson, Cov. & Lich. dio. Disp. for marriage (4th degree consang.). 26s 8d.

Jo. Warde & Agnes Greatike, Chich. dio. Disp. for marriage (3rd & 4th degrees consang.). 30s.

26 Peter Stradlyng & Helen verch Lewes, Lland. dio. Disp. for marriage (3rd & 4th degrees affin.). 30s.

27 Wm Maynarde & Jane Godarde, of London. Disp. for marriage, the banns read once. 6s 8d.

f. 175^v

Jan. 27 Tho. Godolffen of the par. of St Breaca, Cornwall, & Kath. Bonythyn, of St Martin, Ludgate, London. Disp. for marriage in Kath.'s par. ch. without banns. 10s.

22 Meredith ap David & Ingrada verch Gruffith, St David's dio Disp. for marriage (4th degree consang.). 26s 8d.

Jo. ap Jenkyn & Gwenllyan verch Gruffuth, St David's dio. Disp. for marriage (4th degree consang.). 26s 8d.

28 Geo. Grene, sch., Cov. & Lich. dio. Disp. to take all h.o. within the prohibited times. 20s.

29 Peter Ellarde & Cecily Leton, widow, of Southwark, Winton dio. Disp. for marriage, the banns read once. 6s 8d.

1537 Sept. 20 Tho Tasshe, B.C.L. Disp. to enjoy the privileges, &c., of a D.C.L. £4.

f. 176^r

1538 Jan. 27 Tho. Soresby & Alice Raynolds, of Boston, Linc. dio. Disp. for marriage, the banns read once. 6s 8d.

1537 Dec. 16 Tho. Foster & Eliz. Prestene, York dio. Disp. for marriage (4th degree consang.). 26s 8d.

1538 Jan. 20 Ric. Talbott, r. of Drayton Bassett, Cov. & Lich dio. Disp. to hold a benef. with the above; permut. but not non-res. cl. £6 10s.

Feb. 1 Jo. Collyns & Eliz. Rogers, Linc. dio. Disp. for marriage (Jo. was godfather to a child of Eliz.). Arb. 40s. Warrant of the lords shown.

2 Rob. Gregorye & Joan Ivynwode, widow, Linc. dio. Disp. for marriage (Rob. was sponsor at the confirmation of a child of Joan). Warrant of the lords under the signet shown. 'Remittitur gratis quia pauperes.'

10 Jas Car & Kath. Hesketh, Cov. & Lich. dio. Disp. for marriage (3rd & 4th degrees consang.). 30s.

f. 176^v

4 Ant. Deny, gent. of the Kg's hsehld, & Joan Champernowne, dau. of Sir Philip Champernowne. Disp. for marriage in any ch. without banns. 10s; 10s.

Francis Bedyngfeld & Eleanor Wodehouse, Norw. dio. Disp. for marriage in their par. ch. without banns. 10s.

Jan. 28 Jo. Rolde, Cov. & Lich. dio. Disp. to take all h.o. within the prohibited times & from any bp. 20s.

Jan. 31 Rob. Blynkynsope, r. of Hartlebury, Worc. dio., & Houghton, Winton dio. Disp. for non-res. for 3 yrs. 'Pro quolibet anno 6s 8d et p.s.r. 5s.'

Feb. 4 Edm. Champyon & Alice Johnson, of London. Disp. for marriage in their par. ch. without banns. 10s.

7 Francis Bonyngton & Helen Porte *alias* Perpoynt, Cov. & Lich. dio. Disp. for marriage (Helen's mother was Francis' godmother). 30s.

f. 177^r

6 Jas Blythe, clk, Kg's chapl., r. of Horton & v. of Shipton, Linc. dio.; v. of St Alban's, London. Disp. to hold a benef. with the above. £8.

8 Wm Culverhouse & Marg. Birche, Linc. dio. Disp. for marriage (Marg.'s father was sponsor at Wm.'s confirmation). 26s 8d.

Wm Glosshope, literate, Cov. & Lich. dio. Disp. to practise as notary & tabellion. 13s 4d.

7 Jo. Ruggell & Helen Rooper, Norw. dio. Disp. for marriage in their par. ch., the banns read once. 6s 8d.

8 Tho. Ellis, pr., canon of Wormsley, Heref. dio. Disp. to wear the habit of his Order beneath that of a sec. pr. £4.

f. 177^v

Jo. Say & Edith Moresbye, Lond. dio. Disp. for marriage (Jo. was godfather to a child of Edith). Arb. 40s. Bill shown sealed with the sign manual of the lords.

5 Hy Bekynsall & Jane Bothe, Cov. & Lich. dio. Disp. for marriage (4th degree double consang.). 50s.

7 Rob. Wylsey, canon. Disp. to hold a benef., he asserts that he already has a disp. to wear the habit of his Order beneath that of a sec. pr.; permut. & non-res. cl. £4 10s.

8 Hy Howarde & Ann Bramyngham, of London. Disp. for marriage, the banns read once. 6s 8d.

11 Wm Vessey, sch., York dio. Disp. to take all h.o. within the prohibited times & 2 on the same day. 26s 8d.

8 Rob. Blakeney, pr., prior of Tynemouth, Durham dio. Disp. to wear the grey almuce of a cath. canon. 10s.

f. 178^r

5 Wm Hopkyns, pr., recently canon of Caldwell, Linc. dio. Disp. to hold a benef. with change of habit. Also for Jo. Carter, Wm Tyde, Wm Benyngton, Ric. Rey, Wm Hoghley, canons of the same hse. Suppr.

Feb. 20 Tho. Hornell, pr., recently prior of Nocton Park, Linc. dio. Disp. to hold a benef. with change of habit. Also for Jo. Trussell, pr., & Jas Parke, pr., recently canons of the same hse. Suppr.

10 Jo. Dobbys, pr., recently abbot of Boxley, Cant. dio. Disp. to hold a benef. with change of habit. Also for Geo. Donham, Jo. Rede, Jo. Packe, Wm Lorkyn, Geo. Squyer, Jo. Godfrey, Amphibole Mamorn, Jo. Graver, Alex. Wymstherst, canons of the same hse. Suppr.

12 Chris. Reper, pr., recently abbot of Covenham, York dio. Disp. to hold a benef. with change of habit. Suppr.

f. 178ᵛ

Tho. Rowlande *alias* Penthecoste, recently abbot of Abingdon, Sarum dio. Disp. to hold a benef. with change of habit. Also for Ric. Evynsham, Jo. Cliffe, Jo. Cornyshe, Jo. Russell, Jo. Cristall, Rob. Burye, Jo. Eton, Wm Ashendon, Ric. Burall, Wm Bucklande, Nich. Redyng, Jo. Tewkesbury, Geo. Bekorye, Ric. Pamphilion, Gabriell Clement, Jo. Mylton, Tho. Radley, Wm Perth, Tho. Hardington, priests and monks; Tho. Rowlande, Giles Salley, Tho. Freman, Tho. Shottisbroke, Heme Kyngeston, Jo. Marshall, monks of the same. Suppr.

f. 179ʳ

10 Tho. Yonge & Alice Mede, Linc. dio. Disp. for marriage (Tho. was godfather to a child of Alice). 'Remittitur gratis quia pauperes'; warrant of the lords shown.

11 Sir Jo. Chaworthe & Mary Paston, gentw., York dio. Disp. for marriage without banns & not in their par. ch. 10s; 10s.

12 Jo. Suliarde, esq., & Eliz. Jernyngham, Norw. dio. Disp. for marriage (2nd & 3rd degrees affin.) & within the prohibited times, but not during Lent. £8; 20s.

15 Hy Morgan, D.C.L., Kg's chapl., r. of Up Lyme, & v. of Alvington, Ex. dio. Disp. to hold a benef. with the above, or 2 others without. £8.

14 Wm Webbe & Eliz. Butts, Lond. dio. Disp. for marriage without banns & not in their par. ch. 10s; 10s.

f. 179ᵛ

20 Gawin Boradall, recently abbot of Holmcultram, Carl. dio. Disp. to hold a benef. with change of habit. Also for Ant. Richardeson, Chris. Nevynson, Wm Marshall, Rob. Langton, Wm Symondeson, Ric. Robynson, Jo. Jackeson, Rob. Clement, Ric. Wittey, Tho. Grane, Tho. Browne, Arthur Nicholson, Jo. Anlabye, Nich. Pynghnay, Jo. Ydell, Ric. Godfrey, Rob. Bancke, Ric. Patenson, Jo. Wyse, priests; Ric. Adamson, Tho. Hoge, Wm Marten,

monks under h.o.; Jo. Ryton & Tho. London, monks of the same hse. Suppr.

June 20 Jo. Yardeley, recently monk of Studley priory, Worc. dio. Disp. to hold a benef. with change of habit. Suppr.

f. 180ʳ

Feb. 20 Ellis Ambrose, pr., Kg's chapl., incumbent of the par. ch. of ?Wennington, Linc. dio., & of Eversley, Winton dio. Disp. to hold another benef. £8.

10 Jo. Crane, pr., recently monk of Coggeshall, Lond. dio. Disp. to hold a benef. with change of habit. Also for Wm Love, Jo. Sanndeforde, Tho. Brikelsey, Ric. Brayntrey, Rob. Gosfelde, Tho. Bysham, Jo. Bockyng, Jo. Thaxsted, Geo. Cockerell, monks of the same. Suppr.

16 Tho. Grenewode, D.Th., pr., v. of Standish, Worc. dio. Disp. to hold another benef. £6 10s.

f. 180ᵛ

17 Confirmation of composition made on Jan. 15 1537 (8) between the prior & convent of Christchurch, Twyneham (Hants), Winton dio., & v. of Fleet, Dorset. 40s; p.s.r. 5s.

15 Tho. Wolpytt & Helen Baker, Bath & W. dio. Disp. for marriage (Helen's father was Tho.'s godfather). 30s.

12 Tho. Hughes, O.P., Heref. Disp. to wear the habit of his Order beneath that of a sec. pr. £4.

Jo. ap David, pr., r. of More, Heref. dio. Disp. for non-res. while his various ailments last, & for 6 months after recovery. 20s.

15 Wm Manne, r. of Hayfield, Linc. dio., & Morton, Worc. dio. Disp. for non-res. for 2 yrs. 13s 4d.

f. 181ʳ

18 Jo. Darbye, sch., Sarum dio. Disp. to take all h.o. & 2 on the same day. 26s 8d.

16 Tho. Let, M.A., chapl. to the Bp of Carlisle, incumbent of Melbury Abbas, Sarum dio. Disp. to hold a benef. with the above, or 2 without; permut. cl. £6 10s.

18 Jo. Fermer, acol., Chich. dio. Disp. to take all h.o. outside the statutory times. 20s.

Jo. Griffithe & Kath. verch Howell, of Holywell. Disp. for marriage (2nd & 4th degrees affin.). 33s 4d.

Feb. 29 Tho. Wedrelt, Gilbertine canon. Disp. to wear the habit of his Order beneath that of a sec. pr. Arb. 20s. Warrant of the lords shown.

f. 181ᵛ

20 Jo. Pecke *alias* Aylessham, O.S.B., of Hulme. Disp. to wear the habit of his Order beneath that of a sec. pr. & hold a benef. £8.

Wm Ugge *alias* Hornyng, chapl. to the Bp of Norw., r. of Harpley, Norw. dio. Disp. to hold a benef. with the above, or 2 without it; permut. cl. £6 10s.

18 Jo. Thorpe, acol., York dio. Disp. to take all h.o. & 2 on the same day, within the prohibited times. 26s 8d.

20 Tho. Grene, chapl. to the Earl of Shrewsbury, r. of Poringland, Norw. dio. Disp. to hold another benef.; permut. cl. £6 10s.

22 Jo. Dartyll & Beatrice Sannders, Linc. dio. Disp. for marriage within the prohibited times. 20s.

f. 182ʳ

23 Jo. Tyms, recently canon of Canon's Ashby, Linc. dio. Disp. to hold a benef. with change of habit. Also for Jo. Burley, Ric. Smythe, Wm Bromley, canons of the same hse. Suppr.

26 Tho. Audeley & Eliz. Parett, Linc. dio. Disp. for marriage in their par. ch. without banns; also during the prohibited times but not in Lent. 10s; 20s.

1537 Nov. 10 Rob. Pygott, pr., chapl. to Ld Hastings. Disp. to hold any 2 benefices for life; permut. cl. £6 10s.

1538 Feb. 26 Jo. Dyer, M.A., v. of Bampton, Linc. dio., chapl. to Ld Tho. Audley, Ld Chancellor. Disp. to hold any benef. with the above; permut. & non-res. cl. £7 13s 4d.

f. 182ᵛ

16 Tho. Dudley, gent., of the Kg's hsehld, & Alice Aliatt, gentw., of the par. of St Tho. the Apostle, London. Disp. for marriage within the prohibited times; also without banns, & not in their par. ch. 20s; 10s.

27 Alex. Barlow, acol., Cov. & Lich. dio. Disp. to take 2 h.o. within the prohibited times. 13s 4d.

Mar. 1 Ralph Goldesmyth *alias* Castleton, pr., monk of Vale Royal, Cov. & Lich. dio. Disp. to wear the habit of his Order beneath that of a sec. pr. £4.

6 Wm ap Richarde, sch., Lland. dio. Disp. to take all h.o. & hold a benef. despite defect of birth. £4.

Ric. Penyman, O.C. fr., of Norwich. Disp. to hold a benef. with change of habit. £8.

f. 183ʳ

Mar. 6 Geo. Nevell, pr., r. of ——, Carl. dio., natural son of Ld Ric. Nevell, Ld Latimer. Disp. to hold another benef.; permut. cl. £6 10s.

1537 Sept. 20 Tho. Tusshe, D.C.L., r. of ?Thumscoe ('Thornestow'), York dio., v. of Batley, York dio. Disp. to hold a benef. with the above; permut. cl. £8.

1538 Mar. 6 Miles Brathwhete, v. of Carshalton, Winton dio. Disp. to hold a benef. with cure with the above, or 2 without; permut. & non-res. cl. £7 13s 4d.

14 Laurence Sayler, acol., Cov. & Lich. dio. Disp. to take all h.o. without l.d. from his diocesan bp. 6s 8d.

f. 183ᵛ

15 Wm Haynes, B.Th., r. of Walgrave, Linc. dio. Disp. to hold a benef. with the above, or 2 without; permut. & non-res. cl. £7 13s 4d.

Jo. Hotchkynson, sch., Cov. & Lich. dio. Disp. to take all h.o. without l.d. from his diocesan bp. 6s 8d.

16 Confirmation of composition dated Aug. 10 1534 at York Minster, by Ric. Thorne, then resident canon & Vicar-General of York, & witnessed by Wm of Calton, clk & public notary, between the inhabitants of the village of Armin, Hook, and Goole, in the par. of Snaith, & the inhabitants of Snaith, & with the consent of the abbot & convent of Selby. 40s; p.s.r. 5s.

f. 184ʳ

15 Jo. ap Howell *alias* Penwyn, pr., v. of Llantrisant, Lland. dio. Disp. for non-res. on account of discharge of blood & other ailments for their duration, & for six months after recovery 20s; p.s.r. 5s.

Tho. Alynson, acol., Linc. dio. Disp. to take all h.o. within the prohibited times, & 2 on the same day. 26s 8d.

Jo. Saverham, pr. Disp. for non-res. for 3 yrs the hse provided with his benef. being unfit to live in; a suitable curate to be appointed; 20s.

14 Edm. Mawnde *alias* Mawne, sch., Heref. dio. Disp. to take all h.o. within the prohibited times, & 2 on the same day. 26s 8d.

16 Humfrey Segewyke, literate. Creation as public notary & tabellion. 13s 4d.

f. 184ᵛ

Feb. 24 Wm Lumbarde, B.C.L., chapl. to the Bp of Chich., r. of Shimpling, Norw. dio. Disp. to hold another benef. with the above, or 2 without; permut. & non-res. cl. £7 13s 4d.

Mar. 20 Tho. Herby, r. of Ufford, Linc. dio., chapl. to Wm, Bp of St David's. Disp. to hold a benef. with cure with the above, or 2 without; permut. cl. £6 10s.

23 Rhes ap Thomas ap Ritherch & Helen verch Jenn ap David ap Jean Lloid, St David's dio. Disp. for marriage (4th degree consang.). 26s 8d.

26 Jo. Gybson & Kath. Baynbrike, Durham dio. Disp. for marriage (4th degree consang.). 26s 8d.

20 Jo. Nich. Wynterborn, literate, Sarum dio. Creation as public notary. 13s 4d.

f. 185ʳ

23 Wm Stoderede, pr., v. of ?Rainham ('Redensham'), Linc. dio. Disp. readmitting him to the ministry, now he has performed penance & been absolved for the irregularities which caused him to be suspended by the Bp of Linc. £4.

28 Ric. Chapman & Alice Foxcroft, York or another dio. Disp. for marriage (3rd & 4th degrees affin.). 30s.

16 Hy Streynsham, O.F.M., & Hy King, Austin fr. Disp. to change their habits & hold benefices. 'Gratis quia pauperes'; two warrants of the lords shown.

10 Wm Balame, pr., r. of Musbury, Ex. dio. Disp. for non-res. during illness, & for 6 months after recovery. 20s; p.s.r. 5s.

f. 185ᵛ

7 Tho. Parre & Marg. Leylonde, Cov. & Lich. dio. Disp. for marriage (3rd degree consang.). Arb. £4. Warrant of the lords shown.

20 Lewis Williams *alias* Vaughan, sch., St Asaph dio. Disp. to take all h.o. despite defect of birth. 'Gratis quia pauper'; warrant of the lords shown.

30 David ap Hughe ap Jean & Marg. verch David ap Robert, St Asaph dio. Disp. for marriage (4th degree affin.). 26s 8d.

Edm. Perpoynt, B.A., York dio. Disp. to take all h.o. within the prohibited times. 26s 8d.

31 Jo. Bredforde, Crutched fr. Disp. to leave the religious life & become a sec. pr. Gratis; warrant of the lords shown.

Apr. 2 Geo. Amys, subdcn, monk of St Augustine's, Canterbury. Disp. to take the rest of h.o. although in his 24th yr. 16s.

f. 186ʳ

Geo. Amys, subdcn, monk of St Augustine's, Canterbury. Disp. to take dcn's & pr.'s orders on the same day, outside the statutory times. 15s.

Apr. 2 Rob. Glastonburye, subdcn, monk of St Augustine's, Cant. Disp. to take dcn's & pr.'s orders within the prohibited times. 15s.

4 Rob. Archdayll & Jenet Bromehede, York dio. Disp. for marriage (4th degree consang.). 26s 8d.

Brian & Marg. Gey, of Dent, York dio. Disp. for marriage (4th degree consang.). 26s 8d.

Jenkyn ap John, & Joan verch Llen, Lland. dio. Disp. for marriage (4th degree affin.). 26s 8d.

1537 Nov. 30 Jo. Cawte, pr., v. of Streatley, Linc. dio. Disp. for non-res. for 2 yrs. 13s 4d. p.s.r. 5s.

f. 186ᵛ

1538 Mar. 20 Ric. Quyen, r. of ?Welford-on-Avon ('Welnesford') Worc. dio., chapl. to the Ld Privy Seal. Disp. to hold a benef. with the above, or 2 without. £6 10s.

31 Rob. Larke, r. of Millbrook ('Mellesbroke') chapl. to the Bp of Winchester. Disp. to hold a benef. with the above, or 2 without; permut. cl. £6 10s.

Apr. 6 Wm Gray, O.P., recently of Ipswich. Disp. to hold a benef. with change of habit. 'Gratis quia pauper'; warrant of the lords shown.

Peter Stanwey, O.F.M. Disp. to leave the religious life & become a sec. pr. £4.

Mar. 31 Christin(us) Wilson, O.P. Disp. to leave the religious life and become a sec. pr. £4.

Apr. 7 Tho. Cowper & Ann Swaynt, of ?Offerton ('Affreton'), Durham dio. Disp. for marriage (Ann was godmother to a child of Tho.). 'Remittitur gratis ob paupertatem'; warrant of the lords shown.

f. 187ʳ

Mar. 31 Rob. Stickeforde, pr., recently abbot of Revesby, Linc. dio. Disp. to hold a benef. with change of habit. Also for Jo. Sawer, Rob. Pedder, Hy Hardye, Jas Tyldesley, Ric. Lanton, Adam Putterell, Chris. Sherwyn, Wm Warner, Jo. Fylay, Geo. Williamson, Tho. Longbottom, Jas Sothbye, Jo. Clerke, Hy Laton, Tho. Hare, Rob. Birell, Wm Eston, Wm Watson, Jo. Crosse, monks of the above hse. Suppr.

Apr. 1 Tho. Mannyng, recently prior of Butley, Norw. dio. Disp. to hold a benef. with change of habit. Also for Jo. Dennye, Jo. Norwiche, Jas Warner, Rob. Norman, Reg. Westfield, Nich. Palmer, Tho. Rooe, Tho. Spilman *alias* Wodebridge, Hy Johnson *alias* Dunyngton, canons of the above hse. Suppr.

f. 187ᵛ

Apr. 4 Wm. Huddelston, recently abbot of Stratford Langthorne, London dio. Disp. to hold a benef. with change of habit. Also for Wm Persons, Jo. Riddesldale, Ant. Clerke, Jo. Meryott, Jo. Gybbys, Chris. Snowe, Wm Danyell, Wm Pyerson, Tho. Selbye, Wm Symonde, Jo. Stott, Ric. Stannton, Tho. Drake, monks of the same hse. Suppr.

12 Francis Abre, pr., recently prior of St Andrew's, Northampton, Linc. dio. Disp. to hold a benef. with change of habit. Also for Jo. Leth, Tho. Smythe, Tho. Goldeston, Rob. Marten, Jas Hopkyns, Ric. Cooke, Jo. Rote, Jo. Horolde, Tho. Barbor, Tho. Atterbury, Wm Suckar, Wm Warde, monks of the same hse. Suppr.

30 Edw. Jay, pr., recently prior of Hexham, Durham, dio. Disp. to hold a benef. with change of habit. Also for Jas Whiteskales, canon of the above hse. Suppr.

f. 188ʳ

8 Jo. Shurlande, literate, York dio. Disp. to practise as a public notary. 13s 4d.

10 Wm Whitwame & Isabella Blakey, of Colne, Cov. & Lich. dio. Disp. for marriage (3rd & 4th degrees affin.). 30s.

8 Jas Addyshedde & Margery Whiteworthe, Cov. & Lich. dio. Disp. for marriage (3rd & 4th degrees affin.). 30s.

12 Nich. Gyrdlyngton, Linc. dio., & Alice Aske, York dio. Disp. for marriage (3rd & 4th degrees consang.). 30s.

10 Rich. Sylbecke & Marg. Jackson, of Irton, York dio. Disp. for marriage (3rd & 4th degrees consang.). 30s.

10 Jo. Batler, O.F.M. Disp. to become a sec. pr. with change of habit. Gratis; warrant of the lords shown.

f. 188ᵛ

18 Hy Stafforde, sch., Durham dio. Disp. to take all h.o. & 2 on the same day, within the prohibited times. 26s 8d.

Adam Carne, subdcn, York dio. Disp. to take dcn's & pr.'s orders outside the statutory times & on the same day. 13s 4d.

29 Ant. Frobisher, M.A., v. of Darrington, York dio., chapl. to the Earl of Shrewsbury. Disp. to hold a benef. with cure with the above, or 2 without; permut. cl. £6 10s.

19 Wm Cake, v. of Bishops Canning, Sarum dio., chapl. to Bp of Sarum. Disp. to hold a benef. with the above, or 2 without; permut. & non-res. cl. £7 13s 4d.

Apr. 17 Peter Pyper, O.P. Disp. to become a sec. pr. £4.

f. 189ʳ

20 Wm More, suffragan Bp of Colchester, r. of Bardwell & Westbury, Lond. dio., v. of Bradford, York dio. Disp. to hold a benef.
with cure, so that he may live up to the dignity of his station. £8.

25 Wm Foxcrofte, sch., York dio. Disp. to take all h.o. within the
prohibited times, without l.d. 26s 8d.; 6s 8d.

26 Edw. Braydley & Ann Marburye, Cant. dio. Disp. for marriage
without banns. 10s.

27 Tho. Mannsell, pr., v. of Brayton, York dio. Disp. to hold a benef.
with the above; permut. cl. £6 10s.

Wm Lancaster, literate, Bath & W. dio. Creation as public notary
& tabellion. 13s 4d.

f. 189ᵛ

15 Tho. Ld Audeley, Baron Audeley of Walden, Ld Chancellor, &
Ly Eliz. Grey, dau. of the late Ld Tho. Grey, K.G., Marquess
of Dorset. Disp. for marriage not in their par. ch., without banns,
& outside the statutory times. 10s; 20s; 10s.

20 Ric. Harte, pr., recently O.S.A., prior of Llanthony, Worc. dio.
Disp. to hold a benef. with complete change of habit. Also for
Humfrey Jeram, Tho. Hall, Jo. Edwards, Jo. Horowode, Jo.
Richards, Wm Oreton, Wm Monle, Geo. Pomfrey, Ric. West-
burye, Wm Banks, Roger Fortey, Owen Gleting, Maurice Hooper,
Wm Browne, Edm. Sharpe, Wm Philippis, Wm Adams, Mathew
Wever, David Tympe, Wm Awendon, Wm Fuller, ?Maret
Aylbton, Jo. Jordayn, canons of the same hse. Suppr.

f. 190ʳ

26 Ralph Fuster & Alice Comyng, Durham dio. Disp. for marriage
(4th degree consang.). 26s 8d.

Ric. Marysse, O.F.M. Disp. to leave the religious life, with a
stipend. Gratis; warrant of the lords shown.

20 Rob. Catton, recently abbot of St. Albans, v. of Bawburgh,
Norw. dio. Disp. for non-res. for 2 yrs. 13s 4d; p.s.r. 5s.

30 Peter Browne, M.A., acol. Disp. to take subdcn's & pr.'s orders
within the prohibited times & on the same day. 13s 4d.

May 1 Jo. Neve & Marion Marling, Ely dio. Disp. for marriage (Jo's
mother was Marion's godmother). 30s.

f. 190ᵛ

Jo. Shelyt, literate, York dio. Disp. as public notary & tabellion
13s 4d.

May 2 Tho. Watkyn *alias* ap Watkyn & Kath. Lewys *alias* verch Lewys, Heref. dio. Disp. for marriage (4th degree consang.). 26s 8d.

Tho. Bryan, clk, Linc. dio. Disp. to take all h.o. although in his 24th yr. 20s.

5 Tho. Tycheborne, of Winchester, & Ann Chaffyn, of Bulford, Sarum dio. Disp. for marriage despite pre-contract (Tho. was betrothed to Agnes Chaffyn, sister of Ann).' 26s 8d.

6 Tho. Hans, O.S.B., of Hulme, Norw. dio., pr. Disp. to hold a benef. with change of habit. 'Gratis quia pauper'; warrant of the lords shown.

f. 191ʳ

10 Stephen Wateryng & Eliz. Serle, Winton dio. Disp. for marriage (Stephen's mother was Eliz.'s godmother). 30s.

Hugh Wall & Eleanor Wynde, Heref. dio. Disp. for marriage (2nd & 3rd degrees affin.). £8.

Ric. Freyston, esq., & Ann Pecksall, Winton dio. Disp. for marriage without banns. 10s.

Roger Watson, pr., York dio., holder of a benef. or eccles. office, without cure, not yielding £8 p.a. Disp. to hold another. £4.

Wm Poull, O.P. Disp. to become a sec. pr. Gratis; warrant of the lords shown.

f. 191ᵛ

Wm Bewdeley, recently abbot of Kingswood, Worc. dio. Disp. to hold a benef. with change of habit. Also for Tho. Bedyng, Jo. Gethyn, Jo. Westburye, Wm Wotton, Jo. Sodbury, Wm Hughes, Wm Parker, Tho. Archarde, Nich. Acton, Edw. Erlingham, Jo. Stonley, Nich. Hampton, Wm Wyllyngton, monks of the same hse. Suppr.

5 Tho. Stephens, abbot of Beaulieu (spelt 'Bewdeley'), Winton dio. Disp. to hold a benef. with change of habit. Also for Tho. Seall, Griffith Hampton, Walter Bartilmew, Wm Coventre, Ric. Guyldeforde, Wm Baskerley, Ric. Curlew, Harmand Hampton, Alex. Alen, Jo. Bere, Rob. Pyckton, Jo. Somerfelde, Tho. Evaw, Tho. White, Simon Halker, Tho. Burton, Laurence Parker. Suppr.

f. 192ʳ

8 Wm Noxton, recently prior of Southwark, Winton dio. Disp. to hold a benef. with change of habit. Also for Jas Gonwyn, Peter Elton, Wm Dunnan, Simon Wales, Philip Raye, Philip Halse, Tho. Leymer, Jo. Trym, Simon Palmer, Miles Man, Jo. Caredell, Jo. Yonge, religious of the same hse. Suppr.

May 10 Tho. Cowper, O.P. Disp. to become a sec. pr. 'Gratis quia pauper'; warrant of the lords shown.

12 Tho. Ipeswell, v. of Warlingham with the annexed chapel of Chelsham, Winton dio., chapl. to the Bp of St Asaph. Disp. to hold a benef. with the above, or 2 without; permut. cl. £6 10s.

Tho. Whyte, Kg's chapl., v. of Heston & Hampton-on-Thames, Lond. dio. Disp. to hold 3rd benefice with the above. £8.

f. 192ᵛ

13 Hy Jakys & Joan Banester, Linc. dio. Disp. for marriage (3rd and 4th degrees consang.). 30s.

14 Rob. Carnocke & Alice Hynton, Linc. dio. Disp. for marriage (Alice was godmother to a child of Rob.). £6.

Lewis Philpott & Alice ap John, Lland. dio. Disp. for marriage (3rd & 4th degrees consang.). 30s.

15 Jo. Fermery, acol., Linc. dio. Disp. to take subdcn's & pr.'s orders on the same day, within the prohibited times. 13s 4d.

16 Jo. Turman *alias* Turner & Helen Barker, Lond. Disp. for marriage (Jo.'s mother was Helen's godmother). 30s.

17 Jo. Bellott & Joan Cheseman, Cant. dio. Disp. for marriage without banns. 10s.

f. 193ʳ

Jo. Plughe, sch., York dio. Disp. to take all h.o. outside the statutory times, & 2 on the same day. 26s 8d.

Confirmation of the annexation allowed by the Bp & Dean & Chapter of Ferns (Ireland) of the free chapel of Kyllalocke & All Saints, Bellator. 40s; p.s.r. 5s.

Wm Slake and Emms More, Cov. & Lich. dio. Disp. for marriage (4th degree consang.). 26s 8d.

Tho. Chalys & Joan Mynott, Ely dio. Disp. for marriage (Joan's father was Tho.'s godfather). 30s.

18 Tho. Wyatt & Alice Kyngam, Linc. dio. Disp. for marriage (4th degree consang.). 26s 8d.

f. 193ᵛ

Tho. Whisteler & Alice Hobbe, Sarum dio. Disp. for marriage (Tho.'s father was Alice's godfather). 30s.

19 Nich. Peckocke, recently canon of Guisborough, York dio. Disp. to hold a benef. with complete change of habit. Also for Tho. Blythe, canon of the same hse. Arb. £4; warrant of the lords shown.

May   20 Tho. Wyllyams, pr., recently canon of Binham, Norw. dio. Disp. to hold a benef. with change of habit. Suppr.

Wm May, D.C.L., r. of Hatfield, Linc. dio. Disp. to hold a benef. with the above, or 2 without it. £9.

14 Edw. Reveley, B.Th., O.F.M. Disp. to become a sec. pr. 'Gratis, per litteram Thome domini Cromwell.'

f. 194ʳ

20 Confirmation of the statutes of the coll. of Kirk Oswald ('Kirks-wold'), Carl. dio., founded by Ld Wm Dacre, at the request of Jo. Heryng, D.C.L., master of the above coll. 40s; p.s.r. 5s.

Tho. Devicke & Thomasina Beauvoir, of the island of Guernsey, Coutances dio. Disp. for marriage (3rd degree affin.). 'Gratis quia pauperes'; warrant of the lords shown.

19 Tho. Walcott, subdcn, monk of Pershore, Worc. dio. Disp. to take dcn's & pr.'s orders within the prohibited times & 2 on the same day. 13s 4d.

Wm Wright, subdcn, Linc. dio. Disp. to take dcn's & pr.'s orders outside the statutory times. 13s 4d.

20 Jo. Godderde & Alice Rosse, Ely dio. Disp. for marriage (Jo.'s former wife was godmother to a child of Alice). Arb. £4; warrant of the lords shown.

Tho. Carter & Joan Wyllys, Cov. & Lich. dio. Disp. for marriage (3rd & 4th degrees affin.). 30s.

f. 194ᵛ

19 Wm Taylboys, v. of Billinghay, r. of Aswarby, Linc. dio. Disp. for non-res. during illness. 20s.

Geo. Meres, Carl. dio. Disp. to practise as a public notary. 13s 4d.

20 Ant. Myddelton, v. of Sutton, York dio., chapl. to Ld Jo. Scrope. Disp. to hold a benef. with the above; permut. cl. £6 10s.

Jo. Coke, Observant fr. Disp. to become a sec. pr. 'Gratis quia pauper'; warrant of the lords shown.

Jo. Musarde *alias* Walker, pr., O.S.B., recently of Worc. priory. Disp. to change his habit. 'Gratis quia pauper'; warrant of the lords shown.

19 Tho. Gregory & Eliz. Warde, of Coventry. Disp. for marriage without banns. 10s.

f. 195ʳ

18 Laurence Rayne & Jane Preston, York dio. Disp. for marriage (Laurence's mother was Jane's godmother). 30s.

May 15 German & Joan Pole, Cov. & Lich. dio. Disp. for marriage (German's father was Joan's godfather). 30s.

22 Jo. Jenyns & Joan Aspolle *alias* Marks, of London. Disp. for marriage without banns. 10s.

20 Ant. Bellecys, D.C.L., r. of Wickham, Durham dio., in the service of Ld Tho. Cromwell, K.G. Disp. to hold 2 benefices with the above, or 3 without, of which only 2 may be par. chs. £9.

24 Ric. Atkynson & Janet Gye, York dio. Disp. for marriage (3rd and 4th degrees consang.). 30s.

25 Jo. Wade & Eliz. Tyler, Heref. dio. Disp. for marriage (3rd & 4th degrees affin.). 30s.

f. 195ᵛ

20 Oswald Metcalf, v. of Catterick, York dio. Disp. to hold a benef. with the above, or 2 without it; permut. cl. £6 10s.

25 Rob. Felton, subdcn, Cov. & Lich. dio. Disp. to take dcn's & pr.'s orders within the prohibited times & 2 on the same day. 15s.

26 Roger Tempest & Jenet Wedow *alias* Hertple, Durham dio. Disp. for marriage (Roger was godfather to a child of Jenet). £6.

25 Jo. & Isabella Robynson, Cov. & Lich. dio. Disp. for marriage (3rd & 4th degrees affin.). 30s.

26 Hugh & Grace Savill, York dio. Disp. for marriage (3rd degree consang.). £6.

27 Walter ap Jevan ap Watkyn & Joan verch Jenn ap Glyllym. Disp. for marriage (4th degree affin.). 26s 8d.

28 Jo. Scotte, r. of Hulme, York dio., chapl. to Ld Latimer. Disp. to hold a benef. with cure with the above; permut. cl. £6 10s.

f. 196ʳ

27 Patrick Chillam & Agnes Bathe, of Armagh dio. Ireland. Disp. validating their marriage (contracted in ignorance of 4th degree consang.). 26s 8d.

28 Tho. Caldebeke, one of the chanters in the Scrope chantry, York Minster. Disp. to hold another benef. if he does not receive more than £8 p.a. as chanter £4. Also for Martin Warde, the other chanter. £4.

18 David ap Howell ap Gryffithe & Marg. verch William John Owen, St David's dio. Disp. for marriage (4th degree consang., 3rd & 4th degrees affin.). 26s 8d.; 30s.

May 27 Jo. Pyen, O.C. fr., of Bristol. Disp. to change his habit. Gratis; warrant of the lords shown.

28 Gilbert Melborne, O.F.M., of Ware. Disp. to hold a benef. with change of habit. Arb. £4; warrant of the lords shown.

f. 196ᵛ

30 Ric. Makeyn, O.C. fr., recently of Burnham (Norton), Norw. dio. Disp. to become a sec. pr. £4.

Tho. Nix, O.F.M., of Winchelsea. Disp. to leave the religious life. 'Gratis quia pauper'; warrant of the lords shown.

Apr. 30 Jo. Coke, reg. canon of Bibury, Worc. dio. also of Osney. Disp. to hold for life the custody of the chapels annexed to Bibury. £4.

Jo. Swalow, gent. of London & Agnes Pynner, gentw. of Stepney. Disp. for marriage without banns. 10s.

May 30 Wm Fennewike, r. of Litton, Bath & W. dio. Disp. to hold a benef. with the above, which does not yield over £8 p.a. £4.

28 Wm Cartewright & Ann Copeledike, York dio. Disp. for marriage (4th degree consang.). 26s 8d.

f. 197ʳ

Ant. Browne, O.F.M. Disp. to follow the life of a hermit of St Paul. 40s.

Tho. Page & Joan Bere, Linc. dio. Disp. for marriage, the banns read once. 6s 8d.

Jo. Wm Roberts & Alice Richarde Selman, Lland. dio. Disp. for marriage (3rd & 4th degrees consang.). 30s.

21 Lewis ap John, subdcn, Lland. dio. Disp. to take all h.o. although in his 22nd yr. 23s 4d.

31 Rob. Rawlyng, acol., Norw. dio. Disp. to take all h.o. within the prohibited times, & 2 on the same day. 26s 8d.

Wm Norman & Marg. Rede, Lond. dio. Disp. for marriage within the prohibited times. 20s.

f. 197ᵛ

Nich. Stratton *alias* Parkyns & Margery Judde, of Higham Ferrers, Lond. dio. Disp. for marriage (Nich.'s mother was Margery's godmother). 30s.

30 Tho. Tayler, recently abbot of Robertsbridge, Chich. dio. Disp. to hold a benef. with change of habit. Also for Rob. Thurgoode, Stephen Warre, Wm Squyer, Jo. Wyke, Laurence Thrower, Tho. Sprotte, Wm Seynden, Rob. Cowper, monks of the same hse. Suppr.

May 31 Margery Hill, recently prioress of Cheshunt, Lond. dio. Disp. to leave the religious life. Suppr.

June 1 Ric. Hudson, recently prior of Beeston, Norw. dio. Disp. to hold a benef. with change of habit. Also for Nich. Wodeforde & Wm Ellys, of the same hse. Suppr.

2 Jo. Burtham, O.F.M., recently of Salisbury. Disp. to hold a benef., with cure retaining his habit. £4.

f. 198ʳ

3 Rob. Laurence, chapl. to Ld Windsor. Disp. to hold any 2 benefices; permut. & non-res. cl. £7 13s 4d.

Wm Tayllour, pr., recently abbot of Halesowen, Worcs. dio. Disp. to hold a benef. with complete change of habit. Also for Nich. Grayves, Rob. Boolde, Tho. Cannte, Wm Poole, Tho. Bromley, Adam Grene, Jo. Aysheley, Tho. Richards, Wm Mashrudder, Hy Corser, Roger Sherman, Ric. Warynges, Jo. Turnour, canons of the same hse. Suppr.

May 29 Jo. Dyckeson & Marg. Hopkynson, York dio. Disp. for marriage (3rd & 4th degrees affin.). 30s.

20 Peter Vannes, Kg's sec. for Latin Letters, Dean of Sarum, archdcn of Worcester &c. Disp. to postpone taking h.o. for 5 yrs. 50s.

f. 198ᵛ

June 1 Jo. Saylsbury of Henllan St Sadwm ('Hentham imnore'), St Asaph dio., & Joan Myddelton, of Chester, Cov. & Lich. dio. Disp. for marriage (4th degree consang.). 26s 8d.

29 Oliver Halsted & Ann Barcrost, Cov. & Lich. dio. Disp. for marriage (4th degree affin. or consang.). 26s 8d.

28 Nich. Lampen & Marg. Nyell, Ex. dio. Disp. for marriage (Marg.'s mother was Nich.'s godmother). 30s.

4 Ric. Nycholls & Rose Madog, Heref. dio. Disp. for marriage (Rose's father was Ric.'s godfather). 30s.

May 25 Ric. Worthington & Joan Leyner, Cov. & Lich. dio. Disp. for marriage (3rd & 4th degrees consang.). 30s.

June 4 Ric. Payge, canon & prebendary of Salisbury, r. of Clutton, Bath & W. dio. Disp. for non-res. on account of various ailments. 20s; p.s.r. 5s.

f. 199ʳ

20 Lewis Johns, pr., B.C.L., subdean of the coll. ch. of Westbury-on-Trym, Worc. dio. Disp. to hold any other benef. with the above; permut. cl. £6 10s.

May 31 Tho. Gale, B.Th., monk of St Saviour's, Bermondsey, Winton dio. Disp. to hold a benef. with change of habit. Arb. £4; warrant of the lords shown.

Apr. 30 Wm Castelton, prior of Norw. cath. priory. Disp. to wear the habit of a sec. pr. & hold the deanery of Norw. cath & 2 other benefices, conditional upon his residing in Norw. & appointing suitable curates. £20; warrant of the lords shown.

June 3 Tho. Spilman, Cant. dio., & Isabella Brett, Lond. dio. Disp. for marriage in their par. ch. without banns. 10s.

f. 199ᵛ

Apr. 30 Walter Gryme *alias* Crowmere, pr., O.S.B., of Norw. cath. Disp. to wear the habit of a sec. pr. & to hold a canonry & prebend. of Norw. cath. & any other benef. with or without cure, & be non-res. £10. Also for Wm Harydans, £10; for Hy Mannell, Edm. Drake, Nich. Thurkyll, monks, similar faculties, 30s; for Rob. Thwaties, recently monk of the same hse, similar disp. £6 13s 4d. For Stephen Darsham, Tho. Leman, Rob. Bowgyn, Rob. Bennys, Francis Atmere, Rob. Grene, Rob. Stannton, Geo. Beawchyn, Francis Yaxley, Jo. Sherve, Tho. Jolye, Wm Kegell, Adam Barker, Botolph Parker, Andrew Tooke, monks of the same hse, similar faculties. £100; warrants of the lords shown in all cases.

f. 200ʳ

Jo. Toller *alias* Wells, recently monk of Norwich. Disp. to wear the habit of a sec. pr.; also for Wm Wodows & Rob. Smythe. £4 each.

June 6 Jo. Coddenham, O.P., of Norwich. Disp. to change his habit. Gratis; warrant of the lords shown.

Jo. Myll, chanter of Wooton-Glanville, Sarum dio. Disp. for non-res. for 2 yrs on account of various infirmities. 6s 8d.

May 21 Tho. Southwike, chanter in the chantry of St Mary the Virgin, in the ch. of St. Laurence, Hungerford. Disp. for non-res. for 2 yrs because the building is in disrepair. 13s 4d.

June 6 Tho. Colyn & Joan Thorpe, of the par. of Longnewton, Durham dio. Disp. for marriage (3rd & 3rd degrees of consang.). Arb. 40s; warrant of the lords shown.

Tho. Handeley *alias* Senagyr, pr., O.S.B., of St Peter's, Gloucester, Worc. dio. Disp. to wear the habit of a sec. pr. £4.

f. 200ᵛ

May 3 Jo. Bowle, recently prior of Merton. Disp. to hold any benef. with the above office. Similar letters patent for Jo. Debenham,

Tho. Colson, Jo. Codington, Ric. Todd, Jo. Heywarde, Geo. Curson, Ric. Benese, Tho. Mychell, Tho. Paynell, Jo. Page, Edw. Honyber, Jo. Meryvale, Jo. Saling, Rob. Knight. Suppr.

June 3 Tho. Spilman of Ulcombe, Lond. dio., & Isabella Brette, of Cant. dio. Disp. for marriage without banns. 10s.

8 Wm Harris & Helen Houghe, Cov. & Lich. dio. Disp. for marriage (Wm was godfather to a child of Helen). Arb. £3; warrant of the lords shown.

1 Wm Whitte, pr., v. of Fressingfield, Norw. dio. Disp. to hold a benef. with cure with the above, or 2 without. £6 10s.

May 31 Wm Burges, subdcn, monk of St Augustine's, Canterbury. Disp. to take dcn's & pr.'s orders within the prohibited times & on the same day, from any bp. 15s. Also for Wm Horsmenden & Edw. Hales, monks of the same hse. 15s; 15s.

f. 201ʳ

June ? Jo. Brownwiche, pr., r. of Abberton, Worc. dio. Disp. to hold a benef. with the above, or 2 others without it; permut. cl. £6 10s.

10 Ric. Paynter, canon of St Osyth, Lond. dio. Disp. to hold a benef. with change of habit. Arb. £5; warrant of the lords.

Tho. Radforde, literate, Cov. & Lich. dio. Disp. to practise as public notary & tabellion. 13s 4d.

12 Jo. Hamonde, recently abbot of Battle, Sussex. Disp. to hold a benef. with change of habit. Also for Ric. Salehurst, Clement Westfeld, Jo. Hasting, Jo. Henfylde, Jo. Austen, Tho. Levett, Vincent Dunstane, Jo. Benyng, Clement Gregorie, Tho. Cuthbert, Wm Ambrose, Tho. Bede, Jo. Heronne, Edw. Clement, Batholomew Ciprian, Jo. Newton, Ric. Dartmouth. Suppr.

Jo. Wright, acol., Linc. dio. Disp. to take all h.o. without l.d. & at any time. 6s 8d; 26s 8d.

f. 201ᵛ

13 Rob. Oles, B.Cn. & C.L., v. of Firle, Chich. dio. Disp. to hold another benef. with the above, or 2 without; permut. & non-res. cl. £7 13s 4d.

10 Clement Aglionby, v. of Mirfield, York dio. Disp. for non-res. as he asserts he is 60 & is almost blind. 20s.

1 Hy Tayler, monk of Evesham, Linc. dio. Disp. to change his habit. £4.

17 Gavin Carlun, gent., & Mary Gwidforde. Disp. for marriage without banns, in any ch. 10s; 10s.

June 16 Tho. Villirs, Linc. dio., & Eliz. Browne, of St Olave's, Lond. Disp. for marriage without banns. 10s.

20 Wm Knotton of the Order of the Holy Saviour of Syon, Lond. dio. Disp. to hold a benef. with change of habit. 'Gratis; per litteram domini Cromwell.'

2 Tho. Lee, fr. of Newcastle-under-Lyme. Disp. to wear the habit of a sec. pr. £4.

f. 202^r

Chas Waywright, r. of ?Feering ('Fayng'), Lond. dio., chapl. to Ld Hy Parker, Ld Morley. Disp. to hold another benef. with the above, or 2 without; permut. & non-res. cl. £7 13s 4d.

3 Wm Asshefeld, pr., r. of Oddington-on-Otmoor, Linc. dio. Disp. to hold another benef. with the above, or 2 without; permut. cl. £6 10s.

10 Jo. Facett, Austin fr., St Botulph's, Boston, Linc. dio. Disp. to hold a benef. with some change of habit. £8.

18 Wm Law of Hempunstald (?) & Eliz. Culpon of Halifax, York dio. Disp. for marriage (4th degree consang.). 26s 8d.

20 Wm Spendeley, canon of Alvingham, Linc. dio. Disp. to hold a benef. £4.

23 Wm Selman & Joan Turner, Cov. & Lich. dio. Disp. for marriage (4th degree consang.). 26s 8d.

20 Wm Coke & Marg. Lowe, York dio. Disp. for marriage (Tho. Lowe, Marg.'s late husband, was godfather to a child of Wm). Arb. £4; warrant of the lords shown.

f. 202^v

26 Jenn ap Thomas ap Inon & Kath. verch Jenkins, of Bryngwyn, St David's dio. Disp. for marriage (4th degree consang.). 26s 8d.

Jo. Hopton, D.Th., O.P., Prior Provincial in England. Disp to hold any benef.; permut. cl. £4.

Paul Dotrell, Linc. dio., & Susan Treveram, Ex dio. Disp. for marriage in any ch. without banns. 10s; 10s.

10 Roger Colley, master of grammar, Cov. & Lich. dio. Disp. to receive the privileges of his status in a university. £3.

26 Andrew Ryvet & Eliz. Huntingfeld *alias* Tyvame, Norw. dio. Disp. for marriage, the banns read once. 6s 8d.

27 Mich. Mekems, Carth., prior of Axholme, Linc. dio. Disp. to hold a benef. with change of habit. Also for Jo. Popill, Ric. Crakkill, Tho. Alrede, Brian Ree, Hy Wilson, Tho. Broke, Tho. Dobson. Suppr.

f. 203ʳ

June 26 Jo. Harvie & Marg. Gouche, Norw. dio. Disp. for marriage (4th degree consang.). 26s 8d.

Rob. Troubelfeld & Mary Bonham, Wells dio. Disp. for marriage (3rd & 4th degrees affin.). 30s.

Wm Newman, Austin fr., of Norwich. Disp. to change his habit. £4.

27 Ric. Clerkeson, B.Th., canon & prebendary of Wells cath., v. of St Cuthbert's, Wells. Disp. to hold a benef. with the above; permut. cl. £8.

Hugh Robynson & Marg. Blande, York dio. Disp. for marriage (3rd & 4th degrees consang.). 30s.

July 29 Martin Langrishe, Winton dio. Disp. to take pr.'s orders outside the statutory times. 10s.

June 27 Jo. ap Henrye & Cecily verch Jenkyn, Lland. dio. Disp. for marriage (4th degree consang.). 26s 8d.

25 Hy Crewche & Marg. Heydon, Norw. dio. Disp. for marriage without banns. 10s.

f. 203ᵛ

27 Jo. Harleston & Mildred Mundye, of London. Disp. for marriage, the banns read once. 6s 8d.

Vincent Mundye & Juliana Gadburye, of London. Disp. for marriage (the banns read once & 4th degree consang.). 6s 8d; 26s 8d.

July 30 Cornelius Gate, O.P., of Winchelsea. Disp. for change of habit. Gratis; warrant of the lords shown.

26 Walter Hele, B.Th., r. of Harford, Ex. dio. Disp. to hold a benef. with the above, or 2 without. £6 10s.

1 Wm Parpoyente, B.C.L., York dio. Disp. to practise as a notary & tabellion. 13s 4d.

Rob. Thomason & Marg. Nyxon, Cov. & Lich. dio. Disp. for marriage (3rd & 4th degrees affin.). 30s.

June 29 Oliver Halstede & Ann Harecrost, Cov. & Lich. dio. Disp. for marriage (4th degree affin. as well as 4th degree consang. for which they were previously dispensed). 26s 8d.

f. 204ʳ

July 2 Hy Bright & Joan Onstey, Chich. dio. Disp. for marriage (3rd & 4th degrees consang.). 30s.

July   1 Tho. Saywell & Cecily Woode, York dio. Disp. for marriage (3rd
& 4th degrees consang.). 30s.

June   29 Jo. Carter, subdcn, York dio. Disp. to take dcn's & pr.'s orders
on the same day within the prohibited times. 15s.

       28 Howel ap Thomas & Cristine verch William, Lland. dio. Disp.
for marriage (4th degree consang.). 26s 8d.

July   1 Jo. Awse, pr., monk of Buckfast, Ex. dio. Disp. to change his
habit. £4.

        2 Oswald Myers, B.Cn.L. Disp. to hold any 2 benefs; permut.
cl. £6 10s.

June   29 Ric. Hill, sch. & acol., Heref. dio. Disp. to take all h.o. within
the prohibited times. 20s.

f. 204ᵛ

Maurice ap John, acol., Heref. dio. Disp. to take all h.o. outside
the statutory times. 20s.

Geoffrey ap Owen, acol., Heref. dio. Disp. to take all h.o. within
the prohibited times. 20s.

July   4 Wm Lawnde & Ursula Aylonde, of London. Disp. for marriage
without banns. 10s.

Jo. Pole, O.P. Disp. to change his habit. Gratis; by warrant of
the lords.

Jo. Cordrayn, recently abbot of Bisham, Sarum dio. Disp. to hold
a benef. with complete change of habit. Also for Wm Walter,
Laurence Hodgeson, Jo. Church, Jo. Butts, Jo. Walter, Wm
Rooke, Wm Rugisse, Tho. Potter, Jo. Roffe, Edw. Stephenson,
Jo. Myllist, Rob. Knight, Ant. Simonson, Ric. Wachett, Geo.
Nydigate. Suppr.

f. 205ʳ

        5 Jo. Benton & Cecily Hone, of London. Disp. for marriage with-
out banns, in any ch. 10s; 10s.

        6 Tho. Fayrhaye, r. of Rawmarsh, York dio. & v. of Iping. Disp.
to hold a 3rd benef. with the above, or 2 without. £8.

        7 Rewer Wolf & Joan Cook, of London. Disp. for marriage without
banns. 10s.

        8 Jo. Marye & Alice Stentforde, Ex. dio. Disp. for marriage (Jo.'s
late wife was godmother to Alice). Arb. £4; warrant of the
lords shown.

        6 Wm Fawnte & Barbara Cave, Linc. dio. Disp. for marriage with-
out banns. 10s.

July   9 Tho. Moresbye *alias* Stottowe, monk of Hulme, Norw. dio. Disp. to hold a benef. with some change of habit. Arb. £4; warrant of the lords shown.

       10 Jo. Gregorye, recently Trinitarian fr. of Mostenden, Cant. dio. Disp. to hold a benef. with change of habit. Also for Jo. Hardyman, Ric. Hede, Ric. Bukherst, Wm Berker, Andrew Petynden, Geo. Rede, Tho. Wellis. Suppr.

ff. 205ᵛ–206ʳ   blank.

f. 206ᵛ

        9 Tho. Nora, r. of Belleau ('Hellow'), Linc. dio. Disp. to hold a benef. with the above, or 2 without; permut. cl. £6 10s.

June 28 Tho. & Joan Cornysshe, Ex. dio. Disp. for marriage (3rd & 4th degrees consang.). 30s.

       10 Rob. Reding *alias* Goday, canon of Notley, Linc. dio. Disp. to change his habit. £4.

       11 Jas Aysshe, B.Cn. & C.L., r. of Staunton in Corpe Lawn ('Consland'), Worc. dio. Disp. to hold a benef. with or 2 without the above; permut. cl. £6 10s.

        6 Jo. Wigge, r. of Puttenham, Linc. dio. Disp. for non-res. on account of near-blindness & other ailments. 20s.

       10 Jo. Alon, Norw. dio. Disp. to take all h.o. within the prohibited times. 20s.

        7 Rob. Haynes, O.P., of Winchester. Disp. to change his habit. Gratis; warrant of the lords shown.

f. 207ʳ

       25 Wm Golding, M.A., Norw. dio. Disp. to take all h.o., & 2 on the same day, at any times. 26s 8d.

July   8 Howell ap Howell & Kath. verch Leyson, Lland. dio. Disp. for marriage (4th degree consang.). 26s 8d.

       10 Rob. Keling & Marg. Froste, Linc. dio. Disp. for marriage (Rob.'s recent wife was sponsor at the confirmation of a child of Marg.). Arb. £4; warrant of the lords shown.

        5 Rob. Haclynne, O.F.M., incumbent of Horsington (Lincs.). Disp. to retain this benef. & give up his religious habit. Arb. £4; warrant of the lords shown.

       10 Roger Genyns & Agnes Alporte, Cov. & Lich. dio. Disp. for marriage (Roger was sponsor at the confirmation of a child of Agnes). £5.

July 12 Ric. Smythe, v. of Tathwell, Linc. dio., chapl. to the Bp of Dublin. Disp. to hold a benef. with the above, or 2 without; permut. cl. £6 10s.

3 Lewis ap Moryce, acol., St David's dio. Disp. to take all h.o. within the prohibited times. 20s.

f. 207ᵛ

Rhes ap Jenn, acol., St David's dio. Disp. to take all h.o. from any bp within the prohibited times. 20s.

Hy Watkins, acol., Heref. dio. Disp. to take all h.o. within the prohibited times. 20s.

20 Wm Boys & Joan Bright, Chich. dio. Disp. for marriage (Wm was godfather to a child of Joan). Arb. £4; warrant of the lords shown.

13 Edm. Farleye, Heref. dio. Disp. to practise as notary & tabellion. 13s 4d.

14 Jo. Marten & Eliz. Langley, Lland. dio. Disp. for marriage (3rd & 4th degrees consang.). 30s.

10 Stephen Johnson, O.P. Disp. to hold any benef.; permut. cl. £4.

19 Jo. Dawne & Kath Dutton, Cov. & Lich. dio. Disp. for marriage (4th degree consang.). 26s 8d.

f. 208ʳ

May 21 Audley, Tho., Ld Chancellor. Disp. (given in full) dated at Lambeth confirming the grant by royal letters patent to the above of the monastery of Walden, Essex, Lond. dio. with all manors, lands, patronage, & other appurtenances. 'Gratis per warrantum domini Regis domini Cancellario inde concessam.'

f. 208ᵛ

July 20 Jo. Matthew & Agnes Wake, Durham dio. Disp. for marriage (Agnes was godmother to a child of Mathew). Arb. £4; warrant of the lords shown.

Tho. Pannott, O.C. fr. Disp. to wear the habit of a sec. pr. Gratis; similar warrant.

17 Jo. Chamberlayne, recently fr. of Dunwich. Disp. to change his habit. Gratis; similar warrant.

20 Jo. Mowson & Isabella Waterman, York dio. Disp. for marriage (Jo. was sponsor at the confirmation of a child of Isabella). Gratis; similar warrant.

Wm Walker, O.F.M. Disp. to become a sec. pr. Gratis; similar warrant.

July 20 Ric. Bentley, recently abbot of Welbeck, Linc. dio. Disp. to hold a benef. with change of habit. Also for Wm Haytefeld, Tho. Syssow, Ric. Austen, Jo. Raicleson, Jo. Stone, Tho. Hill, Ric. Hogleye, Edw. Tomson, Jo. Buklande, Jo. Marshall, Wm Byrde, Nich. Saxton, Wm Almonde, Roger Baron, Ric. Danke, Tho. Holme. Suppr.

f. 209ʳ

Hy Cundall, recently monk of Roche, York dio. Disp. to hold a benef. with change of habit. Also for Tho. Twellis, Jo. Deddesworth, Ric. Drax, Nich. Collis, Jo. Chappe, Tho. Camdall, Tho. Wellis, Ric. Fishborne, Tho. Myddelton, Tho. Herryson, Hy Wilson, Chris. Herste, Wm Carter, Wm Hylye. Suppr.

22 Tho. Bright & Joan Clerke. Disp. for marriage without banns. 10s.

23 Inhabitants of the village of Torrer, in Ulverston par., nr Furness, York dio. Disp. to have the chapel & cemetery of Torrer consecrated by any bp for the burial of the dead. 13s 4d.

20 Jo. Berwike, recently prior of Thurgarton, Notts. Disp. to hold a benef. with change of habit. Also for Wm Chase, Jo. Champney, Jo. Langhstar, Jo. Rylye, Ric. Leke, Ric. Hopkin, Rob. Cante, Hy Gaskyn. Suppr.

f. 209ᵛ

26 Jo. Damporte & Christine Millener, Cant. dio. Disp. for marriage, the banns read once. 6s 8d.

25 Chris. Mores, r. of Pimperne, Sarum dio. Disp. to hold a benef. with the above or 2 without; permut. cl. £6 10s.

Tho. Welde & Marg. Pratye, Linc. dio. Disp. for marriage (3rd degree consang.). Gratis; warrant of the lords shown.

26 Jo. Molley & Anastasia Shaplondon *alias* Smythe, Ex. dio. Disp. for marriage (2nd & 3rd degrees affin.). £8.

27 Tho. Takersall & Helen Waterton, York dio. Disp. for marriage (4th degree affin.). 26s 8d.

26 Chris. Parker, subdcn, canon of Carl. cath. Disp. to take dcn's & pr.'s orders within the prohibited times. 15s.

Wm Tomlynson *alias* Lowther, subdcn, canon of Carl. cath. Disp. to take dcn's & pr.'s orders within the prohibited times. 15s.

f. 210ʳ

Jo. Richerdson *alias* Danerton, acol., canon of Carl. cath. Disp to take h.o. within the prohibited times. 20s.

July 20 Jo. Typtow, O.P. Disp. to give up his habit. £4.

25 Jo. Pennyngton & Eliz. Bedill, Lond. dio. Disp. for marriage without banns. 10s.

31 Edm. Smeton, pr., recently monk of Woburn, Linc. dio. Disp. to hold a benef. with change of habit. Also for Tho. Toller, Ric. Newport, Ric. Hopworth, Rob. Salforth, Rob. Nede, Wm Stratford, Wm Hampton, Jo. Croxton, Jo. Grace, Jo. Forde, Edw. Woborne, Ric. Hawnes, Ric. Salford, Rob. Evershote, Rob. Slingesbye, Rob. Woborne, Wm Peck. Suppr.

Aug. 1 Jas Gunter & Ann Yonge, of London. Disp. for marriage without banns, & in any ch. 10s; 10s.

f. 210ᵛ

July 1 Jo. Shepey, recently abbot of Faversham, Kent. Disp. to hold a benef. with complete change of habit. Also for Rob. Chillenden, Tho. Deve, Dunstan Goodhew, Jo. Tayler, Ralph Ulcom, Jo. Fylpotte, Peter Mynt, Wm Coyden. Suppr.

31 Ric. Chase, O.C. fr., of Oxford. Disp. to hold a benef. with change of habit. Also for Jo. Tyndall, Laurence Senner, Rob. Charlys, Tho. Sedall, Jo. Haynes, Jo. Bacons, Bartholomew Blythman, Ant. Foxston, Rob. Eston. Suppr.

Wm Waterman, O.P., of Oxford. Disp. to hold a benef. with change of habit. Also for Tho. Borell, Ric. Brokilbank, Guy Welshe, Wm Glenton, Peter Flecher, Jas Norys, Hugh Cordwen, Edw. Bampton, Hy Matthew, Wm Dyngleye, Jo. Low, David Jones, Hy Benett. Suppr.

f. 211ʳ

Edw. Baskerveld, O.F.M., Oxford. Disp. to hold a benef. with complete change of habit. Also for Brian Sandon, Ric. Roper, Jas Smyth, Tho. Withman, Jo. Billing, Ralph Kirswell, Rob. Newman, Wm Browne, Jo. Emerye, Jo. Stafforthshire, Tho. Phillips, Jas Conor, Jo. Thornam, Jo. Butler, Tho. Tanner, Jas Cantwell, Wm Bowghtnell, Tho. Capper, Philip Lane, Jo. Hendeley, Francis Jones, Jo. Trevilian, Zachary Carpenter, Jo. Hoskins, Wm Broke, Jo. Morgan, Jo. Richerds, Jo. Duke, Jo. Oliff, Simon Ludforde, Tho. Barley, Wm Coke, Jo. Coke. Suppr.

Aug. 5 Wm ap Madocke ap Jenn ap Griffith & Joan verch Hughe ap Owen ap Meryke, Bangor dio. Disp. for marriage (3rd and 4th degrees consang.). 30s.

f. 211ᵛ

July 31 Ric. Johnson, recently Austin fr., of Oxford. Disp. to hold a benef. with complete change of habit. Also for Geoffrey Tompson, Edw. Foxesgill, Wm Morrys, Wm Myrrey, Edm. Hyans, Mich.

Simpson, Tho. Griffith, Geo. Allysdon, Rob. Yorke, Rob. Bay-lye. Suppr.

Aug. 6 David Mathew, sch., Heref. dio. Disp. to take all h.o. despite defect of birth. £5.

7 Wm Walforde, r. of Old Cleeve, Bath & W. dio., chapl. to the Earl of Bath. Disp. to hold a benef. with the above, or 2 without; permut. cl. £6 10s.

9 Oliver Danbney & Eliz. Pans, Lond. dio. Disp. for marriage without banns. 10s.

Jo. Vawdye & Marion Hussey, of London. Disp. for marriage without banns & in any ch. 10s; 10s.

f. 212ʳ

10 Jas Prowdlow & Joan Williamson, Cov. & Lich. dio. Disp. for marriage (3rd & 4th degrees consang.). 30s.

Tho. Patrike, O.F.M. Disp. for change of habit. Gratis; warrant of the lords shown.

12 Tho. Gaskyn, M.A., Norw. dio. Disp. to take all h.o. outside the statutory times & 2 on the same day. 26s 8d.

10 Roger Wade, r. of 2 parts of the par. ch. of Clipston, Linc. dio., chapl. of Ld Vaux of Harrowden. Disp. to hold a benef. with the above, or 2 without; permut. cl. £6 10s.

18 Tho. Houghton, B.C.L., r. of Charlton, Roch. dio. Disp. to hold a benef. with the above, or 2 without it; permut. cl. £6 10s.

20 Ric. Whatley, O.F.M. Disp. to change his habit. Gratis, warrant of the lords shown.

Jo. Pope, B.C.L., chanter in St Peter's chantry, Linc. cath. Disp. to hold 2 benefices with the above, or 3 without, of which only 2 may be par. chs. £9.

f. 212ᵛ

21 Edw. Popleye, B.Cn.L., r. of Cricksea, Lond. dio. Disp. to hold a benef. with the above; permut. cl. £6 10s.

Peter Efforde, literate. Creation as public notary & tabellion. 13s 4d.

Tho. Molyneux & Marg. Irlande, Cov. & Lich. dio. Disp. for marriage (3rd & 4th degrees consang.). 26s 8d.

Gilbert Waterhouse & Eliz. Dikeson. Disp. for marriage (3rd & 4th degrees consang.). 30s.

Wm Damperte & Marg. Bothe, Cov. & Lich. dio. Disp. for marriage (4th degree consang.). 26s 8d.

Aug. 22 Jo. Bell & Marg. Garett, of London. Disp. for marriage, the banns read once. 6s 8d.

Edw. & Marg. Whithede, Carl. dio. Disp. for marriage (4th degree affin.). 26s 8d.

Ric. Johnson & Eliz. Attcoke, York dio. Disp. for marriage (3rd & 4th degrees consang.). 30s.

f. 213ʳ

Miles Federgill & Mabel Blande, of the archdcnry of Richmond. Disp. for marriage (4th degree consang.). 26s 8d.

23 Tho. Glover & Eliz. Southerne, Cov. & Lich. dio. Disp. for marriage (Tho.'s father was Eliz.'s godfather). 30s.

22 Ric. Myche & Alice Coppyn, Lond. dio. Disp. for marriage (4th & 4th degrees affin.). 26s 8d.

22 Wm Kidd & Marg. Nussaye, York dio. Disp. for marriage (4th degree consang.). 26s 8d.

Tho. Smyth & Matilda Lorde, Cov. & Lich. dio. Disp. for marriage (4th degree consang.). 26s 8d.

23 Meredeth ap Thomas & Marg. ap verch Philippe, Lland. dio. Disp. for marriage (4th & 4th degrees consang.). 26s 8d.

July 23 Jo. Richardson & Margery Rede, Linc. dio. Disp. for marriage (Margery was godmother to a child of Jo.). Arb. 40s; warrant of the lords shown.

f. 213ᵛ

Aug. 21 Jo. Styles & Agnes Harbye, Linc. dio. Disp. for marriage (3rd & 4th degrees consang.). 30s.

23 Arthur Whitley & Kath. Sale, Cov. & Lich. dio. Disp. for marriage (3rd & 4th degrees consang.). 30s.

Rob. Elmore, monk of Malmesbury, Sarum dio. Disp. to take all h.o., 2 on the same day, within the prohibited times. 26s 8d.

26 Ric. Srigley & Joan Jackson, Cov. & Lich. dio. Disp. for marriage (4th degree consang.). 26s 8d.

24 Miles Burton & Alice Wethererd, York dio. Disp. for marriage (3rd & 4th degrees affin.). 30s.

26 Tho. Cardyn, v. of West Hythe, Cant. dio., chapl. to the Archbp of Cant. Disp. to hold another benef.; permut. cl. £6 10s.

24 Geo. Hobson, Gilbertine canon, v. of Saltby. Disp. to wear the habit of a sec. pr. £4.

f. 214ʳ

26 Wm Leye *alias* Dukeson, canon (*sic*) of St Mary's, Selby. Disp. to hold any benef. £4.

Aug. 25 Morgan Hewes, B.C.L., r. of Llanbeulan, Bangor dio. Disp. as he is in his 80th yr, to have any good woman of 60, not suspected of the vices of the flesh, to live with him. 20s.

22 Nich. Robynson & Joan Bulcoke, Cov. & Lich. dio. Disp. for marriage (3rd & 4th degrees consang.). 30s.

Tho. Nowell & Bennetta Downeley, Cov. & Lich. dio. Disp. for marriage (4th & 4th degrees consang.). 26s 8d.

26 Cuthbert Fell, subdcn, Carl. cath. Disp. to take the rest of h.o. within the prohibited times. 15s.

Sept. 3 Philip ap Phillip ap Howell & Helen verch Jenn ap Philip, St David's dio. Disp. for marriage (4th degree consang.). 26s 8d.

5 Ric. Farington & Agnes Cover, Chich. dio. Disp. for marriage (4th degree consang.). 26s 8d.

f. 214ᵛ

Aug. 31 Wm Griffith, recently prior of St Kath.'s by Lincoln. Disp. to hold a benef. with change of habit. Also for Wm Browne, Jo. Stotte, Ric. Tyson, Tho. Lame, Jo. Stevenson, Jo. Thriston, Tho. Bemonnte, Ric. Wilson, Rob. Swieste, Ric. Bank, Ric. Jervatt, Jo. Colman, Tho. Graye, Rob. Dewesbery, Ada Raynthorpe, Tho. Jackeson. Suppr.

Sept. 5 Jo. Corbette of Hereford & Ann Bereton of Cov. & Lich. dio. Disp. for marriage (3rd & 4th degrees affin.). 30s.

1 Jo. Toser, r. of St Gregory's, Canterbury. Disp. to hold a benef. with the above, which does not yield over £8 p.a. £4.

10 Hy Westote & Marg. Gunter, of London. Disp. for marriage without banns. 10s.

f. 215ʳ

1 Jo. Sturrey, recently of St Augustine's, Canterbury. Disp. to hold a benef. with change of habit. Also for Jo. Wildebore, Tho. Ware, Edw. Wymes, Jo. Dyer, Wm Okenfeld, Rob. Whitte, Jo. Burden, Jo. Hawle, Tho. Edmonds, Jo. Banes, Ric. Stonende, Rob. Davison, Ric. Orgar, Rob. Breacher, Wm Jordeyne, Wm Curle, David Frankeleyn, Wm Mylles, Jo. Hichecoke, Laurence Marden, Jo. Snoweth, Jo. Gilmon, Jo. Lynge, Ralph Butler, Tho. Croston, Wm Mynor, Geo. Amys, Edw. Sawere, Wm Burges, Rob. Winstanley. Suppr.

14 Morgan ap Nicholas *alias* Kiddwelly, subdcn, St David's dio. Disp. to take dcn's & pr.'s orders within the prohibited times, on the same day. 13s 4d.

f. 215ᵛ

6 Tho. Chapman, O.F.M., of London. Disp. to hold a benef. with

complete change of habit. Also for Ric. Quickhope, Jo. Thornall, Jo. Mathew, Gavin Jonys, Rob. Best, Jo. Parker, Nich. Newman, Hugh Norrys, Ric. Hopkins, Rob. Froste, Jo. Bakar, Geo. Howeye, Jo. Thomson, Jo. Sharpe, Edm. Tompson, Tho. Collyns, Jas Kellow, Wm Clerke, Jo. Wyett, Lewis Hollywell, Geoffrey Turner, Lewis Pestell, Wm Holydaye. Suppr.

Sept. 20 Wm Ducket, r. of Pinkney, Heref. dio. Disp. to hold a benef. with the above, or 2 without; permut. cl. £6 10s.

14 Griffin Hygon & his wife Salma, St David's dio. Disp. to keep a portable altar in their home, & to have masses & other services celebrated there by any suitable pr., without depriving the par. ch. 20s.

f. 216ʳ

10 Jo. Dey, recently abbot of Bordesley, Worc. dio. Disp. to hold a benef. with change of habit. Also for Tho. Wall, Tho. Baxter, Tho. Byllye, Ric. Sandforde, Ric. Weston, Ric. Baker, Rob. Moreton, Tho. Yerdeley, Tho. Taylour, Tho. Phillips, Wm Stewerde, Jo. Johnson, Ric. Evans, Wm Edwards, Wm Augustyne, Roger Shakespere, Jo. Penney, Tho. Taylour, Jo. Hampton. Suppr.

16 Tho. Palmer, recently Austin fr., of Norwich. Disp. to hold a benef. with change of habit. Also for Wm Typeshede, Jo. Haddon, Rob. Fetune, Jo. Whitte, Rob. Wudehouse, Tho. Sandwiche, Wm Durye, Jo. Gibson, Rob. Clerke, Jo. Saunders, Ambrose Palmer, Jo. Clemente, Chris. Bronne, Tho. Riches, Tho. Warnes, Rob. Codling. Suppr.

f. 216ᵛ

23 Rob. Walker & Marg. Vicars, York dio. Disp. for marriage (3rd & 4th degrees affin.). 30s.

3 Edw. Games & Eliz. verch William Vaughan, St David's dio. Disp. for marriage (3rd & 4th, & 4th & 4th degrees consang., & 4th & 4th of affin.). 30s; 26s 8d; 26s 8d.

19 Jo. Sheldon, subdcn, Cov. & Lich. dio. Disp. to take dcn's & pr.'s orders within the prohibited times on the same day. 13s 4d.

20 Hopkin ap Jenn & Alice verch Walker, Lland. dio. Disp. for marriage (3rd degree affin.). Gratis.

21 Jo. Taverner & Rose Copley, Linc. dio. Disp. for marriage without banns. 10s.

24 David ap Llan ap Eynon & Gwenlian verch Gruffith. Disp. for marriage (4th degree consang.). 26s 8d.

26 Jo. Marten & Ann Lamberte, Lond. dio. Disp. for marriage, the banns read once. 6s 8d.

Sept. 26 Tho. Stoketh & Alice Holme, Linc. dio. Disp. for marriage without banns. 10s.

29 Gilbert Longtre & Isabella Standische, Cov. & Lich. dio. Disp. for marriage (4th degree consang.). 26s 8d.

Ric. Dareling & Margery Taylour, Linc. dio. Disp. for marriage (3rd degree affin.). £6.

26 Wm ap Griffith ap Llan ap Meredith & Laura verch John ap Hoell, Bangor dio. Disp. validating their marriage (contracted in ignorance of 4th degree consang.). 26s 8d.

Jo. ap Robert ap John ap David ap Llan & Marg. verch Griff ap Ean ap Jollyn, Bangor dio. Disp. for marriage (4th degree consang.). 26s 8d.

30 Clement Thorpe, O.C. fr, recently of Canterbury. Disp. to hold a benef. with change of habit. Also for Peter Alan, Wm Smyth, Wm Wilson, Edw. Eyllesley, Tho. Mayer. Suppr.

Jo. Holte & Agnes Nable, Cov. & Lich. dio. Disp. for marriage (4th degree consang.). 26s 8d.

Peter Shefforde, O.F.M., of Reading. Disp. to hold a benef. with change of habit. Also for Giles Coventre, Hy Alen, Peter Howche, Tho. Hefeld, Nich. Marten, Rob. Lambert, Hy Singleton, Jo. Newerke, Jo. Brewer, Wm Thomson, Jo. Rossell, Ric. Kyreson, Wm Goodbodye, Lewis Bot. Suppr.

Oct. 5 Rob. Madocke & Eliz. Spencer. Disp. for marriage without banns. 10s.

6 Ralph Notoghe & Eliz. Rawstorne, Cov. & Lich. dio. Disp. for marriage (4th degree consang.). 26s 8d.

4 Wm Barkworth & Alice Bromefelde, of London. Disp. for marriage without banns. 10s.

6 Griffin ap Evan ap David & Kath. verch Jenan ap David Lloid Vaughan. Disp. for marriage (3rd & 4th degrees consang.). 30s.

Tho. ap Gett & Janet verch Morgan ap Res, St David's dio. Disp. for marriage (4th degree consang.). 26s 8d.

8 Chris. Elye & Clement Sheldon, Cov. & Lich. dio. Disp. for marriage (3rd & 4th degrees consang.). 30s.

4 Jo. Burcher, recently abbot of Leicester. Disp. to hold a benef. with change of habit. Also for Ric. Duckett, Ric. Webbe, Ric.

Clerke, Jo. Eynsworth, Tho. Lonsdon, Jo. Boworthe, Tho. Mordall, Tho. Hanswate, Rob. Sapcote, Gregory Lang, Jo. Laycey, Jo. Revell, Wm Clerk, Jo. Buxum, Wm Billisbye, Jo. Law, Tho. Westis, Wm Permyter, Hugh Shapye. Suppr.

Aug. 1 Jo. Whitt, r. of Chilcombe, Winton dio. Disp. to take h.o. within 3 yrs. 30s.

f. 218ᵛ

Oct. 6 Wm Walker, monk of Guisborough, York dio. Disp. to hold a benef. with change of habit. Arb. 53s 4d; warrant of the lords shown.

Wm Brogden, recently prior of St Jas by Northampton. Disp. to hold a benef. with change of habit. Also for Tho. Edwards, Ric. Calley, Ric. K[e]lmer, Jo. Cotton, Rob. Lambe. Suppr.

Tho. Chalmer, recently abbot of Croxton, Staffs. Disp. to hold a benef. with change of habit. Also for Rob. Clerke, Rob. Cadde, Tho. Keling, Jo. Thorneton, Tho. Edon, Jo. Orpe, Jo. Alman, Ric. Mayre, Wm Beche, Hy Rothewell, Jo. Standeley. Suppr.

10 Jo. Comberstede, r. of Wootton Glanville, Sarum dio. Disp. to hold a benef. with the above, or 2 without; permut. cl. £6 10s.

15 Wm Wilson, r. of Hillington, Norw. dio., chapl. to the Earl of Worcester. Disp. to hold a benef. with the above, or 2 without; permut. cl. £6 10s.

f. 219ʳ

12 Hugh Olever, recently prior of Huntingdon. Disp. to hold a benef. with change of habit. Also for Wm Williams, Rob. Mayle, Tho. Stoughton, Mich. Bonne, Nich. Gates, Jas Hande, Jo. Harford, Wm Lutter. Suppr.

15 Wm Piers, canon of Guisborough, York dio. Disp. to leave off the habit of his Order. Gratis; warrant of the lords shown.

16 Chris. Lamhede, r. of ?Beckham ('Bacham'), Norw. dio. Disp. to hold a benef. with the above, or 2 without; permut. cl. £6 10s.

Sept. 4 Wm Walton, v. of West Markham, York dio. Disp. to hold another benef. if the above does not yield over £8 p.a. £4.

Oct. 17 Roger Ponsonbye, pr., r. of ?Rotherfield ('Rutterfelde') Greys or Peppard, Oxon., Linc. dio. Disp. to hold a benef. with the above, or 2 others without it; permut. cl. £6 10s.

19 Geo. Baker, pr., r. of Wentnor, Heref. dio. Disp. to hold a benef. with the above if the above does not yield over £8 p.a. £4.

f. 219ᵛ

18 Nich. Butler, of York dio., & Ann Bradshaye, of Cov. & Lich. dio. Disp. for marriage (4th degree consang. & affin.). 26s 8d; 26s 8d.

Oct.   22 Edw. Whithede & Eliz. Bradbere, Cov. & Lich. dio. Disp. for marriage (3rd & 4th degrees affin.). 30s.

18 Jo. Edwards & Ann Croke, of London. Disp. for marriage without banns. 10s.

16 Jo. Maners, r. of Eakring (Akinge), York dio., chapl. to the Earl of Rutland. Disp. to hold 2 benefs with the above, or 3 without, of which not more than 2 may be par. chs. £9.

20 Rob. Austyn, O.C. fr., recently of Winchester. Disp. to hold a benef. with change of habit. Suppr.

Kath. Digbye, recently nun of Shouldham, Norw. dio. Disp. to leave the religious life. Suppr.

23 Wm Manser & Alice Empson, Cant. dio. Disp. for marriage (Alice was godmother to a child of Wm). Arb. 53s 4d.; warrant of the lords shown.

f. 220ʳ

20 Ric. Vowell, recently prior of Walsingham, Norw. dio. Disp. to hold a benef. with change of habit. Also for Jo. Tharlow, Edm. Ponyer, Wm Novell, Wm Rede, Ric. Garnett, Jo. Watson, Tho. Nevell, Edw. Merstone, Jo. Clerke, Tho. Mershull, Humfrey Wilson, Simon Brande, Geoffrey Penneye, Wm Potkyn, Martin Clapton. Suppr.

Loe Ferreys, recently abbot of Wymondham, Norw. dio. Disp. to hold a benef. with change of habit. Also for Tho. Lyme, Tho. Thaxstede, Jo. Harleston, Rob. Colchester, Edw. Sowthons, Jo. Windham. Suppr.

Roger Forman, recently abbot of West Dereham, Norw. dio. Disp. to hold a benef. with change of habit. Also for Wm Snell, Jo. Herperley, Jo. Jackson, Ric. Cressey. Suppr.

f. 220ᵛ

Jo. Grene, recently prior of Clattercote, Linc. dio. Disp. to hold a benef. with change of habit. Also for Wm Perne, Chris. Silbane, Tho. Furnes. Suppr.

Hugh Glasner, O.F.M., recently prior of Greenwich friary. Disp. to hold a benef. with change of habit. Also for Jo. Daye, Jo. Inmer, Ric. Pronte, Nich. Locke, Jo. Herth, Jo. Richerdson, Tho. Yonge, Mathew Jefferey, Wm Hall, Jo. Baddye, Jo. Winchippe, Jo. Smyth. Suppr.

24 Tho. Bradley, Worc. dio., & Margery Russell, Cov. & Lich. dio. Disp. for marriage (3rd & 4th degrees consang.). 30s.

22 Jo. Mychell & Cristine Buknall, Ex. dio. Disp. for marriage (3rd & 4th degrees consang.). 30s.

Oct. 23 Rob. Hull *alias* Thomson, canon of Thornton, Linc. dio. Disp. to hold any benef. £4.

f. 221ʳ

24 Jo. Stephenson & Kath. More, Cov. & Lich. dio. Disp. for marriage (3rd & 4th degrees affin.). 30s.

25 Ric. Curton & Joan Savell, York dio. Disp. for marriage (3rd & 4th degrees consang.). 30s.

24 Rob. Johns, v. of Llan Carfan, Lland. dio. Disp. to hold another benef. with the above, or 2 without; permut. cl. £6 10s.

16 Griffin ap Res ap Griffith & Kath. verch Grigorye ap Jenkyn, St Asaph dio. Disp. for marriage (Kath.'s mother was Griffin's godmother). 30s.

18 Jo. Harryson, O.Cist., of Byland, York dio. Confirmation of disp. by the abbot & convent to hold for life the ch. of Old Byland. 40s; p.s.r. 5s.

26 Tho. Dallaman & Kath. Templeman, Bath & W. dio. Disp. for marriage (3rd & 4th degrees consang.). 30s.

f. 221ᵛ

28 Tho. Hemmesley & Eliz. Lostonsse, York dio. Disp. for marriage (2nd & 3rd degrees affin.). Arb. £4; warrant of the lords shown.

21 Wm Darnell & Margery Doghson, Cov. & Lich. dio. Disp. for marriage (4th degree consang.). 26s 8d.

28 Wm Pullande, subdcn, York dio. Disp. to take all h.o. within the prohibited times. 13s 4d.

Wm Brydge & Agnes Holden, Cov. & Lich. dio. Disp. for marriage (4th degree consang.). 26s 8d.

Rob. & Marg. Holte, Cov. & Lich. dio. Disp. for marriage (3rd & 4th degrees consang.). 30s.

Ric. Shetelworth & Joan Shirborne, Cov. & Lich. dio. Disp. for marriage (4th degree affin.). 26s 8d.

Ric. Chaterton, r. of St Swithin's, London, chapl. to Earl of Southampton. Disp. to hold a benef. with the above, or 2 without; permut. cl. £6 10s.

f. 222ʳ

30 Wm Stannfforde, O.P., recently of Stamford. Disp. to hold a benef. with change of habit. Also for Wm Wakefelde, Hy Rede, Wm Shele. Suppr.

31 Arthur Meverell, recently prior of Tutbury, Chich. dio. Disp. to hold a benef. with change of habit. Also for Tho. Sutton, Tho.

Smyth, Tho. Shele, Rob. Stafforde, Nich. Glassan, Tho. Rymer, Ric. Arnolde, Roger Hilton. Suppr.

Oct. 31 Edw. Wilkins, recently abbot of Hilton. Disp. to hold a benef. with change of habit. Also for Wm Asshenhurst, Wm Norton, Jo. Bucknall, Jo. Smyth, Wm Chalmer, Jo. Johnson, Ric. Cradocke, Geoffrey Heyth. Suppr.

Nov. 4 Jo. Mantell & Ann Fynes. Disp. for marriage without banns. 10s.

f. 222ᵛ

Oct. 31 Ralph Armough, recently abbot of Sulby, Northants. Disp. to hold a benef. with change of habit. Also for Rob. Bukler, Tho. Hill, Simon Kneton, Jo. Haryson, Miles Wydd, Wm Spyns, Rob. Burton, Wm Bagge, Hy Haxton, Jo. Arcleye. Suppr.

Nov. 2 Tho. Hebbes, acol., Sarum dio. Disp. to take all h.o. within the prohibited times, & 2 on the same day. 26s 8d.

Oct. 27 Tho. Knight, recently monk of Spalding. Disp. to hold a benef. with change of habit. Gratis; warrant of the lords shown.

28 Owen Clethorpe, D.Th. Disp. to hold 2 benefices with cure; permut. cl. £6 10s.

Nov. 4 Jo. Griffith, pr., St Asaph dio. Disp., as he already has a disp. to take all h.o., to hold any benef. Arb. 20s; warrant of the lords shown.

f. 223ʳ

Oct. 29 Leonard Reresby, r. of Asshor? Linc. dio., chapl. to Earl of Southampton. Disp. to hold a benef. with the above, or 2 without; permut. cl. £6 10s.

Nov. 6 Chris. Butterwyke & Kath. Maskall, Chich. dio. Disp. for marriage without banns. 10s.

7 Ric. West, B.Th., r. of Donnington, Linc. dio. Disp. to hold a benef. with the above, or 2 without; permut. cl. £6 10s.

Oct. 31 Jo. Edmunds, B.Th., v. of Albourne, Sarum dio., Kg's chapl. Disp. to hold a benef. with or 2 without the above; permut. cl. £6 10s.

Nov. 6 Jo. Massey, recently abbot of Combermere, Cov. & Lich. dio. Disp. to hold a benef. with change of habit. Also for Tho. Humorde, Ralph Smyth, Jo. Olyver, Jo. Cokest, Humfrey Lightsoke, Gilbert Grene, Tho. Lee, Edm. Dugdall, Rob. Furber. Suppr.

f. 223ᵛ

Jo. Casson, recently monk of Furness, Staffs. Disp. to hold a benef. with change of habit. Suppr.

Nov. 6 Wm Hull, recently abbot (prior) of Hougham, Linc. dio. Disp. to hold a benef. with change of habit. Also for Hy Butlar, Geo. Hall, Jo. Braye, Ric. Golding, Ralph Robinson, Ric. Kirke, Giles Wodnett. Suppr.

2 Laurence Irland & Helen Bonde. Disp. for marriage (2nd & 3rd degrees affin. & consang., & without banns). 53s 4d; 10s.

3 Nich. Morreye, B.C.L., v. of Furneaux Pelham, Lond. dio. Disp. to hold a benef. with the above; permut. cl. £6 10s.

8 Chris. Benteley, acol., York dio. Disp. to take all h.o. outside the statutory times. 20s.

Rob. Ingham, Cov. & Lich. dio. Disp. to take all h.o. within the prohibited times. 20s.

f. 224ʳ

Rob. Amayne & Joan Bancroste, Cov. & Lich. dio. Disp. for marriage (4th degree consang.). 26s 8d.

Jas Fletcher, acol., Cov. & Lich. dio. Disp. to take all h.o. outside the statutory times. 20s.

9 Humfrey Darell, r. of Drayton Beauchamp, Linc. dio. Disp. to hold a benef. with the above; permut. cl. £6 10s.

7 Ric. Estbroke & Dorothy Paforde, Ex. dio. Disp. for marriage (Dorothy's father was Ric.'s godfather). 30s.

10 Wm Thomas, r. of Merthyr-Dyfan, Lland. dio. Disp. to hold another benef. if the above does not yield over £8 p.a. £4.

22 Tho. Chockanstall & Eliz. Inman, York dio. Disp. for marriage (3rd & 4th degrees affin.). 30s.

11 Ric. Lodge, Lond. dio., & Joan Cokytt, Norw. dio. Disp. for marriage without banns. 10s.

f. 224ᵛ

10 Jo. Baynbrige & Eliz. Parkins, Durham dio. Disp. for marriage (4th degree consang.). 26s 8d.

7 Tho. Cheyney, r. of Paston, Linc. dio., chapl. to Sir Nich. Carew, K.G. Disp. to hold another benef.; permut. cl. £6 10s.

12 Alex. Mason & Joan Ussher, of London. Disp. for marriage without banns. 10s.

10 Roger Marshall, recently abbot (prior) of Sempringham, Linc. dio. Disp. to hold a benef. with change of habit. Also for Rob. Bell, Reg. Sawbridge, Jo. Jackson, Nich. Gill, Jo. Leyghe, Jo. Wattes, Tho. Crawfort, Ant. Laughton, Rob. Chalymer, Ric. Settell, Tho. Hake, Wm Pygott, Otewell Godebehere, Hugh Griffington, Hy Walker, Jo. Pagett, Rob. Backer, Chris. Robynson. Suppr.

f. 225ʳ

Nov. 10 Wm Graston, recently abbot of Rocester, Staffs. Disp. to hold a benef. with change of habit. Also for Geo. Davy, Jo. Snape, Ric. Hethe, Wm Bonde, Ralph Corke, Jo. Bryckilbancke. Suppr.

Rowland Blyton, recently abbot of Rievaulx. Disp. to hold a benef. with change of habit. Also for Tho. Richemonte, Wm Yersley, Stephen Burgh, Rob. Staynthorpe, Rob. Pykering, Wm Storer, Ric. Skarborgh, Tho. Yarom, Ric. Allerton, Ric. Ripon, Roger Whitbye, Jo. Malton, Wm Bedall, Ric. Gilling, Hy Thriske, Jas Gisborne, Chris. Helmsley, Oliver Broughton, Wm Farlington, Mathew Ampleforde, Wm Wadell, Tho. Capron, Jo. Whalley. Suppr.

8 Wm Singleton & Ann Becansall. Disp. for marriage (4th degree double consang., previously disp. for simple consang.). 26s 8d.

f. 225ᵛ

10 Tho. Stockes, recently prior of Worksop, York dio. Disp. to hold a benef. with change of habit. Also for Wm Nutt, Tho. Richardson, Wm Ingham, Geo. Oxley, Ric. Astleye, Laurence Sherkbone, Alex. Bothe, Tho. Beall, Geo. Bernesleye, Edm. Robynson, Jas Windebricke, Rob. Ernestede. Suppr.

Ric. Stradewicke, recently canon of Durford. Disp. to hold a benef. with change of habit. Also for Tho. Skaffe (formerly canon of Corsham), Tho. Marten (formerly canon of Abergavenny), Jo. Thomas (formerly fr. of Stamford), David Johns (formerly observant fr. of Greenwich), Ric. Robynson (formerly Austin fr. of Grimsby). Suppr.

12 Rob. Edwards & Agnes Boywer, Linc. dio. Disp. for marriage (Rob.'s mother was Agnes' godmother). 30s.

Rob. Denysse, Worc. dio., & Ann St John, Linc. dio. Disp. for marriage in any ch., without banns. 10s; 10s.

f. 226ʳ

10 Griffin Lloid ap Elissa ap More & Marg. verch Griffith Lewis, Bangor dio. Disp. for marriage (3rd & 4th degrees consang.). 30s.

12 Ld Wm Dacre, Baron Greystoke. Confirmation of foundation by the above of the coll. of Greystoke, Carl. dio., with one master, six priests, & two clerks. 40s; p.s.r. 5s.

28 Jo. Lews & Marg. Barow, Durham dio. Disp. for marriage (3rd & 4th degrees consang.). 30s.

12 Jo. Seton, M.A. Disp. to take all h.o. within the prohibited times & 2 on the same day. 26s 8d.

Nov. 14 Ralph Hartley, recently prior of Wetheral, Cumberland. Disp. to hold a benef. with change of habit. Also for Jo. Whitfeld, Tho. Hertley, Jo. Clyston, Jo. Gayle. Suppr.

Rob. Maye & Isabella Ruge, Winton dio. Disp. for marriage (Rob.'s mother was Isabella's godmother). Gratis; warrant of the lords shown.

f. 226ᵛ

Sept. 20 Jo. Hatfeld, Fellow of the coll. of Bonshommes at Ashridge, Linc. dio. Disp. to practise medicine anywhere. £4.

Nov. 15 Jo. Blandell & Alice Methwolde, of London. Disp. for marriage without banns. 10s.

Edm. Wordesworthe & Marg. Foxcrofte, York dio. Disp. for marriage (3rd & 4th degrees consang.). 30s.

Tho. & Eliz. Holwey, Cov. & Lich. dio. Disp. for marriage (4th degree consang.). 26s 8d.

12 Rob. Slade, r. of Skidbrooke, Linc. dio. Disp. for non-res. during illness. 20s.

16 Jo. Mychell & Eliz. Butler, of London. Disp. for marriage without banns, but within the statutory times. 10s.

18 Ric. Rigge & Eliz. Fallowfelde, Carl. dio. Disp. for marriage (3rd & 4th degrees affin.). 30s.

f. 227ʳ

Marg. Vernon, recently nun of Malling, Kent. Disp. to leave the religious life. Also for Rose Morton. Suppr.

15 Roger Gunthorpe, acol., York dio. Disp. to take h.o. & hold a benef. although lame. 40s.

12 Wm Bunnyng & Agnes Wilshare, Linc. dio. Disp. for marriage (Wm was godfather to a child of Agnes). Arb. £4; warrant of the lords shown.

Wm Ludforde, Linc. dio., & Eliz. Birmycham, Cov. & Lich. dio. Disp. for marriage without banns & not in their par. ch. 10s; 10s.

18 Geo Hunter, M.A., Ely dio. Disp. to take all h.o. within the prohibited times & 2 on the same day. 26s 8d.

Jo. ap Robert Walbisse & Marg. verch John, St David's dio. Disp. for marriage (4th degree consang.). 26s 8d.

f. 227ᵛ

Jo. ap Jenkyn & Janet verch Richare, St David's dio. Disp. for marriage (4th degree consang.). 26s 8d.

Nov 12 Pancras Shere & Margery Hamlyn, Ex. dio. Disp. for marriage (Margery's father was Pancras's godfather). 30s.

16 Wm Dodycott, B.C.L., v. of Bromsgrove, Worc. dio. Disp. to hold a benef. with the above; permut. cl. £6 10s.

13 David ap Llan ap Tuder & Lucy Mathew, St Asaph dio. Disp. for marriage (4th degree consang.). 26s 8d.

20 Rob. Sherlee & Margery Swayen, Winton dio. Disp. for marriage (4th degree consang.). 26s 8d.

Tho. Cottisforde, r. of Walpole, Norw. dio., chapl. to Bp of Ely. Disp. to hold a benef. with the above, or 2 without; permut. cl. £6 10s.

f. 228ʳ

Wm Wise, recently prior of Catley, Linc. dio. Disp. to hold a benef. with complete change of habit. Also for Tho. Weste & Chris. Hudson. Suppr.

Wm Austen, recently monk of St Peter's, Gloucester. Disp. to hold a benef. with complete change of habit. Also for Tho. Hartlond, Wm Newporte, Wm Ambrose, Edw. Emvey, Wm Chadworthe, Walter Stanley, Jo. Hacborme, Tho. Kyngeswode, Edw. Benett, Ric. Cicetour, Wm Dene. Suppr.

Tho. Bysseley, recently prior of a cell of Hereford. Disp. to hold a benef. with change of habit. Also for Tho. Forest, Tho. Baskerfeld, Hugh Bowles, Chris. Horton, Rob. Jerome, Tho. Tuckye. Suppr.

22 Roger Walkar, recently prior of Marmont, Kent. Disp. to hold a benef. with change of habit. Also for Wm Cristall, Humfrey Spenceley (recently prior of ?Stunden, Kent), Jo. Monnton (recently prior of Bigging, Herts.). Suppr.

f. 228ᵛ

20 Roger Holte & Laura Adlington, Cov. & Lich. dio. Disp. for marriage (Roger was godfather to a child of Laura's). £6.

18 Jo. Colwill & Joan Atawpole, Ex. dio. Disp. for marriage (3rd & 4th degrees consang.). 30s.

19 Jo. Senocke *alias* Denan, D.Th. Disp. to hold another benef. with the above, or 2 without; permut. cl. £6 10s.

24 Jo. Whitte & Sibil Banes, of London. Disp. for marriage without banns & in any ch. 10s; 10s.

21 Ric. Caye & Marg. Rede, Cov. & Lich. dio. Disp. for marriage (3rd & 4th degrees consang.). 30s.

Nov. 25 Jas Fletcher & Mary Harrison. Disp. for marriage without banns. 10s.

Rob. Bibbye & Gertrude Herbert. Disp. for marriage without banns. 10s.

12 Jo. Smyth & Kath. Bayly, Lond. dio. Disp. for marriage (2nd & 4th degrees consang.). 33s 4d.

f. 229ʳ

20 Wm Lupton & Eliz. Parkynson. Disp. for marriage (Eliz. was godmother to a child of Wm). £6.

26 Tho. Modye, v. of Bottisham, Ely dio., chapl. to Ld Dacre. Disp. to hold a benef. with the above; permut. cl. £6 10s.

20 Rob. Walshaye & Isabella Hilton, Linc. dio. Disp. for marriage (Isabella was godmother to a child of Rob.). Gratis; warrant of the lords shown.

Edw. Bashe & Thomasina Ager, of London. Disp. for marriage without banns. 10s.

28 Wm Phillip, cantor in the par. ch. of Mortehoe, Ex. dio. Disp. for non-res. for 2 yrs. 13s 4d.

22 Jo. Coyette, O.F.M., of Stamford. Disp. to hold a benef. with change of habit. Suppr.

28 Tho. Langton & Mary Wolley, of London. Disp. for marriage without banns. 10s.

f. 229ᵛ

26 David ap Morgan & Dorothy verch Rhes, St David's dio. Disp. for marriage (3rd & 4th degrees affin.). 30s.

Rob. Watson, recently abbot of Lilleshall, Salop. Disp. to hold a benef. with complete change of habit. Also for Jo. Hall, Chris. Ledys, Tho. Dawson, Jo. Ponseburye, Roger Knowsall, Wm Senthe, Ric. Overton, Tho. Maynerde, Wm Massye, Peter Robynson. Suppr.

28 Confirmation of disp. issued by Ric., formerly Bp of Linc., for the consecration of the graveyard & chapel of Gravenhurst in Shillington par. for the inhabitants of Gravenhurst to bury their dead there. 40s; p.s.r. 5s.

Dec. 6 Wm Crispe & Ann Brente, Roch. dio. Disp. for marriage within the prohibited times. 20s.

f. 230ʳ

Nov. 30 Rob. Shwiste, recently prior of Shouldham, Norfolk. Disp. to hold a benef. with change of habit. Also for Ric. Foster, Jo. Holme, Ric. Tayler, Laurence Russell, Ric. Wade, Wm Thorpe, Wm Elderick, Rob. Lussum. Suppr.

Nov. 30 Tho. Gilman, recently abbot of Pipewell, Northants. Disp. to hold a benef. with change of habit. Also for Jo. Baforde, Chris. Hotnett, Rob. Davye, Jo. Godfraye, Tho. Alen, Jo. Harcote, Tho. Ball, Tho. Hadley, Tho. Chester, Jo. Benet, Tho. Gavitins, Jo. Webster, Geo. Wodnett. Suppr.

Jo. Baldocke, recently abbot of Barnwell, Ely dio. Disp. to hold a benef. with change of habit. Also for Ric. Hernam, Wm Raynes, Rob. Wisse, Edw. Ball, Tho. Palmer, Tho. Rawlyns. Suppr.

f. 230ᵛ

Jo. Orrey, recently prior of Chicksands, Beds. Disp. to hold a benef. with change of habit. Also for Jo. Whitte, Tho. Crosdall, Parsivall Sympson, Rob. Harryson, Miles Gill, Peter Husbande. Suppr.

Edw. Stubbes, O.C. fr., recently of Doncaster. Disp. to hold a benef. with change of habit. Also for Jerome Leonarde, Geo. Sanderson, Wm Swanne, Jo. Burton, Hugh Hennyche, Jo. Dyckson, Ric. Crone. Suppr.

Jo. Bebe, recently abbot of Dale, Derbys. Disp. to hold a benef. with change of habit. Also for Ric. Whetley, Jo. Godman, Ric. Hawslen, Tho. Bagshaw, Wm Smyth, Jo. Banks, Geo. Coke, Rob. Harney, Ralph Haryson, Jo. Shermoulde, Rob. Wilson, Jas Cheyneholme, Jas Cleyton, Jo. Batman, Rob. Jerrett, Roger Page Wm Carter, Ric. Banks. Suppr.

f. 231ʳ

Laurence Gopserler, recently fr. of St Tho. of Acon, Lond. Disp. to hold a benef. with change of habit. Also for Tho. Lynne. Suppr.

Tho. ?Witney, recently abbot of Dieulacres, Cov. & Lich. dio. Disp. to hold a benef. with change of habit. Rob. Bageley, Hy Bennett, Geo. Fernys, Ralph Motersett, Ralph Barneys, Wm Crosse, Rob. Seerington, Edm. Bolton, Wm Prowloffe, Tho. Lok, Ric. Cordon, Jo. Bykerton. Suppr.

Dec. 1 Wm Call, O.F.M., recently prior of Norwich friary. Disp. to hold a benef. with change of habit. Also for Ric. Morleye, Tho. Godderd, Tho. Foote, Jo. Woode, Jo. Cause, Tho. Grimston, Edw. Wellis, Rob. Lakeham, Wm Harwoode, Tho. Calye, Tho. Bentleye, Rob. Shereman, Walter Austen, Barnaby Whiting, Tho. Palling, Jo. Albon, Hy Joynte, Ric. Smyth, Tho. Bowth, Jo. Marsley. Suppr.

f. 231ᵛ

2 Tho. Ragg, recently monk of Derby. Disp. to hold a benef. with change of habit. Also for Wm Stanbanke, Walter Reye, Hy Heye, Nich. Johns, Ric. Machyn, Hy Toste, Wm Sutor, Tho. Trypett, Tho. Coste, Edw. Cradocke, Tho. Haryson, Wm Holyleye. Suppr.

Dec. 3 Wm Trasforde, recently prior of the Charterhse, London. Disp. to hold a benef. with change of habit. Also for Edm. Skene, Tho. Barmughame, Jo. Evys, Ric. Tregose, Wm Wayte, Tho. Baker, Everard Digby, Jo. Bardeyne, Jo. Foxe, Wm Broke, Bartholomew Burgon, Jo. Thomson, Jo. Bulleyne, Clement Batemanson, Jo. Nicholson, Maurice Chayme, all priests. Suppr.

f. 232ʳ

Ralph Clerke, recently canon of Repingdon. Disp. to hold a benef. with change of habit. Also for Tho. Skynger, Jas Yong, Jo. Asshebye, Tho. Pratt, Tho. Webster, Rob. Warde, Tho. Branston, Tho. Cordall. Suppr.

6 Leonard Hyde & Ann Butler, Linc. dio. Confirmation of their marriage (contracted in ignorance of 4th degree consang.). 26s 8d.

Jo Baxter, recently prior of Elsham ('Estham'), Linc. dio. Disp. to hold a benef. with change of habit. Suppr.

Rob. Dagkelby, recently monk of Alvingham, Linc. dio. Disp. to hold a benef. with change of habit. Also for Rob. Whitting, Rob. Forman, Jo. Bowton, Geo. Elwoode, Wm Huttson, Edm. Tate. Suppr.

Tho. Norman, monk of Mattersey. Disp. to hold a benef. with change of habit. Also for Tho. Bell, Jo. Garton, Wm Shilton, Ric. Watson. Suppr.

f. 232ᵛ

10 Ric. Brettane, recently canon of Bullington, Linc. dio. Disp. to hold a benef. with change of habit. Also for Jo. Franke, Tho. Byggs, Wm Longhorne, Jo. Boyes, Tho. Spenceley, Tho. Tyssam, Jo. Tyssan, Tho. Dyxon. Suppr.

Jo. Chichester, r. of Stoke-Rivers & Shirwell, Ex. dio. Disp. to postpone taking h.o. until he is 28 in order to study, in spite of holding the above; previously he held disp. until he was 25. 30s.

Rob. Watlington & Eliz. Barnes, Sarum dio. Disp. for marriage (Eliz. was godmother to a child of Rob.). £6.

11 Alan Smyth & Eliz. Pollerde, Cov. & Lich. dio. Disp. for marriage (3rd & 4th degrees affin.). 30s.

14 Chris. Arundell & Joan Beller, Linc. dio. Disp. for marriage without banns. 10s.

f. 233ʳ

Reg. ap William & Kath. verch Howell, St Asaph dio. Disp. for marriage (4th degree consang.). 26s 8d.

20 Roger Comper & Joan Sympson, York dio. Disp. for marriage (3rd & 4th degrees affin.). 30s.

Aug. 20 Wm Pynnake, Cov. & Lich. dio., & Eliz. Badger, Worc. dio. Disp. for marriage without banns & within the prohibited times. 10s; 20s.

Baldwin Smyth & Alice Walker, Cov. & Lich. dio. Disp. for marriage (4th degree affin.). 26s 8d.

Jo. Stilman, literate, Bath & W. dio. Disp. to practise as a public notary. 13s 4d.

Jo. Tyrrey, O.F.M., recently of Winchester. Disp. to hold a benef. with complete change of habit. Suppr.

Wm Bate, O.F.M., of Carmarthen. Disp. to hold a benef. with complete change of habit. Suppr.

23 Jo. White & Sibil Banes, of London. Disp. for marriage without banns & within the prohibited times. 20s.

f. 233ᵛ

Sept. 30 Ric. Caunton, D.Cn.L., canon of St David's, commissary of Tho., former Bp of St David's, v. of Llangham, St David's dio. Confirmation of a decree by which the above vicarage should receive an additional ¼ of all tithes of corn, lambs, cheese, & wool, beyond the portion previously enjoyed. 40s; p.s.r. 5s.

Dec. 20 Jo. Cotton, O.P., recently of Sudbury. Disp. to hold a benef. with change of habit. Also for Tho. Ellys, Rob. Rede, Ric. Pyke, Wm Ellys, Jo. Koo, Jo. Horsenayle, Ralph Terre, Wm Richerds, Jo. Adamson, Jo. Laurence. Suppr.

Jo. Haward, recently abbot of Vale Royal, Cov. & Lich. dio. Disp. to hold a benef. with change of habit. Also for Alex. Sidome, Wm Herryson, Roger Gardener, Tho. Bawdon, Nich. Lawrenson, Tho. Fletcher, Wm Clerke, Jo. Banion, Ric. Benion, Ralph Bente, Jo. Daye, Wm Wright, Jo. Meltham, Nich. Lancaster. Suppr.

f. 234ʳ

Sept. 10 Jo. Raynolds, B.Th., O.P., of Gloucester. Disp. to hold a benef. with change of habit. Also for Jo. Houper, Ric. Bylande, Wm Walton, Ranulph Hoell, Tho. Meykens. Suppr.

Tho. Knyght, O.C. fr., of Gloucester. Disp. to hold a benef. with change of habit. Also for Wm Plesoms, Hy Birche. Suppr.

Wm Lightfote, O.F.M., recently of Gloucester. Disp. to hold a benef. with change of habit. Also for Jo. Barclaye, Hy Jackett, Geo. Couper, Jo. Kebull. Suppr.

Tho. Wroxall, O.C. fr., of Bristol. Disp. to leave his Order & hold a benef. Also for Tho. Clyston, Simon Vaughan, & Jo. Houper. Suppr.

f. 234ᵛ

Sept. 10 Tho. Goldysborowe, recently O.C. fr., of Marlborough. Disp. for change of habit. Also for Chris. Hill, Martin Brasye, Augustine More, Jo. Arnolde. Suppr.

Tho. Parys, O.F.M., recently of Winchester. Disp. to hold a benef. with change of habit. Also for Wm Kenett, Ric. Forde. Suppr.

Ric. Chessham, O.P., recently prior of Winchester friary. Disp. to hold a benef. with change of habit. Also for Rob. Browne, Jo. George, Nich. Barker, Rob. Hayms, Jo. Ingilbye, Wm Petts, Jo. White (Austin fr.). Suppr.

Ric. Edwards, O.P., of Worcester. Disp. to hold a benef. with change of habit. Also for Ric. Elmeley, Wm Crane, Jo. Poskessen, Ant. Corken, Jo. Hatton, Tho. Rogers, Jo. Hogeys. Suppr.

f. 235ʳ

3 Tho. Lynsey, O.F.M., of Worcester. Disp. to hold a benef. with change of habit. Also for Tho. Russell, Ric. Homms (?Homins), Nich. Danyell, Wm Hill, Jo. Carhill, Ric. Davys, Rob. Darynton, Wm Gosnell. Suppr.

Wm Hanlay, O.F.M., of Bridgnorth. Also for Tho. Woode, Jo. Scarsbrike, Jo. Wilkens. Suppr.

Ric. Manson, O.F.M., of Lichfield. Disp. to hold a benef. with change of habit. Also for Wm Wryxham, Ric. Lovett, Hy Whyte, Wm Davynson. Suppr.

Wm Hamonde, O.F.M., of Atherston. Disp. to hold a benef. with change of habit. Also for Rob. Spayn, Wm Eton. Suppr.

f. 235ᵛ

10 Wm Trym, O.F.M., of Stafford. Disp. to hold a benef. with change of habit. Also for Wm Massey, Tho. Preston, Nich. Brige, Ric. Nasche, Jo. Sill. Suppr.

Jo. Hare, Austin fr., of Stafford. Disp. for change of habit. Also for Jo. Sawbrige, Jo. Hawcocke, Philip Stubbis, Wm Castell. Suppr.

Geoffrey Davie, O.P., of Newcastle-under-Lyme. Disp. to hold a benef. with change of habit. Also for Ric. Stage, Tho. Standys Suppr.

Hy Underwode, O.F.M., recently of Shrewsbury. Disp. to hold a benef. with change of habit. Also for Tho. Haris, Ric. Smythe, Jo. Beche, Jo. Porter, Roger Bolt, Jo. Walker. Suppr.

Sept. 10 Jo. Tonne, Austin fr., of Shrewsbury. Disp. to change his habit & hold a benef. Also for Denis Obryn, Edm. Aspoll, Walter Franke. Suppr.

f. 236ʳ

Wm Wall, Prof. Th., O.F.M., prior of Chester friary. Disp. to hold a benef. with change of habit. Also for Wm Dykenson, Ralph More, Edm. or Edw. Godman, Jo. Wenall, Jo. Roole, Wm Amynson. Suppr.

Jo. Hurleton, O.C. fr., of Chester. Disp. to hold a benef. with change of habit. Also for Rob. Drake, Geo. Palmer, Ric. Baswell, Rob. Browne, Tho. Tayler, Ric. Glasyer, Ric. Alcocke, Nich. Segewike, Raffe Batha, Jo. Strypys, Tho. Thornton, Raiff Griffith. Suppr.

Hugh Brekenocke, O.P., prior of Chester friary. Disp. to hold a benef. with change of habit. Also for Jo. Sergiant, Rob. Remsay, Jo. Byrde, priests, David Gryffet, dcn. Suppr.

f. 236ᵛ

Jas Thomas, O.P., of Rhuddlan. Disp. to hold a benef. with change of habit. Also for Wm Holforde, Elis ap Howell, Owen Kenverike, David Griffith, David Lloid, Hugh Benkerth. Suppr.

Jo. Lewys, O.P., of Bangor. Disp. to hold a benef. with change of habit. Also for Tho. Willyams. Suppr.

Jo. Bachelor, O.F.M., of Beaumaris. Disp. to hold a benef. with change of habit. Also for Rob. Bacheler, Peter de Mangcroke, Jo. Sclye. Suppr.

Roger David, O.C. fr., of Denbigh. Disp. to hold a benef. with change of habit. Also for Ric. Browne, Jo. Blakon, Ric. Conwey. Suppr.

Ric. Willett, recently O.C. fr., of Ludlow. Disp. to hold a benef. with change of habit. Also for Humfrey Wenlocke, Patrick Leyster, Wm Burgis, Ric. Frenoll. Suppr.

f. 237ʳ

Giles Pykering, Austin fr., of Ludlow. Disp. to hold a benef. with change of habit. Also for Jo. Pratte, Wm Higgs, Chris. Gogeson. Suppr.

Ric. Gray, O.P., of Hereford. Disp. to hold a benef. with change of habit. Also for Jo. Smythe, Roger Madley, Tho. Pynner, Roger Webbe, Rob. Hore, Tho. Pyers. Suppr.

Jo. Barnarde, O.F.M., of Hereford. Disp. to hold a benef. with change of habit. Also for Zachary Carpenter, Jo. Morgan, Rob. Preston, Jo. Trevilian, Tho. Tanner, Jo. Hoskyns, Jo. Duke,

Rob. Warmoth, Jo. Elkens, Jo. Richards, Jo. Butler, Wm Screven, Wm Broke, Rob. Richards, Wm Hiller (anchorite). Suppr.

f. 237ᵛ

Dec.   4 Gregory Dods, O.P., recently of Cambridge. Disp. to hold a benef. with change of habit. Also for Rob. Pare, Tho. Pulner, Stephen Byston, Jo. Frynde, Rob. Cresmer, Ric. Sturtener, Wm Scalflite, Tho. Pykering, Nich. Hasilwoode, Tho. Cocke, Jo. Fyse. Suppr.

Wm White, O.F.M., recently of Cambridge. Disp. to hold a benef. with change of habit. Also for Rob. White, Tho. Dysse, Jo. Dunne, Jo. Facon, Laurence Draper, Wm Caterike, Wm Cresse, Jo. Arnolde, Jo. Yonge, Ric. Scaffe, Rob. Willingford, Wm Meyn, Tho. Scotte, Damascene Dale, Jo. Brake, Jo. Gyldar, Jo. Vyncent, Jo. Strawling, Wm Canvis, Mathew Lameson, Wm Thurleborne. Suppr.

f. 238ʳ

Jo. Hardyman, Austin fr., recently prior of the Cambridge friary. Disp. to hold a benef. with change of habit. Also for Tho. Watison, Jo. Barbor, Tho. Norley, Rob. Joyne, Rob. Garston, Ric. Kinge. Suppr.

Ric. Claye, O.P., recently of Thetford. Disp. to hold a benef. with change of habit. Also for Rob. Baldrye, Edm. Dyar, Hy Skepar, Edm. Palmer, Rob. Newham, Simon Anderson. Suppr.

Nich. Pratt, Austin fr., of Thetford. Disp. to hold a benef. with change of habit. Also for Tho. Parmyter & Roger Sheroode. Suppr.

Nov. 10 Tho. Lynett, O.P., of Lynn. Disp. to hold a benef. with change of habit. Also for Rob. Scott, Tho. Rosse, Laurence Curtes, Jo. Harbart, Tho. Carton, Wm Brewster, Alex. Traishe, Jo. Tyndall, Tho. Vyncent, Wm Robynson, Tho. Becke, Tho. Ebbes. Suppr.

f. 238ᵛ

Edm. Bryket, O.F.M., of Lynn. Disp. to hold a benef. with change of habit. Also for Wm Mychell, Tho. Person, Walter Harewode, Rob. Audeley, Jo. Heyleye, Jo. Spycer, Wm Cappes. Suppr.

20 Wm Walson, Austin fr., of Lynn. Disp. to hold a benef. with change of habit. Also for Wm Wrytte, Jo. Wadnow, Tho. Fuller, Jo. Potter, Rob. Wilson, Tho. Watson, Edm. Jackson, Jo. Botrayle, Rob. Wartoppe, Jo. Fylles. Suppr.

Rob. Newman, O.C. fr., of Lynn. Disp. to hold a benef. with change of habit. Also for Wm Collyns, Jo. Heye, Rob. Jarvis, Wm Pallett, Wm Pulo, Hy Baraune, Adam Poynter, Rob. Newton. Suppr.

f. 239ʳ

Nov. 20 Jo. Partriche, O.P., of [King's] Langley. Disp. to hold a benef. with change of habit. Also for Jo. Ingworth, Jo. Scobye or Scoteye?, Jo. Dogett, Wm Bery, Roger Grene, Tho. Robson, Edw. Hobson, Jo. Cowper, Tho. Wetherid, Gilbert Glyssen, Tho. Brabon, Wm Bedome. Suppr.

4 Ric. David, O.P., of Brecon. Also for Hy Coke, Roger Thomas, Owen ap Res, Leyson David, Ric. Willyams, Matthew Hary, Geo. White, Tho. Eve. Suppr.

20 Jo. Trahern, O.F.M., of Cardigan. Disp. to hold a benef. with change of habit. Also for Lewis Richards, Ric. Griffett, Morgan David, Ric. Philipps, Tho. Marksfelde, Ric. Ore, Evan Philippe, Wm David, Hy Morgan, Bernard Blakborne, Jo. Williams, Jo. Geiffrey, Jo. Brygan, Jo. David. Suppr.

f. 239ᵛ

Dec. 4 Lewis Johns, O.P., of Haverfordwest. Disp. to hold a benef. with change of habit. Also for Maurice Johns, Hugh Says, Ric. Wade, Roger Rogers, Jo. Baker. Suppr.

Ric. Nicholson, O.P., of Cardiff. Disp. to hold a benef. with change of habit. Also for David Llin, Tho. Stannton. Suppr.

Tho. Gwyn, O.F.M., of Cardiff. Disp. to hold a benef. with change of habit. Also for Roland Johns, Owen Jonys, Rob. Castell, Ric. Mellyn, Jo. Browne, Wm Barboure, Hugh Sawyer, Ric Bate (Austin fr., of Newport). Suppr.

1 Tho. Parker, O.P., of Bristol. Disp. to hold a benef. with complete change of habit. Jas Jermon, Ralph Dolle, Wm Gardyner. Suppr.

10 Tho. Lewis, O.F.M., of Bristol. Disp. to hold a benef. with change of habit. Also for Hy Lawme, Jo. Duke, Tho. Looe, Hy Philipps, Jo. Geiffrey. Suppr.

f. 240ʳ

6 Nich. Sandforde, Austin fr., of Bristol. Disp. to hold a benef. with change of habit. Also for Jo. Clerke, Jo. Ynman, Roger Felion, Tho. Parker, Jo. Pynder, Laurence Frakische, Jo. Stere, Rob. Persey. Suppr.

20 Rob. Sandwiche, O.P., of Ilchester. Disp. to hold a benef. with change of habit. Also for Wm Cotton, Roger Norman, Ric. Archepoll, Ric. Bonde, Jo. Witmarche, Adam Garett. Suppr.

Jo. Harrys, O.P., of Bridgwater. Disp. to hold a benef. with change of habit. Also for Jo. Wake, Ric. Harrys, Gerard Morley, Jo. Cogam, Tho. Howell, Andrew Gonyt, Rob. Olyver. Suppr

f. 240^v

Dec. 4 Jo. Watts, O.P., of Exeter. Disp. to hold a benef. with change of habit. Also for Peter Barett, Rob. Sprange, Jo. Wenarde, Jo. Curties, Nich. Hamlyn, Laurence Godfrey, Nich. Keman, Hugh Collyns, Edw. Helmer, Jo. Forde, Jo. Kilbery, Rob. Tucke, Tho. Hatherstalle, Jo. Adam. Suppr.

Oct. 29 Gregory Bassett, O.F.M., of Exeter. Disp. to hold a benef. with change of habit. Also for Tho. Gardner, Tho. Tucke, Jo. More, Jo. Vele, Wm Hethfeld, Tho. Skynner, Rob. Sinner, Ric. Pyrrye, Jo. Skyrling. Suppr.

Dec. 12 Jo. Morys, O.F.M., of Plymouth. Disp. to hold a benef. with change of habit. Also for Jo. Hunt, Roger Sparnall, Wm Sherwill, Jo. Bowge, Rob. Ellis, Wm Barre, Tho. Tykberd, Adrian Cornelis, Guy Etonne. Suppr.

f. 241^r

5 Wm Millyn, O.C. fr., of Plymouth. Disp. to hold a benef. with change of habit. Also for Simon ap Howell, Jo. Harrys, Jo. Bonde, Hugh Hawyn, Wm Lobbe, Jo. Edwards. Suppr.

8 Walter Rode, O.F.M., of Bodmin. Disp. to hold a benef. with change of habit. Also for Jo. Collyns, Ric. Keserum, Jo. Bowroode, Jo. Colyn, Rob. Skille, Hy Tarwey, Ric. Peter, Jo. Mayne. Suppr.

3 Jo. Reskerman, O.P., of Truro. Disp. to hold a benef. with change of habit. Also for Jo. de Coloribus, Jo. Cooke, Peter Tomkyn, Ric. Cossyn, Martin Geiffrey, Ric. Martyne, Davy Porter, Jo. Woode. Suppr.

Oct. 31 Wm Germyn, O.F.M., of Dorchester. Disp. to hold a benef. with change of habit. Also for Edm. Dorett, Tho. Clas, Jo. Treginzian, Jo. Clement, Jo. Laurens, Tho. Hill, Stephen Popynioye, Tho. Wyre, Wm Barbor. Suppr.

f. 241^v

Jo. Morles, O.P., of Melcombe. Disp. to hold a benef. with change of habit. Also for Rob. Bowreman, Tho. Stacye. Suppr.

Nov. 30 Jo. Heskyns, O.P., of Salisbury. Disp. to hold a benef. with change of habit. Also for Jo. Churchegate, Lewis Marmery, Tho. Browne, Wm Preston, Tho. Marden, Ralph Cooke, Jo. Robey, Roger Philips, Jo. Bentley, Ric. Stonys, Jo. Butler, Hy Crosse, Peter Treurna. Suppr.

Dec. 7 Jo. Burtham, B.Th., O.F.M., of Salisbury. Disp. to hold a benef. with change of habit. Also for Tho. Man, Wm Redyng, Tho. Pope, Wm Yonge, Wm Turnor, Wm Newman, Vincent Tuttye, Bertrand Billing, Rob. Walker. Suppr.

Dec. 2 Jo. Teill, Austin fr., of Southampton. Disp. to hold a benef. with change of habit. Also for Jas Johnson, Jas ?Smante (or Sucante), Wm Sympson, Tho. Senocke, Jo. White. Suppr.

f. 242ʳ

9 Jo. Antony, O.P., of Chichester. Disp. to hold a benef. with change of habit. Also for Jo. Layart, Wm Halle, Tho. Senthill, Tho. Wilson, Jo. Holyday, Jo. Cutforde. Suppr.

11 Wm Still, O.F.M., of Chichester. Disp. to hold a benef. with change of habit. Also for Rob. Bruynton, Andrew Pepper, Cornelius Smythe, Ric. Hoode, Jo. Perkis, Walter Leger. Suppr.

13 Jo. Colwill, O.P., of Arundel. Disp. to hold a benef. with change of habit. Also for Wm Cosynton, Wm Welche, Ric. David, Tho. Mathew. Suppr.

Oct. 20 Wm Combden, O.P., of Guildford. Disp. to hold a benef. with change of habit. Also for Wm Dale, Rob. Moton, Philip Stawforde, Jo. Hyns, Jo. Forte, Tho. Hopkyn. Suppr.

f. 242ᵛ

Nov. 30 Hugh Burtley, O.C. fr., recently prior of Coventry friary. Disp. to hold a benef. with change of habit. Also for Jo. Fysher, Ric. Wodecoke, Wm Walker, Tho. Vicars, Jo. Pastie, Wm Haryson, Ric. Cooper, Jo. Hurse, Ric. Cooper, Wm Kinge, Wm Madder, Jo. Newbolde, Jo. Eckelson. Suppr.

Jo. Stafforde, O.F.M., recently prior of Coventry. Disp. to hold a benef. with change of habit. Also for Tho. Malerie, Tho. Sanderson, Jo. Able, Jo. Woode, Roger Kellie, Tho. Alcoke, Rob. Walker, Tho. Banester, Matthew Walker. Suppr.

Dec. 12 Jo. Ike, O.F.M., recently warden of Stamford friary. Disp. to hold a benef. with change of habit. Also for Jo. Newthropp, Jo. Chadworthe, Jo. Clerke, Jo. Coytte, Jo. German, Ric. Pye, Jo. Yonge, Tho. Lovell, Wm Watsons. Suppr.

f. 243ʳ

Jo. Kyrton, O.C. fr., recently warden of Stamford friary. Disp. to hold a benef. with change of habit. Also for Geo. Borwyne, Tho. Geofrey, Otwillus Preston, Rob. Bolam, Hy Hyvys, Andrew Richerdson, Wm Watsons, Ric. Harrys. Suppr.

Wm Stafforde, O.P., recently warden of Stamford friary. Disp. to hold a benef. with change of habit. Also for Ralph Oliff, Wm Wakefelde, Hy Rede, Jo. Langleye, Wm Shell, Hugh Tryton, Cuthbert Willie, Tho. Ashewell, Jo. Cotys, Ralph Gryffyne, Tho. Chapman. Suppr.

Dec. 31 Tho. Mendar, O.F.M., recently warden of Bedford friary. Disp. to hold a benef. with change of habit. Also for Tho. Roberts, Octavian Blakborne, Jo. Notyngham, Alex. Clerke, Ric. Smythe, Ric. Elmer, Rob. Rufforde, Wm Knight, Tho. Morishe. Suppr.

21 Jo. Amerey, Trinitarian fr. of Mottenden. Disp. to hold a benef. with change of habit. Also for Peter Johnson. Suppr.

f. 243^v

23 Jo. Walcotte & Mary Acton, Heref. dio. Disp. for marriage (3rd degree affin.). £6.

31 Ric. Warner, Austin fr., recently prior of Stamford friary. Disp. to hold a benef. with change of habit. Also for Roger Lightfote, Ralph Jordan, Peter Cicell, Tho. Alen, Jo. Thomas. Suppr.

ff. 244^r-7^v blank.

f. 248^r

1539 Jan.   1 Wm Dyxe & Alice Smythe, of St Giles, Cripplegate, London. Disp. for marriage in their par. ch. within the prohibited times. 20s.

2 Edw. Dryer & Joan Halet, Sarum dio. Disp. for marriage (2nd & 3rd degrees affin.). £8.

4 Edm. Alexander & Alice Dyngley, of London. Disp. for marriage within the prohibited times without banns. 30s.

Rob. Davye & Joan Verges, Winton dio. Disp. for marriage without banns, in Joan's par. ch. 10s.

f. 248^v

6 Alex. Hadfelde & Marg. Boythe, Cov. & Lich. dio. Disp. for marriage (4th degree consang.). 26s 8d.

9 Lewis ap John, subdcn, Lland. dio. Disp. to take dcn's & pr.'s orders within the prohibited times, although in his 22nd yr. 15s.

10 Peter Bradshawe *alias* Pers & Helen Heskey, Cov. & Lich. dio. Disp. for marriage (4th degree affin.). 26s 8d.

9 Sir Tho. Gamage and Joyce Crose, gent. Disp. for marriage (4th degree consang.). 26s 8d.

10 Tho. Talbott of Malahide, esq., & Ly Alison Wade *alias* Warde, widow, of Dublin, & resident in Ireland. Disp. for marriage (3rd & 4th degrees affin.). 30s.

f. 249^r

6 Simon Jekys, recently abbot of Kenilworth, Warwks. Disp. to become a sec. pr. & hold a benef.; permut. cl. Also for Wm Warwyke, Jo. Rogers, Ric. Bager, Geo. Redell, Ralph Baxster, Ric. Heythe, Jo. Raves, Wm Clare, Ric. Palmer, Tho. Stone, Ric. Todde. Suppr.

Jan. 10 Ric. Lypston, recently Superior of Newark (?Austin friary). Disp. to hold a benef. with change of habit. Also for Wm Thetcher, Wm Blundell, Nich. White, Ric. Woode, Tho. Snelling, Jo. Mertyn, Tho. Garlande, Jo. Rose. Suppr.

12 —— Maye & Joan Adeson, of London. Disp. for marriage without banns. 10s.

f. 249ᵛ

13 Ric. Mylton & Eliz. Atchinson, Cov. & Lich. dio. Disp. for marriage (4th degree consang.). 26s 8d.

14 Tho. Brightman & Kath. Hary, of the par. of St Marg., Westminster. Disp. for marriage without banns. 10s.

12 Tho. Werberton & Joan Williams, Cov. & Lich. dio. Disp. for marriage (4th degree consang.). 26s 8d.

10 Jas Jeskyn, gent. of the Kg's hsehld, & Joan Whitehed, of St Pancras par., London. Disp. for marriage in Joan's par. ch. without banns. 10s.

18 Francis Cave, D.C.L., & Marg. Aysheton, widow of Edw. Aysheton, of Godston. Disp. for marriage without banns, & not in their par. ch. 10s; 10s.

Sir Jo. Seyntlove & Marg. Audeley. Disp. for marriage without banns. 10s.

f. 250ʳ

Hugh Hollande & Marg. Lancaster, Cov. & Lich. dio. Disp. for marriage (4th degree consang.). 26s 8d.

Wm & Joan Tredwell, Linc. dio. Disp. for marriage (3rd & 4th degrees consang.). 30s.

20 Tho. Leyson, recently abbot of Neath, Glam. Disp. to hold a benef. with complete change of habit. Also for Jo. Thomas, Tho. Beste, Wm Keyns, Jo. Richards, Tho. Legate, David Thomas, Jo. Roderike. Suppr.

Dennis Sutton & Joan Barker, Cov. & Lich. dio. Disp. for marriage (3rd & 4th degrees consang.). 30s.

Wm Trigolde & Helen Illyarde, Cant. dio. Disp. for marriage (Wm was Helen's godfather). Arb. 26s 8d; warrant of the lords shown.

f. 250ᵛ

Jo. Walcott & Mary Acton, of Acton-on-the-hill, Heref. dio. Disp. for marriage in Mary's par. ch. without banns. 10s.

Jan. 21 Chris. Downys, M.A., Cov. & Lich. dio. Disp. to take all h.o. within the prohibited times, & 2 on the same day, without l.d. from his diocesan bp. 26s 8d; 6s 8d.

20 Wm Haymes, B.Th., r. of Walgrave, Linc. dio., Kg's chapl., v. of Cholsey, Sarum dio. Disp. to hold a 3rd benef. with cure. £8.

22 Tho. Taverham & Alice Clerk, of Shelford, York dio. Disp. for marriage in Alice's par. ch. without banns. 10s.

Jo. Cocks *alias* Chaundeler & Kath. Wynterhay, of Winterbourne Carne, Sarum dio. Disp. for marriage (4th degree consang.). 26s 8d.

f. 251ʳ

20 Peter Wever, r. of Sutton Mandeville ('Manfelde'), Sarum dio., chapl. to Ly Ann Clynton. Disp. to hold a benef. with cure with the above; permut. cl. £6 10s.

22 Jo. ap Jo. ap David ap Dyo & Jenet verch Shone ap Meredith, Bangor dio. Disp. validating their marriage (4th degree affin.). 26s 8d.

23 Jas Bymynton & Alice Walker, York dio. Disp. for marriage (3rd & 4th degrees consang.). 30s.

Thos. Gason, Fellow of All Saints (*sic* for All Souls) Coll., Oxford. Disp. to take all h.o. outside the statutory times, 2 on the same day, without l.d. from his diocesan bp. 26s 8d; 6s 8d.

Wm Newton & Joan Mallacke, Ex. dio. Disp. for marriage (Joan's father was Wm's godfather). 30s.

f. 251ᵛ

24 Wm Crome & Eliz. Whytley, Winton dio. Disp. for marriage in Eliz.'s par. ch., the banns read once. 6s 8d.

Rob. & Alice Chapman, of Westerham, Roch. dio. Disp. for marriage (3rd degree affin.). £6.

25 Wm Whatelo & Alice Glover, Cant. dio. Disp. for marriage (4th degree consang.). 26s 8d.

David ap Howell & Gwellian verch Harrye, St David's dio. Disp. for marriage (4th degree consang.). 26s 8d.

27 Tho. Branwode & Joan Smythe, of London. Disp. for marriage in Joan's par. ch., without banns. 10s.

Jo. Sheparde & Eliz. Gybson, of St Botolph's without Bishopsgate, London. Disp. for marriage in the above ch. without banns. 10s.

f. 252ʳ

Jan. 28 Nich. Marks & Alice Henmershe, of St Botolph's without Aldgate, London. Disp. for marriage in the above ch. without banns.
10s.

29 Ric. Tayllor, recently Austin fr. of Tickhill, York dio. Disp. to
become a sec. pr. & hold any benef. Also for Rob. Ackers, Tho.
Hankok, Hy Isabell. Suppr.

30 Jo. Swanne & Agnes Brewster, of St Mary Abchurch par., London. Disp. for marriage in their par. ch. without banns. 10s.

31 Jas Walles, recently canon of Sixhill. Disp. to become a sec. pr.
& hold a benef. Also for Chris. Errington, Wm Walker, Ric.
Byllisbye, Jo. Shalyes, Leonard Philippe, Jo. Obrey, Hy Yonge,
Rob. Jackeson, Chris. Cuthberde, canons of the same hse. Suppr.

f. 252ᵛ

20 Wm Selye & Cristine Wilkinson of London. Disp. for marriage
within the prohibited times & without banns. 30s.

Jo. Compton *alias* Tele, B.Th., r. of ——, Worc. dio. Disp. to
hold another benef.; permut. cl. £6 10s.

31 Rob. Hill, O.C. fr., recently prior of Beverley friary, Yorks. Disp.
to hold a benef. with complete change of habit. Suppr.

Wm Merton, recently monk of Bardney, Lincs. Disp. to hold a
benef. with complete change of habit. Also for Jo. Ponnfret, Rob.
Cambridge, Peter Barton, Ric. Furisbye, Chris. Kerton, Tho.
Mawre, Ottwell Bottolle, Roger Skipwith, Wm Bowrowe, Jo.
Morpeles, & 4 other monks of the above hse. Suppr.

f. 253ʳ

Ant. Dunstan, recently monk of Evesham. Disp. to hold a benef.
with complete change of habit. Also for Edm. Raynforde, Geo.
Boddhyrste, Rob. Forde, Tho. Mylle, Tho. Philipps, Tho.
Knowllis, Jo. Bockseter, Wm Bucke, Jo. Hedgys. Suppr.

Jo. Botler, formerly O.C. fr., of Hitchin. Disp. to hold a benef.
with change of habit. Also for Jo. Lamkyne, Rob. Colyngwode,
Jo. Coke, Tho. Pratte. Suppr.

Chris. Walker, formerly canon of Bullington. Disp. for change of
habit. Also for Jo. Gybson & Geo. Bentham. Suppr.

f. 253ᵛ

Feb. 1 Wm Gery & Eliz. Plume, Lond. dio. Disp. for marriage within
the prohibited times. 20s.

Tho. Grene, recently abbot of Croxton. Disp. to hold a benef.
with complete change of habit. Also for Ric. Foxe, Wm Ger-

mayne, Jo. Ripewithe, Wm Halydaye, Tho. Tayllor, Peter Anderson, Jo. Stewbese, Chris. Nightingalle, Geo. Perkyn, Tho. Perkyn, Tho. Hylley, Tho. Horner, Geo. Cawme, Ric. Estrycke, Rob. Laughton, Chris. Beckwith, Hy Halle, Wm Person, Jas Charocke, Jo. Consalte, Jo. Fletcher, Tho. Edmershaw. Suppr.

f. 254ʳ

Feb. 1 Jo. Arthure, O.F.M., of Exeter. Disp. to hold a benef. with complete change of habit. Suppr.

2 Philip Cooper & Sibil Rosse, Chich. dio. Disp. for marriage (Philip was godfather to a child of Sibil). £6.

3 Giles Smythe *alias* Sevalle, monk of Abingdon. Disp. to take pr.'s orders without l.d. from his diocesan bp. 6s 8d; 10s.

Tho. Dunnyng, B.Cn.L., r. of North Tuddenham, Norw. dio. Disp. to hold a benef. with the above, or 2 without. £6 10s.

4 Jo. & Agnes Clerke, Linc. dio. Disp. for marriage (3rd & 4th degrees consang.). 30s.

f. 254ᵛ

6 Jo. Sympson, recently prior of St Marg.'s, nr Marlborough, Wilts. Disp. to hold a benef. with complete change of habit. Also for Edw. Sparke, Jo. Radley, Tho. Welbourne, Jo. Tangal. Suppr.

7 Ric. Laurence & Marg. Gurdon, Lond. dio. Disp. for marriage within the prohibited times. 20s.

8 Jo. Lyllyngton, pr., r. of ?Ravenstone ('Raweston'), Sarum dio. Disp. for non-res. for 2 yrs, particularly on account of the rectory hse having been burnt down and there is no other nearby hse available. 13s 4d.

Wm Hutton, B.Th., v. of Sparsholt, Sarum dio. Disp. to hold a benef. with the above; permut. cl. £6 10s.

9 Chris. Andrew, pr., v. of Bishop's Frome, Heref. dio. Disp. if the above does not yield over £8 p.a. to hold another benef. £4.

f. 255ʳ

8 Tho. Hynton & Marg. Moreton, Cov. & Lich. dio. Disp. for marriage (4th degree consang.). 26s 8d.

Ellis Ferrers, B.Th. Confirmation (given in full) of faculty conceded by word of mouth of Wm, Bp of Norw. for the above to enjoy the status of D.Th. £4.

f. 255ᵛ

10 Rob. Hawton, pr., v. of ?Worletby ('Wolbrigbye'), Linc. dio., chapl. to Jo. Vere, Ld Bulbecke. Disp. to hold a benef. with the above, or 2 without; permut. cl. £6 10s.

Feb. 10 Jo. Creche, pr., r. of Melbury, Sarum dio. Disp. to hold a benef. with the above, which does not yield £8 p.a. £4.

Edw. Clyston, v. of Leyton, Lond. dio., chapl. to Ld Morley. Disp. to hold a benef. with the above. £6 10s.

Jo. Coxall *alias* Roydon, recently monk of Coggeshall, Essex. Disp. to hold a benef. with change of habit. Suppr.

Wm Sparhawke, recently monk of Chertsey. Disp. to hold a benef. with change of habit. Suppr.

Ric. Benett, B.Th., O.S.B. Disp. to hold any benef. with cure; permut. cl. £4.

f. 256ʳ

Tho. Henaige, minor, & Eliz. Heton, of Dagenham, Lond. dio. Disp. for marriage without banns, within the prohibited times, & not in their par. ch. 10s; 20s; 10s.

Ric. Rydge, recently abbot of Notley. Disp. to hold a benef. with complete change of habit. Also for Valentine Bouwde, Jo. Kenye, Wm Walter, Wm Ball, Jo. Pole, Tho. Webbe, Jo. Lichepole, Jas Alborawe, Wm Catesbie, Jo. Tymmes, Jo. Wheler, Ric. Smythe, Ric. Barbor. Suppr.

Ant. Molyneux, D.Th., incumbent of ?Chellaston ('Cheston'), Cov. & Lich. dio. Disp. to hold a benef. with the above; permut. cl. £6 10s.

13 Ric. Barbor, Cov. & Lich. dio. Disp. to take all h.o. at any time & 2 on the same day. 26s 8d.

ff. 256ᵛ–7ʳ

12 Ric. Whertley, v. of Earlham, Norw. dio. Confirmation (given in full), of letters issued by Ric., Bp of Norwich, Sept. 22 1529, admitting him also to the vicarage of Colney, Norw. dio, vacant by resignation of Augustine Thirkelde, on the presentation of Eliz. Yaxley, widow, patroness of the above. 40s; p.s.r. 5s.

f. 257ʳ

13 Jo. Halle & Agnes Smythe of London. Disp. for marriage within the prohibited times. 20s.

15 Wm Grene & Joan Wormeston, Lond. dio. Disp. for marriage without banns, within the prohibited times & not in their par. ch. 10s; 20s; 10s.

Edm. Shether, sub-warden of All Souls Coll., Oxford. Disp. to take dcn's & pr.'s orders outside the statutory times. 13s 4d.

f. 257ᵛ

Feb. 7 Wm Houghton, B.C.L., chapl. to the Bp of London, v. of Apple-
         ton, York dio. Disp. to hold any other benef. with the above;
         permut. & non-res. cl. £7 13s 4d.

      20 Jo. Sturton, recently abbot of Keynsham, Somerset. Disp. to hold
          a benef. with change of habit. Also for Wm Heron, Wm Typpett,
          Jo. Arnolde, Jo. Fowler, Jo. Gilforde, Tho. Bede, Jo. Browne,
          Tho. Parker, Jo. Partriche, Wm Dune, Ric. Adams. Suppr.

          Chris. Cartwright, recently prior of Ormsby. Disp. to hold a
          benef. with change of habit. Also for Jo. Jackson, Wm Grege,
          Wm Harewike, Wm Watson, Jo. Doo. Suppr.

f. 258ʳ

      22 Jo. Rogerson & Ann Smythe, Cov. & Lich. dio. Disp. for mar-
          riage (4th degree consang.). 26s 8d.

      20 Wm Gibbes, recently prior of Bath, Somerset. Disp. to hold a
          benef. with change of habit. Also for Jo. Pytte, Tho. Sexton,
          Ric. Griffithe, Nich. Jobbyn, Alex. Bull, Ric. Bigge, Jo. Romsey,
          Tho. Powell, Ric. Gybbes, Tho. Stilband, Wm Clement, Jo.
          Browne, Jo. Sudbury, Edw. Stile, Wm Bewchyn, Jo. Parnell,
          Jo. Longe. Suppr.

      24 Rob. Davye, v. of Icklington, Ely dio., chapl. to Ld Mountjoy.
          Disp. to hold a benef. with cure with the above; permut. cl.
          £6 10s.

f. 258ᵛ

1538 Oct. 20 Tho. Cameswell, recently prior of Coventry (cath. priory). Disp.
              to hold a benef. with change of habit. Also for Ric. Barnade, Wm
              Wenter, Tho. Chambers, Tho Leke, Humfrey Celar, Jo. Eccul-
              sall, Rob. Wilde, Jo. Evance, Nich. Bremyshe, Wm Foster.
              Suppr.

              Jo. Bocharde, recently prior of the Charterhouse, Coventry. Disp.
              to give up his habit & hold a benef. Also for Jo. Todde, Rob.
              Bolde, Wm Abell, Tho. Corbyn, Ric. Apulbye, Ric. Craste, Tho.
              Lekbarowe, Ric. Slader, Jo. Todde, Ric. Wall. Suppr.

          26 Humfrey Ludlow & Eleanor Vernham, Heref. dio. Disp. for
              marriage (3rd & 4th degrees consang.). 30s.

f. 259ʳ

1539 Feb. 22 Wm Byronne & Marg. Rysley, Cov. & Lich. dio. Disp. for mar-
              riage (3rd & 4th degrees affin.). 30s.

              Jo. Buxum, pr., r. of Eastwell, Linc. dio., aged about 30. Disp.
              for non-res. for 3 yrs to study. 6s 8d 'pro quolibet anno'.

           3 Jo. Granocke *alias* Hole, subdcn, Bath & W. dio. Disp. to take

pr.'s orders despite defect of birth, having lost his previous letters of disp. for h.o. despite this impediment. 40s. Arb. 'quia non taxatur in libro'.

f. 259ᵛ

Feb. 4 Jo. Browne, Linc. dio., & Ann Grene, Ely dio. Disp. for marriage in Ann's par. ch. without banns. 10s.

15 Wm Powell, literate. Creation as public notary & tabellion. 13s 4d. Also for Tho. Rede, B.C.L. 13s 4d.

10 Tho. David ap Hopkyn, pr., r. of Llanilid, Lland. dio. Disp. to hold a benef. if the above does not yield over £8 p.a. £4.

28 Roger Nayler & Helen Birchall, Cov. & Lich. dio. Disp. for marriage (4th degree consang.). 26s 8d.

Rob. Thomson, recently Crutched fr., of Colchester. Disp. to hold a benef. with change of habit. Suppr.

f. 260ʳ

26 Humfrey Ludlow & Eleanor Vernham, Cov. & Lich. dio. Disp. for marriage within the prohibited times, without banns, & not in their par. ch. 20s; 10s; 10s.

28 Rob. Bate, abbot of Combe. Disp. to hold a benef. with change of habit. Also for Oliver Adams, Ric. Symmyngs, Humfrey Starke, Tho. Sutton, Wm Sutton, Ric. Wastell, Wm Freman, Ric. Bradacke, Oliver Hardwyn, Wm Perse, Tho. Holme, Tho. Clerk, Geoffrey Damell, Rob. Hipworth, monks of the same hse. Suppr.

Mar. 1 Tho. Otes, acol., York dio. Disp. to take all h.o. within the prohibited times, 2 on the same day, without l.d. from their diocesan bp. 26s 8d; 6s 8d.

4 Wm Whythede & Marg. Sledall, Carl. dio. Disp. for marriage (4th degree consang.). 26s 8d.

f. 260ᵛ

3 Tho. Crane, chanter in the chantry of St Mary the Virgin, Bridgwater, Bath & W. dio. Disp. to hold another benef. with the above, as it does not yield over £8 p.a. £4.

6 Jo. Moone *alias* Sparke & Alice Glover, Cant. dio. Disp. for marriage (Jo. was godfather to a child of Alice; & not in their par. ch., within the prohibited times). £6; 10s; 20s.

4 Ric. Whitell, recently prior of Stafford. Disp. to hold a benef. with complete change of habit. Also for Wm Pyckestoke, Ric. Harvye, Chris. Sympson, Tho. Bagaley, Wm Stapleston, Wm Bowndon, canons of the same. Suppr.

Mar. 6 Jo. Baylye, recently canon of St Kath.'s priory by Lincoln. Disp. to hold a benef. with change of habit. Also for Ric. Jackson. Suppr.

f. 261ʳ

10 Ric. Cotton, literate, Cov. & Lich. dio. Creation as public notary & tabellion. 13s 4d.

Rob. Holstede, of Cov. & Lich. dio. & Marg. Dene, York dio. Disp. for marriage (4th degree consang.). 26s 8d.

Edm. Brudenell & Agnes Bussye, Linc. dio. Disp. for marriage not in their par. ch. without banns & within the prohibited times. 10s; 20s; 10s.

Tho. Smythe, gent. of the Kg's hsehld, & Eliz. Smythe, Lond. dio. Disp. for marriage within the prohibited times & without banns. 20s; 10s.

Jo. Lyne & Eleanor Moryshe, Ex. dio. Disp. for marriage (4th degree consang.). 26s 8d.

f. 261ᵛ

12 Hy Knowlis & Grace Farrande, York dio. Disp. for marriage (4th degree consang.). 26s 8d.

Ric. Hobson, recently canon of Newstead, Lincs. Disp. to hold a benef. with change of habit. Also for Rob. Rayle, Rob. Thornall, Jo. Middelton, Geoffrey Vele, Jo. Haggas. Suppr. Gratis.

Jo. Darley, pr., r. of Skelton in Malters (*sic* for forest of Galters, nr York?) York dio. Disp. to hold a benef. with the above, as it does not yield over £8 p.a. £4.

10 Walter Bayne, Knight Hospitaller, resident in the preceptory of Willoughton, Linc. dio. Disp. to hold any benef.; permut. cl. £4.

18 Jo. Williamson & Agnes Chwatnes, York dio. Disp. for marriage (3rd & 4th degrees affin.). 30s.

f. 262ʳ

Ric. Cletter & Eliz. Besbrowne, York dio. Disp. for marriage (4th degree consang.). 26s 8d.

Ric. Johns, sch., Lland. dio. Disp. to take all h.o. outside the statutory times, & 2 on the same day. 26s 8d.

Tho. Constantyne & Agnes Walton, York dio. Disp. for marriage (3rd & 4th degrees consang.). 30s.

Sir Jo. Willoughbye & Alice Stubbes, widow, Norw. dio. Disp. for marriage within the prohibited times, not in their par. ch. 20s; 10s.

Mar 22 Edw. Kyrbye *alias* Cooper, recently monk of Rievaulx. Disp. to hold a benef. with change of habit. Suppr.

24 Jo. Traves & Cecily Peyfolde, of London. Disp. for marriage without banns & in the prohibited times. 20s; 10s.

f. 262ᵛ

27 Humfrey Luce & Agnes Philipps, of Stratford 'super portum'. Disp. for marriage without banns. 10s.

1538 Nov. 30 Jo. Thixhill, D.Th., Kg's chapl. Disp. to hold a benef. with several others, provided they do not yield over £300 p.a. £13 6s 8d, by warrant of the lords.

1539 Mar. 28 Ric. Kendall & Alice Wyse, Ex. dio. Disp. for marriage (3rd & 4th degrees affin.). 30s.

Jo. Hall, B.A., chapl. to Jo. Rosse, Earl of Rutland. Disp. to hold any 2 benefices; permut. cl. £6 10s.

Apr. 1 Miles Bens, B.A., York dio. Disp. to take all h.o. outside the statutory times, & 2 on the same day. 26s 8d.

11 Rob. Baxter & Joan Pallerton, of London. Disp. for marriage, the banns read once. 6s 8d.

f. 263ʳ

4 Tho. Pernell & Cristine Karkett, of London. Disp. for marriage in Cristine's par. ch. without banns. 10s.

July 5 Geo. Deynes, literate, Norw. dio. Disp. to practise as a public notary & tabellion. 13s 4d.

June 24 Tho. Garrade, r. of the par. ch. of Honey Lane, London. Disp. to hold a benef. with the above; permut. cl. £6 10s.

Apr. 16 Jo. Meyricke, acol., Bangor dio. Disp. to take subdcn's & dcn's orders on the same day, outside the statutory times. 13s 4d.

18 David Deare & Eliz. Lewys, Ex. dio. Disp. for marriage in their par. ch. without banns. 10s.

f. 263ᵛ

Geoffrey Cartewright & Marg. Redyshe, Cov. & Lich. dio. Disp. for marriage without banns. 10s.

20 Jo. Tucker, recently abbot of Buckland, Ex. dio. Disp. to hold a benef. with complete change of habit. Also for Rob. Topy, Jo. West, Wm Alforde, Wm Gye, Tho. Hooper, Tho. Maynerde, Benedict Lovege, Hugh Hervye, Wm Milforde, Simon Rugewike, Jo. Jurden, Wm Ellisworthe. Suppr.

21 Rob. Moreton, reg. pr., Worc. dio. Disp. to have a portable altar & celebrate masses in his private oratory. 20s.

Apr. 21 Ric. Michell, sch., of Cambridge University. Disp. to take all h.o. without l.d. 6s 8d.

f. 264ʳ

22 Jo. Whetham, pr., r. of Worlington ('Wollington'), Ex. dio. Disp. to hold another benef.; permut. cl. £6 10s.

23 Ralph Burrell, recently prior of Leicester. Disp. to hold a benef. with complete change of habit. Also for Wm Hopkyns, Jo. Harforthe, Jo. Coke, Ric. Ingelbie, Ric. Blakewin, Ellis Gevere, Andrew Nyke. Suppr. Gratis.

24 Ric. Tyllye & Eliz. Richardson. Disp. for marriage in Eliz.'s par. ch. without banns. 10s.

Chris. Blande & Marg. Cooper, York dio. Disp. for marriage (4th degree consang.). 26s 8d.

Jo. Harison & Marg. Holme, York dio. Disp. for marriage (4th degree consang.). 26s 8d.

f. 264ᵛ

26 Edw. Bidgelveye & Joan Hanson, Cov. & Lich. dio. Disp. for marriage (3rd & 4th degrees consang.). 30s.

24 Jo. Gruffithe, gent., & Ellen Bulkeley, widow, Bangor dio. Disp. for marriage (3rd & 4th degrees consang.). 30s.

Walter Gluyn & Marg. ap David ap Mead, St David's dio. Disp. to contract or remain in marriage (4th degree affin.). 26s 8d.

26 Rob. Hamlyn, recently abbot of Athelney, Somerset. Disp. to hold any benef., with complete change of habit. Also for Ric. Wells, Jo. Athelweyne, Hy Ambrose, Rob. Edger, Jo. Laurence, Tho. Genyns. Suppr.

f. 265ʳ

29 Tho. Bradsall *alias* Smythe & Eliz. Barlow, Linc. dio. Disp. for marriage (Eliz. was godmother to a child of Tho.). £6.

1538 Nov. 20 Hy Marten, O.F.M., Warden of Aylesbury friary. Disp. to hold a benef. with change of habit. Also for Wm Meye, Jo. Dannell, Jo. Gymbar, Rob. Bynks, Tho. Hucoll, Jo. Molars. Suppr.

30 Ric. Grene, recently abbot of Biddlesden. Disp. to hold a benef. with complete change of habit. Also for Tho. Todde, Rob. Northampton, Jas. Shalstone, Ric. Shiphede, Rob. Westone, Jo. Northampton, Jo. Bradleye, Jo. Anklande, Ric. Brackley, Ric. Benett. Suppr.

1539 Jan. 1 Tho. Norman, O.P., of Warwick. Disp. to hold a benef. with complete change of habit. Also for Nich. Alexander, Ric. Walton, Jo. Watts, Ric. Perse, Jo. Tove, Roger Peke, Rob. Stephenson. Suppr.

f. 265^v

Jan.   2 Jo. Goodwyn, recently prior of the Austin friary of Northampton. Disp. to hold a benef. with complete change of habit. Also for Stephen Barwike, Jo. Browne, Jo. Wilson, Geo. Yewell, Philip Mecar, Ric. Clerke, Jo. Colmyn, Rob. Barret, Rob. Caylie. Suppr.

Edm. Davye, Trinitarian fr. of Thelsford. Disp. to hold a benef. Also for Jas Browne. Suppr.

Jo Wyndelow, O.F.M., of Northampton. Disp. to hold a benef. with change of habit. Also for Rob. Norton, Jo. Hilton, Wm Hardgrow, Jo. Sprotton, Nich. Awdwyn, Jo. Harboo, Rob. Twyne, Jo. Coocke, Wm Staffley. Suppr.

Jo. ap Howell, O.C. fr., of Northampton. Disp. to hold a benef. with change of habit. Also for Jo. Harison, Wm Swayne, Hy Nele, Ric. Dekyn, Philip Bostonne, Jo. Pyckarde, Jo. Pavie, Edw. Jenyn. Suppr.

f. 266^r

Wm Dyckens, O.P., of Northampton. Disp. to change his habit for that of a sec. pr. Also for Ric. Payne, Jo. Lynche, Stephen Wilson, Jas Stywarde, Tho. Mecocke, Rob. Eyre. Suppr.

Mar. 10 Peter Brynckley, B.Th., O.F.M., of Babwell. Disp. to hold a benef. with change of habit. Also for Tho. Hempston, Tho. Warde, Peter Kilborne, Tho. Haywarde, Andrew Lanye, Jo. Gardyner, Tho. Cornell, Rob. Curteys, Tho. Atkynson, Roger Malton, Jo. Hempston, Jo. Flecher, Ric. Ryce. Suppr.

Wm Smythe, O.P., of Norwich. Disp. to hold a benef. with change of habit. Also for Wm Stywarde, Rob. Stapleton, Rob. Corbett, Wm Rede, Rob. Crabe, Ralph Salmon, Rob. Sporgen, Jo. Walsingham, Edm. or Edw. Laurens. Suppr.

f. 266^v

12 Jo. Kempe, O.C. fr., recently of Norwich. Disp. to hold a benef. with change of habit. Also for Wm Fysche, Rob. Schinkewyn, Jo. Reder, Nich. Thorpe, Wm Garnishe, Peter Louse, Tho. Kenett, Jo. Wilson, Francis Renett, Jo. Pynchyn, Wm Burwell, Ric. Lamnothe, Rob. Thewe. Suppr.

Edm. Hiche, O.P., recently of Ipswich. Disp. to hold a benef. with change of habit. Also for Jo. Humfrey, Jo. Gawge, Wm Rede, Rob. Drewe, David Benett, Laurence Johns. Suppr.

Jo. Fowxe, O.P., of Chelmsford. Disp. to hold a benef. with change of habit. Also for Wm Wynter, Roger Elonde, Peter Waly, Wm Newton, Wm Hardye, Wm Bull. Suppr.

f. 267^r

20 Wm Browne, recently prior of Monk Bretton. Disp. to hold a benef., with complete change of habit. Tho. Normanton, Wm

Royston, Geo. Whitacres, Rob. Kyrkebye, Jo. Croston, Wm
Barwike, Tho. Bolton, Ric. Tykhill, Wm Breton, Ric. Wolley,
Tho. Silston, Jo. Pontiffract, Wm Thormre. Suppr.

Mar. 21 Jo. Lexyngton, recently prior of St Andrew's ?by Northampton.
Disp. to hold a benef. with change of habit. Also for Wm Byssett,
Leonard Sharpe, Jo. Hogesonne. Suppr.

23 Jo. Alanebridge, recently abbot of Byland. Disp. to hold a benef.
with change of habit. Suppr.

f. 267ᵛ

Rob. Barker, monk of Byland. Disp. to hold a benef. with com-
plete change of habit. Also for Marmaduke Cristlo, Ric. Letheley,
Tho. Poulton, Ric. Pierson, Jo. Moyser, Wm Baxter, Hy Topin-
ger, Tho. Metcalf, Tho. Hogarde, Rob. Baynton, Rob. Webster,
Rob. Wilkinson, Rob. Lerisse, Peter Jackson, Jo. Clevelonde,
Chris. Cramoke, Wm Hirde, Bernard Bradley, Wm Wederlet,
Wm Wanton, Hy Pierson, Ric. Judson. Suppr.

24 Jo. Bylkwik, recently prior of Kirkham. Disp. to become a sec.
pr. and hold a benef. Suppr.

f. 268ʳ

Rob. Lowson, recently monk of Kirkham. Disp. to hold a benef.,
with change of habit. Also for Jo. Blackett, Tho. Catton, Stephen
Chapman, Jo. Howthorpe, Ric. Lyme, Ric. Baleton, Jas Parkin-
son, Ric. Morwyne, Edw. Newton, Wm Beckfeld, Ant. Watson,
Jo. Hugheson, Rob. Atkinson, Peter Williamson, Jo. Smelte,
Jo. Neville. Suppr.

25 Tho. Knett, recently minister of the dissolved house of the Invoca-
tion founded by Ld Robert (sic). Disp. to hold a benef. with
change of habit. Also for Jo. Turnbill, Jo. Tristame, Tho. Yake,
Jo. Starkvone, Ric. Welshe, Jo. Alemer, Rob. Gibson, Tho.
Grene, Ric. Malling, Ric. Burniston. Suppr.

f. 268ᵛ

Jo. Golding, recently prior of Ellerton. Disp. to hold a benef.
with change of habit. Suppr.

20 Tho. Warde, recently master of the dissolved Trinitarian house
of Wall Knoll (Newcastle-on-Tyne). Disp. to hold a benef. with
change of habit. Also for Roger Dowe, Ric. Simpson, Rob.
Michelson, Wm Spenser. Suppr.

26 Rob. Blakney, recently prior of Tynemouth. Disp. for a change
of habit & to hold a benef. Also for Jo. Castelle, Hy Woddall,
Rob. Bollande, Rob. Forman, Rob. Halle, Tho. Benett, Wm
Carlioll, Rob. Gatisheede, Wm Erisdenne, Stephen Hopham,

Ant. Gardyner, Geo. Jasper, Clement Westmynster, Rob. London, Wm Facett, Tho. Durham, Rob. Charitye, Geo. Faythe. Suppr.

f. 269ʳ

Mar. 27 Wm Lenewoode, recently prior of Newburgh. Disp. to hold a benef. with change of habit. Also for Wm Barker, Jo. Wraugham, Wm Browne, Tho. Barker, Jo. Flyntte, Wm Edwards, Chris. Richardson, Tho. Rypon, Ric. Dawnyng, Wm Johnson, Rowlande Forster, Rob. Temide, Ric. Lolye, Jas Barwike, Tho. Warmouthe, Tho. Grayson, Wm Graye. Suppr.

31 Ric. Mone, recently prior of Bolton. Disp. to hold a benef. with complete change of habit. Also for Chris. Leedys, Tho. Fontayn, Tho. Castle, Geo. Richmonde, Jo. Cromboke, Wm Wilkys, Wm Malhome, Tho. Pyckring, Edw. Hill, Jo. Boltonne, Rob. Knaresburghe, Jo. Halyfaxe, Laurence Plumton, Rob. Burdeux. Suppr.

f. 269ᵛ

1 Wm More, O.F.M., of Dublin, Ireland. Disp. to hold a benef. with change of habit. Gratis.

6 Laurence Sponer, O.P., of Derby. Disp. to hold a benef. with change of habit. Also for Wm Remyngton, Tho. Colton, Jo. Edmunds, Rob. Sadeler, Maurice Manigton, Wm Hepworth. Suppr.

Roger Cappe, O.C., fr., recently of Nottingham. Disp. to hold a benef. with change of habit. Also for Wm Smythe, Wm Froste, Rob. Wilson, Jo. Roberts, Wm Cooke, Wm Thorpe. Suppr.

Tho. Basforde, O.F.M., of Nottingham. Disp. to hold a benef. with change of habit. Also for Tho. Ripton, Rob. Hampton, Rob. Jarvys, Francis Brice, Jo. Chester, Rob. Moreton, Roger Stanley, Wm Thorpe. Suppr.

f. 270ʳ

7 Rob. More, recently canon of Oswestry. Disp. to hold a benef. with change of habit. Suppr.

Apr. 1 Jo. Shere, recently prior of Launceston, Disp. to hold a benef. with change of habit. Also for Jo. Hamme, Jo. Morle, Jo. Hicks, Stephen Gourge, Tho. Webbe, Ric. Orewenyk, Jo. Lawrence, Jo. Fycke, canons of the same hse.

12 Hy More, recently abbot of St Mary Graces by the Tower, London. Disp. to hold a benef. with change of habit. Also for Wm Smythe, Wm Harper, Wm Robynson, Ric. Davye, Ric. Laneroke, Ric. Lawrence, Tho. More, Mathew Davye, monks of the same hse. Suppr.

f. 270ᵛ

Apr. 12 Rob. Swymmer, recently prior of St Germans, Ex. dio. Disp. to hold a benef. with complete change of habit. Also for Stephen Sagynor, Ric. Trotte, Jo. Rythe, Rob. Vian, Wm Lawerye, Rob. Capell. Suppr.

20 Jo. Gybbys, O.C. fr., of London. Disp. to hold a benef. with change of habit. Also for Tho. Lempster, Wm Andrewes, Nich. Maston, Hy Crowder, Tho. Waterhouse, Philip Deye, Jo. Semyngs, Tho. Dubdike, Tho. Phandon, Tho. Illiarde, Tho. Rowdis, Jo. Warmyngton. Suppr.

28 Leonard Spence & Eliz. Robinson, York dio. Disp. for marriage (4th degree consang.). 26s 8d.

f. 271ʳ

29 Wm Adoke & Joan Huchin, Linc. dio. Disp. for marriage (Joan was sponsor at the confirmation of a child of Wm). £5.

30 Jo. Forster, gent., Winton dio., & Jane Wadeham, of Barton, Bath & W. dio. Disp. for marriage in Jane's par. ch., the banns read once. 6s 8d.

30 Tho. Woode & Alice Rowke, Lond. dio. Disp. for marriage in Alice par. ch. without banns. 10s.

May 3 Rob. Sulbys *alias* Fysher & Jane Dyconson, of Marlborough, Sarum dio. Disp. for marriage without banns. 10s.

4 Rob. Stonys, sch., of Corpus Christi Coll., Cambridge, & of York dio. Disp. to take all h.o. outside the statutory times & 2 on the same day without l.d. 26s 8d; 6s 8d.

f. 271ᵛ

5 Jo. Jenyns & Eliz. Cuange(?). Disp. for marriage not in their par. ch., the banns read once. 10s; 6s 8d.

Jo. Loge & Eliz. Tenn, York dio. Disp. for marriage (4th degree consang.). 26s 8d.

Chris. Procter & Alison Laycoke, York dio. Disp. for marriage (Alison's father was godfather to a child of Chris.). 30s.

7 Jo. Nicolle, sch., York dio. Disp. to take all h.o. without l.d. from his diocesan bp. 6s 8d.

8 Jo. Metcalfe & Marg. Dixson, of Newbiggin, York dio. Disp. for marriage (Jo.'s mother was Marg.'s godmother). 30s.

12 Tho. Carns & Kath. Preston, York dio. Disp. for marriage (4th degree consang.). 26s 8d.

f. 272ʳ

Jas Facett & Barbara Redman, York dio. Disp. for marriage (3rd & 4th degrees consang.). 30s.

May 12 Tho. ap Morgan and Jane verch Robert Flemyng, Lland. dio.
Disp. for marriage (4th degree consang.). 26s 8d.

13 Edw. ap Hughe ap John & Janet verch Thomas ap Griffithe, St
Asaph dio. Disp. for marriage (Edw.'s mother was Janet's godmother). 30s.

Jo. Catton & Marg. Magoode, of West Harling, Norw. dio. Disp.
for marriage (Marg.'s mother was Jo.'s godmother). 30s.

23 Jo. Lanerton, r. of East Worlington, Ex. dio., chapl. to the Earl
of Bridgwater. Disp. to hold a benef.; permut. cl. £6 10s.

f. 272ᵛ

20 Jo. Perkyn, recently canon of Kirby Bellars. Disp. to hold a benef.
with change of habit. Suppr.

Apr. 26 Jo. Roo, v. of All Saints, Oyssage, Sarum dio. Disp. to hold
another benef., as the above does not yield over £8 p.a. £4.

27 Jo. Brabam, r. of Wolverton, Winton dio., chapl. to the Bp of
Chich. Disp. to hold a benef. with the above; permut. cl. £6 10s.

Chas Persons, B.Th., incumbent of Collington. Disp. to hold a
benef. with the above; permut. cl. £6 10s.

May 1 Edw. Telinge & Eleanor Barnewall, of Meath dio., Ireland. Disp.
for marriage (3rd degree consang. & 3rd & 4th degrees affin.).
£6; 30s.

f. 273ʳ

6 Tho. Oles, v. of Barnwell, York dio. Disp. to hold another benef.
as the above does not yield over £8 p.a. £4.

10 Confirmation of licence (given in full) issued to the inhabitants of
Bilton, in the par. of Slyne, York dio. to hear masses & other
offices at the chapel of St Mary Magdalen, Bilton, and bury their
dead in the graveyard there, when it has been consecrated, as the
par. ch. of Slyne is 2 miles distant. 13s 4d; p.s.r. 5s.

f. 273ᵛ

4 Tho. Philips & Agnes Sutton, St David's dio. Disp. for marriage
(3rd degree affin.). £6.

13 Wm Smythe & Helen Walker, Lond. dio. Disp. for marriage
within the prohibited times, not in their par. ch., & without banns.
20s; 10s; 10s.

16 Polidore Warmyngton, M.A. Disp. to practise as public notary
& tabellion. 13s 4d.

18 Ric. Maners, esq., & Ly Marg. Coffyn, widow. Disp. for marriage
without banns. 10s.

May 19 Tho. Yardeley, clk, Worc. dio. Creation as public notary &
tabellion. 13s 4d.

f. 274ʳ

12 Tho. Stocboll, v. of Dunboyne, Meath dio., Ireland. Disp. as
he asserts he already has a disp. to take h.o. & hold a benef. despite
defect of birth, to hold the deanery of Cashel cath. & to be chapl.
to Jas Butler, Viscount Thurles, Ld High Treasurer of Ireland;
permut. cl. £6 10s.

19 Ralph Carter & Isabella Burditt, Linc. dio. Disp. for marriage
(Ralph was godfather to a child of Isabella). 'Gratis quia pauperes'; warrant of the lords shown.

21 Wm Yoxall, sch., Norw. dio. Disp. to take all h.o. although in
his 23rd yr & to hold a benef. 40s.

Gilbert Burstow & Helen Marberye. Disp. for marriage without
banns. 10s.

f. 274ᵛ

20 Chas Akerman & Joan Carter, dau. of Wm Carter, Ex. dio. Disp.
for marriage (3rd & 4th degrees consang.). 30s.

22 Confirmation of licence issued under the royal seal to the inhabitants of Bishop's Hull, Bath & W. dio., for the consecration by
any bp of the chapel & cemetery of St Mary in the above village
for the burial of their dead. 13s 4d; p.s.r. 5s.

10 Rob. Gouge & Marg. Mantell, gentw., Cant. dio. Disp. for marriage in Marg.'s par. ch. without banns. 10s.

21 Jo. Chaundeler & Marg. Cradoke, Lond. dio. Disp. for marriage
(4th degree affin.). 26s 8d.

24 Sir Tho. Chayney, K.G., & Ann Broughton, gentw. Disp. for
marriage without banns. 10s.

f. 275ʳ

Peter Baker, pr., v. of Brookland, Cant. dio., chapl. to the Master
of the Rolls. Disp. to hold another benef., permut. cl. £6 10s.

25 David Mathew, sch., Heref. dio. Disp. to take all h.o. within the
prohibited times & 2 on the same day. 26s 8d.

Jo. Verney, esq., & his wife Dorothy. Disp. to have the Eucharist
in their private oratory, though without depriving the par. ch.
10s.

30 Rob. Salmon & Mary Crowte of London. Disp. for marriage in
in their par. ch. without banns. 10s.

Evan Morice & Alison Howell, Lland. dio. Disp. for marriage
(4th degree consang.). 'Gratis quia pauperes'; warrant of the
lords shown.

f. 275^v

<blockquote>

May 31 Jo. Fermerye, dcn, Linc. dio. Disp. to take pr.'s orders outside the statutory times & on any day. 10s.

</blockquote>

1538 Nov. 18 Leonard Fawleighe, gent., of Fulwell, Linc. dio., & Eliz. Pore, of London. Disp. for marriage in Eliz.'s par. ch. without banns. 10s.

<blockquote>

20 Ralph Persall, v. of Halstow, Cant. dio. Disp. to hold another benef., as the above does not yield £8 p.a.; permut. cl. £4.

</blockquote>

1539 June 6 Jo. Laurens, B.C. & C.L., r. of Whittington, Worc. dio. Disp. to hold another benef. with the above, or 2 without it. £6 10s.

<blockquote>

12 Jo. Sawer & Marg. Blande, York dio. Disp. for marriage (4th degrees consang. & affin.). 26s 8d; 26s 8d.

10 Rob. Berison, Cov. & Lich. dio. Disp. to take pr.'s orders outside the statutory times. 10s.

</blockquote>

f. 276^r

<blockquote>

4 Hy Spurre & Agnes Colbye, Linc. dio. Disp. for marriage (2nd & 3rd degrees affin.). Arb. £3; warrant of the lords shown.

5 Rob. Padde, recently prior of St Bees. Disp. to hold a benef. with change of habit. Suppr.

3 Jo. Wyse & Margery Noble, Ely dio. Disp. for marriage (3rd degree affin.). £6.

9 Leonard Barray & Ann Sympson *alias* Hornehede, Carl. dio. Disp. for marriage (3rd & 4th degrees consang.). 30s.

12 Ric. Hyde & Helen Grene, Linc. dio. Disp. for marriage without banns. 10s.

</blockquote>

f. 276^v

<blockquote>

15 Jo. Wilkock & Kath. Lewys, of London. Disp. for marriage without banns, & in Kath.'s par. ch. 10s.

Wm Couper & Jane Penyngton, Cov. & Lich. dio. Disp. for marriage (4th degree consang.). 26s 8d.

</blockquote>

May 10 Jo. Tyldesley, r. of Norton, Lond. dio., chapl. to Rob. Ratcliff, Earl of Sussex. Disp. to hold another benef.; permut. cl. £6 10s.

June 15 Ric. Wright, subdcn, York dio. Disp. to take all h.o. outside the statutory times. 13s 4d.

<blockquote>

16 Howell ap Gwalter & Janet verch David, St David's dio. Disp. for marriage (3rd & 4th degrees consang.). Gratis; warrant of the lords shown.

</blockquote>

f. 277^r

<blockquote>

6 Jas More, B.Th., r. of Haltham-on-Bayne, Linc. dio. Disp. to hold another benef. with cure with the above; permut. cl. £6 10s.

</blockquote>

June 16 Jo. Norden & Isabella Holdefelde, York dio. Disp. for marriage (4th degree consang.). 26s 8d.

14 Jo. Burton, pr., reg. canon of Shap priory, Carl. dio. Disp. to hold any benef. with cure & to change his habit. £8. (Note in left-hand margin: 'nota que taxa £12 vel arbitrabitur.')

20 Jo. Cawarde, recently prior of Leominster. Disp. to hold a benef. with complete change of habit. Suppr.

19 Tho. Goughe & Agnes Donne, Cov. & Lich. dio. Disp. for marriage (3rd & 4th degrees consang.). 30s.

f. 277^v

20 Ric. Chapman, recently of Scarborough. Disp. to hold a benef. with complete change of habit. Also for Roger Smythe, Jo. Bayker, Ric. Wynder, Jo. Frannce, Tho. Browne, Rob. Roper, Tho. Coots, Jo. Williamson, Jo. Jobe. Suppr.

27 Jo. Wylde & Joan Mathew, Linc. dio. Disp. for marriage (Joan was godmother to a child of Jo.). Gratis; warrant of the lords shown.

22 Jo. Broke & Marg. Soome, widow. Disp. for marriage without banns & in a private oratory instead of their par. ch. 10s; 10s.

Tho. Johns & Gwenllian verch David ap Rice, St David's dio. Disp. for marriage (4th degree consang.). 26s 8d.

f. 278^r

24 Ant. Flemyng & Jane Rigemayden, York dio. Disp. for marriage (4th degree consang.). 26s 8d.

Wm Chamber & Jane Fredesbery, Roch. dio. Disp. for marriage (Wm was sponsor at the confirmation of a child of Jane). Arb. 40s; warrant of the lords shown. (Note in left-hand margin: 'notaque tax 100s et non arbitrabitur.')

20 Ralph Blakestone, monk of [West] Dereham. Disp. to hold a benef. with complete change of habit. Gratis; warrant of the lords shown.

24 Rob. Blower & Edith Geste *alias* Verebye, Bath & W. dio. Disp. for marriage (4th degree consang.). 26s 8d.

28 Edw. Bacon, r. of Evelden, Norw. dio. Disp. not to take h.o. for a yr. 10s ('Notaque null taxatur in libro taxe').

26 Rob. Tayllor, M.A., Worc. dio. Disp. to take all h.o. outside the statutory times, & 2 on the same day. 26s 8d.

f. 278^v

Tho. Ayer, M.A., Sarum dio. Disp. to take all h.o. outside the statutory times & 2 on the same day. 26s 8d.

June 28 Jo. Alowes & Kath. Shorte, Durham dio. Disp. for marriage (Jo.'s mother was Kath.'s sponsor at confirmation). 26s 8d.

18 Jo. Hamonde & Kath. (in margin Ann) Brograve, Lond. dio. Disp. for marriage without banns. 10s.

26 Wm Turnor & Alice Clerke, Bath & W. dio. Disp. for marriage (3rd & 4th degrees consang.). 30s.

28 Tho. Holforde, esq., & Jane Dutton, gentw. Disp. for marriage (3rd equal & 3rd & 4th mixed degrees affin.). £6; 30s.

f. 279ʳ

July 1 Ant. Haryson & Ann Butler, York dio. Disp. for marriage (3rd & 4th degrees affin.). 30s.

Wm Cradocke & Marg. Lovet, Cov. & Lich. dio. Disp. for marriage (3rd & 4th degrees affin.). 30s.

Simon Carowe & Marion Corye, Ely dio. Disp. for marriage (Marion was godmother to a child of Simon). £6.

June 28 Tho. Wilson & Eliz. Thurisbye, Carl. dio. Disp. for marriage (3rd & 4th degrees consang.). 30s.

July 1 Jo. Wendover & Agnes Agar, Winton dio. Disp. for marriage (Jo.'s father was sponsor at Agnes' confirmation). 26s 8d.

f. 279ᵛ

July 1 Jo. Olyver, D.C.L. Disp. to receive h.o. on account of holding several benefices, within 3 yrs after the end of the 3 yrs for which he was previously dispensed. 30s.

18 Walter Cocks, r. of Lymington, Bath & W. dio., Kg's chapl., r. of Buckland St Mary or South Buckland. Disp. to hold any 3rd benef. with cure with the above. £8.

June 24 Jo. Wilson, r. of Titsey, Winton dio., chapl. to the Bp of Lland. Disp. to hold another benef.; permut. cl. £6 10s.

July 1 Jo. ap Robert Pye & Ann Vaughan, Heref. dio. Disp. for marriage (3rd & 4th degrees affin.). 30s.

f. 280ʳ

4 Chris. Person *alias* Parson & Isabella Marten, Carl. dio. Disp. for marriage (3rd degree consang.). 'Gratis quia pauperes'; warrant of the lords shown.

Rob. Pricklove, r. of Iping, Chich. dio. Disp. to hold a benef. with cure with the above. £6 10s.

Jo. Sharrocke, Cov. & Lich. dio. Disp. to take pr.'s orders outside the statutory times. 10s.

July   2 Jo. Maltebye, M.A. Disp. to take all h.o. outside the statutory times & 2 on the same day. 26s 8d.

4 Edm. Pymonde, v. of Laughton, York dio. Disp. to hold another benef., as the above does not yield £8 p.a. £4.

f. 280ᵛ

1 Nich. Layburne, York dio., & Eliz. Warcope, Carl. dio. Disp. for marriage (4th degree consang.). 26s 8d.

Jo. Johnson & Alice Crostone, of London. Disp. for marriage without banns & in Alice's par. ch. 10s.

2 Ric. Buller, B.A., Linc. dio. Disp. to take all h.o. outside the statutory times & 2 on the same day. 26s 8d.

Edw. Mershe & Agnes Norwiche, Cov. & Lich. dio. Disp. for marriage (4th degree consang.). 26s 8d.

6 Jo. Cawnde, B.Th., r. of Icklingham ('Oklingham'), Norw. dio. Disp. to hold a benef. with cure with, or 2 without the above; permut. cl. £6 10s.

f. 281ʳ

Tho. Watson, r. of Richmond, archdcnry of Richmond, York dio., chapl. to the Bp of Llandaff. Disp. to hold a benef. with the above, or 2 without it; permut. cl. £6 10s.

16 Wm Lowe, v. of Witham, Lond. dio., chapl. to the Earl of Hertford. Disp. to hold another benef. with the above; permut. cl. £6 10s.

7 Tho. ——, v. of Hornchurch, Lond. dio. Disp. to hold a benef. with the above. £6 10s.

6 Edw. Heynes, literate, Heref. dio. Disp. to practise anywhere as a public notary & tabellion. 13s 4d.

f. 281ᵛ

5 Jo. Knollis, r. of Musgrave, Carl. dio., chapl. to Ld Cromwell. Disp. to hold any benef. with cure with the above; permut. cl. £6 10s.

6 Tho. & Sibil Harper, Heref. dio. Disp. for marriage (3rd & 4th degrees consang.). 30s.

Jo. Armested & Kath. Hall, York dio. Disp. for marriage (Kath.'s father was sponsor at Jo.'s confirmation). 26s 8d.

Jo. White & Eleanor Pecoke, Winton dio. Disp. for marriage (the late husband of Eleanor was godfather to a child of Jo.). Gratis; warrant of the lords shown.

8 Ric. Bacon & Marg. Rowbotham. Disp. for marriage (3rd & 4th degrees simple ?consang. or affin.). 30s.

f. 282^r

July 8 Owen Thomas & Gwenllyan verch Jamys, St David's dio. Disp. for marriage (4th degree consang.). 26s 8d.

Howel ap Jenkyn Lewis & Matilda verch John, St David's dio. Disp. for marriage (4th degree affin.). 26s 8d.

6 Jo. Whetheryke, recently abbot of St Osyth. Disp. to hold a benef. with change of habit. Also for Jo. Russill, Jo. Harwiche, Cornelius Byne, Ralph Dale, Jo. Sherman, Jo. Thorpe, Edw. or Edm. Grove, Geo. Thurston, Ric. Simpwell, Rob. Sprott, Tho. Heywode, Wm Newman, Nich. Busche, Ric. Woode, Wm Joylie. Suppr.

11 Hugh Hopkyns, acol., Heref. dio. Disp. to take all h.o. outside the statutory times & 2 on the same day. 26s 8d.

f. 282^v

8 Roger Higham & Alice Edwards, Lond. dio. Disp. for marriage without banns & in Alice's par. ch. 10s.

11 Nich. Hawcoke, recently prior of St Kath. Cree, London. Disp. to hold a benef. with change of habit. Gratis; by warrant.

9 Edw. Vaughan & Emma Stewkley, Linc. dio. Disp. for marriage without banns. 10s.

10 Tho. Browne, v. of Tilehurst, Sarum dio. Disp. to hold another benef.; permut. cl. £6 10s.

11 Ric. & Alice Crosfelde, of Lincoln. Disp. for marriage (3rd & 4th degrees affin.). 30s.

12 Edm. Chedwicke & Agnes Herdman, Cov. & Lich. dio. Disp. for marriage (4th degree consang. or affin.). 26s 8d.

f. 283^r

15 Rob. ap Richerede ap Meredithe & Matilda verch Jevan ap Meredith, St Asaph dio. Disp. for marriage (3rd & 4th degrees consang.). 30s.

16 Ric. Vaughan, son of Jo. Vaughan, & Matilda Filpott, Heref. dio Disp. for marriage (Mary's [sic] mother was Jo.'s godmother). 30s.

19 Rob. Mosley & Ann Rocheley, Cov. & Lich. dio. Disp. for marriage (3rd & 4th degrees affin.). 30s.

21 Tho. Wynter & Joan Bease, Worc. dio. Disp. for marriage (4th degree consang.). 26s 8d.

12 Wm Snedon & Helen Dowen, of Calais. Disp. for marriage without banns. 10s.

f. 283ᵛ

July   18 Ric. Snowe & Eliz. Candishe, Lond. dio. Disp. for marriage without banns. 10s.

      19 Rob. ap Gruffithe & Gwenllian verch John David. Disp. for marriage (4th degree consang.). 26s 8d.

          David Bedo & Gwenlian verch Harry. Disp. for marriage (4th degree consang.). 26s 8d.

      25 Lancelot Covert & Jane Corney, of the par. of St Andrew Undershaft, London. Disp. for marriage without banns in Jane's par. ch. 10s.

      26 Ric. Sidgrave, r. of Sutton, Sarum dio. Disp. to take all h.o. outside the statutory times & 2 on the same day. 26s 8d.

      31 Roland Taillor, dcn, Worc. dio. Disp. to take pr's orders outside the statutory times. 10s.

f. 284ʳ

          James Mors & Eliz. Perching *alias* Mors, of the peculiar of Dorchester. Disp. for marriage without banns. 10s.

Aug.   1 Wm Bradshaw & Alice Gilbert, Cov. & Lich. dio. Disp. for marriage (Alice was godmother to a child of Wm). £6.

       2 Jo. Wyat & Joan Hallat *alias* Holes, Cov. & Lich. dio. Disp. for marriage (2nd & 3rd degrees consang.). Arb. £4; warrant of the lords shown.

       3 Wm Brymley, v. of ?Uttoxeter ('Vesetter'), Cov. & Lich. dio. Disp. to hold another benef. as the above does not yield £8 p.a. £4.

       4 Jo. Snow & Kath. Edrige, Lond. dio. Disp. for marriage without banns. 10s.

f. 284ᵛ

July   4 Wm Gybeley & Eleanor Fitzherbert, Linc. dio. Disp. for marriage in Eleanor's par. ch. without banns. 10s.

          Tho. Shene & Helen Benett, of the par. of ?Elsham ('Elson'), Linc. dio. Disp. for marriage (Helen's father was Tho.'s sponsor at his confirmation). 26s 8d.

      30 Jo. Roberts & Agnes Trowers, Lond. dio. Disp. for marriage without banns & not in their par. ch. 10s; 10s.

Aug.   8 Tho. Burnell & Julia Brigons, Lond. dio. Disp. for marriage in Julia's par. ch. without banns. 10s.

       9 Jo. Lyon & Marg. Thomson, York dio. Disp. for marriage (4th degree consang.). 26s 8d.

Aug. 10 Jo. Thorneton & Joan Mocke, Cant. dio. Disp. for marriage without banns. 10s.

f. 285ʳ

12 Gilbert Petybrige & Joan Hunt, Ex. dio. Disp. for marriage (3rd & 4th degrees consang.). 30s.

Jo. Atkyns, literate. Creation as public notary & tabellion. 13s 4d.

14 Peter Shakerley & Eliz. Manweryng, Cov. & Lich. dio. Disp. for marriage (4th degree consang.). 26s 8d.

15 Wm Ebysworthe, subdcn, Ex. dio. Disp. to take dcn's and pr.'s orders outside the statutory times & on the same day. 13s 4d.

18 Jo. Rypington, Linc. dio. Disp. to take all h.o. outside the statutory times & 2 on the same day. 26s 8d.

23 Edw. Burchall & Eliz. Knowlis, Cov. & Lich. dio. Disp. for marriage (3rd & 4th degrees affin.). 30s.

f. 285ᵛ

25 Ralph Baguley & Eliz. Bothe, Cov. & Lich. dio. Disp. for marriage (3rd & 4th degrees consang.). 30s.

Wm Iveson & Eliz. Twysolton, York dio. Disp. for marriage (4th degree consang.). 26s 8d.

26 Ric. Philipps & Kath. Benbowe, of the par. of St Botolph without Bishopsgate, London. Disp. for marriage without banns. 10s.

Hy Haye, dcn, Heref. dio. Disp. to take rest of the h.o. outside the statutory times. 10s.

Hugh Maholum & Sibil Hebbe, Heref. dio. Disp. for marriage (4th degree consang.). 26s 8d.

Jo. Athaughe & Isabella Taylboure, York dio. Disp. for marriage (Isabella's father was Jo.'s godfather). 30s.

f. 286ʳ

20 Nich. Mayow, B.A. Disp. to hold a benef. with cure despite defect of age, being in his 21st yr, & to take all h.o. on reaching his 22nd yr. £4 6s 8d; 23s 4d.

Wm Gille, recently prior of St Saviour's [Southwark], Winton dio. Disp. to hold a benef. with change of habit. Also for Tho. Gaynsbrogh, Jo. Pynder, Peter Luke, Jo. Cuthbert, Tho. Rocley, Wm Paynter, Tho. Stonbake. Suppr.

24 Alice Edwards, recently nun of the Minories, outside Aldgate, London. Disp. to leave the religious life. Suppr.

28 —— Sweiste, of York dio., & Agnes Molle, Lond. dio. Disp. for marriage without banns. 10s.

f. 286ᵛ

Aug. 28 Wm Prystley & Alice Thornehill, of Elland, York dio. Disp. for marriage (4th degree consang. & Alice's father was sponsor at Wm's confirmation). 26s 8d; 26s 8d.

Hy Hepworthe & Cecily Hall, of Mirfield, York dio. Disp. for marriage (Hy's mother was Cecily's godmother or sponsor at her confirmation). 30s.

26 Geo. Marten, sch., Worc. dio. Disp. to take all h.o. outside the statutory times & 2 on the same day. 26s 8d.

29 Rob. Leye & Ann Prestlonde, of Banbury, Cov. & Lich. dio. Disp. for marriage (3rd & 4th degrees affin.). 30s.

Francis & Barbara Boothe, Cov. & Lich. dio. Disp. for marriage (3rd & 4th degrees consang.). 30s.

Sept. 1 Wm Egleston & Eliz. Senner, of London. Disp. for marriage in their par. ch., the banns read once. 6s 8d.

f. 287ʳ

Jo. Palmer & Kath. Bayle, of London. Disp. for marriage in Kath.'s par. ch. the banns read once. 6s 8d.

3 Ric. Southe, canon of Christchurch, Twyneham (Hants), Winton dio. Disp. to hold any benef.; permut. cl. £4.

Ralph Alderige & Joan Hill, of Stow, Cov. & Lich. dio. Disp. for marriage (4th degree consang.). 26s 8d.

4 Jo. Wode & Agnes Store, of Ditchling, Chich. dio. Disp. for marriage in Agnes' par. ch. without banns. 10s.

Rob. Gyer & Joan Turney, Winton dio. Disp. for marriage in their par. ch. without banns. 10s.

Wm Jamyson & Marg. Lantwhat, Cov. & Lich. dio. Disp. for marriage (3rd & 4th degrees consang.). 30s.

f. 287ᵛ

Ralph Kingeston & Marg. Whiton, of Horsington, Linc. dio. Disp. for marriage in Marg.'s par. ch. without banns. 10s.

11 Roger Arche & Joyce Pene *alias* Sparran, Worc. dio. Disp. for marriage (3rd & 4th degrees consang.). 30s.

14 Tho. & Dorothy Spenser, Linc. dio. Disp. for marriage without banns & not in their par. ch. 10s; 10s. Also disp. on account of 3rd & 4th degrees consang. 30s.

Aug. 12 Tho. Ambrose & Joan Browne, of Deal, Cant. dio. Disp. for marriage without banns. 10s.

f. 288ʳ

Sept. 17 Chris. Barly, B.Th., v. of Wragby, Linc. dio. Disp. to hold another benef.; permut. cl. £6 10s.

Aug. 10 Roland Tayllor, D.C.L., r. of ?Brandby, Worc. dio. Similar disp. £6 10s.

Sept. 4 Maurice Johns, r. of Bawdeswell, Norw. dio. Disp. to hold another benef. as the above does not yield £8 p.a. £4.

Aug. 27 Rob. Sweiste & Agnes Molle, York dio. Disp. for marriage (Rob. was godfather to a child of Agnes). £6.

30 Wm Baston, r. of Whaddon, Ely dio. Disp. to hold another benef. £6 10s.

f. 288ᵛ

Sept. 15 Jo. Freir & Kath. Clerke, of Knebworth, Linc. dio. Disp. for marriage (3rd & 4th degrees consang.). 30s.

18 Wm Muschampe, esq., of Camberwell, Winton dio. & Eliz. Bacon, lady of Pr. Edw.'s hsehld. Disp. for marriage without banns. 10s.

23 Jo. Elyson & Joan Anderson, Durham dio. Disp. for marriage (3rd & 4th degrees affin.). 30s.

25 Also disp. on account of Jo. having been sponsor at the confirmation of a child of Joan. £5.

24 Abraham Robynson, v. of Lastingham, York dio., chapl. to Ld Latimer. Disp. to hold another benef.; permut. cl. £6 10s.

f. 289ʳ

Aug. 26 Chris. Bassatt & Marg. Willyam, widow, Lland. dio. Disp. for marriage (3rd & 4th degrees affin.). 30s.

Sept. 24 Jo. Banke & Ann Remyngton, York dio. Disp. for marriage (3rd & 4th degrees affin.). 30s.

6 Hy Malery *alias* Malyvery, B.Cn.L., v. of Anderby, in the archdcnry of Richmond, York dio. Disp. to hold a benef; permut. cl. £6 10s.

29 Rob. Belcher & Eliz. Beawso, Linc. dio. Disp. for marriage without banns. 10s.

Oct. 2 Tho. Uston & Alison Hemslaye, York dio. Disp for marriage (3rd & 4th degrees consang.). 30s.

f. 289ᵛ

Ant. Cave, gent., of Newport, & Eliz. —— of Easton, Linc. dio. Disp. for marriage not in their par. ch. & the banns read once. 10s; 6s 8d.

Oct. 3 Ric. Greslande, acol., Heref. dio. Disp. to take all h.o. outside the statutory times, from any bp, & 2 on the same day. 26s 8d.

Sept. 30 Francis Coppilston *alias* Brige, pr., Ex. dio. Disp. to take h.o. & hold a benef. despite defect of age, he having previously obtained a disp. for this by the pretended authority of the Bp of Rome. £4.

f. 290ʳ

Oct. 4 David ap Howell & Eliz. Morgan Thomas, St David's dio. Disp. for marriage (3rd & 4th degrees consang.). 30s.

Sept. 30 Jo. Baldocke & Alice Lace, Cant. dio. Disp. for marriage (Jo. was godfather to a child of Alice). Gratis; by warrant of the lords.

Oct. 4 Wm Chamberlayne, subdcn, Cov. & Lich. dio. Disp. to take all h.o. outside the statutory times on the same day. 13s 4d.

6 Ric. Mayssey & Joan Hokenell, Cov. & Lich. dio. Disp. for marriage (3rd & 4th degrees consang.). 30s.

Sept. 24 Ric. Barlowe & Kath. Almo, of London. Disp. for marriage without banns. 10s.

f. 290ᵛ

Oct. 6 Hy Everingham & Agnes Fayrefax, York dio. Disp. for marriage (3rd & 4th degrees affin.). 30s.

Sept. 26 Hy Manimper, pr., prior of the Charterhouse of Sheen, Winton dio. Disp. to hold a benef. with change of habit. Also for Edm. Fletewode, Wm Rilberye, Rob. Chaffer, Jo. Bromeley, Ric. Tilsley, Hy Ball, Jo. Crabtree, Geo. Hornbye, Tho. Manfelde, Jo. Pysant, Wm Marshall, Tho. Lawe, —— Thirlebye, Tho. Hyne, Jo. Clement, Wm Woode. Suppr.

Oct. 8 Chris. Nayllor & Kath. Padley, Linc. dio. Disp. for marriage (Chris.'s mother was Kath.'s godmother). 30s.

f. 291ʳ

6 Roger Redman & Joan Gye, York dio. Disp. for marriage (4th degree consang.). 26s 8d.

8 Wm Jenyns & Beatrice Raynwicke, of London. Disp. for marriage in Beatrice's par. ch. without banns. 10s.

9 Ric. Tutte & Joan Foster, Chich. dio. Disp. for marriage (Joan's father was sponsor at Ric.'s confirmation). Gratis; by warrant of the lords.

10 Jo. Smythe, O.F.M., recently warden of Lincoln. Disp. to hold a benef. with complete change of habit. Also for Bernard Brandon, Tho. Sympson, Jo. Sparhawke, Gabriel Peycocke, Hy Preston, Tho. Hyrm, Ric. Toodde, Wm White, Hugh Wieghte, Ant. Fyshe, Rob. Nycolson. Suppr.

f. 291ᵛ

Oct. 10 Andrew Natares, r. of Carleton with Willingham, Ely dio., chapl. to the Earl of Westmorland. Disp. to hold another benef. with the above, or 2 others without; permut. cl. £6 10s.

Tho. Pott, recently Austin fr., of Lincoln. Disp. to hold a benef. with change of habit. Also for Wm Jackson, Jo. Feryman, Rob. Feryman, Ric. Heyton, Wm Marshall. Suppr.

Walter Smythe, O.P., of Lincoln. Disp. to hold a benef. with change of habit. Also for Jo. Lewett, Geo. Stephinson, Jo. Wyllocke, Jo. Hall, Tho. Highe, Rob. Pikerton, Jo. Dayley, Tho. Griffith, Patrick Symson. Suppr.

f. 292ʳ

Sept. 12 Rob. Tree, r. of Westerfield, Norw. dio., chapl. to Jo. Tutchet, Ld Audley. Disp. to hold another benef.; permut. cl. £6 10s.

Oct. 10 Jo. Blaydes, O.C. fr., recently prior of Lincoln friary. Disp. to hold a benef. with change of habit. Also for Jo. Till, Nich. Derbye, Laurence Griffithe, Tho. Redman, Rob. Drury, Jo. Handell, Bernard Wright, Tho. Johnson, Jo. Dykeson. Suppr.

Sept. 12 Tho. Harlakynden & Marg. Draper, of London. Disp. for marriage without banns & not in their par. ch. 10s; 10s.

Maurice Lloid, acol., St Asaph dio. Disp. to take 2 h.o. on the same day outside the statutory times. 13s 4d.

f. 292ᵛ

Jo. ap Thomas ap Jevan, sch., Heref. dio. Disp. to take h.o. outside the statutory times. 20s.

Oct. 12 Rob. Shetleworthe & Jane Townleye, Cov. & Lich. dio. Disp. for marriage (3rd & 4th degrees consang.). 30s.

6 Tho. Tadgill, O.F.M., of Preston. Disp. to hold a benef. with change of habit. Also for Jo. Jarvys, Rob. Thornall, Hy Maison, Jo. Perkyns, Roger Leyn, Jo. Lewes, Oliver Herden, Edw. or Edm. Paynter, Tho. Gosnell. Suppr.

10 Jo. Benett & Amice Roto, Linc. dio. Disp. for marriage (Amice's former husband was godfather to a child of Jo. & recently Jo.'s former wife was godmother to a child of Amice). Gratis; by warrant of the lords.

f. 293ʳ

13 Miles Bowes & Janet Robynson, York dio. Disp. for marriage (3rd & 4th degrees affin.). 30s.

9 Jo. Willughbye, r. of Norton, Bath & W. dio., Kg's chapl. Disp. to hold another benef.; permut. cl. £6 10s.

Oct. 16 Jo. Turner & Eliz. Selman, Cov. & Lich. dio. Disp. for marriage (4th degree consang.). 26s 8d.

Edm. Dey & Marg. Cottrell, of London. Disp. for marriage without banns. 10s.

f. 293ᵛ

2 Tho. Peyrson, r. of Knapwell, Ely dio., chapl. to the Bp of Lincoln. Disp. to hold another benef. with the above, or 2 without it; permut. cl. £6 10s.

18 Rob. Percyvall, chanter in the Evers chantry in Linc. cath. Disp. to hold another benef. as the above does not yield £8 p.a. £4.

Ric. Forster, York dio. Disp. for marriage (Marg.'s father was Ric.'s godfather). 30s.

20 Ric. Beste, v. of Middleton, Norw. dio. Disp. to hold another benef. as the above does not yield £8 p.a. £4.

f. 294ʳ

1 Jo. Freman, literate, of Westminster. Disp. to practise as public notary & tabellion. 13s 4d.

20 Jo. Paige & Joan Hall, Lond. dio. Disp. for marriage (Jo. was godfather to a child of Joan). Gratis; warrant of the lords shown.

23 Nich. Saige, recently Observant fr., of Guernsey, Coutances dio. Disp. to hold a benef. with change of habit. Also for Geo. Chevaler, Jo. Humffrey, Augustine Bauden, Chas. Marett, Nich. Marre, Edm. or Edw. Gosse, Gervase Chers, Mathew Pageot. Suppr.

f. 294ᵛ

Ric. Gascoigne, gent., & Eliz. Skergill, widow, York dio. Disp. for marriage (3rd & 4th degrees consang.). 30s.

24 Jo. Fawkener, acol., Cov. & Lich. dio. Disp. to take all h.o. from any bp. outside the statutory times. 26s 8d.

25 Rob. Revell, esq., & Helen Savage of London. Disp. for marriage in Helen's par. ch. without banns. 10s.

July 12 Wm Bolton, pr., keeper of the chapel of St Andrew by St Albans monastery, Linc. dio. Disp. to hold another benef. £6 10s.

f. 295ʳ

Oct. 20 Ralph Fayrfax, recently prior of Kyme, Lincs. Disp. to hold a benef. with change of habit. Also for Jo. Forman, Jo. Wake, Jo. Baryce, Jo. Favell, Jo. Baxter, Ric. Browne, Oliver Edwards, Rob. Elington, Rob. Lounde, canons of the same hse. Suppr.

12 Disp. to the inhabitants of the village of St Day, Cornwall, to have the holy Eucharist reserved by night & day in the chapel built there to the honour of God & the Holy Trinity. 10s.

Oct. 20 Chris. Tenworthe, precentor of Linc. cath., Kg's chapl. Disp. permitting him to exchange benefices he may subsequently obtain. £4.

f. 295ᵛ

26 Tho. Darling & Cicily Knyght, Linc. dio. Disp. for marriage (Tho. was godfather to a child of Cicily). Gratis; warrant of the lords shown.

Rob. Burton, r. of Lawshall ('Laushull'), Norw. dio., chapl. to the Bp of Winchester. Disp. to hold another benef. with the above. £6 10s.

Aug. 6 Tho. Awtye & Alice Felde, Worc. dio. Disp. for marriage (Alice was sponsor at the confirmation of a child of Tho.). Gratis; warrant of the lords shown.

July 10 Jo. Wyat, B.Th., r. of Kegworth, Linc. dio. Disp. to hold a benef. with cure, with the above; permut. cl. £6 10s.

Oct. 31 Hy Symkeley & Agnes Catchmaide, of London. Disp. for marriage without banns. 10s.

f. 296ʳ

Hy Devenyshe & Juliana Hillyarde, of Charminster, Sarum dio. Disp. for marriage (Julia's father was Hy's godfather). 30s.

Nov. 5 Tho. Cottum, acol., Cov. & Lich. dio. Disp. to take all h.o. outside the statutory times. 20s.

Geo. Saterthwatte & Eliz. Rige, York dio. Disp. for marriage (3rd & 4th degrees consang.). 30s.

6 Ric. Bullocke & Jane Atkyns, Cov. & Lich. dio. Disp. for marriage (4th degree consang.). 26s 8d.

f. 296ᵛ

4 Jo. Porter, M.A., Carl. dio. Disp. to take all h.o. outside the statutory times & 2 on the same day. 26s 8d.

Apr. 8 Rob. Newton, pr. Disp. to hold another benef., as his present one does not yield £8 p.a. £4.

Oct. 12 Tho. ap John ap Howell & Gwenllyan verch David, St David's dio. Disp. for marriage (3rd degree affin.). Arb. £4; warrant of the lords shown.

Nov. 6 Nich. Rastell, acol., Cov. & Lich. dio. Disp. to take all h.o. outside the statutory times. 20s.

9 Ric. Tayller & Helen Steyde, York dio. Disp. for marriage (Ric.'s father was sponsor at Helen's confirmation). 26s 8d.

f. 297^r

Nov. 7 Jo. Trerys, pr., r. of Luccombe, Bath & W. dio., chapl. of Ld
Zouche ('Suche'). Disp. to hold another benef. with the above,
or 2 without; permut. cl. £6 10s.

9 Jo. Perkynson & Eliz. Swillinghurste, York dio. Disp. for marriage (Jo.'s brother, Chris. Perkynson, was betrothed to Eliz.
when he was 14 & she 9 yrs old). 26s 8d.

Ric. Clerke & Marg. Lawson, York dio. Disp. for marriage (4th
degree consang.). 26s 8d.

Jo. Wakeham & Joan Collyn, Ex. dio. Disp. for marriage (4th
degree consang.). 26s 8d.

Wm Hamylden & Agnes More, Linc. dio. Disp. for marriage (3rd
& 4th degrees consang. & without banns). 30s; 10s.

f. 297^v

10 Jas Rokeley, gent., & Eliz. Myners, widow, Heref. dio. Disp. for
marriage in Eliz.'s par. ch. without banns. 10s.

Wm Jameson & Marg. Laytwat, Cov. & Lich. dio. Disp. for
marriage (3rd & 4th degrees affin., previously dispensed for 3rd
& 4th degrees consang.). 30s.

12 Chas & Helen Bradshaye. Disp. for marriage (4th degree consang.). 26s 8d.

10 Chris. Proctor, pr. Disp. to hold another benef. with cure as the
one he has obtained does not yield £8 p.a.; permut. cl. £4.

15 Wm Jenkyn & Alice Person, Norw. dio. Disp. for marriage (3rd
degree consang.). £6.

13 Tho. Downyng, v. of Besthorpe, Norw. dio. Disp. to hold
another benef. as the above does not yield £8 p.a. £4.

f. 298^r

14 Jas Roberts, pr., v. of Silverley, Norw. dio. Disp. to hold another
benef. £4.

16 Jo. Carelell, Austin fr., of Warrington. Disp. to hold a benef.
with complete change of habit. Also for Geoffrey Halgode, Jo.
Byrkbecke, Hy Audelyn, Hugh Burrell, Nich. Williamson, Tho.
Bee, Alex. Crafurth, Ric. Blaschurste.

Ric. Knyght, O.P. of Dartford. Disp. to hold a benef. with change
of habit. Also for Jo. Forer, Wm Langley, Rob. Emley, Tho.
Grante, Mich. Estfelde, Wm Olyver. Suppr.

12 Wm Taillor, dcn, Worc. dio. Disp. to take pr.'s orders outside
the statutory times. 10s.

f. 298^v

Nov. 12 Tho. Buller, sch., York dio. Disp. to take all h.o. outside the statutory times & 2 on the same day. 26s 8d.

15 Jo. Yeldman & Eliz. Smithe, Lond. dio. Disp. for marriage in any ch. or chapel without banns. 10s; 10s.

27 Jo. Conwey Inmore & Jane Salisbury, St Asaph dio. Disp. for marriage (4th degree consang.). 26s 8d.

16 Rob. Hale, pr. of Buckingham, Linc. dio., chapl. to Ld Windsor. Disp. to hold any 2 benefices; permut. cl. £6 10s.

20 Ric. Lutley & Jane Jenks, Cov. dio. Disp. for marriage (2nd & 3rd degrees affin.). £8.

f. 299^r

10 Ric. Golder, r. of Layer Breton ('Lyerebreton'), Lond. dio. Disp. to hold another benef., as the above does not yield £8 p.a. £4.

9 Chris. Rook, r. of Hartwell, Linc. dio., chapl. to Ld Clinton. Disp. to hold another benef.; permut. cl. £6 10s.

17 Jo. Jaks, Kg's chapl., incumbent of Rishangles, Norw. dio. Disp. to hold another benef.; permut. cl. £6 10s.

18 Rob. Wheitley, acol., Worc. dio. Disp. to take all h.o. outside the statutory times & 2 on the same day. 26s 8d.

16 Jas & Marg. Wilson, Carl. dio. Disp. for marriage (3rd degree consang.). 'Gratis quia pauperes'; warrant of the lords shown.

f. 299^v

20 Disp. to the inhabitants of the village or hamlet of Northpedele, Worc. dio., to hear divine service & bury their dead in the par. ch. of the above village, when it has been consecrated. 13s 4d.

Rob. Strudle, D.Th., v. of Sutton, Roch. dio. Disp. to hold another benef. with the above; permut. cl. £6 10s.

22 Oliver Dawbney & Thomasina Thomas, of London. Disp. for marriage without banns. 10s.

Jo. Glynne & Eliz. Tremorkyn, Ex. dio. Disp. for marriage (3rd & 4th degrees consang. or affin.). 30s.

f. 300^r

20 Ric. Kensley & Eliz. Acars, Chich. dio. Disp. for marriage (Ric. was godfather to a child of Eliz.). 'Gratis quia pauperes'; warrant of the lords shown.

23 Rob. Sturgys & Marg. Jenyngs, of Hackney, Lond. dio. Disp. for marriage in the bride's par. ch. without banns. 10s.

Nov. 24 Tho. Corvyser, recently abbot of Haughmond, Cov. & Lich. dio. Disp. to hold a benef. with complete change of habit. Also for Jo. Collfox, Wm Rollffye, Roger Mekeyn, Wm Owen, Hugh Cocke, Jo. Wright, Wm Ridge, Wm Rylande, Jo. Mathoos, Tho. Lye, Tho. Clerke, canons of the same hse. Suppr.

25 Disp. to the inhabitants of Holflete, Linc. dio., in the par. of Wigtoft, to have the chapel of Holflete consecrated for masses & other services, on account of the distance & dangers of the road to Wigtoft, the par. ch. of which they have been accustomed to attend. 13s 4d.

f. 300ᵛ

24 Tho. Stone & Joan Butterye, Lond. dio. Disp. for marriage in Joan's par. ch., the banns read once. 6s 8d.

12 Nich. Hall, r. of Ilmington, Worc. dio., & of Pitt, Cant. dio. Kg's chapl. Disp. to hold a 3rd benef. with cure; permut. cl. £8.

23 Wm Tomys & Joan Cooper, Linc. dio. Disp. for marriage (Wm was sponsor at the confirmation of a child of Joan). Gratis; warrant of the lords shown.

17 Ric. Dyason & Marg. Batriche, Cov. & Lich. dio. Disp. for marriage (4th degree consang.). 26s 8d.

7 Jo. Yardeley, chapl. to Bp of St Asaph, r. of Finchcray, Roch. dio. Disp. to hold another benef. £6 10s.

27 Jo. Maskall & Dorothy Trowesdale, of London. Disp. for marriage, the banns read once. 6s 8d.

f. 301ʳ

28 Jo. Croste & Eliz. Morice, of London. Disp. for marriage in Eliz.'s par. ch. without banns. 10s.

27 Stephen ap Rice & Sibil ap Owen ap Griffithe, Heref. dio. Disp. for marriage (4th degree consang.). 26s 8d.

30 Wm Whelhed, O.P., of London friary. Disp. to hold a benef. with change of habit. Also for Edm. Preston, Jo. Cheltham. Suppr.

Jo. Roke & Eliz. Hampden, of the par. of St Martin Vintry, London. Disp. for marriage within the prohibited times. 20s. Also disp. for marriage without banns & in Eliz.'s par. ch. 10s.

f. 301ᵛ

Dec. 1 Ric. Venables & Marg. Decke, of London. Disp. for marriage within the prohibited times. 20s. Also disp. for marriage without banns. 10s.

ff. 301ᵛ–2ʳ

Sept. 2 Disp. (given in full) to the inhabitants of Aberstoithe in Blaenau Gwent, Lland. dio., being about 8 Welsh miles liable to flood from the par. ch. of Llanwenarth, to have the chapel of St Peter in the above hamlet consecrated for the hearing of divine service. £4.

Dec. 3 Wm Inolde, v. of Boughton Aluph, Cant. dio. Disp. to hold another benef., as the above does not yield £8 p.a.; permut. cl. £4.

8 Tho. Buller, acol., York dio. Disp. to take all h.o. without l.d. from his diocesan. 6s 8d.

f. 302ᵛ

1 Rob. Palmer & Agnes Willes, Carl. dio. Disp. for marriage (3rd & 4th degrees consang.). 30s.

7 Alan Coke *alias* Betryn, D.C.L., incumbent of the par. ch. of Bygrave, Linc. dio., & Boxford, Sarum dio. Disp. to hold a 3rd benef.; permut. cl. £8.

Nov. 24 Rice ap William ap Rice & Gwenllian verch Morgan, St David's dio. Disp. for marriage (4th degree consang.). 26s 8d.

11 Avery Copley & Jane Reamonde, York dio. Disp. for marriage (4th degree consang.). 26s 8d.

Dec. 14 Tho. Stephenson, literate, Durham dio. Creation as public notary & tabellion. 13s 4d.

Ric. Dyghton, sch., Linc. dio. Disp. to take all h.o. outside the statutory times. 20s.

f. 303ʳ

11 Wm Ledys & Philippa Fuller, widow, of London. Disp. for marriage within the prohibited times. 20s.

12 Ric. Stephenagis, recently abbot of St Albans. Disp. to hold a benef. with complete change of habit. Also for Tho. Kingesbury, Stephen Bayley, Wm Est, Wm Rickmansworthe, Tho. Newman, Jo. Albonne, Tho. Iyslam, Wm Hemyngforde, Wm Ayshewell, Wm Estriche, Jo. Wendover, Ralph Bury, Wm Albonne, Geoffrey Sterkey, Jo. Whethamstede, Rob. Moreton, Ralph Campion, Hy Burye, Wm Wyat, Tho. Merchant, Edw. Hill, Rob. Burye, Tho. Curteys, Jo. Brightwise, Rob. Gregory, Jo. Saller, Tho. Albon, Rob. Giles, Wm Adams, Ric. Wynne, Ric. Milner, Peter Calton, Edw. Sibley, Ric. Benett, Tho. Bartilmew, Tho. Bynham, Roger Mighell, Wm Leonarde, Wm Alen, monks in the same hse at the dissolution. Suppr.

f. 303ᵛ

Dec. 11 Wm Ledys & Philippa Fuller, widow, of London. Disp. for marriage in Philippa's par. ch. without banns. 10s.

16 Roger Collyns & Ellen Perkins, of London. Disp. for marriage within the prohibited times, the banns read once. 20s. Also disp. for marriage without banns. 10s.

23 Jo. Stryngfelow & Ann Mors, of London. Disp. for marriage, the banns read once, & within the prohibited times. 6s 8d.; 20s.

15 Jo. Gynson & Marg. Harrison. Disp. for marriage (3rd & 4th degrees affin.). 30s.

26 Philip Bale, r. of (St Michael's) Queen hithe ('apud ripam Reginam'), London, chapl. to Archbp of York. Disp. to hold another benef.; permut. cl. £6 10s.

ff 304ʳ–6ᵛ blank.

f. 307ʳ

1540 Jan. 6 Roger Gorstillow, r. of Lexden, Lond. dio., chapl. to the Earl of Sussex. Disp. to hold another benef. with the above, or 2 without; permut. cl. £6 10s.

Wm Gwaller ap Llin ap John & Nesta verch Griffithe, St David's dio. Disp. for marriage (4th degree consang.). 26s 8d.

Tho. Bothe & Marg. Robynson, widow, of Shap, Carl. dio. Disp. for marriage (3rd & 4th degrees consang.). 30s.

Geo. Handforde & Eliz. Kelsall, Cov. & Lich. dio. Disp. for marriage (4th degree affin.). 26s 8d.

f. 307ᵛ

4 Jo. Tomlyn & Mary Hogge, Ex. dio. Disp. for marriage (3rd & 4th degrees consang.). 30s.

8 Geoffrey & Marg. Molynex, Cov. & Lich. dio. Disp. for marriage (3rd & 4th degrees consang.). 30s.

9 Tho. Monke & Mary Fitzhew, of St Bartholomew's par., London. Disp. for marriage outside the statutory times. 20s.

11 Wm Reskemer & Alice Densell, of London. Disp. for marriage the banns read once. 6s 8d.

12 Tho. Ld Burgh & Alice Benyngfelde, widow, Norw. dio. Disp. for marriage without banns not in their par. ch. 10s; 10s.

May 11 Jo. Merick, dcn, Bangor dio. Disp. to take pr.'s orders outside the statutory times. 10s.

f. 308ʳ

   Jan. 12 Jo. Stansfelde & Eliz. Sutliff, York dio. Disp. for marriage (4th degree consang.). 26s 8d.

         Jo. King & Ann Ambres, Lond. dio. Disp. for marriage in Ann's par. ch. without banns. 10s.

      11 Jo. Compley, clk. Disp. to practise as public notary & tabellion. 13s 4d.

      14 Rob. Pakenham, gent., & Eliz. Bertlett, of London. Disp. for marriage without banns & not in their par. ch. 10s; 10s.

         Jo. Huxley & Eliz. Foxley, of London. Disp. for marriage in Eliz.'s par. ch. without banns. 10s.

f. 308ᵛ

         Roger Pakenham, of the Kg's hsehld, & Eliz. Bartelett, of London. Disp. for marriage without banns & outside Eliz.'s par. ch. 10s; 10s.

1539 June 11 Ric. Chaundeler, v. of Piddletrenthide, Sarum dio., chapl. to the Bp of Bangor. Disp. to hold another benef.; permut. cl. £6 10s.

1540 Jan. 15 Jo. & Ann Howell John, Lland. dio. Disp. for marriage (4th degree consang.). 26s 8d.

      16 Wm Wymprey & Ann Alsope, Linc. dio. Disp. for marriage without banns. 10s.

f. 309ʳ

      7 Jo. Warner, Warden of All Souls Coll., Oxford, chapl. to Ld Parr. Disp. to hold another benef.; permut. cl. £6 10s.

      6 Jo. Hall, recently canon of St Mary Overy, Southwark Winton dio. Disp. to hold a benef. with change of habit. Also for Wm Blande. Suppr.

      12 Jo. Halywell & Isabella Gawkeroger, York dio. Disp. for marriage (3rd degree affin.). £6.

      17 Tho. Goode & Marge. Kempe, Linc. dio. Disp. for marriage in Marg.'s par. ch. without banns. 10s.

f. 309ᵛ

   Jan. 13 Tho. Waterhouse, recently r. of the Augustinian hse of Bonshommes, Ashridge, Linc. dio. Disp. to hold a benef. with complete change of habit. Also for Tho. Hill, Mich. Draper, Jo. Hatfelde, Wm Knyghton, Rob. Huchyn, Rob. Bircheley, Joseph Stepenyth, Ric. Gardyner, Ric. Bedforde, Ric. Canan, Wm Donnamer, Wm Yonge, Ric. Saunders, Wm Broke, Jo. Axtell. Suppr.

      16 Jo. Slannyng & Eliz. Skuynner, widow, of London. Disp. for marriage in their par. ch. without banns; 10s.

Jan. 21 Jo. Cordall & Isabella Overton, under the jurisdiction of the Hospital of St Jo. of Jerusalem. Disp. for marriage in Isabella's par. ch. without banns. 10s.

f. 310ʳ

17 Jo. Anwike *alias* Vestell, recently monk of Peterborough. Disp. to become a sec. pr. & hold a benef. Also for Rob. Kyrton, Wm Thornton, Edw. Bardeney, Wm Clyffe, Rob. London, Ric. Clynton, Jo. Holbiche, Roger Byrde, Jo. Morton, Wm Ramsey, Ric. Notyngham, Jo. Ryall, Ambrose Caster, Ric. Grannte, Chris. Croiland, Ric. Depyng, Griffin Gloceter, Geoffrey Lynne, Jo. Croylande. Suppr.

22 Tho. Ansey & Agnes Damell. Disp. for marriage in Agnes' par. ch. without banns. 10s.

Nich. Ladde & Cicily Wright, Cant. dio. Disp. for marriage (Nich.'s father was godfather to Cicily). 'Gratis quia pauperes'; warrant shown.

f. 310ᵛ

17 Maurice Carter, recently monk of Thorney, Linc. dio. Disp. to hold any benef. with complete change of habit. Also for Tho. Jacke, Wm Lee, Alan Kendell, Wm Stalward, Tho. Noble, Jo. Gymlot, Roger Bucke, Rob. Huyte, Rob. Thacker, Wm Chamberleyn, Jo. Smyth, Simon Lewis, Martin Clipsham, Jo. Evererde, Rob. Bate, Griffin Stephenson, Rob. Harpyn. Suppr.

22 Tho. Richemonde & Elthreda Sampson, Roch. dio. Disp. for marriage in Elthreda's par. ch. without banns. 10s.

Rob. Lawrence & Ann Harpeney. Disp. for marriage in Ann's par. ch. without banns. 10s.

23 Jo. Hamond & Eliz. Hardwicke, Winton dio. Disp. for marriage in Eliz.'s par. ch. without banns. 10s.

Jo. Ownstede & Joan Woode, Winton dio. Disp. for marriage without banns in Joan's par. ch. 10s.

f. 311ʳ

24 Tho. King & Alice Hewson, of London. Disp. for marriage without banns, in Alice's par. ch. 10s.

Jo. Alcocke, literate, Cov. & Lich. dio. Disp. to practise anywhere as notary public & tabellion. 10s.

Nich. Hornby, dcn, Linc. dio. Disp. to take pr.'s orders outside the statutory times. 10s.

22 Tho. Richemonde & Elthreda Sampson. Disp. for marriage within the prohibited times. 20s.

Jan. 24 Ritherch ap Gwillym ap Ritherghe & Marg. verch Rice Ethan, St David's dio. Disp. for marriage (4th degree consang.). 26s 8d.

Tho. ap David ap Evan ap Rice & Matilda verch Bedo David Ethane, St David's dio. Disp. for marriage (4th degree consang.). 26s 8d.

20 Sir Humfrey Fers & Dorothy Dokeyn, gentw., Cov. & Lich. dio. Disp. for marriage within the prohibited times. 20s.

25 Mich. Chaterton & Alice Cristyan, Cant. dio. Disp. for marriage within the prohibited times, the banns read once. 20s; 6s 8d.

Ric. Patrike & Ann Fysher, Cant. dio. Disp. for marriage within the prohibited times. 20s.

24 Ric. Jolye & Marg. Anderson, Durham dio. Disp. for marriage (3rd & 4th degrees consang.). 30s.

26 Andrew Brownyng & Kath. Rogers, Cant. dio. Disp. for marriage within the prohibited times. 20s.

Wm Brownyng & Kath. Golde, Cant. dio. Disp. for marriage in Kath.'s par. ch. without banns. 10s. Also disp. for marriage within the prohibited times. 20s.

Andrew Brownyng & Kath. Rogers. Disp. for marriage without banns. 10s.

27 Stephen Carsleghe & Joan Ryanyn, Bath & W. dio. Disp. for marriage within the prohibited times. 20s.

Wm Whiterton, B.Th., v. of Stogursey, Bath & W. dio. Disp. to hold another benef. £6 10s.

30 Rob. Gurdon & Rose Apleton, Norw. dio. Disp. for marriage within the prohibited times. 20s. Also disp. for marriage in Rose's par. ch. 10s.

26 Ric. Talley, recently abbot of Strata Florida. Disp. to hold a benef. with change of habit. Also for Wm Johns, Tho. Durham, Jo. Becwithe, Lewis David, Morgan Johns, David Morgan. Suppr.

Wm Vayn, recently monk of Whitland. Disp. to hold a benef. with change of habit. Also for Wm Vayn, Jo. Smyth, Tho. Says, Hy Norton, Jo. Conowey. Suppr.

30 Ralph Standishe & Mary Tildesley, Cov. & Lich. dio. Disp. for marriage (4th degree consang.). 26s 8d.

f. 313ʳ

Jan. 26 Jo. Sentclere & Eliz. Culpeper, Lond. dio. Disp. for marriage in their par. ch. within the prohibited times. 20s.

Wm Rowthe, recently canon of Thornton Curtis, Linc. dio. Disp. to hold a benef. with complete change of habit. Also for Tho. Exfurthe, Edw. Hudson, Jo. Hilton, Edw. Ednanne, Rob. Huwett, canons of the same hse. Suppr.

27 Ric. Palmer, recently prior of Spalding, Lincs. Disp. to hold benef. with complete change of habit. Also for Rob. Hoode, Jo. Stiward, Tho. Felde, Jo. Herry, Jo. Dickman, Nich. Miller, Ric. Dawber, Jo. Robynson, Ambrose Irbye, Ric. Johnson. Suppr.

f. 313ᵛ

29 Jo. Laurence, recently abbot of Ramsey, Linc. dio. Disp. to hold a benef. with change of habit. Also for Jo. Driver (Prior), Jo. Paky, Rob. Huchyn, Jo. Avison, Jo. Nicols, Laurence Bardney, Wm Silke, Wm Rogers, Wm Alwyn, Stephen Baldwyn, Tho. Bakere, Wm Cooke, Tho. Polley, Jo. Parke, Jo. Hodingsells, Jo. Fannte, Jo. Palmer, Tho. Andrew, Wm Prick, Jo. Bridgeman, Rob. Haris, Ric. Halwyn, Hugh Philipp, Wm Ireland, Tho. Feild, Jo. Pycherd, Jo. Smythe, Tho. Whitwell, Geo. Marshall. Suppr.

f. 314ʳ

Feb. 1 Ric. Jamys & Marg. Hall, of St Antony's par., London. Disp. for marriage in Marg.'s par. ch., within the prohibited times. 20s.

4 Jo. Chapman, gent., & Marg. Petman, Ely dio. Disp. for marriage in Marg.'s par. ch. without banns. 10s. Also for marriage within the prohibited times. 20s.

5 Ant. Bedingfelde & Eliz. Danyell, Norw. dio. Disp. for marriage without banns. 10s. Also for marriage within the prohibited times. 20s.

f. 314ᵛ

6 Jo. Beche & Isabella Meyre, Cov. & Lich. dio. Disp. for marriage (3rd & 4th degrees affin.). 30s.

Tho. Conwey & Jane Penant, St Asaph dio. Disp. for marriage or validating marriage contracted in ignorance of 4th degree consang. 26s 8d.

7 Jo. Tarlington, recently of the dissolved hse of Sion. Disp. to hold a benef. with complete change of habit. Also for Wm Bartelett. Suppr.

11 Tho. Ley & Fortune Freman, of London. Disp. for marriage within the prohibited times. 20s.

Feb. 9 Hy Mercer & Marg. Werall. Disp. for marriage (4th degree consang.). 26s 8d.

10 Jo. Ramshaw, r. of the par. ch. of St Edm. or St Edw., Linc. dio., chapl. to Ld Windsor. Disp. to hold another benef. with the above. £6 10s.

f. 315ʳ

7 Jo. Wells *alias* Brigeis, recently abbot of Crowland, Linc. dio. Disp. to hold a benef. with complete change of habit. Also for Wm Pynsbeck, Ant. Overton, Ric. Waplode, Ric. Coventre, Jo. London, Jo. Boston, Ric. Usfurthe, Jo. Ramsey, Wm Toste, Wm Sidney, Tho. Crowland, Tho. Stoke, Wm Bardney, Nich. Sutton, Jo. Harlington, Wm Birkenall, Jo. Rotheram, Jo. Usfurthe, Tho. Grantham, Peter Freston, Wm Bouthe, Jo. Cotheman, Wm Chesterton, Rob. Portington, Wm Denton, Rob. Stanforde. Suppr.

f. 315ᵛ

12 Tho. Park, r. of Westwell, Linc. dio. Disp. to hold another benef., as the above does not yield £8 p.a. £4.

Tho. Devye, v. of Welford, Sarum dio., chapl. to Ld Wm Howard, son of the former & brother of the present Duke of Norfolk. Disp. to hold another benef., permut. cl. £6 10s.

13 Tho. Babdike & Marg. Moysett, Linc. dio. Disp. for marriage in Marg.'s par. ch. within the prohibited times. 20s.

16 Wm Bynham, r. of Gt Parndon ('Paringdon'), Lond. dio., chapl. to Ly Eliz., dau. of the Kg. Disp. to hold a benef. with the above. £6 10s.

Riv. Bible & Joan Herger, Cov. & Lich. dio. Disp. for marriage (4th degree affin.). 26s 8d.

f. 316ʳ

Jo. Laurence, r. of Whittington, Cov. & Lich. dio. Disp. to hold another benef. as the above does not yield £8 p.a.; permut. cl. £4.

19 Stephen Sagar, pr., recently abbot of Hales, Worc. dio. Disp. to hold another benef. Also for Philip Brode, B.Th., Wm Chao, Jo. Silvester, Tho. Farre, Jo. Gruffs, Ric. Edmonds, Raynold Lane, Adam Tyler, Wm Nethertune, Tho. Hopkyns, Ric. Dawnsar, Ric. Woodward, Roger Rede, Wm Halydaye, Tho. Rede, Jo. Holme, Ric. Deane, Rob. Shakelton, Elyas Dugdale, Jo. Halle, Chris. Hogeson. Suppr.

f. 316ᵛ

12 Geo. Cotes, M.Th., v. of Godshill, Winton dio. Disp. to hold another benef.; permut. cl. £6 10s.

Feb. 20 Wm Toste, O.P., of London. Disp. to leave the religious life &
to hold a benef. Suppr.

28 Wm Wells & Julia Pyckle of the par. of Newington, Cant. dio.
Disp. for marriage (Wm was sponsor at the confirmation of a
child of Julia). Gratis; warrant of the lords shown.

Mar. 2 Wm Antony & Joan Westwicke, Linc. dio. Disp. for marriage
(2nd & 3rd degrees affin.). £8.

Tho. ap David, acol., Bangor dio. Disp. to take all h.o. outside
the statutory times. 20s.

David Mydelton & Cicily Rogerson, Cov. & Lich. dio. Disp. for
marriage (David was godfather to a child of Cicily). Arb. £3;
warrant of the lords shown.

f. 317ʳ

3 Jo. Worthwell, clk., recently dispensed to hold 2 benefs. Disp.
to hold a 3rd benef. with cure. £8.

4 Jo. Dynes & Agnes Huneborne, Linc. dio. Disp for marriage
(3rd & 4th degrees consang.). 30s.

6 Wm Constable, r. of Bottesford in the vale of Beauvoir, Linc.
dio., son of Sir Marmaduke Constable. Disp. to hold another
benef. £6 10s.

10 Rob. Rice, esq., & Marg. Walgrave, gentw. Disp. for marriage
without banns in Marg.'s par. ch. 10s.

15 Wm Rowsa & Ellen Julian, Linc. dio. Disp. for marriage (Wm's
mother was sponsor at Ellen's confirmation). 26s 8d.

f. 317ᵛ

10 Rob. Rice & Marg. Walgrave. Disp. for marriage within the
prohibited times. 20s.

15 Jo. Lewes & Gwenllian verch Jevan, Lland. dio. Disp. for marriage (4th degree affin.). 26s 8d.

17 Rob. Knosley & Janet verch Robert ap Tuder ap Jevan, St Asaph
dio. Disp. for marriage (3rd & 4th degrees consang.). 30s.

18 Adam Richardeson, subdcn, Carl. dio. Disp. to take the rest of
h.o. outside the statutory times. 13s 4d.

Jo. Pyther, acol., Linc. dio. Disp. to take all h.o. & 2 on the same
day. 26s 8d.

Ralph Grymston & Jane Vavaysor, York dio. Disp. for marriage
(3rd & 4th degrees affin.). 30s.

f. 318ʳ

20 Wm Thornebrughe & Thomasina Billingham, York dio. Disp.
for marriage (3rd & double 4th degrees consang.). £6; 50s.

Mar. 20 Rob. Rogers, recently abbot of Selby, York dio. Disp. to hold a benef. with complete change of habit. Also for Rob. Mitley (Prior), Wm Andrew, Jas Laxe, Tho. Harison, Wm Cartwright, Chris. Tayllor, Geo. Gude, Chris. Beste, Jo. Hardewick, Tho. Acton, Jo. Morice, Wm Marshall, Edw. Pepper, Rob. Leades, Denis Huntington, Nich. Rayner, Rob. Brachbrige, Tho. Lightfote, Chris. Flecher, Ric. Thomson, Wm Moore. Suppr.

f. 318v

22 Wm Powtrell, sch., Cov. & Lich. dio. Disp. to take all h.o. within the prohibited times. 26s 8d.

Tho. Lloid, B.Cn. & C.L., precentor of St David's cath. & holder of other benefices requiring residence. Disp. to hold another benef., or a chaplaincy in the service of Prince Edw. or any duke, marquess, earl, or bp, non-res. 53s 4d.

Tho. Mynton & Marg. Leighton, Heref. dio. Disp. for marriage (Marg.'s mother was Tho.'s godmother). 30s.

f. 319r

20 Jo. Huntley, r. of Oxsted, Winton dio., chapl. to the Bp of Chich. Disp. to hold another benef. with cure; permut. cl. £6 10s.

24 Jo. David ap Evan Lloid & Alison verch Rice Gwyn, St David's dio. Disp. for marriage (4th degree consang.). 26s 8d.

1539 Nov. 7 David ap David & Eliz. Lloid, St David's dio. Disp. for marriage (3rd & 4th degrees affin.). 30s.

1540 Mar. 30 Sir Ralph Waren, alderman of London, & Joan Lake, gentw. Disp. for marriage within the prohibited times, in a private oratory of their choice, without banns. 20s; 10s; 10s.

f. 319v

31 Rob. Meredith & Eliz. Hutton, of London. Disp. for marriage without banns & not in their par. ch. 10s; 10s.

Apr. 5 Hy Markham, acol., Linc. dio. Disp. to take all h.o., 2 on the same day, without l.d. from his diocesan bp. 26s 8d; 6s 8d.

Nich. Bakon & Jane Farley. Disp. for marriage in Jane's par. ch. without banns. 10s.

Wm Midgeley & Agnes Shaw, York dio. Disp. for marriage (4th degree consang.). 26s 8d.

6 Jo. Lewys, literate, Cant. dio. Creation as public notary & tabellion. 13s 4d.

f. 320r

7 Hy Yonge of St Mary's, Southwark, & Joan Whiting, of All Saints, Lombard St., London. Disp. for marriage without banns. 10s.

Apr. 9 Philip Morice & Marg. Wyat, Lond. dio. Disp. for marriage without banns. 10s.

10 Ric. Kinge & Eliz. Melle, of London. Disp. for marriage without banns. 10s.

Jas Porter & Isabella Welliche, Waterford dio., Ireland. Disp. for marriage (3rd & 4th degrees consang.). 30s.

12 Edw. Shell & Joan Rowell, York dio. Disp. for marriage (3rd & 4th degrees affin.). 30s.

13 Francis Alen, sch., Norw. dio. Creation as a public notary & tabellion. 13s 4d.

f. 320ᵛ

7 Mathew Gilbye, dcn, Linc. dio. Disp. to take pr.'s orders outside the statutory times. 10s.

10 Edw. Walker, acol., Carl. dio. Disp. to take all h.o. outside the statutory times. 20s.

7 Hy Banaster & Alice Rushewurthe, Cov. & Lich. dio. Disp. for marriage (3rd degree consang.). £6.

10 Edm. Butler & Cicily Fitzgarett, of Ireland. Disp. for marriage (2nd & 3rd degrees consang.). £8.

6 Chris. Willy, B.Th., v. of Bourn ('Bone'), Ely dio. Disp. to hold another benef.; permut. & non-res. cl. £7 13s 4d.

f. 321ʳ

14 Tho. Eliott & Kath. Hering, Sarum dio. Disp. for marriage (Tho.'s mother was Kath.'s godmother). 30s.

15 Tho. Becke, dcn, Linc. dio. Disp. to take pr.'s orders within the prohibited times. 10s.

12 Jervase Marham, recently prior of Dunstable. Disp. to hold a benef. with complete change of habit. Also for Tho. Cheybroke, Ric. Kent, Geo. Edwards, Edm. Grene, Peter Whippe, Jo. Stalworthe, Ric. Bowlstrede, Augustine Curtes, Rob. Somer. Suppr.

15 Jo. Nicolls & Cristine Thomson. Disp. for marriage without banns & not in their par. ch. 10s; 10s.

f. 321ᵛ

Peter Nicolson & Alice Thomlynson, York dio. Disp. for marriage (4th degree consang.). 26s 8d.

Jo. Johnson & Marg. Leynoldes, of London. Disp. for marriage in Marg.'s par. ch. without banns. 10s.

Rob. Chester & Joan Wellis, of gentle birth. Disp. for marriage without banns, not in their par. ch. but in a private oratory of their choice. 10s; 10s.

Apr. 15 Wm Bog & Alice Sherleghe, Linc. dio. Disp. for marriage (Agnes Bog, formerly wife of Wm, was sponsor at the confirmation of a child of Agnes Sherleghe). £5. Also disp for marriage without banns. 10s.

20 Ric. & Marg. Harrys, Worc. dio. Disp. for marriage (2nd & 4th degrees affin.). 33s 4d.

f. 322ʳ

Apr. 21 Wm Coke, D.C.L., & Mary Wilde, of London. Disp. for marriage in Mary's par. ch. without banns. 10s.

Edm. Stote, literate, Lond. dio. Disp. to practise anywhere as notary & tabellion. 13s 4d.

20 Hy Duppa & Joyce Smith, Heref. dio. Disp. for marriage (Hy's mother was sponsor at Joyce's confirmation). 26s 8d.

21 Roger Hill, acol., Ex. dio. Disp. to take all h.o. outside the statutory times & 2 on the same day. 26s 8d.

f. 322ᵛ

20 Francis Dawntre & Ann Danaster, Winton dio. Disp. for marriage in Ann's par. ch. without banns. 10s.

17 Tho. Pope, recently abbot of Hartland. Disp. to hold a benef. with complete change of habit. Also for Jo. Hirwell, Hy Kyne, Neot Bere, Roger Stone, Jo. Norman. Suppr.

22 Jo. Williamson & Rose Bayle, Lond. dio. Disp. for marriage in their par. ch. without banns. 10s; 10s.

20 Hy Sayvell & Dorothy Lacye. Disp. for marriage (4th degree consang.). 26s 8d.

21 Gilbert & Eliz. Ramysden, York dio. Disp. for marriage (3rd degree consang.). £6.

f. 323ʳ

23 Nich. Titerington & Isabella Harper, York dio. Disp. for marriage (Nich.'s mother was Isabella's godmother). 30s.

May 26 Wm Stanton & Agnes Walshefurthe, York dio. Disp. for marriage (3rd & 4th degrees consang.). 30s.

Jo. Staple, esq., & Marg. Yorke, widow, Sarum dio. Disp. for marriage in any ch. without banns. 10s; 10s.

Oliver Dawbeny & Ann Forde, of London. Disp. for marriage in Ann's par. ch. without banns. 10s.

Apr. 22 Jo. Dawson & Agnes Clerke, Carl. dio. Disp. for marriage (3rd & 4th degrees consang.). 30s.

f. 323ᵛ

Apr. 27 Chris. Spence & Dorothy Metcalfe, York dio. Disp. for marriage (4th degree consang.). 26s 8d.

28 Ric. Smythe & Eliz. Bushope, of London. Disp. for marriage, the banns read once. 6s 8d.

7 Jo. Hodsolde & Julie Carew, Lond. dio. Disp. for marriage (Jo. was sponsor at the confirmation of Julia). Arb. 30s; warrant of the lords shown.

24 Tho. ap Owen & Agnes Turner *alias* Kemmys, Lland. dio. Disp. for marriage (4th degree affin.). 26s 8d.

28 Tho. Bateman & Alice Smythe, York dio. Disp. for marriage (3rd & 4th degrees consang.). 30s.

f. 324ʳ

Mathew William & Janet verch Rice, St David's dio. Disp. for marriage (4th degree consang.). 26s 8d.

26 Rob. Curven & Marg. Thornburghe, York dio. Disp. for marriage (3rd degree consang.). £6.

Jo. Frosdyke, r. of Keswick, Norw. dio. Disp. to hold another benef. as the above does not yield £8 p.a. £4.

29 Tho. Standishe & Ann Dingley of Calbourne, Isle of Wight. Disp. for marriage without banns. 10s. Also disp. for marriage within the prohibited times. 20s.

f. 324ᵛ

29 Geoffrey Holland & Jane verch John Owen, St Asaph dio. Disp. for marriage (4th degree consang.). 26s 8d.

David ap Llin & Gwenllian verch Robert, Lland. dio. Disp. for marriage (3rd & 4th degrees consang.). 30s.

May 1 Tho. Payne & Kath. Reade, Ely dio. Disp. for marriage within the prohibited times. 20s.

Geo. Gifforde, esq., & Philippa Shawe, of the par. of St Mich. Cornhill, London. Disp. for marriage within the prohibited times, the banns read once. 20s; 6s 8d.

4 Hy Brither, acol., Sarum dio. Disp. to take subdcn's and dcn's orders on the same day, within the prohibited times. 13s 4d.

f. 325ʳ

5 Hy Brither *alias* Becher, B.Th., v. of Brenzett, Cant. dio. Disp. to hold another benef. £6 10s.

3 Rob. Whitmore, subdcn, Cov. & Lich. dio. Disp. to take dcn's & pr.'s orders outside the statutory times & on the same day. 13s 4d.

Apr. 27 Tho. Ld Wentworthe. Disp. for he & his wife, & any 3 other persons of their choice, to eat meat, butter, eggs, cheese, &c. during Lent & at other prohibited times. 40s; 40s; 40s; 40s; p.s.r. 5s.

f. 325ᵛ

30 Humfrey Darell, r. of Drayton & ?Totternhoe, Linc. dio., chapl. to the Archbp of Cant. Disp. not to proceed to h.o. for 3 yrs, although holding the above benefices, in order to study letters, or to serve the Archbp. Suitable curates must be appointed. 30s; 'pro quolibet anno 6s 8d' (left-hand margin: 'Nota que taxa 13s 4d causa studii').

May 3 Rob. Marten & Agnes Osney, Linc. dio. Disp. for marriage (Agnes' father was Rob.'s godfather). 30s.

4 Ric. Skalcrose & Ann Trafforde, York dio. Disp. for marriage (Ric.'s father was Ann's godfather). 30s.

f. 326ʳ

Tho. Gawdye & Eliz. Stenyngs, of London. Disp. for marriage within the prohibited times, without banns. 20s; 10s.

Hugh Godard & Marg. Falowe, Cov. & Lich. dio. Disp. for marriage (4th degree consang.). 26s 8d.

Ric. Brabye & Marg. Cersant, Norw. dio. Disp. for marriage (4th degree consang.). 26s 8d.

8 Jo. Unghtrede & Alice Stokys, Roch. dio. Disp. for marriage without banns & not in their par. ch. 10s; 10s. Also disp. for marriage within the prohibited times. 20s.

f. 326ᵛ

Apr. 2 Nich. Hethe, M.Th., Bp-elect of Rochester, archdcn of Stafford, Lich. dio., & incumbent of the parishes of Cliff & Shoreham, Cant. dio., also of the chapels of Otford & Barham, annexed to the same. Disp. upon being consecrated Bp, to hold the above archdcnry until the following Feast of St John Baptist, & the above par. churches for life. £26 13s 4d 'per litteram Regis et warr[antum] domini Cancellarii ostens[um]'.

26 Tho. Lawney, v. of Bersted, in the peculiar jurisdiction of Canterbury, chapl. to the Duke of Suffolk. Disp. to hold another benef.; permut. cl. £6 10s.

f. 327ʳ

25 Wm ap Thomas & Marg. verch Thomas, Lland. dio. Disp. for marriage (3rd degree affin.). £6.

May 6 Oliver Solye, r. of ?Colcreke, Norw. dio., chapl. to Jo., Bp of Worcester. Disp. to hold another benef. £6 10s.

May 8 Jas Bell & Alice Dull, Heref. dio. Disp. for marriage (Jas' father was Alice's godfather). 30s.

10 Jo. Nicolson, recently Austin fr. of Woodhouse, Cov. & Lich. dio. Disp. to leave the religious life & hold a benef. Also for Wm Harington & Wm Chaundeler. Suppr.

f. 327ᵛ

Tho. & Agnes Lowe, Heref. dio. Disp. for marriage (3rd & 4th degrees consang.). 26s 8d.

Apr. 26 Jo. Armorer, pr., v. of Sutton, Cant. dio. Disp. to hold another benef.; permut. cl. £6 10s.

May 10 Hy & Joan Wilkinson, York dio. Disp. for marriage (3rd degree consang.). Gratis; warrant of the lords shown.

Hugh Robinson & Isabella Henda *alias* Haden, York dio. Disp. for marriage (3rd & 4th degrees consang.). 30s.

Tho. Couper, literate, York dio. Creation as public notary & tabellion. 13s 4d.

f. 328ʳ

12 Wm Locke & Eleanor Mershe, widow, of London. Disp. for marriage within the prohibited times. 20s.

Wm Leving, v. of Tudenham, Heref. dio. Disp. to hold another benef., with cure with the above, as it does not yield £8 p.a. £4.

14 Jo. ap Edwarde & Ellen verch Piers, Cov. & Lich. dio. Disp. for (3rd degree affin.). 'Gratis quia pauperes'; warrant of the lords shown.

Apr. 24 Ric. Chamber & Edith Prior, Winton dio. Disp. for marriage (Ric.'s mother was Edith's godmother). 30s.

f. 328ᵛ

May 12 Wm Calewhill & Joan Kyndar, Worc. dio. Disp. for marriage (Joan was godmother to a child of Wm). £6.

13 Tho. Cudwerth & Marg. Botrey, Linc. dio. Disp. for marriage without banns. 10s.

7 Hy Beckham, pr., v. of Appleton, Norw. dio. Disp. to hold another benef. as the above does not yield £8 p.a. £4.

10 Jo. Smarte & Joan Alwey, Sarum dio. Disp. for marriage (Jo.'s mother was Joan's godmother). Gratis; warrant of the lords shown.

Jo. Broughton, gent., & Eliz. Grenston, widow. Disp. for marriage without banns. 10s.

f. 329ʳ

May 13 Also disp. for the above, of Lond. dio., to be married not in their par. ch., & within the prohibited times. 10s; 20s.

14 Feltam Humfrey & Eliz. Selffe, Sarum dio. Disp. for marriage (Eliz. was godmother to a child of Humfrey). £6.

20 Ric. Gill, recently abbot of Newenham, Devon. Disp. to change his habit & hold a benef. Also for Rob. Corgan, Wm Westmon (*sic* for Westminster?), Wm Pedo, Tho. White, Jo. Baker, Jo. Rooper, Tho. Male, Jo. Riche, Ric. Alforde. Suppr.

f. 329ᵛ

24 Jo. Mare & Eliz. Seben, of London. Disp. for marriage in Eliz.'s par. ch. without banns. 10s.

?1539 Oct.   Tho. ap Howell ap John & Agatha verch James ap Enyon, St David's dio. Disp. legitimizing their marriage (contracted in ignorance of 4th degree double consang.). 50s.

1540 May 18 Wm Byrrye & Cristine Cely, of London. Disp. for marriage without banns. 10s.

10 Reg. Hendra, pr., v. of Cubert ('Cuthberte'), Cornwall, Ex. dio. Confirmation of licence issued under the royal seal Feb. 18 1537, for non-res. during illness. 5s 'pro sigillo'.

f. 330ʳ

20 Wm Gibbes, O.F.M., recently prior of Leicester friary. Disp. to hold a benef., with complete change of habit. Also for Jo. Standishe, Simon Harryes, Rob. Aysheton, Tho. London, Hy Webster, Ric. Holmes. Suppr.

May 21 Paul Butler & Ann Porter, of the par. of St Patrick, Waterford dio., Ireland. Disp. for marriage (4th degree consang.). 26s 8d.

22 Ralph Sacheverell & Philippa Willobie, of London. Disp. for marriage without banns. 10s. Also disp. for marriage despite 4th degree consang. 26s 8d.

f. 330ᵛ

Jo. Prescote, gent. & Eliz. Gravenor, of London. Disp. for marriage in Eliz.'s par. ch. without banns. 10s.

26 Geo. Tresham, gent., & Eliz. Savage, of Middle Claydon, Linc. dio. Disp. for marriage without banns. 10s.

27 Jo. ap Ivan & Joan verch Harre, Lland. dio. Disp. for marriage (Joan's father was Jo.'s godfather). 30s.

28 Wm Mason & Ann Wynwode, Heref. dio. Disp. for marriage (4th degree consang.). 26s 8d.

Edw. Saltonstall & Christabel Oldenfelde, of Halifax, York dio. Disp. for marriage (4th degree consang.). 26s 8d.

f. 331^r

May 20 Jo. Berscable, recently abbot of Sherborne, Dorset. Disp. to hold a benef. with complete change of habit. Also for Jo. Donser, Jo. Herte, Jo. Paynter, Tho. Cabull, Jo. Stile, Roger Perye, Jo. Bushope, Wm Vowell, Tho. Eliott, Gilbert Saunder, Jo. Kinge, Wm Erode, Jo. Clerke, Rob. Pytman, Augustine Grene, Bartholomew Strete. Suppr.

Jan. 12 Jo. Whiteharte, pr., r. of St Laurence, Winchester. Disp. to hold another benef. as the above does not yield £8 p.a. £4.

May 31 Peter Horseman, acol., York dio. Disp. to take all h.o. outside the statutory times. 26s 8d.

f. 331^v

June 1 Tho. Fitzwilliams & Janet Fingeas, of Dublin dio., Ireland. Disp. for marriage (3rd & 4th degrees consang.). 30s.

2 Wm Roberteson, York dio. Disp. to take all h.o. outside the statutory times. 20s.

Rob. Jackson & Eliz. Wytfelde, York dio. Disp. for marriage (4th degree consang.). 26s 8d.

May 28 David ap Rice ap Thomas & Agnes Thomas ap David, St Asaph dio. Disp. for marriage (3rd & 4th degrees consang.). 30s.

June 4 Ric. Williot, M.A. Disp. to take all h.o. outside the statutory times & 2 on the same day. 26s 8d.

f. 332^r

7 Wm Harrys, gent. of Mondon (*sic* for Maldon?) & Agnes Crymby, of Rochford, Lond. dio. Disp. for marriage without banns. 10s.

Hugh Steventon & Agnes Orne, Cov. & Lich. dio. Disp. for marriage (4th degree affin.). 26s 8d.

9 Hy Grover & Jane Plome, Roch. dio. Disp. for marriage without banns. 10s.

7 Geo. Fawcett & Marg. Blande, York dio. Disp. for marriage (3rd & 4th degrees consang.). 30s.

9 Tho. Leiche & Kath. Comanudrey, of London. Disp. for marriage in Kath.'s par. ch. without banns. 10s.

f. 332^v

21 Geo. Newdigate, dcn, Lond. dio. Disp. to take the rest of h.o. outside the statutory times. 10s.

24 Jo. Stokys & Alice Edwards, Linc. dio. Disp. for marriage (Jo.'s father was Alice's godfather). 30s.

2 Rob. Harys & Marg. Chapell, Ex. dio. Disp. for marriage (Rob.'s former wife was godmother to a child of Marg.). £6.

June 10 Ric. Talbott & Eliz. Whiteacre, Dublin dio. Disp. for marriage
(Eliz.'s former husband was godfather to a child of Ric. & afterwards Eliz. was sponsor at the boy's confirmation). Arb. £4;
warrant of the lords shown.

2 Jo. Howlen & Kath. Rochell, Cant. dio. Disp. for marriage (3rd
degree consang.). Arb. £4; warrant of the lords shown.

f. 333ʳ

21 Rob. Curven & Marg. Thorneburghe, York dio. Disp. for marriage (3rd & 4th degrees affin; disp. already granted for 3rd
degree consang.). 30s.

Apr. 26 Miles Hasebrigge & Brigitt Gruffithe, Linc. dio. Disp. for marriage without banns. 10s.

May 16 Jo. Brickenden, v. of Mitcham, Winton dio. Disp. to hold
another benef. £6 10s.

20 Ric. ap Owen & Marg. Oteley, Cov. & Lich. dio. Disp. for marriage (2nd & 3rd degrees affin.). 'Remittitur gratis quia pauperes';
warrant of the lords shown.

June 25 Sir Tho. Lisley, Winton dio., & Ly Marg. Darell, widow. Disp.
for marriage without banns. 10s.

f. 333ᵛ

20 Jo. Margaretson & Joan Sparhawke, of London. Disp. for marriage without banns. 10s.

May 31 Ric. Haryson & Cristabel Fawcett, York dio. Disp. for marriage
(4th degree consang. & 3rd & 4th degrees affin.). 'Gratis ob
paupertatem'; warrant of the lords shown.

June 10 Oswald Metcalf, clk, York dio. Disp. to take h.o. within 3 yrs, on
account of certain benefices he holds or is about to hold, provided
the cure of souls is not neglected in them. 30s.

19 Rob. Chapman, acol., York dio. Disp. to take all h.o. & 2 on the
same day, outside the statutory times. 26s 8d.

f. 334ʳ

20 Ric. Smythe & Edith Brunsden, Sarum dio. Disp. for marriage
(3rd & 4th degrees consang.). 30s.

21 Hy Johns & Joan Braylonde, of London. Disp. for marriage in
their par. ch. without banns. 10s.

14 Jo. Robson & Emotte Secarquam, Durham dio. Disp. for marriage (Jo.'s father was Emotte's godfather). 30s.

22 Wm Bromefelde & Agnes Hall, Ely dio. Disp. for marriage
without banns. 10s.

June 22 Jo. Edmunds & Olive Nonne, Lond. dio. Disp. for marriage without banns. 10s.

Wm Bynsley, B.C.L., Linc. dio. Creation as public notary & tabellion. 13s 4d.

f. 334ᵛ

25 Gabriel Maistera & Letice Cocks, of St Olave's, Southwark. Disp. for marriage without banns. 10s.

Roger Boithe & Eliz. Muttow, of Bury, Cov. & Lich. dio. Disp. for marriage (4th degree consang.). 26s 8d.

Tho. Kaye & Alice Genogle, Cov. & Lich. dio. Disp. for marriage (4th degree consang.). 26s 8d.

27 Tho. Somerton & Amy Marche, Lond. dio. Disp. for marriage (3rd & 4th degrees consang.). 30s.

Tho. Elis, v. of Chirk, St Asaph dio. Disp., in addition to previous disp. for pr.'s orders despite defect of birth, to retain the above vicarage and minister. 40s.

f. 335ʳ

28 Rob. Colle & Marg. Dewe, Winton dio. Disp. for marriage (Marg.'s father was Rob.'s godfather or his sponsor at confirmation). 26s 8d.

21 Jo. ap Evan & Gwenheyver verch Richard, St David's dio. Disp. for marriage (Jo.'s father was Gwenheyver's godfather). Gratis; warrant of the lords shown.

27 Wm Sapcoite, v. of Edenson, York dio., ?chapl. to Bp of Bangor. Disp. to hold another benef.; permut. cl. £6 10s.

Tho. Hollocke & Joan White, Chich. dio. Disp. for marriage (Joan was godmother to a child of Tho.). £6.

f. 335ᵛ

July 1 Brian Sunderlande & Marg. Hale, of Halifax, York dio. Disp. for marriage (4th degree consang.). 26s 8d.

2 Wm Oxston *alias* Walles & Emma Tailor, of All Saints, Lombard St, London. Disp. for marriage without banns. 10s.

4 Jo. Rither & Mary Baldry, Norw. dio. Disp. for marriage without banns, & not in their par. ch. 10s; 10s.

5 Jo. Bursley & Marg. Badeley. Disp. for marriage in Marg.'s par. ch. without banns. 10s.

29 Jo. Sharpe & Margery Baylie, Winton dio. Disp. for marriage (Margery was godmother to a child of Jo.). Gratis; warrant of the lords shown.

f. 336ʳ

July 9 Wm Whisken & Joan Anderson, of Anglisforde, Cant. dio. Disp. for marriage in their par. ch. without banns. 10s.

5 Rob. Seyton & Ann Westhamton, Linc. dio. Disp. for marriage (2nd & 3rd degrees affin.). £8.

6 Hy Wydenstall & Kath. Seston, Cov. & Lich. dio. Disp. for marriage (Hy was godfather to a child of Kath.). Arb. 40s; warrant of the Ld Chancellor shown.

7 Hy Bate & Alice Coke, Linc. dio. Disp. for marriage (Hy's mother was Alice's godmother). 30s.

9 Ric. ap Owen & Isabella Pakenham, Lond. dio. Disp. for marriage without banns. 10s.

ff. 336ᵛ–7ʳ

1539 July 12 Jo. Brandesbye, D.Th., Master or r. of the coll. ch. of Lowthorpe, York dio. Disp. (given in full) to hold incorporated with the above the prebend of Dunham in the coll. ch. of Southwell, as Lowthorpe yields only £6 p.a. Confirmation under the royal seal Nov. 12. £4 'ultra medietatem beneficii uniti'; £3 'medietas beneficii uniti'.

f. 337ᵛ

1540 July 10 Tho Bryan, sch., Lond. dio. Disp. to take all h.o. outside the statutory times & 2 on the same day. 26s 8d.

Apr. 16 Tho. Hall, pr., r. of Balingham in the march of Calais. Disp. for non-res. on account of ill-health and the bad climate there, until 6 months after recovery. 20s.

July 11 Jo. Fryer & Alice Slynger, York dio. Disp. for marriage (4th degree affin.). 26s 8d.

f. 338ʳ

10 Wm Marshall, sch., Ely dio. Disp. to take all h.o. & 2 on the same day, outside the statutory times. 26s 8d.

1539 Nov. ? Rob. Emeley, O.P., of Dartford friary. Disp. to hold a benef. with change of habit. Also for Tho. Grannte, Wm Langley, Wm Olyver, Jo. Forrer, Mich. Estfelde. Suppr.

1538 Dec. 10 Hy Lace, O.F.M. Disp. to leave the religious life & hold a benef. Suppr.

1540 July 12 Tho. Johnson & Marg. Hawthorne, of St Botolph's without Aldersgate, London. Disp. for marriage without banns. 10s.

f. 338ᵛ

1 Jo. Plunkett, Ld Killeen & Ellen Barnwell, both of gentle birth & of Meath dio., Ireland. Confirmation of disp. legitimizing

marriage contracted in knowledge of 4th degree double consang., 3rd degree simple affin., 4th double & 3rd & 4th mixed degrees affin. 50s; £6; 50s; 30s.

July 14 Ric. Johnson, r. of ?Dolgeyney, Dublin dio. Disp. to hold an additional benef. within the jurisdiction of this part of the kingdom of England. £6 10s.

15 Jo. Andrew & Clementa Browne, Linc. dio. Disp. for marriage (4th degree consang. or affin.?). 26s 8d.

f. 339ʳ

17 Hugh Hudson, pr., r. of Kettleburgh, Norw. dio. Disp. to hold another benef.; permut. cl. £6 10s.

Nich. Gerlade, O.P., recently of Kilmayn friary, Ireland. Disp. to leave the religious life & hold a benef. Suppr.

Wm Lunde, pr., r. of Chalston, Linc. dio. Disp. to hold another benef. £6 10s.

Tho. Bradwall, recently prior of Trentham, Cov. & Lich. dio. Disp. to leave the religious life and become a sec. pr. with a benef. and to change his habit. Suppr.

f. 339ᵛ

Jo. Gedge & Eliz. Waller of London. Disp. for marriage without banns & in Eliz.'s par. ch. 10s.

Jo. Boythe & Agnes Brereton, Cov. & Lich. dio. Disp. for marriage (4th degree consang.). 26s 8d.

18 Edw. Hampden & Milicent Sands, Linc. dio. Disp. for marriage in any ch. without banns. 10s; 10s.

22 Jo. Wright, literate, Linc. dio. Disp. to practise as a public notary & tabellion. 13s 4d.

18 Geo. Blage & Dorothy Badbye, Cant. dio. Disp. for marriage in a private chapel or oratory. 10s.

f. 340ʳ

26 Jo. Knollis, pr., v. of Ashleworth, Worc. dio. Disp. to hold another benef. with the above, or 2 without it. £6 10s.

23 Wm Burwell, pr., v. of Gayton, Norw. dio. Disp. to hold another benef.; permut. cl. £6 10s.

27 Rob. Andrew & Helen Kent, of the par. of St Mich., Hogen Lane, London. Disp. for marriage without banns. 10s.

Aug. 2 Ric. Reade, D.C.L., & Ann Tregunwell, gentw., Linc. dio. Disp. for marriage without banns. 10s.

f. 340ᵛ

July 22 Edm. Whalley, pr., B.Th., r. of Workington, York dio. Disp. to hold an additional benef. £6 10s.

ff. 340ᵛ–1ʳ

14 Nich. Wotton, D.Cn. & C.L., Commissary of Stephen, Bp of Winchester & by royal authority deputed to hear cases of matrimony & divorce. Confirmation (given in full) of sentence of divorce between Christine Bulbecke *alias* Southwode of the above dio. & Tho. Southwode of the same or another dio. 40s.

f. 341ʳ

29 Wm ap Rice, v. of Swansea, St David's dio., chapl. to the Earl of Worcester. Disp. to hold another benef. with the above, as it does not yield £8 p.a. £4.

f. 341ᵛ

Aug. 7 Peter Aysheton, M.A., Kg's chapl., incumbent of Shillington, Broughton, Aysheley, & Houghton with Whitton, Linc. dio. Disp. to hold a 4th benef. £8.

11 Wm Brian & Joan Godericke, Ely dio. Disp. for marriage without banns & not in their par. ch. 10s.

13 Jo. Gonnell & Agnes Myrthe, of St Laurence par., Reading. Disp. for marriage without banns. 10s.

14 Walter Jobson & Eliz. Page, of the par. of St Mary Arches, London. Disp. for marriage without banns. 10s.

f. 342ʳ

Aug. 18 Jo. Shorden & Batlina Stokwode, of the par. of St Martin's in the Fields, nr Charing Cross, Westminster. Disp. for marriage in the par. ch., the banns read once. 6s 8d.

Oliver Wellisburne, esq., & Ann Yate, Sarum dio. Disp. for marriage without banns, in Ann's par. ch. 10s.

Edw. Raynes, sch., Cambridge University. Disp. to take all h.o. within the prohibited times. 20s.

July 14 Jo. Knight & Eliz. Jakeman, of London. Disp. for marriage outside Eliz.'s par. ch. & without banns. 10s; 10s.

Aug. 31 Ric. Whitill, student, of Cambridge University. Disp. to take all h.o. outside the statutory times. 20s.

f. 342ᵛ

July 14 Jo. Knight & Eliz. Jakeman, of London. Disp. for marriage without banns. 10s.

Aug. 22 Jo. Fowle, gent. of the Kg's hsehld, of Cant. dio., & Eliz. Stedhill, widow, of Chich. dio. Disp. for marriage without banns. 10s.

Sept. 26 Jo. Gwynnethe, pr., v. of ?Enstone (Enton), Linc. dio. Disp. to hold another benef. with cure. £4.

Aug. 27 Tho. Collins of St Andrew's par., Worcester, & Marg. Dulwyn of St Laurence par., Old Jewry, London. Disp. for marriage without banns. 10s.

f. 343ʳ

  28 Rob. Molson & Ann Inderwell, of All Hallows the Gt ('ad fenum'), London. Disp. for marriage without banns. 10s.

Sept. 1 Wm Coke & Kath. Haymonde, of London. Disp. for marriage without banns. 10s.

  4 Jas Creyffe, sch. Disp. to take all h.o. without l.d. from his diocesan bp. 6s 8d.

   Hector Stywarde, subdcn, York dio. Disp. to take the rest of h.o. without l.d. from his diocesan bp. 6s 8d.

  10 Jas Birche, sch., Cov. & Lich. dio. Disp. to take all h.o. outside the statutory times & 2 on the same day. 26s 8d.

f. 343ᵛ

  12 Ric. Maddon, sch., Norw. dio. Disp. to take all h.o. outside the statutory times & 2 on the same day. 26s 8d.

  14 Geo. Thomson, gent., of London, & Eliz. Cocks, of Deptford, Roch. dio. Disp. for marriage without banns.

  19 Geo. Bulstrode, esq., & Faith Oxonbridge, Linc. dio. Disp. for marriage without banns. 10s.

Aug. 28 Nich. Bradshawe, B.C.L., of Sudbury, Cov. & Lich. dio. Disp. to hold another benef. £6 10s.

Sept. 24 Philip Longe & Eliz. Breyn, Winton dio. Disp. for marriage without banns. 10s.

f. 344ʳ

   Geo. Forman & Ann Haymonde, Lond. dio. Disp. for marriage without banns. 10s.

  25 Oliver Selbye, of Branxton, Durham dio. Disp. to hold an additional benef. £6 10s.

  28 Giles Mothersbye & Agnes Beynton, of London. Disp. for marriage in their par. ch. without banns. 10s.

   Geo. Breme & Marg. Waldiffe, Cov. & Lich. dio. Disp. for marriage in Marg.'s par. ch. without banns. 10s.

   Tho. Wodes, chanter in St Paul's, London. Disp. to hold another benef. as well as the chantry, which does not yield £8 p.a. £4.

f. 344ᵛ

Oct.   5 Jo. Gunner, sch., Linc. dio. Disp. to take all h.o. outside the statutory times. 20s.

Sir Clement Hurleston & Joan Colcell, widow, of St Stephen's, Colman St, London. Disp. for marriage without banns in a private oratory of their choice. 10s; 10s.

Apr. 30 Rob. Clapman, literate. Creation as public notary & tabellion. 13s 4d.

Oct.   5 Geo. Nevell, clk, son of Ld Ric. Nevill, Ld Latimer, incumbent of the par. ch. of Bolton, Carl. dio. & ?Northelovy, Ex. dio. Disp. to hold a 3rd benef. £8.

· 345ʳ

Oct.   9 Tho. Harrys, sch., Worc. dio. Disp. to take all h.o. outside the statutory times & 2 on the same day. 20s.

11 Sir Geo. Carew, of the Kg's hsehld, & Mary Norice, of the Qn's hsehld. Disp. for marriage without banns. 10s.

8 Bernard Jennyns & Ellen Curtes, of St Mary Bothaw's par., London, in the peculiar jurisdiction of Canterbury. Disp. for marriage without banns. 10s.

9 Jo. Allington & Marg. Hunte, of Lenham, Norw. dio. Disp. for marriage in their par. ch. without banns. 10s.

f. 345ᵛ

Jas Dixie & Helen Northe, of the par. of Essendine, Linc. dio. Disp. for marriage without banns & not in their par. ch. 10s; 10s.

24 Patrick Welshe & Joan Sherlocke, of Waterford dio., Ireland. Disp. for marriage (4th degree consang.). 26s 8d.

Nov. 4 Rob. Sheperde & Eliz. Uteride, Lond. dio. Disp. for marriage in Eliz.'s par. ch. without banns. 10s.

6 Hy Browne, v. of Harlow, Lond. dio., chapl. to Ld Morley. Disp. to hold another benef. with cure with the above; permut. cl. £6 10s.

f. 346ʳ

8 Jo. Blomevile, pr., of the Hospital of St Giles, Norwich. Disp. to hold a benef. as well as belonging to the above community. £6 10s.

Edw. Saxbie, B.C.L., v. of Laughton, Linc. dio. Disp. to hold another benef. £6 10s.

7 Edm. Meide & Joan Rescue, of London. Disp. for marriage in Joan's par. ch. without banns. 10s.

10 Denis Hockleton, vicar choral of York, and Fellow of St Peter's coll., Bedarme. Disp. to hold another benef. as the above vicarage does not yield £8 p.a. £4.

f. 346ᵛ

Nov. 13 Hugh White & Mary Mering, of the par. of St Mary's, Beverley, York dio. Disp. for marriage without banns & not in their par. ch. 10s; 10s.

Feb. 10 Hy Morgan, Master of Law, Qn's chapl., holder of 3 benefices with cure. Disp. to hold a 4th benef. with cure. £8.

Apr. 8 Rob. Robynson, chanter in the chantry of Wm Coke, Beverley, York dio. Disp. to hold a benef. with the above which does not yield £8 p.a. £4.

Nov. 16 Rob. Preston, gent., & Ly Denisa Sandis. Disp. for marriage without banns. 10s.

f. 347ʳ

12 Jo. Pollarde, M.A., Kg's chapl. Disp. to hold any number of additional benefices with or without cure, not exceeding the value of £40 p.a. £14 6s 8d; warrant of the lords shown.

16 Hy Grymsshawe, pr., r. of Saxham, Norw. dio., chapl. to the Bp of Norwich. Disp. to hold another benef. £6 10s.

Jo. Farthyn & Eliz. Reynoldes, of the par. of St Laurence, London. Disp. for marriage without banns. 10s.

f. 347ᵛ

Jo. Tayllor, D.Th., Kg's chapl. Disp. to hold a 3rd benef. £8.

10 Confirmation under the royal seal of licence issued on Nov. 20 1539 to the inhabitants of the village or hamlet of Northpidele, Worc. dio. for burial of the dead in the newly consecrated cemetery; p.s.r. 5s.

17 Jo. Williamson, v. of Althorne, Lond. dio., chapl. to Rob., Earl of Sussex. Disp. to hold another benef. £6 10s.

Rob. Troile & Jean Coke, of the par. of All Saints, Lombard St, London. Disp. for marriage without banns. 10s.

f. 348ʳ

19 Tho. Gilham, r. of Ashley, Linc. dio., chapl. to the Earl of Rutland. Disp. to hold an additional benef. with the above. £6 10s.

Tho. Grenewode, sch., York dio. Disp. not to take h.o. for a yr, although his tenure of a benef. requires it. 10s.

20 Nich. Hogarde, chanter in the chantry of St Kath. in St John's, Beverley, York dio. Disp. to hold another benef. as the above does not yield £8 p.a. £4.

f. 348ᵛ

Nich. Archiebolde, r. of Harlaxton, Linc. dio., Kg's chapl. Disp. to hold an additional benef.; permut. cl. £6 10s.

Nov. 21 Alan Charleton, B.C.L., v. of Wellington, Cov. & Lich. dio. Disp. to hold an additional benef. £6 10s.

22 Jo. Hopton, D.Th., r. of St Ann's & St Agnes's, London. Disp. to hold another benef. as the above do not yield £8 p.a. £4.

24 Sir Tho. Tresham & Ly Letice Lee, widow. Disp. for marriage in their par. ch. without banns. 10s.

f. 349^r

23 Tho. Reynoldes, v. of Lambourn, Sarum dio., chapl. to the Bp of Salisbury. Disp. to hold another benef. £6 10s.

27 Mich. Malett & Joan Stawell, of London. Disp. for marriage within the prohibited times. 20s.

20 Jo. Dun, M.A., v. of Altarnon, Ex. dio., chapl. to Bp of Exeter. Disp. to hold another benef. £6 10s.

23 Geoffrey Crispe, pr., chapl. to Ld Tho. Audley, Ld High Chancellor. Disp. to hold 2 benefices. £6 10s.

f. 349^v
Dec. 1 Ant. Burbanke, r. of Cleburn, Carl. dio., chapl. to Ld Conyers. Disp. to hold a benef. with the above. £6 10s.

2 Jo. Britten, v. of ?Sock Dennis, Bath & W. dio. Disp. to hold another benef. £6 10s.

3 Roger Hillary, pr., r. of Leigh St Mary (Light), Roch. dio. Disp. to hold another benef. if the above does not yield £8 p.a. £4.

Jo. Broke & Ann Bealle, of London. Disp. for marriage within the prohibited times. 20s.

f. 350^r

2 Wm Fitzwilliams, sch., York dio. Disp., although only 18 yrs old, to hold the office of clk & hold a benef. or ecclesiastical office until his 25th yr, without h.o.; permut. & non-res. cl. £5 13s 4d; 20s.

f. 350^v

10 Tho. Sherle & Eleanor Stone, Heref. dio. Disp. for marriage within the prohibited times. 20s.

11 Geo. Holcroste, acol., Cov. & Lich. dio. Disp. to take all h.o. outside the statutory times, & 2 on the same day. 26s 8d.

10 Edm. Sprynt & Joan Hobbe, Lond. dio. Disp. for marriage in Joan's par. ch. within the prohibited times. 20s.

Jo. Caplyn & Margery Percharde, of Southampton, Winton dio. Disp. for marriage within the prohibited times. 20s.

f. 351^r

1540 Dec. 12 Jo. Warley & Marg. Smytton, of London. Disp. for marriage within the prohibited times. 20s.

1541 Jan. 7 Chris. Hales, sch., Cant. dio. Disp. to hold a benef. although in his 21st yr & not to proceed to h.o. until his 24th. £4 6s 8d; 40s.

1540 Dec. 10 Ralph Ade & Marg. Wydow, of Gt Yarmouth, Norw. dio. Disp. for marriage within the prohibited times. 20s.

f. 351^v

13 Edw. Newporte & Marg. Litleton, of Frankley, Worc. dio. Disp. for marriage within the prohibited times. 20s.

17 Abraham Metcalf & Joan Boyes, of St Clement Danes, London. Disp. for marriage within the prohibited times. 20s.

20 Rob. Reve, B.C.L., v. of Collingbourne, Sarum dio. Disp. to hold an additional benef. £6 10s.

Tho. Wilson, B.A., York dio. Disp. to take all h.o. outside the statutory times & 2 on the same day. 26s 8d.

21 Geoffrey Baynbrige, sch., York dio. Disp. to take all h.o. & 2 on the same day, outside the statutory times. 26s 8d.

f. 352^r

20 Wm Matens, chanter in Linc. cath., chapl. to Tho., Duke of Norfolk. Disp. to hold an additional benef. £6 10s.

26 Ric. Godericke & Mary Blacke, of London. Disp. for marriage within the prohibited times, but not in Lent. 20s.

Sir Tho. Pope & Eliz. Basforde, widow. Disp. for marriage within the prohibited times. 20s.

20 Chris. Lambarde, of the Kg's hsehld & Christine June, Norw. dio. Disp. for marriage within the prohibited times. 20s.

f. 352^v

27 Jo. Shether, B.Th., r. of Woolnoth, London. Disp. to hold an additional benef.; permut. cl. £6 10s.

Jo. Mason, gent. of the Kg's hsehld, & Eliz. Hill, widow. Disp. for marriage within the prohibited times. 20s

ff. 353^r–67 blank.

p. 1

1543 Nov. 17 Jo. Tayler *alias* Cardmaker, B.Th., v. of Branscombe, Ex. dio. Disp. to hold a benef. with or 2 without the above; permut. cl. 7s 2d.

15 Wm Rawlyns, acol., Heref. dio. Disp. to take all h.o. on the same day from any bp outside the statutory time. 3s 4d.

22 Jo. Dene, M.A., chapl. to Jo. Vere, Earl of Oxford, v. of Earls Colne, Lond. dio. Disp. to hold a benef. with or without cure with or 2 without the above. 7s 2d.

Wm Bramton & Agnes Squier, of Bewdley, Worc. dio. Disp. for marriage by any pr. within the prohibited times. 3s 4d.

p. 2

26 Jo. Shery, archdcn of Lewes, Chich. dio. Disp. to hold a benef. with or without cure with or 2 without the above. 7s 2d.

27 Hugh Shadwalle, literate, Lich. dio. Disp. to hold the office of notary & tabellion. 4s 5d.

Dec. 2 Jo. Traherne, B.Th., r. of Robertstone, St David's dio. Disp. to hold another benef. with or without cure with the above, if it does not yield over £8 p.a. 4s 5d.

Oct. 1 Edm. Coterell, pr., v. of ?Windrush ('Wynsrishe') Worc. dio. Similar disp. 4s 5d.

p. 3

Dec 12 Alan Clyffe, v. of Kinlett, Heref. dio., chapl. to Jo., Bp of Lincoln. Disp. to hold another benef. with or without cure with the above; permut. cl. 7s 2d.

13 Ric. Byrche, v. of Husborne Crawley, Linc. dio., chapl. to Ly Eliz. Hungerford. Disp. to hold another benef. with or without cure with the above; permut. cl. 7s 2d.

Ric. Thurkettyll, v. of Eye, Norw. dio., chapl. to the bp of Hereford. Similar disp. 7s 2d.

p. 4

11 Jo. Sturley & Agnes Barbor, of St Leonard Eastcheap, London. Disp. for marriage by any pr., & within the prohibited times. 3s 4d.

31 Jo. Markeley & Eliz. Owtrede, both of gentle birth, of Tonbridge, Roch. dio. Similar disp. 3s 4d.

Dec. 13 Disp. for the above to marry, the banns read once. 2s 2d.

9 Roger Lambe, sch., Linc. dio. Disp. to take all or 2 h.o. outside the statutory times, 2 on the same day, from any bp. 3s 4d.

14 Jo. Taylor, M.Th., Dean of Lincoln, Kg's chapl. Disp. to hold a benef. with or without cure with 3 others with cure; permut. cl. 8s 10d.

p. 5

1544 Jan.   1 Jo. Averell & Eliz. Gilpyn, of All Saints the More, London. Disp. for marriage within the prohibited times by any bp. 3s 4d.

1543 Dec. 24 Hy Bradshawe, pr., r. of Aspall Stonham, Norw. dio., chapl. to Ld Tho. Wentworth. Disp. to hold another benef. with or without cure with the above, or 2 without; permut. cl. 7s 2d.

1544 Jan.   3 Wm Rokebye, B.C.L., Chester dio. Disp. to take minor orders & the orders of subdcn & dcn from any bp, outside the statutory times, on any day. 4s 5d.

1543 Dec. 24 Hy Hall, pr., r. of Halsham in Holderness, York dio., chapl. to Hy, Earl of Bridgwater. Disp. to hold another benef. with or without cure with the above, or 2 others without it; permut. cl. 7s 2d.

p. 6

1544 Jan.   3 Wm Hodgis *alias* Hall, B.A., r. of Wharkleigh, Ex. dio., chapl. to Jo. Bourchier, Earl of Bath. Similar disp. permut. cl. 7s 2d.

2 Ric. Starkey, gent., & Eliz. Allen, of the Qn's hsehld, & the par. of St Bartholomew, London. Disp. for marriage in the bride's par. ch. by any suitable pr. without banns. 3s 4d.

11 Roger Sondeforth, subdcn, Winton dio. Disp. to take dcn's & pr.'s orders on the same day. 4s 5d.

15 Jas Hargreaves, Chester dio., student at Qns' Coll., Cambridge. Disp. to take pr.'s orders from any bp without l.d. from his diocesan bp. 2s 2d.

p. 7

11 Gilbert Holrod, York dio., sch., of Michaelhse Coll., Cambridge. Similar disp. 2s 2d.

15 Nich. Corbricke, v. of Paulet, Wells dio., chapl. to Paul, Bp of Bristol. Disp. to hold any other benef with the above or 2 without; permut. cl. 7s 2d.

Cuthbert Warcuppe & Ann Wylkynson, widow, of London. Disp. for marriage in the bride's par. ch., by any pr. & without banns. 3s 4d.

p. 8

Jan. 19 Tho. Rydley, Ely dio. & Alice Daye, Lond. dio. Disp. for marriage in the bride's par. ch., by any pr. & after the banns have been read once. 2s 2d.

24 Tho. Guilyem *alias* Guylyem. Licence to preach anywhere. Gratis.

26 Rob. Palmer, citizen & mercer of Christchurch par., London. Disp. to eat meat & milk foods during Lent, as he is 60 & afflicted with the stone & other ailments. 3s 4d.

p. 9

24 Percival Hethe & Alice Lacy, of St Pancras par., London. Disp. for marriage in the bride's par. ch. by any pr. & without banns. 3s 4d.

1543 May 26 Jo. Goodeman, B.C.L., chapl. to Edw., Earl of Hertford, K.G., r. of Charlton, Ex. dio. Disp. to hold another benef. with or without cure with the above, or 2 others without it; permut. cl. 7s 2d.

1544 Jan. 26 Cuthbert Wytham, of Chester dio., student of Cambridge. Disp. to take pr.'s orders from any bp without l.d. from his diocesan bp. 2s 2d.

p. 10

27 Geo. Rolle & Eliz. Aysshton, of the par. of St Olave, London. Disp. for marriage in any ch., chapel, or oratory, by any pr., without banns. 6s 8d.

26 Ric. Tayler, chanter in the Cantilupe chantry, Lincoln cath. Disp. to hold another benef. with or without cure with the chantry if it does not yield over £8 p.a. 4s 5d.

Hy Spylman & Anne Thursby, of Norw. dio. Disp. for marriage in any ch., chapel, or oratory, by any pr. & without banns. 6s 8d.

p. 11

28 Jo. Share, pr., r. of Ingram, Durham dio., chapl. to Hy, Earl of Cumberland. Disp. to hold another benef. with or without cure with the above, or 2 others without it, permut. cl. 7s 2d.

27 Ric. Colyer, r. of Rotherfield, Chich. dio., Kg's chapl. Disp. to hold another benef. with the above, or 2 with or without cure, without; permut. cl. 7s 2d.

29 Jo Bryne *alias* Bruyne & Joan Wynkefeld, both of gentle birth, of Linc. dio. Disp. for marriage in Joan's par. ch. by any pr. & without banns. 3s 4d.

p. 12

29 Rob. Parker & Alice Grannt, of St Gregory's par., London. Cancelled disp. for marriage in the bride's par. ch. by any pr., the banns read once.

Jan. 27 Paul Darell & Dorothy Sanders, widow, Peterborough dio. Disp. for marriage in any ch., chapel, or private oratory by any pr. & without banns. 6s 8d.

30 Also disp. for the above to be married within the prohibited times. 3s 4d.

Leonard Stubbis & Eliz. Wymmyngton, of Boston, Linc. dio. Disp. for marriage in the bride's par. ch. by any pr. & without banns. 3s 4d.

p. 13

29 Hugh Ions, B.C.L., r. of Trerenock (*sic*), Lland. dio., chapl. to Jo., Bp of Gloucester. Disp. to hold another benef. with the above, or 2 with or without cure without it; permut. cl. 7s 2d.

Feb. 1 Humfrey Colles, esq., of London, & Eliz. Boys, widow. Disp. for marriage in the bride's par. ch. by any pr. & within the prohibited times. 3s 4d.

4 Disp. for the above to be married in any ch., chapel, or oratory, by any pr., without banns. 3s 4d.

p. 14

1543 Sept. 16 Jo. Butler, B.C.L., Kg's chapl., r. of St Peter's by Calais, & St Jas of Colham?, Thérouanne dio., by previous disp. Disp. to hold another benef. with or without cure; permut. cl. 8s 10d.

1544 Feb. 3 Jo. Page, v. of Stardbroke, Norw. dio., chapl. to Chas, Duke of Suffolk. Disp. to hold another benef. with the above or 2 with or without cure, without it; permut. cl. 7s 2d.

5 Percival Leygon, r. of Spenden, Linc. dio., chapl. to Hy, Marquess of Dorset. Disp. to hold another benef. with or 2 with or without cure, without the above; permut. cl. 7s 2d.

p. 15

Wm Sentell & Marg. Serland, Winton dio. Disp. for marriage in any ch., chapel, or oratory, without banns, & by any pr. 6s 8d.

Jo. Apharry, r. of Church Eaton, Lichfield dio., & v. of St Mary the Virgin, Lichfield, Kg's chapl. Disp. to hold another benef.; with or without cure; permut. cl. 8s 10d.

Ric. Welche & Marg. Gowre, of St John's par., Worcester. Disp. for marriage by any pr. within the prohibited times. 3s 4d.

p. 16

1543 Aug. 2 Ant. Belassys, D.C.L., Kg's chapl. Disp. to hold a 3rd benef. with or without cure. 8s 10d.

1544 Feb. 5 Edw. Vaughan, esq. Disp. to eat butter & other milk foods & meat in Lent, on account of many ailments. 3s 4d.

Feb. 6 Jo. Kyttowe & Eliz. Bland, Lond. dio. Disp. for marriage in the bride's par. ch. without banns & by any pr. 3s 4d.

pp. 16–17

4 Hy Springe, Norw. dio., sch., of Cambridge University. Disp. to hold a benef. with or without cure although only in his 22nd yr, & neither to reside nor take pr.'s orders until he is of the correct age, as he is engaged in study. 3s 9d.

p. 17

1543 Apr. 12 Tho. Bull, B.Th., v. of Northfleet, Cant. dio. Disp. to hold another benef. with or without cure with or 2 others without the above. 7s 2d.

1542 May 12 Nich. Cartewright, D.Th. Disp. to hold a 3rd benef. with or without cure; permut. cl. 8s 10d.

p. 18

1544 Feb. 9 Wm Marks & Frances Willoughbie, of All Saints par., London. Disp. for marriage within the prohibited times, in the bride's par. ch. & by any pr. 3s 4d.

3 Wm Todde, v. of Waresley, Linc. dio., Kg's chapl. Disp. to hold another benef. with the above, or 2 with or without cure, without. 7s 2d.

10 Jo. Colcell, sch., Linc. dio. Disp. to take all h.o. from any bp on any day outside the statutory times. 3s 4d.

pp. 19–20

2 Peter Vannes, Dean of Salisbury, Kg's secretary for Latin letters. Disp. (given in full) to hold the canonry & prebend of Shipton-under-Wychwood, together with the above deanery & its revenue. 5s 7d.

p. 21

10 Rob. Thacker, pr., prebendary or canon of Stone & ?incumbent of the free royal chapel or coll. ch. of All Saints, Derby, Linc. dio. Disp. to hold another benef. with or without cure with the above, if it does not yield over £8 p.a. 4s 5d.

Chris. Goldingham & his wife Ann, both of gentle birth, of Norwich. Disp. on account of medical evidence of his melancholy humour, palpitations of the heart, & other infirmities, to avoid eating fish during Lent & at other prohibited times, & to eat milk foods or meat on medical advice. 3s 4d.

p. 22

13 Edw. Saunders, sergeant at law, & his wife Margery, of Peterborough dio. Disp. on account of medical evidence of Margery's many ailments, not to eat fish & to eat meat & milk foods during Lent & at other prohibited times. 3s 4d.

Feb. 10 Jo. Roberts, r. of Fovant, Sarum dio., chapl. to Ld Tho. Audley, Ld of Walden, Ld Chancellor. Disp. to hold another benef. with or 2 others with or without cure, without the above. 7s 2d.

p. 23

13 Rob. Rudston & his wife Ann. Disp. on account of medical evidence of Rob.'s dropsy, indigestion, excessive wind, & various other ailments, to eat meat & milk foods during Lent. 3s 4d.

14 Jo. Harward & Cecily Havelande, of gentle birth, Bristol dio. Disp. for marriage in the bride's par. ch. within the prohibited times by any pr. 3s 4d.

15 Tho. Sandeford & Juliana Sandre, Westminster dio. Disp. for marriage in the bride's par. ch. within the prohibited times, & by any pr. 3s 4d.

p. 24

10 Tho. Weste, M.A., r. of Houghton Robert, York dio. Disp. to hold another benef. with or without cure with the above if it does not yield over £8 p.a.; permut. cl. 4s 5d.

13 Wm Benne, Chester dio., student in Cambridge University. Disp. to take all h.o. & pr.'s orders without l.d., & from any bp. 2s 2d.

16 Tho. Darbye & Joan Wodde, of gentle birth. Disp. for marriage in the bride's par. ch. within the prohibited times & by any pr. 3s 4d.

p. 25

23 Jo. White & Joan Lyddem of Whittisham, Cant. dio. Disp. for marriage in Joan's par. ch. during the prohibited times by any pr., without banns. 3s 9d.

1543 May 10 Jo. Weale, r. of St Mildred's, London, Kg's chapl. Disp. to hold another benef. with or 2 others with or without cure without the above. 7s 2d.

1544 Feb. 20 Ant. Bond & Cecily Far, of St Matthew's par., London. Disp. for marriage in Cecily's par. ch. within the prohibited times, & by any pr. 3s 4d.

p. 26

16 Jo. Anderton & Eliz. Smyth *alias* Gregson, of gentle birth, Chester dio. Disp. for marriage in the bride's par. ch. within the prohibited times & by any pr. 3s 4d.

21 Jo. Grenewode, York dio. Disp. to take h.o., including pr.'s orders, without l.d. 2s 2d.

22 Tho. Wood & Joan Croche, widow, of London. Disp. for marriage in the bride's par. ch. within the prohibited times & by any pr., without banns. 3s 9d.

Feb. 24 Walter Benwell & Joan Barnes, Lond. dio. Similar disp. 3s 9d.

p. 27

1543 Aug. 2 Jo. Gwynneth, Kg's chapl. Disp. to hold another benef. with or without cure, with the one he already holds, or 2 others without it. 5s 7d.

1544 Feb. 23 Rob. Sanders & Eliz. Breyttayne, of London. Disp. for marriage in the bride's par. ch. by any pr., the banns read once. 2s 2d.

27 Ric. Busshop, v. of Brailes, Worc. dio., chapl. to Wm. Earl of Essex. Disp. to hold a benef. with or 2 with or without cure without the above; permut. cl. 7s 2d.

p. 28

26 Eliz. Baker, wife of Sir Tho. Baker, Chancellor of the Court of First Fruits & Tenths. Disp. on account of illnesses, not to eat fish, & to eat cheese, butter, & meat during Lent & at other times. 3s 4d.

27 Tho. Mychell, sch., Ex. dio. Disp. to take h.o. & hold a benef. with cure despite lameness of the foot with partial deformity. 3s 4d.

Tho. Jones, B.Th., r. of Johnson, St David's dio. Disp. to hold another benef. if the above does not yield over £8 p.a., or 2 others with or without cure, without it. 4s 5d.

p. 29

19 Jas Hill, of the Kg's hsehld, & his wife Mary. Disp. to eat meat & milk foods during Lent & at other times of the yr.

27 Andrew Streche, B.A., Dean of Limerick, chapl. to Sir Ant. St Leger, Chief Deputy or Justiciar in Ireland. Disp. to hold another benef. with or 2 others with or without cure, without the above. 10s.

20 Tho. Barnadiston & his wife Mary, Chich. dio. Disp. to eat meat & milk foods during Lent & at other prohibited times. 3s 4d.

p. 30

Maurice Gruffith, chanter in the chantry of St Anne, St Paul's cath., London, chapl. to Arthur, Bp of Bangor. Disp. to hold another benef. with or 2 with or without cure, without the above; permut. cl. 7s 2d.

Mar. 1 Agnes Nantfonnt, widow, Lond. dio. Disp. to eat meat, cheese, & milk foods during Lent & at other prohibited times. 3s 4d.

Tho. Dere, esq., Wells dio. Disp. to eat cheese, butter, & milk foods during Lent & at other times. 3s 4d.

p. 31

Feb. 1 Sir Brian Tuke, Treasurer of the Kg's Chamber. Disp. to eat cheese, butter, meat, & milk foods during Lent & at other times, on medical advice. 3s 4d.

Feb. 25 Simon Sampson, esq., & his wife, Eliz. Disp. to eat cheese, butter, meat, & milk foods during Lent & at other times, on medical advice. 3s 4d.

Mar. 8 Tho. Barne, subdcn, Carl. dio. Disp. to take dcn's & pr.'s orders on any day. 4s 5d.

July 1 Jas Vinfrey, r. of St Mary's, Paynestown, Meath dio., Ireland, chapl. to Sir Ant. St Leger, First Deputy or Chief Justiciar of Ireland. Disp. to hold another benef. 7s 2d.

p. 32

Mar. 8 Rob. Stodcatt *alias* Stodantt, subdcn, Carl. dio. Disp. to take dcn's & pr.'s orders on the same day. 4s 5d.

Otto Rompello, born in 'terra Vergensi' (*sic*), subject of the Kg*. Disp. to hold any number of benefices, with or without cure not exceeding 4 par. churches & not yielding more than £40 p.a. 7s 9d.

Ric. Robynson, subdcn, Carl. dio. Disp. to take dcn's & pr.'s orders on any day from any bp. 4s 5d.

10 Wm Robinson, dcn, Sarum dio., chapl. to the Bp of Carlisle. Disp. to take pr.'s orders on a Sunday or Feast Day from any bp. 3s 4d.

p. 33

6 Edw. Booden, M.A., r. of Eastling & Newton, Cant. dio., chapl. to Sir Tho. Cheyney, K.G., Treasurer of the Hsehld. Disp. to hold a 3rd benef. with or without cure; permut. cl. 5s 7d.

14 Jo. James, acol., Lland. dio. Disp. to take subdcn's & dcn's orders outside the statutory times on any day from any bp. 4s 5d.

Feb. 20 Sir Geo. Gruffith & his wife Ly Mary, Cov. & Lich. dio. Disp. to eat meat & milk foods during Lent & at other times on medical advice. 3s 4d.

p. 34

Ralph Bagenolde, esq., of the Kg's hsehld. Disp. to eat meat & milk foods during Lent & at other times. 3s 4d.

Mar. 17 Wm Rogers, acol., of Lland. dio. Disp. to take subdcn's & dcn's orders on any day from any bp. 4s 5d.

13 Wm Rogers, sch., of Lland. dio. Disp. to take pr.'s orders from any bp without l.d. 2s 2d.

18 Disp. for the above to take pr.'s orders in spite of being in his 24th yr, & to hold a benef. 3s 4d.

---

* Letters of denization dated 1 June 1543 describe him as clk, born in 'terra vergensi' under the obedience of the Duke of Berg. (*L.P.* xviii. i. 802, no. 5).

p. 35

Mar. 18 Walter Wright, D.C.L., archdcn of Oxford. Disp. to take pr.'s orders within 2 yrs. 3s 4d.

17 Ly Eliz. Taylbois, Linc. dio. Disp. to eat meat & milk foods during Lent. 3s 4d.

1541 June 15 Jo. Greves, v. of Ashby de la Zouch, Linc. dio., chapl. to Geo., Earl of Huntingdon. Disp. to hold another benef. with or without cure with the above, or 2 without; permut. cl. 7s 2d.

p. 36

1544 Mar. 23 Wm Feneux & his wife Frideswide, Cant. dio. Disp. to eat meat & milk foods during Lent & at other prohibited times. 3s 4d.

10 Roger Lewes, B.Cn.L., r. of Marnhull, Bristol dio. Disp. to hold another benef. with or 2 with or without cure, without the above. 7s 2d.

24 Hy Scors, literate, York dio. Disp. to practise as a public notary & tabellion. 4s 5d.

p. 37

26 Tho. Rogers, r. of Mersham, Cant. dio., ?Archbp's chapl. ('capel-lano nostro'). Disp. to hold another benef. with or without cure with, or any 2 without the above; permut. cl. 7s 2d. ('fortuna fetat', note in margin).

27 Wm Manndefild, v. of Fleet, Bristol dio. Disp. to hold another benef. with the above if it does not yield over £8 p.a. permut. cl. 4s 5d.

p. 38

Apr. 1 Gordon Bales, Chester dio., B.A. studying at Cambridge. Disp. to take all h.o. without l.d. 2s 2d.

Mar. 31 Ric. Goodriche & his wife Mary. Disp to eat meat & milk foods during Lent & at other prohibited times. 3s 4d.

Apr. 1 Francis West, dcn, York dio. Disp. to take pr.'s orders despite being only in his 23rd yr. 3s 4d.

2 Disp. for the above to take pr.'s orders on any day from any bp. 3s 4d.

p. 39

Tho. Brynckeley, subdcn, Norw. dio. Disp. to take dcn's & pr.'s orders on any day from any bp. 4s 5d.

3 Tho. Thompson, r. of Hasketon & Garboldisham, Norw. dio., chapl. to Tho. Howard, Duke of Norfolk, Ld Treasurer. Disp. to hold a 3rd incompatible benef. without cure; permut. cl. 8s 10d.

Feb. 25 Tho. Palmer, gent., of the royal fortress of 'Le Crowe', & Treasurer at Guisnes. Disp. to eat meat & milk foods during Lent & at other prohibited times, on medical advice, due to injuries received in the Kg's service, viz. a fractured shin bone (*tibia*) & tormenting pain (*angore cruciatus*). 3s 4d.

p. 40

26 Rob Cresswell, gent., Winton dio. Disp. to eat meat & milk foods during Lent & at other prohibited times, on account of his suffering from quartan fever. 3s 4d.

Mar. 24 Sir Edw. Baynton, Vice-Chamberlain of the Qn, & his wife Ly Eliz. Disp. to eat meat & milk foods during Lent & at other prohibited times. 3s 4d.

1 Tho. Nuthake, r. of Little Stambridge, Lond. dio., pr., chapl. to Tho., Ld Audley de Walden. Disp. to hold another benef. with or without cure with the above, or 2 without. 7s 2d.

p. 41

3 Wm Newton, pr., r. of ?Bugthorpe ('Burithorpe'), York dio. Disp. to hold another benef. with or without cure, with, or 2 others without the above, if it does not yield over £8 p.a. 4s 5d.

Apr. 29 Philip Wharton & Joan Johnson, Lond. dio. Disp. for marriage in the bride's par. ch. by any pr., without banns. 3s 4d.

30 Wm Bevyn & Alice Wylde, of Leckhampstead, Linc. dio. Disp. for marriage at any time, by any suitable pr., without banns. 3s 4d.

10 Francis Francleyn & Alice Colnett, Cov. & Lich. dio. Disp. for marriage in any ch., chapel, or oratory, without banns. 6s 8d.

p. 42

May 3 Griffin Leyson, D.C.L., & Ly Joyce Gammage, widow, Linc. dio. Disp. for marriage in any ch. or chapel & by any suitable pr., without banns. 6s 8d.

2 Wm Marshall, sch., Linc. dio. Disp. to take all h.o. including pr.'s orders from any bp, outside the statutory times. 3s 4d.

Edm. Cooper, M.A., v. of Swanbourne, Linc. dio., chapl. to Jo., Ld Bray. Disp. to hold another benef. with or 2 without cure, without the above. 7s 2d.

p. 43

3 Andrew Browne, r. of Skulton, Norw. dio., chapl. to Hy Howard, Earl of Surrey, K.G. Disp. to hold another benef. with or 2 with or without cure, without the above; permut. cl. 7s 2d.

9 Edm. Edwards, acol., student at Cambridge University. Disp. to take all h.o. including pr.'s orders in spite of being in his 22nd yr. 3s 4d.

May 10 Edm. Edwarde, student at Cambridge University. Disp. to take h.o. from any bp on any day. 3s 4d.

p. 44

11 Tho. Hildersham & Frances Bladwell, Norw. dio. Disp. for marriage in the bride's par. ch. without banns & by any suitable pr. 3s 4d.

13 Tho. Audeley & Kath. Southwell, Lond. dio. Disp. for marriage in a ch., chapel or oratory of their choice, by any suitable pr. 6s 8d.

12 Jo. White Payne, citizen & merchant of London, & Agnes Hall. Disp. for marriage in any chapel or oratory without banns, & by any suitable pr. 6s 8d.

Feb. 23 Wm Rede, r. of St Botolph's, Sheringham, Norw. dio. Disp. to hold another benef. with or without cure, with the above if it does not yield over £8 p.a. 4s 5d.

p. 45

May 14 Miles Rotherey, v. of Bubwith, York dio. Disp. to hold another benef., with or without cure, if the above does not yield over £8 p.a. 4s 5d.

2 Griffin Williams, v. of St Leonard's, Shoreditch, Westminster dio., chapl. to Hy Earl of Rutland. Disp. to hold another benef., with or 2 with or without cure, without the above. 7s 2d.

pp. 45–46

17 Tho. Swetnam, v. of Bradburne, Cov. & Lich. dio., chapl. to Rob., Bp of Down & Connor, Ireland. Disp. to hold another benef. with or without cure, with or 2 without the above; permut. cl. 7s 2d.

p. 46

19 Jo. Fyssher, B.Th, v. of Milton, Oxford dio., chapl. to Ld Jo. Russell, K.G., Ld Privy Seal. Disp. to hold 2 additional benefices with the above, or 3 others with or without cure, 2 of which may be par. churches; permut. cl. 10s.

20 Ant. Fortescue & Kath. Poole, both of gentle birth, Chich. dio. Disp. for marriage in any ch., chapel, or oratory, without banns, & by any suitable pr. 6s 8d.

p. 47

21 Jo. Symson, pr., r. of Hanby, York dio. Disp. to hold a benef. with or without cure with the above, if the latter does not yield over £8 p.a.; permut. cl. 4s 5d.

20 Ric. Wotton, pr., r. of Hope Solars, Heref. dio. Disp. to hold another benef. with or without cure with the above if it does not yield over £8 p.a.; permut. cl. 4s 5d.

May 22 Jo. Garrett, sch., Linc. dio. Disp. to take all h.o., including pr.'s orders, outside the statutory times, & from any bp. 3s 4d.

p. 48

  20 Tho. Moke, r. of Cardynham, Ex. dio., v. of Hatfield, Lond. dio., Qn's chapl. Disp. to hold another benef. with or without cure with the above, or 2 others without; permut. cl. 8s 10d.

  22 Rob. Tanfilde & Wilgeforda Fitzherbert, both of gentle birth, Westminster dio. Disp. for marriage in Wilgeforda's par. ch. during the prohibited times, & by any pr. 3s 4d.

  23 Also disp. for marriage in any ch., chapel or oratory, without banns, but during the statutory times, by any suitable pr. 6s 8d.

p. 49

Apr. 28 Simon Atkyns, B.Th., r. of Sutcombe, Ex. dio. Disp. to hold another benef. with or 2 with or without cure, without the above. 7s 2d.

Feb. 1 Emery Tuckfilde, Kg's chapl. Disp. to hold another benef. with or without cure, with the 2 he asserts that he already holds by disp. 8s 10d.

p. 50

June 1 Rob. Spenley & Agnes Wryght, of the par. of St Vedast, London, peculiar of Cant. dio. Disp. for marriage in the bride's par. ch. without banns, during the prohibited times, & by any suitable pr. 6s 8d.

p. 51

1543 Oct. 5 Edm. Weston, B.Cn.L., r. of Upton Pine, Ex. dio. Disp. to hold another benef. with or 2 with or without cure, without the above; permut. cl. 7s 2d.

1544 May 23 Jo. Warner, M.D., r. of Houghton, Peterborough dio., Kg's chapl. Disp. to hold another benef. with or 2 or 3 others with or without cure without the above; not more than 2 of the latter may be par. churches. 10s.

p. 52

June 4 Jo. Brandesbye, D.Th. Disp. to hold another benef. with or without cure together with the rectories of Byforthe, York dio., & Kir(k)by Wiske, Chester dio. 8s 10d.

   Ant. Lysley, M.A., pr., r. of Bonyng (*sic*), in the March of Calais, Therouanne dio., chapl. to Jo., Ld Braye. Disp. to hold another benef. with or 2 with or without cure without the above. 7s 2d.

p. 53

May 26 Emery Tuckfylde, Kg's chapl. Disp. to hold a 3rd benef. with or without cure with the 3 he already holds; permut. cl. 8s 10d.

June 4 Rob. Chechestre & Ann Philipps, both of gentle birth, of London. Disp. for marriage in Ann's par. ch. without banns, & by any suitable pr. 3s 4d.

p. 54

June 14 Rob. Essington & Jane Cawet, of London. Similar disp. 3s 4d.

Wm Dormer & Eliz. Scryven, of London. Similar disp. 3s 4d.

15 Rob. Byrde, B.Cn.L., r. of Melbury Abbas, Bristol dio. Disp. to hold an additional benef. with or 2 with or without cure without the above. 7s 2d.

p. 55

May 20 Tho. Vernon, & Eleanor Sherley, both of gentle birth, Cov. & Lich. dio. Disp. for marriage in Eleanor's par. ch. within the prohibited times & by any suitable pr. 3s 4d.

June 12 Jas Kempe & Ann Powle, both of gentle birth, of London. Disp. for marriage in the bride's par ch. without banns, & by any suitable pr. 3s 4d.

18 Ric. Pronest & Gillian Berington, widow, Winton dio. Disp. for marriage in the bride's par. ch., the banns read once, & by any suitable pr. 2s 2d.

p. 56

19 Nich. Hobbes, M.A., v. of Cherington, Sarum dio., chapl. to Paul, Bp of Bristol. Disp. to hold another benef. with or 2 with or without cure, without the above. 7s 2d.

14 Chris. Pacey, Bristol dio., student at Oxford University. Disp. to take h.o., celebrate the sacraments, & hold benefices despite deformity of the right foot, which is short & thin. 3s 4d.

p. 57

19 Owen Oglethorpe, M.Th., Kg's chapl. Disp. to hold a 3rd benef. with or without cure; permut. cl. 8s 10d.

21 Rob. Brokelbye & Mabel Harney, of gentle birth, Lond. dio. Disp. for marriage in the bride's par. ch. without banns & by a suitable pr. 3s 4d.

p. 58

22 Nich. Calveley & Alice Gybbes, Westminster dio. Disp. for marriage in the bride's par. ch., the banns read once, & by any suitable pr. 2s 2d.

13 Jo. Longlonde, B.A., r. of Stanton St John, Oxford dio., chapl. to Jo., Bp of Lincoln. Disp. to hold another benef. with or 2 with or without cure without the above. 7s 2d.

24 Jo. Holusyer, pr., r. of Gravenhurst, Linc. dio. Disp. to hold an additional benef. if the above does not yield over £8 p.a., or another with or without cure without these. 4s 5d.

p. 59

25 Jo. Standishe, D.Th., r. of St Andrew Undershaft, Lond. dio. Disp. to hold a benef. with or 2 others, with or without cure without the above. 7s 2d.

June 26 Stephen Yevan, pr., v. of St Harmon, St David's dio. Disp. to hold an additional benef. with or without cure, if the above does not yield over £8 p.a. 4s 5d.

27 Jo. Stoks, pr., v. of North Collingham, York dio., chapl. to Jo., Bp of Peterborough. Disp. to hold another benef. with, or 2 others with or without cure without the above; permut. cl. 7s 2d.

p. 60

Tho. Baudry, Linc. dio. Disp. to take all h.o. from any bp. 3s 4d.

May 2 Wm Sanders, r. of Stoke Gaylard, Bristol dio. Disp. to hold another benef. with the above if it does not yield over £8 p.a.; or another benef. with or without cure without it. 4s 5d.

Apr. 12 Hugh Wynnarde, pr., r. of Stradishall, Norw. dio., chapl. to Ld Tho. Audley, K.G., Ld Chancellor. Disp. to hold another benef. with, or 2 with or without cure without the above. 7s 2d.

p. 61
July 1 Jo. Conyers, pr., r. of Burgh(am), Carl. dio., chapl. to Hy, Earl of Cumberland. Disp. to hold another benef. with, or 2 with or without cure without the above; permut. cl. 7s 2d.

2 Adam Stydulff & Kath. Kingesley, Chich. dio. Disp. for marriage in any ch., chapel or oratory, without banns, & by any suitable pr. 6s 8d.

Jo. Stydulffe & Constance Kingesley. Similar disp. 6s 8d.

p. 62
Feb. 28 Nich. Mason, B.Cn.L., v. of Wembdon, Wells dio., chapl. to Jo., Bp of Exeter. Disp. to hold a benef. with the above or 2 with or without cure without. 7s 2d.

July 2 Jo. Weyvant & Isabel Whasshe, of Westminster. Disp. for marriage in the bride's par. ch. without banns & by any suitable pr. 3s 4d.

4 Ric. Edwarde, subdcn, Cov. & Lich. dio. Disp. to take all h.o. outside the statutory times from any bp. 4s 5d.

p. 63
5 Rob. Squyre & Joan Bradforde, widow, of London. Disp. for marriage in the bride's par. ch. without banns & by any suitable pr. 3s 4d.

6 Roger Boydell, M.A., r. of Cleavehanger, Ex. dio. Disp. for non-res. for 6 months on account of near-blindness & other infirmities; his duties to be deputed to a suitable pr. 3s 4d.

8 Hugh Haywarde & Marg. Hornebolt, Westminster dio. Disp. for marriage in Marg.'s par. ch. without banns. 3s 4d.

p. 64

July 8 Ric. Marshall, B.C.L., r. of Stainton-le-Street, Durham dio. chapl. to Ly Ann Conyers, widow of Chris. Conyers, Ld Stainton. Disp. to hold a benef. with, or 2 others with or without cure without the above. 7s 2d.

10 Wm Hand, v. of Gt Shelford, Ely dio., chapl. to his brother. Disp. to hold a benef. with or 2 others without the above. 7s 2d.

17 Simon Nappe, pr., r. of Wentworth, Ely dio., chapl. to Ly Mary, Countess of Sussex, widow. Disp. to hold a benef. with or 2 others with or without cure without the above. 7s 2d.

p. 65

3 Tho. Chippinge, B.A., chapl. to Wm, Bp of St David's, r. of St Mary Magdalene's, London. Disp. to hold another benef. with or 2 others with or without cure without the above. 7s 2d.

22 Tho. Salkyld, Carl. dio., student at Cambridge. Disp. to take all h.o. outside the statutory times, from any bp. 3s 4d.

p. 66

21 Hy Tyndall, B.Th., v. of Wellow, Wells dio. Disp. to hold a benef. with or 2 others with or without cure, without the above; permut. cl. 7s 2d.

23 Hy Baxter & Eliz. Stock. Disp. for marriage in the bride's par. ch. without banns & by any pr. 3s 4d.

pp. 66–67

29 Gabriel Power, M.A., v. of Ivinghoe, Linc. dio. Disp. to hold another benef. with or any other 2 with or without cure without the above; permut. cl. 7s 2d.

p. 67

Jo. Hunte, B.C.L. Disp. to hold a 3rd benef. with or without cure with 2 benefices with cure already held by disp.; permut. cl. 8s 10d.

Rob. Tuckefilde, r. of Holy Trinity par., Ex. dio. (sic). Disp. to hold another benef. with, or 2 others with or without cure without the above; permut. cl. 7s 2d.

p. 68

31 Jo. Aynesey, v. of Tuxford, York dio. Disp. to hold another benef. with, or 2 benefices with or without cure without the above; permut. cl. 7s 2d.

Aug. 4 Chris. Gambull, sch., Linc. dio. Disp. to take all h.o. outside the statutory times, from any bp. 3s 4d.

6 Peter Dormer & Ann Crispe, both of gentle birth, Peterborough dio. Disp. for marriage in the bride's par. ch. without banns & by any suitable chaplain. 3s 4d.

p. 69

Aug. 14 Ant. Stapleton of the Inner Temple, London, & Joan Burlace, widow, of St Martin Vintry, London. Disp. for marriage in the bride's par. ch. without banns & by any suitable chaplain. 3s 4d.

18 Edm. Mervyne, M.A., Winton dio. Disp. to take h.o. on any days from any bp. 3s 4d.

p. 70

21 Nich. Williamson, B.C.L., r. of Wickham, Durham dio., chapl. to the Bp of Carlisle. Disp. to hold a benef. with or 2 others with or without cure without the above. 7s 2d.

27 Wm Newton & Agnes Sutton, both of gentle birth, Lond. dio. Disp. for marriage in any ch., chapel, or oratory without banns & by any suitable chaplain. 6s 8d.

p. 71

26 Hugh Gwyenoke, St David's dio., student at Oxford. Disp. to take all h.o., 2 on the same day, outside the statutory times, from any bp & afterwards to minister at the altar. 3s 4d.

Hugh Phris, Bangor dio., student at Oxford. Disp. to take h.o. outside the statutory times, 2 on the same day, & from any bp. 3s 4d.

pp. 72–73

July 21 Nich. Wutton, D.C.L., Kg's chapl., Dean of Canterbury & holder of various other benefices, Kg's orator with the Emperor. Disp. (given in full) to hold an additional benef. with or without cure not exceeding the value of £500 p.a.; permut. cl. (Also subscribed by Richard Lyell.) No fee mentioned.

pp. 73–74

June 28 Geo. Carewe, Kg's chapl., archdcn of Totnes & holder of various other benefices. Disp. (given in full) to hold any other benef. not exceeding the value of 100 marks p.a. No fee mentioned.

p. 75

Aug. 30 Sir Wm Forman, alderman of the city of London, & Blanche Palmer, widow of London. Disp. for marriage in any ch., chapel, or oratory, without banns & by a suitable pr. 6s 8d.

31 Ric. Marsche, r. of St Pancras, London, chapl. to Chas, Duke of Suffolk. Disp. to hold 2 benefices; non-res. cl. 8s 6d.

Sept. 1 Wm Dix[on] & Denise Neele, both of gentle birth, Lond. dio. Disp. for marriage in the bride's par. ch. without banns & by any suitable pr. 3s 4d.

p. 76

6 Rob. Watson, M.A., r. of Bradley, Linc. dio. Disp. to hold another benef. with the above, or 2 with or without cure without; permut. cl. 7s 2d.

Sept. 8 Jo. Hinde, B.A., Norw. dio. Disp. to take h.o. outside the statutory times, from any bp. 3s 4d.

9 Wm Porter, B.A., Winton dio. Disp. to practise as public notary. 4s 5d.

p. 77

11 Tho. Wallessey, M.A., r. of Denham, Linc. dio. Disp. to hold another benef. with the above or 2 others without it. 7s 2d.

Chris. Alnett, dcn, Oxford dio. Disp. to take pr.'s orders on any day from any bp, outside the statutory times. 3s 4d.

13 Rob. Sharpe, acol., Lich. dio. Disp. to take dcn's & pr.'s orders on the same day outside the statutory times & from any bp. 4s 5d.

p. 78

16 Jo. Wilford, citizen & alderman of London, & Mary Percye, widow, Lond. dio. Disp. for marriage in the bride's par. ch. without banns & by any suitable pr. 3s 4d.

Hy Judde & Mabel Ranff, of London. Disp. for marriage in the bride's par. ch. or in any chapel, without banns & by any suitable pr. 6s 8d.

18 Jo. Fitzherbert, esq., & Marg. Poole, Westminster dio. Disp. for marriage in any ch., chapel, or oratory & by a suitable pr. 6s 8d.

p. 79

Hy Wigstead, M.A., v. of Sidbury, Ex. dio., chapl. to the Bp of St David's. Disp. to hold another benef. with or 2 others with or without cure without the above. 7s 2d.

19 Rob. Cappes, Norw. dio., & Joan Underhill, Westminster dio. Disp. for marriage without banns by any suitable pr. 3s 4d.

p. 80

20 Tho. Huett, B.A., r. of St Michael's, Worcester, chapl. to ——? Cancelled disp. to hold another benef. with or without cure if the above does not yield over £8 p.a.

22 Ralph Jonson, of Rainham, Kent, & Thomasina Copinger, of All Saints par., Rochester, both of gentle birth. Disp. for marriage outside the statutory times without banns & in the bride's ch. 3s 4d.

25 Nich. Hokar, B.C.L., Winton dio. Creation as notary & tabellion. 4s 5d.

Wm Wright, B.Th., v. of Gt Wykeham, Linc. dio., chapl. to Jo., Bp of Lincoln. Disp. to hold another benef. with or 2 with or without cure without the above. 7s 2d.

p. 81

Sept.? Clement Parrett, B.Th., r. of Farthingstone, Northants, Peterborough dio. Disp. to hold another benef. with or 2 others with or without cure, without the above; permut. cl. 7s 2d.

29 Wm Wydington & Brigitt Fortescu, both of gentle birth, & of London. Licence (sic) for marriage by any suitable pr. in the bride's par. ch. without banns. 3s 4d.

Jas Worsley & Anne Oglander, both of gentle birth, & of Norw. dio. Disp. for marriage in the bride's par. ch. without banns & by any suitable pr. 3s 4d.

30 Hugh Grene & Anne Grey, of London. Licence for marriage without banns in the bride's par. ch. 3s 4d.

p. 82

Oct. 2 Owen Oglethorpe, D.Th., Kg's chapl. Disp. to hold another benef., with or without cure, with 3 others, for which he already has a disp. 8s 10d.

11 Jo. Cresse, acol., Linc. dio. Disp. to take all h.o. from any bp, & outside the statutory times. 3s 4d.

12 Jo. Pyerson, M.A., v. of Stanton Harcourt, Oxford dio., chapl. to Rob., Bp of Oxford. Disp. to hold another benef. with the above, or 2 others with or without cure without it; permut. cl. 7s 2d.

Apr. 24 Jo. Grannte, v. of Llanblethyan, Lland. dio., chapl. to Wm, Earl of Essex. Concession (sic) to hold another benef. with the above or 2 others with cure without it. 7s 2d.

p. 83

Oct. 13 Ralph Rokeby & Dorothy Danby, both of gentle birth & Chester dio. Licence for marriage in any ch., chapel, or oratory without banns & by a suitable pr. 6s 8d.

14 Hugh Woodward, pr., r. of Holkby, York dio. Disp. to hold an additional benef. as the above does not yield over £8 p.a.; permut. cl. 4s 5d.

13 Jo. Holbache & Eliz. Danbyscourte, widow, Cov. & Lich. dio. Disp. for marriage in the bride's par. ch. without banns, & by any suitable pr. 3s 4d.

12 Wm Myrycke & Mary Busyfylde, widow, of London. Disp. for marriage without banns in any ch., chapel, or oratory by any suitable pr. 3s 4d.

p. 84

Feb. 25 Tho. Belhouse, r. of West Hanningfield, Lond. dio., chapl. to Eliz., Countess of Kildare. Disp. to hold another benef. with or 2 others with or without cure without the above. 7s 2d.

Oct. 14 Wm Neve, Norw. dio. Creation as notary or tabellion. 4s 5d.

16 Rob. Graggs, pr., v. choral in York Minster. Disp. to hold a benef. with this office, which does not yield over £8 p.a. 4s 5d.

1539 Sept. 30 Jo. Hemsley, formerly Observant fr., of Richmond. Concession (*sic*) to leave his profession as a religious, & hold any benef. 'Gratis quia soluta est domus.'

1544 Oct. 18 Edm. Saynt Quintin, acol., York dio. Disp. to take h.o. & 2 on the same day from any bp, outside the statutory times. 3s 4d.

p. 85

3 Jo. Gregory, literate, Cant. dio. Creation (*sic*) as notary or tabellion. No fee.

18 Jo. God & Eliz. Broke, Lond. dio. Disp. for marriage by any suitable pr. without banns, in the bride's par. ch. 3s 4d.

20 Rob. ap Rice, esq., & Ly Christine Samcoles, widow, Linc. dio. Licence for marriage by any suitable pr. without banns, in the bride's par. ch. 3s 4d.

23 Tho. Wylley, v. of Yoxford, Norw. dio. Disp. to hold an additional benef. as the above does not yield over £8 p.a. 4s 5d.

Humfrey Wever, r. of Morestead, Winton dio. Similar disp. 4s 5d.

p. 86

Ric. Haidon, M.A., r. of St John's, Anthon(y), Ex. dio., chapl. to Jo., Bp of Exeter. Disp. to hold another benef. with or 2 with or without cure without the above; permut. cl. 7s 2d.

22 Tho. Shakylton, sch., Norw. dio. Disp. to take all h.o. from any bp outside the statutory times. 3s 4d.

27 Wm Kyngsmyll, D.Th., r. of Aldershot, Winton dio., Kg's chapl. Disp. to hold 2 benefices with the above or 3 others without it; permut. cl. 14s 9d.

1 Tho. Huett, B.A., v. of Llanarmon-Mawr, St David's dio., chapl. to the Bp of St David's. Disp. to hold a benef. with or 2 others with or without cure without the above. 7s 2d.

p. 87

3 Rob. Wellys, B.Th., v. of Crosthwaite, Carl. dio. Disp. to hold another benef. with or 2 with or without cure without the above. 7s 2d.

Nov. 5 Ric. Fawkan, Winton dio., & Frances Chayney, Sarum dio., both of gentle birth. Licence for marriage in any ch., chapel, or oratory by any suitable pr. 3s 4d.

Nov. 6 Jo. Horner & Mercell Holte, widow, Lond. dio. Licence for marriage without banns. 3s 4d.

Ralph Alway & Mary Bylby, Lond. dio. Licence for marriage without banns. 3s 4d.

9 Wm Dewvet & Michiell Wyngham, widow, Westminster dio. Similar licence. 3s 4d.

p. 88

7 Jo. Mathew *alias* Wyne, formerly canon of Haughmond. Capacity to hold a benef. Fee 'nihil'.

8 Jo. Wyne *alias* Mathewe (*sic*), sch., St Asaph dio. Disp. to take all h.o. from any bp despite defect of birth, & to hold a benef.

11 Jo. Alen & Marg. Knyghton, Westminster dio. Disp. for marriage in the bride's par. ch. by any suitable pr. & without banns. 3s 4d.

12 Jo. Symes, M.A., v. of Sidmouth, Ex. dio., chapl. to Jo., Bp of Exeter. Disp. to hold any 2 benefices; permut. cl. 7s 2d.

p. 89

6 Nich. Langford, esq., & Kath. Holes *alias* Holls, Linc. dio. Disp. for marriage in the bride's par. ch. the banns read once, but during the prohibited times. 3s 4d.

14 Chris. Treder, v. of Wood Ditton, Norw. dio., chapl. to Wm Bp of Norwich. Disp. to hold another benef. with, or 2 others with or without cure without the above; permut. cl. 7s 2d.

15 Tho. Myrfeld, v. of Moutnessing ('King Mouteney'), Lond. dio., chapl. to Mary, Countess of Sussex. Licence to hold 2 benefices with cure. 7s 2d.

18 Jo. Webster, acol., Peterborough dio. Licence to take all h.o. outside the statutory times, from any bp. 3s 4d.

15 Wm More, esq., & Kath. Collects, widow, Lond. dio. Licence for marriage without banns & in the bride's par. ch. 3s 4d.

p. 90

20 Ric. Lyster, sch., York dio. Licence to take h.o. from any bp outside the statutory times. 3s 4d.

18 Rob. Pownde, B.Cn.L., v. of Sutton Courtenay, Sarum dio. Disp. to hold another benef. with or 2 with or without cure without the above. 7s 2d.

21 Wm Polarde, subdcn, Linc. dio. Disp. to take dcn's & pr.'s orders on the same day & from any bp, outside the statuory times. 4s 5d.

20 Wm Sebrande & Agnes Lavell, Westminster dio. Disp. for marriage without banns in the bride's par. ch. 3s 4d.

Nov. 21 Wm Cooke, esq., & Ly Jane Harleston, widow. Disp. for marriage in any ch., chapel, or oratory without banns. 3s 4d; 3s 4d.

22 Tho. Norton & Eliz. Bucfeld, widow, Lond. dio. Similar licence. 3s 4d; 3s 4d.

p. 91

23 Tho. Dryhurst, literate, St Asaph dio. Creation as public notary or tabellion. 4s 5d.

24 Jo. Lamyng, r. of Anderby, Linc. dio., chapl. to Sir Wm Windsor. Disp. to hold another benef. with the above or any 2 others with or without cure without; permut. cl. 7s 2d.

25 Hy Mody & Ann Laurence, both of gentle birth, Lond. dio. Licence for marriage in the bride's par. ch. without banns & during the prohibited times. 3s 9d.

10 Ric. Lyster, sch., York dio. Disp. to take h.o. without l.d. 2s 2d.

27 Morgan Lloyd & Eliz. Elys, Westminster dio. Licence for marriage without banns in any ch., chapel, or oratory. 3s 4d; 3s 4d.

Tho. Wyndesor & Dorothy Dacre, both of gentle birth, Lond. dio. Licence for marriage by any suitable chaplain, the banns read once, & in any ch., chapel, or oratory. 2s 2d; 3s 4d.

Jo. Gryffyth, subdcn, Lland. dio. Disp. to take dcn's & pr.'s orders on the same day from any bp. 4s 5d.

p. 92

Dec. 4 Rob. Whitefeld & Agnes Brownege, widow, of Gravesend, Roch. dio. Disp. for marriage in the above par. ch. within the prohibited times. 3s 4d.

2 Jo. Coseworth & Dorothy Hyll, Lond. dio. Disp. for marriage within the prohibited times. 3s 4d.

6 Geo. Broke, student in Venice, natural & legitimized son of Geo. Broke, Ld Cobham. Disp. to hold the status & privileges of a B.A. 'Concessa per litteras Rmi. dni. Archiepiscopi.' 5s.

Roger Gunter & Ursula Dennyng, Winton dio. Licence for marriage in the bride's par. ch. without banns. 3s 4d.

Geo. Chepyngdale, literate, York dio. Creation as a public notary or tabellion. 4s 5d.

p. 93

3 Edw. Carywitham & Dorothy Gainsford, Westminster dio. Licence for marriage in the bride's par. ch. without banns & within the prohibited times. 3s 9d.

6 Francis Browne & Dorothy Villars, Linc. dio. Licence for marriage in the bride's par. ch. without banns & within the prohibited times. 3s 9d.

Dec. 8 Tho. Rous & Kath. Hansard, Lond. dio. Disp. for marriage in any ch., chapel, or oratory, during the prohibited times, the banns read once. 3s 9d.

11 Jo. Warley, citizen & merchant of London. Licence to eat meat & milk foods during Lent & other prohibited times on account of pains in the head & other members. 3s 4d.

13 Ambrose Blackman *alias* Barker, & Gertrude Wythers, Lond. dio. Disp. for marriage in the bride's par. ch. without banns & during the prohibited times. 3s 9d.

p. 94

15 Wm Smyth, pr., v. of Green, Cant. dio., chapl. to Hy, Bp of Rochester. Disp. to hold another benef. with or 2 without the above. 7s 2d.

14 Rob. Barker & Margerie Pawnfott, Peterborough dio. Licence for marriage in the bride's par. ch. without banns. 3s 4d.

13 Rob. Marshe, v. of Upchurch, Cant. dio. Disp. to hold another benef. with or 2 others with or without cure without the above; permut. cl. 7s 2d.

p. 95

17 Rob. Howe, v. of Newington, Cant. dio., chapl. to Ld. Edw. Clinton, of Clinton & Folstone. Disp. to hold another benef. with or 2 others without the above. 7s 2d.

29 Nich. Bickeforde, B.A., Ex. dio. Disp. to take all h.o. from any bp & without l.d. from his diocesan bp. 2s. 2d.

20 Jo. Faye & Joan Jenkyns, widow, Bristol dio. Disp. for marriage in the bride's par. ch. without banns. 3s 4d.

p. 96

20 Tho. Manbye, v. of Haugham, Linc. dio., chapl. to Sir Tho. Stanley, Ld Mounteagle. Disp. to hold another benef. with or 2 others with or without cure without the above. 7s 2d.

21 Tho. Heskethe & Alice Holcrofte, Westminster dio. Disp. for marriage in the bride's par. ch. within the prohibited times. 3s 4d.

p. 97

26 Jo. Cartemele & Emma Pettingher, of London. Disp. for marriage within the prohibited times. 3s 4d.

27 Disp. for the above to be married during the prohibited times, without banns, & in any ch. or oratory. 6s 8d.

1545 Jan. 2 Nich. Cotman & Barbara Corbet. Disp. for marriage in the bride's par. ch. & during the prohibited times. 3s 4d.

7 Ric. Caldewall, M.A., Fellow of Brasenose Coll., Oxford. Disp. to take h.o. outside the statutory times & from any bp. 3s 4d.

p. 98

Jan. 13 Tho. Smyth, acol., York dio. Disp. to take h.o. outside the statutory times. 3s 4d.

14 Ric. Franncis & Marg. Marchall, Norw. dio. Disp. for marriage without banns in the bride's par. ch. & by any suitable pr. 3s 4d.

Tho. Danyell & Joan Cowlye, widow, Lond. dio. Licence for marriage in any ch., chapel, or oratory without banns. 3s 4d; 3s 4d.

12 Edm. Freke, dcn, Lond. dio. Disp. to take pr.'s orders on any day from any bp. 3s 4d.

17 Rob. Makerell & Alice Auden, Winton dio. Licence for marriage without banns & in the bride's par. ch. 3s 4d.

p. 99

Hy Godderd, Cov. & Lich. dio. Disp. to take all h.o. without l.d. from his diocesan & outside the statutory times. 3s 4d; 2s 2d.

16 Wm Wood & Marg. Pye, Cant. dio. Licence for marriage by any suitable pr., the banns read once. 2s 2d.

Wm Edge & Jane Faux. Similar licence. 2s 2d.

19 Brian Byrte & Alice Walkar, Westminster dio. Licence for marriage in the bride's par. ch., without banns. 3s 4d.

17 Jo. Taylor & Alice Jackson, Westminster dio. Similar licence. 3s 4d.

Ralph Astrye & Alice Rotherham, widow, Linc. dio. Similar licence. 3s 4d.

21 Jo. Hyde & Marg. Hayes, Westminster dio. Similar licence. 3s 4d.

p. 100

Ric. Whitfeld & Marg. White, widow, Lond. dio. Similar licence. 3s 4d.

22 Silvester Blinde & Alice Gawge, Norw. dio. Licence for marriage in the bride's par. ch. within the prohibited time, the banns read once. 3s 4d.

24 Wm Atkynson, dcn, York dio. Disp. to take pr.'s orders without l.d. from his diocesan bp, & outside the statutory times. 3s 4d; 2s 2d.

11 Arthur Dedicot & Emma Butler, Lond. dio. Licence for marriage, the banns read once, in the bride's par. ch. & by a suitable pr. 2s 2d.

10 Jo. Blaxston, B.C.L., chapl. to Jo., Bp of Ex., v. of St Peter's, Hereford. Disp. to hold another benef. with or 2 without the above. 10s.

p. 101

Jan. 23 Jo. Welby & Eliz. Mannyng, Westminster dio. Licence for marriage in the bride's par. ch., the banns read once. 2s 2d.

24 Tho. Stubbes & Eliz. Gray, widow, Cant. dio. Licence for marriage without banns, in the bride's par. ch. 3s 4d.

Jo. Purvey & Eliz. Edwards, Westminster dio. Licence for marriage without banns, in the bride's par. ch. 3s 4d.

Ant. Williams & Kath. Melys, of London. Licence for marriage without banns, in any ch., chapel, or oratory. 3s 4d; 3s 4d.

1539 Dec. 1 Ralph Dey, O.P., formerly of Norwich. Capacity 'in communi forma'. 'Gratis quia soluta est domus.'

1545 Jan. 25 Jo. Murpham & Ann Mannyng, widow, of London. Disp. for marriage without banns & in the bride's par. ch. 3s 4d.

p. 102

27 Hy Jenkyns & Eliz. Mallam, widow, Winton dio. Licence for marriage, the banns read once. 2s 2d.

Simon Cleborn & Ann Rone, widow, Westminster dio. Licence for marriage without banns, in the bride's par. ch. 3s 4d.

Wm Morgan & Eliz. Fyshe, widow, Peterborough dio. Licence for marriage without banns, in the bride's par. ch. 3s 4d.

28 Ric. Rushell, sch., Chester dio. Disp. to take h.o. outside the statutory times & from any bp. 3s 4d.

Augustine Dudley, sch., Peterborough dio. Licence to take h.o. outside the statutory times & from any bp. 3s 4d.

Jo. Wyat & Agnes Sharpe, widow, Westminster dio. Licence for marriage without banns, in the bride's par. ch. 3s 4d.

Geoffrey Newton & Grace Berycke, of London. Similar licence. 3s 4d.

Jo. Cooke & Eliz. Felde, of London. Similar licence. 3s 4d.

p. 103

20 Wm Rokeby, B.C.L., dcn, Chester dio. Disp. to take pr.'s orders on any day outside the statutory times. 3s 4d.

29 Rob. Grace, subdcn, Cov. & Lich. dio. Licence to take dcn's & pr.'s orders on any day outside the statutory times. 4s 5d.

30 Chas Manneryng & Agnes Burleton, Westminster dio. Licence for marriage without banns, in the bride's par. ch. 3s 4d.

Feb. 1 Lawrence Hovett, pr., v. of St Dogmaels, St David's dio. Disp. to hold another benef. with the above, which does not yield over £8 p.a. 4s 5d.

p. 104

Feb. 2 Roger Lovell, v. of Norton Bavent, Sarum dio. Similar disp. 4s 5d.

3 Maurice Denys, esq., & Eliz. Statham, widow, of London. Licence for marriage in the bride's par. ch. during the prohibited times. 3s 4d.

4 Licence for the above to be married without banns, in any ch., chapel, or oratory, & by any suitable chaplain. 6s 8d.

Jo. Burley, esq., & Sibil Skydmore, widow, Linc. dio. Licence for marriage in any ch., chapel, or oratory, within the prohibited times. 3s 4d; 3s 4d.

p. 105

7 Jo. Hache & Ann Taber, Lond. dio. Licence for marriage without banns, in the bride's par. ch. & during the prohibited times. 3s 9d.

Ric. Cherley & Marg. Taylfere, of London. Similar licence for marriage but with the banns read. 3s 4d.

8 Ralph Stepneth & Joan Crowche, widow, Lond. dio. Similar licence without banns. 3s 9d.

10 Philip Cavercannte & Kath. Martyn, of London. Similar licence. 3s 9d.

11 Rob. Gathe & Ann Knyght, of St Clement Danes' par., London. Similar licence. 3s 9d.

13 Wm Alenson, acol., Durham dio. Disp. to take h.o. outside the statutory period from any bp. 3s 4d.

p. 106

1544 Apr. 3 Rob. Garrett, pr. & chanter of a third part of the chantry of St Anne, in St Paul's, London. Disp. to hold another benef. with or 2 other benefices or chaplaincies to noblemen etc. without the above, which does not yield more than £8; permut. & non-res. cl. 4s 5d.

1545 Feb. 3 Rob. Gwyns & Dorothy Swanne, Roch. dio. Licence for marriage in the bride's par. ch. within the prohibited times. 3s 4d.

16 Humfrey Wylson & Joan Hicks, of Stepney, Westminster dio. Disp. for marriage without banns, outside the statutory times & in the bride's par. ch. 3s 9d.

p. 107

18 Nich. Bacon & his wife Jane. Disp. to eat meat during Lent & at other times of the year, on medical advice. 3s 4d.

Feb. 23 Ric. Rutter & Alice Radley, of London. Disp. for marriage without banns, outside the statutory times, & in the bride's par. ch. 3s 9d.

8 Tho. Robynson, Chester dio. Concession to practise as a public notary & tabellion. 4s 5d.

26 Ric. Sutton, sch., Carl. dio. Disp. to take all h.o. outside the statutory times, from any bp, & afterwards to minister at the altar. 3s 4d.

p. 108

Mar. 7 Benjamin Wolley & Agnes Ager, of London. Disp. for marriage in the bride's par. ch. without banns, within the prohibited times though not between Passion Sunday & Whitsun, & by any suitable pr. 3s 9d.

1 Tho. Alyne, B.Th., v. of Grantchester, Ely dio. Disp. to hold a benef. with cure with the above, or any 2 without it; permut. cl. 7s 2d.

7 Jo. Bowdon, pr., r. of Nafford with the chapel of Birlingham, Worcester dio., chapl. to the Bp of Llandaff. Disp. to hold another benef. with or without cure with or 2 without the above. 7s 2d.

p. 109

9 Benjamin Wolley & Agnes Ager, of London. Disp. for marriage in any ch., chapel, or oratory. 3s 4d.

Feb. 17 Jo. Husse & his wife, of Calais. Disp. to eat meat during Lent & at other times during his illness (kidney trouble). 3s 4d.

Mar. 11 Ric. Bydwell & Cecily Pasmere, widow, Ex. or Oxford dio. Disp. for marriage in any ch., chapel, or oratory, without banns. 6s 8d.

p. 110

10 Roger Sterky, of London. Disp. to eat meat during Lent & at other prohibited times during his illness. 3s 4d.

12 Jo. Olyver, D.C.L. Disp. *motu proprio* by the Archbp for prorogation of his taking pr.'s orders for 3 yrs, although he holds benefices. 3s 9d.

p. 111

16 Wm Wigginton, merchant, of London. Disp. to eat meat during Lent & at other prohibited times. 3s 4d.

17 Ric. Fulmerston, esq., & his wife Alice. Disp. to eat meat during Lent & at other prohibited times. 3s 4d.

16 Jas Francis & Alice Pylsdon, of (Bishops) Stortford, Lond. dio. Disp. for marriage in the bride's par. ch. within the prohibited times, though not between Passion Sunday & Whitsun. 3s 4d.

p. 112
Mar. 18 Disp. for the above to be married in any ch., chapel, or oratory, without banns. 6s 8d.

10 Sir Richard Long & his wife, Ly Marg. Disp. to eat meat during Lent & at other prohibited times, during his illness. 3s 4d.

20 Simon Bedill & Marg. Litell, widow, Cov. & Lich. dio. Disp. for marriage in the bride's par. ch. without banns. 3s 4d.

p. 113
Feb. 10 Mary, Duchess of Richmond. Disp., also for 2 guests at her table, to eat meat during Lent & at other prohibited times. 3s 4d.

Mar. 26 Tho. Massy, pr., v. of Eisy & Exton, Sarum dio., chapl. to Edw., Earl of Hertford. Disp. to hold another benef. with or any 2 others with or without cure, without the above; permut. cl. 7s 2d.

p. 114
Jo. Tuchener, pr., M.A., r. of Ashley, Winton dio. Disp. to hold a benef. with or without cure, with the above, which does not yield over £8 p.a.; permut. cl. 4s 5d.

3 Jo. Dene, B.Th., Kg's chapl. Disp. to hold a 3rd benef. with or without cure with 2 others with cure; permut. cl. 8s 10d.

p. 115
28 Roger Smythe & Frances Gryffyn, Peterborough dio. Disp. for marriage in any ch., chapel, or oratory, without banns & by any suitable pr., within the prohibited times. 7s 2d.

25 Jo. Daye, B.Th., r. of Waltham-on-the-Wold, Linc. dio., chapl. to Hy, Marquess of Dorset. Disp. to hold another benef. with the above, or 2 others, with or without cure, without it; permut. cl. 7s 2d.

p. 116
Apr. 1 Jo. Joseph, B.Th., r. of St Martin's, Worcester, chapl. to the Archbp of Cant. Disp. to hold another benef. with or 2 others without the above; permut. cl. 7s 2d.

9 Ric. Willyams, M.A., v. of Letcombe Regis, Sarum dio., chapl. to Tho. Ld Sandys. Similar disp. 7s 2d.

8 Jo. Dicconson, r. of Barrowby, Linc. dio., chapl. to Chas, Duke of Suffolk. Similar disp. 7s 2d.

11 Wm Smyth, gent. & Joan Bettres, widow, Norw. dio. Disp. for marriage in any ch. or oratory without banns & by a suitable pr. 6s 8d.

p. 117
10 Roland Cottney, r. of Starston, Norw. dio., chapl. to Tho., Duke of Norfolk. Similar disp. 7s 2d.

Apr. 11 Edm. Wolfe, r. of Stoke Talmage, Oxford dio., chapl. to the Bp of Oxford. Similar disp. 7s 2d.

15 Nich. Calver, v. of Teynham, Cant. dio., chapl. to Gertrude, Marchioness of Exeter. Similar disp. 7s 2d.

16 Jo. Maygote, M.A., v. of Burton, Linc. dio., chapl. to Jo., Bp of Lincoln. Similar disp. 7s 2d.

p. 118

13 Wm Pykering, gent., of London. Disp. to eat meat during Lent & at other prohibited times. 3s 4d.

16 Nich. Stenytt, r. of Liston, Lond. dio., chapl. to Tho., Bp of Ely. Disp. to hold another benef. with or any 2 without the above. 7s 2d.

13 Edw. Rogyer, gent. of the Kg's hsehld. Disp. to eat meat during Lent & at other prohibited times, while his illness lasts. 3s 4d.

19 Jo. Daulton, Westminster dio., & Ann Bell, widow, Lond. dio. Disp. for marriage without banns, in the bride's par. ch. 3s 4d.

p. 119

1 Lewis Thomas, chapl. to Tho., suffragan Bp of Shrewsbury, r. of ?Llandwrog ('Llandorok'), Bangor dio. Disp. to hold another benef. with or 2 others without the above. 7s 2d.

22 Tho. Monnds & Joan Cope, of St Olave's par., London. Disp. for marriage without banns, in the bride's par. ch. 3s 4d.

23 Adam Copcott & Eliz. Planckney, widow, of Calais. Similar disp. 3s 4d.

1 Jo. Wryght, v. choral (without cure), Ex. cath. Disp. to hold another benef. with the above, or 2 without, one of which must not have cure of souls; permut. cl. 4s 5d.

p. 120

25 Jo. Blackman & Ann Pycke, of the par. of St Mary Colchurch, London. Disp. for marriage without banns, in the bride's par. ch. 3s 4d.

27 Edw. Astwe, esq., of the Kg's hsehld & Marg. Skydwyth, widow, Linc. dio. Disp. for marriage without banns. 3s 4d.

4 Jo. Feckman, B.Th., v. of Feckenham, Worc. dio., chapl. to Edm., Bp of London. Disp. to hold another benef. with or 2 with cure without the above. 7s 2d.

p. 121

27 Hy Boode & Eliz. Byshoppe, Lond. dio. Disp. for marriage without banns, in the bride's par. ch. 3s 4d.

1 Tho. Layton, pr., Qn's chapl. r. of Wolsingham, Durham dio. Disp. to hold another benef. with or 2 without the above. 7s 2d.

Apr. 29 Hugh Whiteforde, sch., son of a pr., St Asaph dio. Disp. to take h.o. & hold a benef. in spite of his defect of birth, even if his father, either r. or v., is still alive; permut. cl. ?11s 1d.

p. 122

30 Rob. Owen & Ann Harman, of St Stephen's, Colman St., London. Disp. for marriage without banns, in any ch., chapel, or oratory. 6s 8d.

2 Geoffrey Thornton, sch., Linc. dio. Disp. to take h.o. from any bp outside the statutory time. 3s 4d.

May   3 Edw. Phetyplace, esq., & Eliz. Moore, widow, Winton dio. Disp. for marriage without banns & in the bride's par. ch. 3s 4d.

Hy Savyll & Marg. Fowler, Westminster dio. Similar disp. 3s 4d.

p. 123

6 Rob. Johnson, Westminster dio., & Joan Huggans, widow, Winton dio. Similar disp. 3s 4d.

3 Jo. Mors, acol., Worcester dio. Disp. to take subdcn's & dcn's orders from any bp, on any day. 5s.

24 Jo. James, M.A., r. of Swerford, Oxford dio., chapl. to the Bp of Llandaff. Disp. to hold another benef. with or any 2 others without the above. 7s 2d.

8 Wm Unedall & Helen Gressham, of the par. of St Mary Aldermary, London. Disp. for marriage in any ch. without banns. 6s 8d.

p. 124

1 Jo Smyth, B.Th. Disp. to hold a 3rd benef. with or without cure; permut. cl. 8s 10d.

9 Jo. Tompson, B.C.L., Sarum dio. Creation as public notary. 4s 5d.

Rob. Gaynsborow, r. of Morningthorpe, Norw. dio. Cancelled disp. to hold another benef. with the above, which does not yield over £8 p.a. 4s 5d.

11 Hugh Basford, sch., Cov. & Lich. dio. Disp. to take h.o. outside the statutory times. 3s 4d.

p. 125

Wm Gerlyng, Norw. dio., & Eliz. Lecknor, Winton dio. Disp. for marriage without banns & during the prohibited times, in the bride's par. ch. 3s 9d.

Jo. Russell, subdcn, Cov. & Lich. dio. Concession to take dcn's & pr.'s orders outside the statutory times from any bp. 4s 5d.

May 12 Tho. Whytehedde & Mary Barnard, Westminster dio. Disp. for marriage in the bride's par. ch. outside the statutory times. 3s 4d.

Walter Marler & Mary Dale, of London. Similar disp. 3s 4d.

p. 126

21 Jo. Goldyng, v. of Wigton, York dio., chapl. to the Archbp of York. Disp. to hold another benef. with, or any 2 others without the above. 7s 2d.

10 Jo. Barker, B.Th., subdean of Chich. cath. Similar disp. 7s 2d.

16 Edw. Ameire, literate, Sarum dio. Concession to practise as notary & tabellion. 4s 5d.

15 Jo. Colburne, pr., r. of Tunstall, Norw. dio., chapl. to Tho. Howard, Duke of Norfolk. Disp. to hold another benef. with or 2 others without the above. 7s 2d.

p. 127

19 Philip Brode, D.Th., v. of Huddersfield, York dio. Disp. to hold another benef. with or 2 others without the above. 7s 2d.

2 Wm Este, pr., Linc. dio., D.Th., Archdcn by royal letters patent of the peculiar of St Albans. Concession to wear the grey almuce of a cath. canon wherever he likes. 3s 4d.

20 Ralph Cockyer, sch., Durham dio. Concession to take h.o. outside the statutory times from any bp on any day without l.d. from his diocesan. 5s 6d.

18 Hy Byssell, M.A., Linc. dio. Concession to take h.o. on any day outside the statutory times, from any bp. 3s 4d.

p. 128

20 Wm ap William, sch., Lland. dio. Concession to take h.o. on any day outside the statutory time, from any bp & without l.d. from his diocesan. 6s 7d.

21 Tho. Chapman, D.Th., r. of St Thomas, Winchelsea, Chich. dio. Disp. to hold another benef. with the above, which does not yield over £8 p.a. or any 2 others without it. 4s 5d.

Roger Fiddes, of the Kg's hsehld, & Margery Storey, widow, Oxford dio. Disp. for marriage without banns, in any ch. or chapel. 6s 8d.

p. 129

Hy Carey & Ann Morgan, both of gentle birth, of the Kg's hsehld. Disp. for marriage in the prohibited times & in the bride's par. ch. 3s 4d.

Disp. for the above to be married in any ch., chapel, or oratory without banns. 6s 8d.

May 23 Tho. Banes, pr., v. of the choral coll. of St Mary's, Southwell, York dio. Disp. to hold another benef. with the above which does not yield over £8 p.a. 4s 5d.

29 Jo. & Eliz. Taylor, of St Margaret's par., Westminster. Disp. for marriage without banns & in the bride's par. ch. 3s 4d.

p. 130

30 Edm. Goodwyn & Joan Danyell, of St Leonard's, par., Shoreditch, Westminster dio. Disp. for marriage without banns, in any ch., chapel, or oratory outside the statutory time. 6s 8d.

June 1 Ric. Powll, M.A., v. of Thatcham, Sarum dio., chapl. to the Bp of Llandaff. Disp. to hold another benef. with or any 2 without the above. 7s 2d.

4 Jo. Baron & Eliz. Mathew, of the par. of St Mary Bow, London. Disp. for marriage in the bride's par. ch. without banns. 3s 4d.

5 Tho. Plaifote & Matilda Castell, of the par. of St Nich. Shambles, London. Disp. for marriage in the bride's par. ch. without banns. 3s 4d.

p. 131

8 Jo. Ponett, M.A., r. of St Michael's, Crooked Lane, London, chapl. to the Archbp of Cant. Disp to hold another benef. with or any 2 others without the above. 7s 2d.

Ric. Cupper & Ann Pakyngton, of London. Disp. for marriage without banns in the bride's par. ch. 3s 4d.

p. 132

13 Simon Sowthorn, pr., r. of Hinton, Glouc. dio., chapl. to the Bp of Gloucester. Disp. to hold another benef. with or 2 others without the above. 7s 2d.

15 Ralph Calfhyll & Ann Crayford, both of gentle birth, of the Kg's hsehld. Disp. for marriage in the bride's par. ch. without banns. 3s 4d.

Hubert Husye, of the par. of St Andrew, Holborn, & Marg. Rushall, widow, Winton dio. Disp. for marriage without banns in the bride's par. ch. 3s 4d.

14 Wm Swyfte, pr., r. of Brokehoole, Peterborough dio., chapl. to Francis, Earl of Shrewsbury. Disp. to hold a benef. with or 2 without the above. 7s 2d.

p. 133

16 Jo. Walker, pr., r. of Evenlode, Worc. dio., chapl. to Wm, Earl of Essex. Similar disp. 7s 2d.

17 Wm Denysson, B.Th., r. of Charlton-on-Otmoor, Oxford dio. Similar disp. 7s 2d.

June 18 Lancelot Rydley, D.Th., v. of Wrawbye, Linc. dio. Similar disp. 7s 2d.

19 Tho. Brounfeld, sch., Linc. dio. Disp. to take all h.o. outside the statutory times from any bp without l.d. from his diocesan bp. 5s 6d.

14 Wm Berton, chanter in the chantry of St Mary the Virgin, in the par. ch. of St Olave, Old Jewry, London. Disp. for absence from the chantry for 5 yrs. 4s 2d.

p. 134

23 Ric. Wheteley, of the King's hsehld, & Ann Wodden, of St Botolph's par., Billingsgate, London. Disp. for marriage in the bride's par. ch. without banns. 3s 4d.

25 Ambrose Dudley & Ann Horwadde, both of gentle birth, Westminster dio. Similar disp. 3s 4d.

Francis Dorcett & Ann Hopper, of St Dunstan's par., London. Similar disp. 3s 4d.

28 Rob. Aston, subdcn, Linc. dio. Disp. to take dcn's & pr.'s orders on any day, outside the statutory times. 4s 5d.

p. 135

Wm Huddy & Brigitt Smyth, both of gentle birth, of London. Disp. for marriage in any ch., chapel, or oratory, without banns. 6s 8d.

Wm Lyghtfote & Agnes Wadder, both of gentle birth, of London. Similar disp. 6s 8d.

30 Wm Jackman & Ann Woodford, Sarum dio. Disp. for marriage without banns in the bride's par. ch. 3s 4d.

31 Elias Price, D.C.L. Disp. to hold the par. ch. of Llan Esthan, Bangor dio., beside 2 benefices with cure previously obtained by disp. if he takes h.o. within 3 yrs. 3s 9d.

p. 136

30 Wm Lowe & Marg. Skave, of St Olave's par., Southwark, Winton dio. Disp. for marriage without banns in the bride's par. ch. 3s 4d.

July 1 Tho. Powell, B.C.L., Kg's chapl. Disp. to hold a 3rd benef. with cure. 8s 1od.

2 Tho. Sanders, M.A., still studying; subdcn. Disp. to take dcn's & pr.'s orders on the same day. 4s 5d.

p. 137

Wm Atkyns, B.A., Oxon, still studying. Similar disp. 4s 5d.

1 Jo. Leghe, pr., r. of Addlethorpe, Linc. dio., chapl. to Frances, Countess of Huntingdon. Disp. to hold another benef. with or 2 without the above. 7s 2d.

July 3 Jo. Ramsey, M.A., r. of Weeby, Linc. dio., chapl. to the Archbp of Cant. Similar disp. 7s 2d.

2 Ric. ap Gryffyth, pr., r. of Cerrig-y-Druidon, St Asaph dio., chapl. to Ly Florence Clifford, wife of Ld Hy Clifford. Similar disp. 7s 2d.

p. 138

6 Jo. Norman, pr., v. of King's Clere, Winton dio., Kg's chapl. Similar disp. 7s 2d.

8 Sir Tho. Fullesthurst, Chich. dio., & Mary Parpoynt, of Mortlake par., Cant. dio. Disp. for marriage in the bride's par. ch. without banns. 3s 4d.

10 Wm Hudson & Alice Pery, widow, of London. Disp. for marriage in any ch., chapel, or oratory without banns. 7s 2d.

pp. 139–40

8 Jo. Crayford, D.Th., Kg's chapl., Chancellor of Salisbury cath., prebendary of Bricklesworth & holder of various benefices with cure by disp. Disp. (given in full & sealed & dated at Lambeth) to hold an archdcnry with the above. 14s 9d.

p. 140

12 Jo. Good & Eliz. Garlande, both of gentle birth, Norw. dio. Disp. for marriage by any suitable chapl. without banns & in the bride's par. ch. 3s 4d.

13 Tho. Kemmeys, literate, Lland. dio. Disp. to practise as tabellion. 4s 5d.

15 Ric. Culverhouse & Marg. Gates, widow, Cant. dio. Disp. for marriage by any suitable pr. in any ch., chapel, or oratory. 6s 8d.

p. 141

18 Jo. Simson, sch., York dio. Disp. to take all h.o. from any bp & without l.d. from his diocesan bp. 2s 2d.

16 Hugh Eglesfylde, Winton dio., & Eliz. Dobbes, Lond. dio. Disp. for marriage by any suitable pr. in the bride's par. ch. 3s 4d.

17 Peter Lede, r. of Nolton, St David's dio. Disp. to hold another benef. if the above does not yield over £8 p.a.; permut. cl. 4s 5d.

p. 142

18 Tho. Whytynge, B.A., v. of Dymocke, Glouc. dio., chapl. to the Bp of Gloucester. Disp. to hold another benef. with, or 2 with or without cure without the above. 7s 2d.

23 Jas Comethop, student at Oxford. Disp. to take h.o. outside the statutory times, from any bp. 3s 4d.

21 Chris. Hyll, B.Th., r. of Alphanston, Lond. dio. Disp. to hold another benef. with or 2 with or without cure without the above. 7s 2d.

p 143

Aug. 1 Ric. Vaughan & Ann Burrowe, of London. Disp. for marriage by any pr. outside the statutory time, without banns, & in the bride's par. ch. 3s 4d.

Walter Sparrey, pr., r. of All Saints, Gt Melton, Norw. dio., chapl. to Jo., Earl of Bath. Disp. to hold another benef. with or 2 others with or without cure without the above. 7s 2d.

4 Wm Clercke & Joan Lyghtfote, of the par. of St Lawrence, Old Jewry. Disp. for marriage the banns read once. 2s 2d.

p. 144

5 Wm Pelsatt & Eliz. Wylkyns, of Ham par., immediately subject to Cant. cath. Disp. for marriage in any ch. or chapel without banns. 6s 8d.

10 Otto Gwynne, B.Th., r. of St Filius *alias* Egglisrose, Oxford, chapl. to the Bp of Oxford. Disp. to hold another benef. with or any 2 others without the above. 7s 2d.

19 Jo. & Alice Marbery, both of gentle birth, Lond. dio. Disp. for marriage in any ch. or chapel without banns. 6s 8d.

pp. 144–5

2 Wm Collman, chantry pr. in the chantry of Tho. Borough, in the ch. of St Mary the Virgin, Gainsborough, Linc. dio. Disp. to hold another benef. with or 2 others with or without cure without the above; permut. cl. 7s 2d.

p. 145

23 Walter Dormer, B.Th., r. of East Reed, Lond. dio. Disp. to hold another benef. with or 2 with or without cure without the above. 7s 2d.

21 Jo. Mayneman, pr., chanter in the chantry of Tho. Alford, Linc. cath. Disp. to hold another benef. with or 2 with or without cure without the above, the value of which does not exceed £8 p.a. 4s 5d.

p. 146

19 Jo. Rawlynson, pr., v. of Wolverton, Linc. dio. Disp. to hold another benef. with or 2 others with or without cure without the above. 7s 2d.

26 Jo. Leveson, esq., & Ann Woodhulf, widow, Lond. dio. Disp. for marriage in any ch. or chapel without banns. 6s 8d.

28 Wm Chamber, literate, of London. Disp. to practise as tabellion. 'Gratis charitatis intuitu.'

31 Alex. Barton, pr., v. of Coldred, Cant. dio. Disp. to hold another benef. if the above does not yield over £8 p.a. 4s 5d.

p. 147

Sept. 1 Edw. Justice, r. of Little Thurrock, Lond. dio. Disp. to hold another benef. with or 2 others without the above. 7s 2d.

Aug. 1 Jo. Gryson & Kath. Sharpe, both of gentle birth. Disp. for marriage in any ch., or oratory, without banns. 6s 8d.

Sept. 4 Wm Salter, v. of Nowton, Norw. dio. Disp. to hold another benef. with or 2 others with or without cure without the above. 7s 2d.

p. 148

6 Hy Matrevers, Earl of Arundel, & Ly Mary Fitzwalter, Countess of Sussex. Disp. for marriage in any ch., chapel, or oratory, without banns. 6s 8d.

7 Jo. Lynell, v. of Sewstern, Peterborough dio. Disp. to hold another benef. with or 2 others with or without cure without the above. 7s 2d.

11 Hy Cole, D.C.L., r. of Chelmsford, Lond. dio. Disp. to hold another benef. with or 2 others without the above. 7s 2d.

p. 149

Tho. Jarmayne & Eliz. Nicholasson, of Calais. Disp. for marriage without banns in the bride's par. ch. 3s 4d.

12 Jo. Symson, acol., York dio. Disp. to take h.o. outside the statutory times. 3s 4d.

10 Osmund Hillyng, M.A., v. of Alveston, Oxford dio., chapl. to Hy, Marquess of Dorset. Disp. to hold another benef. with or 2 others without the above. 7s 2d.

p. 150

14 Wm Page, B.A., Chester dio. Disp. to take h.o. without l.d. from any bp. 3s 2d. Also disp. to take h.o. outside the statutory times & all on the same day. No fee recorded.

6 Jo. Asseton, M.A., r. of Much Lees, Lond. dio., chapl. to Hy, Marquess of Dorset. Disp. to hold another benef. with or 2 others without the above. 7s 2d.

p. 151

16 Jo. Broke & Eliz. Semarke, of the par. of St Jo. the Evangelist, London. Disp. for marriage without banns, in the bride's par. ch. 3s 4d.

17 Roger Ponsobye, B.A., Kg's chapl. Disp. to hold a 3rd benef. with or without cure. 8s 10d.

? (Damaged page). Jo. Long, gent., & ?Joan Bullocke, of the par. of St Botolph without Aldersgate, London. Disp. for marriage without banns & in the bride's par. ch. 3s 4d.

p. 152

Sept. 19 Jo. Elyott & Cecily Ledford, widow, of St Laurence par., Alton, Winton dio. Disp. for marriage without banns in any ch. 6s 8d.

28 Rob. *alias* Joseph Wynnall, D.Th., v. of Glen Magna, Linc. dio. Disp. to hold another benef. with or 2 others without the above. 7s 2d.

29 Jo. & Cecily Frye, widow, Westminster dio. Disp. for marriage in any ch. without banns. 6s 8d.

p. 153

2 Wm Rooper, B.Cn.L., v. of 'Mannden' (*sic* for Maldon?), Lond. dio. Disp. to hold a benef. with the above, or 2 without. 7s 2d.

June 30 Wm Pye, B.Th., r. of Westley, Norw. dio., chapl. to Tho. Wriothesley, Ld Chancellor. Disp. to hold another benef. with or 2 without the above. 7s 2d.

Sept. 30 Adnello Hebburne & Alice Haltt, Westminster dio. Disp. for marriage without banns in any ch. 6s 8d.

p. 154

Oct. 1 Jo. Clarke, sch., Chester dio. Disp. to take h.o. from any bp without l.d. from his diocesan bp. 2s 2d.

2 Jo. Medeshopp, pr., r. of Addingham, York dio., chapl. to Hy, Earl of Cumberland. Disp. to hold another benef. with or 2 without the above. 7s 2d.

3 Wm Leyton, M.A., r. of Broadway, Worc. dio., chapl. to the Bp of Rochester. Disp. to hold another benef. with or 2 without the above. 7s 2d.

p. 155

Oct. 5 Rob. Danyell & Agnes Gowre, widow, Cant. dio. Disp. for marriage without banns in any ch. 6s 8d.

Tho. Bentam, B.A., acol., York dio. Disp. to take h.o. without l.d. from his diocesan bp. 5s 6d.

6 Walter Baron, pr., r. of Long Crichel, Bristol dio., chapl. to Ld Audley. Disp. to hold another benef. with or 2 others without the above. 7s 2d.

p. 156

8 Jo. Ackynson & Eliz. Byghton, of All Saints par., Honey Lane, London. Disp. for marriage without banns in any ch. 6s 8d.

9 Edw. Warton, gent. & Martha Fytz, widow, Oxford dio. Disp. for marriage without banns, in any ch. 6s 8d.

10 Tho. Slanye, pr., r. of Cheriton, Cant. dio., Surveyor of the lands of Sir Tho. Moyle, Kg's chapl. Disp. to hold another benef. with or 2 without the above. 7s 2d.

Oct. 16 Rob. Forman, acol., Linc. dio. Disp. to take h.o. from any bp on any day, outside the statutory times. 3s 4d.

p. 157

Geo. Colcell & Sens Clithero, widow, both of gentle birth, Lond. dio. Disp. for marriage without banns in any ch., outside the statutory times. 6s 8d.

20 Rob. Forman, pr., r. of Ewherst, Chester dio. Disp. for non-res. for 6 months on account of his health. 3s 4d.

11 Wm Parry & Alice Tyson, both of gentle birth, Lond. dio. Disp. for marriage in any ch., without banns. 6s 8d.

18 Wm Stone & Frances Palmer, of St Andrew's par., London. Disp. for marriage in any ch., without banns. 6s 8d.

p. 158

21 Geo. Walton & Kath. Chasmore, widow, Linc. dio. Disp. for marriage without banns in the bride's par. ch. 3s 4d.

26 Huano Quycke, pr., r. of Buckworth, Linc. dio., chapl. to Ld Jo. Mordannt. Disp. to hold another benef. with or 2 others without the above. 7s 2d.

Tho. Barbor & Mary Shaw, widow, Westminster dio. Disp. for marriage without banns in any ch. 6s 8d.

27 Tho. Cooke & Eliz. Whyte, widow, Cant. dio. Disp. for marriage without banns in the bride's par. ch. 3s 4d.

p. 159

28 Wm Bodye, literate, Wells dio. Concession to practise as a public notary & tabellion anywhere. 4s 5d.

29 Jo. Polsgrave, B.Th., Kg's chapl. Disp. to hold a 3rd benef. with or without cure. 8s 10d.

Nov. 2 Wm Anderson, pr., r. of Isham, Peterborough dio., Qn's chapl. Disp. to hold any benef. with cure with the above, which does not yield over £8 p.a.; permut. cl. 4s 5d.

p. 160

Sept. 25 Rob. Richardson, B.Th., r. of Stoke, Linc. dio., Kg's chapl. Disp. to hold another benef. with or 2 with or without cure without the above. 7s 2d.

Nov. 6 Ric. Cooke, pr., r. of Houghton, Winton dio., chapl. to Sir Jo. Wallope, K.G. Disp. to hold another benef. with or 2 without the above. 7s 2d.

7 Ambrose Thruston & Joan Haldryng, of St Dunstan's-in-the-East par., London. Disp. for marriage in the bride's par. ch., the banns read once. 2s 2d.

Nov. 10 Tho. Copplond & Agnes Peton, of Bidford, Worc. dio. Disp. for marriage without banns, in the bride's par. ch. 3s 4d.

p. 161

Wm Gilbert & Eliz. Lincoll, of St Nich.'s par., London. Disp. for marriage in any ch., chapel, or oratory without banns. 6s 8d.

8 Wm Wyllyngton & Ann Mydelmore, of Brailes, Worc. dio. Disp. for marriage without banns, in any ch. 6s 8d.

13 Tho. Lucy, Worc. dio., & Joyce Acten, Heref. dio. Disp. for marriage in the bride's par. ch. without banns. 3s 4d.

Rob. Colmer, M.A., r. of Ellesborough, Linc. dio., chapl. to Rob. Bp of Oxford. Disp. to hold another benef. with or any 2 without the above. 7s 2d.

p. 162

11 Jo. Skydmore, pr., r. of Sherston Magna, Sarum dio. Disp. for non-res. for 6 months on account of illness, a suitable pr. being provided to act as curate. 3s 4d.

17 Hy Worlond & Kath. Awsthorpe, of London. Disp. for marriage in the bride's par. ch. without banns. 3s 4d.

21 Wm Cicile & Mildred Cooke, of gentle birth, Lond. dio. Disp. for marriage in any ch., chapel, or oratory without banns & within the prohibited time. 7s 2d.

p. 163

24 Rob. Alen, literate, Norw. dio. Concession to practise as a notary anywhere. 4s 5d.

19 Wm Bynsley, B.C.L., subdcn, Oxford dio. Disp. to take h.o. outside the statutory time & from any bp. 4s 5d.

27 Hy Plankney & Kath. Johnson, of St Alphage par., London. Disp. for marriage in the bride's par. ch. within the prohibited times. 3s 4d.

Wm Mildnall & Eliz. Taylor, St Ant.'s par., London. Disp. for marriage in the bride's par. ch. without banns. 3s 4d.

p. 164

23 Hy Hollond, sch., Bangor dio. Disp. to take h.o. & hold a benef. despite defect of birth. 5s 7d.

28 Chas Tuke, esq., & Eliz. Nevell, widow, Lond. dio. Disp. for marriage in any ch., or chapel without banns & during the prohibited time. 7s 2d.

27 Jo. Ledes, esq., & his wife. Disp. to eat meat & other prohibited food during Lent & at other times. 3s 4d.

Nov. 29 Jo. Morlay & Helen Tabe, widow, Peterborough dio. Disp. for marriage in the bride's par. ch. without banns & during the prohibited times. 3s 9d.

p. 165

28 Wm Curtnay, esq., & Eliz. Poullett, of gentle birth, Bristol dio. Disp. for marriage in any ch. or chapel, without banns & during the prohibited time. 7s 2d.

Dec. 2 Edm. Atkynson, of the Kg's hsehld, & Mary Lenthroppe, of the par. of St Kath. Cree ('Crechurch'), London. Disp. for marriage in the bride's par. ch. without banns & during the prohibited time. 3s 9d.

3 Ld Jo. Mordaunt & Joan Willford, of the par. of St Martin, Bishopsgate, London. Similar disp. 3s 9d.

p. 166

5 Tho. Holland & Ann Grennston, Norw. dio. Disp. for marriage without banns & in the bride's par. ch. 3s 4d.

6 Jo. Maynns & Margery Fysher, of St Olave's par., Southwark. Disp. for marriage in the bride's par. ch. within the prohibited time. 3s 4d.

Wm Grene & Rose Fysher, widow, of Whaplode, Linc. dio. Disp. for marriage in any ch. or chapel, & during the prohibited time. 6s 8d.

7 Wm Moryce, esq., & his wife Ann. Disp. to eat meat during Lent & at other prohibited times, while his illness lasts. 3s 4d.

p. 167

10 Pers (sic for Piers or Percival?) Slayn, of the Kg's hsehld, & Jane Maye, widow, of the par. of St Marg., Westminster. Disp. for marriage without banns & during the prohibited time. 3s 9d.

1 Wm Hatcliffe, esq., & Ann Skepwyth. Similar disp. 3s 9d.

9 Walter Glesonne, literate, Norw. dio. Concession to practise as a notary anywhere. 4s 5d.

12 Jo. May, B.C.L., r. of Pettaugh, Norw. dio. Disp. to hold another benef. with or 2 without the above. 7s 2d.

p. 168

Gilbert Winter & Eliz. Pomere, both of gentle birth. Disp. for marriage without banns, in the bride's par. ch., & during the prohibited time. 3s 9d.

13 Jo. Hickford, esq., & Mary Lucy, Westminster dio. Disp. for marriage in any ch. or chapel without banns, & during the prohibited time. 7s 2d.

Dec. 14 Jo. Sherye, r. of Worth & Thatcham, Chich. dio., chapl. to Tho., Duke of Norfolk. Disp. to hold a 3rd benef. with or without cure. 8s 10d.

Edw. Maneryng & Alice Jerlond, widow, of Whitmore, Cov. & Lich. dio. Disp. for marriage in the bride's par. ch. without banns & during the prohibited time. 3s 9d.

p. 169

14 Jo. Stapulton, M.A., r. of Little Warley, Lond. dio., & Witham, Sarum dio., Kg's chapl. Disp. to hold another benef. with or without cure with or 2 others without the above. 8s 10d.

16 Jo. Battnall & Eliz. Gosse, widow, of St Saviour's par., Southwark, Winton dio. Disp. for marriage in the bride's par. ch., without banns. 3s 4d.

Rob. Curtes, pr., r. of Wootton, Peterborough dio., chapl. to Sir Ant. Wingfield, K.G. Disp. to hold any benef. with, or 2 others with or without cure without the above. 7s 2d.

15 Jo. Chapman, sch., Bristol dio. Concession to take all h.o. outside the statutory times without l.d. 5s 6d.

p. 170

17 Brian Hole, M.A., r. of Nettleton, Linc. dio., chapl. to Ld Edw. Clinton. Disp. to hold another benef. with, or any 2 others without the above. 7s 2d.

18 Jo. Aiscoughe, Lond. dio., & Grisilla Tuke, Cant. dio. Disp. for marriage in any ch. or chapel & within the prohibited time. 6s 8d.

17 Jas Bacon & Mary Gardinar, of St Mildred's par., London. Disp. for marriage in the bride's par. ch. without banns & within the prohibited time. 3s 9d.

p. 171

20 Sir Francis Hastyngs & Jane Rastold, Linc. dio. Disp. for marriage in the bride's par. ch. without banns & during the prohibited time. 3s 9d.

23 Edm. Cranmer, archdcn of Cant. Disp. to eat meat in Lent & at other prohibited times. 3s 4d.

22 Rob. Shorloke & Marg. Gettens of London. Disp. for marriage in the bride's par. ch. during the prohibited time. 3s 4d.

23 Tho. Skipwith & his wife Joan. Disp. to eat meat during Lent & at other prohibited times during his illness. 3s 4d.

p. 172

31 Ric. Waller & Eliz. Oglander, of London. Disp. for marriage in the bride's par. ch. within the prohibited time. 3s 4d.

Dec. 23 Jo. Buttery, r. of Stoke Charity, Winton dio., chapl. to Ld Chancellor Wriothesley. Disp. to hold a benef. with or any 2 others without the above. 7s 2d.

1546 Jan.   9 Geo. Duke & Philippa Weldon, Cant. dio. Disp. for marriage in the bride's par. ch. during the prohibited time. 3s 4d.

Jo. Botrell, M.A., Lond. dio., student at Cambridge. Disp. to take h.o. outside the statutory time. 3s 4d.

p. 173

11 Chris. Langton & Marg. Chambers, of London. Disp. for marriage in the bride's par. ch. without banns. 3s 4d.

12 Jo. Russell & Alice Rich, of the par. of Bourne, Chich. dio. Disp. for marriage in the bride's par. ch. outside the statutory time. 3s 4d.

16 Ric. Goslyng & Ann Pynfolde, of St Magnus par., London. Disp. for marriage in the bride's par. ch. outside the statutory time. 3s 4d.

17 Nich. Adams & Mary Fissher, Westminster dio. Disp. for marriage in any ch., chapel, or oratory without banns. 6s 8d.

12 Edw. Mourton & his wife Joan, of London. Disp. to eat meat in Lent & at other prohibited times, during their illness. 3s 4d.

p. 174

16 Rob. Warner & Ann Peryent, Lond. dio. Disp. for marriage in any ch. & without banns. 6s 8d.

2 Jas Lodge, M.A., v. of Braintree, Lond. dio., chapl. to Wm, Earl of Essex. Disp. to hold another benef. with or 2 without the above. 7s 2d.

21 Jo. Wynter & Joan Proctor, of Whitechapel, Westminster dio. Disp. for marriage in the bride's par. ch. without banns. 2s 2d.

20 Edw. Hollys & Joan Gryffyn, of St Dunstan's par., London. Disp. for marriage in the bride's par. ch. the banns read once. 2s 2d.

22 Rob. Toy & Eliz. Scampyon, of St Marg.'s par., Westminster. Disp. for marriage in the bride's par. ch., the banns read once. 2s 2d.

p. 175

16 Wm Copplond, B.C.L., Kg's chapl. Disp. to hold a 3rd benef. with or without cure. 8s 1od.

1 Jo. Ryse, pr., r. of Stoke in Teignhead, Ex. dio., chapl. to the Bp of Oxford. Disp. to hold a benef. with or any 2 others without the above. 7s 2d.

23 Ottowell Johnson & Mary Warner, of St Edmund's par., London. Disp. for marriage in the bride's par. ch. without banns. 3s 4d.

p. 176

    Jan. 26 Wm Cateryke, B.Th., v. of Barnwell St Mary, Norw. dio. Disp. to hold a benef. with or any 2 without the above. 7s 2d.

    Feb. 4 Roger Warfelde & Eliz. Tomson, of London. Disp. for marriage in the bride's par. ch. without banns. 3s 4d.

    6 Walter Currye & Eliz. Myddelton, of Islington, Westminster dio. Disp. for marriage in the bride's par. ch. without banns. 3s 4d.

    5 Rob. Hope, pr., r. of St Andrew's by Baynards Castle, London, chapl. to Geo., Bp of Chich. Disp. to hold another benef. with or any 2 without the above. 7s 2d.

p. 177

    6 Jo. Cooke, B.Cn.L., v. of Ditchling, Chich. dio. Similar disp. 7s 2d.

    7 Chris. Waxley, B.A., r. of Gt Holland, Lond. dio., Kg's chapl. Similar disp. 7s 2d.

    8 Jo. Litelton, r. of Munslow, Heref. dio., chapl. to the Bp of Oxford. Similar disp. 7s 2d.

    Ric. Whyte, pr., r. of Peakirk, Peterborough dio., chapl. to the Bp of Peterborough. Similar disp. 7s 2d.

    10 Rob. Lynton & Kath. Jonson, of London. Disp. for marriage in the bride's par. ch. without banns. 3s 4d.

p. 178

    9 Rob. Strenger & Ann Neham, widow, Worc. dio. Disp. for marriage in the bride's par. ch. without banns. 3s 4d.

    10 Nich. Coplond, acol., Chester dio. Disp. to take 2 h.o. on the same day outside the statutory times. 4s 6d.

    9 Wm Gyse & Christine Yomans, of Strand, Westminster dio. Disp. for marriage in the bride's par. ch. without banns. 3s 4d.

    6 Rob. Eliott, B.C.L., r. of Stoke Abbott, Bristol dio., chapl. to Hy, Earl of Bridgwater. Disp. to hold another benef. with or any 2 without the above. 7s 2d.

p. 179

    12 Chris. Rogerson, pr., v. of Askrigg, York dio., chapl. to Jo. Le Scrope, Ld of Bolton. Similar disp. 7s 2d.

    Jo. Hutton & Agnes Curtes, widow, Linc. dio. Disp. for marriage in the bride's par. ch. & during the prohibited time. 3s 4d.

    13 Ric. Houghton & Eliz. West, of Abston, Bath & W. dio. Disp. for marriage in the bride's par. ch. without banns. 3s 4d.

Feb. 13 Rob. Chasye & Marg. Kyngeston, of All Saints par., Lombard St. Disp. for marriage in the bride's par. ch., the banns read once. 2s 2d.

p. 180

Jo. Aubery & Ann Parker of London. Disp. for marriage in the bride's par. ch. without banns. 3s 4d.

Geo. Smyth & Marg. Deane, of St Mathew's par., London. Disp. for marriage in the bride's par. ch. without banns. 3s 4d.

14 Rob. Litton, esq., & Eliz. Borgon, Westminster dio. Disp. for marriage in the bride's par. ch. without banns. 3s 4d.

16 Wm Abbott & Agnes Wilkinson, of St Clement's par., Westminster. Disp. for marriage in the bride's par. ch., the banns read once. 2s 2d.

12 Jo. Chyke, M.A. Disp. to eat meat during Lent & at other prohibited times, during his illness. 3s 4d.

p. 181

Agnes Chyke, widow, Ely dio. Similar disp. 3s 4d.

16 Hy Cumberford, B.Th., r. of Polstead, Norw. dio. Disp. to hold another benef. with or any 2 others without the above. 7s 2d.

15 Jo. Gryme, r. of Barwick, Bath & W. dio. Disp. to hold a benef. with the above, which does not yield over £8 p.a. 4s 5d.

17 Walter Wryght, D.C.L., archdcn of Oxford. Disp. to take h.o. on any days outside the statutory times & 2 on the same day. 3s 4d.

p. 182

Jo. Edwardes & Marg. Lynche, of Bow, London. Disp. for marriage in the bride's par. ch. without banns. 3s 4d.

15 Wm Sakwyle, esq., & Eleanor Browne, Winton dio. Similar disp. 3s 4d.

19 Jo. Frysell & Eliz. Webstar, of St Martin-in-the-Fields par., Westminster. Similar disp. 3s 4d.

20 Ric. Baker & Mary Deryke, of Pentney, Norw. dio. Disp. for marriage in the bride's par. ch. outside the statutory time. 3s 4d.

p. 183

19 Nich. Paver, M.A., Qn Kath.'s chapl., r. of 'Lyntton' (?Linton-in-Craven), York dio. Disp. to hold another benef. with or any 2 without the above. 7s 2d.

1 Simon Nicolls, B.C.L., Kg's chapl. Cancelled similar disp. 7s 2d.

18 Roland Swynburn, B.Th., r. of Little Shelford, Ely dio. Disp. to hold another benef. with or 2 without the above. 7s 2d.

Feb. 21 Simon Nicolls, B.C.L., Kg's chapl. Disp. to hold any 3rd benef. 8s 10d.

p. 184

20 Jo. Rayner, B.Th., v. of Gisburn, York dio. Disp. to hold another benef. with or 2 without the above. 7s 2d.

22 Wm Goodyng & Eleanor Blunt, of St Mary Magdalene par., Southwark, Winton dio. Disp. for marriage in the bride's par. ch. within the prohibited times. 3s 4d.

19 Cuthbert Fawcett, literate, York dio. Disp. to practise as a notary. 4s 5d.

p. 185

3 Ric. Walker, M.A., Kg's chapl. Disp. to hold a 3rd benef. 8s 10d.

23 Sir Edw. Grey, Ld Powes, Lichfield dio. Disp. to eat meat during Lent & at other prohibited times. 3s 4d.

24 Jo. Fetiplace & Eliz. Hungerford, of gentle birth, & Shefford par., Sarum dio. Disp. for marriage in the bride's par. ch. within the prohibited time. 3s 4d.

25 Ant. Copwodde & Mary Betnam, Cant. dio. Similar disp. 3s 4d.

p. 186

Wm Warner & Amy Tye, of Leebury, London dio. Similar disp. 3s 4d.

Matthew Butler & Joan Nottingham, of St Mary's par., Ipswich, Norw. dio. Similar disp. 3s 4d.

26 Ric. Maxey & Anne Stowghton, of Stoke par., Winton dio. Similar disp. 3s 4d.

Wm Dunmer & Alice Wheten, of St Mich.'s, Cornhill, London. Similar disp. 3s 4d.

8 —— Loddyngton, pr., v. of Aldenham, Linc. dio., chapl. to Sir Wm Pagett, Kg's sec. Disp. to hold another benef. with or any 2 without the above. 7s 2d.

p. 187

24 Tho. ap Gryffyth, pr., r. of ?Llandwrog ('Llanwrothen'), Bangor dio. Disp. to hold another benef. with the above, which does not yield over £8 p.a.; permut. cl. 4s 5d.

1 Ric. Gyll, M.A., r. of Toddington, Linc. dio., chapl. to Ld Jo. Russell, Keeper of the Privy Seal. Disp. to hold another benef. with or any 2 without the above. 7s 2d.

28 Ralph Rowlett & his wife Dorothy, both of gentle birth, Linc. dio. Disp. to eat meat during Lent & at other prohibited times during his illness. 3s 4d.

p. 188

Mar. 1 Rob. Browne, of London. Disp. to eat meat during Lent & at other prohibited times during his illness. 3s 4d.

Eustace Suliarde, Lond. dio. Disp. to eat meat during Lent & at other prohibited times during his illness. 3s 4d.

2 Tho. Robinson & Alice Turke, of Rochester. Disp. for marriage in the bride's par. ch. during the prohibited time. 3s 4d.

3 Edw. Peynde & Eliz. Francklyng, of Chart, Cant. dio. Similar disp. 3s 4d.

1 Geo. Feres, of the Kg's hsehld & Jane Sowthtrote, of St Albans. Similar disp. 3s 4d.

5 Wm Monyon & Lettice Hernold, of Melbourn, Ely dio. Similar disp. 3s 4d.

p. 189

6 Jo. Smyth & Agnes Humpstede, of Winchelsey, Chich. dio. Similar disp. 3s 4d.

7 Mich. Prokyng & Eliz. Mardall, Cant. dio. Similar disp. 3s 4d.

Feb. 22 Nich. Lestrange, esq., Norw. dio. Disp. to eat meat during Lent & at other prohibited times during his illness. 3s 4d.

Mar. 8 Ric. Walker, M.A., Kg's chapl. Disp. to hold a 4th benef. 8s 10d.

10 Wm Beckewyth, literate, York dio. Concession to practise as notary & tabellion anywhere. 4s 5d.

Jo. Rayncoke, literate, York dio. Disp. to practise as a notary. 4s 5d.

p. 190

1 Martin Collyn, M.A., r. of Horsmonden, Roch. dio., chapl. to the Bp of Worcester. Disp. to hold another benef. with or 2 without the above. 7s 2d.

11 Wm Hawkyns, merchant, Ex. dio. Disp. to eat meat during Lent & at other prohibited times of the yr during his illness. 3s 4d.

12 Wm Thomas & Alice More, widow, Worc. dio. Disp. for marriage in any ch. or chapel within the prohibited times & without banns. 7s 2d.

8 Fulk Skidmoor, Lond. dio. Disp. to eat meat during Lent & at other times during his illness. 3s 4d.

17 Hy Becham, merchant, Lond. dio. Disp. to eat meat during Lent & at other times during his illness. 3s 4d.

p. 191

Feb. 12 Wm Petre, Kg's sec. Disp. to eat meat during Lent & at other prohibited times during his illness. 3s 4d.

Mar. 23 Jo. Armetredyng & Ann Lye, Westminster dio. Disp. for marriage without banns. 3s 4d.

Jo. Homes & Eliz. Yevar, Westminster dio. Disp. for marriage without banns & outside the statutory time. 3s 4d.

Jo. Cocks & Eliz. Tepytt, Bath & W. dio. Similar disp. 3s 4d.

Jo. Wilson, r. of Colton, Cov. & Lich. dio. Disp. to hold another benef., as the above does not yield over £8 p.a. 4s 5d.

Apr. 2 Edw. Cole & Eliz. Coe, Lond. dio. Disp. for marriage without banns in any ch. & outside the statutory times. 7s 2d.

p. 192

5 Edm. Knyghte, r., of Hardres, Cant. dio. Disp. to hold another benef. as the above does not yield over £8 p.a. 4s 5d.

Mar. 26 Rob. More, r. of Kilworth, Linc. dio. Disp. to hold another benef. with or any 2 without the above. 7s 2d.

23 Jo. Mason & his wife Eliz. Disp. to eat meat during Lent & at other times. No fee.

Apr. 5 Wm Forde & his wife Eliz. Similar disp. 3s 4d.

Mar. 20 Geoffrey Danyell, Sarum dio. Similar disp. 3s 4d.

10 Sir Edw. Darell, Sarum dio. Similar disp. 3s 4d.

p. 193

Apr. 7 Walter Atkyns, B.C., Linc. dio. Disp. to take all h.o. without l.d. & outside the statutory time. 5s 6d.

1 Tho. Goldyng, Lond. dio. Similar disp. 3s 4d.

10 Edw. Bygge, literate, Norw. dio. Concession to practise as tabellion. 4s 5d.

Mar. 24 Ric. Hallyn *alias* ?Ramse, M.A., v. of Wellow, Bath & W. dio., Kg's chapl. Disp. to hold a benef. with or any 2 without the above. 7s 2d.

p. 194

Apr. 12 Jo. Beste, pr., v. of Wrotham, Shoreham deanery, Cant. dio., chapl. to the Bp of St David's. Similar disp. 7s 2d.

16 Jo. Turnor, literate, Peterborough dio. Concession to practise as tabellion. 4s 5d.

13 Ric. Joyner, literate, Oxford dio. Concession to practise as a notary. 4s 5d.

Apr. 13 Roger Dalyson, D.Th., Kg's chapl. Disp. to hold a 3rd benef.

15 Disp. for the above to hold a 4th benef. Combined fee. 17s 8d.

p. 195

16 Ronald Turner & Joan Ourlyme, of Sunbury, Westminster dio. Disp. for marriage without banns. 3s 4d.

17 Arthut Pyttys, Oxford dio., & Marg. Secoll, Worc. dio. Similar disp. 3s 4d.

19 Humfrey Webley, B.Th., v. of Cropthorne, Worc. dio. Disp. to hold another benef. with or any 2 without the above. 7s 2d.

27 Stephen Va[ug]han & Margery Brinclow, widow, of London. Disp. for marriage without banns, in any ch. & within the prohibited time. 7s 2d.

28 Tho. Barnard, M.A., Chester dio. Disp. to take all h.o. without l.d. outside the statutory times. 5s 6d.

p. 196

2 Jo. Holyman, D.Th., r. of Handborough, Oxford dio. Disp. to hold another benef. with or 2 without the above. 7s 2d.

1 Tho. Hodson, pr., r. of Nailstone, Linc. dio., chapl. to Ly Cicilie Dudley. Similar disp. 7s 2d.

May 3 Jo. Aras, literate, Peterborough dio. Disp. to practise as notary. 4s 5d.

April 1 Ralph Boswell, Westminster dio., & Ann Castelton, widow, Winton dio. Disp. for marriage without banns. 6s 8d.

30 Rob. Ame & Eliz. Joyce, Westminster dio. Disp. for marriage without banns. 3s 4d.

p. 197

May 4 Jo. Nethermyll & Winifred Dod, Lich. dio. Disp. for marriage in any ch. & without banns. 6s 8d.

5 Polidore Kyne & Joan Cooke, of London. Disp. for marriage without banns. 3s 4d.

7 Ric. Thomas & Agnes Arnold, of Kingston, Winton dio. Disp. for marriage without banns. 3s 4d.

Jo. Wulsley, pr., v. of Acton, Peterborough dio., chapl. to Qn Kath. Disp. to hold another benef. with or any 2 without the above. 7s 2d.

8 David Sandbroke & Agnes Preston, of London. Disp. for marriage without banns. 3s 4d.

4 Hy Fletcher, B.Th., v. of Town Mallyng, Roch. dio. Disp. to hold another benef. with or 2 others without the above. 7s 2d.

p. 198

May 12 Geo. Doogen, B.Th., v. of Chew, Wells dio. Disp. to hold 2 benefices with or 3 with or without cure without the above. 8s 10d.

6 Ric. Standysh, D.C.L., Chester dio. Disp. to take all h.o. outside the statutory times & without l.d. 5s 6d.

20 Wm Sowrey, B.A., v. of Sedbergh, Chester dio., chapl. to Wm Parr, Earl of Essex. Disp. to hold another benef. with or any 2 without the above. 7s 2d.

21 Ric. Alvey, B.Th., r. of Thorrington, Lond. dio. Similar disp. 7s 2d.

22 Mich. Wilde & Alice Free, of Wendover. Disp. for marriage without banns. 3s 4d.

p. 199

Wm Hall & Joan Gurnell. Similar disp. 3s 4d.

24 Hy Fallowfelde, Lond. dio., & Mary Blake, of Reading, Sarum dio. Similar disp. 3s 4d.

25 Walter Myldmay, Lond. dio., & Mary Walsyngham, Westminster dio. Disp. for marriage in any ch., without banns. 6s 8d.

24 Tho. Bartholomew & Ann Urlyn, of London. Disp. for marriage without banns. 3s 4d.

22 Simon Parrett, M.A., Oxford dio. Concession to practise as a notary. 4s 5d.

Wm Standysh, M.A., Linc. dio. Similar concession. 4s 5d.

p. 200

29 Ralph Tytteley, M.A., v. of Drayton-in-Hales, Cov. & Lich. dio., chapl. to the Bp of Gloucester. Disp. to hold another benef. with or any 2 without the above. 7s 2d.

28 Wm Davyd, pr., r. of Walwyn's Castle, St David's dio. Disp. to hold another benef. with the above, which does not yield over £8 p.a. or another without these. 4s 5d.

June 1 Nich. Hey, pr., r. of Toddington, Linc. dio., chapl. to Ld Wm Howard. Disp. to hold another benef. with or 2 without the above. 7s 2d.

5 Chris. Danncy & Thomasina Ducate, of St Lawrence's par., London. Disp. for marriage without banns & within the prohibited times. 3s 9d.

p. 201

7 Jo. Boye, pr., v. of Waltham, Cant. dio. Disp. to hold another benef. with the above, if it does not yield over £8 p.a., or another without it. 4s 5d.

June 7   Tho. Willey, M.A., v. of Henlow, Linc. dio., chapl. to the Bp of London. Disp. to hold another benef. with or any 2 without the above. 7s 2d.

8   Tho. Wilkynson, sch., York dio. Concession to take h.o. from any bp without l.d. 2s 2d.

Jo. Toolys & Kath. Huntlow, of London. Disp. for marriage without banns & during the prohibited time. 3s 9d.

p. 202

11   Chris. Muschape & Jane Lambert, Winton dio. Disp. for marriage during the prohibited time. 3s 4d.

Rob. Abere & Marg. Nayler, of Canterbury. Disp. for marriage in any ch. & without banns. 6s 8d.

12   Rob. Burnett, acol., York dio. Disp. to take h.o. without l.d. & 2 on the same day. 6s 8d.

8   Benjamin Gunston & Ursula Roberts, of London. Disp. for marriage in any ch. without banns. Fee remitted.

19   Sir Wm Pagett. Disp. to eat meat during Lent & at other prohibited times: also for his wife & 4 other persons at his table. No fee.

p. 203

Rob. Ganisborow, pr., r. of Morningthorpe, Norw. dio. Disp. to hold another benef. with the above, which does not yield over £8 p.a., or another without. 4s 5d.

25   Ric. Stangar, of Boulogne-sur-Mer, & Joan Henry, of London. Disp. for marriage without banns. 3s 4d.

16   Humfrey Wade & Eliz. Fromondys, widow, of Chesham, in the jurisdiction of Cant. dio. Disp. for marriage without banns. 3s 4d.

24   Wm Simbarde, of the Kg's hsehld, & Mary Litell. Disp. for marriage without banns. 3s 4d.

Wm Herbert, sch., Lland. dio. Disp. to take all h.o. on the same day outside the statutory time. 5s.

p. 204

25   Hy Husye & Brigitt Ernley, of East Wittering, Chich. dio. Disp. for marriage without banns. 3s 4d.

Ronald Whitebrede & Eliz. Peyege, of Woodford, Peterborough dio. Disp. for marriage without banns. 3s 4d.

May 27   Jo. Bushe, silversmith of London, & his wife Margery. Disp. to eat meat during Lent & at other prohibited times, while his illness lasts. 3s 4d.

June 17 Tho. Byrchet, gent., Chich. dio. Disp. to eat meat during Lent & at other prohibited times. 3s 4d.

Wm Wymond, gent., Chich. dio. Similar disp. 3s 4d.

25 Hugh Councell, of Calais, Therouanne dio. Similar disp. 3s 4d.

p. 205

26 Ric. Dune & Ann Dencorte, of London. Disp. for marriage without banns. 3s 4d.

Stephen Hales & Ann Bales, of London. Similar disp. 3s 4d.

28 Hugh Tenche, of the Kg's hsehld, & Joan Wilsdon, of Eltham, Roch. dio. Similar disp. No fee.

29 Wm Bramewodde, literate, Winton dio. Disp. to practise anywhere as tabellion. 4s 5d.

July 1 Hugh Wittyngton *alias* Johns, B.C.L., r. of Ulston, Glouc. dio., chapl. to the Bp of Gloucester. Disp. to hold another benef. with or 2 without the above. 7s 2d.

p. 206

June 6 Wm Prety & Alice Laurence, of Danbury, Lond. dio. Disp. for marriage without banns in any ch. 6s 8d.

July 6 Jo. Barrett & Eleanor Stanmer, widow, of South Ambridge, Lond. dio. Disp. for marriage without banns. 3s 4d.

7 Edw. Haydon, B.C.L., Kg's chapl. Disp. to hold a 3rd benef. 8s 10d.

Bartholomew Busfolde, acol., Carl. dio. Disp. to take all h.o. outside the statutory time. 3s 4d.

6 Hugh Sydenham, B.C.L., v. of Ilton, Bath & W. dio. Disp. to hold another benef. with the above, which does not yield over £8 p.a. or another without. 4s 5d.

p. 207

8 Roger Edwarde, r. of Swanton Novers, Norw. dio. Disp. to hold any benef. with the above, which does not yield over £8 p.a. 4s 5d.

9 Tho. Fisher & Jane Fowler, of Islington, Westminster dio. Disp. for marriage without banns. 3s 4d.

12 Ric. Gatefolde, pr., r. of St Peter's, West Lynn, Norw. dio. Disp. to hold another benef. with or any 2 others without the above. 7s 2d.

14 Jo. Sticheford & Helen Beckewyth, of London. Disp. for marriage without banns. 3s 4d.

15 Edw. Pinchester & Kath. Reest, of London. Disp. for marriage without banns in any ch. 6s 8d.

July 15 Jo. Roblyng, pr., v. of Llanstadwell in Rouse, St David's dio. Disp. to hold another benef., which does not yield over £8 p.a., or another without it. 4s 5d.

p. 208

17 Wm Hamerton, Lond. dio. & Marg. Riche, Linc. dio. Disp. for marriage without banns. 3s 4d.

Hy Roberts, Ely dio., & Eleanor Palmer, Linc. dio. Disp. for marriage without banns. 3s 4d.

16 Chris. Twsylton & Ann Bere, of Dartford, Roch. dio. Similar disp. 3s 4d.

29 Ric. Stoke & Eliz. Lenett, of London. Similar disp. 3s 4d.

26 Ric. Hedley, student at Oxford, r. of Badgworth, Bath & W. dio. Disp. to take h.o. within one year, having obtained the above benef. 3s 4d.

p. 209

16 Mark Browthton, literate, Cov. & Lich. dio. Concession to practise as notary. 4s 6d.

23 Chris. Walker, Cov. & Lich. dio. Disp. to take h.o. outside the statutory time. 3s 4d.

Jo. Osborne, of the Kg's hsehld, & Philippa Lufkynne, widow. Disp. for marriage in any ch., without banns. 6s 8d.

p. 210

25 Reg. Whitebrede & Eliz. Peyege, Peterborough dio. Disp. for marriage without banns. 3s 4d.

Aug. 4 Tho. Sclater, B.Th., v. of Wedmore, Bath & W. dio. Disp. to hold any 2 benefices. 7s 2d.

9 Jo. Williams, B.Th., v. of Holy Trinity, Gloucester. Similar disp. 7s 2d.

Rob. Hyndmer, D.C.L. Disp. to hold a 3rd benef. 8s 10d.

21 Wm Radbard, M.A., r. of Kingsbury, Bath & W. dio., chapl. to the Bp of Bath & W. Disp. to hold another benef. with or any 2 without the above. 7s 2d.

p. 211

13 Geo. Stoughton, clk, M.A., r. of Ashe, Winton dio., chapl. to Ly Anne Clynton, widow. Similar disp. 7s 2d.

11 Peter Rowell, B.A., v. of East Clendon, Linc. dio. Disp. to hold another benef. with the above, which does not yield over £8 p.a., or another without it. 4s 5d.

17 Chris. Fisher, Carl. dio. Disp. to take all h.o. after subdcn's outside the statutory times. 4s 5d.

Aug. 12 Humfrey Cavell & Alice Nasshe, of London. Licence for marriage without banns. 3s 4d.

Feb. 1 Sir Jo. Wellysburne & Eliz. Laurence, of Fulwell, Oxford dio. Licence for marriage without banns in any ch. 6s 8d.

Aug. 16 Tho. Dynham & Kath. Rede, of London. Similar licence. 6s 8d.

p. 212

23 Sir Jo Wyett, pr., v. of Allecombe, Ex. dio., chapl. to Hy, Earl of Bridgwater. Disp. to hold another benef. with or any 2 without the above. 7s 2d.

24 Tho. Standysh, M.A., r. of Elworthy, Bath & W. dio., chapl. to Sir Rob. Southwell, Master of the Rolls. Similar disp. 7s 2d.

23 Wm Lee & Joan Walls, of Aylesbury, Linc. dio. Licence for marriage in any ch. without banns. 6s 8d.

26 Chris. Saunders, clk, r. of Lapford, Ex. dio., chapl. to Ld Hy Daubeny, Earl of Bridgwater. Disp. to hold another benef. with or any 2 without the above. 7s 2d.

26 Jo. Warden & Eliz. Morton, Heref. dio. Disp. for marriage without banns. 3s 4d.

p. 213

21 Wm Geffrye, D.C.L., Kg's chapl. Disp. to hold an additional benef. with or without cure with those he holds already, provided they do not yield over £100 p.a.; permut. cl. 14s 9¼d.

6 Tho. Harwell, pr., v. of Taddington, Heref. dio. Disp. to hold another benef. with the above, which does not yield over £8 p.a. or another without it. 4s 5d.

25 Jo. ap Howell & Marg. Creswell, of London. Disp. for marriage without banns. 3s 4d.

28 Wm Fownes, acol., Worc. dio. Disp., after receiving subdcn's orders, to take dcn's & pr.'s orders on the same day & outside the statutory times. 4s 5d; '20d pro suo diaconatu.'

p. 214

27 David Walter, literate, St David's dio. Concession to practise as tabellion. 4s 5d.

28 Tho. Sylvant & Eliz. Russell, of Stepney par., Westminster dio. Disp. for marriage without banns. 3s 4d.

25 Ant. Cowuderston *alias* Jonson & Kath. Vandernote, Lond. dio. Disp. for marriage without banns in any ch. 6s 8d.

30 Wm ap Rhes & Thomasina Myn, of London. Disp. for marriage without banns. 3s 4d.

Aug. 27 Rob. Fells, B.A., York dio. Disp. to take h.o. outside the statutory time. 3s 4d.

30 Jo. Gurley & Ann Hunt, of London. Disp. for marriage without banns. 3s 4d.

p. 215

Edw. Trevor, esq., & Marg. Staneley, widow, York dio. Disp. for marriage in any ch. without banns. 6s 8d.

Sept. 1 Edm. Olyver, r. of Cotterstock, Peterborough dio., chapl. to Frances, Countess of Huntingdon. Disp. to hold another benef. with or any 2 without the above. 7s 2d.

Aug. 30 Jo. Harry, pr., v. of Kenarth, St David's dio. Disp. to hold another benef. with the above, which does not yield over £8 p.a., or another without it. 4s 5d.

Tho. Griffith, St. David's dio. Disp. to take h.o. & hold a benef. although the son of a pr. 5s 6d.

Sept. 4 Wm Harwar, M.A., r. of Brinklow, Cov. & Lich. dio., chapl. to the Earl of Huntingdon. Disp. to hold another benef. with or 2 without the above. 7s 2d.

p. 216

5 Tho. More & Eliz. Fuller, of London. Disp. for marriage without banns, in any ch. 6s 8d.

7 Jo. Nydeham, sch., Cov. & Lich dio. Disp. to take h.o. outside the statutory times. 3s 4d.

4 Jo. Johns, Lond. dio., & Joan Cromwell, Westminster dio. Disp. for marriage without banns. 3s 4d.

6 Benedict Mulsho, M.A., Kg's chapl. Cancelled disp. to hold a 3rd benef. 8s 10d 'ad mandatum reverendi'.

7 Hy, Earl of Arundel & Ly Mary, his wife. Disp. to eat meat during Lent & at other prohibited times. 3s 4d.

p. 217

9 Leonard Dentt, pr., B.A., r. of Riddlesworth, Norw. dio. Disp. to hold another benef. with the above, which does not yield over £8 p.a. or any other without it. 4s 5d.

Jas Brooks, D.Th., r. of Lockinge, Sarum dio. Disp. to hold another benef. with or 2 others without the above. 7s 2d.

10 Tho. Willett, literate, Lond. dio. Disp. to practise as a notary. Gratis.

20 Tho. Pagynton & Dorothy Kytson, of London. Disp. for marriage without banns. 3s 4d.

Sept. 9 Tho. Low & Eliz. Sterkey, of London. Disp. for marriage without banns. 3s 4d.

p. 218

13 Jo. Pagynton & Joan Page, of London. Disp. for marriage in any ch. or chapel without banns. 6s 8d.

14 Geoffrey ap Rice, literate, St Asaph dio. Disp. to practise as notary or tabellion anywhere. Gratis.

2 Humfrey Garthe, pr., r. of St Mildred's, Canterbury. Disp. to hold another benef. with or without cure, with the above, which does not yield over £8 p.a. 4s 5d.

17 Jas Chilester & Christine Hudson, of the par. of St Alphage, Elsing Spital (Cripplegate), London. Disp. for marriage without banns in the bride's par. ch. 3s 4d.

19 Rob. Webbe & Jane Redmayne, of London. Disp. for marriage without banns in any ch. 6s 8d.

p. 219

21 Tho. Hayborne & Joan Eldyng, of London. Disp. for marriage without banns. 3s 4d.

20 Wm Harper, r. of North Pickenham, Norw. dio., chapl. to Qn Kath. Disp. to hold another benef. with the above. 7s 2d.

23 Humfrey Lyghtfote & Dorothy Wattes. Disp. for marriage in any ch. without banns. 6s 8d.

22 Jas Leonard & Alice Barber, of London. Disp. for marriage without banns. 3s 4d.

pp. 219–20

3 Peter Vannes, Kg's Secretary for Latin Letters, Dean of Salisbury. Disp. to postpone taking h.o. for 6 yrs, though holding various benefices. No fee.

p. 221

25 Walter Bucler & Ly Kath. Tanne, Glouc. dio. Disp. for marriage in any ch. without banns.

Jo. Cotterell, D.C.L., v. of Adderbury, Oxford dio. Disp. to hold another benef. with or 2 others without the above. 7s 2d.

24 Jo. Dyneley & Margery Lyn, of London. Disp. for marriage without banns. 3s 4d.

29 Geo. Bewmond & Eliz. Lussher. Disp. for marriage in any ch. or oratory. 3s 4d.

30 Jo. Tinyngton, subdcn, Linc. dio. Disp. to take dcn's & pr.'s orders from any bp. 4s 5d.

p. 222

Oct. 4 Edw. Morren & Eliz. Dakyng, of Streatley, Linc. dio. Disp. for marriage without banns. 3s 4d.

6 Wm Herde, pr., r. of Faversham, Roch. dio. Disp. to hold another benef. with the above, which yields under £8 p.a., or another without it. 4s 5d.

Geoffrey Hosyer & Helen Yarlond, Cov. & Lich. dio. Disp. for marriage without banns. 3s 4d.

5 Rob. Russell, of Shoreham, in the jurisdiction of Cant. dio., & Eliz. Smith, Winton dio. Disp. for marriage without banns. 3s 4d.

10 Tho. Fyldew, B.A., Bath & W. dio. Concession to act as tabellion. 4s 5d.

2 Jo. Carter & Gylian Haverd, Westminster dio. Disp. for marriage without banns. 3s 4d.

p. 223

8 Francis Swanne & Kath. Bryngborne, widow, Cant. dio. Disp. for marriage without banns. 6s 8d.

13 Jas Blande, sch., Chester dio. Disp. to take h.o. without l.d. from any bp on any days outside the statutory time. 5s 6d.

Edw. Pype, acol., Cov. & Lich. dio. Disp. to take h.o. from any bp outside the statutory times. 3s 4d.

Wm Scott, pr., r. of Blackington, Chich. dio. Disp. to hold another benef. with the above, which does not yield over £8 p.a. 4s 5d.

14 Rob. Webster, pr., v. of Alkborough, Linc. dio., chapl. to Jo. de Vere, Earl of Oxford. Disp. to hold another benef. with or 2 others without the above. 7s 2d.

p. 224

16 Ric. Turner, B.Th., chanter in the chantry of Edw. IV, St Geo.'s chapel, Windsor. Disp. to hold another benef. with, or 2 other benefices without the above chantry. 7s 2d.

8 Wm Lorkyn, B.Th., v. of Farnham, Winton dio. Disp. to hold another benef. with or 2 without the above. 7s 2d.

18 Ant. Hall, esq., & Eliz. Ley, widow, Winton dio. Disp. for marriage without banns. 3s 4d.

Jo. Dawdney, pr., v. of Monkleigh, Ex. dio., chapl. to Jo., Earl of Bath. Disp. to hold another benef. with or 2 without the above.

Oct. 20 Brian Sandford, pr., v. of Boston, Linc. dio., chapl. to Hy, Earl of Rutland. Disp. to hold another benef. with or 2 without the above. 7s 2d.

p. 225

22 Tho. Dodsworth & Dorothy Ley, Roch. dio. Disp. for marriage without banns. 3s 4d.

27 Ric. Brasyar, Lond. dio. & Jane Bury, Oxford dio. Disp. for marriage without banns. 3s 4d.

Wm Swyfte & Joyce Raysbye, Roch. dio. Disp. for marriage without banns in any ch. 6s 8d.

Edw. Rochester, acol. Disp. to take h.o. from any bp on any days. 3s 4d.

20 Jo. Barlow, pr., dean of Worcester. Disp. to eat meat during Lent & at other prohibited times. 3s 4d.

p. 226

28 Sir Tho. Hilton, Durham dio. Similar disp. 3s 4d.

Nov. 2 Hy Grey & Benedetta Myddelton, of Stepney, Westminster dio. Disp. for marriage without banns 3s 4d.

Jo. Gray, sch., Linc. dio. Disp. to take h.o. outside the statutory time. 3s 4d.

Sir Ant. Kyngston. Disp. to eat meat during Lent & at other prohibited times. 3s 4d.

3 Jo. Mayster, pr., r. of Stowell, Bath & W. dio. Disp. to hold another benef. with the above, which does not yield over £8 p.a. or any other without it. 4s 5d.

p. 227

4 Geo. Graye, acol., Durham dio. Disp. to take h.o. on any day outside the statutory time. 3s 4d.

Edw. Turner, pr., chanter in the chantry of Edsworth & Worthborow (sic), St Paul's, London, chapl. to Hy, Earl of Cumberland. Disp. to hold another benef. with or 2 without the above. 7s 2d.

5 Jo. Joseffe, pr., B.Th. Disp. to hold a 3rd benef. 8s. 10d.

8 Tho. Rede, sch., Bristol dio. Disp. to take subdcn's & dcn's orders on the same day. 4s 5d.

p. 228

11 Chris. Yorke & Kath. Martin, of Islington, Westminster dio. Disp. for marriage without banns. 3s 4d.

12 Tho. Willyamson, pr., r. of St Mary's, Grimsby, Linc. dio. Disp. to hold another benef. with the above, which does not yield over £8 p.a. 4s 5d.

Nov. 13 Tho. Barnes & Marg. Bawdewyn, of London. Disp. for marriage without banns. 3s 4d.

   6 Hugh Harrys, pr., B.C.L., r. of Waldron, Chich. dio. Disp. to hold another benef. with or 2 without the above. 7s 2d.

  13 Tho. Langton, sch., Winton dio. Disp. to take h.o. outside the statutory times without l.d. & on any days. 5s 6d.

p. 229

   Ric. Morryson, esq., & Brigett Husye, of gentle birth. Disp. for marriage in any ch. without banns. 6s 8d.

  14 Tho. Browne *alias* Cokkove & Eliz. Dannon, Lond. dio. Disp. for marriage in any ch. without banns. 6s 8d.

  16 Tho. ap Rethorgh, sch., St David's dio. Concession to take h.o. on any day without l.d. 5s 6d.

   Ric. Boner, pr., r. of Guisnes, Therouanne dio., chapl. to Sir Wm Grey, of Wilton. Disp. to hold another benef. with or any 2 without the above. 7s 2d.

   Rob. Prydyape, pr., r. of Rose Ash, Devon, chapl. to Jo., Earl of Bath. Disp. to hold another benef. with or 2 without the above. 7s 2d.

p. 230

  21 Edm. Secole & Margery Felps, Worc. dio. Disp. for marriage without banns in any ch. 6s 8d.

   1 Jo. Donne, D.Th., Kg's chapl. Disp. to hold additional benefices not yielding over 200 marks p.a. 14s 9d.

  22 Ralph Wylson, M.A., v. of Throwley, Cant. dio., chapl. to Sir Edw. North, Chancellor of the Court of Augmentations. Disp. to hold another benef. with or any 2 without the above. 7s 2d.

   Wm Chamberlayne, of the Kg's hsehld, & Kath. Lambe, of Wylde. Disp. for marriage without banns. 3s 4d.

  18 Maurice Wogan & Eliz. Atton, widow. Similar disp. 3s 4d.

  24 Tho. Larkyng & Clara Saunders, of London. Similar disp. 3s 4d.

p. 231

   Sir Adrian Poynyngs. Disp. to eat meat during Lent & at other prohibited times. 3s 4d.

  25 David Owen, pr., v. of Aldingborne, Chich. dio., chapl. to Mabel, Countess of Southampton. Disp. to hold another benef. with or any 2 without the above. 7s 2d.

  22 Tho. Tesdell & Joan Foster, widow. Sarum dio. Disp. for marriage without banns. 3s 4d.

Nov. 26 Francis Savage, esq., & Ann Shaldon, Worc. dio. Disp. for marriage within the prohibited time. 3s 4d.

Francis Spylman & Marg. Hill, of London. Disp. for marriage without banns. No fee.

Tho. Smyth & Rose Luce, of London. Disp. for marriage within the prohibited time. 3s 4d.

Ric. Stanfylde & Eliz. Beyston, of London. Disp. for marriage without banns. 3s 4d.

p. 232

Edw. Underhill & Joan Downes, Roch. dio. Similar disp. 3s 4d.

25 Griffin Wyllyams, pr., r. of Bridell, St David's dio., chapl. to the Bp of St David's. Disp. to hold another benef. with or any 2 without the above. 7s 2d.

Jo. Hamner, pr., chapl. to Hy, Marquess of Dorset, r. of Frinton, Lond. dio. Similar disp. 7s 2d.

30 Tho. Dichfylde & Joan Wycks, widow, of London. Disp. for marriage without banns & within the prohibited time. 3s 9d.

Dec. 2 Walter Mugge, pr., Kg's chapl. Disp. to hold a 3rd benef. 8s 10d.

p. 233

Walter Denham & Alice Pryst, widow, Linc. dio. Disp. for marriage without banns, within the prohibited time, & in any ch. 7s 2d.

3 Jas Gosnold & Eliz. Wyllett, of ?Hedingham ('Heddyngton'), Lond. dio. Disp. for marriage within the prohibited time. 3s 4d.

Tho. Hawkyns, sch., Sarum dio. Disp. to take h.o. from any bp without l.d. from his diocesan bp, and outside the statutory time. 5s 6d.

4 Jo. Ripley & Eliz. Hamond, widow, of London. Disp. for marriage without banns & within the prohibited time. 3s 9d.

10 Francis Beyver, pr., v. of Boston, Linc. dio. Disp. to hold another benef. with the above, which does not yield over £8 p.a., or any other without it. 4s 5d.

p. 234

Bartholomew Averell & Felise Harrys, Lond. dio. Disp. for marriage within the prohibited time. 3s 4d.

13 Geoffrey Bayley, M.A., v. of Louth, Linc. dio., Kg's chapl. Disp. to hold another benef. with or any 2 others without the above. 7s 2d.

15 Jo. Woodstocke & Eliz. Taylor. Disp. for marriage within the prohibited time, the banns read once. 3s 4d.

1546 Mar. 11 Simon Low, gent., Lond. dio. Disp. to eat meat during Lent & at other prohibited times, during his illness. 3s 4d.

? Jo. Benet & Edith Blagge, of Warminster, Sarum dio. Disp. for marriage within the prohibited time, the banns read once & in any ch. 6s 8d.

p. 235

? Jo. Hyxston, Durham dio., & Eliz. Raylton, Lond. dio. Disp. for marriage within the prohibited time, without banns, & in any oratory. 7s 2d.

? Drew Saunders & Ann Hatton, of St Pancras par., London. Disp. for marriage in any ch. without banns. 6s 8d.

1547 Jan. 11 Jo. Wodwarde & Marg. Harronden, of Boughton, Cant. dio. Disp. for marriage in any oratory without banns. 6s 8d.

12 Hy Luckyn & Eliz. Hartford, of St Gregory's par., London. Disp. for marriage without banns. 3s 4d.

p. 236

3 Tho. Alman, v. of Mortimer, Sarum dio. Disp. to hold another benef. with or 2 without the above. 7s 2d.

14 Tho. Chapell & Alice Bedyll, of the par. of St Mich. Cornhill, London. Disp. for marriage without banns. 3s 4d.

5 Rob. Nyesbelt & Marg. Hylls, of Lindfield, Chich. dio. Disp. for marriage without banns in any ch. 6s 8d.

13 Stephen Gryne, v. of ? Minting ('Myllyng'), Linc. dio. Disp. to hold another benef. with the above, which does not yield over £8 p.a., or another without it. 4s 5d.

17 Jo. Somer & Eliz. Pyourdye, of London. Disp. for marriage without banns in any ch. or oratory. 6s 8d.

p. 237

20 Clement Cornwell, of London, & Magdalene Raser, of Canterbury. Disp. for marriage without banns. 3s 4d.

24 Ric. Hawes & Ann Pycher, Worc. dio. Disp. for marriage without banns. 3s 4d.

20 Walter Calcot & Alice Marshall, both of gentle birth, Oxford dio. Disp. for marriage in any ch. without banns. 6s 8d.

25 Edw. Napper & Ann Peytoo, both of gentle birth. Disp. for marriage without banns. Gratis.

Jo. Hall, Westminster dio., & Kath. Walker, widow, Lond. dio. Disp. for marriage without banns. 3s 4d.

p. 238

Jan. 26 Jo. Manock & Ellen Brydges, Norw. dio. Disp. for marriage without banns. 3s 4d.

27 Tho. & Ellen Peycock, Norw. dio. Disp. for marriage, the banns read once, in any ch. 5s 6d.

26 Ambrose Farrar & Eliz. Johnson, of London. Disp. for marriage, the banns read once. 2s 2d.

27 Wm & Agnes Hyll, Linc. dio. Similar disp. 2s 2d.

26 Geo. Whythorne, pr., v. of Ruislip, Westminster dio. Disp. to hold another benef. with or any 2 without the above. 7s 2d.

p. 239

29 Jo. Gyfford & Susan Wadeley, Lond. dio. Disp. for marriage without banns. 3s 4d.

30 Tho. Spek. & Mary Freyll, Cant. dio. Similar disp. 3s 4d.

Feb. 3 Jas Goldwell, pr., r. of Addington, Roch. dio. Disp. to hold another benef. with or any 2 without the above. 7s 2d.

4 Jo. Rawlyns & Marg. Corryett, Lond. dio. Disp. for marriage without banns. 3s 4d.

5 Jo. Thoroughgood & Joan Payne, Lond. dio. Disp. for marriage within the prohibited time & in any ch. 6s 8d.

7 Ric. Growdon, pr., v. choral of Exeter cath. Disp. to hold another benef. with the above, or 2 others, one of which must be without cure of souls, without it. 4s 5d.

p. 240

8 Arnold Goldworth, pr., v. of Amberley, Chich. dio. Disp. to hold another benef. with the above, which does not yield over £8 p.a., or another without it. 4s 5d.

2 Wm Thompson, v. of Kympton, chapl. to Ld Edw. Clinton. Disp. to hold another benef. with or 2 without the above. 7s 2d.

6 Roger Wygmore & Cicily Hylaire, widow, both of gentle birth, Bath & W. dio. Disp. for marriage in any ch. without banns & within the prohibited time. 7s 2d.

7 Ric. Whythyll & Jane Kerton, of London. Disp. for marriage without banns & within the prohibited time. 3s 9d.

2 Edw. Loketon, M.A., chapl. to the Bp of St David's, v. of Stogursey, Bath & W. dio. Disp. to hold another benef. with or any 2 without the above. 7s 2d.

p. 241

Feb. 8 Wm Holmes & Eliz. Kydd, of Clerkenwell, Westminster dio. Disp. for marriage within the prohibited time. 3s 4d.

5 Philip Oxford, pr., r. of Calne Rogers, Glouc. dio. Disp. to hold another benef. with the above, which does not yield over £8 p.a. or another without it. 4s 5d.

6 Wm Fawnte & Jane Puressey *alias* Purfrey, both of gentle birth, Linc. dio. Disp. for marriage without banns & within the prohibited time. 3s 9d.

9 Jas Dyer, esq., & Ly Marg. Elyot, widow. Disp. for marriage in any ch., without banns, & within the prohibited time. 7s 2d.

10 Edw. Lloyd *alias* Johans, pr., v. of Hampstead Norris, Sarum dio., chapl. to Sir Ant. Wingfield, K.G. Disp. to hold another benef. with or 2 without the above. 7s 2d.

p. 242

Wm Stacye & Kath. Snowball, Linc. dio. Disp. for marriage within the prohibited time, the banns read once. 3s 4d.

11 Tho. Lee & Mary Morgan. Disp. for marriage within the prohibited time without banns. 3s 9d.

Rob. Davys & Alice Bolloxhyll, of Westminster. Disp. for marriage within the prohibited time without banns. 3s 9d.

9 Ellis Wymark & Florence Kempe, Cant. dio. Disp. for marriage within the prohibited time. 3s 4d.

10 Tho. Lambert & Jane Post, of Wrotham, peculiar of Canterbury. Similar disp. 3s 4d.

11 Tho. Adam & Alice Hyll, Lond. dio. Disp. for marriage within the prohibited time. 3s 4d.

p. 243

Matthew Tortt, pr., v. choral in the coll. ch. of St Mary's, Southwell, York dio. Disp. to hold another benef. if the above does not yield over £8 p.a. 4s 5d.

7 Jo. Sanderson, pr., v. of Dalby Parva, Linc. dio., chapl. to Ly Anne Graye, widow. Disp. to hold another benef. with or 2 without the above. 7s 2d.

11 Jo. Sydeatt, pr., v. choral of Salisbury cath. Disp. to hold another benef. with the above, which does not yield over £8 p.a., or another without it. 4s 5d.

14 Tho. Fyncham & Martha Pelnerton. Disp. for marriage without banns, in any ch. & within the prohibited time. 7s 2d.

Feb. 14 Sir Peter Carew & Ly Marg. Taylebusse. Similar disp. 7s 2d.

p. 244

14 Jo. Pope & Ann Dodmer. Disp. for marriage in the prohibited times. 3s 4d.

15 Roger Huett & Joan Elizander, widow, Westminster dio. Disp. for marriage the banns read once & within the prohibited time. 3s 4d.

13 Wm Crompton & Kath. Richardson, of London. Disp. for marriage within the prohibited time. 3s 4d.

16 Jo. Thronborow & Joan Randall, of Hykeham, Linc. dio. Disp. for marriage without banns in any ch. & within the prohibited time. 7s 2d.

8 Tho. Lyfeld & Frances Braye, Cant. dio. Similar disp. 7s 2d.

20 Jo. Shotter, Winton dio., & Eliz. Corke, Lond. dio. Disp. for marriage within the prohibited time. 3s 4d.

p. 245

20 Andrew Byllysbye, Linc. dio., & Marg. Henney, Lond. dio. Disp. for marriage without banns & in any ch. or oratory. 6s 8d.

21 Rob. Byngley, subdcn, Linc. dio. Disp. to take dcn's & pr.'s orders outside the statutory time, on any day, & from any bp. 4s 6d.

24 Felix Byncke, pr., v. of Felkirk, York dio., chapl. to Ric., Bp of Durham. Disp. to hold another benef. with or 2 without the above. 7s 2d.

26 Jas Langebroke & Grace Abell, Lond. dio. Disp. for marriage within the prohibited time. 3s 4d.

27 Ambrose Dormer & his wife, Oxford dio. Disp. to eat meat during Lent & at other prohibited times. 3s 4d.

p. 246

27 Tho. Bacon & his wife Jane. Similar disp. 3s 4d.

26 Gilbert Dethyke *alias* Nory, Knight at arms. Indult to eat meat during Lent & at other prohibited times. 3s 4d.

Mar. 2 Jo. Holford, sch., Chester dio. Disp. to take all h.o. without l.d. 2s 2d.

Ric. Corbett, gent. & his wife, Cov. & Lich. dio. Disp. to eat meat during Lent & at other prohibited times during his illness. 3s 4d.

3 Sir Ric. Southwell. Disp. to eat meat during Lent & at other prohibited times. 3s 4d.

Mar. 1 Hy Isam, gent. & his wife Ann. Similar disp. 3s 4d.

p. 247

3 Wm Saxye, B.C.L., Kg's chapl. Disp. to hold a 3rd benef. 8s 10d. Also disp. to hold a 4th benef. 8s 10d.

5 Roger More, esq., & his wife Ann. Disp. to eat meat during Lent & at other prohibited times. 3s 4d.

7 Jo. Lysce & Alice Smyth, widow, Lond. dio. Disp. for marriage in any ch. without banns & during the prohibited time. 7s 2d.

Sir Jo. Markham & his wife, York dio. Disp. to eat meat during Lent & at other prohibited times during his illness. 3s 4d.

p. 248

Nich. Lestrange & Kath. Men, Norw. dio. Disp. for marriage in any ch. or oratory without banns & in the prohibited time. 7s 2d.

Feb. 25 Hugh Turnbull, B.Th., r. of Acton, Westminster dio. Disp. to hold another benef. with, or any 2 without the above. 7s 2d.

Mar. 10 Jo. Nedeham, Cov. & Lich. dio. Disp. to take h.o. & hold any benef. despite defect of birth. 4s 5d.

Tho. Carpenter, gent., & his wife. Chich. dio. Disp. to eat meat during Lent & at other prohibited times during his illness. 3s 4d.

8 Wm Harvye, Somerset Herald, & his wife, of London. Disp. to eat meat during Lent & at other prohibited times. 3s 4d.

p. 249

11 Jo. Bretechyurdell, M.A., Chester dio., student at Oxford. Disp. to take h.o. on any day without l.d. from his diocesan. 5s 6d.

13 Tho. Armytage, York dio., student at Cambridge. Disp. to take h.o. on any day. 3s 4d.

14 Jo. Kempe, pr., v. of Burgham, Chich. dio. Disp. to hold another benef. with the above, which does not yield over £8 p.a., or another without it. 4s 5d.

17 Jo. Payne & Marg. Larke, of St Tho.'s par., Southwark. Disp. for marriage without banns & during the prohibited time. 3s 9d.

7 Jo. Fytzwillyam, esq., & his wife, Winton dio. Disp. to eat meat during Lent & at other prohibited times during his illness. 3s 4d.

p. 250

8 Hy, Earl of Bridgwater. Disp. to eat meat during Lent & at other prohibited times. 3s 4d.

10 Walter Moryce, r. of Sutton under Brayles, Gloucs. dio., chapl. to Tho., Earl of Southampton. Disp. to hold another benef. with or 2 without the above. 7s 2d.

Mar. 21 Jo. Prystman, acol., Carl. dio. Disp. to take h.o. from any bp on any day outside the statutory time. 5s.

22 Rob. Catlen & Ann Burgyn, Lond. dio. Disp. for marriage in any ch. or oratory. 6s 8d.

17 Tho. Gresham, citizen of London, & his wife. Disp. to eat meat during Lent & at other prohibited times. 3s 4d.

21 Jas Stoppys & Margery Nuce, of London. Disp. for marriage without banns & in any ch. 7s 2d.

p. 251

22 Ric. Somerskell, acol., York dio. Disp. after taking subdcn's orders to take h.o. on any day outside the statutory time & from any bp. 4s 5d.

23 Ric. Marshall, sch., York dio. Disp. to take dcn's & pr.'s orders after subdcn's on any day, outside the statutory time, from any bp. 4s 5d.

Jo. Maduve, D.Th., r. of Mablethorpe, Linc. dio. Disp. to hold another benef. with or 2 without the above. 7s 2d.

16 Jo. Synger, r. of Charleton, Roch. dio., Kg's chapl. Disp. to hold another benef. with or 2 without the above. 7s 2d.

23 Hy Fyssher & his wife Eliz., of London. Disp. to eat meat during Lent & at other prohibited times. 3s 4d.

Ric. Whawley, esq., & his wife Eliz., York dio. Similar disp. 3s 4d.

p. 252

16 Jo. Hastyngs, Kg's chapl., r. of Bainton, York dio. Disp. to hold another benef. with or 2 without the above. 7s 2d.

27 Wm Edlyngton, acol., Linc. dio. Disp. to take h.o. from any bp on any day outside the statutory time. 3s 4d.

pp. 252–3

16 Sir Jo. Haydon, Norw. dio. Disp. to have a portable altar, & for suitable priests to say offices & celebrate the Eucharist in his chapel or oratory at Baconsthorp Hall. 4s 5d.

p. 253

27 Balwine Hyll, r. of Dowlish Wake, Bath & W. dio., chapl. to Jo. Tuchett, Ld Audley. Disp. to hold another benef. with or 2 without the above. 7s 2d.

Tho. Weste, M.A., Kg's chapl. Disp. to hold a 3rd benef. 8s 10d.

26 Ric. Brayer, gent. of London. Disp. to eat meat during Lent & at other prohibited times during his illness. 3s 4d.

Mar. 26 Wm Chester, merchant, of London, & his wife Eliz. Similar disp. 3s 4d.

p. 254

30 Wm Lane, esq. Disp. to eat meat during Lent & at other prohibited times. 3s 4d.

Matilda Lane, widow, Linc. dio. Similar disp. 3s 4d.

Sir Geoffrey Pole. Disp. to have a portable altar & for suitable priests to say offices & celebrate the Eucharist in his chapel or oratory at Lordyngton, Suffolk. 7s 9d.

p. 255

Jan. 20 Ric. Deane, r. of Acworth, York dio. & St Tho. the Apostle, London, Kg's chapl. Disp. to hold another benef. with, or 3 without the above. 8s 10d.

Mar. 28 Tho. Atkenson, r. of Ormside, Carl. dio., chapl. to Sir Wm Paget, K.G. Disp. to hold another benef. with or 2 without the above. 7s 2d.

31 Wm Quarton, r. of Chiswick, Lond. dio., chapl. to Ld Jo. Russell, K.G., Keeper of the Privy Seal. Similar disp. 7s 2d.

Apr. 1 Geo. Merbery, v. of Rudgwick, Chich. dio. Disp. to hold another benef. with the above, which does not yield over £8 p.a. or another without it. 4s 5d.

p. 256

Edw. Mosley, acol., Cov. & Lich. dio. Disp. to take all h.o. on the same day, outside the statutory time, from any bp & without l.d. 3s 4d.

2 Jo. Woodthorpe, acol., Linc. dio. Disp. to take h.o. without l.d. 2s 2d.

3 Lawrence Harward, B.C.L., v. of South Stoneham, Winton dio., chapl. to Sir Wm Paulet, K.G., Ld St Jo. Disp. to hold another benef. with or 2 without the above. 7s 2d.

14 Ralph Bentley, r. of St Jo. Zachary, London, chapl. to Ld Wm Windsor. Similar disp. 7s 2d.

13 Wm Spenser & Joan Edds, of London. Disp. for marriage without banns. 3s 4d.

1 Hugh Weston, D.Th., r. of St Botolph's without Bishopsgate, London. Disp. to hold another benef. with or 2 without the above. 7s 2d.

p. 257

16 Lancelot Thornton, pr., r. of Syerston, York dio., chapl. to Sir Jo. Conyers, Ld of Skelton & Hornby. Disp. to hold another benef. with, or 2 without the above. 7s 2d.

Apr. 16 Wm Garner, B.Cn.L., chanter in the chantry of St Cuthbert in York Minster. Similar disp. 7s 2d.

15 Tho. Bewly & Agnes Sowthonson, Cant. dio. Disp. for marriage without banns in any ch. 6s 8d.

21 Bartholomew Farres, v. of Down Ampney, Gloucs. dio., chapl. to Jo., Bp of Gloucester. Disp. to hold another benef. with or 2 without the above. 7s 2d.

24 Hamund Hausharte. Disp. to take dcn's & pr.'s orders on any one day, outside the statutory time, from any bp, without l.d. although in his 23rd yr. 9s 11d.

p. 258

Roger Folyat & Dorothy Jenetts, Linc. dio. Disp. for marriage in any ch. & without banns. 6s 8d.

25 Tho. Hubbert & Joan Farrar, Linc. dio. Disp. for marriage without banns. 3s 4d.

26 Jo. Hyde & Eliz. Wyllyams, St David's dio. Disp. for marriage without banns. 3s 4d.

David ap Holl, B.Cn.L., r. of Whitechurch, St David's dio. Disp. to hold 2 other benefices with or 3 without the above. 10s.

27 Tho. Grenelef, pr., r. of Salcott cum Virley, Lond. dio., chapl. to Hy, Earl of Sussex. Disp. to hold another benef. with or 2 without the above. 7s 2d.

p. 259

26 Jo. Payne & Agnes Pynke, Winton dio. Disp. for marriage without banns. 3s 4d.

27 Tho. Whytnall & Dorothy Fane, Roch. dio. Disp. for marriage in any ch. or oratory without banns. 6s 8d.

28 Jo. Hope & Alice Mawde, York dio. Disp. for marriage without banns. 3s 4d.

30 Oliver Lowther & Eliz. Edwards, of Holy Sepulchre, London. Disp. for marriage without banns. 3s 4d.

19 Jo. Clerke, B.C.L., chapl. to Tho., Bp of Ely, r. of Dodington, Ely dio. Disp. to hold another benef. with the above or 2 without it. 7s 2d.

May 2 Wm Talton, gent. & Grace Stanley, widow, Chich. dio. Disp. for marriage without banns & in any ch. 6s 8d.

p. 260

Edm. Ansell & Cristine Ocle, widow, of the par. of Wolchurch, London. Disp. for marriage without banns. 3s 4d.

Apr. 9 Tho. Kente, pr., v. of Wadhurst, Chich. dio., chapl. to Ld Jo. Russell, K.G., Keeper of the Privy Seal. Disp. to hold another benef. with or 2 without the above. 7s 2d.

May 5 Wm Hunerford, M.A., r. of Folke, Bristol dio., chapl. to Ld Jo. Russell. Similar disp. 7s 2d.

Apr. 22 Rob. Wylson, clk, r. of Stadhampton, Linc. dio., chapl. to the Bp of Peterborough. Similar disp. 7s 2d.

May 5 Tho. Ingeson, pr., r. of Whenby, York dio. Disp. to hold another benef. with the above, which does not yield over £8 p.a., or another without it. 4s 5d.

p. 261

     6 Wm Huntt, r. of Dunnington, Worcs. dio., chapl. to Ld Tho. Sandes. Disp. to hold another benef. with or any 2 without the above. 7s 2d.

Simon Throgmorton, gent., & Agnes Marlborowe, widow, Linc. dio. Disp. for marriage in any ch. or chapel without banns. 6s 8d.

Hy Henesyde, sch., Carl. dio. Disp. to take h.o. from any bp without l.d. 2s 2d.

     9 Edw. Welshe & Agnes Hore, of St Saviour's par., Southwark. Disp. for marriage without banns. 3s 4d.

     7 Jo. Hayes & Edith Tenderyng, widow, Lond. dio. Disp. for marriage without banns. 3s 4d.

p. 262

    10 Wm Richard, acol., Linc. dio. Disp. to take subdcn's & dcn's orders outside the statutory times on any day & from any bp. 4s 5d.

Rob. Croste, pr., v. of Masham?, Sarum dio., chapl. to Tho., Earl of Southampton. Disp. to hold another benef. with or 2 without the above. 7s 2d.

    12 Jo. Danyell, gent., & Eliz. Tuke. Disp. for marriage in any ch. without banns & within the prohibited time. 7s 2d.

    13 Wm Hochenson, B.A., student at Oxford. Disp. to take h.o. outside the statutory times & from any bp. 3s 4d.

    14 Tho. Ballander & Ann Scryven, of London. Disp. for marriage without banns. 3s 4d.

p. 263

    13 Jo. Rokbye, D.C.L. Disp. to take all h.o. & 2 on the same day outside the statutory times & from any bp. 3s 4d.

Jo. Syms, B.Th., chapl. to Jo., Bp of Exeter. Disp to hold a 3rd benef. or 3 others instead of those he holds already. 8s 5d.

May 20 Roger Stephenson & Eliz. Packe, Peterborough dio. Disp. for marriage within the prohibited time & in any ch. 6s 8d.

18 Bartholomew Rone & Eliz. Denney, both of gentle birth. Disp for marriage without banns & within the prohibited time. 3s 9d.

21 Wm Cade, of London, & Alice Latham, Chich. dio. Disp. for marriage without banns & within the prohibited time. 3s 4d.

17 Wm Denyson, B.Th., Kg's chapl. Disp. to hold a 3rd benef. or 3 others instead of those he holds already. 8s 10d.

p. 264

22 Justinian Rogers & Ann Haywood. Disp. for marriage in any ch. or oratory, within the prohibited time. 6s 8d.

21 Ric. Lyttelford, subdcn, Cov. & Lich. dio. Disp. to take dcn's & pr.'s orders from his diocesan bp or the latter's suffragan on any day & outside the statutory time. 4s 5d.

22 Wm Payne & Marg. Copynger, of London. Disp. for marriage within the prohibited time. 3s 4d.

20 Rob. Fleccher & Marg. Mollyneux, both of gentle birth, York dio. Disp. for marriage without banns. 3s 4d.

Ric. Papworth & Marg. Gryffyng, of London. Disp. for marriage within the prohibited time. 3s 4d.

25 Wm Woods & Agnes Salyng. Similar disp. 3s 4d.

Tho. Pepys & Alice Sefold, both of gentle birth, Norw. dio. Disp. for marriage without banns in any ch. 6s 8d.

p. 265

24 Chris. Heronden & Joan Nordon, both of gentle birth, Lond. dio. Disp. for marriage without banns during the prohibited time. 3s 4d.

6 Stephen Marryston, pr., r. of Sutton, Lond. dio., chapl. to Hy, Bp of Sodor. Disp. to hold another benef. with or 2 without the above. 7s 2d.

31 Hy Kynge, D.Th., v. of Wyndham, Norw. dio. Similar disp. 7s 2d.

June 3 Ric. Spryngham & Mary Meredyth. Disp. for marriage without banns in any ch. 6s 8d.

2 Rob. Henayge, esq., & Marg. Strangwyshe, widow. Similar disp. 6s 8d.

4 Nich. Morryse, B.C.L., Kg's chapl. Disp. to hold a 3rd benef. with, or 3 others without those he already holds. 8s 10d.

p. 266

June 1 Edw. Redford, pr., r. of All Saints, Southampton, chapl. to Sir Jo. Wallop, K.G. Disp. to hold another benef. with or 2 without the above. 7s 2d.

10 Jo. Howytt & Ann Parker, of the par. of All Saints, Honey Lane, London. Disp. for marriage without banns. 3s 4d.

7 Rob. Porter, of Bedford, Linc. dio. Disp. to practise the art of medicine. 4s 5d.

4 Jo Bruarne, pr., r. of Beesby (Bebye), Linc. dio., chapl. to Hy, Marquess of Dorset. Disp. to hold another benef. with or 2 others without the above. 7s 2d.

14 Wm Wheteley & Clementine Norton, both of gentle birth, London. Disp. for marriage, the banns read once. 2s 2d.

p. 267

21 Jo. Elmer & Ellen Cornell, widow, Roch. dio. Disp. for marriage without banns. 3s 4d.

2 Jo. Hayward, B.A., r. of Padbury, Linc. dio. Disp. to hold another benef. with the above, which does not yield over £8 p.a. or another without it. 4s 5d.

16 Nich. Glademan, B.Th., v. of Fingringhoe, Lond. dio., chapl. to Qn Kath. Disp. to hold another benef. with, or 2 others without the above. 7s 2d.

2 Peter Kytson, York dio. Disp. to take dcn's & subdcn's orders from any bp outside the statutory time. 4s 5d.

25 Jo. Ledyngton & Joan Skydmore, widow, of London. Disp. for marriage in any ch. without banns. 6s 8d.

p. 268

28 Roger Lewes, B.C.L., r. of Marnhull, Bristol dio. Disp. to hold another benef. with, or 2 others without the above. 7s 2d.

25 Tho. Docwrey & Mildred Hales, both of gentle birth, of Stondon, Heref. dio. Disp. for marriage in any ch. without banns. 6s 8d.

29 Ralph Omersham & Joan Elverston, Cant. dio. Disp. for marriage without banns. 3s 4d.

p. 269

July 2 Ric. Kempe & Kath. Catisbye, Worcs. dio. Disp. for marriage in any ch. or oratory within the prohibited time & without banns 7s 2d.

5 Ric. Samwyse, pr., r. of Chideock Ford, Bristol dio., chapl. to Ld Jo. Russell, K.G., Keeper of the Privy Seal. Disp. to hold another benef. with, or 2 without the above. 7s 2d.

July 5 Edw. Lloyd, chapl. to Wm, Ld of Stourton, r. of Little Bromley Similar disp. 7s 2d.

4 Nich. Arscott, subdcn, student at Oxford. Disp. to hold a benef., although not yet beyond his 20th yr, provided he takes dcn's & pr.'s orders after his 21st birthday. 4s 11d.

p. 270

5 Edw. Saxbye & Ann Bolond, widow. Disp. for marriage without banns. 3s 4d.

9 Jo. Ryche & Ann Kelick, of St Mary Abchurch, London. Disp. for marriage without banns. 3s 4d.

13 Tho. Charnell & Joan Thurgood, Lond. dio. Disp. for marriage without banns, in any ch. 6s 8d.

p. 271

July 13 Philip Edwards, B.Cn.L., r. of Chilton, Sarum dio. (*sic*) Disp. to hold another benef. with or 2 without the above. 7s 2d.

15 Tho. Copland & Olive Rosyngton, widow, of Lambeth. Disp. for marriage without banns. 3s 4d.

14 Ric. Cheny, B.Th., r. of St Helen's, Worcs. dio. Disp. to hold another benef. with or 2 without the above. 7s 2d.

16 Tho. Sparcke, B.Th., chapl. to the suffragan Bp of Berwick. Similar disp. 7s 2d.

21 Francis Varneley & Eleanor Cattler. Disp. for marriage without banns & in any ch. 6s 8d.

p. 272

20 Ric. Wollay, M.A., v. of Leytonstone, Lond. dio. Disp. to hold another benef. if the above does not yield over £8 p.a. or another benef. without it. 4s 5d.

25 Jo. Corke, Lond. dio., & Dorothy Tebalde, Cant. dio. Disp. for marriage without banns. Gratis.

29 Wm Page & Alice Cromwell, of the par. of St Giles without Cripplegate, London. Disp. for marriage without banns. 3s 4d.

? Jo. Purvey, Westminster dio., & Agnes Woodley, Lond. dio. Licence for marriage without banns in the bride's par. ch. 3s 4d.

Ric. Best, v. of St Martin's in the Fields, Westminster dio. Licence for plurality. 7s 2d.

Rob. Parkhurst, B.Th., v. of Washington, Chich. dio. Similar licence. 7s 2d.

Owen Morgan & Eliz. Taylor, widow, of London. Licence for marriage in any ch. 6s 8d.

p. 273

Geo. Flower, M.A., chanter in the chantry of Edm. Audley, Salisbury cath. Licence to hold another benef. with or 2 others without the above. 7s 2d.

Ric. Lovidon, v. of Donyngton (probably in Holland, Lincs.), chapl. to Sir Ant. Wingfield. Similar licence. 7s 2d.

Walter Darkenell, v. of Sevenoaks. Similar licence. 7s 2d.

Chris. Wotton & Joan Oland, of London. Licence for marriage without banns. 3s 4d.

Jo. Olde. Creation as public notary. 4s 5d.

Geo. Marin & Philippa Shosmyth, of London. Licence for marriage without banns. 3s 4d.

Mich. Androwe & Anne Walden. Licence for marriage in any ch., the banns read once. 5s 6d.

Wm Bull & Philippa Cawod. Licence for marriage without banns. 3s 4d.

p. 274

Patrick Lenton, r., of Tingrith, Linc. dio. Licence for non-res. during illness. 3s 4d.

Jo. Stones & Millicent Broket. Licence for marriage without banns. 3s 4d.

Jo. Ravessh & Eliz. Sargar, Winton dio. Similar licence. 3s 4d.

Jo. Guyn, B.C.L., v. of ——? Disp. to hold 2 benefices. 7s 2d.

—— Pecocke, r. of Llangham, St David's dio., chapl. to the Bp of Westminster. Disp. to hold 2 benefices. 7s 2d.

? Rob. Arnolld, r. of St Mary Magdalen's, Lincoln. Licence to hold another benef. with the above, which does not yield over £8 p.a. 4s 5d.

Brian Barber & Eliz. Alen. Disp. for marriage in any ch. without banns. 6s 8d.

p. 275

Aug.   ? Tho. Trygg & Eliz. Medcalfe, of Stamford. Similar disp. 6s 8d.

Geo. Foxcote & Joan Snyde, of London. Licence for marriage, the banns read once. 2s 2d.

June   ? Jo. Jones, pr., r. of Talyllyn, St David's dio. Licence to hold another benef. if the fruits of the above do not exceed £8 p.a. 4s 5d.

Aug.   ? Wm Ibry, clk, r. of Chipstead, Winton dio., chapl. to the Earl of Southampton. Licence to hold another benef.; permut. cl. 7s 2d.

Jo. Wrenham & Marg. Gyll, Lond. dio. Disp. for marriage in any ch. 6s 8d.

Tho. Warter & Joan Wilde, of London. Similar disp. 6s 8d.

p. 276

Tho. Utton & Joan Savage, Lond. dio. Disp. for marriage without banns. 3s 4d.

Laurence Manley & Joan Warner, Westminster dio. Similar disp. 3s 4d.

Tho. Chamberlayne, esq. Disp. to eat meat during Lent & at other prohibited times. 3s 4d.

Tho. Walker & Matilda Belchambe, Winton dio. Disp. for marriage without banns. 3s 4d.

Jo. Vicariss & Margerie Gerard, of London. Similar disp. 3s 4d.

Jo. Cooke & Joan Darknall, of London. Similar disp. 3s 4d.

Edw. Mowle, pr., Lond. dio. Disp. to hold another benef. with the one without cure he holds already. 4s 5d.

p. 277

Sept. ? Jo. Smart, r. of Beckley, Oxford dio., chapl. to the Bp of Oxford. Disp. to hold another benef. with or 2 without the above. 7s 2d.

Ric. Benett, v. of St Veep ('Vepe'), Ex. dio., chapl. to the Bp of Exeter. Disp. to hold another benef. with or 2 without the above. 7s 2d.

Wm Pye, D.Th. Disp. for translation. 8s 10d.

Wm Sidey & Mary Flewellen, Lond. dio. Licence for marriage in any ch. without banns. 6s 8d.

Oct. 2 Ralph Newton, r. of Frinsted, Cant. dio., chapl. to Ld Conyers. Disp. to hold another benef. with or 2 without the above. 7s 2d.

11 Jas Marten, r. of Morton, Lond. dio. Disp. to live anywhere in his par. until his recovery from illness. 3s 4d.

p. 278

Chris. Frohocke & Eliz. Mynshull, Westminster dio. Disp. for marriage in any ch. without banns. 6s 8d.

14 Jo. Heth & Agnes Motherbe, widow, of London. Disp. for marriage without banns. 3s 4d.

Geo. Bancroste, pr., r. of Grittleton ('Greatlyngton'), Sarum dio., chapl. to Wm, Marquess of Northampton. Disp. to hold another benef. with or 2 without the above. 7s 2d.

Oct. 10 Ralph Tode, B.C.L., chapl. to the Bp of Durham, v. of Hart, Durham dio. Disp. to hold another benef. with or 2 without the above. 7s 2d.

23 Wm Hamylden & Grace Kechin, of London. Disp. for marriage without banns. 3s 4d.

p. 279

29 Edw. Machell, pr., v. of Aspatria, Carl. dio., chapl. to the Bp of Carlisle. Disp. to hold another benef. with or any 2 without the above. 7s 2d.

Wm Dyon, pr., v. of Cosby, Linc. dio. Disp. to hold another benef. with the above, which does not yield over £8 p.a. or another benef. without it. 4s 5d.

Nov. 1 Jo. Davys, pr., v. of ?Llanelos, Bangor dio. Disp. to hold another benef. with the above, which does not yield over £8 p.a. or another without it. 4s 5d.

2 Ric. Dyngley, gent., & Eliz. Cheseman, widow, Roch. dio. Disp. for marriage without banns in any ch. 6s 8d.

p. 280

3 Jo. Thornton, v. of Leeds, York dio. Disp. to hold another benef. with or 2 without the above. 7s 2d.

2 Jo. Woodthorpe, dcn, Linc. dio. Disp. to take pr.'s orders from any bp outside the statutory times. 3s 4d.

6 Hy Peckham & Eliz. Dakes, both of gentle birth. Disp. for marriage in any ch. 3s 4d.

? Ric. Stradborne, M.A., v. of Kirtlington, Oxford dio., chapl. to the Bp of St David's. Disp. to hold another benef. with or 2 without the above. 7s 2d.

9 Maurice Welshe, gent., Gloucs. dio., & Ly Eliz. Hartcorte, widow, Oxford dio. Disp. for marriage in any ch. without banns. 6s 8d.

14 Roger Androwe, gent., & Helen Bayly, widow, of St Mary's par., Shrewsbury. Similar disp. 6s 8d.

p. 281

3 Ralph Smalepage, r. of Otley, Norw. dio., chapl. to the Earl of Southampton, K.G. Disp. to hold another benef. with or 2 without the above. 7s 2d.

15 Tho. Smythson, r. of West Kingston, Sarum dio., chapl. to Hy Ld Nevill. Disp. to hold another benef. with or 2 without the above. 7s 2d.

Silvester Campien, pr., r. of Mistley, Lond. dio., chapl. to Hy, Earl of Rutland. Disp. to hold another benef. with or 2 without the above. 7s 2d.

Nov. 11 Ric. Unyon & Helen Jones, of St Dunstan's-in-the-West, London. Disp. for marriage without banns. 3s 4d.

12 Ric. Tremayne, B.A., student at Oxford. Disp. to hold a benef., not having yet reached his 21st yr, provided he takes h.o. after his 22nd birthday. 8s 4d.

p. 282

14 Hugh Shadwall, Lond. dio., & Dorothy Wherwood, Cov. & Lich. dio., both of gentle birth. Disp. for marriage without banns. 3s 4d.

16 Walter Fysshe & Eliz. Worthyngton, widow, of the par. of St Dunstan-in-the-West, London. Disp. for marriage without banns. 3s 4d.

18 Rob. Legge, esq., of West Greenwich or Deptford Strand, Roch. dio., Treasurer of the Fleet, & Edith Collowaye, of London. Disp. for marriage without banns in any ch. or oratory. 6s 8d.

Wm Harper & Alice Channtrell, widow. Disp. for marriage without banns. 3s 4d.

Mich. Dunnyng, student at Cambridge. Disp. to take all h.o. outside the statutory times, without l.d. & from any bp. 5s 6d.

p. 283

Tho. Byrche, pr., v. of Leigh, Lond. dio., chapl. to Sir Ric. Rich, Ld Chancellor. Disp. to hold another benef. with or 2 without the above. 7s 2d.

19 Sir Wm Gaskyn & Marg. Wryght, gent., York dio. Disp. for marriage without banns in any ch. or oratory & within the prohibited time. 7s 2d.

20 Jas Bacar & —— Hungerford, of London. Disp. for marriage without banns. 3s 4d.

Rob. Fyssher & Eliz. Robynson, Carl. dio. Disp. for marriage outside the statutory times & in either's par. ch. 6s 8d.

p. 284

21 Hy Partrydge & Alice Newtham, widow, Westminster dio. Disp. for marriage without banns. 3s 4d.

4 Jo. Baker, pr., r. of Allington, Ex. dio., chapl. to Walter Devereux, Ld Ferrers of Chartley, K.G. Disp. to hold another benef. with or 2 others without the above. 7s 2d.

19 Wm Story, clk, r. of Charlton Musgrave, Bath & W. dio., chapl. to Ld Wm Stourton. Similar disp. 7s 2d.

2 Nich. Stone & Agnes Boston, of the par. of St Magnus, London. Disp. for marriage without banns. 3s 4d.

Nov. 23 Rob. Longe & Joan Skargill, both of gentle birth, & of London. Disp. for marriage, the banns read once. 2s 2d.

p. 285

24 Jo. Sone & Lucy Walker, of Sevenoaks, Cant. dio. Disp. for marriage without banns. 3s 4d.

26 Jo. Williams & Mary Blage, of London. Disp. for marriage outside the statutory times. 3s 4d.

24 Tho. Smyth & Alice Hunsdon, Lond. dio. Disp. for marriage without banns. 3s 4d.

25 Arthur Dedycett & Marg. Fulwood, widow, of London. Similar disp. 3s 4d.

p. 286

2 Jo. Hylpe, M.A., r. of Stanford Rivers, Lond. dio., chapl. to Sir Ant. Browne, K.G. Disp. to hold another benef. with or 2 without the above. 7s 2d.

29 Owen Bray & Alice Dannaster, of London. Disp. for marriage outside the statutory times. 3s 4d.

30 Jo. Mathew & Eliz. Bradley, widow, of London. Disp. for marriage without banns & outside the statutory time. 3s 4d.

Dec. 1 Nich. Burton, gent., & Eleanor Fowle, widow, of Mitcham, Winton dio. Disp. for marriage in any ch., the banns read once, outside the statutory times. 6s 8d.

p. 287

2 Tho. Watts & Eliz. Gybbyns, of Benenden, Cant. dio. Disp. for marriage outside the statutory times, the banns read once. 3s 4d.

3 Tho. Rathbone & Marg. Ive, Westminster dio. Disp. for marriage within the prohibited time without banns. 3s 9d.

Hy Marshe & Marg. Hales, both of gentle birth, & of London. Similar disp. 3s 9d.

Tho. Eynns, esq., & Eliz. Nevill. Similar disp. 3s 9d.

4 Jas Wyncles, Lond. dio., & Eliz. Webbe, Winton dio. Disp. for marriage within the prohibited times. 3s 4d.

p. 288

5 Oswald Butler, student at Cambridge. Disp. to take dcn's & pr.'s orders after subdcn's, on any day outside the statutory time, without l.d., & from any bp. 6s 7d.

8 Hy Assheley, esq., & Kath. Basset, gent., of Hever, nr Canterbury. Disp. for marriage within the prohibited time & without banns. 3s 9d.

Dec. 11 Rob. Barns & Kath. Cartar, of Whitechapel. Disp. for marriage outside the statutory time, the banns read once. 3s 4d.

10 Geo. Badcok & Ann Myllys, of London. Similar disp. 3s 4d.

p. 289

Oct. 11 Jo. Croke, esq., of London. Disp. to eat meat during Lent & at other prohibited times, also for his wife & 3 other persons. 13s 4d.

Dec. 9 Wm Hertford & Marg. Stevens, of London. Disp. for marriage within the prohibited times. 3s 4d.

17 Alex. Huys & Ann Wolley, of London. Disp. for marriage within the prohibited time without banns. 3s 9d.

Alex. Wrythyngton & Juliana Wylford, of London. Similar disp. 3s 9d.

16 Tho. Canner, B.Th., Kg's chapl., r. of Stoke sub Hamdon, Bath & W. dio., archdcn of Dorset. Disp. to hold another benef. 8s 10d.

p. 290

3 Phillip Roberts, r. of Ludchurch, St David's dio. Disp. to hold another benef. with the above, which does not yield over £8 p.a., or another without it. 4s 5d.

11 Tho. Mountayne, literate, York dio. Concession to practise as tabellion. 4s 5d.

? Tho. Vycary (or Vincry?) & Alice Buck, of London. Disp. for marriage in any ch. without banns & within the prohibited time. 7s 2d.

? Gregory Harryson & Ellen Badcock, of London. Disp. for marriage within the prohibited time & without banns. 3s 9d.

p. 291

*1 Nich. Archebold, Kg's chapl. Disp. to hold a 3rd benef. 8s 10d.

1548 Jan. 5 Wm Perye, M.A., r. of Caldbeck, Carl. dio., chapl. to the Bp of Carlisle. Disp. to hold another benef. with or 2 without the above. 7s 2d.

10 Francis Pycher & Mary Lylgrave, both of gentle birth, of London. Disp. for marriage in any ch. or oratory without banns, 'Mr Husey debet'. 6s 8d.

17 Hy Whytaires, Westminster dio., & Isabella Hasylwood, Lond. dio. Disp. for marriage without banns. 3s 4d.

p. 292

19 Mich. Apsley & Kath. Huse, Chich. dio. Disp. for marriage without banns. 3s 4d.

* Page heading is 'mense Januarii' but this entry is dated December: perhaps mistakenly.

Jan. 13 Humfrey Darell, M.A., Peterborough dio. Disp. to take h.o. on any day from any bp, outside the statutory time. 3s 4d.

? Wm Dunche & Mary Barons, of London. Disp. for marriage without banns in any ch. 6s 8d.

7 Jo. Yelde & Eliz. Matche, Cant. dio. Disp. for marriage without banns. 3s 4d.

? Jo. Redman & Joan Marse, of London. Disp. for marriage, the banns read once. 2s 2d.

p. 293

24 Wm Barbor & Eliz. Watkynson, of London. Disp. for marriage without banns. 3s 4d.

27 Stephen Andrewes & Marg. Wemys, of the par. of St Botolph's by Billingsgate, London. Disp. for marriage without banns. 3s 4d.

Jo. Pynfold & Cicily Bruerton, of London. Similar disp. 3s 4d.

28 Jo. Marin? Fayre & Eliz. Branche, of London. Disp. for marriage within the prohibited time. 3s 4d.

Wm Lock, citizen & alderman of London, & Eliz. Meredyth, widow. Disp. for marriage without banns in any ch. & within the prohibited time. 7s 2d.

p. 294

29 Edm. Brygett, D.Th., r. of Thorley, Lond. dio. Disp. to hold another benef. with or 2 without the above. 7s 2d.

27 Wm Clyston, of London. Disp. to eat meat during Lent & at other times during his illness. 3s 4d.

31 Polidore Rosse & Joan Gowghe, of the par. of St Botolph without Bishopsgate, London. Disp. for marriage within the prohibited time. 3s 4d.

24 Tho. Goodrich, Bp of Ely. Disp. to eat meat during Lent & other prohibited times, also for 4 other persons. 16s 8d.

p. 295

12 Tho. Whytwell, pr., B.Th. Disp. to eat meat during Lent & other prohibited times. 3s 4d.

28 Geo. Raye & Agnes Blande. Disp. for marriage without banns. 'Familia nostra mason militis nihil solvit.'

31 Barnerd Jenyns & Frances Sawnders, of Ewell, Winton dio. Disp. for marriage within the prohibited time. 3s 4d.

29 Geo. Kyllyngworth & Jane Sanderson, of the par. of St Botolph's by Billingsgate, London. Disp. for marriage without banns & within the prohibited time. 3s 9d.

Jan. 20 Stephen Galthrop & Agnes Mathew, of London. Disp. for marriage without banns. 3s 4d.

p. 296

24 Simon Goodnep & Eliz. Corbet, of London. Disp. for marriage without banns. 3s 4d.

26 Ciriac Petyt & Florence Charnocke, both of gentle birth, of Ightam, Cant. dio. Disp. for marriage within the prohibited time. 3s 4d.

Feb. 1 Jo. Fytzjamys, r. of Horsington, Bath & W. dio., chapl. to Sir Jo. Tuchet, Ld Audley. Disp. to hold another benef. with or 2 without the above. 7s 2d.

2 Sir Jo. Gascoigne. Disp. to eat meat during Lent & at other prohibited times. 3s 4d.

3 Mich. Hall, Cant. dio., & Christine Harman, Norw. dio. Licence for marriage, the banns read once, within the prohibited time. 3s 4d.

p. 297

2 Wm Hunsdon & Margery Wederell, Westminster dio. Licence for marriage within the prohibited time. 3s 4d.

3 Tho. Burbage, Heref. dio., & Eleanor Lee, Lond. dio. Similar licence. 3s 4d.

2 Hy Reppes & Dorothy Jenny, of London. Disp. for marriage within the prohibited time & in any ch. 7s 2d.

3 Jo. de Vere, Earl of Oxford. Disp. to eat meat during Lent & at other prohibited times, also for 4 other persons invited to his table. 16s 8d.

Geo. Myddelton & Sibil Martin, widow, Winton dio. Licence for marriage without banns & within the prohibited times. 3s 9d.

p. 298

Jan. 19 Wm Damsell. Licence to eat meat during Lent & at other prohibited times, also for 4 other persons he may invite to his table. 16s 8d.

Feb. 3 Ric. Carne & Adriana Lynch, widow, Westminster dio. Disp. for marriage without banns & within the prohibited time. 3s 9d.

1 Ant. Calthrope & Joan Harys, of London. Disp. for marriage without banns & within the prohibited time. 3s 9d.

5 Jo. Broxoline & Eliz. Rawlyns, of St Dunstan's-in-the-East, London. Disp. for marriage in any ch., without banns & during the prohibited time. 7s 2d.

p. 299

4 Hy Veysey & his wife, Ely dio. Disp. to eat meat during Lent & at other times. 3s 4d.

Feb. 4 Wm Coton & his wife. Similar disp. 3s 4d.

3 Ric. Browne, Winton dio., & Agnes Bradley, Lond. dio. Disp. for marriage without banns. 3s 4d.

6 Edw. Porter & Clementine Benett, Sarum dio. Licence for marriage within the prohibited time. 3s 4d.

Hy Clyfford & Eliz. Caraunnt, Sarum dio. Disp. for marriage in any ch., without banns, & within the prohibited time. 7s 2d.

p. 300

7 Mich. West & his wife. Disp. to eat meat during Lent & at other prohibited times. 3s 4d.

9 Edm. Pyerson, v. of Helpringham, Linc. dio., chapl. to Ld Wingfield. Disp. to hold another benef. with or 2 without the above. 7s 2d.

Jo. Alshere & Ann Gardiner, Sarum dio. Disp. for marriage within the prohibited time. 3s 4d.

Rob. Grove & his wife. Disp. to eat meat during Lent & at other prohibited times. 3s 4d.

p. 301

8 Roger Ruddyng & Agnes Sampford, Gloucs. dio. Disp. for marriage in any ch., the banns read once. 6s 8d.

11 Wm Garnett & Helen Ledes, of London. Disp. for marriage within the prohibited time. 3s 4d.

7 Nich. Ricthorne & Joan Crymes. Similar disp. 3s 4d.

10 Jo. Dod & Alice Webe, of London. Similar disp. 3s 4d.

9 —— Fermer & Frances Rawley, Peterborough dio. Similar disp. 3s 4d.

p. 302

10 Geo. Zowche & his wife. Disp. to eat meat during Lent & at other prohibited times. 3s 4d.

11 Wm Stevinson, pr., r. of a mediety of Lenton ('Laverton') ch., Linc. dio., chapl. to Ld Edw. Clinton. Disp. to hold another benef. with or 2 without the above. 7s 2d.

12 Jo. Newton & Mary Pygge, Linc. dio. Disp. for marriage in any ch. or chapel & within the prohibited time. 6s 8d.

Ric. Hill & Eleanor Myddelton, of London. Disp. for marriage without banns & within the prohibited time. 3s 9d.

p. 303

Sir Jas Hales & his wife. Indult to eat meat during Lent & at other prohibited times, also for 4 others invited to his table. 16s 8d.

Feb. 14 Jo. Ashby. Disp. to eat meat during Lent & at other prohibited times. 3s 4d.

Rob. Wyeth, gent. Similar disp. 3s 4d.

12 Tho. Benerley, of Boulogne. Similar disp. 3s 4d.

15 Sir Ric. Cotton & his wife. Similar disp., also for 4 other persons invited to his table. 16s 8d.

p. 304

16 Wm Sheryngton. Similar disp. 16s 8d.

17 Wm Clesbroke *alias* Claybroke, pr., B.Th. Licence to preach in any ch. in the Kg's realm. 'Nihil'.

20 Rob. Gosnolde, Norw. dio. Licence together with his wife to eat meat during Lent & at other prohibited times. 3s 4d.

10 Francis Bryght & Barbara Core, of London. Indult for marriage without banns & within the prohibited times. 3s 9d.

1 Ric. Barckston, v. of Chart Sutton. Disp. to hold another benef. with the above, which does not yield over £8 p.a. 4s 5d.

p. 305

11 David ap Powell, of London. Disp. to eat meat during Lent & at other prohibited times. 3s 4d.

19 Rob. Raynbowe, Norw. dio. Similar disp. 3s 4d.

20 Hy, Earl of Rutland. Indult, also for his wife & 7 other persons invited to his table, to eat meat during Lent & at other prohibited times. 26s 8d.

22 Ralph Simons, esq. Licence together with his wife to eat meat during Lent & at other prohibited times. 3s 4d.

21 Tho. Fyscher, gent. Cancelled disp. for the same with his wife & 4 others. 16s 8d. 'Noluit sol[vere].'

p. 306

20 Ric. Forssett, of London. Disp. together with his wife to eat meat during Lent & at other prohibited times. 3s 4d.

Eline Edolff *alias* Eston, Cant. dio. Similar disp. 3s 4d.

23 Tho. Marowe, esq., & his wife. Similar disp. 3s 4d.

Nich. Alcoke, Westminster dio., & Marg. Turner, Lond. dio. Disp. for marriage without banns in any ch. & during the prohibited time. 7s 2d.

25 Wm Smyth, Cant. dio. & Mary Priste, Lond. dio. Disp. for marriage without banns & within the prohibited time. 3s 4d.

Feb. 27 Jo. Core, of London. Disp., also for his wife & 4 other persons invited to his table, to eat meat during Lent & at other prohibited times. 16s 8d.

p. 307

18 Sir Jo. Saynte. Indult, also for his wife & 2 other persons, to eat meat during Lent & at other prohibited times. 10s.

27 Ric. Grevyll & Eliz. Gylpyn, of London. Disp. for marriage without banns & during the prohibited time. 3s 9d.

28 Jo. Morton, pr. Disp. to hold a 3rd benef. 8s 10d.

Tho. Stuard & Mary Renyngton, of London. Disp. for marriage without banns & during the prohibited time. 3s 9d.

p. 308

27 Alan Scott, Carl. dio., student at Oxford. Licence to take subdcn's orders. 20d.

Mar. 2 Sir Jo. Thynne & Christine Gressam, of London. Concession for marriage without banns, in any ch., & during the prohibited time. 7s 2d.

Ric. Trasey, Gloucs. dio. Concession together with his wife to eat meat during Lent & at other prohibited times. 3s 4d.

Feb. 27 Tho. Pyke, of London. Licence together with his wife to eat meat during Lent & at other prohibited times. 3s 4d.

Mar. 3 Sir Tho. Wharton, Ld Wharton. Disp. to eat meat during Lent & at other prohibited times together with his wife & other persons invited to his table. 3s 4d.

p. 309

4 Ric. War Vernon, M.A., r. of Fringford, Oxford dio., chapl. to Ld St Jo. Disp. to hold another benef. with the above. 7s 2d.

5 Hy Augustine, of London. Licence together with his wife & another to eat meat during Lent & at other prohibited times. 6s 8d.

4 Jo. More, Chich. dio. Disp. to eat meat during Lent & at other prohibited times with one person invited to his table. 3s 4d.

20 Tho. Fyscher, esq. Disp. together with his wife & others invited to his table to eat meat during Lent & at other prohibited times. 16s 8d.

p. 310

4 Sir Ralph Vayne. Disp. to eat meat during Lent & at other prohibited times. 3s 4d.

5 Roger Wodhowse, esq. Disp. to eat meat during Lent & at other prohibited times, also for his wife & 4 others. 16s 8d.

Mar. 6 Wm Garrat, of London. Concession together with his wife to eat meat during Lent & at other times. 3s 4d.

1 Sir Wm Candissth. Similar disp. 3s 4d.

11 Jo. Mere, literate, Cant. dio. Concession to practise as a tabellion anywhere. 4s 5d.

p. 311

12 Tho. Sowdly, pr., r. of St Nich. of Cold Abbey, London, chapl. to Ld St Jo. Disp. to hold another benef. with or 2 without the above. 7s 2d.

Feb. 2 Hy Peckham, esq., & his wife, Linc. dio. Disp. to eat meat during Lent & at other prohibited times. 3s 4d.

Mar. 14 Tho. Pynchester & Kath. Reste, both of gentle birth, London. Disp. for marriage in any ch. & without banns, during the prohibited time. 7s 2d.

10 Sir Edw. Wotton. Disp. together with his wife & others invited to his table to eat meat during Lent & at other prohibited times. No fee.

p. 312

16 Wm Hamerton & Benet Castelyn, of London. Disp. for marriage in any ch., without banns, & during the prohibited time. 7s 2d.

21 Hugh Hodgeson, M.A., r. of Titchwell, Norw. dio., chapl. to the Bp of Carlisle. Disp. to hold another benef. with or 2 without the above. 7s 2d.

23 Rob. Cosen, M.A., v. of St Lawrence Old Jewry, London, chapl. to Edm., Bp of London. Disp. to hold another benef. with, or 2 without the above. 7s 2d.

Jo. Pronell & Agnes Ladbroke. Disp. for marriage without banns. 3s 4d.

p. 313

3 Armigill Wade, of London. Disp. to eat meat during Lent & at other prohibited times, also for his wife & 4 others. 16s 8d.

23 Ric. Secoll. Disp. to eat meat during Lent & at other prohibited times. 3s 4d.

31 Geo. Delalyn & Anne Goryng, both of gentle birth, Sarum dio. Disp. for marriage within the prohibited times. 3s 4d.

Apr. 5 Tho. Randolffe, B.C.L. Concession to practise the office of notary anywhere. 4s 5d.

p. 314

Ric. Fryth & Marg. Gravenar, of London. Disp. for marriage without banns. 3s 4d.

Apr. 6 Jo. Hyller & Kath. Hall, of the par. of St Giles without Cripplegate, London. Disp. for marriage without banns. 3s 4d.

8 Wm Hatch, pr., r. of Barley. Disp. to hold another benef. with or
any 2 without the above. 7s 2d.

9 Jo. Sterkye & Marion Edlyn, widow, of London. Disp. for
marriage without banns in any ch. 6s 8d.

13 Nich. West & Joan Russell, Linc. dio. Similar disp. 6s 8d.

p. 315

20 Philip Grannt, dcn, student at Oxford. Disp. to take pr.'s orders
on any day outside the statutory times & from any bp. 3s 4d.

2 Francis Verney & Marg. Poultney, widow, Linc. dio. Disp. for
marriage in any ch. without banns. 6s 8d.

? Rob. Rugge, student at Cambridge. Disp. to hold the archdcnry
of Suffolk or another benef. in spite of being only in his 20th yr.
5s 3d.

2 Rob. Wynter, pr., r. of Kittisford, Bath & W. dio., chapl. to Jo.,
Earl of Bath. Disp. to hold another benef. with or 2 others without the above. 7s 2d.

p. 316

26 Wm Askeryck & Eliz. Ludford, Cov. & Lich. dio. Disp. for
marriage without banns. 3s 4d.

27 Wm Randall, M.A., v. of Blakawton, Ex. dio., chapl. to Ld
Chancellor Ryche (sic). Disp. to hold another benef. with or 2
without the above. 7s 2d.

6 Rob. Sutton. Disp. to practise anywhere as tabellion. 4s 5d.

27 Wm Hall, pr., v. of Gedney, Linc. dio., Kg's chapl. Disp. to
hold another benef. with or 2 without the above. 7s 2d.

23 Jo. Atkynson, Lond. dio., & Agnes Randall, Norw. dio. Disp. for
marriage without banns & in any ch. 6s 8d.

p. 317

May 1 Stephen Bayly, B.Th., v. of Redbourne, Linc. dio. Disp. to hold
another benef. with or 2 without the above. 7s 2d.

3 Ralph Johnson & Marg. Jaxon, of St Alphage par., London.
Disp. for marriage without banns. 3s 4d.

Chris. Leynam, pr., r. of St George's, Southwark. Winton dio.,
& of Huntingfield, Norw. dio. Disp. for non-res. 3s 4d.

1 Wm Jones, Lland. dio. Disp. to practise the office of notary.
4s 5d.

p. 318

May 5 Hy Sheryngton & Ann Paget, both of gentle birth. Disp. for marriage in any ch. or oratory without banns & in the prohibited time. 'Debet.'

6 Chris. Shugden, M.A. Disp. to preach the Word of God anywhere in the realm provided that in his sermons he does not preach anything to the alteration or innovation of religion & ceremonies other than in the Kg's recent Statute. No fee.

7 Geoffrey Hellat, pr., v. of St Martin's, Stamford, Peterborough dio. Disp. to hold another benef. with the above, which does not yield over £8 p.a., or another without it. 4s 5d.

12 Ronald Carter & Joyce Chapman, of London. Disp. for marriage within the prohibited times. 3s 4d.

p. 319

Jo. Haddon & Eliz. Hartt, of London. Disp. for marriage without banns & within the prohibited times. 3s 9d.

10 Wm Cooke & Agnes Tayler. Disp. for marriage without banns & within the prohibited time. 3s 9d.

13 Jo. Sergent & Joan Hery. Disp. for marriage within the prohibited time. 3s 4d.

? Geo. Hausley & Eliz. Stokes, Linc. dio. Disp. for marriage without banns & within the prohibited time. 3s 9d.

Rob. Tomson, literate, York dio. Disp. to take dcn's & subdcn's orders on any day without l.d. 6s 7d.

Edw. Morecrofte, student of Oxford. Licence, being in his 22nd year, to hold a benef., & proceed to dcn's & pr.'s orders after subdcn's. 9s 5d.

p. 320

Jo. Alen & Eliz. Casshyng, of London. Disp. for marriage within the prohibited time. 3s 4d.

Jo. Freman & Alice Caunton, of London. Licence for marriage without banns, during the prohibited time, & in any ch. 7s 2d.

Ric. Bery & Agnes Benyfolde, of London. Disp. for marriage within the prohibited time, & in any ch. 7s 2d.

June 6 Tho. Wyllson, B.Th., r. of Trusthorpe, Linc. dio. Disp. to hold another benef. with or 2 without the above. 7s 2d.

p. 321

8 Tho. Emery & Kath. Dalwodde, of London. Disp. for marriage without banns. 3s 4d.

June 10 Wm Davys, pr., v. of Gt Dunford, Sarum dio., chapl. to Ld Tho. Sandys. Disp. to hold another benef. with or 2 without the above. 7s 2d.

11 Jo. Harrys, pr., r. of Ashwater, Ex. dio., chapl. to Ly Dorothy Mountjoy, recently wife of Ld Mountjoy. Similar disp. 7s 2d.

Ric. Rysbey & Marg. Downall, widow, Linc. dio. Disp. for marriage without banns. 3s 4d.

p. 322

6 Wm Foster, v. of Billingshurst, Chich. dio., chapl. to the Bp of St Asaph. Disp. to hold another benef. with or 2 without the above. 7s 2d.

12 Gabriel Rayne, M.A., Chester dio. Disp. to preach the Word of God anywhere in the realm provided that he does not preach anything to the alteration or innovation of religion & ceremonies other than in the Kg's recent Statute. No fee.

? Jo. Wyatt, B.Th., Linc. dio. Similar disp. No fee.

3 Tho. Chedulton, Cov. & Lich. dio. Disp. to practise the office of notary anywhere in the realm. 4s 5d.

p. 323

16 Wm Nanseglose, r. of Bremhill, Sarum dio., chapl. to Ld Tho. Seymour, K.G., Ld High Admiral. Disp. to hold another benef. with the above. 7s 2d.

18 —— Northye, gent., & Eliz. Payne, widow. Disp. for marriage without banns. 3s 4d.

13 Tho. Balknappe *alias* Stowres & Avis Petye, both of gentle birth, Winton dio. Disp. for marriage without banns in any ch. 6s 8d.

? Mich. Willoughby, & Kath. Tatlocke, Linc. dio. Licence for marriage without banns. 3s 4d.

? Hugh Lewes, dcn, St David's dio. Licence to take pr.'s orders from any bp. 3s 4d.

p. 324

23 Ric. Worley & Isabella Wevant, of the par. of St Martin-in-the-Fields, Westminster dio. Disp. for marriage without banns. 3s 4d.

Wm Rawlynson & Joan Sowraye, Linc. dio. Disp. for marriage without banns. 3s 4d.

28 Tho. Kyng, v. of St Mich.'s by St Alban's, chapl. to the Dowager Ly Kath (i.e. Qn Kath?). Disp. to hold another benef. with the above. 7s 2d.

? Walter Linverson & Eliz. Wodroff, of London. Disp. for marriage without banns. 3s 4d.

? Humfrey Browtston & Dorothy Wheler, Lond. dio. Disp. for marriage without banns. 3s 4d.

? Ric. Broke & Christine Carew. Licence for marriage without banns in any ch. 6s 8d.

p. 325

July 2 Edw. Wyllye, subdcn, York dio. Concession to take dcn's & pr.'s orders from any bp. 4s 5d.

June 30 Jo. Heron & Jane Joslyn, Heref. dio. Disp. for marriage without banns. 3s 4d.

July 2 Wm Samwell, sch., Worc. dio. Concession to take h.o. outside the statutory time, on any 2 Sundays or holy days, without l.d. 5s 6d.

     4 Tho. Rydley & Ellen Austyne, Bath & W. dio. Disp. for marriage without banns in any ch. 6s 8d.

     3 Wm Lovys & Joan Maltby, of London. Disp. for marriage without banns. 3s 4d.

p. 326

? Martin Pugson & Joan Luckyns. Licence for marriage without banns. 3s 4d.

? Jo. Hornby & Joan Sheperd. Similar licence. 3s 4d.

? Jo. Cooke & Mary Badcocke. Similar licence. 3s 4d.

? —— Cook. Licence for non. res. 3s 4d.

? Hy Downe. Licence for plurality. 7s 2d.

? Tho. Pharey & Ann Reid. Licence for marriage without banns, & in any ch. 6s 8d.

Aug. 20 Jas Ruddam & Winifred Mollyner. Disp. for marriage without banns. 3s 4d.

? Tho. Welshe, clk, r. of Langston, Winton dio. Disp. to hold another benef. 7s 2d.

? Hy Jolyff, B.Th., chapl. to the Bp of Worcester, r. of Hewby, Linc. dio. Disp. to hold another benef. 7s 2d.

p. 327

? Bernard Sandford, r. of St Martin's, Ludgate. Similar disp. 7s 2d.

? Rob. Towwde & Kath. Whytyngton, St Leonard's par., London. Disp. for marriage without banns. 3s 4d.

? Florence Seym, chapl. to the Bp of Norwich. Disp. to hold 2 benefices. 7s 2d.

? Dr Perpoynt. Disp. to preach.

? Nich. Nycolls, v. of St Ives, Cornwall, Ex. dio., chapl. to the Bp of Exeter. Disp. to hold 2 benefices. 7s 2d.

p. 328

? Ralph Dodd & Breton ——. Disp. for marriage (*sic*). 6s 8d.

? —— Sudenham & —— Rydon. Similar disp. 3s 4d.

Aug. 24 David ap Llun, v. of Llanybyther, chapl. to Ld Ferrers. Disp. to hold another benef., as the above does not yield over £8 p.a. 4s 5d.

27 Arthur Grene, r. of ? Cokysby, York dio. Similar disp. 4s 5d.

? Gilbert Lawson & Eliz. Madocke. Licence for marriage without banns. 3s 4d.

31 Rob. Sparry, r. of Charfield, Gloucs. dio., chapl. to the Bp of Gloucester. Disp. to hold another benef. with or 2 without the above. 7s 2d.

p. 329

Ralph Standysch & Marg. Flower. Disp. for marriage without banns & in any ch. 6s 8d.

Sept. 2 Wm Brakynbere & Kath. Sober. Disp. for marriage without banns. 3s 4d.

6 Jo. Ryver, Cov. & Lich. dio. Disp. to be a public notary. 4s 5d.

7 Tho. Latham & Marg. Hall, of London. Concession for marriage without banns & in any ch. 6s 8d.

p. 330

12 Roger Pyllyswerth & Ellen Potkynholme. Disp. for marriage without banns. 3s 4d.

14 Jo. Leme & Audrey Simpson, of London. Similar disp. 3s 4d.

17 Jo. Skorye, B.Th., v. of Middleton, Cant. dio. Disp. to hold another benef. with or any 2 without the above. 7s 2d.

18 Jo. Gwynne & Alice Hudson, of London. Disp. for marriage without banns. 3s 4d.

p. 331

23 Chris. Wylton, r. of Garsdon, Sarum dio., chapl. to Tho. Seymour, Ld High Admiral. Disp. to hold another benef. 7s 2d.

Sept. 28 Tho. Parker, r. of Murton. Ex. dio., chapl. to Jo., Earl of Bath. Similar disp. 7s 2d.

Oct. 10 Jo. Dernelly & Joyce Parker, of the par. of St Alban's, Wood St., London. Disp. for marriage without banns. 3s 4d.

Edw. Mylmaye & Joan Awparte, of London. Disp. for marriage in any ch. without banns. 6s 8d.

Hugh Broke & Barbara Chydley, both of gentle birth, London. Disp. for marriage in any ch., & without banns. 6s 8d.

19 Tho. Trape, B.Th., r. of Alderley, Glouc. dio. Disp. for nonres. for 3 yrs while he studies. 4s 6d.

p. 332

31 Tho. Whytlocke & Joan Warner. Disp. for marriage in any ch. & without banns. 6s 8d.

Nov. 4 Tho. Lant, r. of Heslerton, York dio., chapl. to the Archbp of York. Disp. to hold another benef. with or 2 without the above. 7s 2d.

6 Ric. Eston, r. of Edford, Ex. dio., chapl. to the Bp of Exeter. Disp. to hold another benef. with or 2 without the above. 7s 2d.

Dec. 2 Wm Edwards & Joan Heth, widow, of St Mary Magdalen par., London. Disp. for marriage without banns & within the prohibited time. 3s 9d.

p. 333

3 Mathew Farror, sch., Norw. dio. Disp. to take all h.o. outside the statutory times, & any 2 Sundays or holy days, without l.d. 5s 2d.

Nov. 27 Edw. Flowrence, Bristol dio. Disp. to practise as notary & tabellion anywhere in the realm. 'Husey debet.'

20 Jo. Jervys, v. of St Hilary, Cornwall, Ex. dio., chapl. to Sir Ric. Southwell. Disp. to hold another benef. with or 2 without the above. 7s 2d.

Dec. 5 Tho. Webster, pr., v. of Hayton, York dio., chapl. to the Archbp of York. Similar disp. 7s 2d.

4 Tho. Brantime & Eliz. Rockwood, Lond. dio. Disp. for marriage without banns, within the prohibited time, & in any ch. or oratory. 7s 2d.

p. 334

7 Jo. Harman, esq., & Ly Ann Owen. Disp. for marriage within the prohibited time. 3s 4d.

6 Ric. Hareford, archdcn of St David's. Disp. to take h.o. outside the statutory time, on any 2 Sundays or Holy Days. 3s 4d.

Dec. 6 Oswald Rydley, v. of the par. ch. of West Gate, Canterbury, chapl. to Nich., Bp of Rochester. Disp. to hold another benef. with or 2 without the above. 7s 2d.

26 Rob. Rockwood & Ann Stede, widow. Disp. for marriage without banns. 3s 4d.

6 Jo. Barker & Ann Lyster. Disp. for marriage within the prohibited time & without banns. 3s 9d.

11 Chris. Turnbull & ——. Disp. for marriage within the prohibited time. 3s 4d.

p. 335

Jo., Earl of Bath & Ly Marg. Longe, widow. Disp. for marriage in any ch. without banns. 6s 8d.

Jo. Bourchier, Ld Fitzwarin, & Frances Kytson, of London. Disp. for marriage without banns & in any ch. 6s 8d.

15 Wm Tylley & Beatrice Carre, widow. Disp. for marriage within the prohibited time. 3s 4d.

Mar. 28 Tho. Stevyns, r. of Bentworth, Winton dio., chapl. to the Bp of Salisbury. Disp. to hold another benef. with or 2 others without the above. 7s 2d.

Dec. 1 Lancelot Harryson & Thomasina Browne, Lond. dio. Disp. for marriage in any ch. without banns & within the prohibited time. 7s 2d.

p. 336

19 Edw. Torrell, r. of West Bergholt, Lond. dio., chapl. to Ld Edm. Sheffield. Disp. to hold another benef. with or 2 without the above. 7s 2d.

29 Bartholomew Skerne & Jane Cother. Disp. for marriage within the prohibited time. 3s 4d.

1549 Jan. 6 Tho. Myllys. Disp. to practise as tabellion anywhere in the realm. 4s 5d.

18 Edw. Lee & Ellen Awe, Lond. dio. Disp. for marriage without banns. 3s 4d.

1548 Dec. 30 Humfrey Parkyns, D.Th., v. of Staines, Westminster dio. Disp. to hold another benef. with or 2 without the above. 7s 2d.

p. 337

1549 Jan. 28 Alex. Barkley, D.Th., v. of Oake, Bath & W. dio. Disp. to hold another benef. with or 2 without the above. 7s 2d.

29 Edm. Robarts & Frances Welles, of Royston, Lond. dio. Disp. for marriage without banns. 3s 4d.

Feb. 6 Hy Ratclyff, esq., & Una Pounde. Disp. for marriage without banns & in any ch. 6s 8d.

Sir Rob. Lawrence & Ann Knyght, widow. Disp. for marriage without banns & in any ch. 6s 8d.

7 Nich. Semester & Juliana Cave. Disp. for marriage without banns. 3s 4d.

p. 338

7 Tho. Base & Margery Herne, of London. Disp. for marriage without banns. 3s 4d.

? Rob. (Holgate), Archbp of York. Disp. to eat meat during Lent & at other prohibited times. No fee.

Feb. 10 Chas, Ld Stourton & Ly Ann Stanley. Disp. for marriage without banns & in any ch. 6s 8d.

? Sir Edw. Boughton & ——?. Disp. for marriage in any ch. & without banns. 6s 8d.

p. 339

3 Clement Foreman & Emma Cartmole, of London. Disp. for marriage without banns. 3s 4d.

12 Jas Brande, gent., & Anne Dockery. Similar disp. 3s 4d.

14 Hy Wynkfeld, gent., & Mary Boulcher. Similar disp. 3s 4d.

Jo. Comberford & Emma Bollet. Disp. for marriage without banns & in the prohibited time. No fee.

p. 340

20 Rob. Caleway, esq., & Ly Cecily Vinpton, widow. Disp. for marriage without banns, within the prohibited times, & in any ch. 7s 2d.

21 Francis Chawrye, gent., & Alice Tyrell. Disp. for marriage in any ch. without banns & within the prohibited time. 7s 2d.

20 Valentine Geta & Marion Alyn, Cant. dio. Disp. for marriage within the prohibited times. 3s 4d.

Barnard Randolph & Joan Harrys, widow, of London. Disp. for marriage without banns & within the prohibited time. 3s 9d.

21 Simon Appultre & Agnes Rudyck. Cancelled disp. for marriage the banns read once.

p. 341

1 Ric. Pynner, Winton dio. Disp. to practise as tabellion anywhere in the realm. 4s 5d.

23 Jeremy Burdet & Marg. Tottyll, of [St. Mary] Colechurch par., London. Disp. for marriage without banns & within the prohibited time. 3s 9d.

Feb. 26 Hy Bartlet & Juliana Townsende. Disp. for marriage in any ch. & within the prohibited time. 7s 2d.

25 Ric. Jonas & Joan Smyth, of Odiham, Winton dio. Disp. for marriage, the banns read once & within the prohibited time. 3s 4d.

27 Owen Layden & Kath. Grecharste, widow. Disp. for marriage without banns & within the prohibited time. 3s 9d.

p. 342

28 Roger Sheryngton & Ann Haddon. Disp. for marriage in any ch. & without banns. 6s 8d.

Mar. 1 Wm Stacye & Juliana Matarus, of London. Disp. for marriage without banns & within the prohibited time. 3s 9d.

7 Jo. Wetts & Joan Hyams. Similar disp. 3s 9d.

1548 Nov. 20 Chris. Neveson, D.C.L. Disp. to eat meat during Lent & at other prohibited times. 3s 4d.

p. 343

1549 Mar. 2 Jo. Mascye, v. of Chicheley, Linc. dio. Disp. for non-res. during his illness, & for 6 months after his recovery. 3s 4d.

1 Ric. Benson, r. of Kinnersley, Heref. dio., chapl. to Sir Hy Seymour, the Kg's uncle. Disp. to hold another benef. with the above or 2 without it. 7s 2d.

1548 Oct. 1 Jo. Foster, esq., & his wife. Disp. to eat meat during Lent & at other prohibited times. 3s 4d.

15 Jo. Taylor, D.Th. Similar disp. 3s 4d.

p. 344

1549 Mar. 12 Tho. Hare & Patricia ——. Disp. for marriage within the prohibited time. 3s 4d.

1548 Nov. 30 Sir Tho. Wentworth & his wife. Disp. to eat meat during Lent & at other prohibited times. 3s 4d.

1549 Mar. 7 Tho. Boughton. Disp., also for his wife and one guest at his table, to eat meat during Lent & at other prohibited times. 3s 4d.

Ly Eliz. Moryshe, widow, of London. Disp. to eat meat during Lent & at other prohibited times. 3s 4d.

p. 345

1548 Sept. 8 Peter Heyman, gent. Disp., also for his wife & one guest at his table, to eat meat during Lent & at other prohibited times. 6s 8d.

1549 Mar. 14 Ric. Rydge, pr., chapl. to the Bp of Llandaff. Disp. to hold another benef. with or 2 without the above. 7s 2d.

1548 Dec. 30 Clement Clerke & Marg. Lyghtfote. Disp. for marriage without banns. 3s 4d.

1549 Mar. 4 Sir Wm Willoughby, Ld Willoughby. Disp., also for his wife & 4 others, to eat meat during Lent & at other prohibited times. 16s 8d.

1548 Nov. 4 Jo. Poynet, D.Th. Disp., also for his wife, to eat meat during Lent & at other prohibited times. 3s 4d.

p. 346

? Ellis ——, Linc. dio. Disp. to eat meat during Lent & at other prohibited times. No fee.

1549 Mar. 3 Jo. Sutherton, gent. Disp., also for his wife & another person to eat meat during Lent & at other prohibited times. 6s 8d.

Apr. 4 Ric. Brumbrugh, r. of Buttermere, Sarum dio., chapl. to the Bp of Salisbury. Disp. to hold another benef. with or 2 without the above. 7s 2d.

1548 Nov. 1 Sir Jo. Guildeford. Disp. together with his wife & 4 others to eat meat during Lent & at other prohibited times. 16s 8d.

1549 Apr. 25 Wm Crosley & Eliz. Archer. Disp. for marriage within the prohibited times. 3s 4d.

1547 Feb. 28 Jo. Belleme *alias* Bellowe, esq. Disp. together with his wife to eat meat during Lent. 3s 4d.

p. 347

1548 Nov. 4 Wm, Marquess of Northampton. Disp. together with 6 others to eat meat during Lent & at other prohibited times. 23s 4d.

3 Wm Peterson. Disp., also for his wife & 2 others, to eat meat during Lent & at other prohibited times. 10s.

1549 Feb. 2 Ric. Hyllys. Similar disp. 10s.

Apr. 16 Wm Smyth, r. of Wanstead. Disp. to hold another benef. with the above, which does not yield over £8 p.a., or another without it. 4s 5d.

12 Rob. Whythibroke, v. of Spreyton, Ex. dio., chapl. to the Earl of Rutland. Disp. to hold another benef. with the above. 7s 2d.

INDEX TO INTRODUCTION

INDEX OF PLACES

NOTE. This is an index to the religious houses and parishes named in the register; it includes benefices, and places of residence in the case of unbeneficed persons. It does not, however, include general references to dioceses or to London as an individual's place of residence where the parish is unspecified; nor does it give the individual names (patron saints, &c.) of churches and religious houses except in the case of London and seven other places (Cambridge, Canterbury, Lincoln, Norwich, Oxford, Southwark, York) where the large number of references seemed to make this necessary.

Abberton, 138.
Abbey Cwmhir, 101.
Abbey Dore, 98.
Abergavenny, 156.
Aberstoithe, 202.
Abingdon, 38, 50, 123, 173.
Abston, 269.
Aconbury, 97–98.
Acton, 274, 290.
Acton-on-the-hill, 170.
Acworth, 292.
Adderbury, 281.
Addingham, 263.
Addington, 287.
Addlethorpe, 259.
Albourne, 154.
Aldeburgh, 91.
Aldenham, 271.
Alderley, 315.
Aldershot, 246.
Aldingborne, 284.
Aldington, 54.
Alfriston, 54.
Alkborough, 282.
Alkrington, 109.
Allecombe, 279.
Allington, 301.
Alnwick, 52.
Alphanston, 260.
Altarnon, 226.
Althorne, 225.
Althorpe, 48.
Alton, 263.
Alveston, 262.
Alvingham, 139, 161.
Alvington, 123.
Amberley, 287.
Anderby, 194.
Anglisforde, 220.
Anthony, 246.
Appleton, 175, 215.
Archingworth, 28.
Arksey, 16.
Armin, 126.
Arundel, 168.
Ashby, 10, 17, 105.
Ashby de la Zouch, 236.
Ashe, 278.
Ashleworth, 221.

Ashley, 254.
Ashridge, 157, 204.
Ashwater, 312.
Ashwell, 117.
Askrigg, 269.
Aspall Stonham, 229.
Aspatria, 300.
Asshor, 154.
Aswarby, 133.
Athelney, 74, 179.
Atherston, 163.
Awre, 16.
Axholme, 37, 139.
Aykan, 48.
Aylesbury, 179, 279.
Aysheley, 222.

Babistocke, 18.
Babwell, 180.
Badgworth, 278.
Bainton, 44, 291.
Baldock, 1.
Balingham, 220.
Bampton, 125.
Banbury, 193.
Bangor, 12, 66, 164.
Bardney, 35, 172.
Bardwell, 130.
Barham, 214.
Barking, 16.
Barlings, 94, 96.
Barnaby, 50.
Barnardiston, 7.
Barnwell, 160, 184.
Barnwell St Mary, 269.
Barrowby, 254.
Bartlow, 117.
Barton, 183.
Barwick, 270.
Bath, 175.
Batheley, 43.
Batley, 126.
Battle, 50, 60–61, 138.
Bawburgh, 130.
Bawdeswell, 194.
Beauchief, 75.
Beaulieu, 66, 131.
Beaumaris, 164.
Beaumont, 15.

INDEX OF NAMES

Note. Names are indexed only under surnames, except in the cases of bishops and nobility. Cross-references will be found for these under the names of sees and titles. Welsh names with the prefixes 'ap' and 'verch' are listed under A and V respectively, but are only quoted to the first generation (in some cases the text gives several generations of forebears, e.g. p. 104). Identical names which appear with variant spelling (e.g. Fisher, Fissher, Fyscher, Fyssher) are listed as they stand, and without cross-references to all the possible variants, so it is advisable to check these very fully.

Goston, 77.
Gostwike, 92.
Gouche, 140.
Gouge, 185.
Goughe, 187.
Gourge, 182.
Gower, 91.
Gowghe, 304.
Gowland, 81.
Gowre, 231, 263.
Grace, 88, 93, 145, 251.
Graffeham, 116.
Graffon, 66.
Graggs, 246.
Grane, 123.
Granemer, 59.
Grannt, 230, 310.
Grannte, 205, 220, 245.
Granocke, 175.
Grante, 199.
Grantham, 208.
Graston, 156.
Gravenar, 309.
Gravenor, 216.
Graver, 123.
Gravet, 79.
Gray, 42, 66, 128, 164, 251, 283.
Graye, 148, 182, 283.
Graystocke, 109.
Grayves, 136.
Greatike, 120.
Grecharste, 318.
Grege, 175.
Gregg, 119.
Gregorie, 138.
Gregory, 102, 133, 202, 246.
Gregorye, 121, 142.
Gregson, 233.
Grene, 19, 62, 69, 70, 74, 76, 80, 93, 97,
    100, 110, 120, 121, 125, 136, 137, 152,
    154, 166, 175, 176, 179, 181, 186, 211,
    217, 245, 266, 314.
Grenehalgh, 112.
Greneside, 95.
Grenewaye, 29.
Grenewode, 124, 225, 233.
Grenewood, 50, 70.
Grenlef, 293.
Grennston, 266.
Grenston, 215–16.
Grentham, 67.
Gresham, 291.
Greslande, 195.
Gressam, 308.
Gressham, 256.
Grete, 53.
Greves, 1, 236.

Grevyll, 308.
Grewode, 105.
Grey, 43, 71, 89, 245, 271, 281.
Grey, Edw., Ld Powis, 271.
Grey, Tho., Marquess of Dorset, and Ly
    Eliz., 130.
Grey, Hy, Marquess of Dorset, 66, 231, 254,
    262, 285, 296; Frances, Countess of, 5.
Griffet, 166.
Griffington, 155.
Griffith, 9, 11, 12, 35, 53, 92, 120, 146,
    148, 154, 164, 196.
Griffith ap Robert Vaughan, 104.
Griffithe, 95, 124, 175, 179.
Griffiths, 100.
Grifithe, 98.
Grigge, 58.
Grimston, 160.
Grome, 93.
Grove, 190, 306.
Grover, 217.
Grow, 97.
Growannce, 73.
Growdon, 287.
Growte, 81, 116.
Gruffith, 234, 235.
Gruffithe, 218.
Gruffs, 208.
Gryffet, 164.
Gryffyn, 254, 268.
Gryffyne, 168.
Gryffyng, 295.
Gryffyth, 248.
Gryffythe, 8.
Grygell, 16.
Gryme, 87, 119, 137, 270.
Grymesdiche, 35.
Grymsshawe, 225.
Grymston, 209.
Gryndon, 108.
Gryne, 286.
Gryson, 262.
Gude, 210.
Guildeford, 319.
Guilyem, 230.
Guithlike, 38.
Gunner, 224.
Gunston, 276.
Gunter, 145, 148, 248.
Gunthorpe, 157.
Gurdon, 173, 206.
Gurley, 280.
Gurnell, 275.
Guy, 104.
Guyldeforde, 131.
Guylyem, 230.
Guyn, 298.

Heysam, 67.
Heyth, 154.
Heythe, 117, 169.
Heythorne, 68.
Heyton, 196.
Heywarde, 138.
Heywode, 190.
Heywood, 11.
Hibbarte, 32.
Hiche, 180.
Hichecoke, 148.
Hichson, 70.
Hickeling, 44.
Hickford, 266.
Hickling, 23.
Hicks, 182, 252.
Higdon, 59, 71.
Higgs, 48, 164.
Higham, 190.
Highe, 196.
Higwaye, 39.
Hildersham, 238.
Hill, 9, 11, 21, 25, 31, 35, 38, 54, 74, 75, 99, 136, 141, 144, 154, 163, 167, 172, 182, 193, 202, 204, 212, 227, 234, 285, 306.
Hillary, 226.
Hiller, 165.
Hilliun, 80.
Hillyarde, 198.
Hillyng, 262.
Hilsey, Jo., Bp of Rochester, 69, 101.
Hilton, 15, 154, 159, 180, 207, 283.
Hinde, 244.
Hipworth, 176.
Hirde, 181.
Hirwell, 212.
Hobbe, 132, 226.
Hobbes, 25, 240.
Hobson, 147, 166, 177.
Hochenson, 294.
Hockleton, 224.
Hoddington, 78.
Hodgeson, 141, 309.
Hodgis, 229.
Hodingsells, 207.
Hodsolde, 213.
Hodson, 274.
Hoell, 162.
Hogarde, 181, 225.
Hoge, 123.
Hogeson, 60, 63, 208.
Hogesonne, 181.
Hogeys, 163.
Hogge, 203.
Hoggeson, 29.
Hoghley, 122.
Hogleye, 144.

Hokar, 244.
Hokenell, 195.
Hokeson, 96.
Holbache, 245.
Holbeach, Hy, Bp of Rochester, 249, 263.
Holbeme, 18.
Holben, 93.
Holbiche, 205.
Holbyn, 26.
Holcrofte, 249.
Holcroste, 226.
Holdefelde, 187.
Holden, 54, 65, 75, 90, 91, 109, 153.
Holderness, 68.
Hole, 4, 140, 175, 267.
Holes, 191, 247.
Holford, 289.
Holforde, 164, 188.
Holgate, Rob., Bp of Llandoff, Abp of York, 31, 93-94, 188-9, 257, 315, 317.
Holland, 213, 266.
Hollande, 111, 115, 170.
Hollingbourn, 65.
Hollingbourne, 61.
Hollocke, 219.
Hollond, 54, 265.
Hollonde, 17.
Holls, 247.
Hollys, 268.
Hollywell, 149.
Holman, 120.
Holme, 72, 100, 105, 144, 150, 159, 176, 179, 208.
Holmes, 10, 51, 216, 288.
Holrod, 229.
Holstede, 177.
Holte, 19, 68, 112, 150, 153, 158, 247.
Holusyer, 240.
Holwey, 157.
Holyday, 168.
Holydaye, 149.
Holyleye, 160.
Holyman, 274.
Holywell, 117.
Homes, 2, 273.
Homme, 112.
Homms, 163.
Hone, 141.
Honyber, 138.
Honywoode, 38.
Hoode, 168, 207.
Hooper, 130, 178.
Hope, 44, 269, 293.
Hopham, 181.
Hopkin, 144.
Hopkins, 149.
Hopkyn, 68, 168.

Huwett, 207.
Huxeley, 65.
Huxley, 204.
Huys, 303.
Huyte, 205.
Hyams, 318.
Hyans, 145.
Hycklyn, 73.
Hyde, 161, 186, 250, 293.
Hygon, 149.
Hylaire, 287.
Hyll, 3, 248, 260, 287, 288, 291.
Hyller, 310.
Hylley, 173.
Hylls, 286.
Hyllys, 319.
Hylpe, 302.
Hylye, 144.
Hymerforde, 19.
Hynde, 74.
Hyndmer, 278.
Hyne, 3, 195.
Hyns, 168.
Hynton, 43, 132, 173.
Hyrm, 195.
Hyvvys, 168.
Hyxston, 286.

Ibry, 298.
Iden, 44.
Ike, 168.
Illiarde, 183.
Illyarde, 170.
Ilonde, 119.
Inderwell, 223.
Inge, 44.
Ingelbie, 179.
Ingeson, 294.
Ingham, 15, 30, 155, 156.
Ingilbye, 163.
Inglomes, 67.
Ingworth, 166.
Inman, 155.
Inmer, 152.
Inolde, 202.
Ions, 231.
Ipesley, 73.
Ipeswell, 132.
Irbye, 207.
Ireland, 207.
Irland, 155.
Irlande, 146.
Irlham, 8.
Irton, 85.
Isaac, 9.
Isabell, 172.
Isacke, 8, 109.

Isam, 290.
Isode, 94.
Ive, 302.
Iveson, 192.
Ivynwood, 121.
Iyslam, 202.

Jacke, 205.
Jackeson, 148, 172.
Jackett, 162.
Jackman, 25, 259.
Jackson, 11, 41, 76, 87, 95, 113, 123, 129, 147, 152, 155, 165, 175, 177, 181, 196, 217, 250.
Jacobbe, 98.
Jaggis, 97.
Jakeman, 222.
Jaks, 201.
Jakson, 17.
Jakys, 132.
James, 8, 9, 32, 235, 256.
Jameson, 199.
Jamys, 207.
Jamyson, 193.
Jane, 102.
Jane, Qn, see Seymour.
Jarmayne, 262.
Jarvis, 165.
Jarvys, 182, 196.
Jasper, 182.
Jaxon, 310.
Jay, 129.
Jefferey, 152.
Jefford, 78.
Jeffys, 111.
Jekys, 169.
Jenetts, 293.
Jenks, 201.
Jenkyn, 199.
Jenkyns, 249, 251.
Jenn, 28.
Jenny, 305.
Jennyns, 87, 224.
Jenyn, 180.
Jenyngs, 201.
Jenyns, 134, 183, 195, 304.
Jeram, 130.
Jerarde, 108.
Jerlond, 267.
Jermon, 166.
Jermy, 8.
Jernyngham, 123.
Jerome, 98, 158.
Jerrett, 160.
Jervatt, 148.
Jervys, 315.
Jeskyn, 170.

Poole, 67, 136, 238, 244.
Poore, 13.
Poote, 81.
Pope, 10, 33, 63, 65, 88, 146, 167, 212, 227, 289.
Popill, 139.
Popley, 103.
Popleye, 146.
Popynioye, 167.
Pore, 186.
Porte, 122.
Porter, 79, 91, 163, 167, 198, 211, 216, 244, 296, 306.
Portington, 40, 208.
Portyngton, 6, 14.
Poskesson, 163.
Post, 288.
Potkyn, 92, 152.
Potkynholme, 314.
Pott, 196.
Pottenne, 65.
Potter, 19, 141, 165.
Poull, 131.
Poullett, 266.
Poultney, 310.
Poulton, 181.
Pounde, 317.
Poundfold, 79.
Powell, 34, 40, 175, 176, 259.
Powell ap John, 58.
Power, 242.
Powis, Ld, see Grey.
Powle, 240.
Powll, 258.
Pownall, 110.
Pownde, 247.
Powtrell, 210.
Powys, 10.
Poynet, 319.
Poynter, 165.
Poyntz, 114.
Poynyngs, 284.
Prate, 74.
Pratt, 119, 161, 165.
Pratte, 164, 172.
Pratye, 144.
Prescote, 216.
Prest, 8, 44.
Prestene, 121.
Prestlonde, 193.
Preston, 65, 67, 72, 74, 97, 133, 163, 164, 167, 168, 183, 195, 201, 225, 274.
Prety, 277.
Price, 259.
Prick, 207.
Pricklove, 188.
Prior, 215.

Priste, 307.
Procter, 106, 183.
Proctor, 21, 57, 199, 268.
Prokyng, 272.
Pronell, 309.
Pronest, 240.
Pronte, 152.
Prowdlow, 146.
Prowett, 88.
Prowloffe, 160.
Pruste, 24.
Prycklowe, 20.
Prydyape, 284.
Pryst, 285.
Prystley, 193.
Prystman, 291.
Pugson, 313.
Puleston, 38, 40.
Pullande, 153.
Pullen, 3.
Pulner, 165.
Pulo, 165.
Punchin, 41.
Purese, 31.
Puressey, 288.
Purfrey, 288.
Purlee, 87.
Purvey, 251, 297.
Putterell, 128.
Pychar, 111.
Pycher, 286, 303.
Pycherd, 207.
Pyckarde, 180.
Pycke, 255.
Pyckestoke, 176.
Pyckle, 209.
Pyckring, 182.
Pyckton, 131.
Pye, 168, 250, 263, 299.
Pyen, 135.
Pyende, 67.
Pyers, 164.
Pyerson, 129, 245, 306.
Pygge, 108, 306.
Pygott, 125, 155.
Pyke, 162, 308.
Pykering, 156, 164, 165, 255.
Pyllyswerth, 314.
Pylsdon, 253-4.
Pymonde, 189.
Pynchester, 309.
Pynchion, 61.
Pynchyn, 180.
Pynder, 73, 166, 192.
Pynfold, 304.
Pynfolde, 268.
Pynghnay, 123.

Watkins, 143.
Watkyn, 131.
Watkyns, 75.
Watkynson, 304.
Watlington, 161.
Watson, 5, 17, 21, 57, 91, 128, 131, 152, 159, 161, 165, 175, 181, 189, 243.
Watsons, 168.
Watte, 14.
Watterfall, 31.
Wattes, 155, 281.
Watts, 23, 86, 167, 179, 302.
Wawen, 52.
Waxley, 269.
Waye, 70.
Wayte, 161.
Waywright, 139.
Weale, 233.
Webb, 63, 66.
Webbe, 49, 111, 123, 150, 164, 174, 182, 281, 302.
Webber, 16.
Webe, 306.
Webley, 274.
Webstar, 270.
Webster, 71, 160, 161, 181, 216, 247, 282, 315.
Webure, 67.
Wederell, 305.
Wederlet, 181.
Wedow, 134.
Wedrelt, 125.
Weekes, 120.
Welbourne, 173.
Welby, 251.
Welche, 168, 231.
Welde, 48, 144.
Welden, 34.
Weldon, 268.
Welford, 85.
Welles, 37, 39, 83, 84, 95, 316.
Welliche, 211.
Wellis, 74, 142, 144, 160, 211.
Wellisburne, 222.
Wells, 137, 179, 208, 209.
Wellys, 246.
Wellysburne, 279.
Welshe, 39, 145, 181, 224, 294, 300, 313.
Wemer, 69.
Wemys, 304.
Wenall, 164.
Wenarde, 167.
Wendover, 188, 202.
Wenlocke, 164.
Went, 112.
Wenter, 175.
Wentworth, 105.

Wentworth, Ld Tho., 214, 239, 318.
Werall, 208.
Werberton, 170.
Were, 55, 78.
Werner, 80.
West, 15, 41, 154, 178, 236, 269, 306, 310.
Westburye, 130, 131.
Westbye, 98.
Weste, 90, 93, 158, 233, 291.
Westfeld, 138.
Westfield, 128.
Westhamton, 220.
Westis, 151.
Westminster, Bp of, see Thirlby.
Westmon, 216.
Westmorland, Earl of, see Nevell.
Westmynster, 182.
Weston, 26, 39, 149, 239, 292.
Westone, 179.
Westote, 148.
Westwike, 209.
Wetherden, 104.
Wethererd, 147.
Wetherid, 166.
Wetts, 318.
Wevant, 312.
Wever, 130, 171, 246.
Weyvant, 241.
Whaddon, 83.
Whalley, 97, 156, 222.
Whaplot, 68.
Wharton, 8, 24, 237, 308.
Whasshe, 241.
Whatelo, 171.
Whatley, 146.
Whawley, 291.
Wheitley, 201.
Wheler, 45, 78, 81, 88, 174, 313.
Whelhed, 201.
Whertley, 174.
Wherwood, 301.
Wheteley, 16, 259, 296.
Wheten, 271.
Whetham, 179.
Whethamstede, 202.
Whetheryke, 190.
Whetley, 160.
Whiffen, 68.
Whight, 116.
Whippe, 211.
Whisken, 220.
Whisteler, 132.
Whit, 64.
Whitacre, 2, 91, 95.
Whitacres, 181.
Whitbye, 156.

Wylkyns, 5, 261.
Wylkynson, 117, 229.
Wyllett, 285.
Wylley, 15, 22, 246.
Wyllocke, 196.
Wyllsey, 116.
Wyllson, 311.
Wyllyams, 104, 133, 285.
Wyllye, 313.
Wyllyngton, 131, 265.
Wyllys, 133.
Wylsey, 122.
Wylson, 252, 294.
Wylton, 314.
Wymark 288.
Wymbusshe, 40.
Wymes, 148.
Wymmyngton, 231.
Wymond, 277.
Wymprey, 204.
Wymstherst, 123.
Wynbyry, 79.
Wynchelsey, 74.
Wyncles, 302.
Wynde, 99, 131.
Wyndelow, 180.
Wynder, 187.
Wyndesor, 248.
Wyndesore, 78.
Wyndor, 26.
Wyne, 247.
Wyngfelde, 93.
Wyngham, 247.
Wynkfeld, 230, 317.
Wynnall, 263.
Wynnarde, 241.
Wynne, 202.
Wynnyngton, 110.
Wynston, 16.
Wyntenstalle, 110.
Wynter, 180, 190, 268, 310.
Wynterborn, 127.
Wynterhay, 171.

Wynterhey, 93.
Wynwode, 216.
Wyralde, 110.
Wyre, 167.
Wyse, 123, 178, 186.
Wyseman, 108.
Wysse, 2.
Wytfelde, 217.
Wytham, 230.
Wythers, 249.
Wyton, 62.
Wytter, 24.

Yake, 181.
Yambson, 69.
Yardeley, 124, 185, 201.
Yarlond, 282.
Yarom, 156.
Yate, 8, 9, 222.
Yaxley, 137, 174.
Ychan, 36.
Ydell, 123.
Yearnton, 25, 31.
Yelde, 304.
Yeldman, 201.
Yerdeley, 149.
Yersley, 156.
Yevan, 241.
Yevar, 273.
Yewell, 180.
Ynman, 166.
Yomans, 269.
Yong, 68, 161.
Yonge, 76, 87, 96, 103, 123, 131, 145, 152,
    165, 167, 168, 172, 204, 210.
York, Abps of, *see* Holgate, Lee.
Yorke, 146, 212, 283.
Young, 59.
Yoxall, 185.

Zouche, Jo., Ld, 199.
Zowche, 306.

PRINTED IN GREAT BRITAIN
AT THE UNIVERSITY PRESS, OXFORD
BY VIVIAN RIDLER
PRINTER TO THE UNIVERSITY